PHARMACEUTICALS AND DRUGS TECHNOLOGY WITH FORMULATIONS

PHARMACEUTICALS AND DRUGS TECHNOLOGY WITH FORMULATIONS

Written By

EIRI BOARD OF CONSULTANTS & ENGINEERS

ENGINEERS INDIA RESEARCH INSTITUTE

4449, Nai Sarak, Main Road, Delhi - 110 006 (India)

Ph:. 91-11- 23918117, 23916431, 23840361, 31082370

Fax: 91-11- 2391 6431, 2391 8117

* E-Mail : eirisidi@bol.net.in

* Website: www.startindustry.com

Sole Distributor :

INDIAN INSTITUTE OF CONSULTANTS, 4/27 ROOP NAGAR, DELHI - 07

PRINTED & PUBLISHED BY

ENGINEERS INDIA RESEARCH INSTITUTE

4449, Nai Sarak, Main Road, Delhi - 110 006 (India)
Ph:. 91-11-23918117, 23916431, 23840361, 31082370
* Fax: 91-11-23916431, 23918117
* E-Mail : eirisidi@bol.net.in
* Website: www.startindustry.com

DISTRIBUTED BY

SMALL INDUSTRY RESEARCH INSTITUTE
INDIAN INSTITUTE OF CONSULTANTS

ISBN : 81- 86732-52-7
Printed in New Delhi (INDIA)

Rs. 950

Printed & Published by Sudhir Gupta for "Engineers India Research Institute" 4449 Nai Sarak, Main Road, New Delhi - 110 006

Preface

The book **Pharmaceuticals and Drugs Technology with Formulations** covers almost all the basic and advanced details to setup own Pharmaceutical and Drugs Unit. The new edition of the book is covering latest technology including Tablet and Capsules, Oral Preparations, External Preparations, Preparations for the Eyes, Antibiotics, Formulations, Packaging, Tablets Formulations, Injectables, Liquid Orals methods, Syrups, Capsules and Dry Syrups with formulae, Eye and Ear Preparations, Topical Preparations. Apart from the above details and formulae, the book also deals with the project profiles on many industries, Suppliers of Plant and Equipments and Chemicals with Packaging materials have also been incorporated in this mega edition.

The book has been written for the benefit and to prove an asset and a handy reference guide in the hands of new entrepreneurs & well established industrialists.

Director

ENGINEERS INDIA RESEARCH INSTITUTE

Nai Sarak, New Delhi (INDIA)

E-Mail : eirisidi@bol.net.in

CONTENTS AND SUBJECT INDEX

Chapter — 12

EYE AND EAR PREPARATIONS .... 411 — 428

Chapter 1

Tablets and Capsules

Solid medicaments may be administered orally as powders, pills, cachets, capsules or tablets. As these contain a quantity of drug which is given as a single unit they are known collectively as solid unit-dose forms even in the case of sustained action preparations which, technically, contain the equivalent of several normal doses of drug. The stringent formulation requirements of modern medicaments, the many advantages of tablet and capsule medication, coupled with expanding health services and the concomitant need for large-scale economic manufacture, have lead to a steady decline in the prescribing of powders and pills. A few medicaments such as the salts of para-aminosalicylic acid are administered as cachets and the production of these dose-forms is described elsewhere in this volume. Tablets and capsules, on the other hand, currently account for well over half the total number and cost of all National Health prescriptions issued in the U.K.

TABLETS

Tablets are solid masses made by the compaction of suitable prepared medicament (granules) by means of a tablet machine. Although it is possible to manufacture tablets in a wide range of shapes, official tablets are defined as circular discs with either flat or convex faces. The *British Pharmacopoeia* 1973 includes monographs for over three hundred tablets.

Advantages of Tablet Medication

When correctly formulated and manufactured tablets provide an accurate, stable dose of drug with the necessary physical and chemical properties for the required duration and intensity of therapeutic action. Modern methods are capable of large scale economic production with a high degree of tablet uniformity both within and between batches. Suitable formulations provide sustained release characteristics and coatings can be applied to improve palatability or reduce the incidence of gastric irritation. Of all dose forms, the tablet presents the medicament in the highest practicable state of compaction. This permits the use of light weight, low cost containers for packaging, while emergency supplies of the drug can be conveniently carried by the patient.

Disadvantages of Tablet Medication

Some patients, particularly children and the seriously ill, may experience difficulty in swallowing tablets. If the tablet is too large, reformulation as two smaller units each containing half the required dose may minimize the problem in some cases. Occasionally a particular property of a medicine, such as the demulcent action of a linctus, cannot effectively be obtained with a tablet. Absorbents are available which allow the production of tablets containing a small amount of liquid, but it is usually more satisfactory to formulate as a soft capsule.

Types and Uses of Tablets

To secure rapid release of drug the majority of tablets are required to break down (disintegrate) rapidly in the stomach, but there are a number of exceptions to this general rule. If the drug is inactivated at low pH, causes gastric irritation, or is intended to exert its effect on the lower part of the gut, an enteric coating is applied to ensure that disintegration does not take place in the stomach but readily occurs in the small intestine. Examples are enteric coated tablets containing erythromycin or the alkali metal halides. Only part of the medicament in a sustained action tablet is released in the stomach to obtain prompt therapeutic action while the remainder is released at a controlled rate as the tablet progresses along the gastrointestinal tract. As an alternative to enteric coating for the minimization of gastric irritation, the drug e.g. aspirin, may be formulated as a soluble tablet to be dissolved in water prior to administration ; an effervescent base, as in Effervescent Potassium Tablet BPC, improves palatability. If the preferred site of absorption is the oral mucosa the tablet is directed to be dissolved in the mouth (isoprenaline), under the tongue (ethisterone) or chewed (phenolphthalein). For lozenges slow solution in the mouth, rather than disintegration, is required.

A number of preparations, not intended for oral administration, are also prepared by compression, examples being Mouth-wash Solution Tablets BPC, Testosterone Implants BP and Acetarsol Pessaries BPC. Solution tablets are dissolved in water and the solution applied to mucous surfaces or externally. A distinctive shape and colour is used for solution tablets that contain a poison.

GRANULATION

The Tablet Compression Cycle

Further processing, that is, granulation, is usually required before a drug can be tabletted. To a large extent the requisite physical properties of the granules are determined by the design of the tablet machine and the nature of the compaction process. Details of machine design are given later, but a brief discussion of the compression cycle, specifically that of the single punch tablet press, is relevant at this point to a proper understanding of the objectives to be attained by granulation.

Granules flow from hopper (Fig. 1.1) into a feedshoe which oscillates over the die to promote uniform flow of material into the die-cavity. For a given granule the volume of the cavity, which is adjustable, governs the weight of the tablet. At the end of the filling stage the toe of the feedshoe is deflected so that it smooths the surface of the granules in the die and cannot

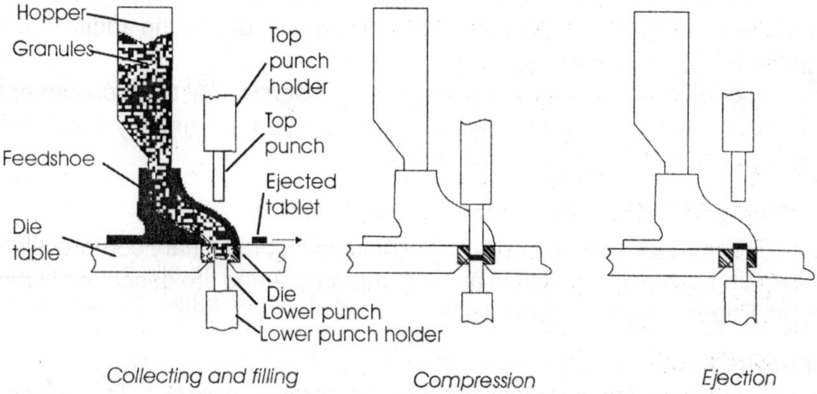

Fig. 1.1. The compression cycle for a single punch tablet machine.

foul the top punch as it is lowered to compact the granules. The penetration of the top punch into the cavity can be adjusted to regulate the degree of compaction, that is the tablet hardness. The top punch is then quickly raised and, after a short delay, the bottom punch moves upward to eject the tablet. Finally, the bottom punch drops to the filling position and the ejected tablet is pushed towards the collection chute by the toe of the feedshoe as it moves forward to commence the filling cycle of the next tablet.

ESSENTIAL GRANULE PROPERTIES

From the foregoing it should be clear that for the successful production of tablets the granules must fulfil a number of requirements. With both single punch and rotary tablet presses only about a fifth of a second or less is available for filling the die-cavity. Rapid, reproducible, flow of granules is essential if the tablet weight is to remain constant throughout the batch. Furthermore, particles of different size of density must not separate in the hopper as a result of machine vibration if both tablet weight and composition are to be maintained. Granules of uniform size minimize difficulties due to separation, but yield tablets with an inelegant pitted surface. A broader size distribution, with a proportion of fines to fill the inter-granule spaces, avoids the latter problem. The conflicting requirements for tablets uniformity and finish must be carefully balanced by rigid control of the granulation process.

During compaction inter-granule bonds must be formed to allow the production of a tablet which combines the required disintegration characteristics with sufficient firmness to withstand damage due to packaging, transport and other hazards. The volume of the tablet into which they are compacted. The reduction in volume is due to removal of air and this must readily escape for the proper development of the inter-particle bonds. Compaction also forces the tablet material into very close contact with the wall of the die. Excessive die-bore wear the damage to the edges of the tablet result if the die-wall friction is not reduced, usually by the addition of a lubricant to the granules.

In addition to the above it is, of course, essential that the medicament in a tablet is stable and released at the required rate. Primarily these are matters of correct formulation and processing.

Granulation Processes

Three processes namely, moist granulation, preliminary compression or slugging and dry granulation are in common use and are described in the *British Pharmaceutical Codex*, 1973.

Moist Granulation

This is steel the most widely used of the three processes. The mixed, powdered, tablet constituents are converted to a moist cohering mass by the incorporation of granulating fluid. Granules formed by passing the moist mass through a screen are dried, rescreened to break down agglomerates and blended with other tablet adjuvants such as lubricant and disintegrant. Although the majority of drugs are available as powders suitable for direct use in the moist granulation process, in a few cases the particle size of the powder affects the eventual compression characteristics of the granules. Smith (1950), for instance, reports that a powder finer than 80 mesh should be used for the production of tablets containing either phenacetin or phenobarbitone. Often the dose of the drug is very small and an inert diluent (bulking excipient) should be added before granulation to give, as a minimum, a 50 mg tablet. Some diluents will absorb small quantities of liquids (absorbent excipients); others may be used in the dry granulation process (see Table 1.1). Although the inertness of diluents is generally assumed, there have been reports of their adverse effect on product performance. Stephenson and Humphreys-Jones (1951) examined a number of formulations for glyceryl trinitrate tablets and demonstrated the superior stability of preparations using a lactose base. Richman et al. (1965) noted that microcrystalline cellulose permits dry granulation of this drug and yields a more stable product than that obtained with a lactose—sucrose diluent. A carbonyl-amine reaction causes darkening of tablets containing lactose or other reducing sugars together with a primary amine (Duvall et al. 1965). The BPC 1968 states that calcium phosphate may interfere with the absorption of calciferol.

TABLE 1.1

SOME DILUENTS USED IN TABLETTING

Diluent	Use and comments
Calcium Phosphate BPC	Absorbent diluent, Increases granule density but some grades are abrasive.
Calcium Hydrogen Phosphate USP	Used for direct compression formulations.
Colloidal silica	Small proportion used as an absorbent diluent or to improve granule flow by glidant action.
Anhydrous Dextrose BP	Absorbs moisture at high relative humidity—see BPC.
Dextrose (spray dried)	Useful for direct compression formulations but absorbs moisture at high relative humidity.
Lactose BP	Inert, tasteless, odorless, inexpensive and gives granules by moist granulation which have good tabletting properties. Incompatable with primary incompatable with primary amines.
Lactose (spray dried)	Used for direct compression formulations but tablets may assume a brown tinge on storage (Brownley and Lachman 1963). Is also incompatable with primary amines.
Lactose (anhydrous)	Used for direct compression formulations. Care should be taken to prevent moisture uptake. Is also incompatible with primary amines.
Mannitol BP	Dissolves readily and has a 'cooling' effect in the mouth.
Microcrystalline cellulose	Mainly used for direct compression formulations; has some lubricant and disintegrant effect and may improve the behaviour of granules made by other methods.
Sodium Chloride BP	Oral tablets containing this substance must be dissolved in water before administration to avoid gastric irritation—see BP. Usually reserved for the formulation of solution tablets. To avoid binding during compression, dry thoroughly and compress while still warm.
	Starch BP

Mixing. To ensure batch uniformity it is essential that the dry powders are thoroughly mixed before moistening. It must be stressed that mixing problems are particularly acute where one or more of the constituents forms only a small proportion of the tablet weight. Such minor components should, if possible, be dissolved in the granulating fluid or other suitable solvent and incorporated during the moistening stage. This method is included in the *British Pharmacopoeia* 1973 monograph on tablets and was specified for Soluble Paediatric Atropine Sulphate Tablets BPC 1968. Train (1960) pointed out that solute migration during the drying stage, analogous to separation on a chromatographic column, will lead to unequal distribution of solute within the granule mass, that is, to virtual demixing and this may be difficult to rectify in subsequent processing. With soluble dyes the effect is visually apparent in the uneven coloration of the dried granules and the mottled appearance of the finished tablet. Jaffe and Lippman (1964) studied the migration of F.D. and C. Blue No. 1 dye in lactose and noted that tragacanth, acacia and talc tended to 'fix' the dye so reducing its migration. The problem may be circumvented by the use of lake dyes, that is, soluble dyes bonded to an inert base. Lake dyes usually exhibit greater stability to light than the corresponding soluble colorant and are now much used, particularly for tablet coating.

A further mixing difficulty may arise if the drug is physically adsorbed on to the surface of the granules and these have a broad size distribution. A large fraction of the drug will be adsorbed on the fines since these make a disproportionately large contribution to the total granule surface. Should separation of fines occur this again is equivalent to demixing. The deliberate removal of fines to improve the tabletting properties of the granules is particularly suspect in these circumstances as this could lead to the production of low potency tablets. Where solvent dispersion of the minor components is not feasible a concentrated triturate may be prepared and subsequently diluted, in steps, with the remainder of the tablet ingredients. This should improve mixing, as comparable quantities of materials are blended at each stage of the process.

Batches up to a few hundred grams may be mixed in a mortar. Larger quantities of powders require power driven mixers, e.g., Y-cone, Roto-cube, or ribbon blenders. The transference of large quantities of material from the mixing to the moistening equipment may be obviated by the use of trough or change-pan mixer (Fig. 1.2) which are capable of performing both operations. The change-pan mixer is so called because the mixing blades and pan are detachable. Only one drive unit is required to service a number of blades and pans in which separate products may be prepared according to the needs of production. In this way the mixer is utilized more efficiently, transport of granules for further processing is facilitated and cleansing of the blades and pan simplified.

Moistening. This involves the gradual addition of granulating fluid to the dry mixed powders. A pestle and mortar is suitable for small batches, but power driven equipment such as the trough or change-pan mixer is essential for thorough blending action on a larger scale. Initially most of the fluid is held by capillary forces at the points where particles are in contact (Fig. 1.3, Stage 1). Further liquid builds up a continuous film on the external surfaces of the particles and at this second stage the powder is obviously damp and is very coherent. A quite small addition of fluid is now sufficient to produce a film of such thickness that the inter-particle friction is lowered to an extent that close packing of the particles can take place. At this third stage of moistening, air in the voids is displaced by fluid and a wet paste, technically a very concentrated suspension, is formed. This can however be produced once the second stage of granulation has been reached, by prolonged or more efficient blending, without the further addition of granulating fluid, owing to more uniform distribution of existing moistening medium and the mechanical removal of air from the mass. For production of tablet granules the volume of granulating fluid, mixing time and efficiency must be adjusted to give a second stage mass which just coheres when lightly compressed in the hand. Often, this condition may be anticipated by observing the behaviour of the mass which breaks away from the walls of the mixer, while the powder shows obvious signs of aggregation as a result of the greater cohesiveness of the particles.

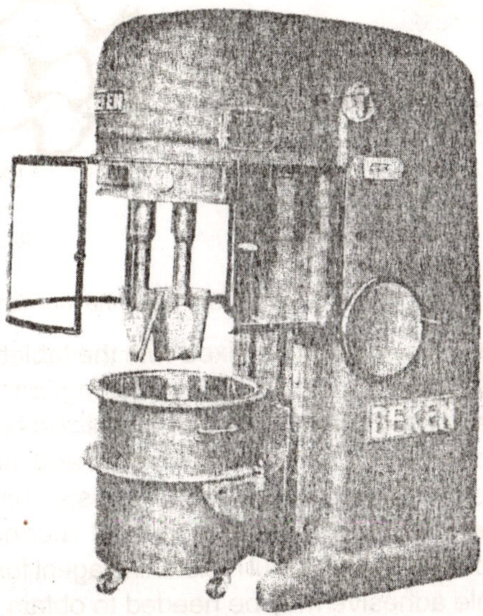

Fig. 1.2 The Beken change pan mixer with working capacity of about 0.1 m³. The machine is shown with the pan lowered and the guard open (Beken Engineering Ltd.)

In some cases moistening may be carried out with a solvent which causes partial dissolution of one or more components. With suitable materials the finished granules retain their structure, as the individual particles have been cemented together with solute deposited by the removal of solvent on dying. Reversion to the original powdered state will occur if substances of low natural cohesiveness are solvent granulated and a binding or adhesive granulating agent is required in these circumstances. The adhesive may be

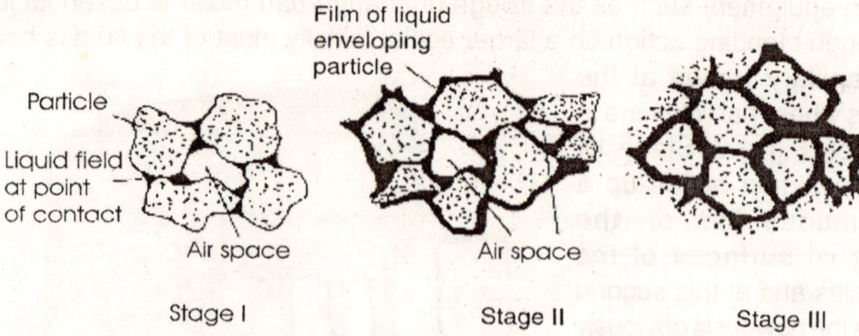

Fig. 1.3. Stages in the moistening of a powder.

added as a solution or mixed with the tablet ingredients as a dry powder for subsequent activation by moistening with solvent. The latter method is sometimes less effective, as many binders are hydrophilic colloids requiring for complete hydration more solvent and mixing time than is normally used at the moistening stage. Table 1.2 lists some of the more commonly used binders. Ethyl alcohol, isopropyl alcohol, acetone, and chlorinated hydrocarbons are useful moistening agent for water-sensitive drugs; a solvent soluble adhesive may be needed to obtain firm granules. Due to their high cost, the use of anhydrous solvents is usually restricted to those situations where other methods are not feasible. Attention must be given to fire and toxicity hazards and efficient vapour extraction is mandatory.

The most suitable granulating fluid, the volume to be used and the optimum operating conditions are best selected by the production of trial batches of granules. In the early stages of developing a suitable process, when even an approximate value for the volume of granulating fluid is not known, the time taken for moistening may be unduly protracted. Significant amounts of solvent may be lost by evaporation in these circumstances and should be allowed for in subsequent trials. Clearly, the volume of fluid must be sufficient to produce a second stage moistened powder mass and at the same time add sufficient binder to ensure the production of suitable granules. Powdery granules which do not compress well are obtained if the adhesive is too 'weak', is employed in too low a concentration, or if the volume of granulating fluid is inadequate. The converse conditions lead to hard granules which produce excessive amounts of fines when dry-screened. Symptoms of over-moistening are clogging of the screen and agglomeration of the wet granules. Scale-up calculations based on data obtained from small trial batches often overestimate the concentration and volume of granulating fluid on account of the higher blending efficiency of equipment used for large scale manufacture. Finally, granules must be evaluated on a press of the type used for production as their performance may to some degree be affected by mechanical features such as the method for filling the die-cavity, speed of operation and compaction conditions.

TABLE 1.2

ADHESIVE GRANULATING AGENTS

Material	Concentration in the granulating fluid % w/v	Concentration in the dried granules % w/v	Uses and comments
Acacia	5–15	1–5	Use high quality gum to avoid the darkening of white tablets. Clarify the solution. Excess gives very hard granules.
Ethylcellulose	2–5	0.5–3	Soluble in water or alcohol, the latter being used for water-sensitive drugs. Is relatively expensive.
Gelatin	5–20	1–3	Dissolve in hot water and use warm, as the cold solution gels. Produces hard tablets which dissolve slowly—useful for lozenges.
Liquid glucose	10–30	5–20	Strong adhesive action. Tablets may soften under humid conditions.
Methylcellulose	2–10	0.5–3	Use low viscosity grades. May prolong disintegration time.
Polyethylene glycol (Macrogol)	Solvent activated	2–15	Use grades with molecular weight in excess of 5000. Soluble in water and some anhydrous solvents. Has some lubricant action and helps to counteract effects due to the hydrophobic nature of some materials.
Polyvinyl pyrrolidone (P.V.P.)	2–10	0.5–3	
Sodium alginate	2–10	0.5–3	
Sodium carboxymethylcellulose	2–10	0.5–3	
Starch	5–15	1–5	Mucilage prepared with boiling

			water and used as warm as possible, as the mucilage gels on cooling. Efficient blending action is essential.
Sucrose	10–50	5–30	Strong adhesive, but tablets tend to harden on storage.
Tragacanth	0.5–2	up to 0.5	Not generally used as an adhesive but is added to lozenges for its demulcent effect. Often solvent activated.

Wet Screening. Granules will not readily flow into a cavity with which they are comparable in size due to crowding at the entrance of that cavity. On the other hand very fine granules often exhibit poor flow characteristics. Both conditions lead to excessive weight variation in the manufactured tablets. In addition, tablets which are too thin relative to their diameter are prone to breakage when handled. For these reasons the screens used for granulation and the die size for compression are selected (Table 1.3) according to the final tablet weight. The Table must be regarded as a guide only since, for example, a smaller die size may be required if the material to be tabletted is unusually dense, while screens somewhat larger or smaller than those recommended may give granules with better characteristics.

Small batches of moistened mass may be screened by hand, the material being lightly rubbed, rather than forced, through the screen. Too vigorous manipulation at this stage is equivalent to highly efficient blending which, as already explained, may result in the formation of a third stage pasty mass and consequent difficulties due to screen clogging. Hand screening is tedious for more than a few kilograms of moist material, power driven equipment such as the Apex comminutor or the Fitz mill

TABLE 1.3

A GUIDE TO THE SIEVE NUMBER, PUNCH SIZE AND MAXIMUM PUNCH LOAD FOR THE PRODUCTION OF TABLETS

Tablet load(2) weight (mg)	Sieve number[1] for wet screening	dry screening	Punch diameter (mm)	Maximum punch load Flat or normal concave (kg)	Deep concave or flat bevelled edge (kg)
50	16	20	5–6.5	2000	1300
100	16	20	7	3000	1500
150	12	16	8	3800	1800

200	12	16	8.5	4800	2000
300	10	12	10.5	6500	2500
500	10	10	12	8800	3500
1000	8	8	16	15300	6500

(1) Meshes per inch (2.54 cm.)
(2) Applies to special steels used for tabletting punches; for other materials refer to the manufacturer.

being employed for larger batches. The oscillating granulator (Fig. 1.4) also finds considerable industrial use. The base of the hopper is closed by a semi-cylindrical interchangeable screen just above which a rotor oscillates about a horizontal axis. Blades parallel with the axis and integral with the rotor push the moist mass through the screen on to a receiver below. In a recent study Fonner et al. (1966) found that this type of granulator gave smoother, more nearly spherical granules of a starch-lactose formulation than either hand screening or three other commonly used power-driven granulating machines.

Drying. The drying temperature for granules is usually about 60°C but may be lower if thermolabile substances are involved. With tray dryers, air exchange is essential to prevent saturation of the oven atmosphere with solvent vapour. By spreading the granules as thin layers on the trays and raking these layers over from time to time, agglomeration of granules and migration of solutes is minimized and even drying of the granules promoted. If different products are to be dried in the oven at the same time care must be taken to avoid cross-contamination. Up to 24 h may be required for the drying of large batches of granules.

The fluid-bed dryer (Fig. 1.5) is now widely used in the pharmaceutical industry because the drying time is only 20 to 30 min, irrespective of batch size which may be 60 kg or more. The amount of granulated solvent to be evaporated decreases as drying proceeds; thus the temperature of the air leaving the fluidized bed rises until it is constant and approximates to that of the input air stream. With experience the effluent air temperature provides a convenient means of establishing the optimum drying time. If drying is prolonged beyond this point attrition of the granules leads to an increase in the proportion of fines. The overdried granules have inferior compressing characteristics and consequently difficulties are encountered in the production of the tablets. On large scale equipment an automatic timer is provided to shut off the heaters and air flow at the end of the pre-determined drying time. Generally, less fluid is needed for granules which are to be dried in fluid-bed equipment as the amount of granulating fluid suitable for tray-dried granules gives a moist mass which is too dense and cohesive for correct fluidization of the bed. On the other hand, undermoistening should be avoided as fines may clog the output air filters and impede the air flow.

Dry-screening. This breaks down agglomerates and reduces them to a size compatible with the tablet diameter. Too vigorous dry-screening causes granule structure to be lost with the production of excessive quantities of fines. Although a proportion of these is required to fill the voids between larger granules, so giving a smooth tablet surface, and excess causes trouble at the compression stage.

Other methods of moist granulation. The conventional process has a wide range of application but is time consuming and involves a large number of separate operations. Alternative methods of moist granulation have been developed whereby granule manufacture can be carried out as a single integrated process. Fluid-bed granulation (and drying) stems form the work of Wurster (1959, 1960) who had earlier patented a fluid-bed method for tablet coating. One equipment in current use for moist granulation has a downwards directed atomizer placed centrally above the fluidization chamber. Correct circulation of material is brought about by the special shape of the perforated base and the progressive expansion of the upper part of the chamber. The powders are mixed, granulated by the spray of warm granulating solution and dried while in a fluidized state. Lubricant, disintegrant and any other necessary tablet adjuvants are then added and blended by a further short period of fluidization. Granule size is controlled by the volume, temperature and rate of addition of granulating fluid together with the air flow-

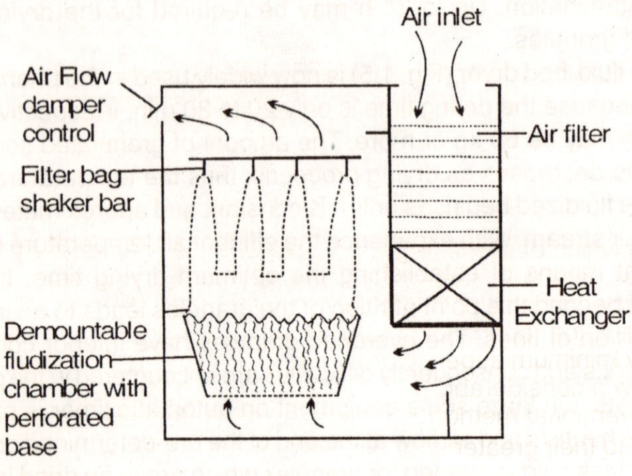

Fig. 1.5. The fluid-bed drier.

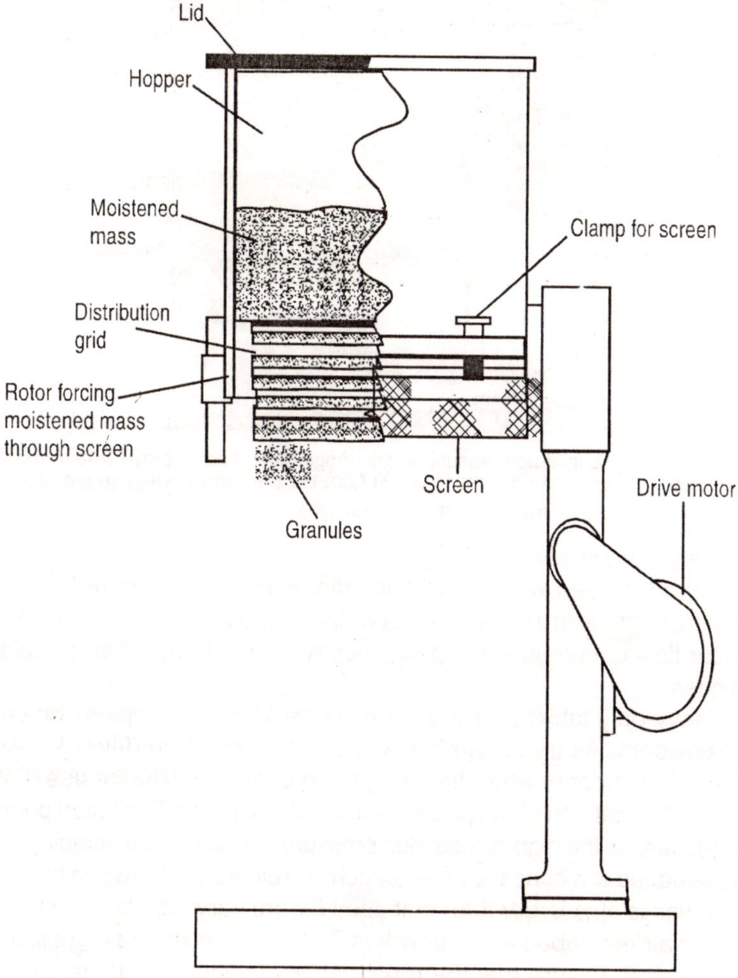

Fig. 1.4. The oscillating granulator

rate,which determines the expansion and circulation of the bed. Normally, these parameters are automatically controlled by presetting a programming device on the basis of data obtained from previous development batches. A granulator capable of processing up to 60 kg of material in under 2 hr with only minimum supervision, is shown in Fig. 1.6. The foregoing methods all show a considerable saving in time and labour costs as compared with the conventional method: the granules often possess superior flow properties due to their greater smoothness and sphericity.

Fig. 1.6. The Calmic fluid-bed granulator. The programming panel may be seen top left. This controls application of granulating agent from the pressure vessel (centre bottom) to the material in the fluidizing chamber.

Preliminary Compression or Slugging

This method is used where the tablet ingredients react chemically when moistened, degrade in the presence of water or when heated, or yield granules with poor flow or compression properties when made by other granulation techniques.

Heavy-duty tablet presses are employed for the compression of dry, mixed powders. As these rarely flow well, vibratory feed devices may be attached to the hopper while die-cavity filling is facilitated by the use of large (2–5 cm) punches and slow speed operation of the press. Flat faced punches are necessary as the high compaction pressures employed for slugging would splay the edges of a concave faced punch: the clearance between the punch and die-wall is also larger than that used for ordinary tablets to allow rapid escape of air entrapped in the powders. The compaction pressure must be high enough to ensure that the rough tablets (slugs) give material with a granular structure when forced through a screen. It is usually advantageous to add some lubricant and disintegrant prior to slugging, further quantities of these being added to the granules before final compression. Talc is frequently employed as lubricant, since powder flow rather than die-wall friction is usually the major problem in the preliminary compression stage. Adhesive-containing granules, prepared by moist granulation, tend to retain their structure for long periods in contact with aqueous media. The absence of adhesives from tablets prepared by slugging however usually results in good disintegration.

Paediatric Ampicillin Tablets BPC and the official soluble analgesic tablets containing aspirin may be prepared from granules made by preliminary compression.

Dry Granulation

This is the simplest of the three granulation techniques. The material to be tabletted is screened if necessary, mixed with any additional adjuvants and is then ready for compression. Tablets made in this way are said to have been prepared by direct compression.

Formerly, the alkali metal and ammonium halides, hexamine and potassium chlorate were the only commonly used medicinal substances which could be dry granulated. More recently the list has been extended by the commercial production of suitably granular forms of Dried Yeast, Dry Cascara Extract, Aspirin, some ferrous salts and a few other substances. Provided an increase in the tablet weight can be tolerated, the addition of spray-dried lactose or anhydrous lactose to the medicament, together with lubricant and disintegrant, will often yield granules which may be directly compressed. As Lactose BP does not promote free powder flow, act as a dry binder or possess good compaction properties it would appear that these characteristics reside in the spherical shape of the spray-dried sugar. The applications of this material to tabletting technology have been reviewed by Gunsel and Lachman (1963). Tablet containing spray-dried lactose may assume a brown tinge on storage due, it has been suggested, to the presence in the sugar of 5-hydroxymethyl-furfural (Brownley and Lachman 1963). This darkening should be distinguished from that resulting from the reaction of primary amines and lactose. Other excipients which may be used in direct compression formulae are listed in Table 1.1. Of these, microcrystalline cellulose is of particular interest since, as reported by Reier and Shangraw (1966), this material also possesses marked lubricating and disintegrating properties.

In those cases where one or more ingredients are present in low concentration, efficient mixing may be more difficult with dry than with moist granulation. The problem has a two-fold origin. Firstly, solvent dispersion cannot be used and, secondly, fine powders are essential to secure efficient mixing—but fine powders lack the good flow and compaction characteristics essential to tablet manufacture. The magnitude of the problem may be appreciated by applying the methods described by Train (1960) to the example of 50 mg tablets containing 1 per cent by weight of drug. If the density of the material from which the tablet is formed is 1.5 gm^{-3} the particle size should not exceed 20 microns and at least 10^7 particles per tablet are necessary to ensure that 99.7 per cent of tablets in the batch comply with a ± 10 percent tolerance in the content of the drug.

Dry granulation is the most economical of the three processes in terms of time, labour and equipment. The availability of the drug for absorption should be good due to the absence of adhesive granulating agents while the elimination of drying and moistening stages obviates many of the stability problems associated with the moist granulation process. Against these advantages must be set the relatively high cost of some diluents used in direct compression formulae and the restricted range of materials manufactured in a suitable granular form. It seems likely however that the more widespread adoption of devices for promoting uniform die-filling with difficult materials will reduce the cost and extend the applicability of the dry granulation process.

Flavours, Lubricants and Disintegrants

When moist granulation is employed, these adjuvants are normally added to dry, screened granules, but the incorporation of internal lubricant or a proportion of disintegrant prior to moistening, as described below, are exceptions. For slugging and dry granulation the addition of these adjuvants has been discussed in the relevant sections.

Flavours

Essential oils are included in a few official tablets. They may be mixed with a small quantity of fines or absorbent excipient and the triturate thoroughly blended with the rest of the granules. Dissolution in a volatile solvent aids dispersion if the volume of flavouring agent is small or, alternatively, the solution may be directly sprayed on to the granules. In both cases solvent must be completely removed before compaction. For non-official tablets a wide range of flavours in powder form is available. Flavours may not, of course, be added prior to an operation involving the use of heat.

Lubricants

These may promote granule flow (glidants), minimize die-wall friction (die-wall lubricants) or prevent the adhesion of granules to the punch faces (anti-adherents). Talc, for example, is a good glidant but is inferior to magnesium stearate as a die-wall lubricant. In addition to their mode of action, lubricants may also be classified according to the way in which they are added to the granules. External lubricants are incorporated immediately before compression and function by coating the granule surface while internal lubricants are mixed with the dry powders prior to moistening with granulating fluid. Granules prepared in this manner are described as self-lubricating. One step in the moist granulation process can be eliminated by the use of an internal lubricant in conjunction with polyethylene glycol as the binding agent. In suitable cases the water solubility of the glycol permits the formulation of tablets with good disintegration properties. Commonly used lubricants are listed in Table 1.4.

Disintegrants

These assist the disintegration of the tablet by swelling (bursters), by improving the penetration of aqueous liquids (Table 1.5), or by the liberation of gas from an effervescent base. For a number of medicaments, disintegration of the tablet is improved if part of the disintegrant is added to the powders prior to moistening; the disintegrant within the granules assists the disruption of these in contact with aqueous media. Powdered disintegrants e.g., starch, methylcellulose, etc., are normally employed in proportions which significantly increase the fines content of the granules and in unfavourable circumstances this can give rise to compression difficulties. Additionally, premature disintegration of the tablet may occur in the mouth if excessive amounts of disintegrant are employed and, apart from difficulty in swallowing the powdery mass, any unpleasant taste due to the medicament may prove objectionable. In a few cases an effervescent base is used to promote disintegration. This consists of citric or tartaric acid together with sodium bicarbonate, potassium bicarbonate or calcium carbonate. These react in contact with water to liberate carbon dioxide which disrupts the tablet. A slight trace of moisture is sufficient to initiate the reaction which produces further water and is thus potentially self-perpetuating. For stability, very dry materials, rigorous exclusion of moisture during manufacture and efficient sealing of the packages are essential—the use of *anhydrous* citric acid in official preparations of this type should be noted.

TABLE 1.4

LUBRICANTS USED IN TABLETTING

Material	Type	Concentration in the granules per cent w/w	Uses and comments
Boric acid	E, L	1–5	Toxic orally, reserve for solution-tablet.
Colloidal silica	E, G	0.1–0.5	Promotes granule flow but has little effect on die-wall friction.
Hydrogenated vegetables oils	I, L	1 –5	May prolong disintegration time. 'Hard' grades must be used to avoid punch face adhesion.
Magnesium stearate	E, L	0.1–1	Use minimum effective amount as excess may impede granule flow, reduce tablet hardness, or prolong disintegration. Some grades are slightly 'alkaline' —this causes discoloration of aminophylline tablets (Castello and Mattocks 1962)

			and promotes the hydrolysis of aspirin (Ribeiro et al. 1955 ; Kornblum and Zoglio 1967).
Polyethylene glycol	I, L	2–15	Use grades with molecular weight in excess of 5000. Soluble in water and some anhydrous solvents. Has some lubricant action, helps to counteract effects due to the hydrophobic nature of some materials, but main use is as a binder.
Stearic acid	E, L I, L	0.1–1 0.2–2	Use finely powdered grade. Effect on tablet hardness and disintegration not so marked as with the magnesium salt.
Talc	E, G	1–5	Promotes granule flow and inhibits punch face adhesion but is much less effective than the stearates as a die-wall lubricant. Low quality grades may be abrasive causing punch and die wear.

E — External lubricant
I — Internal lubricant
L — Lubricates die-wall
G — Glidant

TABLE 1.5

DISINTEGRANTS USED IN TABLETTING

Material	Concentration in the granules per cent w/w	Uses and comments
Alginic acid	2–10	Burster which may prove better than starch for 'difficult' materials (Berry and Ridout 1950). May be incorporated prior to moistening to improve disintegration. If added to the dry granules, avoid finely powdered grades as these form a

		coherent gel on the tablet surface and may prolong disintegration time.
Magnesium aluminium silicate	1–10	Burster; Veegum is one variety.
Methylcellulose	2–10	Burster. Use medium viscosity grade in a not too fine powder.
Microcrystalline cellulose	1–10	Has some lubricant properties, higher concentrations used as dry-binding diluent
Sodium lauryl sulphate	0.1–0.5	Wetting agent which improves penetration of the tablet pore system by aqueous liquids. Will counteract the water-repellent effect of, for example, phenothiazine and the stearate lubricants. May minimize the increase in disintegration time which often occurs as tablets age.
Starch	2–10	Burster. Potato and maize starch are usually considered superior to the other varieties. Part may be incorporated prior to moistening.

The Compressing Weight

This is the weight of granules which must be fed into the die-cavity to give a tablet containing the nominal amount of drug. The most direct method is to assay the granules and from the result calculate the compressing weight. Alternatively, this may be derived form data obtained during the manufacture of the granules and allows production of tablets to proceed without the delay due to the time taken to assay the granules. Whichever method is used, the finished tablets must be examined for medicament content, weight uniformity etc.

Dry granulation. The compressing weight is the sum of the weights of the individual ingredients in each tablet:

Codeine Phosphate	20.00 mg
Stearic acid, in fine powder	0.06 mg
Potato Starch	0.60 mg
Spray dried lactose	39.34 mg
Compressing weight	60.00 mg

As given, this formula would not be adopted for the commercial production of large batches, due to the possible darkening of the spray-dried lactose. It is suitable for the extemporaneous preparation of small batches. If a specified number of tablets must be supplied, an allowance must be made for losses incurred when adjusting the machine for correct tablet weight and hardness.

Preliminary compression. Here, an allowance must be made for losses which occur when slugging and rescreening. Consider typical production data for 100000 Soluble Aspirin Tablets BP:

	per tablet	*for 100000 tablets*
Aspirin, in fine powder	300 mg	31.00 kg
Anhydrous Citric Acid	30 mg	3.10 kg
Calcium Carbonate	100 mg	10.33 kg
Saccharin Sodium	3 mg	0.31 kg
Talc	4 mg	0.41 kg
Theoretical weight of ingredients	437 mg	45.15 kg
Weight of granules after slugging and rescreening		44.30 kg
Weight of talc added prior to final compression		0.80 kg
Total weight of granules for final compression		45.10 kg

Actual number of tablets which may be prepared from the slugged and rescreened material is:

$$\frac{44300}{0.437} = 101373$$

Compressing weight

$$= \frac{\text{Total weitght of granules for compression}}{\text{Number of tablets}}$$

$$\frac{45100}{101373} = 0.445 \text{ g}$$

Talc, rather than magnesium stearate, is used to avoid hydrolysis of aspirin and to improve powder flow. Disintegrant is not required as an effervescent base and finely powdered aspirin ensures rapid dissolution when the tablet is placed in water. The use of anhydrous citric acid avoids premature reaction of the ingredients.

Moist granulation. When calculating the compressing weight of granules prepared by this process it cannot be assumed that the starting materials are perfectly dry or that all moistening solvent is removed by drying. By keeping a record of the weight of the product at each stage of the granulating process calculation of the compressing weight is feasible. The following data might be typical for the manufacture of, say, about 200000 tablets each containing 0.5 g of medicament:

Medicament	101.0 kg
Adhesive granulating fluid	10.6 kg
Theoretical weight of mass	111.6 kg
Actual weight of moist granules	111.1 kg
Weight of granules after drying	104.6 kg
Weight of granules after screening	104.3 kg
Formula of granules for compression:	
Screened granules	104.3 kg
Disintegrant	8.0 kg
Lubricant	0.5 kg
Weight of granules for tabletting	112.8 kg

Number of tablets which could be produced from 101 kg of medicament is:

$$\frac{101000}{0.5} = 202000$$

Weight of moist mass per tablet:

$$\frac{111600}{202000} = 0.5525 \text{ g}$$

Number of tablets that may be prepared from the actual weight of moist granules:

$$\frac{111100}{0.5525} = 201095$$

After drying 104.6 kg of material contains the medicament present in 111.1 kg of moist granules and 104.3 kg of dried material is available for tabletting after screening. The number of tablets that may be produced from the screened granules is:

$$\frac{201086 \times 104.3}{104.6} = 200518$$

The final compressing weight after addition of disintegrant and lubricant is:

$$\frac{112800}{200518} = 0.5625 \text{ g}$$

In the previous two examples large quantities of materials are being handled and losses can be kept to a minimum. Much greater losses are incurred when the moist granulation technique is applied to small batches; moistened mass which cannot be recovered from the granulating screen and tablets lost when adjusting the tablet press may represent a large proportion of the total batch. A loss of up to 10 per cent is possible in these circumstances and should be allowed for when calculating the weights of materials required to produce the batch.

PRODUCTION OF TABLETS

The Single Punch Tablet Machine

Assembly

Clean the punches and die, set the machine by hand to the filling position, insert the bottom punch in its holder (Fig. 1.7), making sure that the locking notch faces the locking bolt, and lightly secure in position. Carefully fit the die, check that the die-face is flush with the table and then securely tighten the locking bolt. The top punch may now be fitted, lightly secured, and this operation followed by the assembly of the feedshoe with not the connecting rod. Fill the feedshoe with granules, adjust the weight regulating collar so that the punch face is 0.5 to 1 cm below the die table and then fill the cavity with granules. Carefully lower the top punch into the die-cavity and at the same time adjust the hardness control such that the machine drive cannot be turned by hand past the compression position; maintain the load on the punches while their locking bolts are finally tightened. This procedure ensures that the punches are firmly locked in their holders and cannot work loose during tablet manufacture. Finally, reduce the compression control and eject the compact.

Adjustments

Tablet weight. For the filling and compression stages the lifting block pulls down the weight-regulating collar and holds it in contact with the main frame of the machine. The position of the bottom punch face in the bore determines the volume of the die-cavity and hence the tablet weight. For preliminary weight adjustment the collar is adjusted on its thread so that a weighed quantity of granules just fills the cavity. Final weight adjustment is made with the press running normally, as die filling is affected by the dynamic flow properties of the granules under operating conditions.

Ejection. After the compression stage the lifting block moves to its top position and raises the lower punch assembly by engagement with the ejection regulating collar. This is set to bring the punch face flush with the upper surface of the die. Too low a setting will cause part of the tablet to be sliced off as the feedshoe moves forward, while the punch will foul the base of the shoe if the setting is too high. The feedshoe is fabricated from a soft metal to minimize damage in the even of machine malfunction. A locking device is provided to make sure that the regulating collars cannot move during machine operation.

Tablet hardness. The top punch is locked in a holder which moves in a guide to ensure accurate registration of the punch and die-bore. During operation of the press an eccentric cam imparts a vertical movement to the punch holder. Since the amplitude of the upper punch stroke and the centre of rotation of the cam drive are fixed by the machine design, die penetration is controlled by an adjustment which, effectively, alters the distance between the centre of rotation of the cam drive and the face of the upper punch at the bottom of its stroke. If this distance is increased the punch penetrates further into die-cavity; thus, for a given fill, the granules are more highly consolidated and a harder tablet is formed. The mechanisms used to adjust tablet hardness vary considerably and are best understood by examination of actual equipment. One method is shown in Fig. 1.7; as the holder is moved down the adjusting thread punch penetration is increased.

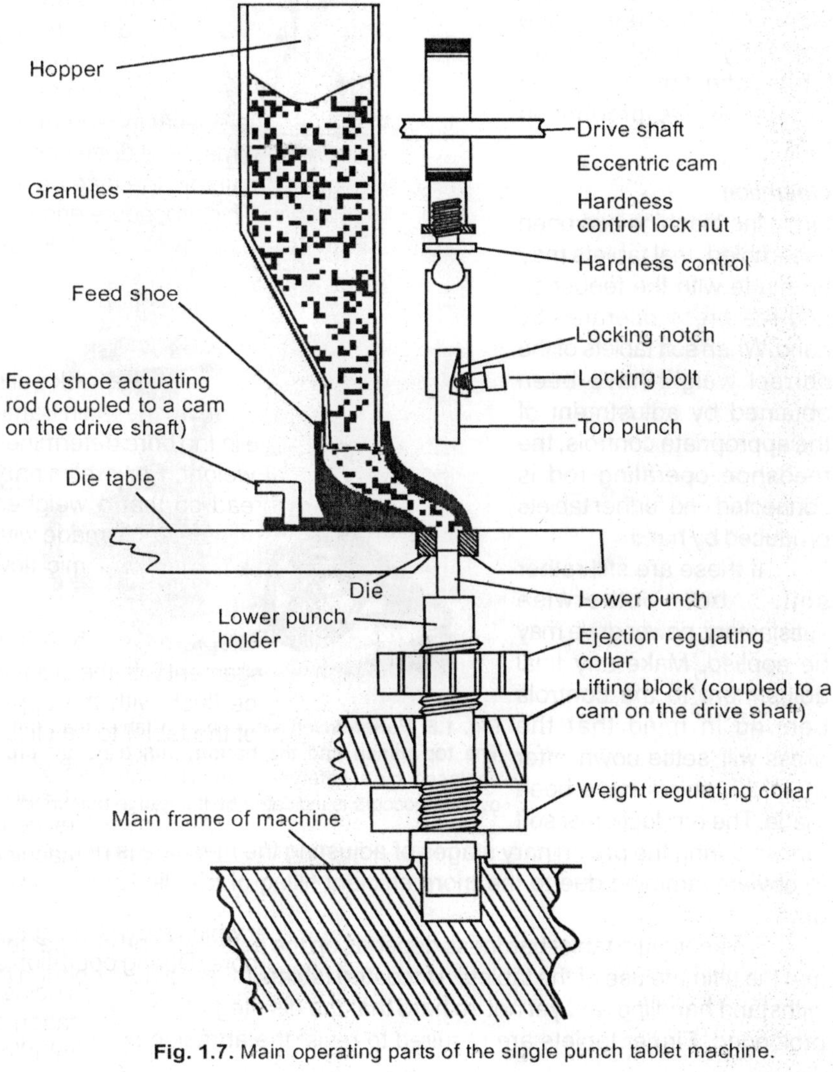

Fig. 1.7. Main operating parts of the single punch tablet machine.

Feedshoe movement. A rod connects the shoe to its actuating mechanism, transverse oscillation of the feedshoe relative to the die-cavity being controlled by the length of the rod. This should be adjusted to ensure that the cavity is uniformly filled with granules, the top punch does not foul the shoe and the ejected tablet is pushed well away from the vicinity of the die. Once correctly adjusted, little further attention is required for successive production runs.

Operation

Once the machine has been assembled, trial tablets may be made with the feedshoe and the press operated by hand. When soft tablets of the correct weight have been obtained by adjustment of the appropriate controls, the feedshoe operating rod is connected and further tablets produced by hand.

If these are still rather soft, but otherwise satisfactory, power drive may be applied. Make any final adjustment to the controls bearing in mind that the press will 'settle down' after 20 to 30 tablets have been made. The production of soft tablets during the preliminary stages of adjusting the machine is necessary to obviate jamming due to the more efficient filling of the die under power drive.

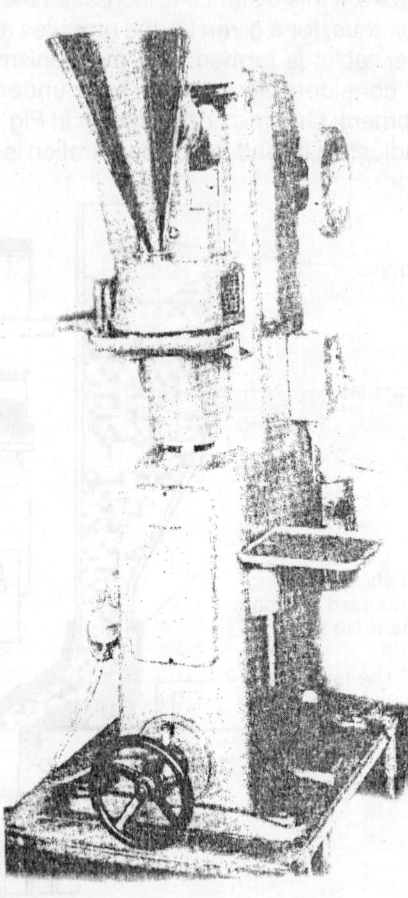

Fig. 1.8. Power-driven single punch tablet machine. The top punch and the bottom punch holder are enclosed by a safety screen. The value at which overload occurs is indicated by the gauge bottom left.

The optimum tablet hardness depends on the material to be compacted and the ultimate use of the tablets. Uncoated tablets must be hard enough to withstand handling and yet not so hard that the disintegration time is unduly prolonged. Firmer tablets are required to resist the abrasion normal to the film or pan coating processes, but cores for compression coating must be somewhat soft to allow further consolidation when the coating is applied. A crushing test is used to ensure compliance with predetermined specifications for tablet hardness.

There is, obviously, a limit to the compaction force which may be safely developed by a given model of tablet press. Some are fitted with an adjustable overload release whereby the weight regulating collar rests on a spiring loaded stop which is deflected downwards should the pre-selected compacting force be exceeded. In this way jamming and machine damage is avoided. The medium duty press shown in Fig. 1.8 is provided with means for varying the production rate from 40 to 90 tablets a minute and overload release for loads up to 4 tons (4000 kg).

Fig. 1.9. Medium duty 16-station rotary tablet press. The upper turret and punches are visible beneath the plastic dust screen (Manesty Machines Ltd.).

It is essential that precautions are taken to preclude accidental connection of the power supply during assembly and initial adjustment of the press. As large compaction forces are developed, even by hand tablet machines, it should not be necessary to emphasize that the hands must be kept clear of the compressing area during production. On some presses in interlocking switch isolates the power supply until the moving parts are enclosed by a safety screen. The machine must never be operated so that the punch faces come into contact: if it is to be left for a short period the die-cavity must be filled with granules. Finally, the feedshoe connecting rod must be removed and the shoe deflected away from the die area, if it becomes necessary to operate the press in the reverse direction.

The Rotary Tablet Machine

The most important factor limiting the production capacity of a tablet press is the rate at which the die-cavity can be filled with granules. For the single punch machine the limit is probably of the order of 8000 tablets/hr but by mounting the punches and dies in a rotating holder (turret) which passes them in sequence through the filling, compression and ejection stages much larger outputs are possible. This is the principle of the rotary tablet machine (Fig. 1.9).

The top and bottom punches move freely in guides bored in the upper and lower sections of the turret (Fig. 1.10) while the centre section forms the die-table. Cam tracks govern the positions of the punches by engaging with the head or the under surface of the 'mushroom' head of the punch. The die-cavity is over-filled with granules as it passes below a flat feedframe (Fig. 1.11) fed from a hopper

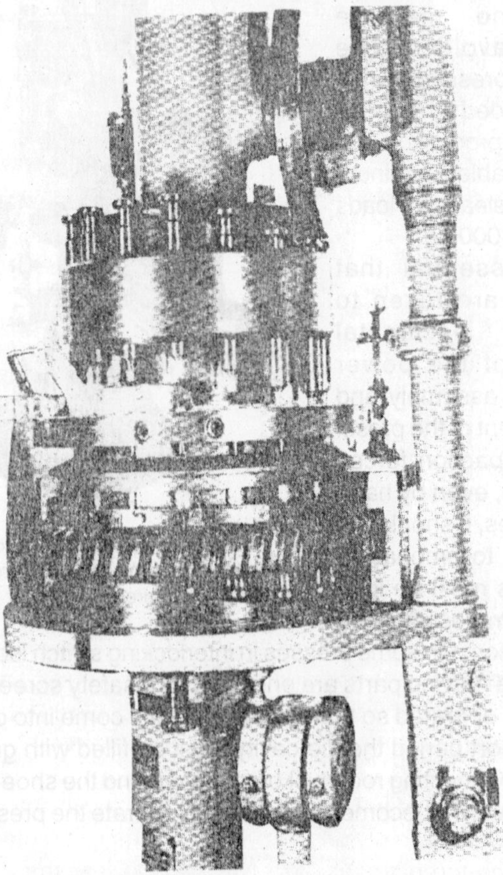

Fig. 1.10. 16-station rotary tablet press. The perspex screens and hopper and lower guard have been removed to show the upper and lower turrets and die table. The upper and lower cam tracks and the upper pressure roller are also visible.

Fig. 1.11. Close-up view of rotary press. The output of the hopper may be seen (left) feeding granules into the feed frame. Ejected tablets are being directed towards the collection chute bolted to the end of the feed frame. The upper cam track for lifting the top punch clear of the feed frame is also visible.

Tablet weight is regulated by an adjustable section of the lower cam track which, towards the end of the filling period, causes the bottom punch to rise slightly. The excess granules are removed by a scraper bar and retained in the feed frame. The method gives a more consistent die fill than would be obtained by setting the bottom punch at the correct level for the whole of the filling period. Weight adjustment is followed by a slight but sudden drop in the bottom punch level both to remove air by tamping action and lower the level of the granules in the die. This facilitates subsequent compaction and at the same time obviates spillage from the die-cavity due to the centrifugal forces developed by the rotating turret.

At the start of the compression stage the top punch is rapidly lowered to penetrate the die-cavity and then both punches pass between pressure rollers which 'squeeze' the punches towards one another. The position of the upper roller is fixed and it is adjustable lower roller that controls the separation of the punch faces at the point of maximum compression, that is, the tablet hardness. The lower roller is fitted with adjustable overload protection. Following compression, the top punch is raised rapidly to clear the feed frame and allow the tablet to be ejected as the lower punch rides up the lower cam track which may be adjusted to set the correct height of the punch for tablet ejection. The lower punch is then pulled down for the filling stage on the next revolution of the turret. A scraper bar directs the ejected tablet towards the collection chute. Any granules which have seeped out of the feed frame are carried round on the die-table and returned to the frame behind the scraper bar. With 16 punch and die positions (16 station machines) the output is of the order of 50 000 tablets/hr. Double rotary machines produce two tablet per revolution of the turret; outputs in excess of half a million tablets/hr may be obtained with 69-station double rotary machines (Fig. 1.12).

Fig. 1.12. 69-station rotary tablet machine (Manesty Machines Ltd.).

It is inherent in the processing of particulate solids that dust will be liberated into the environment, a problem which is particularly acute with rotary tablet machines. With highly potent medicaments toxicity hazards must be considered, while inter-product contamination is ever present problem in all tablet production processes. Modern rotary machines are provided with clear plastic covers over themoving parts and dust extraction. In difficult cases the only complete solution may be the provision of individual dust-extracted cubicles for each machine. Finally, as discussed earlier, it should be remembered that granules which 'run' well on a single punch machine may need reformulation for good performance on a rotary machine (and vice versa) due to differences in the modes of die feed and compression.

Developments in the Design of Rotary Tablet Machines

Granule Flow

The flow of granules into the feed frame is controlled by the height of the hopper outlet above the die-table. A number of materials flow erratically or may even block the hopper outlet. Vibratory devices for attachment to the hopper offer a partial solution to these problems but where a very high flowrate is required—this may be as much as 2 kg/min for ultra high-speed presses producing half a million tablets/hr—more positive feeding is essential. The Stockes metering hopper minimizes blocking by allowing the granules to flow down a wide straight section at the base of the hopper on to an inclined plate which in turn directs the granules on to a metering wheel. The form of the latter i.e. perforated disc, mesh or paddle, its rotational speed and the height of the baffle above the wheel, control the flowrate of the granules out of the hopper and into the feed frame.

Die Filling

Even flow of granules from the feed frame into the die-cavity is essential if tablets of uniform weight are to be produced. Even at low operating speeds filling of the die with 'difficult' materials may be erratic with conventional feed frames. A number of devices have been designed to give 'forced', 'assisted' or 'induced' feed of granules into the cavity. The Manesty Rotaflow feeder employs contrarotating vaned rotors in an enclosed feed frame to assist granules into the dies. Some removal of air and slight compaction of the granules in the die-cavity is obtained by the use of this feeder which is so designed that excess granules are automatically returned to the die-feed area. Gold et al. (1968) have reported that with a normal 16-station press the coefficient of weight variation for 500 mg tablets was 0.7 to 2.4 per cent when a granule with good flow properties was used and 3.4 to 3.9 per cent for a poor granule. Using an ultra high speed machine with induced die-feed they found that the coefficient of variation fell to 2 per cent or less irrespective of the type of granule, in spite of a lower tablet weight of 200 mg and a rate of production (3000 to 4000 tablets min) at least five times that attained with the conventional machine.

Removal of Air

The time taken for compression may not be sufficient for the complete removal of air from the granules in the die-cavity. The air which remains hinders inter-granule bonding and may result in capping, lamination and other difficulties.

Many rotary presses are now fitted with precompression rollers for light compaction of the granules ahead of main compressing position. In this way most of the air is removed from granule bed which is partially compacted before final compression takes place.

The introduction of devices for improving granule flow, die-filling and the removal of air has made feasible the ultra high-speed production of tablets. These devices will, undoubtedly, find wide application in the direct compression of a wider range of substances than has hitherto been possible with conventional tablet machine.

Multilayer Tablets

One further development, not directly concerned with overcoming flow and compaction problems, has been the introduction of equipment for making multi-layer and compression coated tablets. The latter are discussed in the section on coating techniques. Layer presses are used where chemically incompatible materials, or those which separate in a mixed granulation, must be presented in the same tablet. For sustained action products each layer may be formulated for different release characteristics. The presses employ three filling and compression stages found the turret and as each layer is filled into die-cavity in sequence the granules are lightly compressed to remove air. When the final layer has been deposited the whole is compressed into a firm tablet in the normal way. Since each layer is thinner than in normal tabletting, fine granules (16 mesh or smaller) must be employed. Excessive fines and lubricants must be avoided to promote good inter-layer adhesion. A sampling device is provided so that the weight of each layer may be checked without stopping the machine. For the successful production of multilayer tablets the granules must not be too dense and should compact to less than half their original volume, otherwise the depth of fill is unmanageably small and difficult to control.

Punches and Dies

These are usually fabricated from special steels, the working surface being accurately machined and highly polished to ensure proper mechanical operation and well finished tablets. For single punch machines the punches are held, firmly seated in their holders, by wedge action of the locking notches against the tips of the locking bolts; notches or circumferential channels serve the same purpose for the dies. For the manufacture of specially shaped product, such as pessaries, registration of the upper punch and the die must be exact. In the case of rotary tablet machines a key inserted in the guide prevents free rotation of the upper punch. The clearance between the upper punch and die-bore is normally 0.0013–0.004 cm (0.5–1.5 thousandsth of an inch) but for slugging this is increased of 0.008 cm to allow rapid escape of air from the granules. Fines seeping downwards between the lower punch and die-bore would become highly compacted and impede free punch movement but for a slight reduction in the shank diameter some 0.5 cm below the punch face.

In most English speaking countries and some others, punch diameters were, until recently, quoted as multiples of a thirty-second of an inch, but metric sizes have been adopted by the *British Pharmacopoeia* 1973 and *British Pharmaceutical Codex* 1973. The majority of tablets are produced with flat, flat bevelled edge or normal concave punches (Fig. 1.13) but where tablets are to be pan or film coated deep concave punches must be used to facilitate the coating process. Punch faces may be embossed so that tablets with engraved letters or other devices are produced. Diametrical scoring permits more ready subdivision of the tablet by the patient should this be required. The load which may safely be applied to punches is limited by the material from which they are fabricated and by the type of punch face. A load of 8×10^7 kg/m^2 (50 tons/in^2) is permissible for flat or normal concave steel punches but must be reduced to half this figure, or less, depending on the punch diameter and face contour where the edge of the punch face is very thin as is the case with deep concave, bevelled edge and ball punches. This is because the lateral forces developed during compression would splay the thin weak edges of these types of punches. The maximum loads quoted in Table 1.3 are average figures of the special steels used in punch manufacture; where other materials are employed the manufacturer of the punches should be consulted.

Punches and dies (tooling) must be stored, lightly oiled, in containers which prevent accidental contact. The ease of manufacture and the final appearance of the tablet depend on unblemished, highly polished working surfaces; punch edges must be sharp and free from burrs. As compaction usually occurs in the middle section of the die-bore, wear 'rings' are formed at this point and hinder tablet ejection. Inversion of the die for alternate tablet batches minimizes ringing and extends the life of the die. Tapered dies may facilitate the compaction of 'difficult' materials, as the progressive increase in clearance (about 0.004 cm in the centre to 0.008 cm at the die-face) permits more ready escape of air and gradual reduction of die-wall friction as ejection proceeds. Tungsten carbide inserts, having greater resistance to wear are particularly useful for the compaction of abrasive materials. Non-metallic tooling may be required for the compaction of corrosive substances. Agate may be employed for this purpose, for instance in the production of tablets containing mercury salts. All stations of a rotary machine must produce tablets of uniform weight and hardness. Maintenance must, therefore, ensure that all punches in a given upper or lower set are of identical length as the weight, hardness and ejection controls are common to all stations of a rotary.

The comprehensive range of tooling required for even a modest tablet manufacturing department represents a large capital investment which rapidly depreciates in the absence of proper maintenance. Additionally, the inferior tablets produced by defective punches and dies do little to enhance the reputation of the manufacturer. Swartz et al. (1962) and Swartz and Anschel (1968) indicate that extended life and improvements in the quality of tooling supplied by the manufacturer are positive advantages which may be expected from a well organized punch and die quality control programme.

Tabletting Problems

Tablets may exhibit a number of defects which are immediately apparent or, as is often the case with capping, appear only after storage. It is important therefore that the appropriate tests be applied at start of and during a production run in order that remedial action may be promptly taken.

Binding in the Die

When this occurs ejection of the tablet is difficult and is often accompanied by a characteristics 'grunting' noise; the tablet edges are rough or scored. The problem results from those conditions which give rise to high die-wall friction namely, poor lubrication, underdried granules and a dirty or blemished die. Poor lubrication includes inefficient blending of the lubricant with the granules as well as the wrong quantity or choice of this adjuvant. An alternative source of trouble is too large a clearance between the lower punch and the die-bore as a result of excessive wear. Fines seep downwards through the gap and compact to form a tough film which hinders free movement of the punch.

Picking and Sticking

Here the problem is caused by adhesion of material to the punch faces. If localized, portions of the tablet surface are seen to be missing; this is called picking. The tablet has a dull rough appearance when 'sticking' occurs due to adhesion of the tablet to the whole punch face. In either case, if not corrected, the defect worsens progressively and a layer of compacted granules builds up on the punch face. This effectively, is equivalent to an increase in punch length that causes high compaction pressure and eventual jamming of the press if not promptly rectified. The fault can usually be traced to under-dried granules, poorly maintained punch faces or the use of a lubricant lacking in anti-adherent properties.

Capping and Lamination

These faults can often be traced to inadequate removal of air from the granules in the die-cavity before and during compression. The entrapped air interferes with granule bonding while its subsequent expansion at the ejection stage detaches the top, the 'cap', of the tablet. In other cases the tablet splits into a number of layers (laminates). Excessive fines, incorrectly prepared or overdried granules or too small a top punch/die-bore clearance all hinder escape of air from the die cavity and may be the cause of capping or lamination.

A second cause of the problem is associated with due elastic compression of the tablet due to the use of too high a pressure at the compaction stage. During ejection, elastic recovery of that part of the tablet protruding from die gives rise to both lateral and longitudinal forces (Fig. 1.21) which rupture the intergranule bonds and the tablet then caps or laminates. Finally, on occasion, these faults may be traced to distortion of the tablet during ejection from a 'ringed' die or to the use of burred punches.

Excessive Weight Variation

This problem is associated with poor granule flow and separation of granule constituents. Thus granules which are under-dried, too large (see wet-screening, p. 274), too fine or contain a large proportion of fines, are incorrectly lubricated or comprise elements with widely differing densities or sizes, may all be suspected as possible causes of excessive weight variation. If the fault occurs with a rotary machine and granule flow appears to be satisfactory, then it is worth considering the possibility that one or more punches are of different length to the others due, for example, to inadvertent mixing of bottom punch sets. Occasionally, 'difficult' granules are produced in spite of care in processing and tablets of more uniform weight and improved appearance may be obtained at a slower machine speed that allows more time for die-cavity filling.

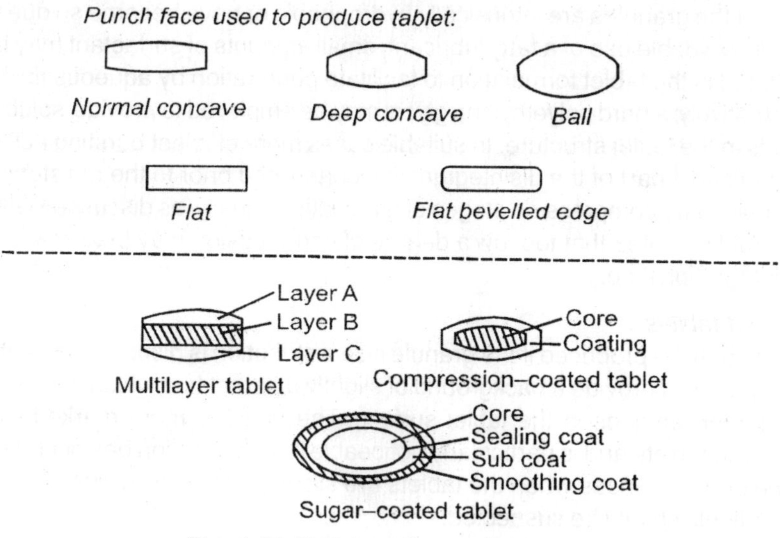

Fig. 1.13. Tablet profiles and structure.

Fissured or Pitted Surface

If this is not due to sticking or picking the most likely cause is the presence of granules which are uniform in size and lack the fines necessary to fill the voids. Generally, the problem may be cured by the use of granules with a broader size distribution but care must be taken to see that this does not lead to other problems such as capping or lack of uniformity in the tablet weight.

Soft Tablets

Apart from the use of too low a compaction pressure this problem usually arises when granules have been inadequately dried or the intergranule bonds have been weakened either by traces of air in the granule bed (insufficient to cause capping) or by excessive proportions of fatty lubricant such as magnesium stearate.

Protracted Disintegration

In this case the tablet either rapidly breaks down to form large particles that persist for a long period, or fine particles are produced, but the overall disintegration time is excessive. The fault can usually be traced to:

(i) an adhesive granulating agent which is too 'strong'.

(ii) conditions that inhibit the penetration of water; high degree of compaction, hydrophobic tablet ingredients, excessive quantities of fatty lubricant or gelling of the granulating agent, or

(iii) inefficient bursting action resulting from the use of the wrong type of disintegrating agent, or insufficient of it.

If the granules are intrinsically hydrophobic or have become so due to the unavoidable use of a fatty lubricant, small amounts of surfactant may be included in the tablet formulation to facilitate penetration by aqueous fluids. Alternatively, a hard polyethylene glycol may be employed to provide 'soluble' points in the tablet structure. In suitable cases more efficient bursting action is obtained if part of the disintegrant is incorporated prior to the moistening or preliminary compression stages of granulation. Finally, as discussed later, it should be noted that too *low* a degree of compression may lead to a long disintegration time.

Mottled Tablets

These may be produced if the granule size distribution is discontinuous; the finer particles provide a background of slightly different hue which shows up the larger granules in the tablet surface. The effect is more marked with coloured tablets and is particularly noticeable if dye migration has occurred. If the problem arises when the tablets are stored, instability of one of more ingredients should be suspected.

Variation of Medicament Content

Standards will eventually be set for the drug content of individual tablets. If the content shows excessive variation and those factors contributing to weight variation can be eliminated as a cause, the most likely sources of trouble are migration of solute, physical adsorption with separation at some stage of the production process and inefficient mixing.

Drug Instability

This topic is discussed in detail elsewhere in this volume. The majority of air-dry drugs and tablet excipients contain water and this is also deliberately added, and may not be completely removed, in the moist granulation process. Moisture content must be controlled not only for purely technical reasons associated with the physical processes of tablet production, but also to ensure drug stability. The subject was reviewed by Griffiths (1969).

TABLET COATING

Tablet coatings perform one or more of the following functions. They may: *mask* the taste of unpalatable drugs, *protect* the drug from deterioration due to light, oxygen or moisture, *separate* incompatible ingredients, *control* the release of medicament in the gastrointestinal tract, and *provide* an elegant or distinctive finish to the tablet.

The materials used for coating may largely comprise sucrose (sugar coating), water-soluble film-forming polymers (film coating) or substances which are soluble in the intestinal secretions but not in those of the stomach (enteric coating). These types of coating can all be applied by the pan or fluid-bed processes; the compression coating technique is suitable for sugar and enteric coatings, but not for film coating.

Pan Coating

In this process the tablets are tumbled in a bowl or pan which rotates about an axis inclined about 30° to the horizontal (Fig. 1.14). With the correct pan load a three dimensional circulation is established and sufficient coating solution is added to wet the tablet surfaces. Internal baffles (Sutaria 1968) or hand manipulation of the wetted tablets ensures that the solution is evenly distributed and a satisfactory tumbling action maintained while the coating is dried by a stream of warmed air. Small amount of dusting powder may be applied to reduce tackiness and cohesion of the tablets during the drying stage. The volume of coating solution for each application is critical;inadequatewetting leads to irregular coating, whereas with too large a volume the tablets agglomerate and do not tumble well. The cycle of alternate wetting and drying is continued to build up a coating of the required properties. Initially, the tablets are subject to considerable abrasive action and for this reason should be more highly compressed than the corresponding uncoated tablets.

Sugar Coatings

This traditional coating imparts a smooth, rounded, elegant appearance to the tablet. Stephenson and Smith (1951) have given a detailed discussion on the composition of sugar coatings.

Sealing. After all dust has been removed from the tablets a dextrin, gelatin or acacia coat may be applied to ensure good coating adhesion. Where protection against the effects of water in subsequent coating solutions is required a 30 to 50 per cent solution of shellac in alcohol or other suitable solvent is employed for sealing, care being taken to avoid over generous application as this leads to a prolongation of the disintegration time.

Fig. 1.14. Production model pan coating machine. The diameter of the bowl is about 1 m (Manesty Machines Ltd.).

Subcoating. To minimize the amount of material which must be used to round the tablet edges the cores are made on deep concave punches. The subcoat is built up in successive layers by wetting the tablets with an adhesive solution, dusting with filler and then thoroughly drying, as retained moisture may cause later cracking of the coat or deterioration of the core. The subcoating solution is usually an aqueous solution of sucrose to which is added acacia, gelatin or both, to impart adhesive properties. Talc and precipitated calcium carbonate are widely used in the subcoating filler together with some sucrose and a small proportion of acacia. A small proportion of inert filler, e.g., talc, may be added to the subcoating solution, which, if it contains gelatin, should be used warm to avoid gelling. Too heavy an application of filler must be avoided as the excess forms 'granules' with the coating solution and these interfere with the formations of a smooth subcoat. This stage of the process is continued until the tablets have a rounded appearance and the edges are well covered. When complete, the tablets are removed from the pan and thoroughly dried.

Smoothing and polishing. The application of a smoothing solution (60 per cent sucrose in water is satisfactory) causes limited wetting of the subcoat, which has been hardened by drying, so that it is smoothed out by the tumbling action. Soluble dye or a lake colour may be added to the smoothing solution if a coloured coating is required. As soon as the coat has become comparatively smooth the volume of smoothing solution per application should be reduced and the tablets dried without the aid of heat. In the final stages, tumbling is limited by 'inching' rather than rotating the bowl so that the coating is not scratched or otherwise damaged. At this stage the tablets will have a perfectly smooth but matt appearance and are thoroughly dried before polishing in a pan specially set aside for the job and coated with a beeswax-carnauba wax or similar waxy mixture.

Film Coating

Sugar coating doubles the weight and increases the size of a tablet and this is obviously undesirable if the tablet, in the uncoated state, is already large. Film coating provides an alternative means of masking the taste of the medicament and providing protection against adverse climatic conditions without significantly altering the tablet weight or size. The obvious advantages of excluding water from the coating process may be secured with film-forming polymers, such as ethylcellulose, polyvinylpyrrolidone or hydroxymethyl propyl cellulose, that are soluble in both water and anhydrous organic solvents. Some 3 to 10 per cent of the foregoing materials can be dissolved in an acetone-alcohol mixture together with 5 to 10 per cent of diethyl phthalate or other plasticizer to produce a film coating solution which may be applied by the pan technique. The plasticizer stops the film becoming brittle with age. Methylene chloride is often added to the solvent to reduce fire hazards, while undue absorption of expensive film forming agent is prevented by the prior application of a shellac sealing coat to the core tablets.

Enteric Coating

Tablets are enteric coated if the medicament is decomposed in the acid secretions of the stomach, if it causes gastric irritation, or if it is intended to exert its main effect only on the intestine. Some official tablets coated in this way include those containing biscodyl, bismuth and emetine iodide, and erythromycin. Enteric coatings resist the acid conditions of the stomach but readily dissolve in the more nearly natural fluids of the small intestine. They are also used in the formulation of sustained action preparations as the release of medicament is delayed by the time taken for the tablet to pass from the mouth to the intestine.

Formalized gelatin, keratin, salol, shellac, sandarac, stearic acid and cetyl alcohol have all been used to produce enteric coatings but are either difficult to apply or erratic in their action. The compositions of the fluids in the gastrointestinal tract are not constant but vary with time and from person to person. It is clearly important that the enteric action shall largely be independent of such variations in compositions. Cellulose acetate phthalate is widely used for enteric coating and was reported by Antonides and DeKay (1953) to be the only cellulose derivative of the fourteen evaluated that was satisfactory for this purpose. Only one of the phthalic acid carboxyl groups is attached to the cellulose, the other being free for reaction. The polymer dissolves in a variety of solvents, gives water-soluble salts with a number of bases and forms coatings which are insoluble in, but slightly permeable to, water (Malm et al. 1951). An important feature is the solubility of cellulose acetate phthalate films in buffers having a pH as low as 5.8; thus the requirements for enteric action are a medium with a pH higher than this value which can contribute ions to the coating to form a soluble salt. Such conditions are found in the intestine but not in the stomach.

In addition to 5 to 15 per cent of cellulose acetate phthalate the enteric coating solution may contain a plasticizer such as castor oil or butyl stearate together with a soluble or a lake dye if a coloured finish is required. The materials are dissolved or dispersed in a volatile solvent comprising alcohol, acetone, and, to reduce flammability, methylene chloride.

Automated Pan Coating

Successful use of the pan coating technique depends, in large measure, on the skill of the operator: it is also time consuming. Due to their higher volatility the solvents used for film coating permit rapid drying of tablets after each addition of the coating solution. As with moist granulation, spraying rather than pouring the coating solution is a more controllable technique that relies less on the operator's skills and which is more readily adapted to automatic control. In the case of enteric coated tablets, performance is determined by the thinnest part of the film and for reproducible characteristics between and within batches the coating must be of known uniform thickness. According to Lachman and Cooper (1963), enteric coatings complying with the foregoing criteria may be obtained by means of an automated film coating process. The tablets are tumbled in a baffled pan and a solution of cellulose acetate phthalate together with fillers in suspension is sprayed on to the tablets in repetitive 'bursts' alternating with longer drying periods. The spray gun for applying the coating solution and the hot or cold air flow for removing solvent are controlled by a punched tape programming device. The coating time for an 85 kilogram batch of tablets (90 minutes) is half that required by the corresponding manual procedure, and the weight of the coating is reduced and is more uniform.

Fully automated equipment for pan coating is now commercially available. Provision is made for programmed control of the coating composition, spray application and drying air-flow at each stage of the process. The different paths taken by tablets in a pear-shaped bowl leads to a lack of uniformity in the thickness of coating applied to tablets within the batch. This problem is avoided in the Manesty Autocota by the adoption of a cylindrical coating vessel rotating about a horizontal rather than inclined axis.

Fluid-bed Coating

Wurster (1959) first described the application of sugar or film coatings to tablets suspended in an air stream. In that equipment the coating solution is introduced into the fluidizing airstream at the base of a tall vertical tube in which tablets circulate as they are coated. Evaporated solvent and air are removed at the top of the chamber. The fluid-bed moist granulation equipment described earlier has now been modified by the makers for fluid-bed coating. As the tablets circulate in the air stream they are subjected to considerable abrasive action and for this reason they are compressed with extra firmness on punches which give a well rounded profile.

Compression Coating

As noted earlier it is desirable on occasion to separate tablet ingredients to avoid incompatabilities, to facilitate manufacture or to produce a sustained action product. Layer tablets provide an acceptable means for ingredient separation but the protective effect of the coat enveloping the tablet is lacking. It is not an easy matter to ensure a sugar coat of the same thickness for all tablets in a batch by pan coating and although reasonable variation in coat thickness and weight is not significant in plain sugar coating such variation cannot be tolerated if the coat contains a potent medicament. The idea of applying granular coating materials to a preformed core was conceived by Noyes in 1896 but could not be commercially exploited until the problem of core centration and the automatic rejection of coreless tablets had been solved. The expected advantages of a compression coating process are:

(i) core tablets are not subjected to abrasive action and need not be especially hard,
(ii) the process is 'anhydrous' and sealing coats are not required,
(iii) the disintegration time of a coated tablet can be comparable with that of the uncoated variety, due to the above,
(iv) good control of coating weight can be obtained,
(v) chemically incompatible ingredients may be separated,
(vi) the core and coat may be formulated for different properties e.g., for a sustained action tablet the coating would provide the prompt dose and the core the sustaining dose,

(vii) the process is continuous, completely mechanized and removes much of the element of skill from tablet coating.

Compression Coating Machines

The essential stages of coating by compression are (Fig. 1.15), deposition of the bottom fill of coating granules, transfer and centration of the core tablet, deposition of the side and top fill and finally compression to bond the coat to the core. The machine described by Whitehouse (1954), the Kilian Prescoter, used preformed cores which were fed into holes on the periphery of a transfer disc and deposited on the lower fill of coating granules as the lower punch dropped in readiness for the top fill. The core was centred by a light tap of the top punch, the top fill deposited and the coating bonded to the core by compression. The force developed during compaction in the presence of a core was sufficient to cause slight deflection of the overload release but failed to do so in the absence of a core. A switch connected to the overload release provided an electrical signal which, when fed to a memory unit, actuated a gate on the collection chute such that coreless tablets were rejected.

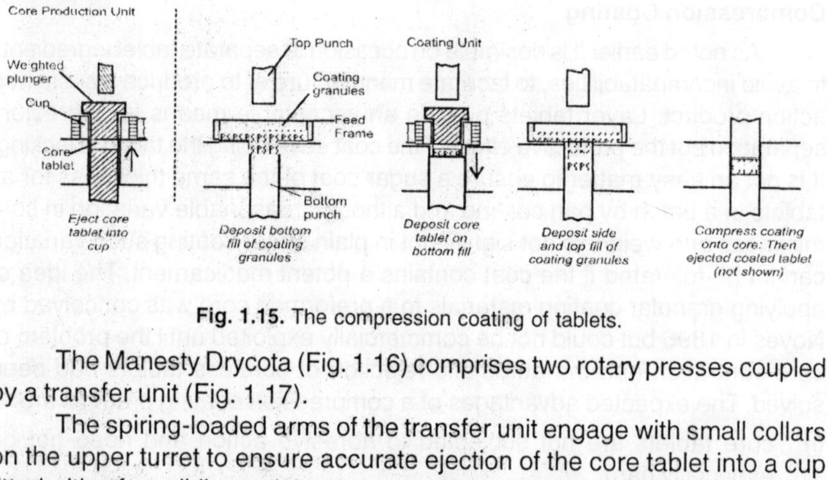

Fig. 1.15. The compression coating of tablets.

The Manesty Drycota (Fig. 1.16) comprises two rotary presses coupled by a transfer unit (Fig. 1.17).

The spiring-loaded arms of the transfer unit engage with small collars on the upper turret to ensure accurate ejection of the core tablet into a cup fitted with a free sliding weighted plunger. Next, the cup passes over a 'bridge' where dust is removed to avoid contamination of the coating granules and then engages with the collar on the upper turret of the coating press. As the bottom punch drops, the tablet is pushed out of the cup on to the centre of the bottom fill of coating granules by the action of the weighted plunger. The cavity is then filled with granules for the sides and top of the coating, which are bonded to the core by compression. As the cups pass round the transfer unit the plungers are examined by feelers which operate microswitches. If a cup fails to pick up or deposit a core at the appropiate stage in the cycle the signal from the microswitches initiates action for the rejection of coreless tablets.

Requirements for Core Tablets and Coating Granules

Core tablets should be prepared from rather large granules and should be lightly compressed. The surface of a soft tablet made from large granules is somewhat porous and provides a good 'key' for adhesion of the coating. There is a second reason for light compression of the core tablet. Residual stresses in a tablet are not instantaneously relieved when that tablet is ejected from the die. Large residual stresses induced by a high degree of compression may be sufficient to split the coating some time after manufacture has been completed.

Fig.1.16. Compression coating machine. The core tablet formed by the left hand unit is carried by the central transfer unit to the coating press or the right.

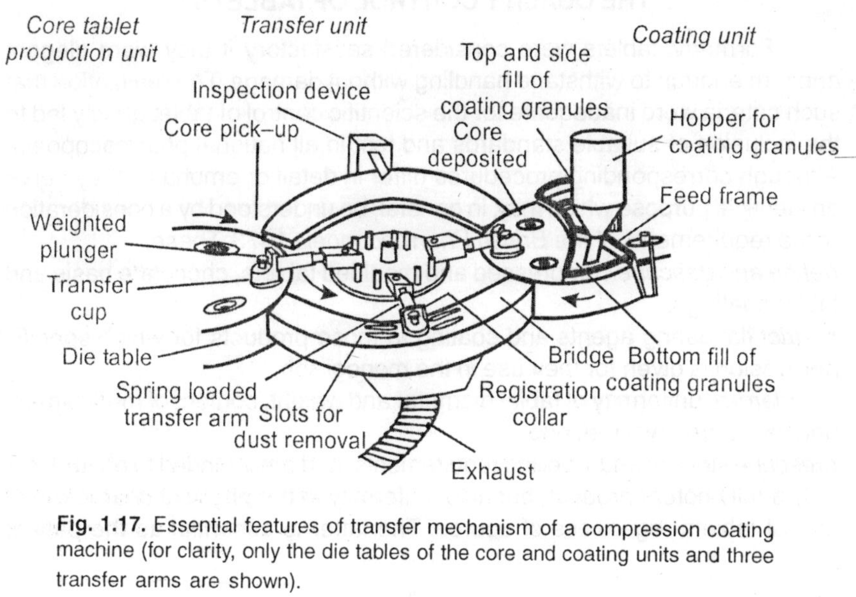

Fig. 1.17. Essential features of transfer mechanism of a compression coating machine (for clarity, only the die tables of the core and coating units and three transfer arms are shown).

The gap between the core and die-wall should be least 0.13 cm to facilitate uniform deposition of coating granules round the edges of the coretablet and hence to ensure adequate coating strength. For these reasons too, the granule size should not exceed a quarter of the edge coating thickness. On the other hand, excessive amounts of fines or fatty lubricants should be avoided, as these lead to poor coating strength and poor adhesion to the core.

Performance

Provided the requirements for edge thickness are met, the weight of the coating is maintained with considerable precision and may be varied over a wide range. It may be noted that the official test for weight variation applies to compression coated tablets but not to those having a film or conventional sugar coat. Centrifugal and tangential forces due to turret rotation may slant the bottom fill of coating granules and displace the core from its central position. Lachman et al. (1966) concluded that coating granules which gave minimum weight variation also tended to give less core displacement.

Coating may be formulated for a wide range of properties but of these, enteric coatings are of particular interest. Blubaugh et al. (1958) have described the preparation of coating granules containing triethanolamine cellulose acetate phthalate which, when applied by compression, produce a coating with enteric properties. In a more recent paper Srinivas et al. (1966) have reported on the use of a number of carboxylated polymers for the production of entire coating granules.

THE QUALITY CONTROL OF TABLETS

Formerly, tablets were considered satisfactory if they were elegant and firm enough to withstand handling without damage. The realization that such criteria were inadequate for the scientific control of tablet quality led to the inclusion of suitable standards and test in all national pharmacopoeia. Although corresponding procedures differ in detail or emphasis they serve an identical purpose which may, in general, be understood by a consideration of the requirements of the *British Pharmacopoeia* 1973. These:

define and describe compressed and moulded tablets, chocolate basis and tablet coatings,

restrict flavouring agents and coating to those products for which specific permission is given for their use in the monograph,

standardize uniformity of tablet diameter and weight, content of medicament and disintegration time, and

prescribe storage and labelling requirements, and are intended to ensure, not only a fully potent product, but also uniformity in the physical characters of official tablets regardless of source. The latter is essential as the patient quickly perceives, and is concerned about, differences in the appearances of nominally identical tablets.

Uniformity of Diameter

The standard specifies the punch diameter to be employed for a given tablet and the permitted tolerance on the specified size, thus securing dimensional uniformity between tablets of the same kind from different manufacturers. The standards apply only to uncoated and compression coated tablets. They make allowance for the manufacturing tolerances in die fabrication and for tool wear by allowing a deviation about the stated diameter. Generally, the manufacturing tolerance is proportionately less for large than for small dies and the deviation is reduced from ± 5 per cent to ± 3 per cent for diameters in excess of 12.5 mm.

Tests for Uniformity of Weight and for Medicament Content

The combined effect of these tests is to ensure that all tablets in a batch are, within reasonable limits, of the same potency. A perfect manufacturing procedure would yield a batch of tablets having identical weight and medicament content; in practice the values of these parameters for individual tablets deviate about the mean values for the whole batch. Such deviation will be of acceptable magnitude if correctly formulated and prepared granules are compressed on properly maintained equipment but will be larger, and probably unacceptable, if the converse conditions apply.

Ideally, the quality of a batch of tablets would be assessed by determining the potency of each tablet in a truly representative sample. The analysis of a large number of tablets by conventional means would be both costly and time-consuming while automated techniques for the analysis of the majority of drugs have still to be developed. At the present time therefore the reasonable assumption is made that the variation of the weight of individual tablets is a valid indication of the corresponding variation in the drug content.

Test for Uniformity of Weight

This test does not apply to sugar or enteric coated tablets. The weight of each tablet and the average weight of all tablets in the sample are determined. The standard, summarized in Table 1.6, limits the number of tablets in the sample which may deviate from the average weight by more than specified amounts. Rogers (1956), on the basis of production data then available, showed that the coefficient of variation of tablet weight was reasonably constant for tablets weighing more than 0.2 to 0.3 g but rose steeply for smaller tablets; a similar observation has been made by Smith et al. (1963). This is not unexpected as there is greater practical difficulty in ensuring the flow, die-filling and air release characteristics necessary for low weight variation, with the finer granules which must be used for the production of small tablets. This factor is recognized by making the weight variation tolerances wider for small than for large tablets.

Twenty tablets represent a very small fraction of a manufacturing batch that will generally exceed 10 000, and may be as large as 1000 000. If the tablet weights in a batch of, say, 0.3 g tablets are normally distributed and 10 per cent deviate from the average weight by more than 5 per cent, then 0.1 per cent of the tablets in that batch could be expected to deviate by more than 10 per cent from the average weight. Smith (1955) has calculated that there is a 67 per cent probability that the examination of a sample of twenty tablets by the official method would lead to the acceptance of such a batch. With a rotary machine, if the weight variation derives from a few punches of significantly different length from the others in the set, the foregoing calculations that are based on an assumed normal distribution do not apply. Nevertheless, the unsatisfactory nature of a batch of tablets produced under these conditions should be relaxed as indicated in Table 1.7. This table may

TABLE 1.6

SUMMARY OF THE BP 1973 TEST FOR THE UNIFORMITY OF TABLET WEIGHT

Number of tablets in sample	Average weight of tablets in sample	Percentage deviation about average weight	
	80 mg or less	± 10.0	± 15.0
	More than 80 mg, less than 250 mg	± 7.5	± 12.5
20			
	250 mg or more	± 5.0	± 10.0
	Number of tablets in the sample that may deviate by more than the above percentages	Not more than two	None
	80 mg or less	± 10.0	± 15.0
	More than 80 mg, less than 250 mg	± 7.5	± 12.5
10			
	250 mg or more	± 5.0	± 10.0
	Number of tablet in the sample that may deviate by more than the above percentages	Not more than one	None

intended to detect abnormal weight variation. While the stringency of the official test could be improved, for instance, by specifying narrower weight tolerances, it is important to remember that the discrimination level must provide a reasonable balance between the risks to the patient arising from over or under dosage and the performance that can reasonably be expected with the currently available manufacturing methods. Although the manufacturer must ensure that the completed batches of tablets comply with official requirements, samples would be examined during production as an extra check on quality and for the early detection and rectification of any faults which may develop.

Content of Medicament

The standards are framed to take into account processing difficulties, variations in the purity of the drug, accuracy of the assay methods and the size of the sample relative to that of the typical manufacturing batch. The stated limits for drug content given in the individual monographs apply to the examination of a sample of 20 tablets; where less than this number is available the sample must comprise at least 5 tablets and the limits are relaxed as indicated in Table 1.7. This table may be used directly where the limits specified in the monograph are *between* 90 and 110 per cent. Thus, for a sample of 20 Promazine Tablets each containing 25 mg of Promazine Hydrochloride the monograph limits are 92.5 to 107.5 per cent of the nominal content of drug

TABLE 1.7

BP 1973 STANDARD FOR THE CONTENT OF MEDICAMENT IN TABLETS

Sample size	Instruction	Weight of drug in each tablet		
		0.12 g or less	More than 0.12 g Less than 0.30 g	0.3 g or more
15	Subtract from lower limit	0.2	0.2	0.1
	Add to upper limit	0.3	0.3	0.2
10	Subtract from lower limit	0.7	0.5	0.2
	Add to upper limit	0.8	0.6	0.4
5	Subtract from lower limit	1.6	1.2	0.8
	Add to upper limit	1.8	1.5	1.0

Allowances to be made when examining samples containing less than 20 tablets where the monograph limits for content of medicament between 90 and 110 per cent.

and would be widened in the case of a sample of 5 tablets to 90.9 to 109.3 per cent. To comply with official requirements the tablets must therefore contain between 22.73 and 27.33 mg of drug.

Where the monograph limits fall outside the 90 to 110 per cent range the *Pharmacopoeia* directs that proportionately larger allowances should be made for samples of less than 20 tablets. A method for the calculation has been suggested by Hadgraft (1945).

It is now recognized that although a *sample* of tablet may comply with given standards for drug content, this may not be so for *individual tablets* within that sample. From theoretical considerations, Train (1960) concluded that if 20 tablets are examined and as a whole comply with ± 10 per cent limits, a variation as large as ± 40 per cent might be expected if each tablet was separately assayed. This variation could be due to solute migration and adsorption, granule separation and other effects. As discussed earlier, such variation is more likely to occur where the weight of the medicament is only a small proportion of the total tablet weight. Even a reduction in the proportion of medicament from 90 per cent to 23 per cent doubled the standard deviation of drug content for the tablets examined by Smith et al. (1963). On the other hand, Robinson et al. (1968) failed to detect a deviation greater than ± 15 per cent when examining over 1000 imipramine and desipramine tablets and capsules. In a number of cases the United States *Pharmacopoeia* includes a standard for the drug content of individual tablets; Feldman (1969) has indicated that the number of products affected by this standard will be increased in the future. The BP 1973 requires that, for tablets and capsules described in its monographs, no gross deviation from the stated amount of medicament is permissible when each dose unit is individually assayed. The term 'gross deviation' is not defined. If a formal standard for drug content per tablet is included in future editions of the *Pharmacopoeia*, automated analytical techniques of sufficient rapidity, sensitivity, accuracy and precision will be required. It is evident from the review by Kuzel et al. (1969) that considerable progress has been made in the field of automated analysis since 1960 when Stephenson concluded that for Digoxin Tablets the methods of mixing were probably superior to the then available assay methods.

Test for Disintegration

Methods

Features common to the tests described in the literature are: an aqueous disintegration medium, agitation of the tablet or medium to simulate peristalsis and means for recognizing the end point, that is, complete disintegration. The many proposed methods may be classified into three types:

(i) The tablet, supported on a frame, is immersed in water and the time determined for a weighted wire to pass through the tablet (Berry 1939). The method was abandoned because it gave anomalous results if the tablet disintegrated into large particles or yielded a hard core (Berry and Smith 1944). This stricture on the method might not be so relevant at the present time when, for efficient drug release, it is considered desirable that a tablet should disintegrate completely into very fine particles.

(ii) A tube filled with water except for a small headspace and containing the tablet, is rotated end over end (Berry and Smith 1944; Mapstone 1952).

(iii) A wire mesh cage (Hoyle 1946) or a tube closed by a wire mesh at the lower end (Prance et al. 1946) is moved up and down in the disintegration medium so that the tablets are constantly agitated. Disintegration is complete when all particles from the disintegrated tablet pass freely through the mesh.

The reader is referred to the BP 1973 for details of the official apparatus which, essentially, is that described by Prance and coworkers. Tablets may fail the test because, for instance, they form a gummy mass in contact with water or a resistant core is left after the rest of the tablet has disintegrated. If tablets fail the test for any reason, it may be repeated with a guided disc (Fig. 1.18)

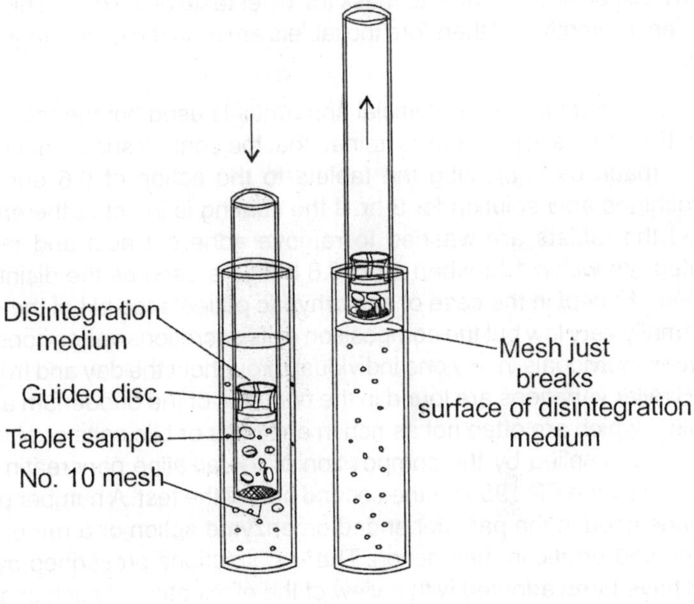

Fig 1.18. Essential features of apparatus for the BP 1968 disintegration test showing guide disc in use.

placed in the disintegration tube above the tablet sample. The light percussive action of disc as it rises and falls in the tube assists the breakdown of the tablets.

Requirements

Uncoated and compression coated tablets. The general requirement is that these shall disintegrate within 15 min. There are a number of exceptions. Tablets which are to be dissolved in water prior to administration e.g., Sodium

Citrate, Soluble Aspirin, must disintegrate within 3 min. Calcium Lactate Tablets harden on storage and 30 min is allowed for these. The same period is specified for Thyroid Tablets and Prepared Digitalis Tablets as these form a gummy mass which is not easily persuaded through the mesh even with the aid of a guided disc. The test does not apply to products which should dissolve slowly in the mouth, e.g. lozenges, Compound Sodium Bicarbonate Tablets, Glyceryl Trinitrate Tablets, or to those which must be masticated, e.g. Phenolphthalein, Aluminium Hydroxide, or to Effervescent Potassium Tablets BPC. The official apparatus is not used for the latter; they are required to dissolve completely within 3 min when placed in water at 20°.

Sugar and film coated tablets. As these coatings may increase the disintegration time, 1 h is allowed. One exception is Quinalbarbitone Tablets which must be sugar coated to mask the bitter taste of the drug. This hypnotic acts very promptly and therefore the tablets are required to disintegrate within 15 min.

Enteric coated tablets. The official apparatus is used but the test is carried out in two stages. It is first ascertained that the coating should not rupture in the stomach by subjecting the tablets to the action of 0.6 per cent v/v hydrochloric acid solution for 3 hr. If the coating is intact at the end of this period the tablets are washed to remove adherent acid and must then disintegrate within 1 hr when a pH 6.8 buffer is used as the disintegrating medium. Except in the case of achlorhydric patients the pH of the stomach is normally very low but the composition of its secretions varies considerably between individuals in any one individual throughout the day and from day to day. Similar variations are found in the contents of the duodenum and small intestine which are often not as rich in enzymes or bile salts or of as high a pH as was implied by the composition of the alkaline pancreatin solution specified by the BP 1963 for the second part of the test. A number of enteric coatings used in the past depended on enzyme action or a rather high pH and proved erratic in their action. The test solutions prescribed by the BP 1968 have been adopted with a view of the elimination of such coatings.

Comments on the Test

The choice of water as the disintegrating medium is open to criticism. Among others Abbott et al. (1959) observed that the addition of mucoid substances to the test solution had a marked effect on disintegration time, which was often doubled and on occasion increased by a factor of 16. However, as Hartley (1950) has commented, the selection of 15 min for the disintegration time of uncoated tablets is, itself somewhat arbitrary and may be quite unrelated to the rate at which the drug is absorbed. Generally, prompt action is required but the optional coating of, for example, Benzylpenicillin Tablets leads to the anomalous situation that the permitted maximum disintegration time may be 15 or 60 min depending on whether uncoated or coated tablets have been supplied to the patient. Benzylpenicillin Tablets (Ashby et al. 1954), those of Quinalbarbitone and a number of others (Howard 1951) can be sugar coated without extending the disintegration time beyond 15 min. The coating methods used for these tablets could, presumably, be more widely employed with the consequent potential advantage of more prompt therapeutic action. It is well known that although a tablet may comply with official requirements, the particles freely passing the mesh of the disintegration tube may remain intact for periods in excess of 15 min. Furthermore a number of factors, such as the physical state of the medicament used to produce the tablet, may have a marked effect on therapeutic response. For these reasons it is probably the dissolution rather than the disintegration behaviour which should be tested.

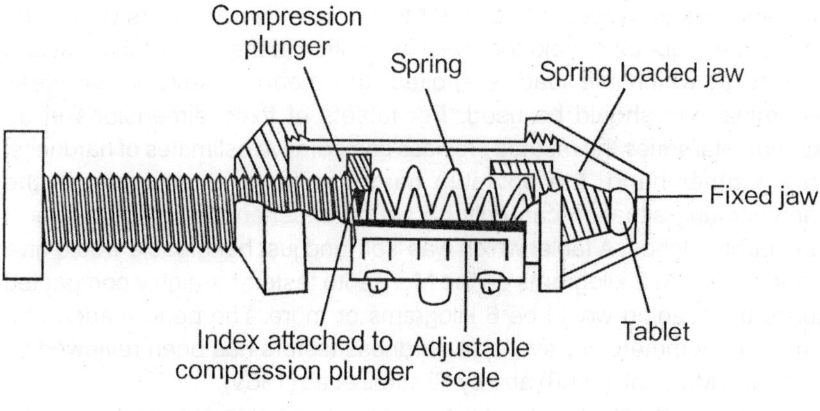

Fig. 1.19. The Monsanto tablet hardness tester.

Colour

Rolfe (1956) has argued the case for and against the addition of colourants to tablets. Such arguments were, presumably, involved in the decision to remove all former restrictions, in the BP 1968, but the BPC 1973 still prohibits the use of colours except for specific tablets and those which are enteric or compression coated. The colour to be employed for a given tablet is not stated in either book of standards. Even if the proportion of a named colourant were to be specified for a given tablet, considerable difficulties would still arise when attempting to standardize the final shade and depth of colour as these are markedly affected by processing conditions. The problem is obviously more acute if the same product is to be produced by a number of manufacturers.

Hardness

Although there is no official test for tablet hardness this property must be controlled during production to ensure that the product is firm enough to withstand handling without breaking, chipping or crumbling and yet not so hard that the disintegration time is unduly prolonged. Most testers apply a load to the edges of the tablet across a diameter. The load is gradually increased until the tablet fractures, the value of the load at this point (the crushing force) giving a measure of the hardness of the tablet. In the Monsanto Hardness Tester (Fig. 1.19) the tablet is held between a fixed and a moving jaw. The force applied to the edge of the tablet is gradually increased by turning the compression screw. The body of the instrument carries an adjustable scale which can be set to zero against an index mark fixed to the compression plunger when the tablet is lightly held between the jaws. With the Strong Cobb tester the load is applied pneumatically, while a pliers mechanism is employed in the Pfizer tester. To minimize errors due to the small force required to hold the tablet in position at the start of the test and the rate at which the load is applied, the mean of several hardness determinations should be used. For tablets of fixed dimensions in an experimental series the method provides comparative estimates of hardness. On the other hand, the optimum hardness for a given tablet in the manufacturing situation can only be set by experience extending over a number of batches. A tablet which was 'soft' and just handleable would give a reading of 1 to 2 kilograms on the Monsanto tester; for highly compacted tablets the reading would be 6 kilograms or more. The performance of a number of commercially available hardness testers has been reviewed by Brook and Marshall (1968) and by Ritschel et al. (1969).

Tablets are usually subjected to a second type of test which, essentially, measures the surface hardness. The Vickers test measures the size of the indentation produced on the tablet surface by a specially shaped loaded point. More usually the tablets are tumbled in a controlled manner and the change in the average weight of the tablets determined after a specified length of treatment. Such a test provides an indication of the likely edge damage that would occur when the tablets are handled during packaging and dispensing. The equipment designed by Webster and Van Abbe (1955) uses a vertical jogging action, whereas in the Roche Friabilator the tablets drop through a fixed distance during each revolution of a horizontally disposed plastic drum. The permissible loss in weight is obviously set by production experience, but with the Friabilator is usually in the range 1 to 5 per cent for 10 min treatment. Incipient capping and lamination usually show up on a tumbling test.

THEORETICAL STUDIES IN TABLETTING TECHNOLOGY

Although a great deal of information on the practical aspects of tabletting had appeared in the literature prior to 1952, very few papers had been concerned with theoretical studies. In that year, however, Higuchi and his associates (1952, 1953, 1954) published the first in a series of papers relating to the physics of tablet compression. Subsequently, as may be seen from the extensive bibliographies of Evans and Train (1963, 1964), many workers have reported the results of studies in this field.

The Compaction Process

Both tablet machines and ram presses have been used to investigate the compaction behaviour of pharmaceutical substances. Pressure in the range 300 to 3000 kg/cm^2 are usual for tablet machines, but the upper limit may be higher for mechanical, or hydraulic ram presses. The use of flat-faced punches simplifies subsequent treatment of the data. Where the time taken for compression is short, as with the tablet machine, transducers must be used to convert the compaction forces, punch displacements, etc. into electrical signals which can be recorded, usually by an ultraviolet oscillograph. The necessary instrumentation has been described by Higuchi et al. (1952, 1954a), Shotton and Ganderton (1960a), Shotton et al. (1963), Goodhart el al. (1968) and by other workers. Fig. 1.20 shows typical results that are obtained using an instrumented tablet machine.

The downwards thrust of the top punch in the die-bore during compaction causes movement of material relative to the wall of the die. The movement is resisted by frictional effects, in part within the bed of material but mainly between that material and the die-wall. As a result, the maximum force transmitted to the lower punch (F_b) is less than the maximum force (F_a) applied by the top punch to the contents of the die-cavity by an amount F_d' that is, the force 'lost' to the die-wall. As compaction also squeezes the compacting material into close contact with the wall of the die this latter experiences a maximum radial force F_r. Even when the top punch has been removed from the die, residual stresses within the tablet give rise to a load normal to die-wall and therefore an ejection force, maximum value F_e' must be applied to the compact by the lower punch to overcome friction and initiate ejection. The extent to which the material in the die has been compacted may be evaluated from the relative volume (V_r), relative density (ρ_r), or porosity (ε) of the tablet. By loading the edges of the tablet across a diameter the minimum crushing force (F_c), just sufficient to rupture the tablet, may be found. If, as is often the case, the tablet dimensions are maintained in an experimental series, F_c provides a comparative measure of tablet hardness. The foregoing parameters, together with a number of others commonly used in tabletting theory, are defined in Table 1.8.

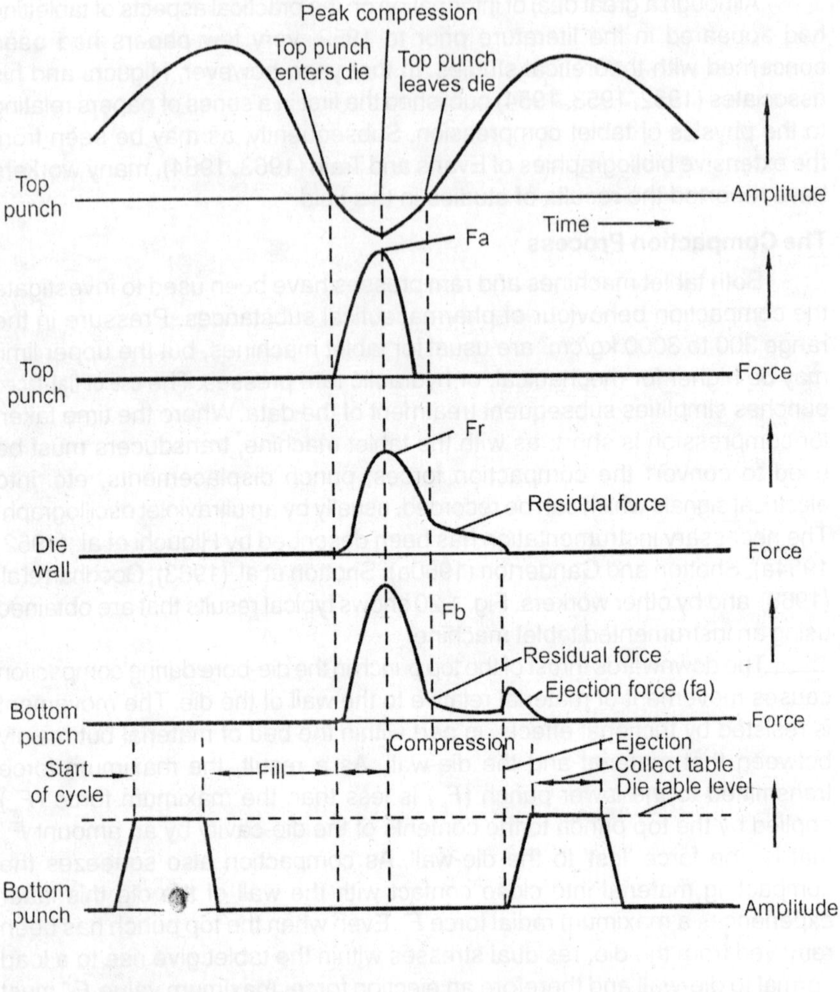

Fig. 1.20. Punch displacements and forces developed during tablet compression.

By finding the values of the parameters described in the previous paragraph at a number of pre-selected maximum upper punch pressures the compaction behaviour of a substance may be studied. Higuchi et al. (1953) determined these values for sulphathiazole compacts made in a ram press. In each case the upper punch pressure (P_a) was raised to its preselected maximum value over a period of 20 to 60 s. Whereas the logarithm of the disintegration time was found to be proportional to P_a' the crushing force (F_c)

was linearly related to log P_a. Thus, the compaction pressure had a much greater effect on the disintegration time than on hardness as is shown in Table 1.9. The porosity of the tablets progressively decreased as the pressure was increased but the specific area rose to a maximum at about 1600 kg/cm^2 and subsequently decreased. This was attributed to fragmentation of granules during the initial stages of compaction followed by bonding of the freshly formed surfaces at higher pressures. Further studies with aspirin, lactose and sulphadiazine (Higuchi et al. 1954b) gave results qualitatively similar to those obtained with sulphathiazole.

Train (1956) compacted alternate layers of normal and coloured magnesium carbonate. When the die-wall was lubricated with graphite the layers compressed evenly, whereas, in the absence of the lubricant, the layers curved downwards from the wall of the die towards the centre of the compact indicating that friction had restricted movement of the particles near the die-wall. Due to intense local shear action a hard 'skin' of distorted strongly bonded particles was formed where the compact had been in contact

TABLE 1.8

DEFINITIONS OF SOME PARAMETERS USED IN TABLETTING THEORY

Symbol	Definition	Derivation
A	Area of tablet in contact with die-wall	πDL
A_p	Area of punch face	$\pi D^2/4$
D	Diameter of punch face	
F_a	Maximum upper punch force applied to compact	
F_b	Maximum force transmitted to lower punch by compact	
F_c	Crushing force applied across a diameter to edges of compact, just sufficient to cause rupture	
F_d	Force loss to the die-wall	$F_a - F_b$
F_e	Maximum force applied by lower punch to initiate ejection	
F_r	Maximum radial force at die-wall during compaction	
F_r'	Force normal to die-wall during ejection	
k_d	Die-wall coefficient of friction during compaction	
k_e	Die-wall coefficient of friction during ejection	
L	Observed length of compact	
L_o	Length compact would assume if	

	compressed to zero porosity	$W/A_p\rho_o$
P_a	Maximum upper punch pressure	F_a/A_p
P_b	Maximum lower punch pressure	F_b/A_p
P_m	Mean compaction pressure	$(P_a+P_b)/2$
P_r	Maximum radial pressure during compaction	F_r/A
P'_r	Radial pressure during ejection of compact	F'_r/A
R	Punch force ratio	F_b/F_a
T	Transmission ratio	P_b/P_a
V	Observed volume of tablet	A_pL
V_o	Volume compact would assume if compressed to zero porosity	W/ρ_o
V_r	Relative volume of compact	V/V_o
W	Weight of tablet	
ε	Porosity—ratio of void to total volume	$(V-V_o)V$, $1-\rho_r$
ρ	Observed density of compact	W/V
ρ_o	True density of material used in compaction study	
ρ_r	Relative density of tablet	ρ/ρ_o, $1/V_r$

It is assumed that the punches are flat faced and circular in section.

with the die. This 'skin' is often formed on tablets and provides resistance to abrasive damage. The degree of compaction was assessed by measuring the thickness of the layers in each region and was found to be higher in a peripheral ring near the top punch and in a lower central region (Fig. 1.21). The latter may explain why the 'core', often seen towards the end of a disintegration test, breaks down more slowly than the rest of the tablet. A plot of V_r as a function of log P_a was not a smooth curve but showed several abrupt changes of slope (Fig. 1.22). The initial decrease in V_r was due to closer packing of the magnesium carbonate but this was eventually limited

TABLE 1.9

THE EFFECT OF COMPACTION PRESSURE ON THE PROPERTIES OF SULPHATHIAZOLE COMPACTS

Compaction pressure (P_a) kg/cm²	Specific surface area m²/g	Porosity (ε) per cent	Crushing force (F_c) kg*	Disintegration time s
319	0.25	30	2.9	50
638	0.75	23	5.8	150

957	0.85	17	8.8	285
1276	0.95	15	10.2	560
1595	1.00	11	11.0	1180
1914	0.90	10	12.4	3000
2552	0.70	9	13.1	15000
3828	0.45	5	16.1	—
5104	0.30	4	16.8	—

* Strong-Cobb units × 0.73—see Brook and Marshall (1968).

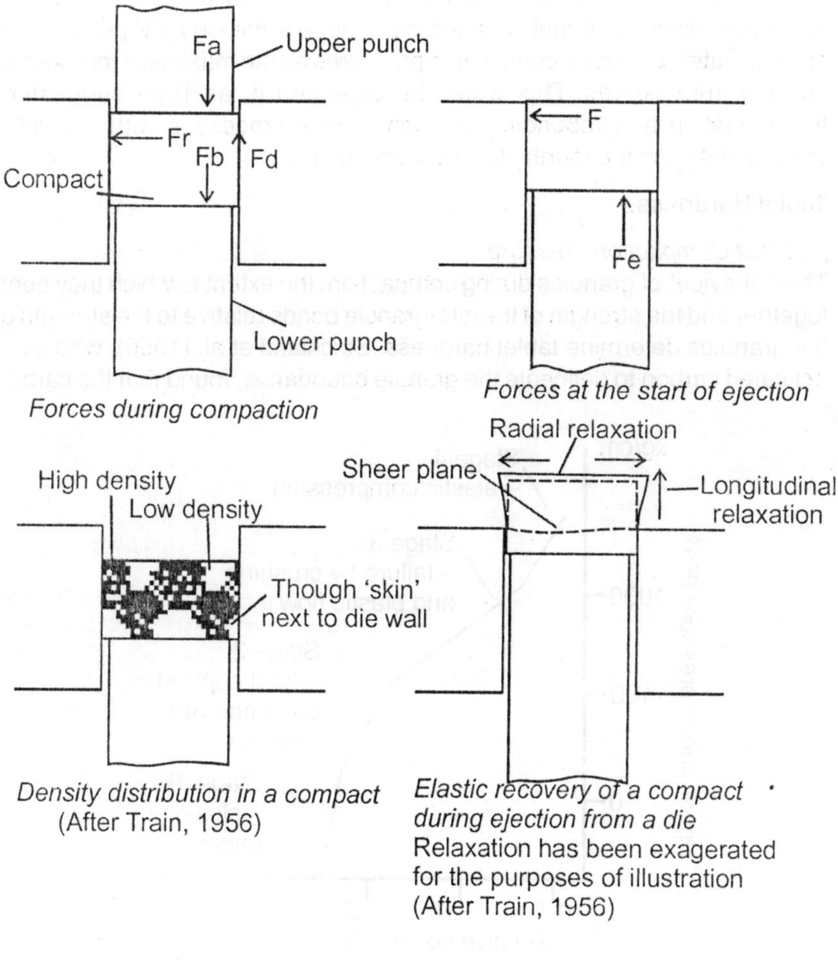

Fig. 1.21. Physical conditions during tabletting.

by the available space in the die-cavity. Thereafter, the slope increased abruptly and during the second stage the load was supported by temporary structures of compacting material. At still higher pressure the structures collapsed and the material failed by crushing and plastic flow (third stage) until, in the fourth stage, there was sufficient rebonding of the freshly created surfaces to give a compact with enough strength to involve the normal compression characteristics of solid magnesium carbonate in any further reduction of volume. The data of Higuchi et al. (1953, 1954b) and Shotton and Ganderton (1960a), when plotted in the form used by Train, show that the third and fourth stages of compaction also occur with aspirin, lactose, sulphadiazine, sulphathiazole and sodium chloride. In the cases of the first four substances the abrupt changes in the slope of the log P_a/V_r plot occur at approximately the same compaction pressures as the maxima in the specific surface area curves. This would be expected if, as Train suggested, fragmentation and rebonding are competitive processes with the latter predominating in the fourth stage of compaction.

Tablet Hardness

Effect of Compaction Pressure

The behaviour of granules during compaction, the extent to which they bond together and the strength of the intergranule bonds relative to the strength of the granules determine tablet hardness. Strickland et al. (1956), who used activated carbon to delineate the granule boundaries, found that the carbon

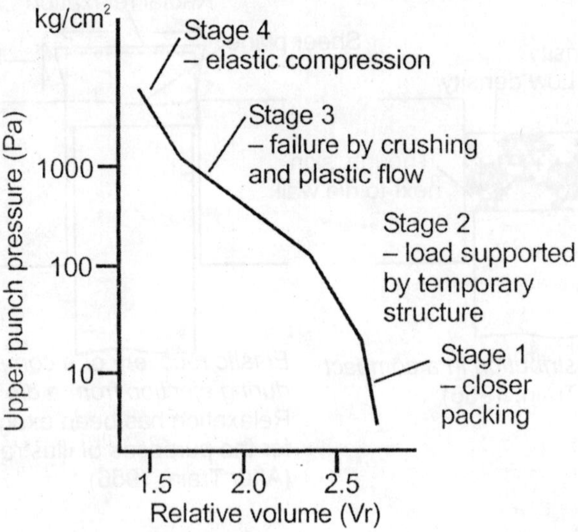

Fig. 1.22. Stages in the compaction of magnesium carbonate.

did not penetrate the interior of the granules even though these were laterally deformed by compaction. Shotton and Ganderton (1960b) applied a vividly coloured sucrose coating to preformed spherical granules of that material. The coating remained intact and the granules largely retained their shape at low compaction pressure but as this was increased the granules distorted progressively until, at the highest compaction pressures, the coating had ruptured to such an extent that it appeared as coloured fragments against the white underlying sucrose. The strength of the intergranule bonds formed by light compression was less than that of the granules with the result that the tablet failed along, rather than across, the granule boundaries when submitted to a crushing force. When this was applied to the more heavily compressed tablets the bond strength was large enough to permit the development of faults within the granules which spread across the boundaries and led to failure of the tablet. The rebonding of surfaces formed by fragmentation, rather than granule interlocking, was apparently the more important factor determining the hardness of these tablets.

Effect of Materials Used and Tablet Dimensions

For given compaction conditions the intergranule bond strength is highly dependent on the nature of the base material. Strong bonds offer resistance to the propagation of faults across the grain boundary in which case, according to Orewan (1949) and others, the strength of the compact formed at a particular compaction pressure should be greater with fine than with coarse granules. This effect was noted with sodium chloride and hexamine compacts (Shotton and Ganderton 1961). Aspirin granules, however, formed weak bonds and softer tablets and, since fault propagation was not involved, granule size had little effect on tablet hardness. Coating sodium chloride and hexamine granules with stearic acid to weaken the intergranule bonds, reduced the hardness of the compacts, and abolished the particle-size effect observed with hexamine, but in the case of sodium chloride the hardest tablets were formed by the coarsest granules. Shotton and Ganderton suggested that the particle to particle contact pressure was greater in coarse sodium chloride grains than in fine ones since, for a given weight of that substance, fewer contacts were available to support the applied load. The higher contact pressure with the coarsest granules allowed penetration of the stearic acid film, the formation of strong bonds and, consequently, the production of the hardest tablets.

The majority of tabletting studies have used a constant die size for an experimental series and the thickness of the tablet, over a range of compaction pressures, has been maintained at a particular value by varying the compressing weight of the base material. Rees and Shotton (1969) reported preliminary studies on the effect of tablet dimension on the crushing strength. For sodium chloride their data indicated a relation of the form:

$$\frac{F_c V_r}{D L_o} = k_c P_m + C_c \qquad (1.1)$$

where D is the tablet diameter, L_o the length the compact would assume if compressed to zero porosity and k_c and C_c are constants.

Capping and Lamination

Granule Bonding and Relaxation Stresses

Occasionally, at the start of a disintegration test, small radiating cracks appear on the upper face of the tablet and small bubbles of air are released. If air does not freely escape from the granules in the die-cavity, for example, where the fines content is high, the force created by the expansion of entrapped air may be sufficient to disrupt the bonds between the 'cap' and the rest of the tablet when the top punch is removed at the initiation of the ejection stage although, as will be seen later, capping and lamination can occur under conditions which preclude the implication of air as the causative agent. It is well known that too high a compaction pressure may lead to capping and lamination and has been shown to occur, for example, with hexamine (Shotton and Ganderton 1961) and sodium chloride (Rees & Shotton 1969).

In 1956, Train pointed out that on removal of compacting force the elastic recovery of the dense peripheral ring (Fig. 1.20) would be larger than that of the adjacent, less dense, part of the tablet. The differential stress in this region is aggravated by both longitudinal and radial relaxation of that part of the tablet extruded from the die during the initial stages of ejection (Fig.1.20). Both effects would increase the tendency to capping and lamination. It may be noted that the increase in tablet dimensions that is due to elastic recovery is usually sufficient to prevent re-insertion of the tablet into the die from which it has just been ejected. Clearly, the strength of the granule bonding may be critical in determining whether the tablet will cap or laminate. According to Shotton and Genderton (1961) the bonds in sodium chloride compacts were strong enough to support relaxation without laminar failure although this can occur if extreme compaction pressures have been employed (Rees and Shotton 1969). The weaker bonds in aspirin compacts allowed the relaxation stresses to be dissipated by bond weakening and partial separation of the granules within the tablet. Undoubtedly, some loss of hardness must have occurred but the bonding was still sufficient to give a firm tablet. Hexamine tablets capped and laminated by fault propagation across the granule boundaries. This was not due to entrapped air as compacts prepared in vacuo behaved in a similar manner. Coating the hexamine granules with stearic acid eliminated the fault entirely and this was attributed to the bond weakening effect of the fatty acid which permitted dissipation of the relaxation stresses by the mechanism postulated for aspirin.

Residual Die-wall Pressure

Practical experience has shown that some tablets do not cap or laminate immediately, but may do so on storage. Higuchi et al. (1965) studied the decay of die-wall pressure for a number of materials. In addition to an immediate elastic recovery in the die there was also a residual die-wall pressure (Table 1.10) which decayed slowly over a period of a minute or more, during which time the tablet 'flowed' in a direction opposite to that in which the compacting pressure had been applied. Addition of lubricant lowered the residual die-wall pressure due, presumably, to the 'softer' nature of the tablets (see the values for crushing strength) and to reduced die-wall friction. The fact that a radial pressure persisted at the end of the decay period showed that there was an elastic deformation which could only be relaxed by ejection of the tablet from the die. Internal strains within the tablet might also provide a further source of stress energy which could be dissipated at any time during the life of the tablet. For single punch and rotary tablet machines, upper punch pressure release and ejection take only a fraction of a second. Even if a tablet with a tendency to cap survived the rapid elastic recovery stage on extrusion from the die, the subsequent slower relaxation may cause capping when the tablets are handled and packed. Incipient capping and lamination of this type is usually apparent if a few tablets are shaken in the cupped hands, dropped on to a hard surface or subjected to a friability test.

Hardness of Materials and Tablet Properties

Prior to compression, a granule porosity exceeding 60 per cent would not be unusual. As shown in Table 1.9, porosity is reduced to about 20 per cent with light compression and decreases to 5 per cent or less at much higher compaction pressures. The reduction in porosity is due to granule fragmentation giving smaller particles which may be more closely packed, and plastic deformation which allows the granules to 'flow' into the void spaces. The contribution of each process depends on the hardness of the substance being compressed. If it were possible to compress a liquid in a tablet machine P_a, P_b and P_r would be equal i.e., the transmission ratio would be unity. Rubber and silicone putty show 'liquid' behaviour and are used for die-wall pressure calibration. For other materials the transmission ratio will be less than unity. When sodium bicarbonate or sulphathiazole were compressed, Nelson (1955) observed that about a third of the upper punch pressure was transmitted to the die-wall. Windheuser et al. (1963) distinguished three distinct stages in the development of die-wall pressure increasing values of upper punch pressure. The initial steep rise of P_r was due to the reduction of void space by the removal of air. This was followed by a less rapid rise in P_r during which granule fragmentation and consolidation took place. In the third stage, Pr increased more rapidly than in the second stage and represented the compression of an essentially void-free material, the 'yield value' of which was estimated by extrapolating the third portion of the curve to the abscissa (Fig. 1.23). Generally, the first ascending portion of the curve was steeper, the second stage more extended and the yield value higher for the harder materials examined. The reduced hardness of potassium chloride and sulphathiazole tablets containing magnesium stearate (Tables 1.10 and 1.11) was reflected in the smaller yield value obtained when that lubricant was employed. For phenacetin and acetanilide a measurable radial pressure could not be obtained until a significant upper punch pressure had been

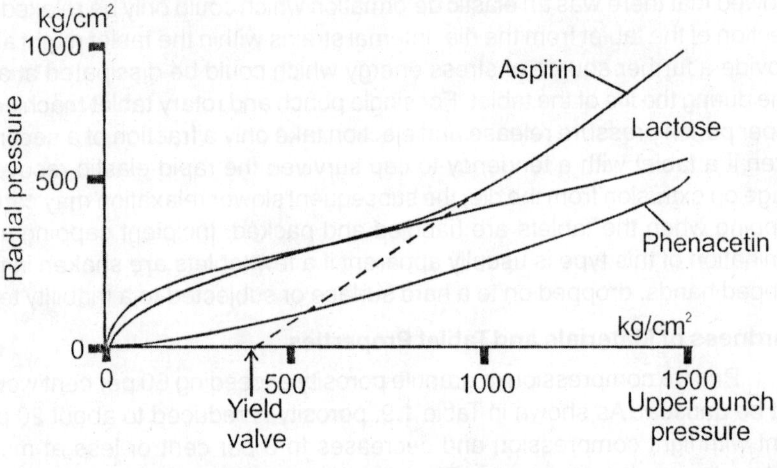

Fig. 1.23. Radial pressure as a function of upper punch pressure (after Windhesuer et al. 1963).

applied: the second stage was virtually absent. These materials produced poor tablets due to the fact that the crystals were plate-like and tended to compact into layers with poor interlayer bonding. Although there were considerable experimental difficulties, Ridgeway et al. (1969a) obtained values for Youn'gs modulus and the surface hardness for a number of pharmaceutical materials; these values were then related (Ridgeway et al. 1969b) to the transmission ratio and to the surface hardness of the compact. The result of these studies (together with data from other sources) are summarized in Table 1.10 where it will be seen that, as anticipated, the transmission ratio was large for soft materials such as aspirin, and vice versa. Overall, the data in the table generally support the view that the hardness of a substance is an important factor determining its behaviour both during and after compression.

TABLE 1.10

THE RELATION OF THE HARDNESS OF SOME PHARMACEUTICAL SUBSTANCES TO THEIR TABLETTING BEHAVIOUR

Substance	Hardness		Compaction behaviour			Properties of compacts prepared at 1000 kg/cm^2	
	Young's modulus (kg/mm^2)	Vickers surface hardness (kg/mm^2)	Transmission ratio: T	Yield value (kg/cm2)	Die-wall coefficient: of friction K_d	Vickers surface hardness (kg/mm^2)	Crushing strength: F_c (kg)
Aspirin	9	8.7	0.67	410	0.17	11.6	3.6
Urea		9.1	0.60			8.6	
Hexamine	90	13.3	0.56		0.31	12.8	5.4
Salicylamide	130	15.1	0.50				
Potassium chloride		17.7	0.45	440		16.1	
Sodium chloride	190	21.2	0.40	640	0.40	27.4	9.1
Sucrose	220	63.6	0.33	700			2.8
Reference	(1)		(2)	(3)	(4)	(2)	(5)

Substance	Lubricant	per cent	Transmission ratio T	Properties of compacts prepared at 1290 kg/cm^2		
				Residual die-wall pressure (kg/cm^2)		Crushing strength F_c
				Initial	Equilibrium	(kg)
Aspirin	—		0.73	36	23	9.4
Sodium chloride	—		0.59	307	200	>19.0
Sucrose	—		0.49	141	119	8.0
Potassium chloride	—		0.71	301	149	14.6
Potassium chloride	Magnesium	2	0.80	178	118	7.3
Potassium chloride	stearate	5	0.84	135	92	7.3
Reference	(6)					

References: (1) Ridgeway et al. (1969a) (2) Ridgeway et al. (1969b)
(3) Windheuser et al. (1963) (4) Lewis and Shotton (1965a)
(5) Shotton and Lewis (1964) (6) Higuchi et al. (1965)

Lubrication

Lubricants are used to improve granule flow (glidants), minimize die-wall friction (die-wall lubricants) and prevent adhesion of the granules to the punch faces (anti-adherents). The extent to which they possess these properties varies; talc is a better glidant than magnesium stearate but is an inferior die-wall lubricant. Excessive proportions of the stearate may actually impede granule flow.

Glidants

The effect of a glidant on the flow properties of a granule may be assessed by measuring the angle of repose, flow-rate through an orifice or by the other methods. A number of mechanisms have been proposed to account for glidant action. The flow properties of smooth, nearly spherical particles are known to be better than those of more irregular shape: it has been suggested that glidant may fill surface depressions and thereby reduce roughness. If the coefficient of friction of the glidant is less than that of the granules then inter-particle friction may be lowered. Alternatively, the glidant may physically separate the solid particles so that inter-molecular attractive and capillary adhesion forces are reduced. The latter derive from the thin film of moisture normally present on solid surfaces. A proportion of fines will often improve granule flow, presumably by a combination of the foregoing effects although, as discussed earlier, an excess of fines often has an adverse effect on tabletting properties. Some materials acquire a frictional electrostatic charge when handled. The mutual repulsion of particles due to this effect is sufficient to impede proper die-filling during the production of hexoestrol implants. Although the solution to this specific problem resides in recrystallization from a suitable solvent, glidant action may in some cases be attributed to the reduction of electrostatic charges. A detailed review of glidant action is given by Jones (1969).

Die-wall Lubricants

The effects of die-wall lubricants on tabletting behaviour may be seen by inspection of Tables 1.10, 1.11 and 1.12. They reduce the force lost to the die-wall, the ejection force, the crushing strength and the residual die-wall pressure. The relative density, punch force ratio, transmission ratio and disintegration time are increased. In part, the lubricant effect appears to reside in the formation of a tough film on the die-wall. If a die 'conditioned' by the production of tablets from lubricated granules is subsequently used to compact unlubricated granules, easy tablet ejection persists for a short period. Strickland et al. (1956) expressed the view that the reduction of force lost to the die-wall as a result of lubrication (ΔF_d) may be related to the fractional coverage of the die-wall–compact interface. At low concentrations (c) of lubricants they reported an apparent agreement with a Langmuir-type adsorption equation i.e.

$$\Delta F_d = c/(k + c) \qquad (1.2)$$

TABLE 1.11

THE EFFECT OF LUBRICANTS ON TABLETTING PROPERTIES

Substance	Lubricant	Per cent	Force lost to die-wall F_d (kg)	Punch force ratio: R	Die-wall coefficient of friction K_d	Ejection force: F_e (kg)	Crushing force: F_c (kg)	Relative density: ρ_r	Ref.
Aspirin	—		438	0.71	0.17	60	3.6	0.975	
Hexamine	—		392	0.74	0.31	144	5.4	0.987	
Hexamine granules	—		392	0.74	0.31	156	14.6	0.965	
Sodium chloride	—		362	0.75	0.40	165	9.1	0.895	
Sucrose	—		Could not be measured—the machine				2.8		
Sucrose granules	—		jammed during the preparation of compacts				2.8		1 and 2
Aspirin	Magnesuim stearate	2	129	0.91	0.051	62	2.7	0.982	
Hexamine	Magnesuim stearate	2	90	0.94	0.051	59	1.3	0.995	
Hexamine granules	Magnesuim stearate	2	174	0.87	0.093	145	10.5	0.985	
Sodium chloride	Magnesuim stearate	2	90	0.94		26	2.6	0.940	
Sucrose	Magnesuim stearate	2	90	0.94		26	1.4	0.890	
Sucrose granules	Magnesuim stearate	2	90	0.94		48	4.0	0.860	
Sucrose granules	—		682	0.55		371			
Sucrose granules	Stearic acid	2	78	0.94		22			
Sucrose granules	Magnesuim Stearate	2	104	0.93		50			3
Sucrose granules	Talc	2	664	0.59		353			
Sulphathiazole granules	—		367	0.69		100	18.3		
Sulphathiazole granules	Magnesuim stearate	0.1	105	0.90		20	17.5		
Sulphathiazole granules	Magnesuim stearate	0.2	86	0.92		15	17.2		
Sulphathiazole granules	Magnesuim stearate	0.4	74	0.93		14	16.1		
Sulphathiazole granules	Magnesuim stearate	0.6	65	0.94		11	15.1		
Sulphathiazole granules	Magnesuim stearate	1	72	0.93		10	13.9		
Sulphathiazole granules	Magnesuim stearate	2	51	0.95		8	11.0		4
Sulphathiazole granules	Stearic acid	0.2	266	0.77		72	17.2		
Sulphathiazole granules	Stearic acid	0.4	187	0.83		50	16.8		
Sulphathiazole granules	Stearic acid	0.6	156	0.85		43	16.4		
Sulphathiazole granules	Stearic acid	1	124	0.88		35	15.9		
Sulphathiazole granules	Stearic acid	2	102	0.90		30	15.3		

(1) Shotton and Lewis (1964)—mean compaction pressure 1000 kg/cm²
(2) Lewis and Shotton (1965a)—mean compaction pressure 1000 kg/cm²
(3) Lewis and Shotton (1965b)—mean compaction pressure 1033 kg/cm²
(4) Strickland et al. (1956)—mean compaction pressure 1390 kg/cm²
Data is quantitatively comparable within, but not between groups due to different operating conditions.

TABLE 1.12

EFFECT OF LUBRICANTS ON THE DISINTEGRATION TIME OF SODIUM BICARBONATE TABLETS COMPACTED AT APPROXIMATELY 1300 Kg/CM²

Lubricant concentration per cent	Disintegration time (s) Stearic acid	Magnesium stearate
0	200	200
0.25	370	1500
0.50	520	2000
0.75	680	2200
1.00	900	2300
2.00	1400	2900
4.00	2500	3800

From Strickland et al. (1956)

Materials used as lubricants must shear readily even when highly compressed. In this connection it may be noted that he slip and orientation of layers within the crystal lattice, on which the action of laminar lubricants such as talc depends, are compaction. Under these conditions the shear strength of talc is high (Train and Hersey 1960) which undoubtedly accounts for the poor die-wall lubricant action of that substance.

Compression and ejection processes involve movement of material relative to the die-bore surface. The frictional force (F) resisting motion of one surface over another is proportional to the load (L) applied normally to those surfaces, that is:

$$F = kL + C \quad (1.3)$$

where k is the coefficient of friction applicable to the particular conditions. For consolidation of granules the maximum force resisting further reduction in the length of the compact is related to F_d and the normal load is the die-wall force (F_r). During ejection the resistance to motion of the compact is related to the ejection force (F_e) whilst F'_r, the radial force operating as ejection takes place, constitutes the normal load. As $F_r = P_r A$ and $F'_r = P'_r A$, by analogy with equation (1.3):

$$F_d = k_m P_r A + C_m \quad (1.4)$$

$$F_e = k_n P'_r A + C_n \quad (1.5)$$

If it is assumed that P_r and P'_r are proportional to a generalized compaction pressure (P) the appropriate substitution in equations (1.4) and (1.5) yields expressions with a common factor (PA), which implies that F_e and F_d are linearly related. This has been confirmed by, for instance, Train (1956), Lewis and Shotton (1965a) and by other workers. Clearly, this is a simplification of a very complex process and could not be expected to apply directly to all materials and compaction conditions. Train's data for the ejection of magnesium carbonate compacts was best represented by a power law, but Lewis and Shotton used linear expression:

$$F_d = k_d P_m A + C_d \tag{1.6}$$

$$F_e = k_e P_m A + C_e \tag{1.7}$$

to describe the compression and ejection of aspirin, hexamine sodium chloride and sucrose compacts. In these equations k_d and k_e were coefficients which depended on the frictional conditions at the die-wall. They found that whereas the values of k_d (Table 1.11) were different for each of the unlubricated substances, they assumed (except in the case of hexamine granules) a virtually identical and lower value when 2 per cent magnesium stearate was added to the base materials. The values of k_e showed a similar but less marked trend. In these circumstances the lubricant governed the frictional characteristics of the die-wall–compact interface regardless of the properties of the material being compacted or ejected. The absolute magnitudes of P_r and P'_r are determined by the transmission ratio (T) and this would not be identical for all lubricated substances which explains why these produced different values of F_d and F_e at a given mean compaction pressure.

In common with the investigations described above, most compaction studies have employed a constant compact diameter and thickness in an experimental series. Sometimes when tabletting 'difficult' granulations, it is found that there is an optimum die-size which minimizes e.g., F_d, F_e, capping, lamination, etc. The effect of thickness and diameter on tabletting properties is therefore of considerable technical interest. From Table 1.8 it can be seen that:

$$\frac{P_r}{P_a} = T \quad \text{and} \quad \frac{F_a}{A_p} = \text{Pa}$$

and substituting these in equation (19.4) and rearranging, then:

$$\frac{F_d}{A} = \frac{k_1 F_a}{A_p} + C_1 \tag{1.8}$$

Also, if the assumption is made that P'_r is proportional to P_a:

$$\frac{F_e}{A} = \frac{k_2 F_a}{A_p} + C_2 \tag{1.9}$$

Equations (1.8) and (1.9) fitted the results of Rees and Shotton (1969) for the compaction of sodium chloride. As these workers pointed out, these equations are not applicable when the length of the compact is sufficient to prevent proper consolidation of granules near the bottom punch—a condition which should rarely be encountered in normal pharmaceutical tabletting operations. Further studies will be necessary to show whether the expressions are valid ɔr a wider range of materials.

It is implicit in the reduction of residual die-wall pressure and improvement of transmission ratio (Table 1.10) by die-wall lubricants that they facilitate the movement of material in the die-cavity both during and after compression. The more ready elimination of voids is reflected in the higher relative density of the compacts (Table 1.11). Die-wall lubricants are not, however, without adverse effects on other tablet properties such as disintegration time (Table 1.12). Also, as has been noted earlier, they may reduce the strength of the bonds between particles in a tablet. While this has the beneficial effect of reducing capping and lamination in the case of hexamine, with other substances an undesirable reduction in tablet hardness may occur. Clean surfaces are known to produce the strongest bonds but, as hard tablets can be prepared with lubricated granules, it seems reasonable to suppose that enough of the clean surface produced by fragmentation during compression remains uncontaminated by lubricant and capable of forming strong bonds. If this is so, lubricants should affect the hardness of tablets produced from crystals more than those produced from granules. This is because the crystals, being harder than granules, would tend to fragment to a lesser extent under pressure. In confirmation of this, Shotton and Lewis (1964) found that the strength of hexamine and sucrose tablets prepared from crystalline material was reduced by 76 per cent and 50 per cent respectively by the addition of 2 per cent magnesium stearate. The corresponding reduction in hardness was 28.1 per cent and 18.4 per cent respectively for tablets formed from granulated hexamine and sucrose.

Disintegration

In the context of tablet technology, disintegration implies penetration of the tablet by an aqueous liquid, disruption of internal bonds and the subsequent breakdown of the tablet. It is reasonable to suppose that rapid penetration of liquid is an essential requirement for rapid disintegration of conveniently formulated tablets.

Theory

A pressure differential P is required to cause liquid of viscosity η to flow with a velocity dL/dt in a horizontal pore of hydraulic radius m at a time t when the meniscus has moved a distance L along the pore.

$$\frac{dL}{dt} = \frac{Pm^2}{k_0 \eta L} \qquad (1.10)$$

Here, k_0, a pore shape factor and m, the hydraulic radius, are used because the pore in a compact has an irregularly shaped rather than a circular cross-section. In all other respects the equations is of the same form as the used to describe the flow of liquids in circular pipes. The pressure differential derives from the drop in pressure across a meniscus:

$$P = \frac{\gamma \cos\theta}{m} \qquad (1.11)$$

where γ is the surface tension of the liquid and θ the contact angle with the pore wall (cf. the corresponding expression for a liquid meniscus in a capillary of circular section). From the foregoing:

$$\frac{dL}{dt} = \frac{m\gamma \cos\theta}{k_0 \eta L} \qquad (1.12)$$

If $L = 0$ when $t = 0$ on integration

$$L^2 = \frac{2m\gamma \cos\theta}{k_0 \eta} t \qquad (1.13)$$

If the pore is part of a network that is uniform throughout the compact, for penetration into one face of that compact, the volume of liquid in the pores (V) is proportional to L and at any time:

$$V^2 = kt \qquad (1.14)$$

k being a coefficient representing the properties of the liquid and of the pore network within the compact.

Effect of Granule Properties

For a compact of given porosity the void space may comprise a few large diameter pores as many fine ones. Fine pores are most likely to be formed from soft friable granules that readily fragment into much smaller particles during compression. In these circumstances the size of the pores should be largely independent of the size of the granules used to prepare the compact. Conversely, hard granules do not collapse to the same extent during compaction and thus the pore network will be coarser and dependent on the original granule size. According to equation (1.13) such a network would be more readily penetrated by liquids than that resulting from the compaction of soft materials. Ganderton and Selkirk (1969) made granules from lactose and sucrose by massing with water and found that the hardness and bulk density increased with the amount of water used for granulation. They suggested that this was due to a reduction in intra-granule pore volume. Sucrose granules, which were harder and less friable than those prepared with lactose, gave compacts with a coarser pore structure that was more readily penetrated by liquid. Initially, the imbibition rate for all compacts conformed to equation (1.14), but on many occasion slowed down or stopped abruptly before the theoretical volume of liquid had been absorbed. This was more frequently observed with sucrose compacts, particularly in those circumstances where the porosity was high and the largest, hardest, granules had been used. These conditions were essential for the effect to occur with lactose compacts. It was postulated that compacts showing this type of behaviour had a broad and perhaps discontinuous distribution of pore sizes. Rapid penetration of the wider pores isolated some regions of the compact, occluded air prevented subsequent penetration of the isolated regions and, as a result, a lower than theoretical degree of saturation was attained. By compressing the compacts to a lower porosity the size and lack of uniformity in size distribution was reduced and higher fractional saturation obtained.

In the foregoing experiments liquid penetrated one face of the compact. However, complete immersion of the tablet during disintegration exposes the whole surface to penetrant liquid. In this situation the geometry of the system demands a reduction in the total pore cross-sectional area available for flow as liquid approaches the centre of the tablet. Furthermore, as the pore entrances on all surfaces of the tablet will be sealed by liquid, air entrapment will occur. Liquid will penetrate until the increase in the pressure of the occluded air is equal to the capillary pressure. A larger fraction of the total pore length will be penetrated with fine rather than coarse pores, but this need not necessarily imply good disintegration characteristics. It is quite possible that the back pressure of the occluded air as it compresses in the pore and the decreasing area available for flow could act in concert with the normally operative viscous forces so that the rate of penetration was too low for a short disintegration time.

Effects of Die-wall Lubricants

Some medicaments e.g., phenothiazine, and most die-wall lubricants are hydrophobic and impart this property to the pore walls in the tablet. The resultant increase in the contact angle reduces the value of $\cos\theta$ in equation (19.13) and therefore the pore is less readily penetrated by an aqueous liquid. This is reflected in the longer disintegration time which is found when, for instance, the stearate lubricants are used (see Table 1.12). For magnesium carbonate compacts there was rough proportionality the concentration of magnesium stearate and the time taken for the uptake of a given amount of water (Ganderton 1969). This time was extended, other conditions being constant, by increasing the efficiency of the process whereby the lubricant was blended with the granules. When 1 per cent of magnesium stearate was incorporated during the moist granulation stage penetration of water was completely inhibited: the pores were so well coated that the contact angle was greater than 90° and probably approached that of the solid lubricant. As the cosine of an angle greater than 90° is negative, V^2 in equation (1.14) is also negative and penetration cannot occur. Where such a situation arises in tablet manufacture, due either to the intrinsic water repellency of the medicament or the lubricant, a water soluble surfactant may be added to the granules to reduce the contact angle. Surfactants also facilitate the displacement of air from blind pores in a tablet under the conditions of a dissolution test. Studies by Wurster and Seitz (1960) with benzoic acid compacts into which 1 mm diameter artificial holes had been formed by drilling, demonstrated that the total pore surface was not available for attack by simple aqueous dissolution fluids, due to occluded air. This effect was abolished when air was removed from the pores by vacuum treatment or by addition of a surfactant to the dissolution medium.

Mode of Disintegrant Action

Starch has been used for many decades as a disintegrating agent. Since instrumented tablet machines were not available to Berry and Ridout (1950) they used the compression ratio, that is the ratio of the weight of a tablet to its thickness, as a measure of the degree of compaction in their studies. The disintegration time of tablets containing 15 per cent of starch, dry mixed with phenacetin granules, fell linearly from 15 min at a compression ratio of 0.57, to 6 min as that ratio was raised to 0.7; further compaction to 0.75 brought about a steep rise in disintegration time to 24 min. They argued that the disintegrating action of starch was due to swelling and that this would be most efficient when the granules were in close contact with the starch grains in a tablet of low porosity. At still lower porosities (higher compression ratios) imbibition of water was restricted by the small pore size. Similar effect have been noted by Higuchi et al. (1954b) with sulphadiazine tablets. Berry and Ridout compared the effect of starch added as described above with that of alginic acid incorporated during the moist granulation stage. This latter substance also swells in contact with aqueous liquids, but, since it was part of the granule structure, disintegration occurred by erosion and breakdown of the granules into the original particles from which they had been prepared. A low disintegration time of approximately 3 min was maintained up to a compression ratio of 0.65 but then, as with starch, further compaction caused a marked increase in the time taken for the tablet to disintegrate. Burlinson (1950) observed that there was little to choose between aliginic acid and starch if part of the latter was incorporated into the granules during moist granulation of the medicaments.

The assumption that starch facilitates tablet disintegration by swelling action (bursting) is based on the known increase in the dimensions of starch grains exposed to aqueous fluids. Patel and Hopponen (1966) found a 70 per cent increase in volume, but Ingram and Lowenthal (1968) quote a lower figure which, they suggest, is not sufficient to account for the disintegrant action of starch. The latter workers suggest that the irreversible swelling of damaged starch grains is much greater but could not establish a correlation between the degree of damage and tablet disintegration time. As an alternative to the 'swelling' theory it has been argued that starch may derive its disintegrant properties from capillary action in the intergranule pore system.

It is possible that it may also prevent the complete collapse of the pore system during compaction or provide a secondary pore surface of low contact angle against aqueous media.

It seems likely that the disintegration time of tablets is determined by the complex interaction of a wide variety of factors. The rate at which liquid penetrates a tablet, the nature and method of incorporation of lubricants, the action of disintegrants, the degree of compaction and the reduction of inter-particle bond strength in the presence of water, are all clearly of major importance. In practice, granules often contain hydrophilic colloids which, apart from their effect on the surface tension, viscosity and contact angle of the penetrant liquid, may dissolve or gel and this may have a profound effect on the rate at which a tablet disintegrates. Finally, some tablets disintegrate by continuous erosion of an outer wetted layer in which case the complete rapid saturation of the pore system by aqueous media may not be an essential initial step in the disintegration process.

CAPSULES

A capsule consists of a dose of drug enclosed in a water-soluble shell or envelope. Although capsules are predominantly used for oral medication, suppositories, consisting of the drug and a suitable dispersion medium enclosed in a flexible gelatin shell, are available (Senior 1969). There are two types of capsule, the hard variety which is intended for the administration of particulate solids and the soft or flexible capsule used for powders, non-aqueous liquids or pastes. As the shell takes several minutes to dissolve, the taste of unpalatable drugs is effectively masked. Officially, capsules may be spherical (perles), ovoid or cylindrical with hemispherical ends—only the last of these descriptions applies to hard capsules. The shell may include an antimicrobial preservative, can be coloured as an aid to identification and may be rendered opaque by dyes or fillers if the drug e.g., some vitamins and Chlorodiazepoxide, is photosensitive. For official preparations, diluents may not be added to the medicament unless this is specifically permitted in the relevant monograph: a similar restriction also applies to the use of coloured shells for capsules described in the Codex. It is possible to coat capsules with cellulose acetate phthalate or a mixture of stearic acid and butyl stearate if enteric action is required, but it is more usual in these circumstances to formulate if possible as an enteric coated tablet.

Soft Capsules

Formerly, these were extemporaneously prepared by filling and sealing shells which had been made by dipping metal formers or 'olives' into a molten aqueous base containing glycerin and gelatin (glycogelatin). The glycerin ensures that a flexible shell is obtained. The first step in mechanizing the production of soft capsules was the development of a process whereby a sheet of glycogelatin was covered with a measured amount of anhydrous fluid drug. A second sheet was then placed over the drug and the 'sandwich ' compressed between plates into which had been set hollow elliptical or hemispherical dies. The pressure forced the glycogelatin sheets and the drug into the dies and formed individual capsules by sealing and cutting at the rims. The capsules were then separated from the residual glycogelatin matrix, washed in solvent to remove traces of oil used as a release agent and dried to give a tough though flexible shell. The process was used until recently but could not complete with the rotary die machine (Fig. 1.24 and 1.25) in terms of economics, continuous, high speed production. In this machine the dies are set in a pair of contra-rotating cylinders. Two continuous glycogelatin ribbons, previously warmed by the filling wedge to make them plastic, are fed between the cylinders. At the moment when opposing dies converge, a measured fill of drug is forced between the ribbons by a metering pump and simultaneously the edges of the dies seal and cut out a complete capsule. These are separated from the matrix, washed in solvent and dried (*Pharmaceutical Journal*, 1960). It is claimed that the fill of drug per capsule can be maintained to within 1 per cent of the mean fill for the batch.

Fig. 1.24. The rotary die soft capsule machine (R. P. Scherer Ltd.).

Depending on machine capacity and capsule size, production rates in excess of 30 000 capsules/h are possible while production lines are available for the formation of the ribbons, sealing of the capsules and their subsequent washing and drying as a continuous integrated process. Rotary die machines have also been developed whereby powders, as such, may be directly encapsulated in a flexible gelatin shell. The ribbon is made to conform to the contour of the die by application of reduced pressure, a 'plug' of powder is forced between the ribbons and the capsules sealed, washed, and dried as described above. Capsules of some tetracycline antibiotics are made by this method.

Virtually any non-aqueous liquid drug or a powdered solid formed into a suspension of suitable consistency by the addition of oil, may be presented as a soft capsule. Vegetable oil, Liquid Paraffin and Soft Paraffin are used when necessary to dilute or suspend the drug. Vegetable oils are specified for the dilution of the oil-soluble vitamins, as the paraffins are known to interfere with the absorption of these medicaments from the gut. As noted in the BPC 1968, drugs containing water or other gelatin solvent cannot be filled into soft capsules due to the resultant pitting, softening and eventual breakdown of the shell; the water should be removed and the residue mixed with an oil prior to encapsulation. Conversely, anhydrous but hygroscopic liquids may withdraw water from the shell which then hardens and has reduced solubility. Glycogelatin softens markedly as the temperature is raised and it is usual to increase the proportion of gelatin for capsules used for tropical climates. Due to changes in the equilibrium moisture content of the shell, the flexibility of soft capsules varies with ambient humidity. They are hard and inflexible at 20 per cent, taut but flexible at 50 per cent, and soft and flaccid at 80 per cent relative humidity. In the latter condition the relatively high moisture content of the shell may encourage the diffusion of any water-soluble substance from the fill into the shell and as a result there may be unwanted reactions between the constituents or changes in the appearance and solubility of the shell.

According to Notton (1956) the oxygen permeability also increases with the moisture content of the glycogelatin envelope. It will be noted that the official storage requirements for both varieties of capsules are framed to prevent moisture uptake and other forms of deterioration as well as crushing and breakage. Sufficient preservative must be used to ensure effective antimicrobial action even where the moisture content of the envelope is high. Additionally, the possibility that preservative may partition between the shell and the capsule content can not be ignored. Studies by Patterson and Lerrigo (1947) showed that beta-naphthol, used extensively at that time as a mould inhibitor, partitioned to such an extent that after approximately 18 months storage the amount of preservative in the capsule contents was more than twice that in the shell. It is unlikely, however, that partitioning would be a serious problem with the ionized antimicrobials, such as potassium sorbate, that are now employed as preservatives for capsule shells.

Hard Capsules

These are made by filling the drug as powder, granules or pellets into a performed cylindrical shell or body, the content being retained by a shorter shell or cap fitted over the body. Wood (1965) has reported that on occasion the cap may disengage from the body during the act of swallowing. This, clearly, is undesirable, and may be avoided by securing the shell components with a narrow sealing strip. Hard capsules provide an alternative to powders, cachets and tablets for the administration of solid medicaments. They are at least as durablè as tablets and correct formulation permits the rapid release and absorption of drug in the gastrointestinal tract.

Hard capsule shells are made by dipping moulds into a gelatin solution, the film on the mould dried, the shell cut to length and then stripped from the mould (*Pharmaceutical Journal*, 1965 and 1966). The shells are made in a range of 8 sizes to accommodate 50 to 1000 mg doses of drug but for veterinary preparations three larger shells are available for 5 to 30 g doses. Particularly where high-speed filling equipment is used there must be no difficulty in removing and replacing the cap, yet the junction of this with the body must form an efficient seal. The necessarily small tolerances on the dimensions of the cap and body are achieved by rigid control of all stages of the manufacturing process. Peck et al. (1964) have described a device utilizing the absorption of β-radiation from a chlorine-36 source for the control of shell thickness.

For large scale production the capsules are sorted and positioned body downwards and sucked into holes in upper and lower rings which, when separated, retain the cap and body respectively. The lower ring is then presented to a head which fills the body with medicament composition, as either a powder or a lightly compacted pellet. Subsequently the rings are recombined, the body pushed into the cap, the capsule ejected and any dust adhering to the outer capsule surface removed. In semi-automatic equipment the rings are separated, transferred to the filling head and recombined by hand, but with fully automatic machines these operations are accomplished by mechanical means.

In common with many other pharmaceutical materials such as bacitracin, magnesium trisilicate and starch (Strickland 1962), the moisture uptakeambient humidity curve for gelatin exhibits marked hysteresis (Strickland & Moss 1962). Thus, the moisture content of the shell, normally 9 to 12 per cent, is determined by both its previous history and the ambient humidity; it may vary between 4 and 16 per cent under extreme conditions. Strickland and Moss concluded that the diffusion of moisture into the capsule contents occures mainly through the shell surface with only a small contribution due to the junction between the body and cap. Moisture will be absorbed from the environment via the capsule wall if the medicament is more hygroscopic than the shell and for this reason such substances should not be dispensed in capsules. The preparation of the drug and its subsequent filling into the body poses many of the problems which have already been discussed in the context of tabletting, for instance, care must be taken to ensure the efficient mixing of minor constituents with other drugs or diluents. The weight of drug in both tablets and capsules is governed by the volume availble for filling and the bulk density of the drug formulation under production conditions, while for low weight variation the powder must flow in a reproducible manner. Unlike the die-cavity of the tablet machine, the volume of the capsule body cannot be adjusted to accommodate a given weight of powder and therefore, with hard capsules, the bulk density of the powder must be adjusted by the addition of an inert diluent such as lactose. Care is necessary in the selection of the diluent as, apart from its effect on powder flow properties there is some evidence, at least in the case of Chloramphenicol Capsules (Withey and Mainville 1969), that high concentrations of lactose may interfere with drug dissolution. In addition to diluent, a lubricant such as magnesium stearate (about 0.5 per cent) may be added for correct operation of the mechanism in the filling head and up to 5 per cent talc may be added to improve the flow properties of the powder. Reier et al. (1968) have reported on preliminary studies to elucidate the effect of medicament type, production rate, capsule size, presence or absence of talc, particle size, specific volume and powder flow on the semi-automatic filling of hard capsules. These studies showed that, for a given capsule size and production rate, the filling weight was largely determined by the specific volume of the powder, while the action of talc in reducing weight variation was attributed to more reproducible, rather than more rapid, flow of the powder. Computer analysis of the data gave equations for filling weight and filling weight variation which included all possible interactions of the factors listed above, except that terms for medicament type and particle size were not required as their effect was reflected in the flow properties of the powder and these were adequately defined by the flowbility and specific volume. As the capsule size is set by the specific volume of the powder, only that parameter and the flowability need be measured, using a small sample, to predict the performance of a given filling composition. Thus, production difficulties may be anticipated and corrected prior to filling trials with large and potentially expensive batches of medicament. Reier and co-workers found excellent agreement between the predicted and observed behaviour of a number of model filling compositons.

Quality Control of Capsules

The reason for controlling the disintegration time, weight variation and medicament content of tablets also apply to capsules and have been discussed in considerable earlier in this chapter.

Disintegration

The tablet disintegration apparatus of the *Pharmacopoeia* is specified for the best test but the guided disc may not be used. With capsules, it is clearly necessary to disinguish, during the course of the test, between particles of shell and drug; the BP 1973 requires that no portion of *drug* shall remain after 15 min which does not freely pass the 10 mesh screen at the base of the disintegration tube. Aguiar et al. (1968) found that hard capsules containing chloramphenicol disrupted sufficiently to release the drug after a few minutes immersion in simulated gastric fluid, but several hours were required for complete solution of the shell. These authors emphasized that both rapid deaggregation (disintegration of powder aggregates into primary particles) and rapid dissolution were necessary conditions for good biological availbility of the drug.

Uniformity of Filling Weight

This cannot be determined by simply weighing the filled capsules as there will be a variation in the weights of the individual shells. For this reason the weight of the content of individual capsule is defined as the different in weight of the intact dose unit and the empty shell. Removal of dry particulate solid from the capsule merely involves detaching the cap or slitting the shell (Method A) but oily contents are squeezed out of the split shell and the remainder removed by washing in solvent (Method B). In all other respects the principle of the test is the same as that applied to tablets: Table 1.13 summarizes official requirements. Only one set of tolerances is specified when Method B is used to determine the weight of the capsule contents as this method applies to soft capsules and it is not usual to fill these with less than about 0.3 g of material.

Content of Medicament

A sample from the bulked contents of the capsules used in the test for weight uniformity is assayed and the dose of medicament per capsule calculated. This must comply with the limits set out in the relevant monograph which is framed to take into account such factors as drug purity, assay accuracy, assay precision and manufacturing difficulties. The general requirements that the drug content of individual dose units shall not show a gross deviation from that stated or prescribed also applies to capsules.

The available literature, see for example Aguiar et al. (1968), Robinson et al. (1968) and Stock (1962), suggests that, provided the capsule contents are correctly formulated and the manufacturing process adequately controlled, there should be few instances where difficulties will be encounted in the large scale production of capsules complying with official requirements.

TABLE 1.13

SUMMERY OF THE BP 1973 TEST FOR UNIFORMITY OF FILLING WEIGHT OF CAPSULES

Method	Applicable to	Sample size	Average weight of contents	Deviation per cent about the average weight	Maximum number of capsules which may exceed the stated weight range
A	Capsules containing particulate solids	20	0.12 g or less	± 10	Two
				± 20	None
			More than 0.12 g	± 7.5	Two
				± 15	None
B	Flexible capsules containing oily filling	10	Not stated — see text	± 7.5	One
				± 15	None

Chapter 2

Oral Preparations

Drugs may be administered by a variety of routes but oral administration is adopted wherever possible. It is the safest, easiest and most economical route of drug administration. There are, however, limitations to the use of the oral route. It is obviously unsatisfactory for substances such as insulin and adrenaline which are inactivated for destroyed by the secretions of the gastrointestinal tract. Other substances, although not destroyed, may not be adequately absorbed from the alimentary tract and if required to produce a systematic effect must be administered by other routes. Such drugs may nevertheless be given by mouth to obtain a localized action in the large intestine and bowel. For example, neomycin and the less soluble sulphonamides are administered orally in the treatment of gastrointestinal infections or to reduce the bacterial flora prior to surgery of the bowel.

Another limitation to oral administration is the fact that some drugs irritate the gastric or intestinal mucosa, but this may be minimized by giving the drug after food. Enteric coating may be applied to tablets or capsules to prevent gastric irritation and some drugs, e.g. phenylbutazone and indomethacin, may be administered rectally as an alternative to the oral route.

SOLID PREPARATIONS

For oral administration there is a choice between solid and liquid medicines. Solid forms of drug presentation include powders, cachets, tablets and capsules.

The most commonly used oral preparations, nowadays, are tablets and capsules. Generally speaking, they are more stable and less prone to microbiological contamination than extemporaneously dispensed liquid medicines. However, liquid preparations have advantages for administering drugs to children and patient who have difficulty in swallowing solid preparations.

Powders

Drugs administered in powdered form are immediately available for absorption. However, the absorption of substances which are only poorly soluble may be affected by the particle size of the drug. The clinical aspects of the fineness of particles in pharmaceutical practice were discussed by Lees (1963). He gave a number of examples of drugs, of which the gastrointestinal absorption is affected by particle size, including the corticosteroids, sulphonamides and griseofulvin. The absorbability of the latter drug is directly related to the logarithm of the specific surface. The efficacy of other drugs acting locally in the gut may be enhanced by reduction of particle size. In veterinary medicine, the anthelmintic activity of phenothiazine has been shown to be related to particle size.

Dispensing of Powders

Powders may be ordered to be individually wrapped in single doses or in bulk. Individually wrapped powders are used for potent drugs and wherever it is necessary to ensure accurate measurement of the dose. They may be either simple (containing only one active ingredient) or compound (containing more than one active ingredient). Individually wrapped powders provide a useful method of drug presentation if the required dose is not available as a standard tablet or capsule.

Powders are administered by placing the contents of one powder paper on the tongue and swallowing with a drink of water. For administration to children, powders are sometimes mixed with jam, treacle or honey. If the drug is likely to be adversely affected by acids, the responsible person should be warned against the use of jam.

Simple Individually Wrapped Powders

Powders are wrapped in white glazed paper, cut to a suitable size, depending upon the bulk of powder contained in a single dose. Machine or guillotine-cut paper is preferable.

Select a number of papers corresponding to the number of powders ordered and of a suitable size. Turn up one of the longer edges of each paper about half an inch and place the papers in a convenient position on the dispensing bench so that each slightly overlaps the next.

Weigh out the total quantity of powdered drug to be dispensed and replace the bottle. If the drug is caked or lumpy, reduce it to a powder by grinding in a mortar. When six or more powders are to be sent, it is advisable to weigh a total quantity corresponding to one more than is required, because during weighing there may be slight losses due to powder adhering to the knife of scale pan. Place the total quantity of powder on a large sheet of paper and weigh from this. The latter procedure prevents too many or too few powders being sent and is a check on the weighing.

Wrap the powders so that they are of a size that will fit loosely in the box (a white glazed, slide or hinge-lid box is generally used). Bend the far border over until it is about half an inch from the near border (Fig. 2.2). Turn the margin upwards with the thumb and bend over to form a flap. Fold the flap loosely over on itself to an extent which makes the packet slightly narrower than the interior of the box. Hold the packet over the drawer section of the box and turn the ends down lightly over the ends of the drawer so as to form a slight crease that will act as a guide to the length of the finished powder. Bend each end in turn sharply over a powder knife, holding made by the ends of the box. Finally, place the folded packet on a sheet of white paper, cover it with another sheet of paper and pass a knife over the upper sheet. This last procedure distributes the powder evenly within the packet and prevents the escape of powder through the folds.

When all the powders have been wrapped, arrange them in pairs, flaps to flaps and encircle the stack with an elastic band before placing them in the box.

Crystalline substances or substances in large or small lumps must be reduced to a fine powder to facilitate administration and hasten solution after administration.

Potent crystalline substances should be powdered in a glass mortar, preferably placed on a black surface. Wedgewood ware or composition mortars are liable to absorb potent drugs to some extent. Iodine is absorbed by composition mortars and stains them badly.

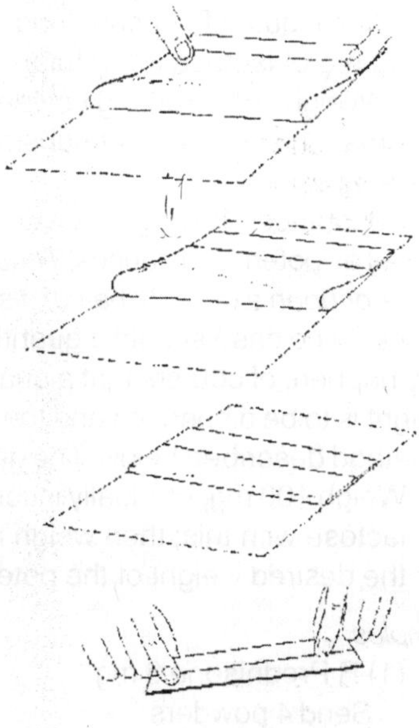

Fig. 2.1. Wrapping a powder.

Hygroscopic substances must be powdered and weighed as rapidly as possible, avoiding undue exposure to moisture.

Powders of hygroscopic substances should be doubly wrapped, the inner wrap consisting of waxed paper to protect the powder from moisture.

Volatile substances must also be doubly wrapped in the same manner.

Triturations

A trituration is the term applied to mixture or dilution of a potent substance with an inert one. Small quantities of finely powdered solids may be mixed on a sheet of white paper by means of a powder knife or spatula. A mortar should be used when the quantities are too large to be conveniently dealt with on paper. The invariable rule is to add a little of the substance present in greater amount to the whole of the substance present in lesser amount (usually the more potent substance), and mix intimately; the remainder of the substance present in greater amount is then introduced into the mixture in very small quantities at first, but gradually increasing the quantities, until the whole has been added. It is impossible to ensure intimate dispersion of one powder in another by mixing the two substances all at once.

Powders weighing less then 100 mg must be made up to 100 mg by adding an appropriate quantity of lactose.

Consider the following prescription:

R Cortisone acetate 15 mg

Send 10 powders

Total quantity of cortisone acetate = 10 × 15 = 150 mg

Add 850 mg of lactose = 1 g total.

Weight 10 × 100 mg powders

Small doses of potent substances must not be weighed on ordinary dispensing scales.

Substances having a maximal dose of less than 60 mg should be regarded as potent substances. *These should be weighed either on a chemical balance or upon a delicate pair of dispensing scales specially reserved for the purpose*. In no case should a quantity less than 50 mg be actually weighed. It may happen, of course, that a quantity of potent substance less than 50mg in weight is to be dispensed and the required amount should be obtained by the method described below. The general procedure is as follow:

Weigh 100 mg; gradually incorporate a convenient weighed quantity of lactose with this; then weigh a portion of the mixture that will contain the desired weight of the potent substance.

Examples

(1) R Prednisone 8 mg

Send 4 powders

Method. Weigh 100 mg of prednisone; mix on paper with 900 mg of lactose = 1 g total. 320 mg of this mixture will contain 32 mg of prednisone. Mix this quantity with 80 mg of lactose and divide into 4 powders each weighing 100 mg.

(2) R Pentobarbitone sodium 15 mg

Send 2 powders

Method. Total required = 2 × 15 = 30 mg. Weight 60 mg of pentobarbitone sodium; mix on paper with 60 mg of lactose = 120 mg total. 60 mg of this mixture will contain 30 mg of pentobarbitone sodium. Mix this quantity with 140 mg of lactose and divide into 2 powders each weighing 100 mg.

Compound Powders in Doses

These are powders containing more than one active ingredient. Small quantities may be mixed on paper by means of a spatula or with a pestle and mortar. Any ingredients that are not finely sub-divided should be reduced to powder form separately before being mixed.

In mixing compound powders it is essential to follow the general rule of gradually incorporating the ingredient present in greatest amount with the whole of the ingredient present in least amount, any other ingredients then being introduced in turn a little at a time. When using a pestle and mortar for mixing, trituration should be light; heavy trituration or grinding tends to make powders denser and less diffusible in fluids. Only hard, crystalline substances require heavy grinding. Caution should be exercised in handling mixtures of oxidizing and reducing agents in a mortar and pestle as an explosion may cccur. If it is necessary to mix such substances, they should be powdered separately and then mixed very lightly on paper.

Sifting. Compound powders containing vegetable substances often require sifting to break up small masses of cohering particles. A no. 44 or no. 60 sieve should be chosen and the mixed powder brushed through or rubbed through with a spatula. Various mixers and sifters are obtainable for small quantities.

After sifting, all powders must again be lightly mixed, as there is sometimes a tendency for the ingredients to be separated by the sieve.

Fractional quantities. In some cases it may happen that after all the ingredients have been mixed an awkward fraction is obtained when the total weight is divided by the number of powders to be sent. This difficulty is easily overcome by adding a small quantity of lactose to bring the weight of each powder to a convenient figure. If the total weight of the ingredients is 3.7 g and this is to be divided into 10 powders, it would be advisable to incorporate 0.3 g of lactose (= 4 g total) and divide into 10 × 0.4 g powders.

Lactose intolerance. It should be noted that there is a rare condition in children which makes them intolerant to lactose. In such cases, an alternative inert diluent must be used (e.g. starch powder).

Powder in Bulk

Sometimes when the dose is not critical, powders may be ordered in bulk. Often powders of this kind are for use as antacids, e.g. Magnesium Trisilicate Powder, Compound BPC. The quantities are usually so large that it is necessary to use a mortar in mixing, even though the ingredients may be already in fine powder. They should be sent out in *perfectly dry,* wide mouthed, glass bottles with plastic screw caps or other suitable closure. If any of the ingredients are deliquescent or volatile, an airtight container should be used.

Cachets

Powders can be enclosed in small containers made of rice flour and water, known as cachets. They are available in various sizes holding from 0.2 to 1.5 g of powder. Such preparations have advantages for the administration of nauseating drugs given in large doses. The cachet prevents the patient from tasting the powder and a large dose can enclosed in a cachet than in a tablet or a capsule. Sodium aminosalicylate, which is given in a dose of 12 g daily in the treatment of tuberculosis, is commonly prescribed in cachets.

Before administration, a cachet should be immersed in water for a few seconds and then placed on the tongue and swallowed with a draught of water. In this way the outer shell of the cachet is softened, but is retains the enclosed powders long enough for the whole to be swallowed without permitting the powder to come into contract with the palate. After being swallowed, the

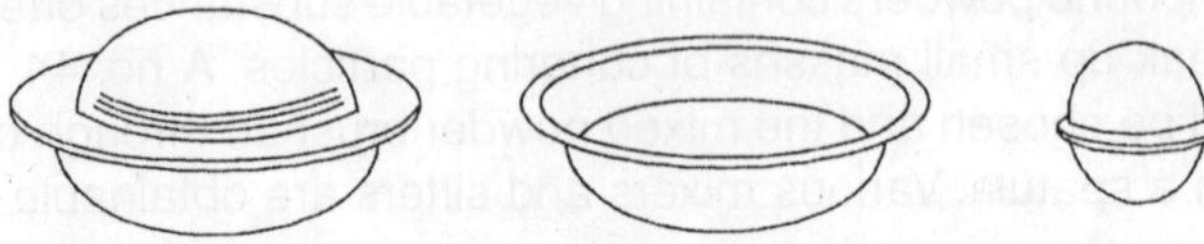

Fig. 2.2. Cachets.

cachet disintegrates and the powder is liberated.

There are two kinds of cachet; 'wet seal' cachets which are sealed by moistening the edges with water, and 'dry seal' cachets which, as the name implies require no moisture for sealing.

Wet seal cachets. A wet seal cachet is composed of two similar concave halves, having flat edges (see Fig. 2.2). The weighed powder is deposited into one half, the edges of the other half are moistened with water, inverted over the first half and the flat edges pressed together so that they adhere and enclose the powder.

Wet seal cachet machine. This consists of three metal plats (Fig. 2.3), the two outermost plates being attached by hinges to the centre one. The halves of the cachets in which the powder is to be inserted are placed in holes in thecentre plate, A, where they fit loosely. One of the other plates, B, is then swung over the placed on top of the cachets. This second plate also has holes, which are congruent with the holes in the first plate, and its object is to protect the edges of the cachets while they are being filled. A funnel, D, of

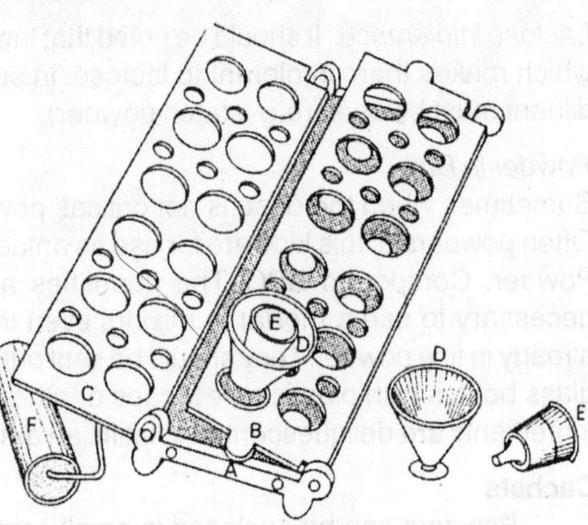

Fig. 2.3. Cachet machine.

the correct size, supplied with the machine, is next placed in each hole of the second plate in turn, and the powder introduced. The powder is pressed down with a small wooden plunger or metal thimble, E, also supplied with the machine.

When the lower halves have been filled, the second plate is folded back. The top halves of the cachets are then placed in the holes of the third plate, C, on the opposite side of the centre plate. The holes in C are somewhat smaller than those of the centre plate, so that the tops of the cachets fit tightly. The edges of the top halves are then moistened with a roller, F, the plate is swung over and pressed down firmly on the centre plate. The top halves of the cachets are thus brought exactly over the lower halves and the edges made to adhere. The upper plate is now lifted, when it brings with it the completed cachets. The finished cachets are finally pushed out gently and boxed.

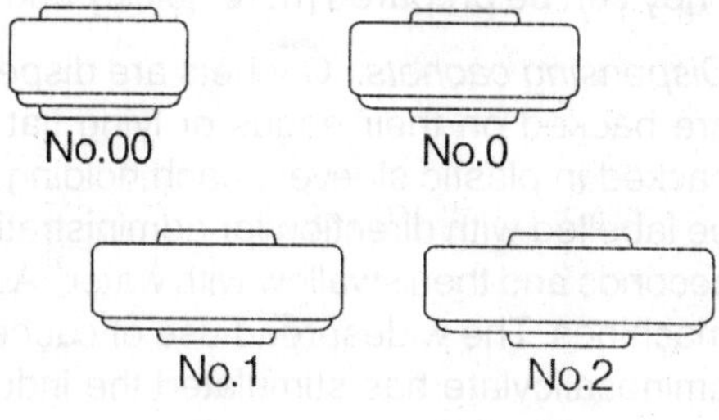

Fig. 2.4. Dry-closing (Secca) cachets.

The amount of moisture used is very important and somewhat difficult to judge correctly. Too much causes the edges to crinkle and become discoloured; too little may produce an imperfect seal and allow the powder to escape at some point on the circumference, or cause the two halves to fall apart completely after the patient has received the cachets.

Dry seal cachets. Dry seal cachets consist of two halves, the upper half fitting over the lower half like the lid on a box (Fig. 2.4). The backs of both lower and upper halves have small projections which fit into the holes of the plates of the machine. Since the projections are the same size on all the sizes of cachets, only one machine is required for the whole range of sizes. The lower halves are fitted into the lower plate (Fig. 2.5) of the machine and filled. The upper halves are filled into the upper plate, D, which is pressed down on the lower one, when the upper halves or 'lids' fit

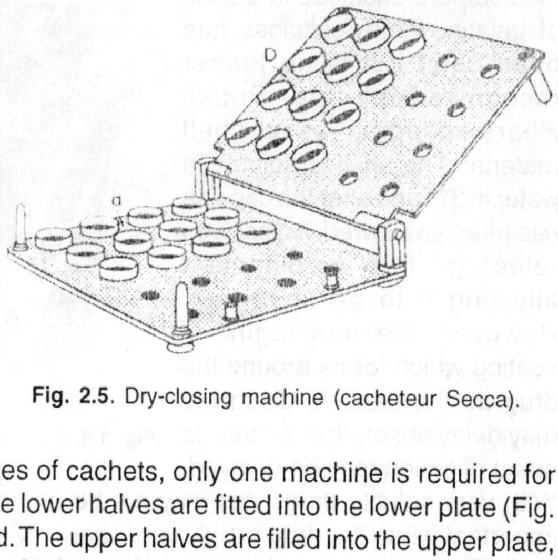

Fig. 2.5. Dry-closing machine (cacheteur Secca).

exactly over the lower halves. These cachets are much more substantial than the ordinary type, and there is no likelihood of the powder escaping. They can be prepared more quickly and are more hygienic.

Dispensing cachets. Cachets are dispensed in boxes or tins in which they are packed on their edges or lying flat. Some manufactured cachets are packed in plastic sleeves, each holding a day's treatment. Cachets should be labelled with direction for administration, e.g. 'Immerse in water for a few seconds and then swallow with water'. Automatic and semi-automatic cachet machines. The widespread use of cachets for the administration of sodium aminosalicylate has stimulated the industrial production of cachets in this country. Bot dry and wet seal cachets may be filled and sealed by automatic (machine-fed) or semi-automatic (hand-fed) machines. Fig. 2.6 shows an automatic machine in which the adjustable fourpunch dosing mechanism delivers a plug of compressed powder to the lower half of the cachet and to this the upper half (automatically moistened if wet sealed) is applied. To achieve consistent dosage from such machines it is essential that the bulk density, particle size and flow characteristics of the powder or blend of powders is accurately controlled.

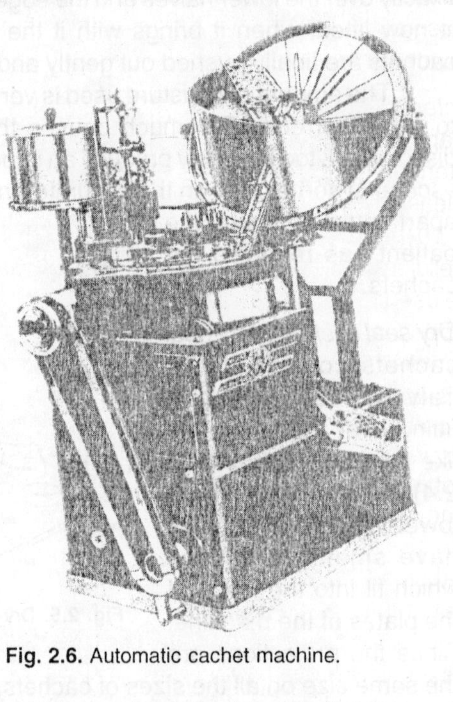

Fig. 2.6. Automatic cachet machine.

Capsules

Capsules consist of a medicament enclosed in a shell of gelatin; methylcellulose has been used but is no longer recognized by the *British Pharmacopoeia* as a shell material. The shell is soluble in water in 37° and after the capsule has been swallowed, it dissolves releases the medicament allowing it to be absorbed. However, the mucilaginous coating which forms around the drug as the capsule dissolves may delay absorption, so that its onset of action may be delayed. With very soluble drugs this may not be an important factor, but is more important when the drug is only very sparingly soluble.

Small quantities of hard gelatin capsules may be extemporaneously dispensed by hand-filling.

Hard Capsules. Hard gelatin capsules are available in a range of sizes to hold varying doses of powdered drugs. They are formed of two cylindrical halves, one slightly larger but shorter in length than the other. The medicament is inserted in the longer narrower half, then the other half is fitted over the open end as a cap, held in place by moistening the edges.

Hand Filling Hard Capsules. The smallest size capsule should be selected that will hold the quantity of medicament prescribed.

The lower halves of the capsules may be supported in the holes of a suppository mould or in a block of wood in which holes of a suitable size have been bored. The powders are prepared in the usual way and are poured into each capsule. This operation is facilitated by the use of a small glass or aluminium funnel and a thin wooden plunger that will pass down the steam of the funnel and prevent it from becoming clogged with powder. The outer edges of the lower halves of the capsules are then moistened with water, using a camel hair brush, and finally the caps are pressed on. This forms a seal which prevents the powder from leaking out of the capsules.

Fig. 2.7. Tevopharm capsule filling machine (Anglo-Continental Machines Ltd.).

Enteric Coated Capsules Enteric coating is applied to gelatin capsules when they are intended to pass through the stomach and release their contents in the small intestine. A 10 per cent solution of cellacephate (cellulose acetate phthalate) in acetone may be used for this purpose. The capsules are dipped in the solution, removed by means of tweezers and allowed to dry on a sieve. It is usually necessary to apply three coats.

Containers for capsules. Capsules are dispensed in small glass screw-cap tablet bottles or in suitable plastic containers. They should be protected from moisture.

Small scale manufacture of capsules. In hospital practice a hand-operated capsule filling machine may be found useful for preparation of capsules, particularly special formulations required in the clinical trial of new drugs. The Tevopharm machine (see Fig. 2.7) is suitable for such purposes, and is essentially a device for locating the capsules into two plates which can be brought together to effect closure. Plates are available to accommodate the different sizes of empty capsules and each plate holds 60 capsules. A sorting device is used to drop the capsules, bottom downwards into the holes in the filling plates. The capsules are pushed firmly into the holes and the lower plate is then fixed by the screw on the front. The upper plate is removed, taking with it the tops of the capsules. The lower halves of the capsules are then pushed flush with the lower plate and are gravity filled with the powdered drug. If the dose required cannot be obtained by filling one of the standard capsules size, a triturate in lactose must be prepared. After filling the capsules, the top plate is replaced and the lever at the side of the machine operated to bottoms of the capsules upwards at the same time as pressure is applied at the top plate is removed bringing away the filled capsules.

LIQUID PREPARATIONS

Drugs administered in aqueous solution or suspension are presented to the gastrointestinal mucosa in a form that is immediately available for absorption. Liquid medicines are, however, generally less stable than solid forms of drug presentation, although, non-aqueous vehicles may be used for drugs which deteriorate in the presence of moisture. Nauseous drugs and those which are irritant to the gastric mucosa are usually unsuitable for presentation in liquid formulations unless well diluted.

Mixtures

Mixture are liquid medicines which the patient divides into doses; he may, or may not be directed to dilute each dose before taking. *A draught* is a liquid medicine consisting of one dose only. *A linctus* is a preparation intended for the treatment of a cough and is rendered viscous by the inclusion of glycerin of syrup; it should be administered undiluted in order to obtain the lubricant effect of the vehicle.

The *British Pharmaceutical Codex* 1973 gives the following metric dose volumes for liquid preparations: for linctuses and elixirs, 5 ml; for adult mixtures, 10 ml, or multiples thereof; and for draughts, 50 ml.

Metric medicine bottles. Mixtures are dispensed in clear glass bottles which comply with British Standard No. 1679/6. The following range of sizes of metric bottles are available: 50, 100, 150, 200, 300 and 500 ml.

If the mixture consists of a simple solution in water, it can be adjusted to volume in a measure before being transferred to the bottle. If the mixture contains an insoluble powder or is viscous, the bottle should be calibrated to the correct volume and the final adjustment to volume made in the bottle. This procedure enables the whole of the insoluble powder or a viscous liquid to be transferred to the final container.

Labelling. The dose should be stated in terms of the metric medicine spoon (B.S. 3221/4). This has a capacity of 5 ml and in the case of medicines having a 5 ml dose-volume the label should read, 'One 5-ml spoonful to be taken...'. In the case of medicines having larger dose volumes, the dose should be stated in units of the 5 ml medicine spoon, e.g. for a 10 ml dose volume, the label should read, 'Two 5-ml spoonfuls'.

For the medicines which are still prescribed in the apothecary system of weights and measures, the prescription must be transcribed into the metric system (see below) and the doses stated in terms of the metric medicine spoon. The use of domestic teaspoons and tablespoons should be abandoned for measuring medicines.

A plastic medicine spoon should be supplied with each bottle of mixture dispensed.

Mixtures containing an insoluble deposit should always be labelled with the direction, 'Shake the Bottle'.

The *British Pharmaceutical Codex* 1973 gives the following directions for labelling mixtures issued on a medical prescription or for an individual patient:

(1) The prescriber's directions
(2) Any special storage conditions
(3) For suspensions, a direction to shake the bottle
(4) A date after which the mixture should not be used if a recommendation is made by the manufacturer, or if a mixture is diluted before issue.

The requirement to state a date after which the mixture should not be used applies to mixtures containing unstable ingredients. For example, elixir of phenoxymethylpenicillin prepared from granules which have been ready made by an industrial manufacturer. The granules are stable if stored in a cool place, but once the elixir has been prepared by addition of water, it must be stored in a cool place and used within 7 days.

Tap water is bacteriologically controlled and is free from pathogenic organisms. Purified water, on storage, can become heavily contaminated with microorganism. Purified water prepared in a de-ionizer is particularly liable to be contaminated if the water is allowed to stagnate in the resin bed. Purified water, prepared by distillation, should not be stored in large volume tanks or containers which permit it to become contaminated. Polythene tubes and containers may become contaminated and form a reservoir of infection which will proliferate and build up a heavy infection in stored water.

Medicinal waters. Medicinal waters such as peppermint water and cinnamon water are used as flavouring agents and carminatives. Chloroform water is used for its sweet taste & also possesses excellent preservative properties.

Infusions. Fresh infusions are no longer used. They are now prepared by diluting concentrated infusions which are 10 times the strength of the original infusions.

Suspending Agents

Many insoluble substances, when shaken up, will remain suspended sufficiently long for a dose to be measured without the use of a suspending agent, but others will not and these require the use of a suspending agent. When no suspending agent is ordered by the prescriber, the pharmacist must use his judgement as to whether it is necessary to include one.

The following are the most commonly used suspending agents:

Compound Tragacanth Powder, BP. This is a mixture of powdered tragacanth, powdered acacia, starch and sucrose. It is used in quantities of 25 to 200 mg for each 10 ml of mixture. It is only in exceptional cases that more than 100 mg for each 10 ml required.

The powder is mixed in a mortar with the substance to be suspended, and the vehicle added gradually with trituration.

Tragacanth Mucilage, BPC. This is employed in quantities up to 1 ml for each 10 ml of mixture, depending on the weight of insoluble matter to be suspended.

Sodium Carboxymethylcellulose BPC. This is available in various viscosity grades, depending upon the degree of polymerization. A medium viscosity grade is preferable for suspending powders in mixtures and is used in a concentration of 0.25 to 1 per cent. It is incorporated in the same manner as compound tragacanth powder.

Powdered tragacanth. This is satisfactory as a suspending agent since it is liable to coagulate into unmanageable lumps unless it is mixed very intimately with an insoluble powder before addition of the vehicle. If it is prescribed in combination with an alcoholic liquid, tragacanth can be made into a mucilage by adding it to the alcoholic liquid in a dry bottle, adding a large quantity of the aqueous vehicle all at once and shaking vigorously.

Liquids in Mixtures

Measurement of volume. The errors involved in measuring volumes of liquids are discussed by Capper and Dare in their report, *Dispensing Tolerances in Liquid Medicines* (1957). Government stamped metric measures complying with British Standard 1922:1953 should be used for dispensing purposes.

Measures are graduated to contain and not to deliver. Consequently after the volume of a liquid has been measured, the measure should be rinsed out with some of the vehicle and the rinsings added to the mixture before adjusting to volume. To measure volume correctly, the bottom of the meniscus should be in line with the graduation on the measure and this should be aligned with the sighting mark on the back of the measure.

If a viscous liquid is to be incorporated in a mixture, it should be measured, and then diluted in the measure with some of the vehicle, and mixed with a glass rod before transferring it from the measure. The measure should be finally rinsed with some more of the vehicle. However, glycerin or syrup if combined with an insoluble substance, should not be too much diluted in the measure; if added to the powder in a mortar, they assist in producing a paste free from lumps and this can then be diluted with the vehicle to produce a uniform suspension.

Volatile, liquids, such as compound spirit of orange, should always be added last to avoid loss of the volatile ingredients.

Soluble Solids in Mixtures

If there is sufficient water present to dissolve the substance completely, a solution can be prepared in a measure with the aid of a stirring rod. The solution should be filtered through sintered glass and the filter washed through with more of the water before making up to volume.

Large crystals such as those of ferrous sulphate should be powdered and dissolved in a mortar. Scale preparations, such as iron and ammonium citrate, dissolve more readily if they are added to water in a measure, small portions at a time with constant stirring.

Stock solutions. For convenience in dispensing solutions of stable soluble salts may be kept ready prepared. However, solutions of some salts may become heavily contaminated with bacteria and fungi if stored for more than a few days.

The use of heat. Some substances dissolve only slowly and the rate of solution may be increased by the use of hot water. Care must be taken to ensure that there is sufficient water present in the mixture to keep the substance permanently in solution; and solution should be allowed to cool at room temperature before the final adjustment to volume. If the substance is present in excess of its solubility, the excess will crystallize out when the solution cools and probably form a mass of crystals at the bottom of the bottle. The method for dealing with substances present in excess of their solubility is described below.

Hot water should not be used for substances decomposed at only moderate temperatures e.g. bicarbonates. It should also not be used if volatile ingredients are present.

Substances present in excess of their solubility. The substance is powdered as finely as possible in a mortar and triturated with some of the cold vehicle. The suspension is then transferred to a previously calibrated bottle and the mortar rinsed with further quantities of the cold vehicle, the rinsings beings added to the contents of the bottle. The mixture is labelled 'Shake the Bottle'.

Small doses of potent substances. The smallest quantity which can be weighed on a dispensing balance is 50 mg and it may sometimes be necessary to make a liquid triturate in order to obtain the required quantity.

Example

Hyoscine hydrobromide 0.5 mg
Chloroform water to 5 ml
Send 100 ml

Hyoscine hydrobromide is freely soluble in water. The required quantity is 0.5 × 20 = 10 mg. Weigh 50 mg; dissolve in 100 ml of chloroform water. Take 20 ml of this solution and dilute with chloroform water to 100 ml.

Insoluble Solids

Diffusible insoluble substances. The general procedure is to reduce the substance to a fine powder in a mortar. The powder is then triturated to a smooth cream with a small amount of the vehicle and this is then diluted by gradually adding about two-third of the vehicle required. The suspension is then transferred to a measure or calibrated bottle and the mixture is made up to volume the with remainder of the vehicle, washing out the mortar with successive small portions and adding to the bulk of the preparation. If syrup of glycerin is present in the mixture, it is diluted with a small portion of the vehicle and used to form the primary smooth cream.

This method can be applied to mixtures containing vegetable powders and diffusible solid drugs such as magnesium carbonate, magnesium trisilicate, light kaolin, etc.

Soluble substances with insoluble solids. The soluble substance can sometimes be mixed with the insoluble powder in a mortar before adding the vehicle. However it is usually preferable to dissolve the soluble ingredient separately and use the solution to triturate the insoluble powder in a mortar.

Indiffusible solids. Substances which do not remain in suspension sufficiently long for a dose to be measured accurately must be suspended by means of a suspending agent. Substances which require the use of a suspending agent include the sulphonamides (e.g. sulphadimidine and succinylsulphathiazole), aspirin and phenacetin. Corticosteroids such as hydrocortisone acetate may sometimes be prescribed as suspensions for administration to children but it is preferable for potent substances such as these to be supplied where possible in tablet form, with instructions that they be crushed and mixed with honey or syrup before administration.

The general procedure for indiffusible solids is to reduce the substance to a fine powder in a mortar, triturate with the suspending agent (usually compound tragacanth powder or sodium carboxymethylcellulose) and form a smooth cream with a small portion of the vehicle. The remainder of the vehicle is then added gradually.

Dispensing in the Metric System

As noted above, the liquid medicines in the *British Pharmaceutical Codex* and *British National Formulary* are formulated to dose of 5 ml or a multiple thereof. When a fractional dose is prescribed, the pharmacist is directed to dilute the medicine with the appropriate vehicle so that the patient is able to measure a full medicine spoonful. Consider the following mixture prescription :

R Tetracycline mixture
2.5 ml four times daily
Send 50 ml

This is dispensed as follows:

Tetracycline mixture 2.5 ml
Syrup to 5 ml
Send 100 ml and label, 'One 5-ml spoonful to be taken four times daily'.

The appropriate diluents for use in each case are stated in the monographs of the *British Pharmaceutical Codex*. Care should be taken to note those preparations which must not be diluted (e.g. Nystatin Mixture). Diluted preparations have only a limited stability and must not be used more than 14 days after the date of preparation. The above mixture therefore should also be labelled 'Do not use after (date)'.

Interpretation of Prescriptions Written in Apothecary System

In order to effect the changeover to dispensing in the metric system, the Weight and Measures (Equivalents for Dealing with Drugs) Regulations, 1968 include six tables specifying how to convert a prescription from the apothecary system into the metric system. A useful series of articles dealing with the changeover to metric dispensing appeared in the Pharmaceutical *Journal*, February, 1969, and a review of the problems involved was given by Thornton Jones (1969).

EMULSIONS

In physical chemistry an emulsion is described as a system in which one immiscible liquid is dispersed in another, but in pharmacy the term is restricted to oil-in-water preparations for internal administration. An emulsion is a particularly convenient form in which to administer oily substances such as liquid paraffin and fixed oils. The oil is dispersed in a continuous surrounding aqueous medium in which flavouring agents may be incorporated to mask the nauseous properties of the oil and improve the palatability of the preparation. This chapter deals with the extemporaneous preparation of small volumes of emulsions.

Small quantities of emulsions may be prepared either in a small emulsifying machine or by the mortar and pestle method. Many machines advertized for cream making can be used for the extemporaneous preparations of emulsions and the results are superior to those produced by the mortar and pestle method. The use of a machine enables a wider range of emulgents to be employed and smaller proportions of emulgents are required.

Hand Emulsifying Machines

The oil, water and mucilage are shaken together to form a coarse emulsion which is poured into the bowl of the machine and pumped by a lever movement of the handle through a fine office at high pressure. This gives the shearing effect which produces a fine emulsion.

Mortar and Pestle Method

The most commonly used emulgent for preparing oil-in-water emulsions in powdered acacia, which can be used for fixed oils, volatile oils, oleo-resins and liquid paraffin. Emulsions may be prepared by hand in a mortar and pestle either by a *dry gum method* or a *wet gum method.*

The dry gum method. A primary emulsion is prepared by mixing the oil, water and gum in the proportions indicated below. When the primary emulsion has been formed it may be diluted with more of the external aqueous phase.

To obtain a good primary emulsion, oil, water and gum must be mixed in the following proportions, depending on the nature of the oil:

Fixed oil	4	Volatile oil	2
Water	2	Water	2
Gum	1	Gum	1

It will be observed that the proportion of gum is twice as great in an emulsion of a volatile oil as in one containing a fixed oil. The ratio of water to gum in the primary emulsion is always 2:1.

In preparing an emulsion by hand, an ample sized mortar should be selected with a corresponding pestle with a broad, flat head to provide the maximum amount of shear in use.

Example:

Olive oil 50 ml

Powdered acacia, a sufficient quantity

Chloroform water to 250 ml

Method. Place in the mortar 12.5 g of powdered acacia; measure 50 ml of olive oil and pour it on to the gum in the mortar, allowing time for the measure to drain. Triturate the oil and gum together to obtain even dispersion of the gum (prolonged triturations is undesirable since it will result in the particles of gum becoming surrounded by oil and they will not readily be hydrated by water). Using a *clean* measure, add 25 ml of chloroform water, *all at once*, and triturate vigorously, working in one direction only and using a whipping action.

As the primary emulsion forms, the preparation changes to a white homogeneous paste and the motion of the pestle produces a cracking sound. The triturations should be continued until a stable primary emulsion has formed. The remaining chloroform water should then be added, in small quantities at first but in increasing quantities as the preparation becomes dilute. Finally, transfer the emulsion to a measure, rinse the mortar with more chloroform water and adjust to volume.

A simple emulsion such as this should be white in appearance and when a few drops are diluted in a large volume of water there should be no visible oil globules on the surface. Emulsions should not cream for several hours and the oily layer should be êasily diffused again by shaking.

Failure to obtain a satisfactory preparation may be due to one or more of the following causes: (i) the use of a mortar which is too small or which is too conical; (ii) the use of a narrow-headed pestle which fails to shear the oil into globules; (iii) measuring the oil in a wet measure; (iv) measuring the water in an oily measure; (v) using an old sample of gum, which has acquired an acid reaction; (vi) bad manipulation; (vii) using incorrect proportions of oil, water and gum; and (viii) diluting the primary emulsion before it is completely formed.

The wet gum method. The proportions of oil water and gum used in the wet gum method are the same as those used for dry gum method. Only the procedure is different.

Example :

Cottonseed oil 50 ml

Powdered acacia, a sufficient quantity

Chloroform water to 250 ml

Method : Weigh 12.5 of powdered acacia and transfer to a suitable sized mortar. Add 25 ml of chloroform water and triturate until the gum has dissolved to form a mucilage. Add the cottonseed oil, drop by drop with constant trituration using a whipping motion. As the oil is added, the liquid in the mortar may acquire a ropy appearance and the oil may not be readily absorbed. When this occurs, add a few drops of chloroform water and triturate the mixture until it becomes homogeneous. Continue to add the oil so long as it is taken up homogeneously, adding a few drops of chloroform water if the preparation shows any tendency to become ropy.

When all the oil has been added, continue triturating until a stable primary emulsion has been obtained. Finally, dilute the primary emulsion with chloroform water, transfer to a measure, rinsing the mortar with further quantities of chloroform water, and adjust to volume.

The wet gum method is more time consuming than the dry gum method. The mucilage should be freshly prepared, since on storage it may become acid in reaction, lose viscosity and render emulsification impossible.

Emulsifying Agents

Powdered Tragacanth

This is inferior to acacia as an emulgent and its emulsifying properties depend mainly upon the viscosity it imparts to the continuous phase. Tragacanth emulsions are coarser than acacia emulsions and do not have their white colour. The main use of tragacanth in emulsions is as an ancillary emulgent in association with acacia. A mixture of tragacanth, 1 part, with acacia, 15 parts, may be used in place of powdered acacia in the extemporaneous preparation of emulsions.

Methylcellulose, BPC

This is a methyl ether of cellulose and is available in various viscosity grades which are denoted by a number following the name. The lower viscosity grades are used as emulsifying agents, methylcellulose 20 being the most commonly used member of the series for this purpose. The suffix '20' indicates the approximate viscosity in centistokes of a 2.0 per cent w/v solution in water at 20°. A mucilage of methylcellulose may be prepared by adding the solid to about one-third the required amount of boiling water stirring constantly and adding the remainder of the water, preferably in the form of ice, when the powder is thoroughly hydrated. The mucilage can be used to make emulsions extemporaneously by the wet gum method but better results are obtained if a mechanical stirrer is used.

Methylcellulose 20 is used as the emulgent in Liquid Paraffin Emulsion, BPC.

Agar

This was formerly used extensively (in association with acacia and tragacanth) for the emulsification of liquid paraffin. It was included for its supposed therapeutic action but was present in too small a quantity to be effective. The *British National Formulary* allows Liquid Paraffin Emulsion to be supplied when Liquid Paraffin and Agar Agar Emulsion is prescribed.

Casein

This is the protein emulsifies fat in milk. Soluble casein or similar products obtained from milk protein may be used as emulgents in the proportion of 12 g of casein for 100 ml of fixed oil. The oil is added to the casein in a mortar and triturated to form a paste and the water is then added gradually with continuous trituration. Emulsions containing casein are particularly liable to microbiological contamination and a preservative should be included. Chloroform, 1:500 may be used for this purpose.

Gelatin Solution
This is an effective emulsifying agent when used on a large scale. A solution containing 120 g of gelatin with 200 g of potassium carbonate in 5 l of water will emulsify 120 l of liquid paraffin.

Substances Requiring Special Treatment

Male fern extract. Add it to its own weight of acacia and triturate thoroughly; then add twice the same amount of water with constant trituration. Take care that the extract does not come into contact with water until it is intimately mixed with gum. Otherwise, the emulsion will contain unsightly black particles.

Paraldehyde. This is now usually given by intramuscular injection but may occasionally be administered orally as a draught. One gram of paraldehyde dissolves in 9 ml of water and it need only be emulsified if present in excess of its solubility. An emulsion can be prepared by adding the paraldehyde to compound powder of tragacanth (100 mg for each 25 ml of paraldehyde) in a dry bottle, shaking gently to disperse the powder and then adding twice the volume of water and shaking vigorously. The remainder of the water can then be added gradually, shaking after each addition.

Chapter 3

External Preparations

LIQUID PREPARATIONS

Liquid preparations for external application can be classified as follows:

(a) *For application to the skin*: applications, liniments, lotions, and paints.
(b) *For application to the ear:* ear drops
(c) *For application to the mouth and throat:* gargles and mouth-washes.
(d) *For application to the naso-pharynx:* nasal drops, spray solutions, and inhalations.

Applications

Applications are liquid or viscous preparations intended for application to the skin. They often contain parasiticides and are intended for only a limited number of applications (e.g. Dicophane Application, BBC). Compound application of Calamine, BPC, is really an oily lotion since it consists of calamine dispersed in a water-in-oil emulsion. Applications should be dispensed in fluted bottles so as to be distinguishable by touch and should be labelled 'For external use only'. The closure of the bottle should be of plastic screw-cap type.

Liniments

Liniments are liquid preparations for external use and may be applied with or without friction. For the relief of pain, they may be applied or warmed flannel or lint, or may be painted on the skin by means of a soft brush. As stimulants, liniments may be massaged into the skin with considerable friction. They should not be applied to areas in which the skin is broken.

Liniments may be: alcoholic solutions (e.g. Aconite Liniment, BPC); oily solutions (e.g. Methyl Salicylate Liniment, BPC); or emulsions (e.g. Turpentine Liniment, BP). They should be dispensed in coloured, fluted bottles and labelled 'For external use only'.

Lotions

Lotions are aqueous solutions or suspensions intended for application to the skin surface. If they contain insoluble solids in suspension, they are sometimes referred to as 'shake lotions'. On application to the skin, the water evaporates leaving a residue of the medicament on the skin surface. The evaporation causes cooling and lotions are applied to acutely inflamed areas. The cooling effect may be enhanced by the inclusion of alcohol. Glycerin may be included to promote adherence of the residual powder on the skin surface. Suspending agents such as sodium carboxymethylcellulose or bentonite may be present to assist the dispersion of insoluble powders in shake lotions (e.g. Calamine Lotion, BP).

Lotions may also take the form of dilute emulsions, usually of the oil-in-water type and containing emulsifying wax. They should contain a preservative to inhibit the growth of microorganisms. When purified water is used for the preparation of lotions, it should be freshly boiled and cooled before use.

Lotions should be dispensed in fluted bottles, closed with a plastic screw-cap. They should be labelled 'For external use only'.

Paints

Paints are another group of liquid preparations for external application, usually for circumscribed areas. They may be aqueous or alcoholic solutions and sometimes are prepared with a collodion basis to form a film on the skin. Compound Tincture of Benzoin BPC is also used as a basis for paints for the same reason (e.g. Compound Podophyllin Paint, BPC).

Paints should be dispensed in coloured fluted bottles, preferably closed by means of glass stoppers.

Ear Drops

Ear drops are often aqueous (sometimes glycerin or alcoholic) solutions dispensed in small quantities (10 or 25 ml) and intended for instillation into the ear. hydrogen peroxide ear drops (5-volume) and phenol ear drops (6 per cent w/w) are typical examples. It should be noted that glycerin phenol (16 percent w/w) becomes caustic if diluted with water. When prescribed in ear drops, glycerin phenol must be diluted with glycerin.

Ear drops should be dispensed in coloured, fluted bottles with a dropper and plastic screw-cap closure.

Gargles

Gargles are aqueous solutions, intended to be used after dilution with warm water. They are intended to bring the medicament into contact with the mucous surface of the throat, but it is now generally recognized that antiseptic substances exert little effect when used in this manner. Gargles may be useful in giving symptomatic relief and may have some analgesic effect. Gargles are usually clear solutions but occasionally aspirin, if the form of a suspension may be used as a gargle and afterwards swallowed.

Gargles should be dispensed in clear, fluted glass bottles closed with a plastic screw-cap. If they are to be swallowed after use, they should be dispensed in clear, plain glass bottles in the same way as mixtures.

Mouth-Washes

Mouth-washes are similar to gargles but are intended to wash out the mouth. They may be of value for local hygiene of the mouth but antiseptic substances used in this way are unlikely to be effective.

Mouth-washes should be dispensed in clear, fluted bottles.

Nasal Drops

Nasal drops are aqueous solution for instillation into the nostrils. They may contain vasoconstrictor drugs to relieve nasal congestion and are often preserved with chlorbutol (0.5 per cent) or other suitable antiseptic substance. Formerly, oily solutions were commonly used as nasal drops but the oil may retard the ciliary action of the mucosa or, if drops of oil enter the trachea, may even cause lipoid pneumonia. For this reason, oily solutions are no longer recommended.

Nasal drops are dispensed in small quantities (10 or 25 ml) in fluted, coloured glass bottles fitted with a plastic screw-cap and dropper. Proprietary nasal sprays are supplied in plastic, squeeze-type containers. The prolonged use of vasoconstrictor drugs in the nose may damage the nasal mucosa.

Spray Solutions

Spray solutions are aqueous, alcoholic or glycerin solutions intended to be applied to the membrane of the throat or nose by means of an atomizer. Oily solutions were formerly used for this purpose but are no longer used for the same reason that oily nasal drops have been discontinued.

The type of atomizer used depends upon the viscosity of the spray solutions; the more viscous the solution the more powerful the atomizer needed. When dispensing a spray solution, the patient should be asked whether he possesses a suitable spray. If not, an appropriate one should be supplied and its use explained.

The drugs most commonly dispensed as spray solutions are adrenaline and isoprenaline, which are both used for the relief of Asthma. The use of spray solutions for this purpose has been superseded to a large extent, by the introduction of metered aerosols. Metered aerosols have the advantage of producing a more accurately controlled dose of the drug in particulate form. The particle size can be controlled to ensure that the drug penetrates the bronchial tree. Such preparations are not without risk and adverse reactions, including fatalities, have followed the too frequent use of such preparations. It is advisable to warm patients that they should follow very carefully the medical directions in the use of these preparations and should resist any temptation to use them more frequently.

Ergotamine tartrate is also sometimes administered by inhalation from a metered aerosol for the relief of attack of migraine.

Inhalations

Inhalations are solutions or suspensions of volatile, aromatic or antiseptic substances, the vapour of which is inhaled from the surface of hot water. The directions are usually to the effect that one teaspoonful of the liquid is to be poured about one pint of hot, but not boiling, water and the vapour inhaled. Inhalations are useful for the relief of nasal congestion and it is probable that the steam contributes mainly to the effectiveness of these preparations.

Inhalations often consist of alcoholic solutions of substances such as menthol, volatile oils or benzoin (e.g. Benzoin Inhalation, BPC). Occasionally, volatile oils are ordered with water as the vehicle, and in these circumstances the oil is triturated with a small amount of light magnesium carbonate in a mortar and the water added gradually, the suspension being finally rinsed into the bottle and made up to volume with more of the water (e.g. Menthol and Eucalyptus Inhalation, BPC). The object of the light magnesium carbonate is to ensure even dispersion of the volatile oil throughout the vehicle and such inhalations should be labelled with directions to shake the bottle before use. Inhalations should be dispensed in fluted bottles of clear glass.

SOLID PREPARATIONS

The solid or semi-solid preparations for external applications are ointments, creams, pastes, poultices, and dusting powders.

Ointments

Ointments are greasy, semi-solid preparations for application to the skin. They are often anhydrous and contain the medicament either dissolved or dispersed in the vehicle. Substances which are dispersed should be in the form of a fine powder and in some cases, notably the corticosteroids, the solid should be in the form of a micronized powder.

The bases that are used mainly in the preparation of ointments may be classified into hydrocarbon bases, absorption bases, emulsifying bases, and water soluble bases.

Hydrocarbon bases These may consist of soft paraffin or a mixture of soft paraffin with hard paraffin and liquid paraffin to produce a suitable consistency. Paraffins are inert substances, chiefly saturated, which are unlikely to react with the medicament and do not develop rancidity on storage.

Paraffin Ointment BP is a mixture of white beeswax, hard paraffin, cetostearyl alcohol and white soft paraffin. The *British Pharmacopoeia* directs that when paraffin ointment is used in a white ointment, it should be prepared with white soft paraffin and when used in a coloured ointment, it should be prepared with yellow soft paraffin. The cetostearyl alcohol is included in paraffin ointment in order to improve its spreading properties on the skin. Paraffin ointment is stiffer in consistency than soft paraffin.

The paraffin bases form a greasy film on the skin surface which remains unabsorbed. They reduce the rate of moisture loss from the skin surface and, in dry scaly conditions of the skin, may improve the hydration of the horny layer.

Absorption bases. Absorption bases contain a water-in-oil emulsifying agent, usually in the form of wool fat or one of its derivatives. Simple ointment BP is a mixture of wool fat, hard paraffin cetostearyl alcohol and white or yellow soft paraffin, depending upon whether it is used in a white or coloured ointment. Simple Ointment will absorb about 15 per cent of its weight of water, forming a water-in-oil emulsion.

Wool Alcohols Ointment, BP contains wool alcohols, hara paraffin, liquid paraffin and white or yellow soft paraffin depending upon whether it is used in a white or coloured ointment. Wool alcohols ointment will absorb an equal weight of water. Wool alcohols is liable to oxidize on storage and when preparing ointment of wool alcohols, the outer film of oxidized material should be removed since the emulsifying properties are reduced on oxidation.

Absorption bases such as simple ointment and wool alcohols ointment form a greasy film on the skin surface which modifies the rate of moisture loss in the same way as the hydrocarbon bases. The wool fat or wool alcohols may also assist in hydrating the horny layer by forming a water-in-oil emulsion on the skin surface, thus prolonging the time during which the moisture may be absorbed by the keratin layer.

Although not included in the *British Pharmacopoeia or British Pharmaceutical Codex* hydrogenated lanolin is sometimes used in preference to wool fat, since it is a more elegant product and more consistent in its performance. However, wool fat and related products are now less favoured in dermatological vehicles, since some individuals are sensitive to them.

Emulsifying bases These bases contain oil-in-water emulsifying agents which render them readily miscible with water or 'self-emulsifying'. Depending upon the nature of the emulsifying agent present, emulsifying bases can be classified into three main groups; anionic emulsifying bases, cationic emulsifying bases, and non-ionic emulsifying bases.

Anionic emulsifying bases contain an anionic emulsifying agent and are exemplified by Emulsifying Ointment, BP. This consists of a mixture of emulsifying wax, white soft paraffin and liquid paraffin. Emulsifying wax is a mixture of cetostearyl alcohol and sodium lauryl sulphate which is incompatible with cationic organic medicaments and the salts of barium and heavy metals.

Cationic emulsifying bases are exemplified by Cetrimide Emulsifying Ointment, BP. This consists of a mixture of cetrimide, cetostearyl alcohol, white soft paraffin and liquid paraffin. Cetrimide Emulsifying Wax BPC is a mixture of cetrimide and cetostearyl alcohol which is compatible with cationic medicaments.

Non-ionic emulsifying ointments are exemplified by Cetomacrogol Emulsifying Ointment, BPC. This consists of a mixture of Cetomacrogol emulsifying wax, white soft paraffin and liquid paraffin. Cetomacrogol Emulsifying Wax BP is a mixture of cetostearyl alcohol and Cetomacrogol 1000 which is compatible with cationic medicaments and fairly high concentrations of electrolytes. Cetomacrogol is a polythylene glycol either of cetostearyl alcohol and is incompatible with pehnolic compounds.

Because of their surface active properties, emulsifying bases may facilitate contact between the medicament and the skin surface. They are also readily washed off the skin and are used when this property is desired, e.g. on scalp areas.

Water soluble bases. Water soluble bases consist of mixtures of macrogols (polyethylene glycols). These are polymers of ethylene glycol which range from mobile liquids to hard waxes, depending upon the number of ethylene oxide units in the polymer. Macrogol 300 BP contains five or six ethylene oxide units and has a molecular weight of 285 to 325. Macrogol 4000 BP contains 69 to 84 ethylene oxide units and has a molecular weight of 3100 to 3700.

Macrogol Ointment, BPC is a mixture of liquid and hard macrogols which has a consistency similar to that of soft paraffin and is completely soluble in water. Macrogol bases are used for local anaesthetics such as lignocaine and are useful when easy washing from the skin surface is desired, but they reduce the activity of phenolic antiseptics.

Preparation of Ointments

Trituration. When the quantity of ointment is not more than about 50 g. a white porcelain or marble ointment slab (about 30 cm square) should be used in conjunction with a flexible steel spatula.

A steel spatula should not be used when there is a possibility that the medicament may react with the metal, e.g. mercury compounds, tannic acid, salicylic acid and iodine. Stainless steel spatulas are suitable for most substances or a flexible vulcanite spatula may be used.

The whole of the medicament is first intimately mixed with a little of the base, and then the remainder of the base incorporated gradually, the spatula being held flat and worked with a side-to-side motion rather than a rotary one. When the medicament is rather gritty or contains large aggregated lumps (e.g. zinc oxide, calamine or mercuric oxide) it should be levigated on the slap with a few drops of liquid paraffin before incorporation into a paraffin base.

Twin roller mills are available for the preparation of small quantities of ointment by hand. The degree of fineness is determined by the setting of the variable roller. Larger, triple-roll mills, motor driven, capable of handling large quantities of ointments and having an output up to 5 to 7 kg per h, are also available.

Crystalline, water soluble substances (e.g. resorcinol), present in small quantities, may be dissolved in a little water before incorporation in the basis. It should be noted that soft paraffin is capable of absorbing up to 10 per cent of its weight of water and wool fat will absorb nearly twice its weight of water.

Fusion. Ointments containing ingredients which are quite solid at room temperature (hard paraffin beeswax, emulsifying wax, wool alcohols) are prepared by melting the ingredients in a procelain dish over a water bath. The usual method is to melt the substance with the highest melting point first and add the other ingredients of the basis in order of their melting points.

When an insoluble substance is to be incorporated into such a base containing an oil, it is advisable to levigate the solid with the oil in a hot mortar and then to add it, with constant trituration, the previously melted mixture of the other ingredients. For small quantities of ointment a heated slab may be used.

If no oil is present, the solid medicament must be finely powdered and sifted into the melted base through fine muslin or a No. 60 mesh sieve, after the base has been removed from the water bath and has just begun to thicken. The mixture is then stirred until cold.

Water soluble bases containing liquid and hard macrogols are also prepared by fusion, using a minimum amount of heat and stirring until cold.

Creams

The term 'cream' in pharmacy and medicine is applied to viscous emulsions of semi-solid consistency intended for application to the skin or mucous membrane. They may be of the water-in-oil (oily creams) or oil-in-water (aqueous creams) type.

Preparation of Creams

Microbiological contamination is liable to occur, particularly in aqueous creams, which should always contain an added preservative. In the presence of an oily phase and emulsifying agents, the activity of preservatives may be reduced and if there is heavy contamination, the preservative may not be capable of preventing bacterial growth. Special care should be taken to avoid contamination of creams with *Pseudomonas aeruginosa,* which is commonly found as a contaminant of purified water. Apparatus used in the preparation of creams should be thoroughly cleansed and rinsed with freshly boiled and cooled purified water before use. Purified water must be freshly boiled and cooled before incorporation into creams and hygienic precautions should be taken both during the preparation of a cream and when filling into containers.

Containers Creams should be dispensed in well-closed containers to prevent evaporation of the aqueous phase. Collapsible metal or plastic containers are preferable, but if a pot with a screw-cap is used, care should be taken to ensure that the liner of the screw-cap is of plastic or is plastic-coated. Bonded cork liners are particularly to be avoided. Creams should be stored in a cool place.

Oily Creams

Oily creams contain a water-in-oil emulsifying agent which may be wool fat, wool alcohols, a fatty acid ester of sorbitan or the salt of a fatty acid and a divalent metal (e.g. calcium)

Oily Cream, B.P. Oily Cream, BP, consists of a mixture of equal parts of wool alcohols ointment and purified water.

Method. Melt the ointment of wool alcohols over a water bath. Warm the purified water, freshly boiled and cooled, to about 50°C and mix with the melted ointment of wool alcohols. Stir constantly until cold, preferably by means of a mechanical stirrer.

Oily Cream, BP is incompatible with phenolic substances and with ichthammol. It is liable to separate on standing, particularly at summer temperature. The water is usually readily reincorporated by stirring. For a discussion of the use of wool alcohols see Clark and Kitchen (1960).

Zinc Cream, BP. Zinc Cream BP consists of zinc oxide suspended in a water-in-oil emulsions of arachis oil. The emulsifying agent is calcium oleate and wool fat.

Method. Mix the zinc oxide with the calcium hydroxide and triturate with the oleic acid and archis oil. Incorporate the wool fat and gradually add sufficient purified water to produce the required weight, stirring vigorously during this addition.

Aqueous Creams

Aqueous creams contain an oil-in-water emulsifying agent which may be one of the emulsifying waxes, and alkali salt of a fatty acid, self emulsifying monostearin or a polyethylene glycol derivative of a sorbitan fatty acid ester.

Aqueous Cream, BP. Aqueous Cream, BP, consists of a mixture of 30 percent of emulsifying ointment with purified water preserved with chlorocresol.

Method. Boil and cool sufficient purified water. Measure the quantity required and dissolve the chlorocresol with the aid of gentle heat. Add the solution to the emulsifying ointment, previously melted over a water bath. Stir gently until cold.

Hydrocortisone Cream, BPC

Method: Boil and cool sufficient purified water and measure the quantity required. Dissolve the chlorocresol with the aid of gentle heat; melt the cetomacrogol emulsifying ointment over a water bath; add the chlorocresol solution warmed to the same temperature and stir the mixture until cold. Incorporate the required amount of hydrocortisone acetate in the cream by trituration on a clean ointment slab using a spatula.

Note: Special care should be taken to avoid introducing heavy contamination during preparation, and creams containing coricosteroids are best dispensed in collapsible metal or plastic tubes so that they do not become contaminated during use.

Dimethicone Cream, BPC

Method: Melt the cetostearyl alcohol with the dimethicone 350 and the liquid paraffin over a water bath. Boil and cool sufficient purified water and measure the required quantity. Dissolve the chlorocresol and cetrimide with the aid of gentle heat. Add the solution to the oily phase at the same temperature and stir mechanically until cold.

Note: Dimethicone 350 is a silicone fluid which is water repellant. Dimethicone cream is used as a protective barrier around colostomies and to prevent bedsores and napkin rash. It is vital, therefore, that is should not be contaminated with microorganisms.

Pastes

Pastes are stiffer preparations than ointments and contain a high proportion of powder dispersed in a fatty basis. They were originally formulated on the principle that the high content of powder would absorb exudate but it is unlikely that a powder which has been preferentially wetted with oil will be capable of absorbing an aqueous fluid. Because of their very stiff consistency, pastes are useful for applying active medicaments (e.g. dithranol and coal tar) to circumscribed areas of the skin since they tend to localize the effect of the active ingredient.

Pastes are usually applied liberally by means of a wooden spatula or palette knife. Zinc and Salicylic Acid Paste, BP (Lassar's paste) is the most commonly used preparation of this type. Medicaments incorporated in zinc and salicylic acid paste are less active than when included in ointments. Higher concentrations of substances such as dithranol may therefore be tolerated if they are combined in zinc and salicylic acid paste. The following example illustrates this:

R, Dithranol 0.1 g.

Zinc and salicylic acid paste to 100 g

Method. This preparation is best prepared on a heated ointment slab.

Triturate the dithranol with a small quantity of the zinc and salicylic acid paste until it is smooth and completely dispersed. Gradually incorporate the remainder of the zinc and salicylic acid paste, with constant trituration to ensure uniform dispersion of the dithranol. The preparation should be carefully inspected to ensure that no discrete agglomerates of dithranol are present.

Poultices

A poultice is a viscous, pasty preparation for external use, usually employed with the object of reducing inflammation and allaying pain. The two most commonly used preparations of this type are Kaolin Poultice, BPC and Magnesium Sulphate Paste, BPC.

In the preparation of Kaolin Poultice, BP, heavy kaolin is first sifted and dried at 100°C to remove moisture. It is then mixed with boric acid and glycerin and the mixture heated to 120°C for 1 h with occasional stirring. After cooling, thymol, methylsalicylate and peppermint oil are added and the mass thoroughly mixed.

Heavy kaolin is liable to be contaminated with bacterial spores (e.g. *Clostridium tetani*) and the heating procedure is necessary to kill these. The temperature is limited to 120°C to prevent decomposition of the glycerin.

Kaolin Poultice is stored in well closed containers to prevent loss of volatile ingredients and absorption of moisture from the atmosphere by glycerin.

In the preparation of Magnesium Sulphate Paste, BPC, the dried Magnesium Sulphate must first be heated at 130°C or 150°C for an appropriate length of time to ensure that the dried power contains at least 85 per cent of magnesium sulphate. This is necessary to ensure that the product complies with the standard and does not form a granular crystalline preparation on storage.

Dusting Powders

Dusting powders are mixtures of fine powders which are applied to the skin folds to prevent friction. They may contain talc, zinc oxide, starch and kaolin. Powders such as talc and kaolin, which may be contaminated with bacterial spores, should be sterilized by heating at 160°C for 1 h before incorporation into a dusting powder. Talc is included for its lubricant properties whereas starch and zinc oxide absorb moisture. Boric acid should no longer be used in dusting powders since it has been found that it may be absorbed in toxic amounts through abraded skin.

Dusting powders are prepared by the same technique as those described for powders. After mixing, they should be passed through a No. 44 mesh sieve or finer; any powder that will not pass the sieve must be further ground until it will. After sifting, the whole must be again lightly mixed.

Chapter 4

Preparations for the Eye

Drugs may be applied to the eye in the form of drops, ointments or lotions. They may also be injected into various regions of the eye. The *British Pharmaceutical Codex* defines the following ophthalmic injections:

Subconjunctival injections– aqueous solutions or suspensions which are injected under the conjunctiva. The volume injected by this route is limited to 1 ml and consequently the amount of soluble drug administered is restricted to the amount which dissolves in that volume.

Intracameral injections – aqueous solutions which are injected into the anterior chamber of the eye during surgery to increase the volume of the chamber, to produce miosis and for zonulysis. Antibiotics are usually satisfactorily administered by subconjunctival injection and rarely need intracameral injection.

Intravitreous injections – used to increase the volume of the vitreous chamber. Reconstituted dried vitreous fluid is used for this purpose and a suitable grade of sterilized silicone oil may also be used.

Retrobulbar injections– aqueous solutions used to produce anaesthesia of the globe and akinesia of the extraocular muscles.

Ophthalmic injections must be sterile and are prepared under the same conditions and by the same methods as other parenteral preparations. Solutions used during surgery must also be sterile and contain no preservative. They must therefore be presented in single-use containers and any solution remaining at the end of an operation must be discarded.

EYE DROPS

Eye drops are sterile aqueous or oily solutions or suspensions intended for instillation into the conjunctival sac. They may contain antimicrobial substances such as antibiotics, anti-inflammatory agents such as the corticosteroids, miotic drugs such as physostigmine sulphate or mydriatic drugs such as atropine sulphate. Oily eye drops are nowadays seldom used but may, nevertheless occasionally be requested. They are usually prepared with sterile castor oil and alkaloids incorporated in such a vehicle must be used in the form of the base; e.g. oily eye drops of pilocarpine consist of pilocarpine base dissolved in sterile castor oil.

Sterility of Eye Drops

Until the Supplement 1966 to the *British Pharmaceutical Codex* 1963, there was no official requirement that eye drops should be sterile. They had previously been regarded as extemporaneously prepared preparations and although precautions were taken to avoid contamination during preparation, they were not subjected to a final sterilizing process. It became evident, particularly in hospital practice, that contaminated solutions could cause serious infections of the eye and various organisms were incriminated including *Pseudomonas aeruginosa*, *Staphylococcus aureus* and *Proteus vulgaris*. Of these, *Pseudomonas aeruginosa* has give rise to the most concern. It is widely distributed and is commonly found contaminant of distilled water. It has simple nutritional requirements and is resistant to the action of many antimicrobial agents antibiotics. Moreover, it can cause serious infections leading to the loss of an eye.

The intact eye has its own defences against infection. The corneal epithelium provides an effective barrier against infection and the tears contain lysozyme which has a powerful antimicrobial action. However, if the eye is damaged, infection can pass into the non-vascular, underlying stroma which provides a good culture medium in which the organisms can proliferate. The cornea may become ulcerated and loss of sight ensue. It is particularly important therefore, to ensure the sterility of solutions which may be used in damaged eyes. Fluorescein eye drops, for example, are used as a diagnostic agent to detect foreign bodies and corneal abrasions. In such circumstances, the need for sterility is vital and it is better that such preparations should be used from single-dose containers.

Sterilization of Eye Drops

The problems of sterilizing eye drops are essentially the same as those involved in the preparation of parenteral solutions. Many of the drugs used in ophthalmology are infected by heat and the amount of heat applied in the sterilization procedure has to take account of the stability of the drug. The *British Pharmaceutical Codex* recommends the three following general methods:

1. The medicament is dissolved in the aqueous vehicle containing one of the prescribed antimicrobial substances, the solution is clarified by filtration, transferred to the final containers, which are then closed to exclude microorganisms, and sterilized by autoclaving.
2. The medicament is dissolved in the aqueous vehicle containing one of the prescribed antimicrobial substances, the solution is sterilized by filtration and transferred, by means of an aseptic technique to sterile containers, which are then closed so as to exclude microorganisms.
3. The medicament is dissolved in the aqueous vehicle containing one of the prescribed antimicrobial substances, the solution is clarified by filtration, transferred to the final containers which are then closed so as to exclude microorganisms and sterilized by maintaining at 98 to 100 for 30 min.

The *British Pharmaceutical Codex* permits eye drops to be prepared by any other method provided that the product is identical in appearance, quality and composition with one prepared by the appropriate method described in the individual monograph. Exposure to ionizing radiations is not a permitted method but it may be used provided that the product is sterile and has not undergone chemical degradation so that it fails to comply with the required standards. It should be pointed out, however, that the effect of ionizing radiations on drugs and bactericides has not yet been fully investigated and unusual pathways of degradation may be involved. Trigger and Caldwell (1968) have reported that both sodium sulphacetamide eye drops and fluorescein eye drops darken in colour on exposure to a dose of 2.5 Mard but this colour change was not associated with any other measurable change in assay, ultraviolet absorption or chromatography. There was also no detectable increase in the irritancy of the eye drops according to the Draize test. The same authors also reported that atropine eye drops and eye ointment bases could be sterilized by exposure to ionizing radiations.

Bactericides in Eye Drops

In order to prevent the growth of microorganisms,. accidentally introduced during use, eye drops which are dispensed in multi-dose containers must contain a suitable preservative. The preservation of ophthalmic preparations has been reviewed by Brown and Norton (1965). These authors state that there is no ideal preservative for eye drops available at present. The properties of an ideal preservative are:

1. It should be rapidly effective against a wide range of organisms, particularly *Pseudomonas aeruginosa.*
2. It should be non-irritant to the eye, non-toxic and should not cause pain or stinging.
3. It should be compatible with the medicaments used in eye preparations.
4. It should be compatible with eye drops containers and closures.
5. It should be stable at the temperatures used for sterilization of eye drops.

The *British Pharmaceutical Codex* permits the use of three antimicrobial agents as preservatives in eye drops namely: (a) phenylmercuric nitrate or acetate (0.002 per cent): (b) benzalk onium chloride (0.01 per cent); or (c) chlorhexidine acetate (0.01 per cent). Phenylmercuric salts are unsuitable for use in eye drops which are used over long periods of time (e.g. pilocarpine and physostigmine) since there is a possibility that with prolonged use they may cuase deposition of minute traces of mercury in the lens. While this condition appears to be symptomless, it is nevertheless undesirable. Benzalkonium chloride is unsuitable for use in eye drops containing local anaesthetics because the latter abolish the blink reflex and the benzalkonium chloride, because of its detergent action, removes the protective oily alyer from the precorneal film. If the blink reflex is normal, the meibomian oily layer is rapidly restored.

Apart from the above considerations, the selection of the preservative to be used in eye drops depends upon its compatibility with the medicament. The preservatives used in the eye drops of the *British Pharmaceutical Codex* are given in Table 4.1.

Table 4.1

Medicament	Preservative
Amethocaine hydrochloride	PMA or PMN 0.002 per cent
Atropine sulphate	PMA or PMN 0.002 per cent or BC 0.02 per cent
Carbachol	BC 0.02 per cent
Chloramphenicol	PMN or PMA 0.002 per cent
Cocaine hydrochloride	PMN or PMA 0.002 per cent or CA 0.01 per cent
Cocaine hydrochloride and Homatropine hydrobromide	CA 0.01 per cent
Fluorescein	PMN or PMA 0.002 per cent
Homatropine hydrobromide	BC 0.02 per cent or CA 0.01 per cent
Hyoscine hydrobromide	BC 0.02 per cent or CA 0.01 per cent
Lachesine chloride	PMN or PMA 0.002 per cent
Neomycin sulphate	PMN or PMA 0.002 per cent
Phenylephrine hydrochloride	BC 0.04 per cent
Physostigmine sulphate	BC 0.02 per cent
Pilocarpine hydrochloride	BC 0.02 per cent
Prednisolone sodium phosphate	BC 0.04 per cent
Sulphacetamide sodium	PMN or PMA 0.002 per cent

BC = Benzalkonium chloride, CA = Chlorhexidine acetate, PMN = Phenylmercuric nitrate, PMA = Phenylmercuric acetate

Hydrogen Ion Concentrations

The lacrimal secretion has a pH value between 7.2 and 7.4 and has a high buffering capacity. Consequently, the eye can tolerate solutions having a wide range of pH values from 3.5 to 10 provided they are not strongly buffered since the tears will rapidly restore the normal pH value of the eye.

Most drugs used in the eye are the salts of weak organic bases (e.g. alkaloids) and are stable at acid pH values. The degree of ionization is affected by the pH value and as this approaches neutrality, the concentration of the unionized organic base is increased. The free base is lipid soluble and will penetrate the cornea more readily than the ionized form of the drug. The therapeutic activity of eye drops may therefore be affected by the pH value but, for reasons of stability, this must usually be kept low.

Tonicity

It was formerly though that, for reason of comfort on instillation, eye drops should be made isotonic with the lacrimal secretion. However, it has been established that the eye can tolerate a range of tonicity from 0.5 to 2% sodium chloride before discomfort is experienced. It is often the nature of the medicament itself which causes pain or stinging on instillation. Amethocaine hydrochloride, for example, has surface active properties which cause pain when solutions are instilled into the eye and for this reason concentrations above 1 per cent should not be used. There is now no general requirement in the *British Pharmaceutical Codex* for eye drops to be made isotonic.

Viscosity

Attempts have been made to prolong the contact time of the drug in the eye by increasing the viscosity of the vehicle. For this purpose, methyl cellulose has been incorporated into eye drops but it is unlikely that the increase in viscosity has any material effect on the efficacy or duration of action of the medicament.

Hypromellose Eye Drops BPC, contain hydroxypropylmethylcellulose which has been selected for the purpose because it produces clearer solutions than methylcellulose. Hypromellose eye drops are intended for use as a substitute for tears in eye conditions in which the lachrymal secretion is deficient. They may also be used as a contact lens solution but may need diluting when used for this purpose. Hypromellose eye drops cannot be used as a general vehicle for eye drops since incompatibilities may arise between the medicament and the bactericide or the hydroxypropylmethylcellulose. Solutions containing cellulose derivatives are coagulated on heat sterilization but will usually go back into solution if shaken while cooling. However, there is usally some reduction is viscosity.

Eye Drop Containers

For use in hospital practice during and after surgery on the eye, eye drops should be dispensed in single-dose containers. Eye drops which are used in damaged eyes (e.g. fluorescein) should be similarly dispensed. In such a container, there is no necessity for eye drops to contain a bactericide and it should be remerbered that solutions used during surgery must not contain any added antimicrobial substance.

Multi-dose containers. For domiciliary use and for intact eyes in hospital practice, eye drops are dispensed in multi-dose containers. The conventional type of eye drops bottle is made of glass and is closed by a screw-cap through which the eye dropper and teat are inserted. The *British*

Pharmaceutical Codex specifies that such containers should comply with British Standard 1679; Part 5: 1965. This requires that the bottle is amber coloured, vertically ribbed and made of neutral glass or soda glass which has been surface treated to limit the amount of alkali released into aqueous solutions. The surface treated bottles are known as `one trip' bottles and should not be autoclaved more than once. Glass droppers are made of neutral glass and the rubber teats must be capable of withstanding autoclaving on one occasion and must not release alkali or other impurities during use. The caps into which the teats are inserted may be made of aluminium or a suitable plastic.

Natural rubber teats not infrequently give rise to difficulty. Certain batches may not withstand autoclaving on a single occasion, while others may be incompatible with the bactericide. On autoclaving in the presence of benzalkonium chloride, they may produce a cloudy solution possibly due to the leaching out of stearates from the rubber. Silicone rubber teats are less likely to absorb the bactericide from solution (see below). Unfortunately, they are considerably more expensive than natural rubber teats and allow considerable loss of water vapour on storage.

Eye drops may also be dispensed with an ordinary screw-cap closure and the sterile dropper provided separatley in a suitable pack to maintain sterility. This method of presentation may be adopted to overcome the difficulty of incompatibility between the bactericide and the rubber closure, in which case the rubber liner of the screw-cap must be protected by a disc ethylene terephthalate (`Melinex'). This method presents practical difficulties since ethylene terephthalate is available only in sheet from and the discs must be hand-cut. Eye drops may also be dispensed in this manner in hospital practice so that a supply or wrapped sterile droppers may be issued with them and a new sterile dropper used every time the drops are applied to the eye in order to minimize the risk of infection.

Aluminium or other metal screw-caps are unsuitable if a phenylmercuric salt is used as the bactericide because of the possibility of chemcial interaction.

The *British Pharmaceutical Codex* also permits the use of `suitable plastics containers' for eye drops. Such containers must be compatible with the preparation and not release undesirable materials (e.g. plasticizers), into the solution. Containers made of nylon have been used for eye drops and are generally satisfactory, but elderly patients may have difficulty in using them to instil the drops iinto the eye. They are used for some proprietary presentations of eye drops.

Preparation of Eye Drops

An account of the small scale preparation of eye drops has been given by Smith (1967). The general precautions with regard to cleanliness of apparatus, working environment etc. are the same as those for parenteral solutions.

Containers

Glass containers must be throughly cleansed by rinsing in detergent solution and purified water. Rubber in detergent solution and purified water. Rubber tests must also be cleansed by boiling in water and detergent followed by rinsing in purified water. They are then impregnated with the bactericide to be used by autoclaving in a closed container in a solution containing twice the concentration of bactericide used in the eye drops and storing them in this solution for 7 days before use. It is preferable to have a stock of rubber tests all ready for use stored in closed screw-cap jars containing each of the bactericides used in the *British Pharmaceutical Codex*.

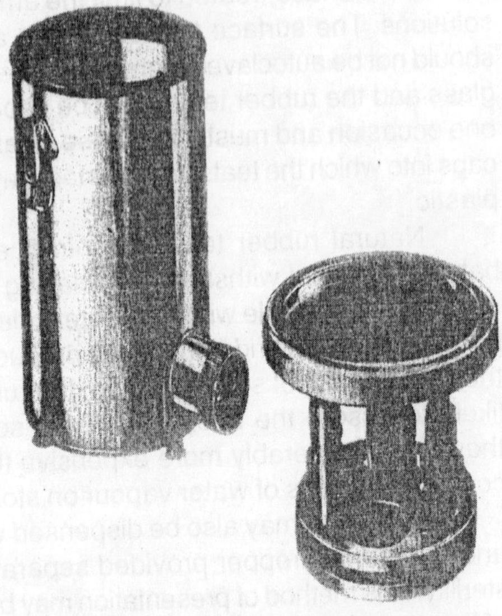

Fig. 4.1 Electrically heated autoclave for small scale preparation of eye drops.

The absorption of bactericides from the solution varies with the quality of the rubber. Natural rubber teats absorb all these bactericides readily from aqueous solution. Silicone rubber teats do not absorb appreciable amount of chlorhexdine acetate and benzalkonium chloride but readily absorb phenylmercuric salts. As mentioned above, benzalkonium chloride may extract stearates from certain grades of natural rubber teats.

Most eye drops are simple solutions in water which should be clarified by filtration before filling into the containers. The *British Pharmaceutical* Codex limits the volume to be supplied in each container to 10 ml so that the eye drops are not in use over too long a period of time.

Sterilization

The sterilization producers are the same as those applied to parenteral solutions, which should prove no problem in a well-equipped hospital pharmacy. In general practice pahrmacy, it may be necessary to obtain a small, electrically heated autoclave especially for the extermporaneous preparation fo eye drops. A suitable autoclave is obtainable from Jacob White and Co. Ltd. and is illustrated in Fig. 4.1

Sterilization by filtration may also be a problem in general practice pharmacy, particularly for the extemporaneous preparation of sodium sulphacetamide eye drops. The small scale preparation of eye drops by filteration has been outlined by Smith (1967) who described different kinds of modified syringes which can be used to sterilize small volumes of aqueous solutions. The most satisfactory is probably the Swinnex filter unit (Fig. 4.2) which is available pre-sterilized from Millipore U.K. Ltd. Swinnex filter units are available in two sizes (filter diameters 13 to 25 mm) and the membrane filters in two porosites (0.45 and 0.22 μm). The smaller diameter filter is usually adequate for eye drops and it is safer to use the lower porosity membrane, although filtration may be slower.

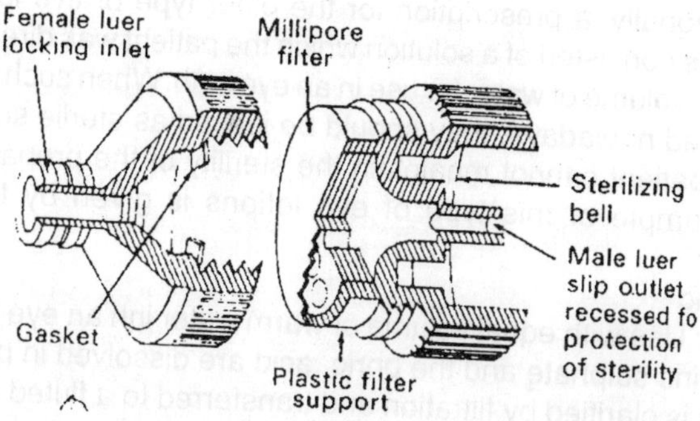

Fig. 4.2 Swinnex-25 filtration unit (Millipore).

The plastic bag holding the Swinnex unit is opened by means of sterile scissors and, with aseptic precautions, the unit is attached to the syringe and a sterile needle is fixed to the other end of the unit. The solution is then forced through the membrane filter into a previously sterilized eye drop bottle by pushing down the plunger of the syringe. The closure is immediately placed on the bottle. It is essential that all operations are carried out as rapidly as possible to minimize the risks of contamination.

Labelling

Eye drops which are not issued to the user (i.e. purchased from a pharmaceutical manufacturer) should state: (1) the concentration of the active ingredients, and (2) the name and concentration of the antimicrobial substances used in the eye drops.

It is customary in hospital practice for this information also be stated on eye drops issued to patients for domiciliary use.

Eye drops which are not extemporaneously dispensed should have a readily breakable seal over the closure to indicate that the container has not been opened. In hospital practice, this usually takes the form of a Viscose ring.

EYE LOTIONS

The *British Pharmaceutical Codex* defines eye lotions as either (1) sterile aqueous solutions containing no bactericide for first-aid purposes over a maximum period of 24 h, or (2) aqueous solutions containing a bactericide for intermittent domiciliary administration for up to 7 days. They therefore hyave only a limited use nowdays, but may nevertheless occasionally be prescribed. Sodium bicarbonate eye lotion is used for the emergency treatment of acid burns of the eye and is known as `Factory Eye Drops No. 2'. Sodium chloride eye lotion is an isotonic solution which is occasionally used for irrigating the eye. Both these preparations are prepared by conventional sterilization procedures.

Occasionally, a prescription for the older type of eye lotion may be received. This consisted of a solution which the patient was directed to dilute with an equal volume of water for use in an eye bath. When such preparations are prescribed nowadays, they should be issued as sterile solutions even though the patient cannot mnaintain the sterility of the preparation during use. An example of this type of eye lotions is given by the following prescription:

R Boric

Label: Use with equal volume of warm water inh an eye bath.

The zinc sulphate and the boric acid are dissolved in purified water, the solution is clarified by filtration and transferred to a fluted bottle, closed with a screw-cap and sterilized by heating in an autoclave.

The patient should be instructed to avoid contamination of the solution during use as far as possible (see also below).

Containers for Eye Lotions

Eye lotions are dispensed in coloured fluted bottles closed with a screw-cap. It is important to ensure that the liner of the screw-cap is not made of cork since this may be a source of microbial contamination. Rubber or plastics liner are suitable and the screw-cap may be either or metal or plastics. Uncoloured or non-fluted bottles may be used if a suitable coloured, fluted bottle is not available.

Labelling

In addition to the words `For external use only', eye lotions which are used for first-aid purposes (e.g. sodium bicarbonate eye lotion) should be labelled to indicate that the preparation should be used on one occasion only, e.g. with the words `Discard any lotion remaining after use when the seal is first broken'.

Eye lotions which are issued for domiciliary purposes should be labelled to indicate that they are not to be used more than 24 h (or 7 days if a bactericide is added) after first opening the container, e.g. with the words

Discard any lotion remaining 24 hours after the container has been first opened'.

EYE OINTMENTS

Eye ointments are required by the British Pharmacopoeia to be sterile and as their preparation involves aseptic handling using a previously sterilized medicament, they are seldom dispensed extemporaneously.

Eye ointment basis of the British Pharmacopoeia consists of a mixture of 80 per cent of yellow soft paraffin with 10 per cent of liquid paraffin and 10 per cent of wool fat. It is prepared by melting the constitutents together, filtering through a coarse filter paper in a heated funnel and sterilizing at 150 for 1 h. It is stored in containers sealerd so as to exclude microorganism before use.

Preparation of Eye Ointment

The *British Pharmaceutical Codex* describes two alternative producers for the preparation of eye ointments. Aseptic precautions must be observed throughout.

Water-soluble medicaments. Medicaments which are readily soluble in water are dissolved in the minimum quantity of purified water. The solution is sterilized by heating in an autoclave or by filtration and the sterile solution incorporated into melted, previouslys terilized basis by stirring until cold and observing aseptic precautions. The preparation is then transferred to previously6 sterilized eye ointment tubes which are immediately closed so as to exclude microorganisms. Many medicaments used in eye ointments ar thermolabile and in these circumstances filtration is used for sterilization.

Sinsoluble medicaments. In this method, it is essential to use a previously sterilized sample of the medicament. Observing aseptic precautions, the medicament is finely powdered and triturated with a small quantity of the melted, previously sterilized basis. The mixture is then incorporated with remainder of the melted basis and the eye ointment transferred to sterile eye ointment tubes which are sealed immediately so as to exclude microorganisms. It is essential that an insoluble medicament should be finely powdered so as to exclude the possibility of a large particle of the drug being introduced into the eye.

Containers for Eye Ointments

Eye ointments should be packed in collapsible metal or plastics tubes or in single-dose containers. Plastics tubes are used for some proprietary formulations of eye ointments but there are no standard empty containers of this type available for dispensing purposes.

Collapsible metal tubes should as far as possible be freed from dust and metal particles before use. This is probably the best achieved by blowing the tubes out with a powerful jet of filtered, dust-free air. Washing the tubes is less effective and often adds more particles than it removes. It has been found that, with present methods of manufacture, it is impossible to produce collapsible metal tubes which are completely particle-free and all the particles may not be removed by cleansing. The particles are not removed until they undergo the shearing action of the ointment as it is expressed from the tubes. Following reports of the occurence of metal particles in eye ointments, a British Standard was devised to limit the particles present in tubes used for eye ointments. Metal tubes used for dispensing eye ointments must comply with the requirements of British Standard 4230:1967.

Certain properitary formulations of eye ointments are available in single-dose containers. These take the form of an elongated, flexible gelatin capsule with one end constricted, and are opened by cutting off the constricted end with sterile scissors.

The container of eye ointments, which are not extemporaneously dispensed, should bge enclosed in a readily breakable sealed package to indicat ethat it has not previously been opened. This can take the form of a sealed paper or plastic envelope or a sealed carton.

Labelling

The *British Pharmaceutical Codex* requires that the label on the tube or outer sealed envelope (except one issued on prescription) should state that the contents are sterile provided that the container has not been opened.

Chapter 5

Antibiotics

Microorganisms produce a great diversity of metabolites with structures as simple as that of ethanol or as complex as that of a polypeptide antibiotic. The biological activity of these metabolites has been long known; Pasteur in 1877 observed that the growth of *Bacillus anthracis* was inhibited by contamination with other bacteria and in 1896 Gosio found that *Penicillium brevi-compactum* produced a substance, mycophenolic acid, which although bacteriostatic towards the anthrax bacillus was too toxic for clinical use.

In 1929 Fleming observed that *Penicillium notatum* produced a substance which inhibited the growth of *Staphylococcus aureus* and other Grampositive organisms. He suggested that the culture filtrate, which was non-toxic, could be used for the treatment of infections and named the active constituent penicillin. With the facilities then available, Fleming was not able to isolate and purify penicillin and it was not until after the outbreak of war in 1939 that the potential of this substance was fully appreciated and it received the intensive investigation necessary to isolate, purify and elucidate its structure. This work was carried out at many centres in the UK and the USA and the results were published in *The Chemistry of Penicillin* (Clarke, Johnson and Robinson 1949).

In 1944 Waksman isolated streptomycin from a culture of *Streptomyces griseus*; the value of this antibiotic lay in its broad spectrum of activity against Gram-positive and negative organisms and *Mycobacterium tuberculosis*. This discovery accelerated the search for other antibiotics, and soil samples from all over the world were screened for the production of biologically active metabolites. Many thousands of moulds and bacteria have been examined and activity has been found in several thousand strains. From many of these the active substance has been isolated and its structure elucidated by chemical degradation and physical studies. Some of the more common antibiotics found in this way are given in Table 5.1.

TABLE 5.1
COMMON ANTIBIOTICS

Antibiotic	Source	Spectrum of activity
Penicillin (1929)	*Penicillium notatum*	Gram-positive
Griseofulvin (1939)	*Penicillium griseofulvum*	Anti-fungal

Streptomycin (1944)	*Streptomyces griseus*	Broad, *Mycobacterium tuberculosis*
Chloramphenicol (1947)	*Streptomyces venezuelae*	Broad, some *Rickettsia*
Polymyxin (1947)	*Bacillus polymyxa*	Gram-negative
Cephalosporin (1948)	*Cephalosporium brotzu*	Broad
Chlortetracycline (1948)	*Streptomyces aureofaciens*	Broad
Neomycin (1949)	*Streptomyces* fradiae	Broad
Oxytetracycline (1950)	*Streptomyces rimosus*	Broad
Erythromycin (1952)	*Streptomyces erythreus*	Gram-positive, some *Rickettsia,* some viruses
Novobiocin (1956)	*Streptomyces spheroides, Streptomyces niveus*	Gram-positive, some negative
Fusidic acid (1962)	*Fusidium coccineum*	Broad, penicillin resistant staphylococci
Gentamicin (1963)	*Micromonospora purpurea*	Broad, particularly Gram-negative

Antibiotic Research and Production

The production of antibiotics proceeds along well-defined lines and the general principles apply for all; details differ, but much of this information is either unpublished or contained within the patent litreature and cannot be included here.

The Search for a New Antibiotic

Most antibiotics are obtained either directly by fermentation, or by chemical modification of a fermentation product. The first stage in the search for a new antibiotic is the screening either of pure cultures obtained from a collection, or of soil samples which contain bacteria and moulds in abundance. In the latter case, soil suspensions are plated out into petri dishes containing different media, and after incubation selected colonies are transferred to a nutrient agar slope to establish the culture. To test these or the pure cultures for antibiotic activity they are then grown in agar media and when growth has been established plugs are cut out and incubated on large agar plates seeded with a test organism (frequently *Staphylococcus aureus*).Where the culture has produced an antibiotic and inhibited the bacterial growth, a clear zone is obtained. Alternatively, the organism may be grown in a liquid medium and the filtered brew placed in cups cut into a seeded agar plate, again giving zones of inhibition similar to those shown in Fig. 5.5.

Having established that an organism produces an antibiotic, it is tested against a range of bacteria in order to obtain an indication of its possible clinical value and the extent to which the activity is novel.

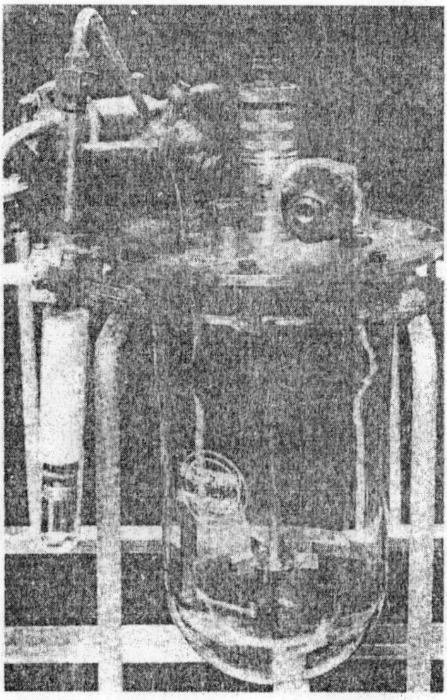

Fig. 5.1. Laboratory fermenter.

The next stage in the study is the growth of the organism on a laboratory scale, using 5- or 10-litre vessels to define some of the conditions required for its production by deep culture. These studies include the effects of medium composition, pH, fermentation time, aeration and stirring rates and inoculum size. Methods for the isolation of the metabolite size. Methods for the isolation of the metabolite are also studied, the usual method being extraction with a variety of water-immiscible solvents over a range of pH. Purification may be achieved by crystallization of a suitable salt, ion exchange chromatography or adsorption followed by extraction, but in the case of a mixture, or a intractable product, it is sometimes only possible to obtain a freeze-dried extract at this stage.

Before proceeding to large scale production it is necessary to carry out pilot plant studies in 100–2000 litre vessels to optimize the conditions and to give sufficient material for the extensive pharmacological and toxicologocal investigations which have to be carried out before an clinical studies can be started. At the same time the structure of the antibiotic is established and possible variants prepared chemically.

A continual search is made for strains of the mould or bacterium which will produce greate yields of the antibiotic; for this purpose mutant are produced by X-ray or ultraviolet irradiation or treatment with radiomimetic substances such a nitrogen mustard.

Antibiotic Production

Originally penicillin was produced by surface culture, the mould being grown is small static containers, the mycelium forming a mat on the surface of the medium. In spite of the extremely cumbersome nature of the process it was used for all the early production of penicillin in the UK. The production of penicillin was revolutionized by the discovery at Peoria, that a strain of *Penicillium chrysogenum* (obtained from an over-ripe Cantaloupe melon) would

Fig. 5.2. Fermentation pilot-plant.

produce high yields of penicillin under conditions of deep or submerged culture. The growth of a mould is aerobic and, in surface culture, growth and production of antibiotic is limited by the rate at which oxygen can diffuse into the medium. In submerged culture the mould is grown in an agitated tank and supplied with a continuous flow of air to give non-limiting conditions.

The medium used in fermentation will vary for the particular antibiotoc being produced but all media contain a source of carbon, which may be lactose or glucose, nitrogen as ammonium salts and trace elements such as phosphorus, sulphur, magnesium, iron, zinc and copper. In addition, cornsteep liquor is added for penicillin production and soya bean meal and dried distillers residues for streptomycin; these provide various factors which increase the yield of product. Before use, the medium as well as the fermentor and associated equipment is steam sterilized, since bacterial contamination could destroy the antibiotic.

The selected culture is transferred from storage as the master culture first to an agar slope, then to culture to give a seed suspension, and finally grown in seed vessels in the plant for 24 to 48 h before transfer to the main fermentors. Fermentation is continued for 3 to 5 days during which period the vessel is cooled to keep the temperature between 23° and 27°, stirred and aerated with sterilized air. The introduction of large volumes of air causes frothing which is controlled by the addition of antifoams such as lard oil, octadecanol or silicones.

When fermentation is complete the mycelium is removed on a rotary filter and the antibiotic extracted with an organic solvent, after adjustment of the pH. Alternatively, as with streptomycin, the brew is passed through a carboxylic acid resin from which it is subsequently removed with dilute acid. The extracted antibiotic is converted into the particular derivative which is to be used, products for injection being rendered sterile by passage of their solution through sterilizing filters followed by final crystallization or precipitation under sterile conditions.

Fig. 5.3. Production fermenters.

Antibiotic Assay

When a new antibiotic has been isolated it is essential to have an assay method available in order to follow the processes of purification, its distribution within the blood and tissues when given to animals and finally humans, and also the potency of the various formulations used. In the absence of a chemical method, a biological assay against a standard sample of agreed potency is performed, using a suitable test organism. A biological assay is also used for the determination of low concentrations of an antibiotic, such as are obtained in blood and urine, where a chemical assay might be insufficiently sensitive.

The cup-plate method, which is preferred, requires the test organism to be very sensitive to the abtibiotic, giving clear zones of inhibition with well marked changes in zone diameter with small changes in concentration. The antibiotic must also diffuse readily through the agar medium; if this is not so, assay is carried out using serial dilution or turbidimetric methods to measure its effect upon the test organism.

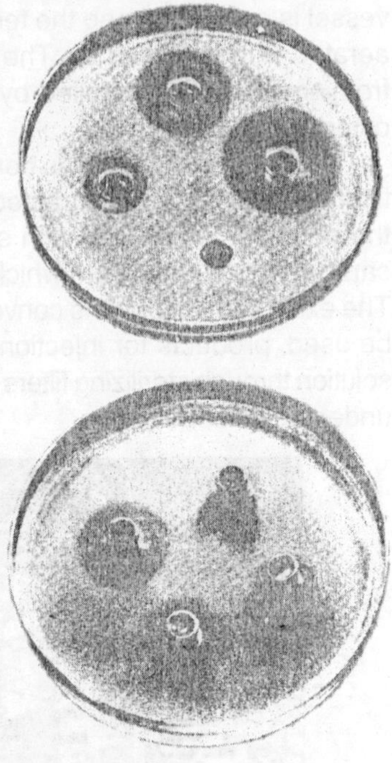

Fig. 5.4. Cup-plate (top) and cylinder-plate (bottom) assay.

Petri dishes or rectangular glass trays are filled to a uniform depth, with nutrient agar medium which has been inoculated with a suitable organism. The *British Pharmacopoeia* 1973 lists organisms to be used, e.g. *Bacillus pumilus* for erythromycin, *Bacillus subtilis* for novobiocin, etc. When the agar has solidified, sterile cylinders of glass, stainless steel, porcelain or aluminium 5 mm in diameter are placed on the surface. Alternatively, holes 5 to 8 mm in diameter are cut into the medium using a sterile borer. Solutions of various concentrations of the standard and also solutions of the preparation under test, presumed to be of similar concentration, are placed in the holes. When petri dishes are used the standard and test solutions are alternated in the dishes, and when rectangular trays are used the solutions are arranged in the form of a randomized Latin square. The plates are then maintained at room temperature for 2 h to allow the antibiotic to diffuse into the medium.

If the agar is uniform, diffusion of the antibiotic will occur uniformly around the cup and a concentration gradient will be established around it and at a certain distance from the cup, depending upon the concentration of the antibiotic within it, the concentration in the agar will be just sufficient to inhibit the growth of the organism. When the plates have been incubated at a suitable temperature (usually 37° to 39°) for 16 h, each cup will be surrounded by a clear zone of inhibition, the diameter of which is proportional to the logarithm of the concentration of antibiotic in the cup. By plotting zone diameter

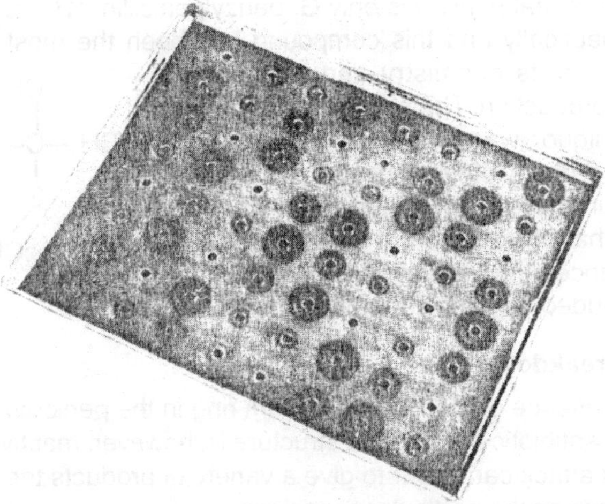

Fig. 4.5. Cup-plate assay in a tray.

against concentration for both standard and test, the potency of the test relative to the standard may be obtained by measuring the horizontal displacement between the two lines which should be parallel. Any lack of parallelism indicates either that the test was faulty or that another antibiotic was present with a different does response curve.

PENICILLINS

From 1940 on, the penicillins were the subject of considerable investigation at a number of industrial and university laboratories in the UK and in 1943 this collaboration was extended to the USA. During the early days of this research, considerable differences in analytical and degradative results were obtained from different laboratories. These were resolved when it was demonstrated that the mould produced six different penicillins. In the UK the medium used was synthetic and penicillin F was the main product while in the USA corn-steep liquor was added to increase the yield of penicillin and here penicillin G was the major product. Early studies on the structure of penicillin were hampered by the low yields and purity of the unstable product. Later when crystalline material became available, the structure was elucidated by degradation and partial synthesis and confirmed by X-ray crystallographic analysis.

The molecule was shown to contain a carboxyl group, a β-lactam ring (four membered cyclic amide) fused to a thiazolidine ring (five membered ring containing nitrogen and sulphur) and an acylamino group, and the various penicillins differed only in the structure of the acyl-group, R, of the side-chain. The general structure is given in the next page:

Of the natural penicillins only G, benzylpenicillin, (R = $C_6H_5.CH_2^-$) is used therapeutically and this compound has been the most extensively studied both in its chemistry and in improving methods of production. The stimulation of yield by corn-steep liquor was shown to be due to the presence of β-phenylethylamine and this provided the side-chain phenylacetyl group. Subsequently, it was found that the addition of phenylacetic acid greatly enhanced the yield of benzylpenicillin and this is now added as a regular practice.

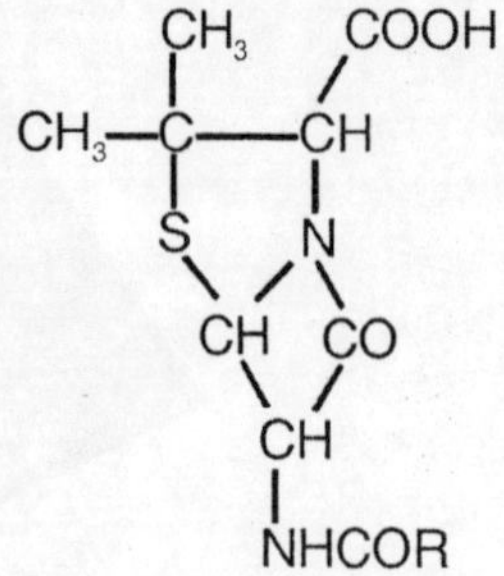

Penicillin Breakdown

The presence of the intact β-lactam ring in the penicillin molecule is essential for antibiotic activity. The structure is, however, reactive and it is at this ring that attack can occur to give a variety of products the structure of which depends on the particular conditions.

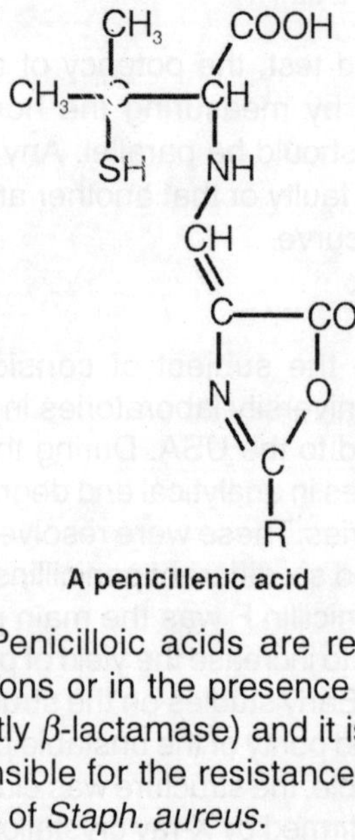

A penicillenic acid

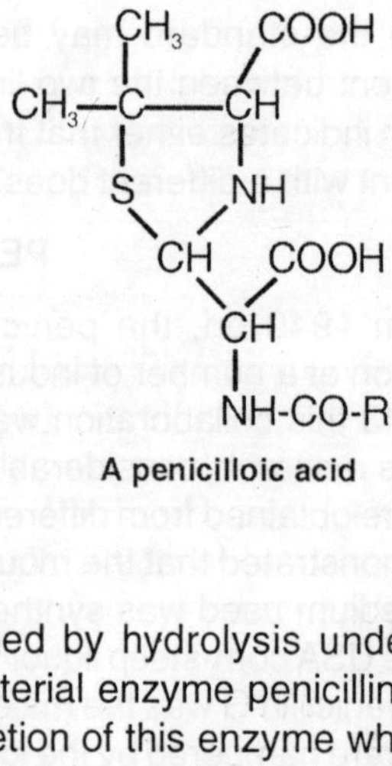

A penicilloic acid

Penicilloic acids are readily formed by hydrolysis under alkaline conditions or in the presence of the bacterial enzyme penicillinase (more correctly β-lactamase) and it is the secretion of this enzyme which can be responsible for the resistance to penicillin by bacteria, for example, some strains of *Staph. aureus*.

Applications of Benzylpenicillin

Benzylpenicillin acts specifically on bacteria by interfering with the mechanism of cell-wall synthesis; it is of very low mammalian toxicity and consequently has been used for the treatment of a wide range of infections. Almost all the Gram-positive and some of the Gram-negative pathogens are sensitive, e.g. *Staph. aureus, Strep. pyogenes, Strep. pneumoniae, C. welchii, B. anthracis,*

N. gonorrhoeae.

In moderately acid solution the carbonyl-group of the side-chain reacts with the β-lactam ring to give a penicillenic acid while at a lower pH, and particularly in the presence of heavy metals, a penillic acid is formed by such a reaction followed by a complex series of rearrangements. Because of the ready decomposition of most penicillins under acid conditions they are usually administered as their neutral salts.

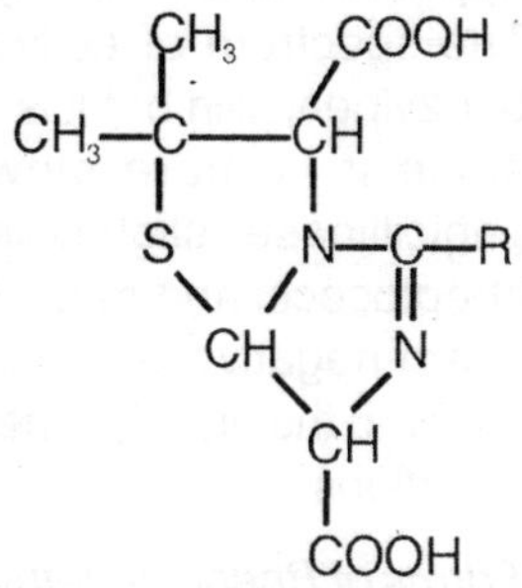

A peniloic acid

N. meningitidis. As it is rapidly destroyed by acid and poorly absorbed from the stomach it is almost invariably administered by injection, although occasionally it is given orally.

Forms of Benzylpenicillin

Benzylpenicillin is official in the *British Pharmacopoeia* as its sodium and potassium salts which give high blood levels for only a few hours unless administered repeatedly. In order to obtain prolonged, but lower, blood levels, the water-insoluble salts with procaine (diethylaminoethyl *p*-amino-banzoate) and benzathine (*N*: *N'*-dibenzyl-ethylene-diamine) are used. Procaine penicillin will give detectable blood levels after 24 h and benzathine penicillin after several weeks.

Assay of Benzylpenicillin

The basis of the chemical assay for benzylpenicillin is that penicillins do not react with iodine in neutral aqueous solution, but their penicilloic acids consume a quantity of iodine, which although non-stoichiometric is reproducible under constant conditions. Thus the difference between the amount of iodine consumed by a sample in neutral solution and one which has been hydrolysed to the penicilloic acid is proportional to the amount of penicillin present. A sample of known potency is assayed concurrently in order to obtain the actual potency of the sample under test.

Phenoxymethyl Penicillin

When it was discovered that phenylacetic acid added to a penicillin fermentation was incorporated in the molecule as benzylpenicillin, large numbers of substituted acetic acids were screened to discover if they were incorporated and if so whether the resulting penicillin had desirable properties. As a result of this investigation, it was found that phenoxyacetic acid was accepted by the mould and the resulting phenoxymethylpenicillin (penicillin V) was acid stable.

Although there was no great change in the antibacterial spectrum or its sensitivity to penicillinase, this reresented a considerable advance in convenience since it could be administered orally in tablets, capsules or syrups.

Applications of Phenoxymethylpenicillin

The spectrum of activity of phenoxymethylpenicillin is similar to that of benzylpenicillin but it is slightly more active against resistant staphylococci since it is more slowly destroyed by penicillinase, slightly less active against streptococci and much less active against Gram-negative bacteria. It is particularly useful in the oral treatment of Gram-positive infections.

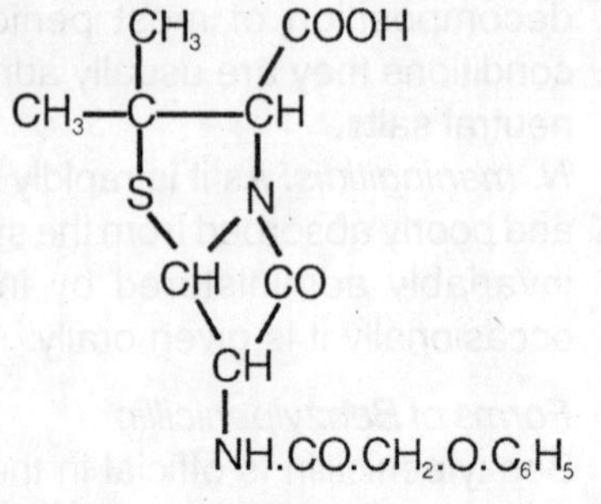

Phenoxymethylpenicillin

Forms of Phenoxymethylpenicillin

Phenoxymethylpenicillin is official as the free acid, its calcium and potassium salts and in the form of tablets and capsules.

Assay of Phenoxymethylpenicillin

The total penicillin content of phenoxymethyl-penicillin is determined iodometrically against a standard sample. As phenoxymethylpenicillin may contain traces of other penicillins, the phenoxymethylpenicillin content is also determined photometrically.

Semi-Synthetic Penicillins

The range of structures accepted by the *Penicillium* mould as precursors is limited to acetic acid derivatives and, of the penicillins which can be prepared by this process, only penicillin V is of therapeutic value. Batchelor et al. (1959) showed that in the absence of any added precursor *Penicillium chrysogenum* produced 6-aminopenicillanic acid, which could be isolated using ion-exchange resins and subsequently it was found that this compound could also be prepared by the enzymic de-acylation of penicilin G ov V.

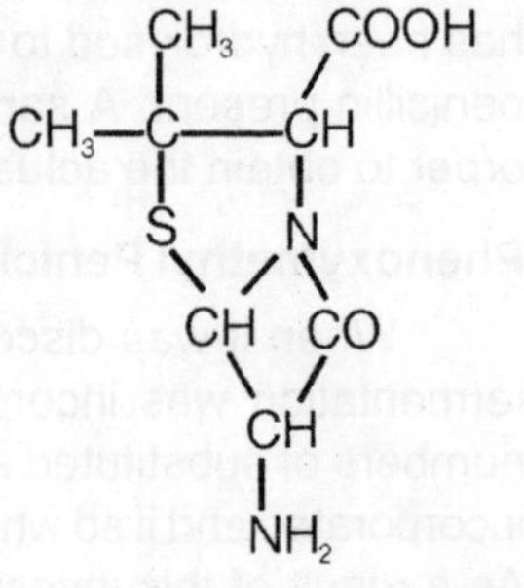

6–Aminopenicillanic acid

Although 6-aminopenicillanic acid itself has only very slight antibiotic activity, it can be acylated chemically to give a penicillin of any desired structure which could not be prepared by the precursor technique. A very large number of penicillins have been prepared and it has been shown that with a suitable side-chain it is possible to obtain compounds which are stable to acid, such as phenethicillin; resistant to penicillinase, such as methicillin and cloxacillin, or with a broad spectrum of activity including Gram-negative organisms, such as ampicillin and carbenicillin, the last having particular value as it is also active against *Pseudomonas aeruginosa*. Further penicillin derivatives are given in Table 5.2.

Applications of the Semi-Synthetic Penicillins

Phenethicillin. This analogue of phenoxymethylpenicillin shows a similar antibacterial spectrum but is better absorbed and so gives higher blood levels. It is always administered orally.

Methicillin. Highly resistant to staphylococcal penicillinase and is consequently clinically effective against penicillinase-producing and penicillin-sensitive strains of *Staphylococcus aureus*. It is readily destroyed by acid and has to be administered parenterally.

TABLE 5.2
PENICILLIN DERIVATIVES

R	Penicillin
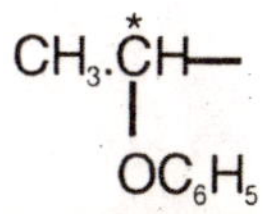 Dl-configuration	Phenethicillin Dl-α-phenoxyethylpenicillin
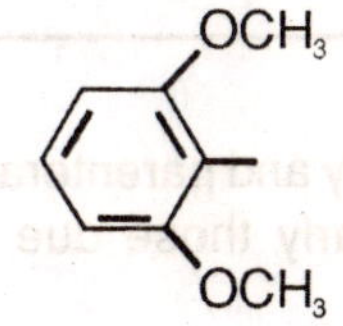	Methicillin 2-6-dimethoxyphenylpenicillin
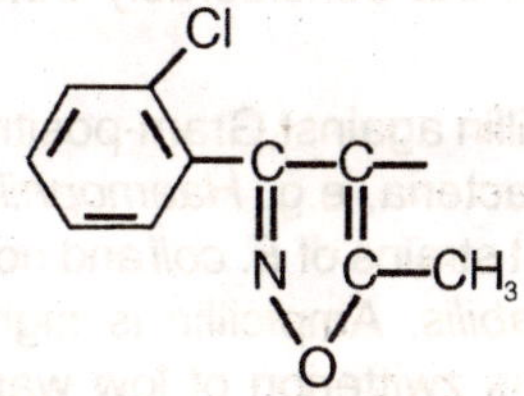	Cloxacilin 3-(2-chlorophenyl)-5-methyl-4-isoxazolypenicillin
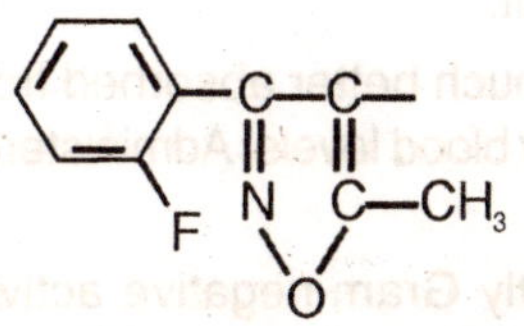	Flucloxacillin 3-(2-chloro-6fluoro-phenyl)-5-methyl-4-isoxazolypenicillin

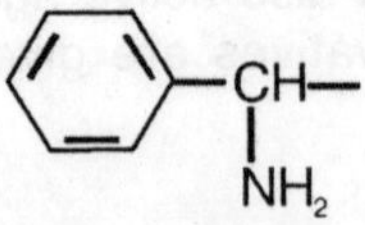

D(-)configuration

Ampicillin
D(-)-α-aminobenzylpenicillin

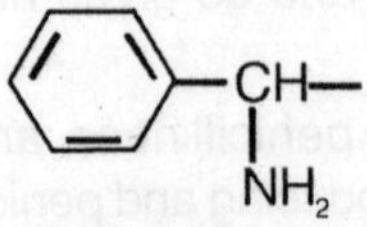

D(-)configuration

Ampicillin
D(-)-α-aminobenzylpenicillin

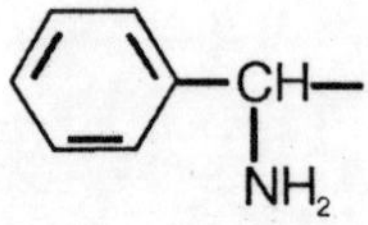

D(-)configuration

Ampicillin
D(-)-α-aminobenzylpenicillin

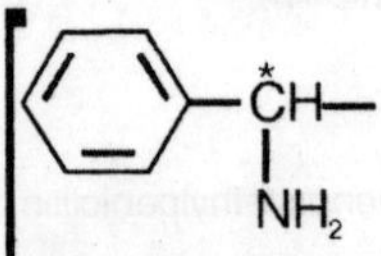

D(-)configuration

Carbenicillin
DL-α-carboxybenzylpenicillin

*Assymetric Carbon

Cloxacillin. Resistant to penicillinase and acid, used orally and parenterally for the treatment of Gram-positive infections particularly those due to penicillinase-producing staphylococci.

Flucloxacillin. Similar in properties to cloxacillin but considerably better absorbed when given orally.

Ampicillin. Slightly less active than benzyl-penicillin against Gram-positive but much more active against Gram-negative bacteria, e.g. *Haemophilus influenzae, Salmonella* and *Shigella* species, most strains of *E. coli* and non-penicillinase producing strains of *Proteus mirabilis*. Ampicillin is highly resistant to acid and is administered orally as its zwitterion of low water solubility or by injection as its soluble sodium salt.

Amoxycillin. Similar in activity to ampicillin but much better absorbed from the gastrointestinal tract, giving considerably higher blood levels. Administered orally as its zwitterion.

Carbenicillin. Broad spectrum with predominantly Gram-negative activity extending to *Escherichia coli, Pseudomonas aeruginosa* and strains of *Proteus vulgaris, Proteus rettgeri* and *Proteus morganii.* Carbenicillin is not absorbed orally and is administered parenterally as its highly soluble disodium salt.

Forms of the Semi-Synthetic Penicillin

Phenethicillin. This is official as the potassium salt and in the form of tablets and capsules.

Methicillin. This is official as the sodium salt which is used for injection.

Cloxacillin. This is official as the sodium salt which is used for capsules and injection.

Flucloxacillin. Is used as its sodium salt for oral and parenteral administration.

Ampicillin. The free acid exists in two forms, as a trihydrate and the anhydrous compound, both of which are official and may be formulated into capsules. The sodium salt is used for injection.

Amoxycillin. The free acid is used as the trihydrate which may be formulated into capsules and a dry syrup mix to which water is added before use.

Carbenicillin. This is official as the disodium salt which is used for injection.

Assay of the Semi-Synthetic Penicillins

Phenethicillin, methicillin, cloxacillin and flucloxacillin. Are assayed by heating with an excess of a known amount of alkali. The penicilloic acid produced by the hydrolysis of the β-lactam ring consumes an equivalent amount of alkali which is determined by titrimetric estimation of the amount remaining. As the formation of the penicilloic acid is stoichiometric this assay is absolute and does not require the use of a standard.

Ampicillin. Determined by acid hydrolysis in the presence of a copper catalyst to give α-amino-benzylpenillic acid which is estimated photometrically against a standard sample of ampicillin of known potency.

Carbenicillin. Assayed by iodometric assay for total penicillins with correction for the trace of benzylpenicillin, produced by decarboxylation, by agar-gel electrophoresis.

CEPHALOSPORINS

In 1945, Brotzu isolated from a sewage outfall in Sardinia a strain of *Cephalosporium* which produced metabolites with some activity against typhoid. Studies by Abraham and Newton (Abraham 1967) showed that the mould produced a complex mixture of antibiotics one of which, cephalosporin C, was active against Gram-negative and penicillinase producing organisms. Chemical degradation followed by X-ray crystallographic analysis showed that the structure was related to the penicillins in that it also contained a *β*-lactum ring bearing an acylated amino-group but it was fused to a dihydrothiazine ring instead of the thiazolidine ring present in penicillins.

The side-chain of cephalosporin C cannot be removed enzymically, but this can be accomplished chemically, for example with nitrosyl chloride to give 7-aminocephalosporanic acid which like 6-aminopenicillanic acid can

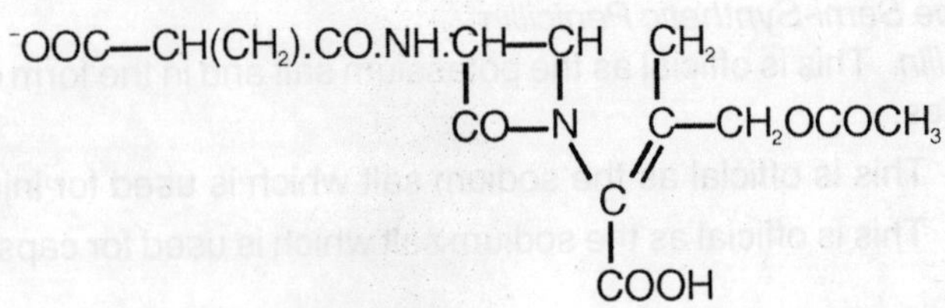

Cephalosporin C

be acylated to give a whole range of semi-synthetic cephalosporins. In addition to acylation, the group at carbon 3 can be modified to improve the properties of the compounds. A large number of cephalosporins have been prepared, of which those in common use are given on following pages.

Applications of Cephalosporins

Cephaloridine. This shows activity against all strains of staphylococci and

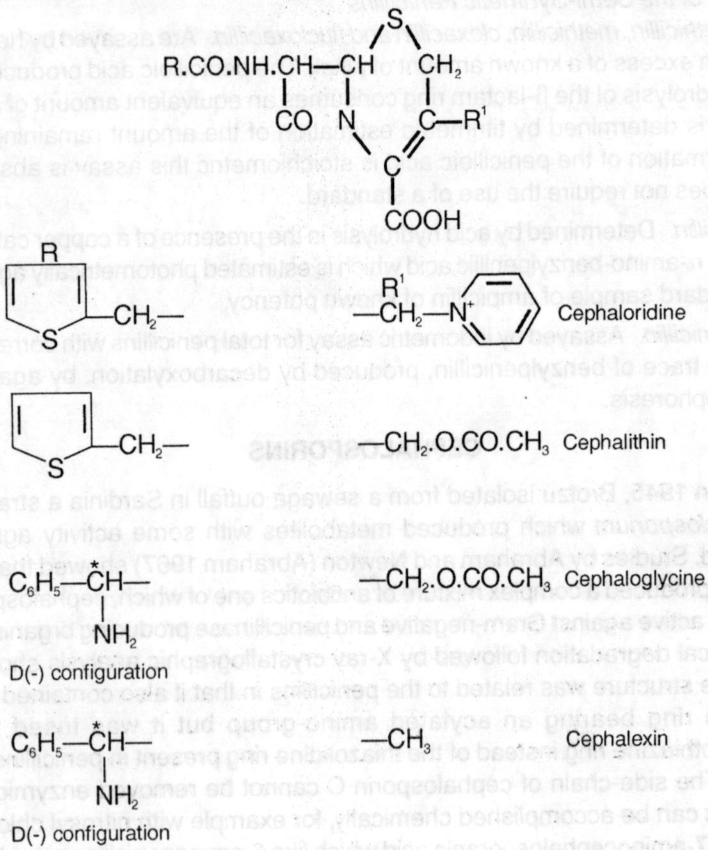

streptococci, except *Streptococcus faecalis*. Of the Gram-negative bacteria *Neisseria* species are highly sensitive, *Haemophilus influenzae, Escherichia coli, Proteus mirabilis, Salmonella* and *Shigella* species less so. Cephaloridine is not absorbed orally and is administered parenterally.

Cephalothin. Similar spectrum of activity to cephaloridine but frequently slightly less active against certain organisms.

Cephaloglycine. Active against many Gram-negative bacteria but enterococci, indole-positive *Proteus* and *Enterobacter* are usually resistant, *Pseudomonas* invariably so. Absorbed from the gastrointestinal tract sufficiently well to be used for urinary tract infections. Metabolized to the desacetyl compound which also has antibacterial activity.

Cephalexin. Similar in spectrum of activity to the parenteral cephalosporins but less active against resistant staphylococci. Well orally absorbed in man, most of the compound being excreted un-changed in the urine.

Forms of the Cephalosporins

Cephaloridine. Official as the betaine (α or δ form) for injection.

Cephalothin. Official as the sodium salt for injection.

Cephaloglycine. Available as zwitterion dihydrate.

Cephalexin. Official as the monohydrate in the form of capsules and tablets.

Assay of Cephalosporins

The β-lactam portion of the molecule is assayed iodometrically by a procedure similar to that used for benzylpenicillin. The pyridine content of cephaloridine is determined by reaction with bromine and potassium cyanide to give a red colour which is estimated photometrically.

CHLORAMPHENICOL

Chloramphenicol was isolated in 1947 from a culture of *Streptomyces venezuelae* and chemical degradation showed that the structure was D(–)*threo*-2-dichloroacetamido-1-*p*-nitrophenyl-1 : 3-propanediol. The most surprising feature of this relatively simple compound was the presence of an aromatic nitro-group which was previously unknown in nature.

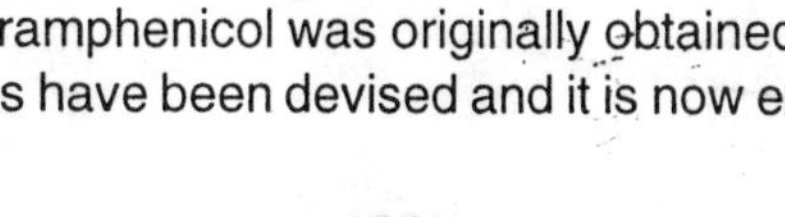

Chloramphenicol

Although chloramphenicol was originally obtained by fermentation, a number of syntheses have been devised and it is now exclusively prepared synthetically. Numerous analogues of chloramphenicol have been synthesized but these have shown reduced activity or increased toxicity.

Applications of Chloramphenicol

Chloramphenicol is bacteriostatic to a broad spectrum of organisms being particularly valuable for the treatment of typhoid and rickettsial infections. It is now less used that formerly since very high doses can produce granulocytopenia and aplastic anaemia. Chloramphenicol is well absorbed orally but it has an intensely bitter taste. To overcome this, the primary hydroxyl group is esterified with palmitic acid to give a bland ester which is very suitable for use in syrups. The water-soluble mono-sodium salt of the hemi-ester of succinic acid is used parenterally.

Forms of Chloramphenicol

Chloramphenicol and chloramphenicol Capsules are official in the *British Pharmacopoeia.* It is assayed photometrically.

POLYPEPTIDE ANTIBIOTICS

The polypeptide antibiotics all consist of amino acids linked by peptide bonds into cyclic structures of some considerable complexity containing unusual amino acids and saturated aliphatic acids.

Bacitracin

Bacitracin was isolated in 1945 from cultures of *Bacillus licheniformis* obtained from the leg wound of a young girl. If has been shown to be a mixture of five related polypeptides, the material which is produced commercially be deep fermentation being predominantly bacitracin A.

Applications of Bacitracin

Bacitracin is active against Gram-positive organisms particularly certain strains of clostridia. Its nephrotoxicity limits its parenteral use but as it is not absorbed its main use is topical, it has been used for sterilization of the gut. It is official as the zinc salt.

Polymyxin

Polymyxin was isolated in 1947 from *Bacillus polymyxa* in a soil sample. Like the other members of this class of antibiotic, polymyxin was found to be a mixture of five antibiotics each of which is separable into two closely related substances. Of the polymyxins only B and E (colistin) are used therapeutically, the other members of the group being too toxic.

THE CARBOHYDRATE ANTIBIOTICS

This group, of which the most important members are streptomycin and neomycin, is produced by streptomycetes. They are basic compounds giving crystalline, water-soluble salts and consist of sugars and amino sugars linked glycosidically.

Streptomycin

Streptomycin was isolated by Waksman in 1944 from a culture of *Streptomyces griseus* obtained from a chicken's throat. Two years earlier, streptothricin had been isolated from *Streptomyces lavendulae* and although it possessed a broad spectrum of activity, it was too toxic for use. Streptomycin was far less toxic and in addition to its Gram-negative activity it was found to be the first useful antibiotic active against *Mycobacterium tuberculosis.*

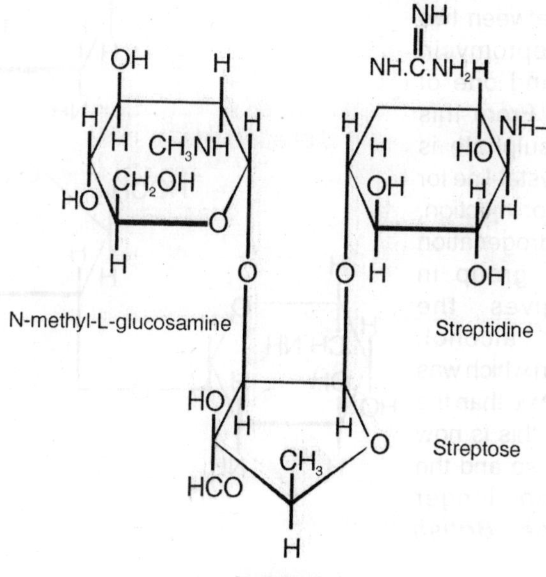

Streptomycin

Early production of streptomycin was by surface culture, meat extract, peptone and sodium chloride being added to the medium. Subsequently, it was found that deep culture techniques were applicable, the meat extract could be replaced by a much cheaper extract of soya bean meal and distillers' solubles and this process is now used on a large scale. After fermentation and clarification of the broth, the antibiotic is absorbed on to a carboxylic acid ion-exchange resin and then eluted from the washed resin with dilute acid. The concentrated streptomycin salt solution so obtained is then purified by crystallization of the complex formed between two molecules of streptomycin trihydrochloride and one of calcium chloride. From this purified salt the sulphate is prepared, either crystal-line for oral use, or sterile for injection.

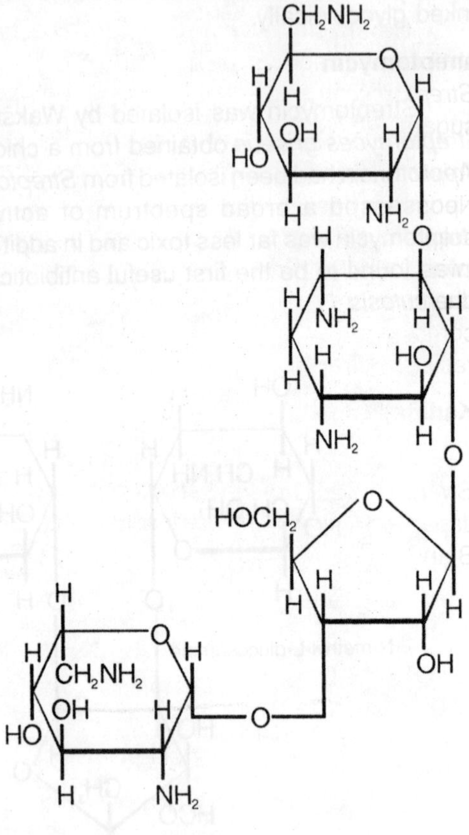

Neomycin B

Catalytic hydrogenation of the aldehyde group in streptomycin gives the corresponding alcohol, dihydrostreptomycin which was thought to be less toxic than the parent compound; this is now believed not to be so and the compound is no longer described in the *British Pharmacopoeia.*

Applications of Streptomycin

Streptomycin is chiefly used in the treatment of tuberculosis, particularly in combination with other drugs such as isonicotinic hydrazide or *p*-amino-salicylic acid, which delay the development of resistance by the bacterium. It is also used for the treatment of plague and tularaemia. Although well absorbed by injection, it is not absorbed orally and has been used for the treatment of gastro-intestinal infections and sterilization of the gut prior to abdominal surgery. The most serious side effect of streptomycin is on the eighth nerve causing vertigo and also deafness.

Assay of Streptomycin
Streptomycin may be assayed biologically using *B. subtilis,* or chemically by heating with sodium hydroxide, when the streptose fragment of the molecule rearranges to give maltol which is estimated colorimetrically by the purple colour produced with ferric ammonium sulphate.

Neomycin

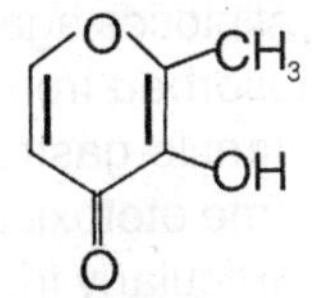

Maltol

Neomycin is a mixture of three closely related antibiotics (neomycins A, B and C) first isolated from *Streptomyces fradiae* in 1949. It consists of three basic sugars and D-ribose linked glycosidically.

Applications of Neomycin
Neomycin has a broad spectum of activity and as it is not absorbed orally its sulphate is used for sterilization of the gut and for the treatment of intestinal infections. It is of considerable value for the topical treatment of infections due to staphylococci and Gram-negative bacteria, and is frequently used in combination with polypeptide antibiotics to prevent the development of resistant strains.

Kanamycin

Kanamycin was isolated in 1957 by Umezawa from a culture of *Streptomyces kanamyceticus* obtained from soil collected in Nagarov in Japan. It is a mixture of predominantly kanamycin A together with kanamycins B and C.

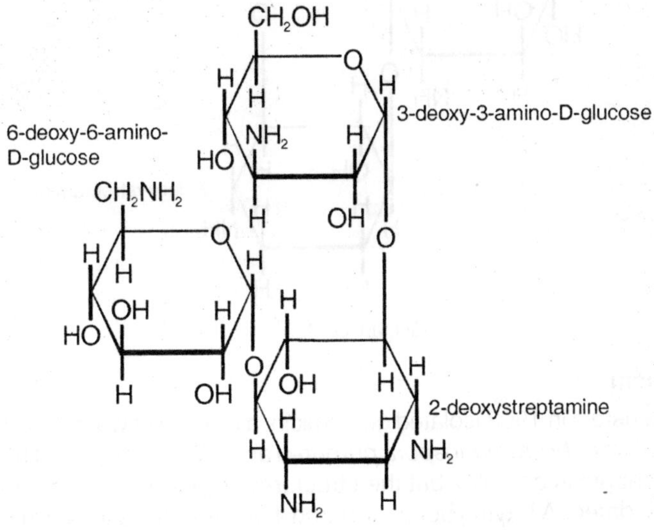

Kanamycin A

Kanamycin A has the structure shown below, B and C differ in the structure of the amino sugar linked to the 2-deoxystreptamine ring. The structures of all three compounds have been confirmed by total synthesis.

Applications of Kanamycin

Kanamycin has a spectrum of activity similar to the other carbohydrate antibiotics against Gram-positive and negative organisms. It is not usefully absorbed from the alimentary tract and hence is used for the treatment of infantile gastroenteritis and for sterilizing the gut. Although it does exhibit some ototoxicity it can be administered by repeated intramuscular injection particularly for the treatment of tuberculosis.

Kanamycin is administered as its readily water-soluble monosulphate (official).

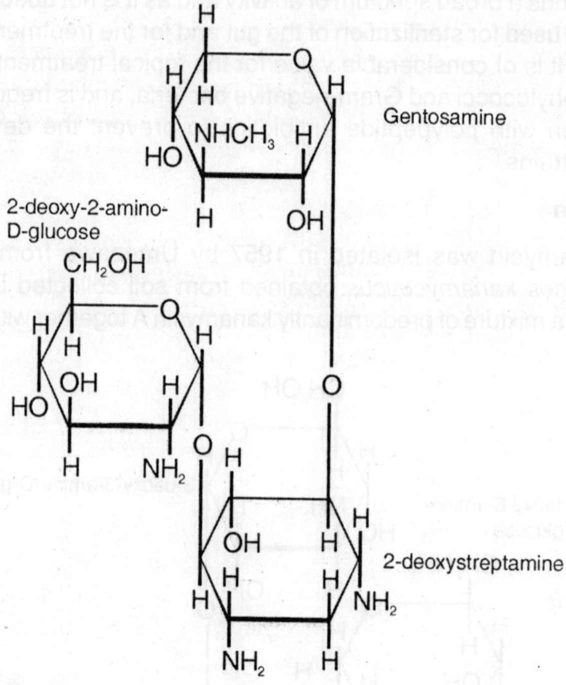

Gentamicin A

Gentamicin

Weinstein in 1963 isolated gentamicin, a mixture of water-soluble basic antibiotics from *Micromonospora purpurea* and *M. echinospora*. The mixture of components is complex but the structures of gentamicins A and C have been elucidated; A having been prepared in a pure crystaline form has been shown to consist of paromamine (a component of the neomycin analogue paromomycin) linked to a novel 3-methylamino-3-deoxy-pentapyranose (gentosamine). Gentamicin forms salts with mineral and strong organic acids, the sulphate (official) being used clinically.

Applications of Gentamicin
An antibiotic with Gram-negative activity particularly against *Aerobacter, Escherichia, Klebsiella, Salmonella* and some *Proteus* species. Its most significant activity is against *Pseudomonas aeruginosa* and it is largely used for the treatment of infections caused by this organism.

Like all the other carbohydrate antibiotics it is not absorbed orally and must be administered by intramuscular injection as its sulphate (official).

THE TETRACYCLINES

The tetracyclines are a group of broad spectrum antibiotics possessing a hydronaphthacene skeleton bearing a wide variety of functional groups. They are amphoteric, forming crystalline salts with strong acids and bases and chelates with many metal ions and it has been suggested that this last property is responsible for their antibacterial action. They are prepared by deep culture fermentation of streptomycetes and have been isolated by a number of methods; as their calcium or mixed barium and magnesium salts, as their iron chelates or as salts with cationic surfactants.

Because of the clinical value of the tetracyclines and the number of functional groups capable of modification, many have been synthesized in attempts to obtain maximum antibiotic activity and blood levels, modified absorption exceretion patterns and improved chemical stability (Blackwood and English 1970). At least eight tertrcyclines are produced commercially of which half are obtained by chemical modifications of fermentation products. The most important at the present are chlortetracycline, oxytetracycline, tetracycline, demethylchlortetracycline, doxycycline and methacycline.

Chlortetracycline

The first member of this group to be isolated was chlortetracycline in 1948 from *Streptomyces aureofaciens.* Its structure was established shortly after Woodward elucidated that of oxytetracycline in 1953. Chlortetracycline hydrochloride is a yellow crystalline solid which is assayed biologically against *B. pumilus* and is usually administered orally in capsules.

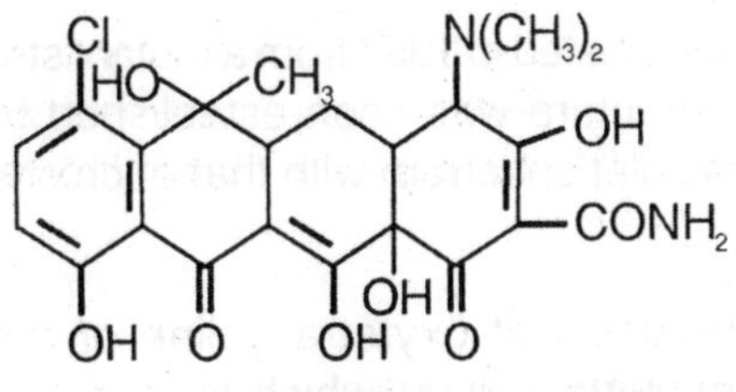

Chlortetracycline

Oxytetracycline

Oxytetracycline was isolated in 1950 from the soil organism *Streptomyces rimosus*. As may be seen it differs from chlortetracycline in the absence of a chlorine and the presence of an additional hydroxyl group. The total synthesis of DL-oxytetracycline has been performed by Muxfeldt and the product shown to possess 50 per cent of the biological activity of the natural, optically active, material (Muxfeldt et al. 1968).

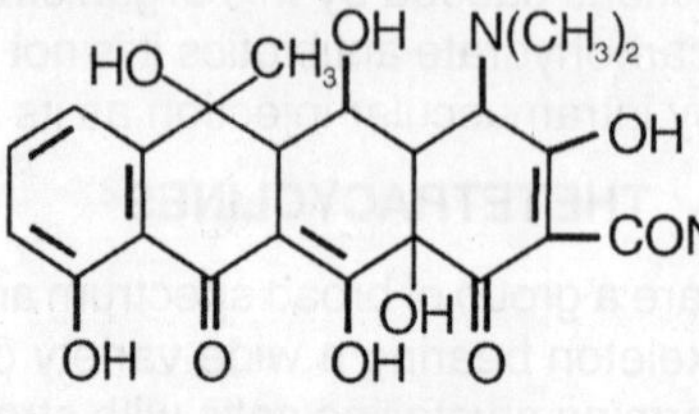

Oxytetracycline

Oxytetracycline is used as its hydrochloride in injections and capsules and as the less soluble dihydrate of the free base in tablets.

Tetracycline

Tetracycline was originally prepared by hydrogenolysis of chlortetracycline or later from oxytetracycline. More recently mutant strains of *Streptomyces* have been isolated which produce tetracycline directly. The antibacterial spectrum of tetracycline is similar to the 'chloro' and 'oxy' derivatives but it is better absorbed orally. Tetracycline hydrochloride is administered orally or by injection.

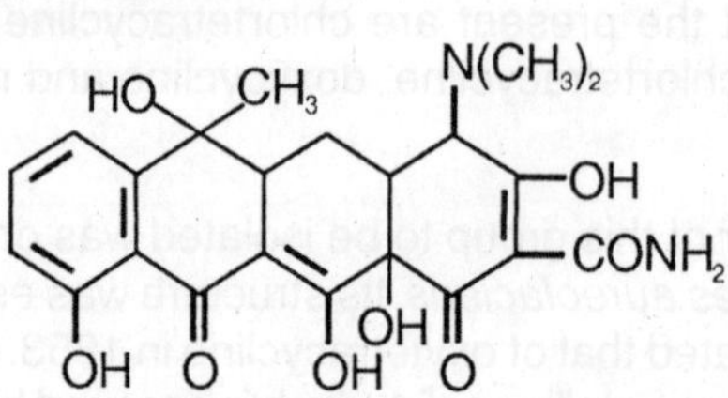

Tetracycline

Demethylchlortetracycline

This antibiotic was isolated in 1957 from a mutant strain of *Streptomyces aureofaciens* and its structure was soon established by degradation and comparison of its ultraviolet spectrum with that of chlortetracycline.

Doxycycline

Chemical modification of oxytetracycline or methacycline yields doxycycline (α-6-deoxytetracycline) which is more active against most bacteria than tetracycline and in addition is well absorbed orally with a prolonged serum half-life.

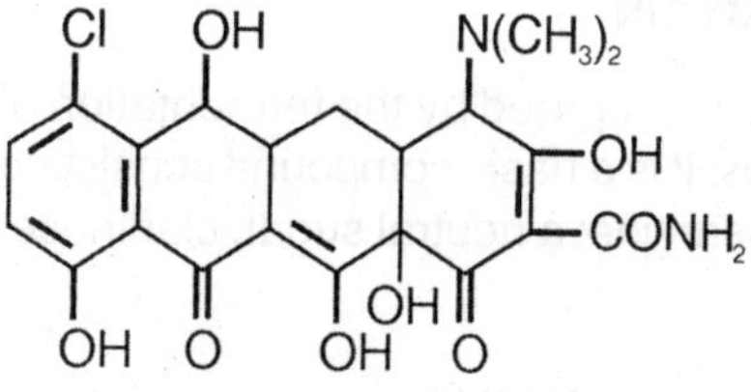
Demethylchlortetracycline

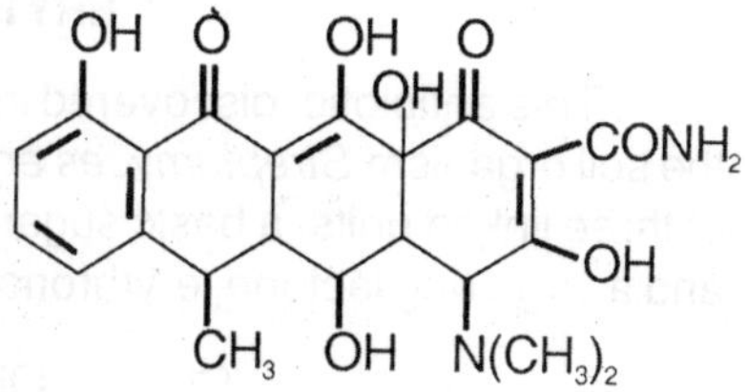
Doxycycline

Methacycline

Methacycline is prepared synthetically from oxytetracycline, its activity and absorption characteristics are similar to those of demethylchlortetracycline with slightly higher blood levels during the first eight hours after administration.

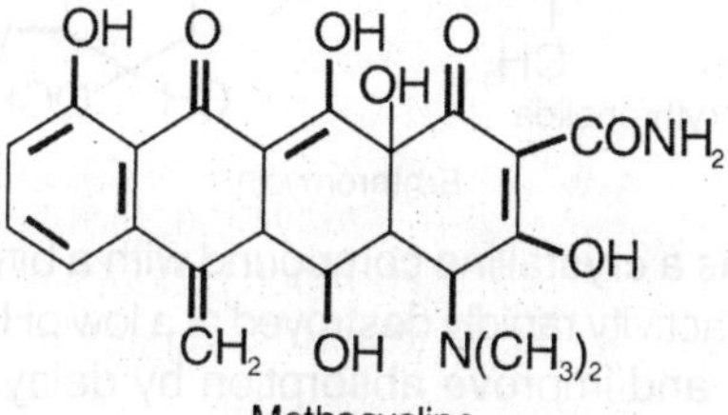
Methacycline

Methacycline is official as its hydrochloride and is administered in capsules.

Applications of the Tetracyclines
The tetracyclines as a group are of considerable value by virtue of their activity against a wide range of Gram-positive and Gram-negative bacteria, rickettsiae, actinomycetes, spirochaetes and the psittacosis virus. The various members differ slightly in their pharmacological properties but all have a low toxicity and are well absorbed orally. They are used particularly for the treatment of brucellosis, chronic bronchitis and other respiratory infections.

Forms of the Tetracyclines
Chlortetracycline. Hydrochloride, capsules.

Oxytetracycline. Hydrochliride for injection and in capsules. The dihydrate of the free base in tablets.

Tetracycline. Hydrochloride capsules, tablets and for injection.

Demethylchlortetracycline. Hydrochloride, capsules.

Doxycycline. Hemihydrate, hemiethanolate of the hydrochloride, capsules.
Methacycline. Hydrochloride, capsules.

ERYTHROMYCIN

This antibiotic, discovered in 1952, is prepared by the fermentation of the soil organism *Streptomyces erythreus.* It is a basic compound consisting of three linked units, a basic sugar, desosamine; a neutral sugar, cladinose; and a large ring lactone, erythronolide.

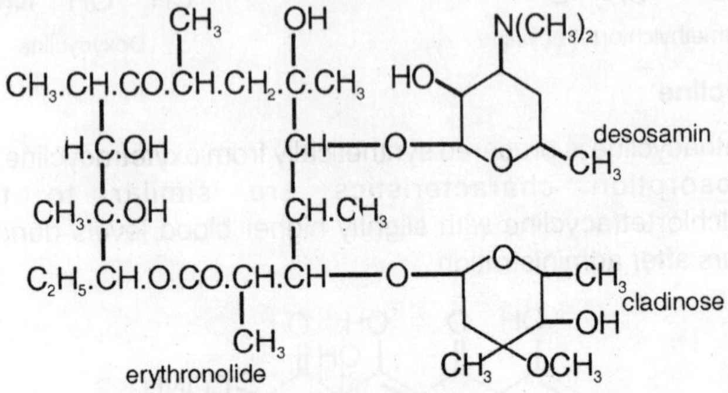

Erhthromycin

Erythromycin is a crystalline compound with a bitter taste, only slightly soluble in water, and activity rapidly destroyed at a low pH. In order to overcome the flavour problem and improve absorption by delaying attack by gastric acid, the hydroxyl group in the desosamine ring can be esterified to give the stearate, propionate or estolate (the lauryl sulphate salt of the latter). Water-soluble salts for injection are obtained with glucoheptonic or lactobionic acids.

Applications of Erythromycin

Erythromycin is an antibiotic of low toxicity with an antibacterial spectrum similar to benzylpenicillin. It is active against many Gram-positive and some Gram-negative bacteria such as *Neisseria, Haemophilus* and *Brucella* strains; also some activity against *Rickettsia*. It was particularly valuable before the advent of penicillinase resistant penicillin, since it is unaffected by this enzyme. Erythromycin is usually administered orally: for parenteral use a soluble salt is used.

Forms of Erythromycin

Erythromycin tablets, erythromycin stearate tablets, erythromycin estolate capsules.

NOVOBIOCIN

Novobiocin has at various times been isolated from several different strains of streptomycetes and is now prepared from *Streptomyces niveus.*

Novobiocin has been shown to consist of a coumarin linked to a substituted benzoic acid and a neutral nitrogen containing sugar.

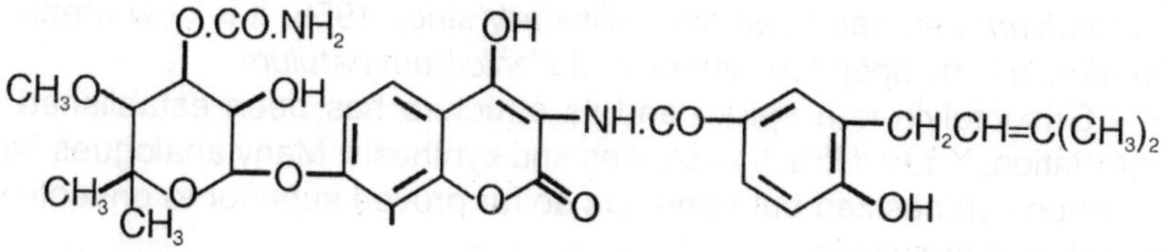

Novobiocin

The hydroxyl group in the coumarin portion of the colecule is acidic and gives salts with strong bases such as sodium or calcium which are used in tablet formulations. Novobiocin is well absorbed orally and is well tolerated and has been used in the treatment of infections due to Gram-positive bacteria resistant to other antibiotics.

FUSIDIC ACID

Fusidic acid was isolated in 1962 from a strain of *Fusidium coccineum* found in monkey dropping in Japan. The structure of fusidic acid is unusual in that antibiotic activity is rarely associated with steroids or triterpenes although recently the antibiotics cephalosporin P_1 and helvolic acid have been shown to possess similar structures.

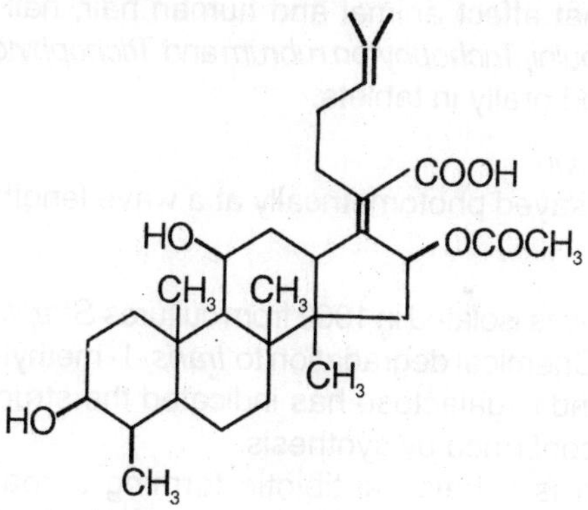

Fusidic acid

Fusidic acid is sparingly soluble in water but the crystalline sodium salt is readily soluble and is administered in capsules.

Applications of Fusidic Acid

Fusidic acid is active against Gram-negative cocci and Gram-positive bacteria particularly *Staphylococcus aureus*. It is of low toxicity, well absorbed orally and has been principally used for treatment of severe staphylococcal infections.

GRISEOFULVIN

Griseofulvin was isolated in 1939 from the mycelium of *Penicillium griseofulvum* and has been used clinically since 1958. It is now prepared commercially by deep fermentation of *Penicillium patulum.*

Griseofulvin is a spiran and its structure has been established by degradation, X-ray diffraction studies and synthesis. Many analogues have also been synthesized but none has so far proved superior to griseofulvin against dermatophytes.

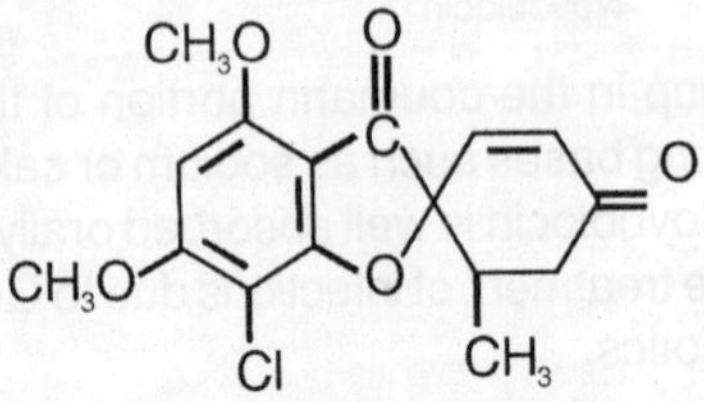

Griseofulvin

Griseofulvin is only very slightly soluble in water and in order to ensure absorption when given orally, it is essential for the material to be very finely divided, the *British Pharmacopoeis* requires a particle size of less than 5 µm.

Applications of Griseofulvin

Griseofulvin has no antibacterial action but it is very active against the dermatophytes that affect animal and human hair, nail and skin such as *Microsporum audouini, Trichophyton rubrum* and *Trichophyton mentagrophytes.* It is a administered orally in tablets.

Assay of Griseofulvin

Griseofulvin is assayed photometrically at a wave length of 291 mm.

Lincomycin

Lincomycin was isolated in 1962 from cultures *Streptomyces lincolnensis* var. *lincolnensis.* Chemical degradation to *trans*-1-methyl-4-*n*-propyl proline, D-allothreonine and D-galactose has indicated the structure shown below, which has been confirmed by synthesis.

Lincomycin is a baisc antibiotic forming a readily water-soluble hydrochloride which is used orally and parenterally. The hydrochloride monohydrate is official in capsules and injection.

Applications of Lincomycin

Lincomycin resembles erythromycin in its activity against Gram-positive organisms, particularly the haemolytic streptococci, pneumococci and staphylococci including those producing penicillinase. It is readily absorbed orally with a low toxicity and is generally used where benzylpenicillin is contra-indicated.

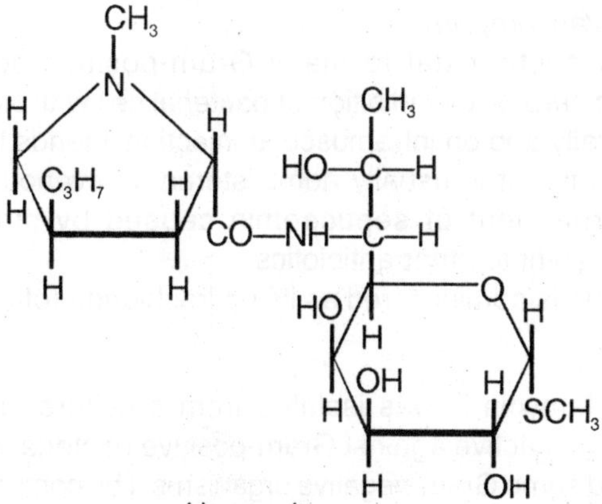

Lincomycin

Clindamycin

Modification of lincomycin by the insertion of chlorine into the allothreonine moiety has yielded clindamycin (7-chloro-7deoxylincomycin) which is considerably more active than the parent compound against staphylococci and pneumococci and of at least comparable activity against other sensitive species. The compound is well absorbed orally and is administered as the hydrochloride hydrate in capsules, as the palmitate ester hydrochloride in syrup formulaltions and as the phosphate for parenteral use.

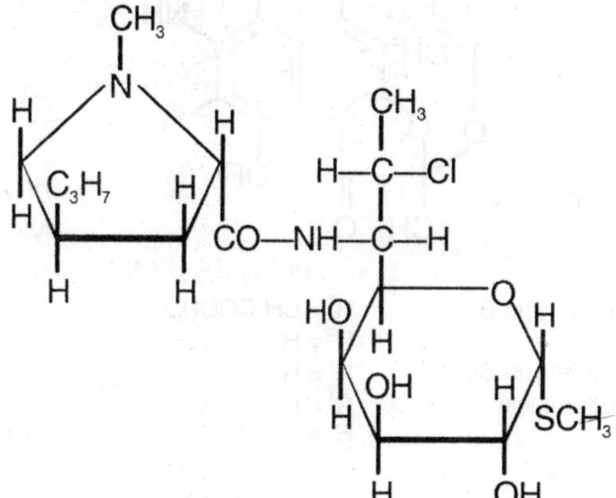

Clindamycin

Vancomycin

Vancomycin was isolated in 1955 from *Streptomyces orientalis*. It is an amphoteric substance but little is known of its structure. Hydrolysis yields a number of amino acids, glucose and a compound containing chlorinated phenyl residues.

Applications of Vancomycin

Vancomycin is bactericidal to many Gram-positive cocci, including *Staphylococcus aureus,* by inhibition of bacterial cell wall biosynthesis. It is not absorbed orally and on intramuscular injection it tends to produce pain and necrosis, hence it is usually administered intravenously. It is mainly used for the treatment of septicaemia caused by staphylococci or streptococci resistant to other antibiotics.

Vancomycin is administered as its hydrochloride (official).

Rifampicin

In 1959 rifamycin B was isolated from a culture of *Streptomyces mediterranei,* it was active against Gram-positive bacteria, *Mycobacterium tuberculosos* and some Gram-negative organisms. The compound was poorly absorbed from the alimentary tract and caused local irritation when injected. In addition, its solution was unstable, increasing in potency on storage. It

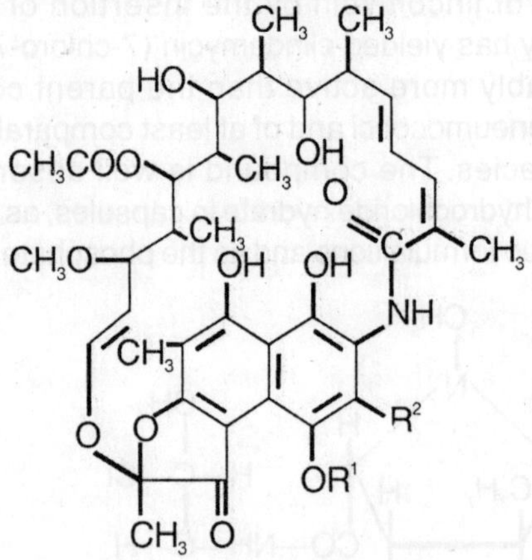

Rifamycin B	$R^1 \equiv CH_2COOH$ $R^2 \equiv H$
Rifamycin SV	$R^1 \equiv R^2 \equiv H$
Rifampicin	$R^1 \equiv H$ $R^2 \equiv$ —CH = N—N N—CH_3

The rifamycins

was established that this change was due to oxidation and hydrolysis to give a quinonoid compound, rifamycin S, which could be reduced with ascorbic acid to the phenolic rifamycins SV. This compound was more active and less toxic than the parent. Over 400 semi-synthetic rifamycins have been prepared by chemical modification in order to obtain optimal activity and oral absorption.

A Mannich reaction between rifamycin S, formaldehyde and dimethylamine followed by ascorbic acid reduction yields the 3-dimethylamino-methyl derivative of rifamycin SV[$R^1 \equiv H$, $R^2 \equiv -CH_2N(CH_3)_2$] from which the aldehyde [$R^1 \equiv H$, $R^2 \equiv -CHO$] is obtained by oxidation. The orally absorbed hydrazone, rifampicin, is obtained by reaction of the aldehyde with 1-amino-4-methyl-piperazine.

Rifampicin acts as an antibiotic by blocking the initiation of ribonucleic acid synthesis, and because of this the compound is also active against various pox and adenoviruses.

Applications of Rifampicin

Rifampicin is well absorbed orally and is used for the treatment of tuberculosis, respiratory, urinary tract and Gram-positive infections.

Chapter 6

Formulations

It is only on relatively few occasions that a drug, as such, may be directly administered to a patient. Usually, the medicament must be mixed with adjuvants, stabilizers, preservatives, etc. and subjected to various process to give a practical dose-form: in other words the medicament must be formulated. The practising pharmacist is ethically and legally required to supply medicines complying with accepted specifications and for this reason must be aware of the relevant formulation and storage requirements for those medicines. These requirements are likely to be particularly stringent for the complex, more recently developed, medicaments, but care is needed even with apparently simple products such as aspirin tablets if all the main aims of formulation are to be satisfied. These aims, not in order importance, are that the product shall be:

(a) economical for large scale manufacture,
(b) acceptable,
(c) chemically and physically stable,
(d) correctly packaged,
(e) preserved against microbial contamination,
(f) able to provide correct dose of drug, and
(g) therapeutically effective.

Economic Large-Scale Manufacture

Earlier formulation studies will have established the main product requirements and possible means by which these may be achieved. Difficulties may arise when bench or even pilot scale methods are translated to full commercial production; Oldshue (1961), for instance, has discussed scale-up problems for solid/liquid mixing processes. Particular attention must be given to those processes which are prolonged on the industrial scale. It may be necessary, for instance, to pass a stream of nitrogen or other inert gas through an industrial comminutor if the drug is heat or oxygen sensitive and its transit time in the equipment is long. Heat-up and cool-down times for a manufactured batch may be increased by a large factor compared with bench experiment, and a degradative reaction that may be ignored during initial studies may assume crucial importance on the large scale. Theoretical treatment of the problem leads to mathematical difficulties, but even a small additional loss, regardless of cause, could be significant within the context of the overall degradation during the life of the product and it may be necessary, for instance, to install cooling coils within the processing vessel.

Alternatively, new equipment might be purchased or a completely original production facility designed. These points require a good knowledge of pharmaceutical engineering and the resources available to the particular organization, as well as an awareness that equipment and manufacturing costs must bear a reasonable relation to the expected throughout and selling price of the product.

Acceptability

A produced must be acceptable to those who handle or use it. The doctor, for instance, will note those features of a product that facilitate administration to the patient. An injection what is so viscous that it cannot readily be drawn into the syringe is unlikely to attract continued use if an alternative more readily administered product is available. Ultimately, it is the patient who uses a product. The success of a treatment often depends on strict adherence to a given dose regimen that may extend over a considerable period of time. The patient may be well find, for example, a gritty ointment or an unpalatable mixture, completely unacceptable, and may abandon treatment or ask the physician for an alternative form of the drug.

Flavour and Perfumes

These are available to the formulator as concentrated extracts and alcoholic or aqueous solutions, or they may be adsorbed on powder carriers or micro-encapsulated. They are usually mixtures of natural and synthetic materials; concertrated fruit extracts or juices are used to prepare fruit syrups. Volatile oils still find use although their solubility tends to be limited by the terpene fractions. These may be removed and the deterpenated oil is more soluble in water and dilute alcohols, has a finer flavour lacking the terpene overtones, and is some 2 to 8 times stronger than the original oil. Short (1960) makes the point that removal of terpenes leads to a less readily oxidized oil. Some flavours, and most perfumes, tend to 'disappear' when first added to a product but develop their full effect later. When deciding the optimum level at which to use these materials, produts having a range of concentrations should be prepared and assessed after a short period of storage.

Only the bitter, sweet, salt or acid elements of a flavour are perceived by the taste buds of the tongue, all other flavours and perfumes being recognized by smell. A heavy cold causes almost complete obliteration of taste and smell. As water–insoluble materials have little or no taste, unpleasant drugs may be rendered more acceptable by administration as a water-insoluble derivative— a classical example is chloramphenicol palmitate— although acceptability obtained in this way may cause problems of sedimentation, bio-availability, etc. If an insoluble derivative cannot be used, a strong perfume or flavour may be required to mask an unpleasant drug but there is the high probability that a strong identifiable perfume or flavour, initially acceptable, may eventually be actively disliked if the treatment is prolonged. It must be remembered that the preferences of the sick adult or child do not necessarily coincide with, and are likely to be more capricious than those of the healthy subject. Where possible it is probably better to use a neutral but nevertheless pleasant and effective flavour or perfume that is not recognized by the patient. The problems of flavouring are most acute for paediatric preparations where a very strong flavour may itself cause nausea and vomiting. Few situations are more difficult than the firmly shut mouth of a child refusing to take a medicine.

There are associations between colours and flavours e.g. yellow with lemon, red with cherry, etc. and between flavours e.g. acids with citrus flavours. It is generally true that lime flavour, for instance, is more appropriate to a pale green, faintly acid product than to one which is neutral and coloured red. With the wide range of flavours available to the formulator it is not surprising that there has been a tendency for the traditional materials to be ignored but there is still a case for the judicious use of pahrmaceutical substances such as oils of dill and caraway, and oleorisins of capsicum and ginger, particularly in those situations where their carmintive action may be useful in allaying any gastric upset caused by the drug. A persistent flavour of the chocolate type, or the local anaesthetic action of menthol, pure or in peppermint oil, is particularly effective in covering bitter unpleasant tastes--a combination of both may be tried if the taste of ferrous salts must be masked. Charnicki and Kober (1957), in describing all stages of the flavouring trials for an aqueous oral penicillin/sulphonamide product, noted that a flavouring agent may also adversely affect product stability. Vanillin accelerated decomposition, whereas clove and aniseed were without effect. As will be seen, sulphur dioxide used to preserve fruit juices and syrups against microbial spoilage has been implicated in the fading of colouring substances.

Apart from flavouring it may be necessary to cover a bitter taste by means of a sweetning vehicle. While sucrose is likely to remain the most widely employed sweeting agent, glycerin and chlorofrom may be of value and have preservative action in sufficient concentration. Alternatively, given suitable preparations, honey, liquorice and treacle have useful sweetening action. Soluble saccharin (the sodium salt) is acid to have a less obtrusive bitter after-taste than saccharin itself and, depending on concentration, is about 200 to 700 times sweeter than sugar; it is best used in conjunction with sugar at trial concentrations of 0.02 – 0.05 per cent. The cyclamates are 20 to 30 times sweeter than sugar but until their freedom from toxicity has been completely established it would be wise to avoid their use in formulation. Sorbitol is recommended as a replacement for sugar in diabetic preparations but has only half the sweetening power, is more expensive and is said to have some laxative action. It is converted to fructose in the liver and is contra-indicated where there is intolerance to that sugar. It may be noted also that lactose used in tables may give trouble with galactosaemic patients. These problems are most acute for children where the dose of carbohydrate related to body weight is higher than for adults. A useful review is given by Leach (1970).

Colours

These may be derived from natural sources (Cochineal) or made synthetically (Tartrazine). They may be soluble in water (Amarnath), in oil (Scarlet Red) or insoluble in both solvents. In the latter group those of pharmaceutical interest include a few pigments (Bole) and the lakes which are insoluble calcium or aluminium complexes of water-soluble dyes. Carmine is the aluminium lake of the colouring matter from cochineal. Lakes are included in tablets and tablet coating because of their greater light stability compared with the corresponding water–soluble dye. Opacification of the shell of capsules of Chlordiazepoxide and some other drugs by lakes etc., is carried out where it is necessary to exclude light and avoid photo-decomposition.

The majority of dyes used in formulation are synthetically produced and are usually salts. The coloured ion may react with substances of opposite polarity; thus both tartrazine and Amarnath give insoluble salts with solutions containing nicotine. Dyes vary in their stability to pH, light and reducing agents as discussed by Swartz and Cooper (1962). Non-ionic surfactants may promote accelerated fading due possibly to interaction between the ethylene oxide moiety of the surfactant and the chromophoric group of the dye (Scott et al. 1962). The effect of such variables should be checked in the formulated product for the proposed range of dyes.

Dyes are used to standardize or improve an existing colour, to mask an innocuous colour change, to complement a flavour or odour or for identification purposes. Unfortunately there is evidence that some dyes may act as carcinogens or are ortherwise undesirable and for this reason are not permitted in foodstuffs or , by implication, in drugs or cosmetics. Dyes must be selected with care as there is no internationally recognized list of permitted colours; a colour which is allowed in one country may be totally banned in another. A useful summary of the situation is given in the Extra Pharmacopoiea (Martindale) (1972). In Great Britain the colouring agents which may be used are given in the Colouring Matter in Foods Regulations, 1996 (S.I. 1996: No. 1203) and for Scotland in S.I. 1996: No. 1384. If it is imperative to include a dye in the formulation, the lowest concentration should be used, especially for paediatric products, since children are likely to vomit with consequent staining of clothes.

Stability

The main causes of physical and chemical instability have been discussed elsewhere in this volume. Here only a number of details in the use of anhydrous vehicles and in the formulation of suspensions will be discussed.

Anhydrous Vehicles

If these are needed for the formulation of water sensitive drugs in oral products,. either a water miscible or an oily vehicle may be considered. The former could comprise various mixtures of ethyl or isopropyl alcohols, glycerol, propylene glycol or the low molecular weight polyoxyethylene glycols. Ethylene glycol must *not* be used as it is metabolized to oxalic acid which is toxic. Generally, vehicles based on alcohol and glycols have an unpleasant burning taste but are much more acceptable if diluted with water immediately prior to administration. If the stability of the medicament is such that it will have a reasonable shelf-life in the presence of a limited amount of water, a combination of the alcohols with a suitable syrup produces an acceptable vehicle of the type used for the official elixirs.

As well as olive and arachis oils, a number of other oils are suitable for the formulation of oily vehicles. Cottonseed, soyabean and corn oils are all used for culinary purposes and are sufficiently bland for consideration as oily vehicles for oral preparations. Fractionated coconut oil is virtuallly colourless, odourless and tasteless; it is used as a diluent for Phenoxymethylpenicillin Mixture BPC. Such vehicles are rather difficult to flavour except with vanillin, volatile oils or other oil-soluble flavours. Sweetness may be improved by the addition of saccharin.

Anhydrous vehicles are also much used for the formulation of ointments, suppositories and parenteral solutions. In the first two types of product a suitable consistency is obtained by the inclusion or exclusive use of fats and waxes. Absorption from topical preparations and the pharmacological basis to topical therapy are discussed by Wagner (1961) and D'Arcy (1965) respectively. Systemic medication per rectum is convenient where oral administration may induce nausea or vomiting, onset of action is usually faster than by the oral route and (in common with buccal absorption) enterohepatic recycling is avoided. The lower efficiency of rectal absorption may dictate a dose larger than that given by mouth. The formulation of suppositories and related matters are discussed by Senior (1969 a and b) and Wagner (1971). Anhydrous injection vehicles have been reviewed by Speigel and Noseworthy (1963), who note that care is needed in selecting the vehicle if unwanted modifications of drug activity is to be avoided. Polyxyethylene glycol vehicles markedly increase the toxicity of nitrofurantoin and are incompatible with many phenolic substances. If the drug is only partially soluble in the vehicle, temperature fluctuation may cause a coarsening of the particle size of the undissolved portion. For completely soluble drugs it is necessary to check that this condition also obtains at a suitably low temperature, say– 5, as material deposited at a lower than normal temperature may not readily redissolve when the temperature rises again.

Suspensions

The stability of these depends both on the properties of the dispersed–solid and on those of the vehicle. Apart from gravitational sedimentation which is a function of particle size, the behaviour of the solid may be determined by the zetpotential. If this is small, say in the range +25 to –25 mV, nett attractive forces cause particles to aggregate and settle rapidly to form a high volume loosely packed sediment which is readily redispersed on shaking. At larger zeta potentials repulsive forces predominate and particles sediment individually and slowly to form a densely packed, clay-like, dilatant sediment which is not easily redispersed by shaking. From the point of view of product formulation neither system is satisfactory but, as discussed by Haines and Martin (1961), it may be possible to adjust the zeta potential of the suspended particles by addition of electrolytes to give the optimum compromise between the slow sedimentation of the deflocculated state and the ready redispersion of sediment that is characteristic of the flocculated system. For this purpose, polyvalent ions are usually most efficient; for example sodium citrate controls the degree of floculation of the bentonite in Calamine Lotion, and hence it consistency, It will also deflocculate a 100 per cent w/w barium sulphate paste to give a thin pourable suspension. Matthews and Rhodes (1968 a and b) reported that satisfactory griseofluvin suspensions may be prepared by zeta potential control with Al^{3+} ions.

Even with correct control of the zeta potential, the size of density of the particles may be such that still settle too rapidly for the proper quantity of medicament to be poured out, drawn into a syringe or topically applied. For *dilute* suspensions the rate v at which a particle of density D and radius r settles in a liquid of viscosity η and density d is given by Stokes' equation in the form:

$$v = \frac{2r^2(D-d)g}{9n} \qquad (6.1)$$

In general, for more concentrated dispersions crowding and other effects will reduce the rate of settling. The densities of the particles and vehicle are fixed by product requirements while processing methods, therapeutic requirements, etc. many determine the optimum particle size in which case it is only by increasing the viscosity of the vehicle that the sedimentation rate may be decreased. For this purpose, as well as traditional suspending agents such as tragacanth and acacia, the alginates and cellulose derivatives should also be considered. As noted elsewhere in this volume, modification of the naturally occurring cellulose chain produced the first commercial plastics; it is also a fruitful starting material for a large number of hydrophilic colloids. Cellulose is an extended open chain some 1000 to 3000 anhydro-β -glucose units long (Fig. 6.1). Steric hindrance near the —O— linkages limits rotation of the glucose units relative to one another. This, together with the rigidity of the glucose units restricts the flexibility of the chain. Interchain attraction is very high due to hydrogen bonding between neighbouring —OH groups and as a result cellulose is not thermoplastic, cannot be plasticized and is insoluble in all but very acid or alkaline aqueous media. If the —OH is modified by the formulation, of an ester, e.g. cellulose acetate, or ether, e.g. methyl cellulose, hydrogen bonding is much reduced and the properties of the resultant product will depend on the degree of substitution, the average chain length and the distribution of chain lengths. In general the degree of substitution controls and solubility (Table 6.1) while the chain

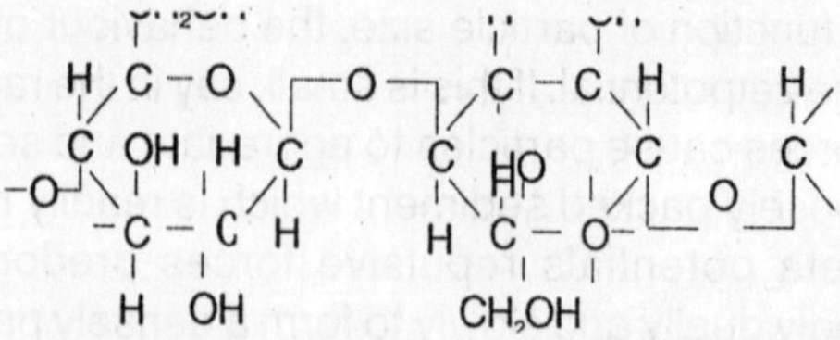

Fig. 6.1. Part of the cellulose chain

TABLE 6.1

THE EFFECT OF SUBSTITUTION ON THE SOLUBILITY OF CELLULOSE ESTERS

Derivative	Alkoxyl groups / Glucose Units		Soluble in
Methyl–	1.6 – 1.8	$-OCH_3$	Water
Ethyl–	0.5	$-OC_2H_3$	10 per cent NaOH solution
	0.8 – 1.3		Water
	1.4 – 2.5		Alcohol
	2.5 – 2.8		Non-polar solvents
Sodium carboxymethyl	0.7 – 0.8	$-OCH_2COONa$	Water
Hydroxy-	1.6 – 1.8	$-OCH_3$	Water–low to
propyl	0.1 – 0.2	$-OC_3H_7OH$	medium viscosity
methyl	0.1 – 1.4	$-OCH_3$	Water-medium
	0.1 – 0.3	$-OC_3H_7OH$	to high viscosity

length and distribution determines the viscosity grade. The propoxyl group is sufficiently hydrophobic for propyl cellulose to be insoluble in water at all levels of substitution. The viscosity grade is indicated by a number after the name, i.e. Hypromellose 20 BPC would be that grade of hydroxypropylmethylcellulose which, at a concentration of 2 per cent in water gives a solution with a viscosity of 20 centistokes. A 2 per cent solution is also used for standardizing methylcellulose but the concentration is 1 per cent for sodium alginate and sodium carboxymethylcellulose. Sodium alginate is a purified substance extracted from *Laminaria* type seaweeds. Alginic acid is a D-mannuronic acid polymer; solutions of the sodium salt at a given concentration become more viscous as the degree of polymerization of the acid is increased. A wide variety of viscosity grades is available but only one (30–60) is official. Carboxypolymethylene is a totally synthetic vinyl polymer with a high degree of carboxyl substitution. The acid powder is dispersed in water and then neutralized with a base to give a viscous solution that is most stable between pH 6 and pH 11. Unless protected by an antioxidant the solutions loose viscosity on exposure to sunlight.

Substances that desolvate the polymer chain of suspending agents reduce the viscosity of their solutions and may, eventually, precipitate the polymer. Typical of such substances are inorganic salts and high concentrations of such hydrophilic materials as alcohol, glycerol and sucrose. Heating solutions of the polymer changes their viscosity reversibility thus solutions of methylcellulose or hydroxypropylmethylcellulose get a certain temperature, the so-called get-point, which is lower for methyl-than for hydroxypropylmethyl cellulose. Above the gel-point the polymer is precipitated. Prolonged heating, however, or most natural and synthetic suspending agents lead to depolymerization and permanent loss of viscosity. This loss of viscosity may amount to some 25 per cent when, for instance, sodium carboxymethylcellulose solutions are sterilized by autoclaving.

Sodium alginate, -carboxymethylcellulose and -carboxypolymethylene give insoluble salts with a number of multivalent metal ions and the acids are precipitated at a sufficiently low pH. Hypromellose is the preferred polymer for thickening ophthalmic solutions as these are clearer and have fewer undispersed fibres. The official preparation is used for the replacement of lachrymal secretion where this is deficient.

The availability of a wide range of viscosity grades permits the selection of the grade and type of polymer best suited to the needs of the product. Assume, for instance that it is required to suspend a power of 50μm maximum diameter and density 1.5 g/cm³. If the mixture is to be taken every four hours an arbitrary decision might be taken that the largest particles must not sediment more than 1 cm in that time. The density of the vehicle may be taken as 1.0 g/cm³. Substituting in equation (37.1):

$$\frac{1}{4 \times 60 \times 60} = \frac{2 \times (25 \times 10^{-4})^2 \times (1.5 - 1.0) \times 981}{n} \tag{6.2}$$

whence $n \approx 10$ poise

From Fig. 6.2 it would appear that the most economical materials for providing a vehicle of this viscosity would be Tragacanth or Sodium carboxymethylcellulose 3500 at a concentration of about 0.7 per cent. Smoother pouring characteristics might result from using a lower viscosity grade suspending agent at a higher concentration. Additionally, less suspending agent than is implied by the above calculation would probably achieve the desired performance as the majority of particles would have a diameter less than 50μm. In any case their concentration is likely to be greater than that for which Stokes' equation is strictly applicable and sedimentation would be hindered by crowding and other effects. Clearly, the foregoing effects would need to be investigated by direct experiment.

For lotions and related products it may be possible to thicken the product with bentonite or related materials that form structured gels with water. The intention is that vigorous shaking would break the structure to give a thin pourable product but on standing the structure would reform and so prevent sedimentation of dispersed solids.

Preservation Against Microbial Spoilage

In the strictest sense microbial spoliage is another form of product instability but is conveniently discussed here as a separate issue. There is an obvious connection with the addition of bacteriostatics to multidose quantities of injections to prevent the development of microorganisms accidentally introduced during use; indeed, this is a specific instance of the general problem of preventing microbial spoliage where failure may have particularly serious consequences. The addition of antimicrobial substances to non-sterile preparations is intended to stop the multiplication of microorganisms present when the product was manufactured as well as those subsequently introduced. It is important that preservative measures should have a broad spectrum of activity because of the wide range of the likely contaminants both bacterial and fungal, the impossibility of predicting the kind of contamination that may occur during the life of the product, and the nutrient properties of many pharmaceutical products.

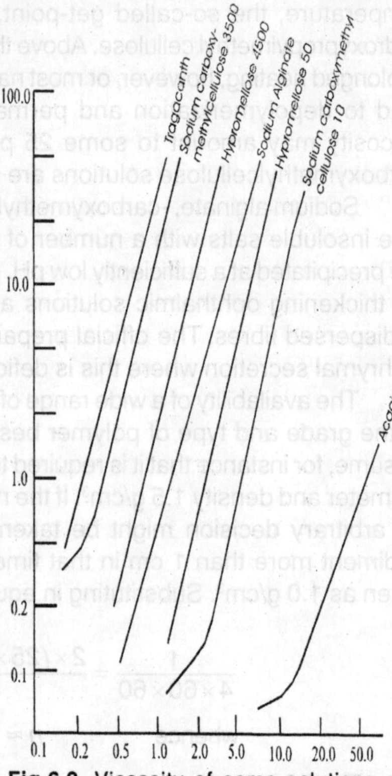

Fig.6.2. Viscosity of some solutions of hydrocolloids as a function of concentration. These curves should be used as a guide only as the viscosity is very dependent on the method of measurement and the technique used to prepare the solutions.

Physical Methods of Protection

These include sterilization and pasteurization, low moisture content, unfavourable pH, low temperature, minimum nutrient content and high osmotic pressure. It may be noted that a number of *Aspergillus* and *Penicillium* spp will grow at a pH as low as 2.0 while osmophilic yeasts are found in honey. However, the major disadvantage with physical methods of protection is that they become inoperative as soon as the particular constraint is removed, for example, the product is stored in a warm rather than cool place or the closure is taken out of a vial of sterile product. It is generally preferable to use a method that is largely independent of the environmental conditions namely the addition of a chemical substance that will kill contaminating organisms or at least prevent their multiplication in the product during storage and use.

Chemical Methods of Preservation

In addition to the specific requirement that an antimicrobial substance shall have a wide range of activity against contaminating organisms it must also comply with the more general requirements for all pharmaceutical adjuvants. It should be:

(a) effective in low concentration
(b) non-toxic, non-irritant and non-sensitizing,
(c) odourless, tasteless, colourless and soluble in the proposed vehicle.
(d) stable and effective, unaffected by pH,
(e) inert, non-volatile, readily prepared in a pure state, easily standardized, and
(f) compatible with all other product constituents.

A list of commonly used preservative is given in Table 6.2

TABLE 6.2
SUBSTANCES USED AS ANTIMICROBIAL PRESERVATIVES

Substance:	*Usual concentration per cent w/v*	*Remarks*
for oral use:		
Ethyl alcohol	At least 10	These hydroxylic material probably act by increased osmotic pressure. Ethylene glycol is toxic and must not be used (see text).
Isoprpyl alcohol	At least 10	
Glycerol	At least 25	
Propylene glycol	At least 25	
Sugar	At least 65	
Sulphur dioxide and sulphites	400 ppm.	Used in foodstuffs
e.g. sodium metabisulphate	0.1	Oxidizes and loses efficiency; may reduce days.
Benzoic acid	0.1	Rapid loss of effectiveness above pH 5.0. Soluble about 0.3 per cent in water at room temperature
Dehydroacetic acid	0.1	More effective in acid products

Sorbic acid	0.1	More effective in acid products. Soluble about 0.15 per cent in water at room temperature
Methyl *p*-hydroxybenzoate	0.2	Less effective about pH 8.0. Soluble about 0.3 per cent in water at room temperature.
Propyl *p*-hydroxybenzoate	0.02	Less effective about pH 8.0. Soluble about 0.03 per cent in water at room temperature
		Mixtures of these esters have a wider range of action. May be used as carbon source by one species of Ps. aeruginosa (Hugo & Foster 1964)
		Solutions of the sodium salts are strongly alkaline.
Chloroform	0.25	Chloroform water
	0.5	Double strength chloroform water
		Has warm sweet taste. Is very volatile and is easily lost from the product
For other use:		
Alcohols and glycols		
Benzoic, dehydroacetic and sorbic acid		See above. Sorbic Acid may cause skin irritation.
p-hydroxybenzoic acid esters		
Formaldehyde		Very effective and highly reactive–may cause skin irritation. Rarely used in pharmaceutical products but 0.05 per cent may be used in shampoos.
Benzyl alcohol	1.0	Has weak local anaesthetic action
Phenylethyl alcohol	0.5	Has been used in ophthalmic preparations
β–Phenoxyethyl alcohol	1.0	Very little action against Gram-positive organisms
Chlorbutol	0.8	Soluble about 0.8 per cent— action is erratic due to losses by volatilisation and hydrolysis– HCL is produced and may acidify the product
Phenol	0.5	
Cresol	0.3	
Chlorocresol	0.1	
Thiomersal	0.01	Unstable at pH lower than 7
Phenylmercuric salts	0.001	Maximum solubility about 0.1 per cent depending on salt used. The highly insoluble chloride may be precipitated if product contains chloride ions.
Chorexidine salts	0.01	Has been used for ophthalmic preparations. Salts of low solubility formed with many anions particularly of the anionic surfactants.
Quatenary ammonium salts e.g. Benzalkonium chloride	0.01	Incompatible with anionic surfactants, alkali hydroxides and carbonates. Benzalkonium chloride has been used in ophthalmic preparations.

Selection of Anti-Microbial Preservatives

In addition to the simple sub-division into oral and other use (Table 6.2) there may be other restrictions that narrow the range of choice when selecting a preservative. Apart from gross incompatibilities that are a number of situations in which activity may be impaired. Either the proportion of the active form of the preservative may be reduced (as with the effect of unfavourable pH) or (as occurs with hydrocolloids, surfactants and oil phases) the active form may be bound and not available for action.

Adjustment of the pH of a solution may affect both the chemical stability and the activity of the preservative. The former effect is, however, usually slight. If it is accepted that most pharmaceutical products will have a pH in the range 3–8, the only commonly used preservative for which serious chemical instability problems are likely to arise is thiomersal which degrades in acid media. Within the assumed pH range there will, however, be a marked variation in the activity of the ionized preservatives. In general, it is the

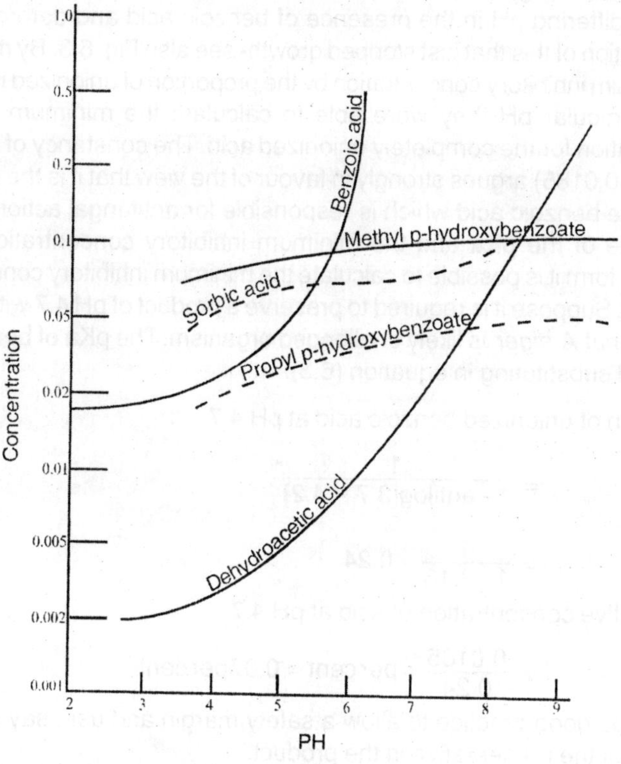

Fig. 6.3. Effect of pH on the minimum inhibitory concentration of some acid preservatives against *Aspergillus niger*. (Winsley & Walters, 1965, Bandelin 1958).

unionized form of these that has antimicrobial activity and the proportion of that form at any pH may be calculated by means of the Henderson-Hasselbalch equation arranged as follows:

Proportion of unionized preservative

$$= \frac{1}{1 + \text{antilog}(\text{pH} - \text{pK}_a)} \qquad (6.3)$$

Bandelin (1958) examined the effect of pH on the activity of a number of ionizable preservatives against *Chaetomium globosum*, *Alternaria solani*, *Penicillium Citrinum* and *Aspergillus niger*. The substances chosen for the study were benzoic, sorbic and dehydroacetic acids and the esters of *p*-hydroxybenzoic acid. As expected, he found that the activity decreased as the pH increased. In general, *A. niger* was the organism most resistant to the antifungal action of the preservatives. His data for that organism is summarized in Fig. 6.3. Winsley and Walters (1965) also grew *A. niger* in media of differing pH in the presence of benzoic acid and determined the concentration of this that just stopped growth- see also Fig. 6.3. By multiplying the minimum inhibitory concentration by the proportion of unionized molecules at the particular pH they were able to calculate the minimum inhibitory concentration for the completely unionized acid. The constancy of this value (0.0169 – 0.0185) argues strongly in favour of the view that it is the unionized form of the benzoic acid which is responsible for antifungal action. When a knowledge of the pKa and the minimum inhibitory concentration for the unionized form it is possible to calculate the minimum inhibitory concentration at any pH. Suppose it is required to preserve a product of pH 4.7 with benzoic acid and that *A.niger* is likely challenged organism. The pKa of benzoic acid is 4.2 and substituting in equation (6.3):

Proportion of unionized benzoic acid at pH 4.7

$$= \frac{1}{1 + \text{antilog}[3.7 - 4.2]}$$

$$= \frac{1}{1 + 3.16} = 0.24$$

Preservative concentration of acid at pH 4.7

$$= \frac{0.0185}{0.24} = \text{per cent} = 0.07 \text{ per cent}$$

It would be good practice to allow a safety margin and use, say 0.1 – 0.15 per cent of the preservative in the product.

The activity of preservatives is reduced if these are bound by another substance. Hydrophilic colloids of the type used for suspending insoluble solids are particularly liable to cause trouble. The hydroxybenzoate esters, for instance, are indifferent to the presence of tragacanth and sodium carboxymethycellulose but show loss activity in the presence of methylcellulose, polyvinylpyrrolidone and gelatin (Miyawaki et al., 1959). On the other hand, methylcellulose, diminishes the activity of cetylpyridinium chloride (Delucca and Kostenbauder 1960). As there is no simple rule by which interaction may be predicted it is advisable directly to check antimicrobial activity where hydrocolloids are employed in a formulation.

In their active form many preservatives are predominantly lipophilic and tend to partition between the hydrophilic and lipophilic phases of a two phase system. The absorption of preservatives by rubber and plastics is discussed elsewhere but it must be remembered that absorption may also occur with any other lipophilic solid. A solution of water-soluble surfactant may be regarded as another type of two-phase system with an aqueous and a lipophilic micellar pseudophase between which the preservative may partition; the effect is well known in the field of phenolic disinfectants. In the presence of polyxyethylene sorbitan oleate loss of activity has been shown to occur with sorbic acid (Blaung and Ahsan 1961a), cetylpyridinium chloride (Delucca & Kostenbauder 1960) and the *p*-hydroxybenzoic acid esters (Pisano and Kostenbauder 1959). The foregoing surfactants at a 5 per cent concentration, caused a four-fold increase in the amount of methyl *p*-hydroxybenzoate required for effective preservative action (Blaug and Ahsan 1961b). It is possible to determine the amount of preservative in the aqueous phase of a surfactant solution; this allows comparison of the activity of solutions with and without surfactant, but having the same concentration of preservative in the queous phase. Humpherys et al. (1968) found a higher than predicted activity for benzoic acid/non-ionic surfactant systems which they ascribed to micelles acting as reservoirs for preservative and to other effect.

Emulsions are more obvious examples of two phase systems. In the simplest model, a mechanical dispersion of oil in water, lipophilic antimicrobial substances will partition between the oil and water until:

$$\frac{\text{Concentration of preservative in oil}}{\text{Concentration in water}}$$

$$= \frac{C_o}{C_w} = \text{the partition coefficient (K)}$$

The weight of preservative in the system is $C(V_o+V_w) = C_w V_w + V_w C_o$ where C is the concentration of preservative in the whole system and V_w and V_o are the volumes of water and oil respectively. If $V_o / V_w = \phi$

$$C(\phi V_w + V_w) = C_w V_w + \phi V_w K C_w$$

$$\text{and} \quad C_w = \frac{C(f+1)}{fK+1} \qquad (6.4)$$

The effect of partitioning in a simple oil-water system is described in paper by Bean & Heman Ackah (1964). For a liquid paraffin-water system at 15° the partition coefficient of phenol is 0.062. If ϕ is 1.0- *i.e.* a 50 per cent v/v dispersion and the overall concentration (C) of phenol in the preparation is 0.5 per cent, the concentration of that substance is the aqueous phase is:

$$C_w = \frac{0.5(1.0+1.0)}{0.062 \times 1.0 + 1.0} = 0.94 \text{ per cent}$$

This is due to the fact that the partition coefficient as defined above is less than 1.0. The efficiency (E) of an antimicrobial substance is given by:

$$E = pC_w^m \qquad (6.5)$$

where p is a constant and n is the concentration exponent; for phenol and chlorocresol n may be put equal to 6. If, arbitrarily, the efficiency of a 0.5 per cent phenol solution is set at 1.0 the relative activity of a 0.94 per cent solution is:

$$\frac{E}{1.0} = \frac{p(0.94)^6}{p(0.5)^6} = (1.88)^6 = 44.2$$

The foregoing enhanced activity may be compared with the decrease that occurs when chlorocresol is employed under similar circumstances. The partition coefficient is 1.34 at 15° and a suitable value for C is 0.1 per cent. The concentration of preservative in the aqueous phase of a 50 per cent *v/v* dispersion may be calculated as 0.086 per cent and the efficiency is reduced to 0.41, that is, less than half the value for the corresponding simple aqueous solution having the same overall concentration of chlorocresol.

Bean and Heman-Ackah point out that the partition coefficient usually changes in favour of the oil as the temperature is raised and this may explain the failure of products in a warm climate that have proved satisfactory in a more temperature environment. Thus, if the temperature of the above dispersion were raised to 35° (when the partition coefficient for chlorocresol at 35° is 1.78) the concentration of preservative in the aqueous phase is only 0.072 per cent and a relative efficiency 0:14 as compared with 0.41.

A real emulsion might include an emulgent which could provide a micellar pseudophase into which the antimicrobial substance would partition. The behaviour of a preservative in a real emulsion is therefore more complex than in the two-phase system described above and a full theoretical treatment would reflect this. By finding experimentally the ratio (R) of the total preservative in the aqueous phase to the free preservative in that phase Bean et al. (1969) where able to simplify the theoretical treatment and derived the expression.

$$C_w = \frac{C(\phi + 1)}{K\phi + R} \qquad (6.6)$$

where the symbols have the previously defined meanings. Extending the previous example with chlorocresol as the preservative ($\phi = 1.0$, $K = 1.34$ and $C = 0.1$ per cent) with $R = 3$ that is, three quarters of the total amount of preservative in the aqueous phase is locked in micelles:

$$C_w = \frac{0.1(1.0 + 1.0)}{1.34 \times 1.0 + 3.0} = \frac{0.2}{4.34} = 0.046 \text{ per cent}$$

and

$$\frac{E}{1.0} = \frac{p(0.046)^6}{p(0.1)^6} = \frac{p(0.046)^6}{p(0.1)^6} = (0.046)^6 = 0.01$$

It will be clear from the above calculation why it is so difficult to preserve emulsions against microbial contamination. In general, the oil and emulgent concentration should be kept to as low a value as possible, the selected antimicrobial substance should have a low concentration exponent and all components should be chosen to minimize the value of K and R. The amount of preservative in the aqueous phase will, of course, by raised by substances that increase its solubility in that phase. Hibbott and Monks (1961), for example, reported that the partition coefficient of methyl hydroxybenzoate is changed in favour of the aqueous phase if this contains glycerol or propylene glycol. These and many other factors that affect the preservation of emulsified preparations and discussed in considerable detail by Wedderburn (1964). It should be noted that many countries now require creams to be supplied in a sterile condition, or at least with a very low level of contamination; this is the main purpose of official instructions for the preparation and packaging of creams. For complete assurance of sterility it may be necessary to heat the cream in which case there will be problems of physical stability superimposed upon those associated with preservative activity.

Assessment procedures usually reveal the minimum concentration needed to protect the product against specific organisms. A safety margin must, however, be provided to take account of manufacturing tolerances. By way of illustration assume that 0.3 per cent phenol is found to be the best preservative for a given lotion. It may be considered that 90 to 110 per cent of the nominal amount of preservative is a reasonable manufacturing tolerance. By substitution in equation 37.5, however, it can be shown that reduction of the concentration of phenol to 90 per cent of the nominal value will have a very marked effect on the bactericidal efficiency of the preparation. Thus for phenol $n = 6$ and:

$$\frac{E}{1.0} = \frac{p(90)^6}{p(100)^6} = 0.53$$

A reduction of the phenol concentration of 10 per cent has therefore reduced the bacterial efficiency to 53 per cent of its original value. Clearly, to provide the the worst conditions of manufacture, the amount of phenol must be increased to:

$$\frac{0.3 \times 1.00}{90} = 0.33 \text{ per cent}$$

In practice an even higher concentration, perhaps 0.5 per cent, would be used to ensure efficient protection during the whole life of the product.

Testing preservative efficiency. There is no standard method for testing the activity of a preservative in a product. Although details vary there is general agreement that performance should be compared in normal and sterilized products when challenged by a variety of bacteria and fungi. These should also include a mixed culture obtained at the manufacturing unit, organisms isolated from failed samples and any special organisms relevant to the end use of the product, e.g., it is advisable to challenge eye-drops with several pseudomonad species and in particular with *Pseudomonas aeruginosa.* This organism is exceptionally resistant to the action of most preservatives which are acceptable for use in ophthalmic preparations (Brown and Norton 1965).

Inoculated samples should be incubated for at least 10 weeks at a variety of temperatures between 20° and 40°. Samples must be examined at intervals appropriate to the product, e.g. an hour or less for ophthalmic preparations as a rapid kill is required, whereas less frequent sampling would be more appropriate to mixtures. If possible the test should be carried out in such a way that quantitative results may be obtained.

Correct Dose

Although every care may be taken in the manufacture of a drug preparation the patient will not receive the correct dose if the product has deteriorated in storage. Chemical degredation leads to a reduction in the amount of the active constituent and low dose follows directly from this. Of the product is physically unstable then the correct total amount of drug may be present but this may be unevenly distributed throughout the product. In this way the patient may receive a variable dose of drug. This situation is potentially dangerous in those cases where the drug forms a dilatant sediment which is not easily dispersed by shaking the full container. Early doses might contain less than correct amount of drug, Later, because shaking may be more efficient with a partially emptied container, the sediment may become dispersed and the patient could be exposed to an overdose.

Uneven distribution may also arise from unsuspected faults in the manufacturing process, particularly, if this involves the dispersion of one solid phase with another. It should be noted that, even if the correct manufacturing procedures have been employed, bulk powders may demix during storage and transport and every care should be taken at the formulation stage to foresee and eliminate this possibility.

Finally, the correct amount of drug in a product, as determined by analysis, does not guarantee that the desired clinical response will be elicited in the patient.

Therapeutic Effectiveness

With very few exceptions a drug must be in aqueous solution to exert its therapeutic action. Often the site of action is remote from the site of administration and therefore a transport system is required; this is provided by the circulation of blood (Fig. 6.4). When administered by buccal, rectal, intramuscular, or subcutaneous routes, the drug directly diffuses into the blood from the absorbing tissue. Onset of action from this route will, therefore, be somewhat slower than by intravenous administration where the drug is directly injected into the blood. Onset of action is even longer by the oral route. This is partly due to the transit time of the drug to that part of the gastrointestinal tract from which it is best absorbed, to the nature of the

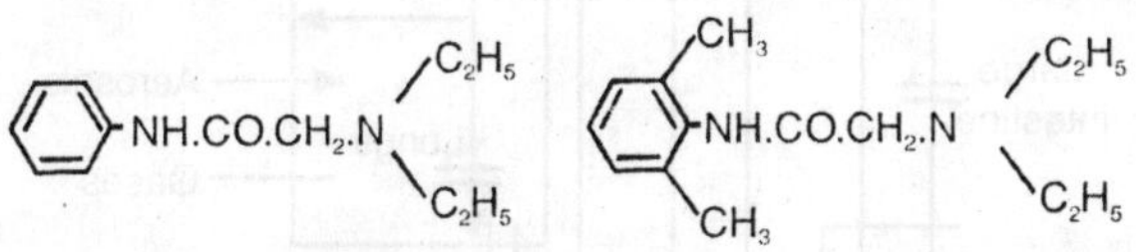

absorbing tissue, hepato-enteric recycling and to the nature of the oral product. Simple solutions tend to act faster than suspensions at time will be required for the suspended solid to dissolve so that it can exert its effect. Similarly, suspensions (fine particles) will act faster than powders (coarse particles) which in turn act faster than capsules and tablets. As far as the body is concerned all drugs are foreign substances and mechanisms are available for their elimination. The drug may be excreted in the faeces, urine or saliva, etc. either unaltered or as metabolites. The therapeutic response is often related to the amount of drug in the blood which in turn is determined by the nett effect of the absorption, transport and elimination processes. Products may therefore be ranked in order of promptness of response and duration of action as in Table 6.3. Each type of product will have a characteristic response, thus without considering the relevant theory at this stage, the graph for the time course of action for an oral product may be sketched as in Fig. 6.5 If the characteristic response of any product is to be modified for whatever purpose, there are three main ways in which this may be done:

Biological — a classic example is the co-administration of adrenalin with local anaesthetics to cause local vasoconstriction which minimizes leakage of anaesthetic from the injection site and therefore prolongs its action.

Chemical — the compound diethylaminoacetanilide (I) is clearly related to lignocaine (diethylaminoacet-2,6-xylidide) (II), and yet has only transient local anaesthetic action. This is due to the absence of methyl groups in the 2,6 positions that allows hydrolytic enzymes to gain access to the –NH,CO– group which is rapidly hydrolysed and the activity of the drug destroyed.

Pharmaceutical — by embedding a drug in wax, the rate of release of the drug may be slowed down and the activity prolonged in suitable cases.

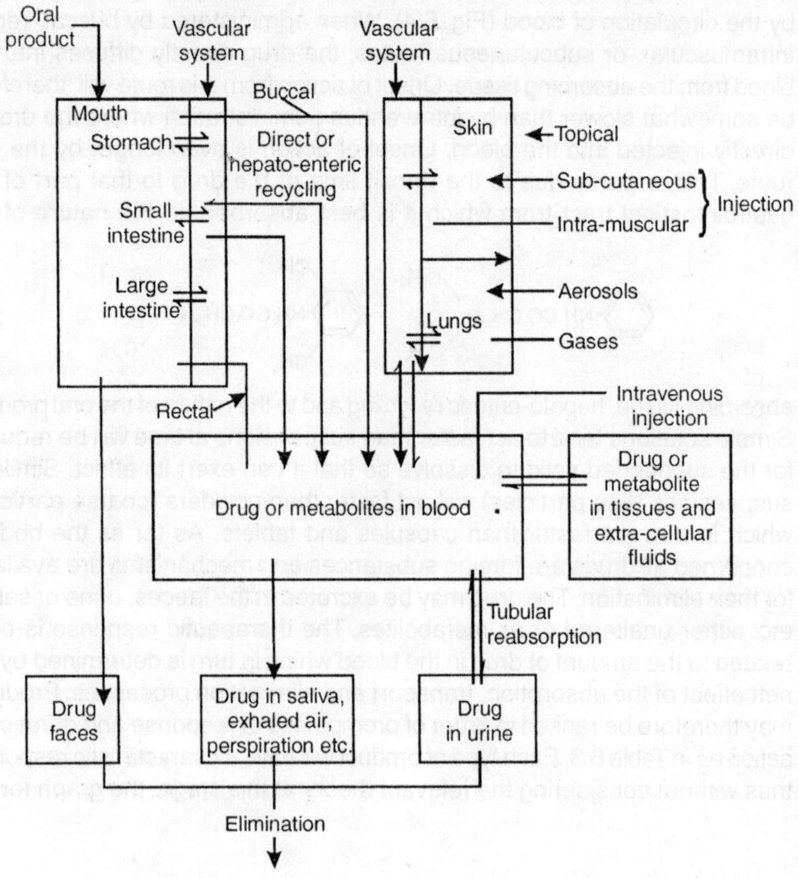

Fig. 6.4. Distribution of drugs in the body.

Most frequently the formulator will use the third method to modify drug action but there are occasions where ethe second method may be more applicable. Two examples will be quoted here. Above a certain dose, level the duration of action of oestradiol by deep intramuscular injection is independent of the dose. The diproprionate ester is the preferred form of the medicament for depot injections as, in vivo, hydrolysis of the ester controls the release of the hormone and the duration of the action is dose dependent. Basic drugs form insoluble tannates from which the base is released in the body at a controlled rate by hydrolysis. The tannates of pheniramine, mepyramine and phenylephrine have been combined in both tablet and

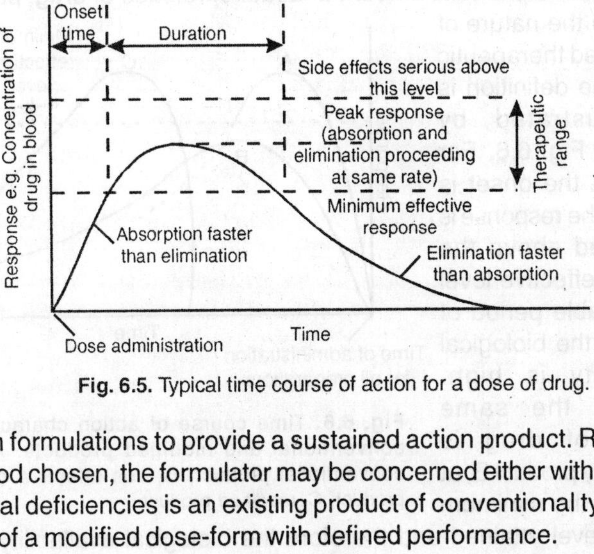

Fig. 6.5. Typical time course of action for a dose of drug.

suspension formulations to provide a sustained action product. Regardless of the method chosen, the formulator may be concerned either with correcting unintentional deficiencies is an existing product of conventional type or with the design of a modified dose-form with defined performance.

TABLE 6.3

THERAPEUTIC EFFECTIVENESS OF PHARMACEUTICAL PRODUCTS

Type	*Product*	*Onset*	*Duration*
Conventional	i/v injection	Immediate– seconds	Normal for drugs by that route usually some four to six hours
	i/m injection. Subcutaneous injection. Buccal tablet, Suppository, Aerosol Gases	Rapid– up to a few minutes.	Normal for drugs by that route
	Oral preparations Solution, Suspension, Powder Capsule. Tablet Topical products	Prompt to slow– a few minutes to more than an hour.	Normal for drug by that route
Modified	Prolonged action tablets,	Varies	Varies

capsules and short term depot injections	Prompt to slow– a few minutes to over an hour	Longer than normal for drug by that route— up to twelve hours
Enteric coated preparations	Delayed up to a few hours	Normal for drug after onset of action
Long term depot injections	Up to a few days	Several weeks
Solid implants	Up to a few days	Several months

In general these objectives may be attained by attention to the biological availability of the drug. Often, this is defined with reference to a `standard' preparation but in quantifying this parameter it is also necessary to take account both of the total amount and rate of release of drug, particularly in relation to the nature of the required therapeutic action. The definition is best illustrated by reference Fig. 6.6. For product A the onset is rapid and the response is maintained above the minimum effective level for a suitable period of time, i.e., the biological availability is high. Although the same amount of drug is released by product B, at no time is the minimum effective level attained and therefore the biological availability is low. On occasion it may be desirable to delay the release of drug because, for instance, it is inactivated by acid gastric secretions. The curve for product C best expresses the type of response that is required for high biological availability under these circumstances.

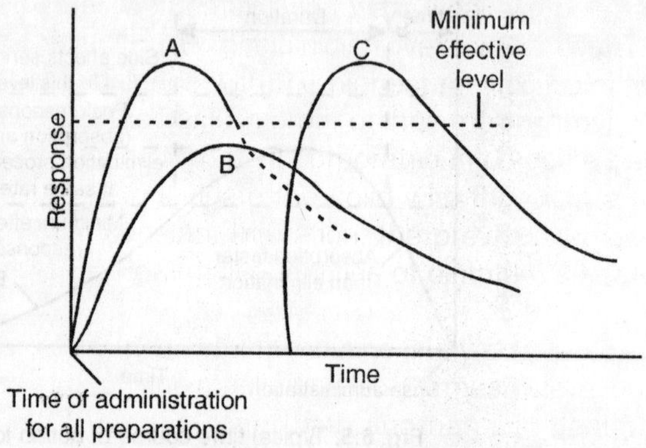

Fig. 6.6. Time course of action characteristics for conventional and modified products. A, effective conventional product; B, non-effective conventional product; C, modified product.

Biological Availability of Drugs from Conventional Preparations

It is axiomatic that a drug preparation shall be therapeutically effective yet only in the past decade or so has it been realized how wide may be the margin between potential activity as inferred from the known drug content and the actual activity observed in clinical use. For example, Anderson (1966) related the low therapeutic activity of a chloramphenicol palmitate preparation to the use of the wrong polymorph (q.v.). As noted earlier, the formulator's efforts are best directed at securing the correct rate of release of drug from the product. Although solutions usually give the highest rate of release, care

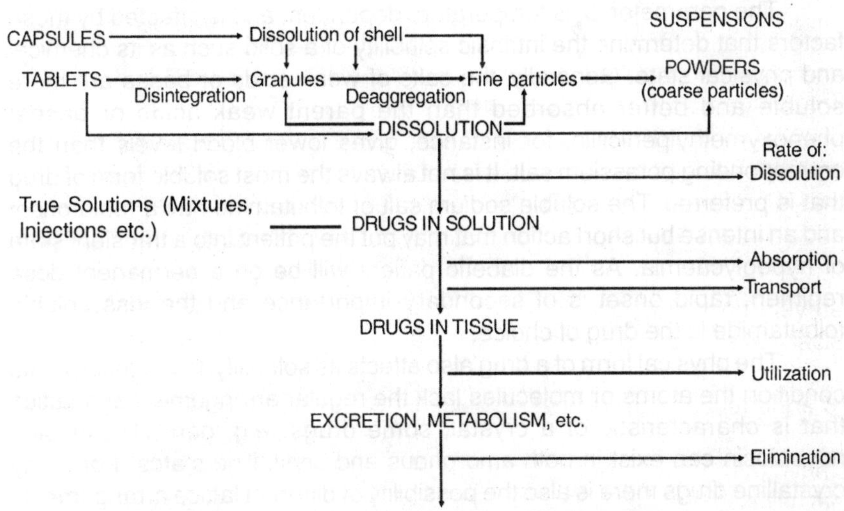

Fig. 6.7. Course of drug utilization for conventional products.

should be taken to ensure that precipitation of active substance does not occur due to dilution of the vehicle or pH changes. When sodium phenylbutazone solution is injected intramuscularly the drug is precipitated at the injection site due to pHY changes and the rate of release is limited by the dissolution rate of the solid material. A part from such examples, biological availability problems are most likely to occur if the product is a solid or a dispersion of a solid in a liquid. In these circumstances there is a high probability that the dissolution rate is the key factor (6.7).

In the Noyes and Witney (1987) model of dissolution, diffusion of solution from the interface to the bulk solution across the stationary film at the surface of the solid was the rate determining step. Alternative models assume that the dissolution process is rate determining or that macroscope packets of solvent transport solute to the bulk solvent. Each model requires a different mathematical treatment, but in all cases the rate of dissolution may be related to the difference between the concentration (C_s) of the solute in solution adjacent to the interface-often assumed to be saturated– and that is the bulk solvent (C), the surface area (S) exposed to attack and other factors (K) such as the viscosity and the degree of agitation of the solvent. The generalized equation may be written:

$$\text{Dissolution rate} = (C_s - C).F(S).f(K) \qquad (6.7)$$

If C is small and is only a small fraction of C_s then $(C_s - C) \approx C_s$ and the dissolution is then said to be proceeding under sink conditions and:

$$\text{Solubility dissolution rate} = C_s.F(S).f(K)$$

The parameter C_s is temperature dependent and is affected by those factors that determine the intrinsic solubility of a solid such as its chemical and physical state. Generally, the salts of weak acids or bases are more soluble and better absorbed than the parent weak acids or bases; phenoxymethylpenicillin, for instance, gives lower blood levels than the corresponding potassium salt. It is not always the most soluble form of drug that is preferred. The soluble sodium salt of tolbutamide has a rapid onset and an intense but short action that may put the patient into a transient state of hypoglycaemia. As the diabetic patient will be on a permanent dose regimen, rapid onset is of secondary importance and the less soluble tolbutamide is the drug of choice.

The physical form of a drug also affects its solubility. In the amorphous condition the atoms or molecules lack the regular arrangement of a lattice that is characteristic of a crystal; some drugs, e.g. penicillin, insulin, novobiocin can exist in both amorphous and crystalline states. For many crystalline drugs there is also the possibility of different lattice arrangements and these amorphous and different crystalline forms are known as polymorphs. Only one polymorph is stable under given physical conditions and all other forms tend to revert more or less rapidly to that stable form. The life-time of some polymorphic forms may be so long that the polymorphs appear to have a separate existence and are said to exist in a metastable state. From the formulator's point of view it is an unfortunate fact that the most stable form is also the least soluble and thereby is potentially the least active. In the case of novobiocin, the amorphous form of the acid is an effective antibiotic whereas the less soluble crystalline variety is inactive at th same dose level (Mullins and Macek 1960). The crystalline sodium salt is converted to the amorphous state under the acid conditions of the stomach and the calcium salt is amorphous state under the acid conditions of the stomach and the and three crystalline forms. Aguiar et al. (1967) showed the administration of 1.5 g of the most stable form of the ester to adults produced a mean peak blood level of about 2.5 μg/ml whereas the most soluble variety of the drug gave a peak concentration nearly ten times higher.

Polymorphic forms of drugs occur more frequently than is generally realized and lack of awareness of their existence can lead to unwelcome therapeutic effects even though chemical analysis would reveal nothing amiss. The low potency of some chloramphenicol palmitate preparations which have been marketed was due to the selection of the most stable but least active polymorph (Anderson 1966). Equally dangerous is the higher activity and incidence of side effects that might occur if a product formulated on the basis of clincial trials with the stable variety was inadevertantly manufactured with the metastable polymorph. The problem is further complicated by the possibility that the metastable variety may revert to the stable state during the lifetime of the product. Such changes may often be prevented by added substances, such as hydrocolloids and surface active agents, that position that crystal lattice. Mullins and Macek found that benzalkonium chloride increased the rate of crystallization of solutions of amorphous novobiocin. Methylcellulose, on the other hand, had the reverse effect and increased the time for crystals to appear in the solution form 22 days at 37° to more than 365 days at the same temperature. Calcium novobiocin, although amorphous, did not revert to the crystalline form at 37° even after storage for two years.

Surface area. Particle size reduction is a familiar pharmaceutical operation employed to secure better dispersion of a drug in its vehicle. The process also increases the surface area per given weight of material (the specific surface area) and can therefore affect the biological availability. As originally submitted to clinical trial, griseofulvin had a specific surface area of 0.4 m^2/g, a particle diameter of about 10 μm and a recommended dose of 250 mg. Subsequently the manufacturing procedure was changed and yielded a powder with a specific surface area of 1.5 m^2/g and a particle diameter of 2.7μm. The more rapid dissolution rate of the finer powder allows the dose to be halved. The official description, a white to pale cream powder the particles of which are generally up to 5 micrometeres in maximum dimension' is framed to give a powder with an average particle size smaller than this to ensure the correct biological availability for the antibiotic. Modern insulin preparations provide a further example of the importance of particle size and polymorphic form as factors controlling the biological availability of a drug. An insulin-zinc complex can be precipitated either as 10–40µm crystals or as amorphous particles upto 2 µm in size. If a mixture of both types is injected the amorphous particles dissolve rapidly for prompt response which is maintained by the slower dissolution of the crystals. The proportions of each type of particle determine the release profile of the preparation and may be varied to suit the individual needs of the patient.

As was the case with tolbutamide it is not always that most rapidly absorbed form of the drug that is most satisfactory for clinical use. A similar situation has arisen with nitrofurantion where the 10 μm powder, in suitable dose forms, gives a satisfactory concentration in the urine at an oral dose level of 50–100 mg but nausea and vomiting is a problem for a significant number of patients. It has been shown (Paul et al. 1967) that although side effects rarely occur if the coarser 100–150μm powder is used, neither the urinary concentration nor the amount of drug absorbed are markedly changed. It may also be necessary to avoid a small particle size powder if local action in the distal parts of the gastrointestinal tract is required and the drug has appreciable water solubility. Premature dissolution and absorption of the drug in say, the stomach might give rise to toxic effects and would certainly reduce the amount available for the required local action.

The Variable (K)

For the three types of dissolution mechanism that have been proposed *K* will include a factor for viscosity and degree of agitation as well as for specific effects peculiar to the particular type of preparation. The viscosity is important in that it determines the speed with which the molecules more away from the interface to the bulk dissolution medium. Hydrocolloids are often included in the formulae of pharmaceutical products to suspend solids, to prevent polymorphic changes or to act as binders during the moist granulation of powders for tableting. At best the hydrocolloid may mix with the dissolution medium, increase viscosity and slow down diffusion of the dissolving molecules: at worst it may absorb onto the solid surface to form a thin layer having an extremely high viscosity which will considerably delay diffusion. If absorption occurs, the effect is out of all proportion to the actual concentration of hydrocolloid in the product. Instead of being absorbed, these materials may be precipitated on to the particle surface by interaction with the contents of the gastrointestinal contents. Whatever the cause the effect is well illustrated by the following data from Davidson et al. (1961).

The degree of agitation is important both from the point of view of drug dissolution in vivo and also for possible tests for dissolution rate in vitro. In any static dissolution system there is a tendency for a stagnant pool of solution to form in the vicnity of the dissolving solid.

As a consequence, the concentration gradient is reduced and further dissolution of the solid is inhibited. Such evidence as is available (Levy 1963) suggests that the degree of agitation in the gastrointestinal tract is only moderate. It will be recalled that large doses of rapidly soluble materials such as the alkali metal halides must be dissolved in water before administration to avoid the nausea and vomiting that would arise from high local concentration of solute in the stomach. Furthermore, if the density of the product is unusually high it may become lodged in lower parts of the stomach and in the case of iron preparation this has led to gastric erosion. In normal situations however the degree of agitation in the stomach is probably sufficient to ensure that the rate of dissolution is not limited by poor mixing.

Dose : 0.72 millimoles of `salicylate' per kg administered orally to rats

Preparation	*Peak level after 30–minutes in*	
	plasma (µg/ml)	*brain (µg/g)*
Aspirin suspended in 2 per cent methylcellulose solution	132	11.6
Sodium acetylsalicylate solution	201	19.6
Sodium salicylate	208	21.1
Sodium salicylate in 2 per cent methylcellulose solution	162	13.3

A part from viscosity and agitation effect it is convenient to include in the variable *K* a number of factors peculiar to certain types of dose form. Suspensions should be free from effects other than those that may be attributed to factors already discussed above. Nevertheless, as an instance of the way quite minor changes may influence the time course of action of griseofulvin it was noted by Duncan et al. (1962), that a suspension prepared by dispersing the antibiotic directly in a solution of wetting agent gave a lower peak blood level than a product containing the same concentration of adjuvant added as a solid to the drug prior to dispersion with water.

The simplest model of a hard capsule comprises a powder mass enveloped in a water-soluble shell. It might be thought that such a system would be free from dissolution problems. The work of Aguiar and co-workers (1968) suggests that this is far from the truth; their examination of four nominally identical brands of chloramphenicol capsules showed peak plasma levels in adults varying from 2.2–9.5 μg/ml. The observed differences were related to the rate of deaggregation of the drug during dissolution. In the wider range of chloramphenicol capsules examined by Withey and Mainville (1969) the time for dissolution of 50 per cent of the dose of drug (t_{50}) varied from 2.4 to 20 minutes and with one brand, a soft capsule, only a quarter of the drug had dossolved in 30 minutes as compared with 60 to 90 per cent for the hard capsule preparations. Several experimental capsules were also studied and confirmed earlier reports that the capsule shell interferes with the initial stages of dissolution. Many hard capsule formulations contain lactose in addition to the drug and in high concentrations this may also depress the dissolution rate. For drug mixtures containing 43 per cent of the sugar t_{50} was about 4 minutes but was increased to about 13 minutes with 80 per cent of the adjuvant in the mixture. On the other hand, when lactose was substituted for calcium sulphate in manufactured batches of phenytoin capsules, enhanced activity and a much higher incidence of side effects were noted. Tyrer et al. (1970) have reported blood serum concentrations (20 to 25 μg/ml) for the formulation with lactose and only about a third of this value for the product with calcium sulphate.

There are so many variable in the production of tablets that it is difficult to disentangle the many possible interactions that may have a bearing on biological availability. On such attempt has been described by Ganderton et al., 1967. In studies with phenylindione tablets they reported a maximum dissolution rate at compaction pressures in the range 400 to 800 kg/cm^2 within which range it is known from other studies that there is also a maximum in the internal surface area of the tablets. At less than about 800kg/cm^2 compaction pressure the dissolution rate is increased by small granule size, surfactant to promote wetting by the dissolution medium, and starch to aid disintegration. Conversely, the hydrophobic nature of magnesium stearate used as the lubricant has the effect of decreasing dissolution rate. It is shown elsewhere that this effect can be put to good use in the formulation of sustained action tablets.

Dissolution Rate Tests

When designing test apparatus means must be provided for agitating the dissolution medium, supporting the sample without impending the flow of liquid and estimating the quantity of drug that has dissolved. Closed circuit systems have been devised by e.g. Marshall and Brook (1969), to take advantage of the methods that now exit for continuously monitoring the concentrations of solutes in liquids. Provision may also be made for replacing part of the dissolution medium from time to time or for changing its nature; both modifications are intended to give a closer simulation of actual conditions within the gastrointestinal tract. A more intractable problem is that of ensuring the right degree of agitation and it would appear that this is probably less than is commonly assumed by designers of test apparatus. Often the dissolution rate becomes sensibly constant above a certain (high) level of agitation— see, for instance, Flanagan et al. (1969). If a high level of agitation is accepted for the sake of experimental reproducibility, it must be recognized that the dissolution may be proceeding under conditions quite different from those which are through to obtain in vivo. Some workers, for example, have used the official tablet disintegration test apparatus with a finer mesh to retain all particles in the oscillating tube. According to Levy (1963) these conditions are too severe, as this method did not distinguish between tablets shown to be different by other methods and by trial in vivo.

That no universally acceptable apparatus has so far been designed is evidenced by the larger number of devices that have been described in the literature; Hersey (1969) has provided a useful review. With proper attention to operating conditions dissolution tests provide valuable in vitro data for the development of pharmaceutical products, an indication of relative potential in vivo performance and means for quality control. Certainly, there is now considerable evidence to show that in a given series of products, the one with the highest dissolution rate will probably produce the most rapid and intense response in vivo. It is not even necessary for the products to be all of the same type: Bates et al. (1969), for example, compared suspension and tablet formulations of salicylamide and demonstrated that their in vivo behaviour ran parallel to their in vitro dissolution rates. It is now also clear that the tablet disintegration time is, in most cases, a poor guide to the biological availability of the drug. In the series of aspirin tablets examined by Levy (1961), the one with the longest disintegration time gave the highest rate of excretion. There was however an obvious correlation between the amount (*E*) of drug excreted in the first hour after the administration of 600 mg of aspirin to adults and the dissolution rate (D) expressed as the weight of drug dissolved from the tablets in 10 minutes under stated conditions. In two series of experiments (A & B) the data were described by the equations:

$$E = 0.074D + 6.2 \quad \text{(A)}$$

$$E = 0.084D + 1.0 \quad \text{(B)}$$

The nearly identical slopes indicated that the mechanisms of absorption and excretion were identical in both series but the author attributed the different values of constant (6.2 and 1.0) to the fact that in the series A experiments, a glass of water was taken half an hour before the administration of the tablets and 200 ml with the dose, whereas in series B a glass of water was taken one hour before and only 100 ml when the tablets were taken. The higher liquid intake for the first series of experiments probably caused more rapid gastric emptying and absorption of the aspirin.

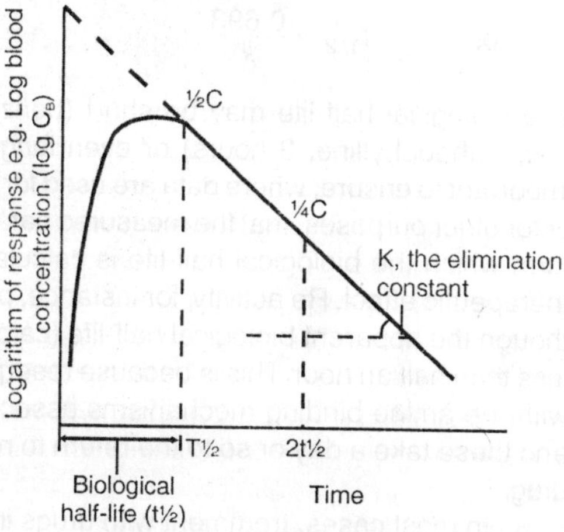

Fig. 6.8. Biological half-life of a drug.

Modification of the Onset, Intensity and Duration of Therapeutic Action

It was noted earlier that the time course of action curve for a drug is a composite of the absorption transport and elimination processes. Frequently, it is found that once the peak response is past, a plot of the logarithm of response e.g., concentration in the blood, is, for all practical purposes, a linear function of time (Fig. 6.8). By analogy with chemical kinetics theory this is a first order process that is, the rate of elimination is effectively proportional to the concentration of drug in the blood, thus:

$$\frac{dC_B}{dt} = kC_B \qquad (6.8)$$

which when integrated gives

$$C_B = C_{Bo}e^{-kt}$$

C_B is the response at time t, C_{Bo} is the response that would be required to produce the observed data in the absence of other processes and k is the elimination constant, which has the dimensions of time^{-1}. The elimination rate is more easily visualized however, in terms of the time taken to eliminate half the drug originally present in the blood. This is called the biological half-life ($t_{1/2}$) and is related to the elimination constant as follows:

$$C_B = C_{Bo}e^{-kt} \quad (6.9)$$

$$\therefore \quad \log e\frac{C_{BO}}{C_B} = \log e2 = 0.693 = kt_{1/2}$$

or

$$t_{1/2} = \frac{0.693}{k} \quad (6.10)$$

The biological half-life may be short (benzylpencillin, 30 minutes), a few hours (theophylline, 3 hours) or even longer (tetracycline, 8 hours). It is important to ensure, where data are used for calculation of the required dose or for other purposes, that the measured parameter e.g. blood concentration, form which the biological half-life is calculated is positively related to the therapeutic effect. Re activity, for instance, persists for about two days even though the apparent biological half-life (calculated from blood level data) is less than half an hour. This is because reserpine probably acts by interfering witht he amine binding mechanisms associated with the biogenic amines and these take a day or so to the return to normal after a single dose of the drug.

In most cases, treatment with drugs involves administration of doses at fixed intervals of time. The activity will, therefore alternately rise and decline as reported, for example, by Drain et al. (1959) for doses of *p*-aminosalicylic acid and its esters. To ensure continuous therapeutic effect each dose must be given at a time when there is still an effective response from the previous administration. Each peak will be higher than its predecessor but will ultimately

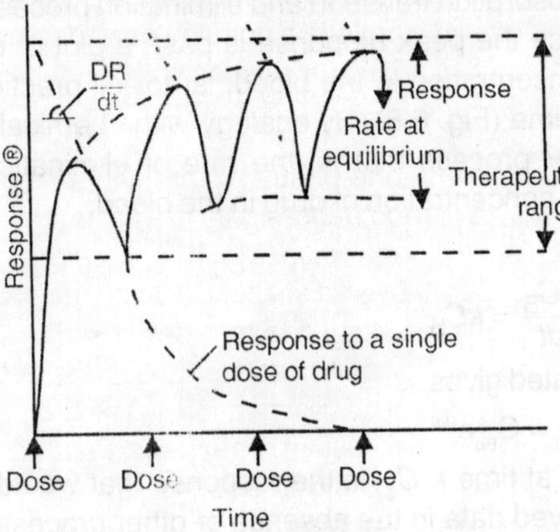

Fig. 6.9. Time course of action for several doses of drug.

attain an equilibrium value as the rate of decline of response is proportional to, and therefore increases with, the peak value of the response. If the correct dose and timing is chosen, the peaks and toughs of response will fall within the upper and lower limits for effective therapy (Fig. 6.9). When doses are too widely spaced, the troughs will fall below the level required for proper treatment but, on the other hand, if they are administered too frequently the peaks may exceed the level for acceptable incidence of side effects.

When thinking of preparation with modified time course of action it is easy to forget that there are situations in which shortened, rather than prolonged, drug action is required. Numerous medium to long-acting genral anaesthetics are known and yet it is only recently that safe short-acting general anaesthetics for use in dentistry and minor surgery have become available. It is worth recalling also hat it is not always easy or convenient to administer medicaments by the intravenous route in very young or very old patients. If large volumes of liquid must be given parenterally in these circumstances, it is possible to inject subcutaneously at up to about 10 ml/ minute provided hyaluronidase is used to increase tissue permeability (Wilson 1959). There are also occasions (the treatment of diabetes by insulin is an obvious example), where a reduction in the frequency of dose administration would be a great conveninence to the patient; but for dose-forms other than injections the argument for reducing the frequency of dose administration is more tenuous. Nevertheless, in suitable cases, there are other good reasons for increasing the duration of action of individual dose units.

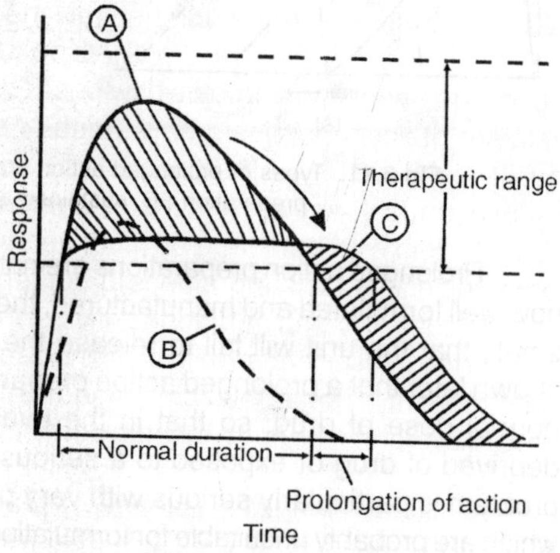

Fig. 6.10. Prolongation of drug action.

For reasonable duration with a normal dose, the response to the drug is likely to be in excess of that necessary for effective therapeutic action (Fig. 6.10, curve A); if the dose is reduced to avoid this situation, the period of effective action is reduced (curve B). The amount of drug in excess of that strictly necessary for effective therapy would be more usefully employed in stretching the period of activity as shown in the shaded portions of curves A and C. The benefits are obvious; curative action has been extended without increasing the total amount of drug while the reduced peak response will probably lower the incidence of side effects. It is unlikely, however, that these factors would extend the useful period of activity by more than about a third; thus, assuming the normal effective period of action to be some four hours, it would be extended to just over five hours.

For a worthwhile prolongation of drug action it is necessary to combine a prompt dose for rapid onset with a maintenance dose or doses to obtain therapeutic action for about twelve hours (Fig. 6.11), but the total amount of drug in the dose unit will be several times the normal dose. In addition to the advantages noted above, such a system would eliminate deficiencies in treatment due to incorrect timing of individual doses.

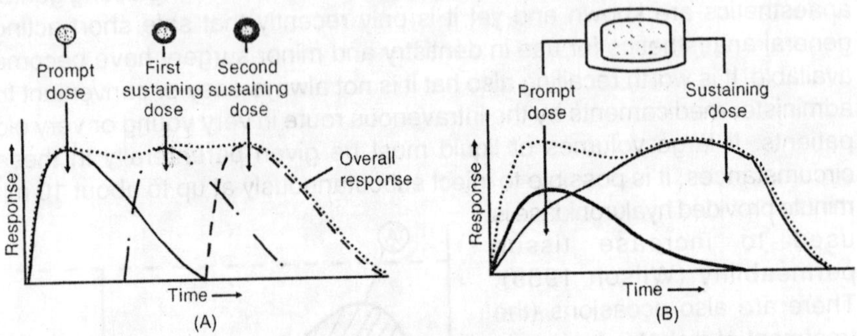

Fig 5.11. Types of prolonged action oral dose forms. A repeat action preparation ; B, sustained action preparation.

Prolonged action preparations are not without disadvantages. No matter how well formulated and manufactured, there is always the chance, however small, that the unit will fail to release the drug in the correct manner. It is shown later that a prolonged action preparation may contain 2 to 5 times the normal dose of drug, so that in the event of failure the patient is either deprived of drug or exposed to a serious overdose for a long period. This problem is particularly serious with very potent short half-life medicaments which are probably unsuitable for formulation as sustained action preparations. If the half-life is very long there is very little point in attempting to extend the duration of action, at least for oral products.

The maximum practical size for a solid dose unit is 1 to $1\frac{1}{2}$ g depending on the density of the product. This value could easily be exceeded with a prolonged action preparation if the normal dose is large, perhaps 0.5 g, and the biological half-life is short. Finally, although products have been specificaily designed to release drugs under specific physiological states or at specific sites in the body, this is not a universally applicable product design philosophy as it is well known that there is always considerable inter-patient variation in the response to medication and also variation from day to day for a particular patient.

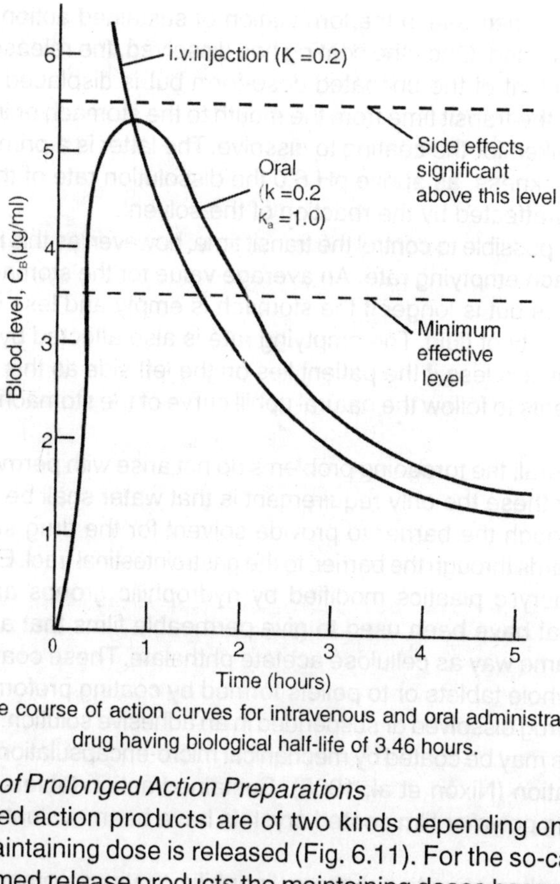

Fig. 6.12. Time course of action curves for intravenous and oral administration 80 mg of drug having biological half-life of 3.46 hours.

Formulation of Prolonged Action Preparations

Oral sustained action products are of two kinds depending on the way in which the maintaining dose is released (Fig. 6.11). For the so-called repeat action and timed release products the maintaining doses become available at discrete time intervals. If the maintaining drug is continuously released, the product is of the prolonged action or sustained release type. Although other names are used for branded products there is no widespread agreement on nomenclature; the terms used in the text should be self-explanatory. In spite of the diversity of names the formulator may use coatings, erosion, diffusion or a limited combination of these to control drug release from oral products. Additionally there is a group of miscellaneous products where biological availability is controlled by the dissolution rate, partitioning, chemical reaction within the body and by other means.

Coating. Enteric and barrier coatings are used. *Enteric* coatings are intended to resist the acid gastric secretions but dissolve in the intestinal fluids. Cellulose acetate phthalate and some other polymeric films avoid most of the problems associated with earlier materials and provide reliable enteric action. Their use in the formulation of sustained action products is less clearly defined. Once the coating has dissolved, the release of drugs is identical with that of the uncoated dose-form but is displaced by a period equivalent to the transit time from the mouth to the stomach or intestine and by the time taken for the coating to dissolve. The latter is a primary function of coating thickness, as above pH 6.0 the dissolution rate of the coating is not markedly affected by the reaction of the solvent.

It is not possible to control the transit time, however, as this is dependent on the stomach emptying rate. An average value for the stomach emptying time is 4 hours but is longer if the stomach is empty and less if the drug is taken with plenty of fluid. The emptying rate is also affected by the posture of the patient; it is less if the patient lies on the left side as this requires the gastric contents to follow the natural uphill curve of the stomach towards the duodenum.

In general, the foregoing problems do not arise with permeable barrier coatings; for these the only requirement is that water shall be available for diffusion through the barrier to provide solvent for the drug so that it may diffuse outwards through the barrier, to the gastrointestinal tract. Ethylcellulose, nylon and acrylic plastics modified by hydrophilic groups are polymeric materials that have been used to give permeable films that are applied in much the same way as cellulose acetate phthalate. These coatings may be applied to whole tablets or to pellets formed by coating preformed sucrose seeds with drug dissolved or suspended in an adhesive solution. Alternatively, drug crystals may be coated by mechanical micro-encapsulation (Nack 1970) or coacervation (Nixon et al. 1968). Sustained action tablets prepared by compressing polymer film coated crystals have been evaluated (Bell et al. 1966).

As an alternative to polymers, lipophilic coatings comprising paraffin waxes, fatty alcohols and acids, glyceryl monostearate and distearate may also be used to form permeable barriers. For a given coating composition the release rate is decreased if the thickness is increased or, for a given coating thickness, the more polar materials allow water to penetrate more rapidly and this results in a faster release of drug (Jack 1961). Release is delayed by the time taken for water to penetrate to the solid and for this to diffuse outwards. In one product using this method of controlling release, the drug is formed into small pellets as described above and these are treated with a wax composition dissolved in a suitable solvent. Normal pan coating is used. The batch of pellets will have a mean value for the delay and release rate. Due to the nature of the pan coating process the values of these parameters will vary by a greater or lesser extent about the mean values for the batch. A typical sustained action preparation consists of a capsule containing untreated drug pellets together with pellets that have been given different thicknesses or compositions of wax coatings. On ingestion the capsule shell dissolves and the uncoated drug pellets provide a prompt dose which is maintained by release from the different coated pellets at timed intervals. The release profile is shown in Fig. 6.11. The statistical release of drug from each batch of pellets smoothes out the peaks and troughs in the response. A dextamphetamine product of this type behaves in the expected manner (Beckett and Tucker 1966).

It is worth nothing that if product performance is to assessed by urinary excretion data, it is necessary in the case of ionized drugs to control the pH of the urine so that tubular reabsorption is avoided.

Erosion control. The finely powdered medicament is embedded in a wax formed from one or more of the following— stearic acid, hydroxystearic acid, hardened castor oil and fatty alcohols. If necessary, water penetration may be controlled by the inclusion of a hard polyethylene glycol in the wax. The drug is dispersed in molten wax, rapidly solidified on a cold drum or in trays and the flakes passed through a swing-hammer granulator. The granules are compressed in the normal manner to give a sustained action core onto which is compressed a dose of the same drug formulated for prompt release. When administered, the coating disintegrates to provide the prompt dose which is maintained by gradual erosion of the core that constantly exposes fresh surface from which drug may be dissolved. Wax embedment has been used to produce sustained action liquid oral products containing sulphaethidole. The molten mixture is containing sulphaethidole. The molten mixture is either spray congealed (Raghunathan and Becker 1968) or dispersed in dilute surfactant solution to 1968) or dispersed in dilute surfactant solution to form a mechanical emulsion and chilled (Robinson and Becker 1968). The wax spheres containing drug formed by these processes are very small and it is likely that a diffusion, rather than erosion, mechanism is responsible for the sustained action properties.

Diffusion control. This may be exerted by a gelled layer of hydrophilic colloid, a plastic matrix or by ion exchange resins. In the first of these methods the drug is mixed with inert filter, hydrophilic colloid and lubricant and compressed in the normal way at high compaction pressure. Tragacanth, hydroxypropylmethyl cellulose and a number of other gums have been used as the gelling agent. The lubricant is usually employed in a higher than normal concentration to raise the contact angle of the pores and thereby control penetration of liquid into the tablet. The initial release of drug is rapid as it is dissolved from the surface but the rate subsequently slows down as the colloid hydrates to form the gelled layer through which drug must diffuse to provide the maintenance dose. It is possible that in vivo there may be some erosion of the gelled layer.

Diffusion governed drug release from an insoluble plastic matrix is also used to provide sustained action products. Polythene, polyvinyl acetate or chloride, ethylcellulose and other plastics have been used. Tablets are prepared by mixing the drug with powdered plastic and compressing in the normal way or, alternatively, the mixed powders may be moist granulated with a solution of the plastic in a suitable organic solvent.

Higuchi (1963) derived equations for the release of drug from matrices and showed that for a range of conditions the amount of drug (Q) released should vary as the square root of time, that is:

$$Q = m.t^{1/2} \tag{6.11}$$

where m is a constant relating to the matrix and elution conditions. In vitro tests have shown that equation 37.11 applies to a wax matrix under noneroding conditions (Schwartz et al., 1968) and to plastic matrices (Desai et al. 1966a and b) provided the dissolution fluid contains a surfactant to promote pore wetting and air is removed by vacuum treatment. The plastic matrix does not disintegrate but is excreted unchanged.

Ion-exchange resins provide a means for binding ionized drugs inside a diffusion controlling insoluble matrix. The maximum size of the molecular that may be accommodated within the molecular mesh of the resin is determined by the degree of cross-linking. This factor and the size of the resin beads determines the rate of release, which is slower for partially saturated resins (Chaudry and Saunders 1956). Drug is released regardless of the nature of the gastrointestinal fluids; taking the case of a cationic drug bound to an anionic sulphonic acid resin the appropriate reactions in the stomach and intestine are:

Stomach:

$$R\text{–}SO_3'X^+ + H{+}Cl' \rightarrow R\text{–}SO_3'H^+ + X^+Cl'$$

Intestine

$$R\text{–}SO'_3X^+ + Na^+Cl' \rightarrow R\text{–}SO'_3NA^+ + X^+Cl'$$

The utility of ion-exchange resins for the formulation of sustained action products is limited in that only ionic drugs are suitable and the capacity of the resin for the drug is small. There is also the possibility that the body electrolyte balance may be disturbed by absorption of ions by the resin. An example of this type of medication is afforded by an anti-tussive mixture, formulated by suspending the ion-exchange resin complexes of pholocodine and phenyltoloxamine in a syrupy vehicle.

Other Long-acting Preparations

It is often pssible to extend the duration of activity by forming a derivative of the drug that has low solubility. The utility of this approach in the case of insulin preparations has been described already. Deep injection into muscle and the use of an oily vehicle may also help to prolong action provided the latter is viscous enough to form a localized depot rather than spread along to muscle fascia.

Early penicillin injections used oil thickened with beeswax but were difficult to use unless thinned by gentle warming prior to administration. According to Buckwalter and Dickison (1958) oily depot injections of procaine penicillin gelled with aluminium stearate give higher and more prolonged blood levels than corresponding products with beeswax or plain oil. Ober et al. (1958) investigated aqueous depot injections of the same antibiotic derivative. Using a high (40 to 70 per cent w/v) concentration of the drug together with sodium citrate as deflocculating agent they produced a series of injections having as a characteristic rheological property a spur in the shear stress/shear rate curve. Suitable products were obtained when the spur had a value which, on their rotational viscometer, was equivalent to a torque in the range 10^5 to 10^6 dyne cm. The shear stress in the needle exceeds the upper value and the product can be withdrawn from the vial and injected into the patient. In muscle, where the shear stress is less than the lower value, structure build-up takes place and the injected material sets to form a depot.

Abroad range of particle size is desirable to provide immediate response by the dissolution of fine particles and a sustained effect lasting several days by the less rapid dissolution of the coarser particles.

It is also possible to control the release of drug by absorption onto insoluble carriers such as zinc or aluminium hydroxides or phosphates. Corticotrophin depot injections are produced in this way: zinc phosphate carriers tend to crystallize on storage and must be produced by precipitation of the carrier in the container just prior to injection. This procedure is not necessary with the zinc hydroxide carrier as the latter does not crystallize when stored.

With suitable drugs it is possible to produce depot injections with an effective duration of several weeks while even longer periods are possible with implants. Preparations of these types are only feasible with drugs that are effective in very low dosage and which are also very insoluble in water. This combination of therapeutic and physicochemical requirements limits the range of medicaments that are worthwhile formulating as ultra long-acting drugs to the steroid hormones and a few other substances. They also form esters that hydrolyse in vivo at rates convenient for formulation purposes, as discussed earlier. Depots of drug are formed by deep intramuscular injection of aqueous suspensions of the drug or oily solutions of these. Oestradiol, testosterone, methylprednisolone and fluphenazine and examples of drugs available as depot injections.

If a longer period of therapy is required the drug may be fused or compressed into a pellet (implant) and inserted into the muscle by a minor surgical operation. The use of additives for the production of implants is prohibited. Obviously, the surface area of the implant will decrease as the drug dissolves. Nevertheless, for the purpose of dose calculation, Edkins (1959) has shown that the average daily dose over a given period may be related to the initial surface area of the implant. Thus, for deoxycortone acetate implants.

Weight (mg)	Surface area (mm^2)	Average daily dose (mg)	Duration (days)
25	49	0.3	83
300	222	1.3	230

If an average daily dose of 1.2 mg of 83 days is required then 4 × 25 mg would be implanted in the muscle. Generally, as in the case of testosterone, the release is sufficiently limited by the dissolution rate that there is no need to employ the ester. It will be appreciated that the complete prohibition of additives and the need for rigorous aseptic precautions during manufacture pose formidable technical problems.

Calculation of doses for sustained action products.

The total dose of drug, D_t, in a prolonged action preparation comprises the normal (prompt) dose, D_n, and the sustaining dose D_s, i.e.,

$$D_t = D_n + D_s \qquad (6.12)$$

If the first order elimination rate constant is k, the rate at which drug is eliminated when a normal dose is given is $D_n k$ which is the rate at which drug must be replaced if the peak blood level is to be maintained. Given a maintenance period t the maintenance dose (D_s) is $D_n kt$. the total dose is therefore:

$$\begin{aligned} D_t &= D_n + D_s \\ &= D_n + D_n kt \\ &= D_n (1 + kt) \\ &= D_n (1 + kt) \\ &= D_n (1 + 0.693\ t/t_{1/2}) \end{aligned} \qquad (6.13)$$

Suppose the biological half-life is 1.73 hours. D_n is 80 mg and t is 10 hours, substituting in equation 13:

$$D_t = 80\left(1 + \frac{0.693 \times 10}{1.73}\right) = 80 + 320 = 400 \text{ mg}$$

For a $t_{1/2}$ of 3.46 hours

$$D_t = 80 + 160 = 240 \text{ mg}$$

The use of the normal dose does not take into account the fact that to obtain a reasonable duration of action it may be necessary to accept a peak response near that at which side effects become noticeable. Nelson (1957) suggested that a factor (f) should be used in calculation to adjust the amount of drug such that lower but still therapeutically effective blood levels are attained. Fig. 6.12 shows the calculated response curve for an 80 mg oral dose of drug having a biological half-life of 3.46 hours and it is assumed that the upper and lower limits of blood concentration for effective therapy are 3.5–5.5 μg/ml respectively. The peak blood level is 5.35 μg/ml, the onset about 35 minutes and the duration about $4\frac{1}{2}$ hours. If a reasonable blood level is 4.0 μg/ml the value of D_n for equation 5.13 must be reduced by the factor (f) equal to 4.0/5.35 = 0.75. The total dose may be recalculated as follows :

$$D_t = 0.75 \times 80\left(1 + \frac{0.693 \times 10}{3.46}\right)$$

$$= 60 + 120 = 180 \text{ mg}$$

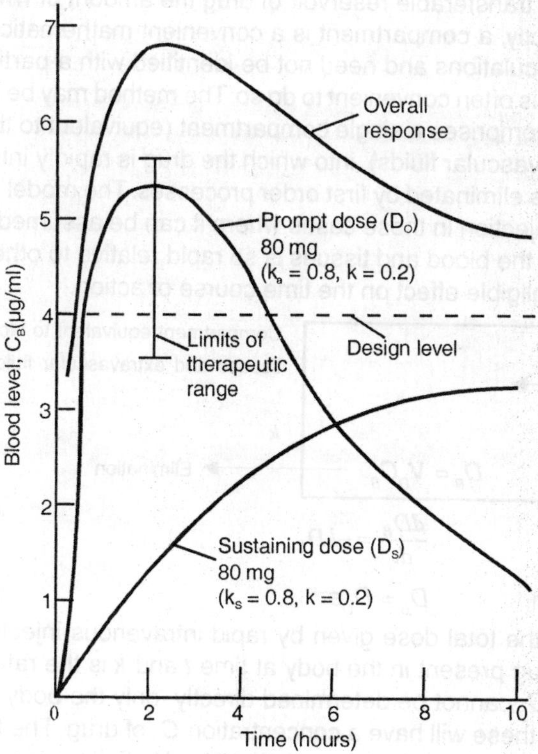

Fig. 6.13. Combined effect of 80 mg of prompt and sustaining doses of drug having a biological half-life of 3.46 hours.

Even with these reduced amounts of drug the concentration in the blood may be higher than intended due to the simultaneous release from both the prompt and maintenance forms. There is also the possibility (Rowland and Beckett 1964) that there may be an initial peaking of the blood level, particularly for drugs with short biological halflives. It must be stressed that some products, for example those of the repeat action type, are not subject to this particular problem. Similarly, the problem may be avoided if the release of drug from the maintenance form is deliberately delayed by, say, the use of film coating.

Further sophistication of the calculations for the amounts of the prompt and sustaining doses requires more elaborate theoretical treatment than has been used so far. A fundamental theory of the time course of action of drugs relies on a knowledge of the effective concentration of drug at the ultimate site of action but this is not accessible. One approach, widely used, is that of compartmental analysis due to Teorell (1937). A compartment may be regarded as a transferable reservoir of drug the amount of which changes with time. Strictly, a compartment is a convenient mathematical device for simplifying calculations and need not be identified with a particular part of the body but it is often convenient to do so. The method may be illustrated by a model that comprises a single compartment (equivalent to the blood, tissue and extravascular fluids) into which the drug is rapidly introduced and from which it is eliminated by first order processes. The model mimics rapid intravenous injection in those cases where it can be assumed that equilibrium between the blood and tissues is so rapid relative to other processes that it has negligible effect on the time course of action.

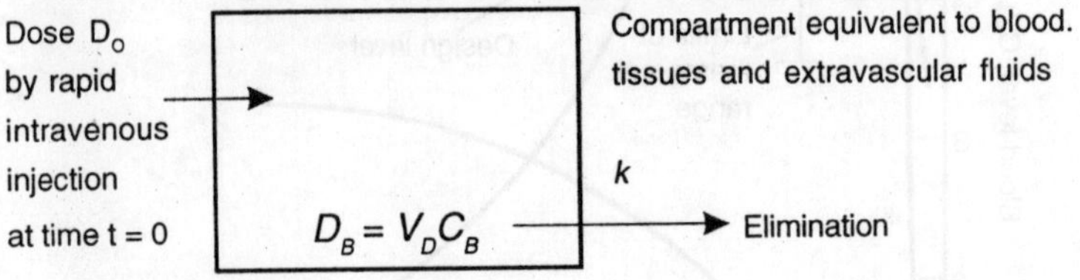

$$\frac{dD_B}{dt} = -kD_B$$

By integration, $$D_B = D_O e^{-kt} \qquad (6.14)$$

where D_O is the total dose given by rapid intravenous injection, D_B is the amount of drug present in the body at time t and k is the rate constant for elimination. D_B cannot be determined directly–only the body fluids are accessible and these will have a concentration C_B of drug. The term V_D is the apparent volume of distribution such that $D_B = V_D.C_B$ it too is a mathematical device used to account for the mass of drug in each part of the model and should not be identified with the total body fluids. The value of V_D is calculated from the data obtained in each particular study of drug action but an acceptable value for the purposes of these calculations is 10 litres (10 000 ml). Substitution gives:

$$C_B = \frac{D_O}{V_D} = e^{-kt} \qquad (6.15)$$

Clearly, equations (6.14) and (6.15) are alternative forms of equation (6.9). Assume the dose of 80 mg (80000 micrograms) used in the previous calculation and a biological half-life of 3.46 hours, that is $k = 0.2$ hours^{-1}. The blood level after 1 hour is:

$$C_B = \frac{80\,000}{10\,000} e^{-0.2 \times 1.0} = 8 \times 0.8187 = 6.55\ \mu g/ml.$$

and for other times is shown in Fig. 6.12.

It must be emphasized that compartmental analysis is applied to the results of in vivo investigations to obtain the mathematical model that best fits the experimental data. Apart from providing information about the mechanisms of absorption metabolism and excretion the model allows the effects of dose size, rate of release, dose frequency and other factors to be calculated. Subsequent in vivo experiments to determine the optimum values for those parameters are thereby reduced and this is of the greatest importance if tests are to be conducted with human volunteers.

Applying the method to the formulation of a sustained action tablet, assume that a single compartment model is known to provide a good fit to the available in vivo data. The model is :

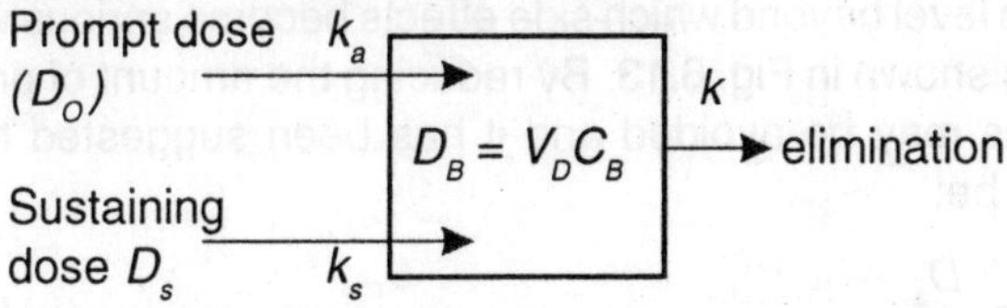

Zero order release from the sustaining dose ensures a constant level of drug in the blood; the rate constant is k_s. If, as before, $k = 0.2$ hr^{-1} the design value of C_B is 4 μg per ml and the drug is completely absorbed, i.e $F = 1$

$$k_s = FkC_B = 1 \times 0.2 \times 4.0 = 0.8\ \mu g \text{ per hour.}$$

If V_D = 10 litres and the sustaining time (T) is 10 hours the sustaining dose D_s is

$$k_s V_D t = 0.8 \times 10000 \times 10 = 80 \text{ mg}$$

For the zero-order sustaining process

$$\frac{dC_B}{dt} = ks - kC_B \qquad (6.16)$$

Which on integration gives:

$$C_B = \frac{k_s}{k}(1 - e^{-kt}) \qquad (6.17)$$

The release and absorption of drug from the prompt dose is first order overall and rate constant is k_a. The appropriate rate equation is:

$$\frac{dD_B}{dt} = Fk_a D_O - kD_B \qquad (6.18)$$

Which, on integration gives:

$$C_B = \frac{Fk_a D_O}{(k_a - k)V_D}\left(e^{-kt} - e^{-k_a t}\right) \qquad (6.19)$$

For $F = 1$, $k_a = 1.0\ hr^{-1}$, $D_O = 80$ mg, $k = 0.2\ hr^{-1}$ and $V_D = 10$ litres the blood concentration at, say, 2 hours is:

$$\frac{1.0 \times 1.0 \times 80\,000}{(1.0 - 0.2) \times 10\,000}\left(e^{-0.2\times 2} - e^{-1\times 1}\right)$$

$= 5.35\ \mu g$ per ml.

The complete curve is given in Fig. 6.12.

Clearly, when the additional drug released from the maintenance dose is also taken into account, at say, 2 hours after administration of the sustained action tablet, the blood level would be very much in excess of the design level. Calculation shows that a peak level of the order of 6.8 μg per ml would be produced thus the level beyond which side effects become serious would also be exceeded as shown in Fig. 6.13. By reducing the amount of prompt dose these problems may be avoided and it has been suggested that a suitable value would be:

$$D_O = \frac{D_s}{Tk} \qquad (6.20)$$

which for the preparation considered here is:

$$\frac{80}{10 \times 0.2} = 40 \text{ mg}$$

Equations 6.17 for the sustaining dose and 6.19 for the prompt dose may be combined to give equation 6.21.

$$C_B = \frac{Fk_a D_O}{(k_a - k)V_D}\left(e^{-kt} - e^{-k_a t}\right) + \frac{k_s}{k}(1 - e^{-kt}) \qquad (6.21)$$

This may be solved for different values of prompt dose (D_O) until the desired release profile is obtained as shown in Fig. 6.14.

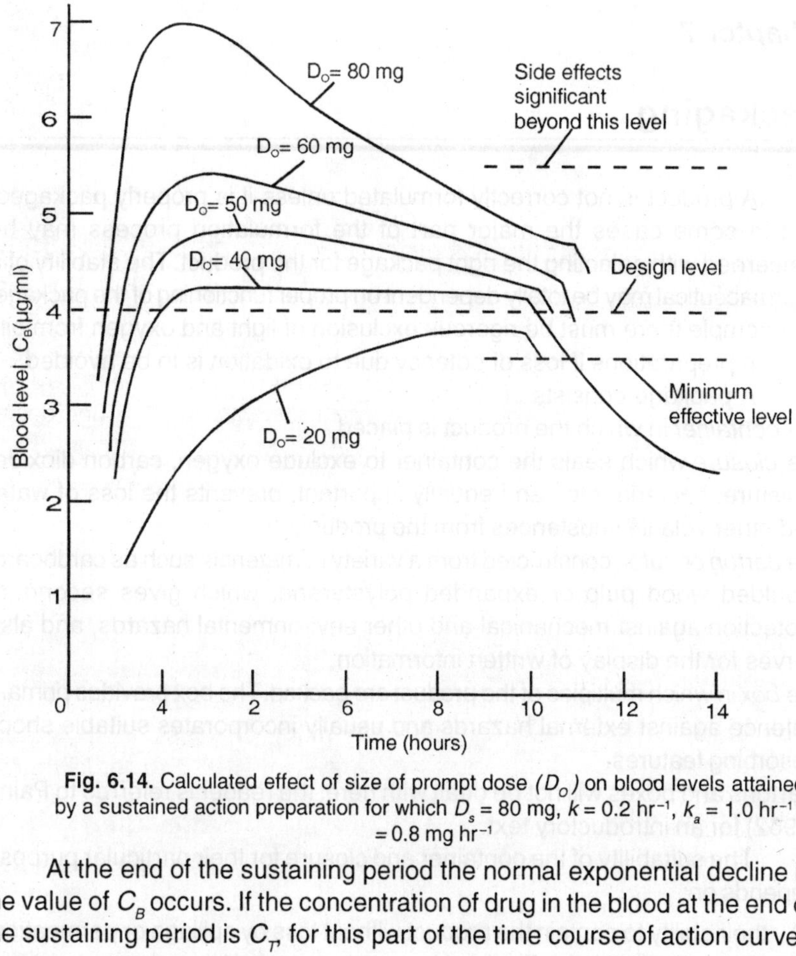

Fig. 6.14. Calculated effect of size of prompt dose *(D_O)* on blood levels attained by a sustained action preparation for which D_s = 80 mg, k = 0.2 hr^{-1}, k_a = 1.0 hr^{-1} k_s = 0.8 mg hr^{-1}

At the end of the sustaining period the normal exponential decline in the value of C_B occurs. If the concentration of drug in the blood at the end of the sustaining period is C_T, for this part of the time course of action curve:

$$C_B = C_T e^{-k(t-T)} \tag{6.22}$$

From these calculations it would appear that a tablet comprising a prompt dose of 40 mg and a sustaining dose of 80 mg should meet the design specification. In practice several trial formulations would be made and then tested in vivo.

Chapter 7

Packaging

A product is not correctly formulated unless it is properly packaged, and in some cases the major part of the formulation process may be concerned with selecting the right package for the product. The stability of a pharmaceutical may be totally dependent on proper functioning of the package, for example there must be rigorous exclusion of light and oxygen from oily vitamin preparations if loss of potency due to oxidation is to be avoided.

A package consists of:
the *container* in which the product is placed,
the *closure* which seals the container to exclude oxygen, carbon dioxide, moisture, bacteria, etc., and equally important, prevents the loss of water and other volatile substances from the product,
the *carton or outer,* constructed from a variety of materials such as cardboard, moulded wood pulp or expanded polystyrene, which gives secondary protection against mechanical and other environmental hazards, and also serves for the display of written information,
the *box* in which multiples of the product are packed. The box provides primary defence against external hazards and usually incorporates suitable shock absorbing features.
Cartons and boxes will not be dealt with here; the reader is referred to Paine (1962) for an introductory text.

The suitability of the container and closure for their particular purpose depends on:

(a) their ability to contain the product without loss by spillage or permeation,
(b) the protection they afford against environmental hazards.
(c) whether they are suited to the function of the product both in form and size, for example a volume of injection intended to provide several doses for use on different occasions should not be packed in an ampoule,
(d) freedom from interaction between product and container,
(e) reasonable cost in relation to the cost of the product and that of alternative packages which may offer some marginal advantages.

This technically formidable specification is derived, in large measure, from the concept of an ideal package. To match this as closely as possible is a function of the materials from which the package is formed and these must first be discussed.

PACKAGING MATERIALS

With very few exceptions containers and closures are fabricated from metals, rubber, plastic, glass or a combination of these. These materials may be divided into two groups. On the one hand the metals are polycrystalline, that is, composed of a large number of small, randomly orientated, crystalline structural units (grains) separated by a grain boundary, about two or three atomic distances wide, in which the atoms do not belong precisely to either of the adjacent lattices. On the other hand plastics, rubber and glass, are all polymers formed by the bonding together of a large number of molecular units. The basic structural elements in polymers are therefore long chains of repeating molecular units which intertwine to form a three dimensional network.

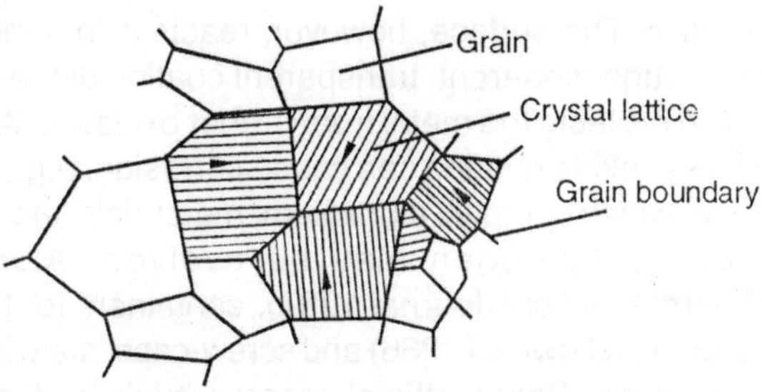

Fig. 7.1. Polycrystalline structure of metals.

Metals

There are over seventy metals in the periodic table but of these only tin, lead, aluminium and iron are of significance in pharmaceutical packaging. In use, small stresses sufficient to cause only elastic deformation are accomodated by changes in the distances between the atoms in he crystal lattices of the grains. Larger stresses bring about relative slippage of the crystal planes (dislocation) and the deformation is permanent.

Tin

This metal is very resistant to chemical attack and readily coats a number of other metals. Tin-coated lead tubes combine the softness of lead with the inertness of tin and for this reason were formerly used for packaging fluoride toothpaste. The high cost of lead has resulted in the use of the much less expensive lacquered aluminium tubes for this purpose. Currently, some eye ointments are still packaged in pure tin ointment tubes.

Iron

Although iron as such is not used for pharmaceutical packaging, large quantities of tin-coated steel are employed for the fabrication of drums, screw-caps and aerosol cans. Tin-coated steel, popularly called 'tin', combines the strength of steel with the corrosion resistance of tin. The performance of tin-coated steel is dependant on the uniformity of the coating. If an aqueous liquid can penetrate a pinhole or other fault in the layer of tin, what is virtually a short-circuited galvanic cell is set up and the intense chemical action which results brings about rapid failure of the underlying steel. As a further protection measure tinned steel packaging components may be given a thin coating of lacquer.

Aluminium

This metal has a very low atomic weight implying that it should be very reactive. The surface, however, reacts with atmospheric oxygen to form a thin, tough, coherent, transparent coating of the oxide, of atomic thickness, which protects the metal from further oxidation. Any substance which reacts with the oxide coating can cause corrosion, e.g., products of high or low pH, those which complex aluminium, mercurials, etc. As a result of the corrosion process hydrogen may be evolved. Aluminium ointment tubes (Pharmaceutical Journal 1957), containers for tablets and other unit-dose products (Glowacki 1966) and screw-caps, are widely used in pharmaceutical packaging. Some official creams such as those containing Cetrimide, Neomycin or Hydrocortisone may be packed in aluminium tubes provided a phosphate buffer is included in the formulation to inhibit corrosion and evolution of hydrogen. Alternatively an internally lacquered tube may be suitable but care must be taken to ensure that the coating if of sufficient thickness and satisfactory composition, and is free from pin-holes and other faults.

Polymers

The polymer chains may be free to glide independently over one another or may be partially constrained in relation to neighbours by chemical cross-links as is shown for silicone rubber in Fig. 7.2. The cross-link is formed, in the example given, from methyl groups attached to silicon atoms in adjacent chains.

The similar form of the molecular structure of plastic, rubber and glass, leads to similarities in their physical behaviour. All three materials have a glass transition temperature (T_g) below which they become hard, rigid, brittle solids and are said to be in the glassy state. In this condition they are not crystalline but are supercooled liquids of high viscosity as explained in the section on glass. If rubber is cooled in liquid air below its glass transition temperature it becomes brittle and shatters like glass if subjected to mechanical shock. Above T_g there is a progressive loss of rigidity. The familiar properties of polymers depend therefore on whether T_g is greater (glass: about 1000°; polymethylmethacrylate: 110°) or less (polypropylene: – 27°; rubber: about – 60°) than the normal ambient temperature. *Thermoplastics,* such as polyethylene, soften and melt if heated to a high enough temperature. Other plastics are very highly cross-linked and for these *thermosetting* plastics T_g is so high that decomposition takes place before the material can soften and melt; urea-formaldehyde plastics are of this type. Below T_g the rotational

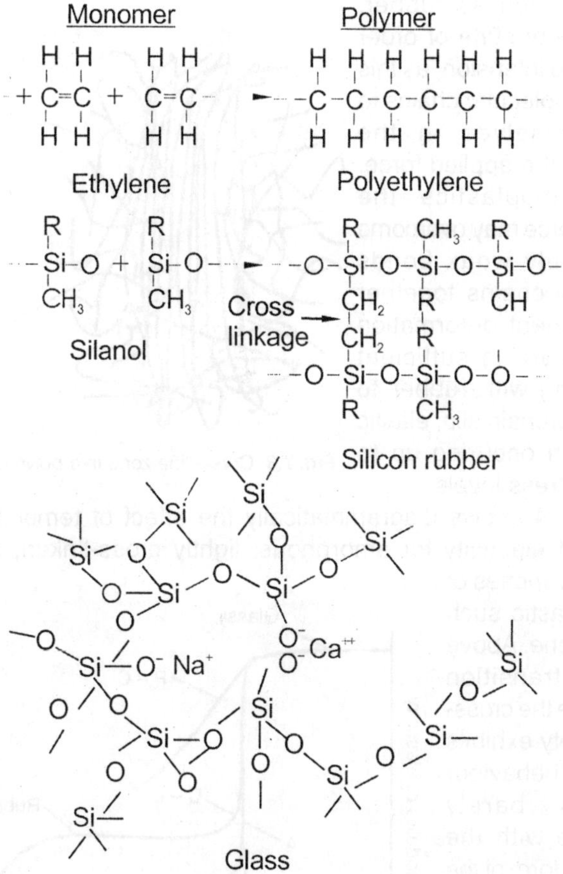

Fig. 7.2. Polymer structure.

freedom of the bonds and relative movement of the molecular chains of thermoplastics are severely restricted. Near the glass transition temperature there are, in addition to greater freedom of movement for the chains, changes in density, refractive index and other physical parameters. Above T_g the molecular chains are able continuously to move about, change their shape and intertwine with neighbours. Nevertheless, there is evidence from X-ray diffraction studies that dis-order is not complete and that zones exist wherein the chains are more regularly aligned than elsewhere (Fig 7.3). Such zones are said to be 'crystalline' but it must be clearly understood that the term in this context refers to the regular arrangement of molecular chains not of atoms. Some polymers, polypropylene for example, can be prepared in a highly crystalline form, and the crystalline polymer has a higher densty than the truly amorphous variety because of closer packing of the chains. Other polymers, such as rubber, attain a higher state of order when placed intension, as this cause the molecular chains to align themselves in the direction of the applied force. With thermoplastics the stretching force may overcome the relatively weak bonds holding the chains together and permanent deformation follows. There is sufficient cross-linking with rubber to prevent interchain slip, elastic deformation occuring up to very high stress levels.

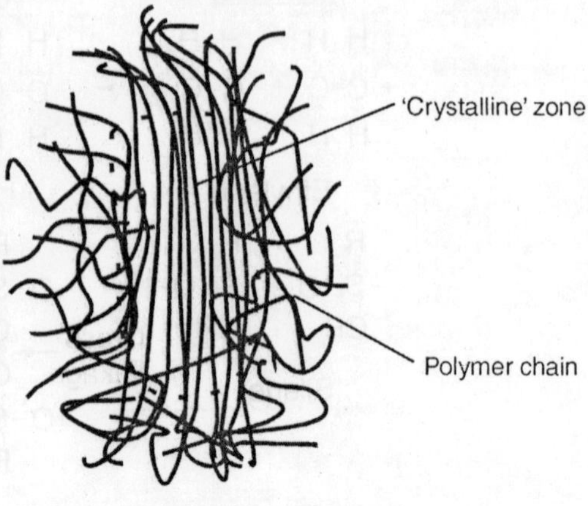

Fig. 7.3. Crystalline zone in a polymer.

Fig. 7.4 shows diagrammatically the effect of temperature on the modulus of elasticity for amorphous, lightly cross-linked, and partially crystalline varieties of a thermoplastic such as polystyrene. Above the glass transition temperature the cross-linked variety exhibits a rubbery 'behaviour which is barely discernible with the amorphous form of the plastic. The partially crystalline form has a glass transition temperature but this is obscured by the modifying influence of the crystalline regions

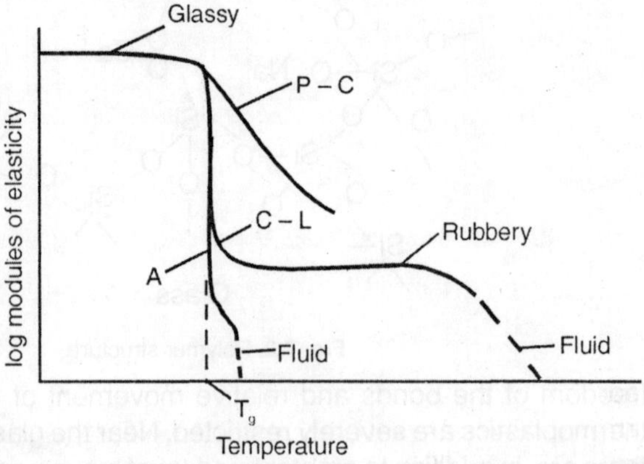

Fig. 7.4. Effect of temperature on elasticity of a polymer. A, Amorphous: C–L, lightly cross-linked; P–C, partially crystalline.

Plastics

Plastics are high molecular weight polymers, usually based on a carbon 'backbone': they are good thermal and electrical insulators and their density falls in the range 0.9 to 1.5. The polymerization process may generate non-functional side-chains that hinder close packing of the polymer molecules. High pressure polymerization of ethylene gives a polyethylene of lower density

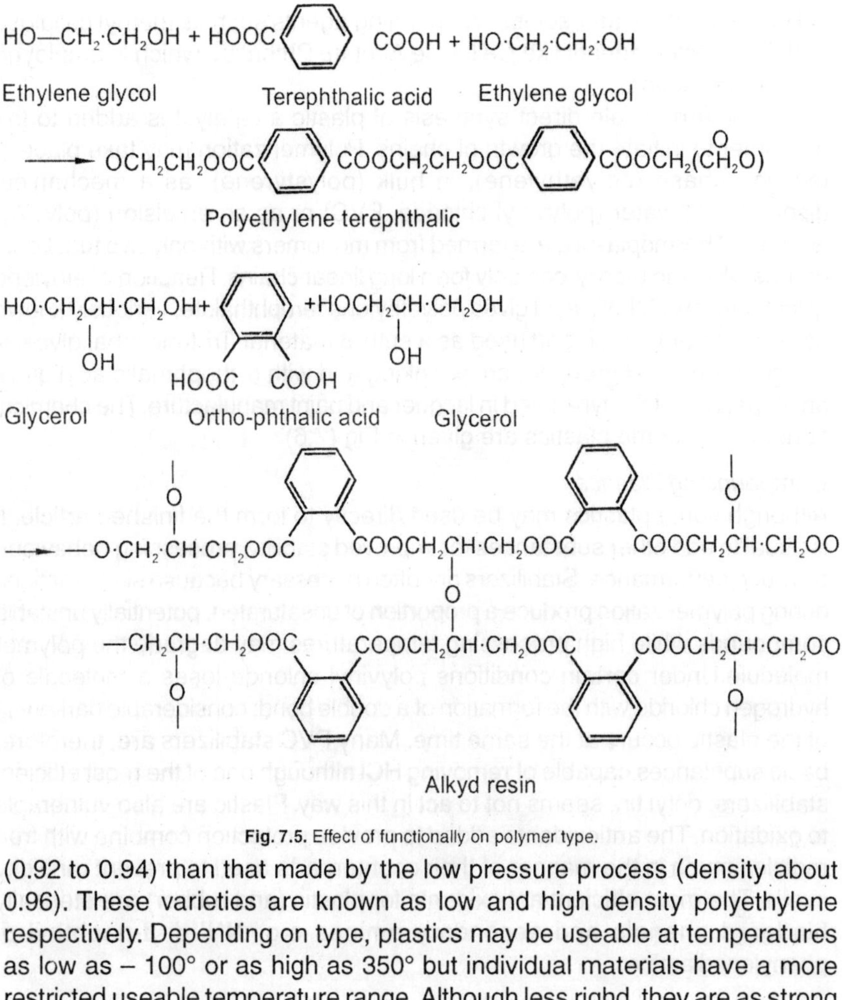

Fig. 7.5. Effect of functionally on polymer type.

(0.92 to 0.94) than that made by the low pressure process (density about 0.96). These varieties are known as low and high density polyethylene respectively. Depending on type, plastics may be useable at temperatures as low as – 100° or as high as 350° but individual materials have a more restricted useable temperature range. Although less righd, they are as strong as metals on a weight to weight basis. Generally, they show a high degree of resistance to attack by inorganic reagents but are usually softened or dissolved by organic solvents (Childs 1955).

The first plastic, celluloid, was obtained by nitrating cellulose. Many different cellulose polymers have been made since and are still important today. If dissolved and reprecipitated, the chain length is shortened and this modified cellulose is suitable for the production of textile products such as rayon dressings—see the BPC 1973. Nitration yields an explosive (gun cotton), a plastic (celluloid) or a lacquer (the official Collodions), depending on the reaction conditions. Other pharmaceutically important polymers derived from cellulose are the water soluble suspending agents such as methyl cellulose and film forming agents like Cellulose Acetate Phthalate which is employed for enteric coating.

For large scale direct synthesis of plastic a catalyst is added to the monomer to initiate the growth of chains. Polymerization may take place in the gas phase (polyethylene), in bulk (polystyrene), as a mechanical dispersion in water (polyvinyl chloride, PVC) or as an emulsion (polyvinyl acetate). Thermoplastics are formed from monomers with only two functional groups which, in theory, can only form long linear chains. Reaction of ethylene glycol with terephthalic acid gives polyethylene terephthalate, variously known as Terylene or Dacron and used as a suture material. Tri-functional glycerol has a 'spare' –OH group for cross-linking and with orthophthalic acid gives an alkyd resin of the type used in lacquer and paint manufacture. The chemical structures of some plastics are given in Fig (7.6).

Compounding Plastics

Although some plastics may be used directly to form the finished article, it is usual to add other substances for improved stability, processing behaviour, or in-use performance. Stabilizers are often necessary because side reactions during polymerization produce a proportion of unsaturated, potentially unstable compounds while high processing temperatures may degrade the polymer molecule.Under certain conditions polyvinyl chloride loses a molecule of hydrogen chloride with the formation of a double bond; considerable darkening of the plastic occurs at the same time. Many PVC stabilizers are, therefore, basic substances capable of removing HCl although one of the most efficient stabilizers, octyl tin, seems not to act in this way. Plastic are also vulnerable to oxidation. The antioxidants added to provide protection combine with free redicles much in the manner of their counterparts used to prevent rancidity in oils. The most efficient antioxidants for plastic (and rubber) are sterically hindered phenols and secondary amines e.g. NN'-di-β-naphthyl-*p*-phenylenediamine:

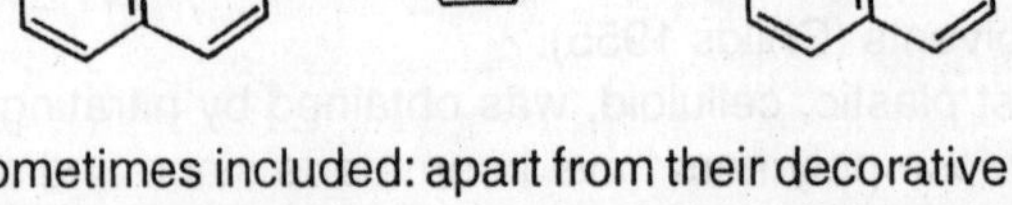

Pigments are sometimes included: apart from their decorative use they may absorb in u.v. region and thereby reduce photodegradation. For clear plastics organic absorbers such as 4-biphenylsalicylate are used. Fillers are often employed to cheapen the product but in some cases may be essential for correct product performance. Bakelite, a pehnol-formaldehyde resin, is a brown brittle material quite unsuited for the manufacture of screw-caps unless mixed with a filler such as wood flour. Among other fillers are whiting, asbestos and mica. Plasticizers are added to lower the glass transition temperature by directly reducing the attractive physical forces between polymer chains, and by increasing the interchain distance. As a result the plastic is softened, it can be processed at a lower temperature and the final product has greater flexibility. Camphor is used as a plasticizer for celluloid, and castor oil for collodion. More generally, high boiling esters are employed as these have low volatility and do not evaporate from the product. Dibutyl sebacate, tritolyl phosphate and dioctyl phthalate are among the many esters employed for this purpose. Cellulose acetate phthalate, used as a film forming agent for enteric coating, may be plasticized with substances such as castor oil or butyl stearate. Thermosetting plastics are compounded by mixing a suitable precursor with a cross-linking agent. For Bakelite the precursor is a phenol-rich partially cross-linked condensate with formaldehyde which when mixed with filler and hexamine (a source of further formaldehyde) may be placed in a suitable mould and heated to complete the cross-linking reaction. One of the curing agents for the epoxy resins is triethylamine tetramine. Activators and accelerators may be added to lower the temperature at which the 'cure' takes place and to reduce the time for its completion. In this way degradation and darkening due to overheating may be avoided. The similarities with the compounding of rubber will be noted.

The substances required for the rough mix of thermoplastics are passed through two or three heated rollers to complete the dispersion process. The resultant crude sheet is chopped up into small cubes or flakes ready for the forming process. Rods, tubes or films are made by heating the compounded plastic to a temperature at which it has the consistency of dough, when it may be extruded under pressure through a suitable nozzle, rather like squeezing ointment out of a tube. If individual articles are required the dough may be squeezed into a closed mould (injection moulding) or extruded tubing may serve as the feedstock for blow moulding whereby a portion of tube is trapped in a hot mould and blown to shape. Extruded sheet may be heated and forced to take the shape of a suitable jig (thermoforming); for thermosetting plastic the compounded material is fed into a mould, compressed and heated to complete the cross-linking (compression moulding).

Moulds must be made to very rigid tolerances if given dimensions are to be maintained throughout a batch. A faulty cavity in a multiple mould would produce a small proportion of faulty articles which might not be detected if the quality control sample was too small, an identical problem is encountered in tabletting. Long (1961) has reported the sporadic failure of polyethylene plug closures due to a fault of this type.

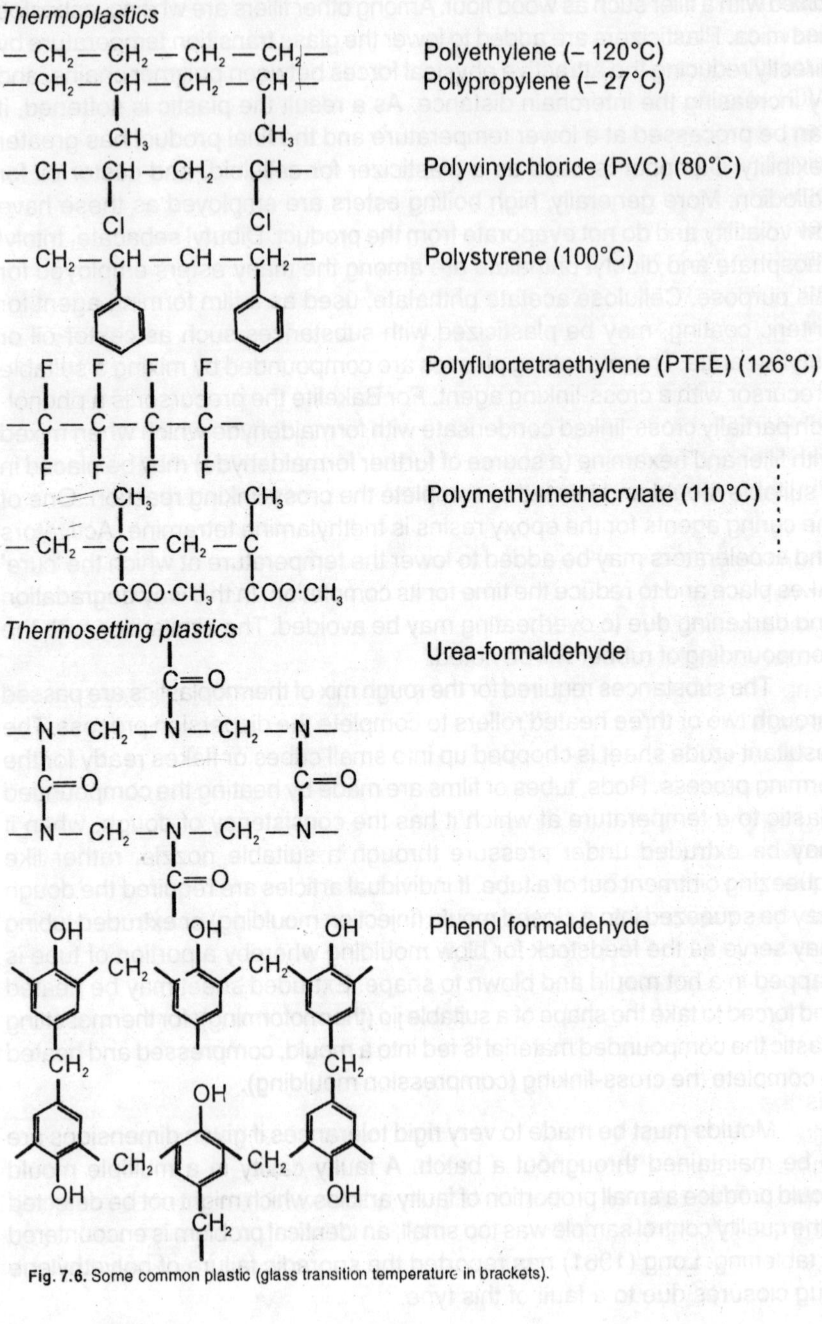

Fig. 7.6. Some common plastic (glass transition temperature in brackets).

Toxicity

Plastic are probably inert physiologically—it is the additives which give rise to toxicity problems. As noted earlier, octyl tin is an excellent stabilizer for PVC but is known to be toxic (Cooper 1966). Biological tests on extractives prepared with different solvents, and implantation of pieces of plastic in animals are among the control procedures proposed. Simpson (1969) has commented that the solvents and the amounts injected into the animal may themselves give rise to biological effects. He suggested that an aqueous extract of the plastic should be examined for pyrogenicity as some of the chemicals used for compounding purposes are known to be pyrogenic. The British Pharmacopoeia 1973 requires that the additives to plastics for pharmaceutical packaging shall be non-toxic and prescribes a test with which containers must comply to ensure freedom from toxic extractives in use, particularly if a sterilization procedure is involved. In particular, autoclaving accelerates the leaching process and represents the most rigorous in-use condition to which the plastic container is ever likely to be exposed.

Permeability

When using plastics for packaging it is necessary to consider not only the permeability to oxygen, water vapour and carbon dioxide but also the permeation or absorption of product constituents. For a flexible pack of dusting powder containing camphor it is the loss of this latter to the environment that is important. On the other hand, if the product is an oxygen sesitive steroid, it is the permeation of oxygen from the environment into the product via the container wall that must be considered.

Assuming here are no cracks or other defects, and that the plastic is not heavily 'filled', the pssage of gases and vapours occurs by diffusion. Above the transition temperature the polymer chains are in continuous thermal motion and the spaces between them constantly form and disappear. If a high concentration is established at one surface of the plastic, diffusing molecules will move from space to space to the low concentration side. Applying Fick's Law:

$$Q = \frac{ADt}{l} \cdot \frac{dc}{dx} \qquad (7.1)$$

Q is the quantity of gas diffusing in time t under the influence of a linear concentration gradient dc/dx. The plastic has a thickness l, area A and diffusion constant D. According to Henry's Law $c = pS$ where p is the partial pressure of the diffusing species and S its solubility coefficient for the plastic. Integrating (7.1), making the appropriate substitutions and rearranging:

$$P = DS = \frac{lQ}{At(p_1 - p_2)} \qquad (7.2)$$

where p_1 and p_2 are the partial pressures at the surfaces of the plastic and P is the permeability constant. If, as was assumed in deriving (7.2), the diffusing gas obeys the gas laws reasonably well, the effect of temperature is given by an Arrhenius type equation:

$$P = P_0 e^{-E/RT} = D_0 S_0 e^{-E/RT}$$

D_0 may be regarded as a measure of the number of interchain 'spaces' in the plastic at a given moment in time. Fewer spaces will be available for diffusion in the crystalline or cross-linked plastic than in the corresponding amorphous form. This is in line with Flück's (1966) observations that amorphous forms of a particular plastic are usually more permeable than the crystalline or cross-linked varieties. Plasticizing also increases permeability—it is well known, for instance, that moist gases permeate nylon films more rapidly than dry gases, as water is adsorbed and acts as plasticizer. The factor S_0 is a function of the relationship of the affinity of the diffusing molecules for plastic molecules of their affinity for each other. In general, low molecular weight, highly polar molecules permeate less rapidly than lipophilic molecules having structural similarities to those of the polymer.

It will be appreciated, therefore, that the physical properties of a given plastic will vary markedly according to the nature of the additives and the treatment it has undergone in manufacture—see, for instance Busse and Hughes (1969). The data in Table 7.1 must be regarded as approximate, but will serve as a comparative guide to the permeability of a number of plastics to oxygen and water vapour.

TABLE 7.1

PERMEABILITY CONSTANT (P) OF PLASTICS TO OXYGEN AND WATER VAPOUR POLYETHYLENE

(P in units of $cm^3/cm^2/mm/sec/cm\ Hg \times 10^{10}$)

	Low density	High density	Poly-propylene	Poly-styrene	Rigid PVC
Water vapour	400	130	250	12000	1600
Oxygen	50	11	23	30	4

Note that water vapour best permeates the more polar plastics whereas the reverse is true for oxygen. The more open molecular structure of low density polythene as compared with the high density variety is reflected in the lower value of P for the latter with both gases.

Plastics in the Packaging of Pharmaceutical Products

Compared with glass, plastics offer the obvious advantages of lightness, resistance to mechanical hazards and low cost. There is also the possibility that a particular property of a plastic, flexibility say, may be exploited to obtain greater package functionality. Against these advantages must be set the problems of permeability and toxicity, neigher of which arise with glass, and of disposal. In selecting plastic containers it is necessaary to check that:

(a) toxic substances are not leached from the plastic into the product,
(b) product constituents are not lost by absorption or permeation,
(c) loss or gain of moisture or permeation by oxygen takes place at an acceptable rate,
(d) no other interactions can occur between product and container.

Large numbers of plastic containers are now employed for dispensing mixtures, tablets, capsules, ointments, etc. Although polyethylene and polypropylene were used for some of the containers examined by Jolly et al. (1970) the majority were fabricated from high impact polystyrene. This is a polystyrene/styrene—butadiene rubber formulation which is as rigid but less brittle than polystyrene. Perfusion fluids and retention enemas are now packaged in plasticized PVC 'sachet' packs. These have the merit of collapsing as fluid is withdrawn and with perfusion fluids this obviates the use of an air bleed which was necessary on the older type of giving set with glass transfusion bottle. Water loss by permeation from sachet type containers can be as much as 10 per cent per annum but may be reduced to a quarter of this value by a polythene wrapper. Single applications of some eye drops are now packed in low density polythene sachets, container and contents being sterilized by g-radiation. A further advantage of the sachet type packages for applications such as these is the reduced amount of particulate matter shed from the container surface, which is a particular problem with the corresponding glass containers. Metal particles are sometimes found in ointments packed in metal tubes in spite of careful cleansing of the tube prior to filling—a difficulty which does not arise with plastic ointment tubes. Because its walls remain in opposition as the contents are removed, it has been said that a metal ointment tube is the only container that is completely full until it is completely empty. The same comment could not be made of the early plastic ointment tubes, which regained their original shape—sucked back—after each removal of contents, leading possibly to oxidation and microbial contamination problems. Such-back is less of a problem with the modern plasticized PVC tubes. Considerable economies are now possible in the manufacture of suppositories since the introduction of a machine that uses a preformed plastic package which alo serves as the mould. Suitable grades of polypropylene (and some other plastics) may be autoclaved. This is possible because the viscosity of the plastic at the autoclaving temperature, which is about 150 above T_g, is still high enough for the article to resist the deforming effect of its own weight. As described in the section on glass, this viscosity is of the order of 10^{13} poises or more.

Finally, two other methods of packaging which do not rely on a primary container and closure should be noted. In strip packaging, the tablet is sandwiched between two layers of foil or paper coated with a thermoplastic meterial such as polyethylene. This is fused together around the periphery of each tablet. Each strip is usually two tablets wide and several tablets long depending on requirements. Water vapour resistance normal to the surface is excellent but is lower round the edges. Where tablets are to be taken in a given sequence, they are deposited into a pocket thermoformed in a sheet of PVC and sealed in position with a foil laminate. The tablet is released by pushing it through the foil.

Rubber

Rubber is an elastic polymer (elastomer), and may be obtained from natural sources or by synthetic methods. It has a glass transition temperature well below the normal ambient temperature; for natural rubber T_g is about — 60.

Natural Rubber

The basic material is a colloidal dispersion (latex) obtained from the rubber tree *Hevea braziliensis,* containing about 30 to 35 per cent rubber hydrocarbons and up to 5 per cent overall or resins, proteins, sugars and salts, the rest being water. The solids may be precipitated by the addition of acid and the coagulum dried in the smoke of a wood fire when it acquires a dark brown colour and absorbs sufficient phenolic substances to prevent microbial spoilage during shipment. If pale crepe rubber is required, bisulphite is added prior to precipitation and the coagulum is dried at air temperature. The bisulphite stops oxidative discoloration and inhibits mould growth. For a number of purposes it is convenient to maintain the rubber in a 'liquid' state. To avoid the expense of shipping water the crude latex is either creamed by the addition of common salt or concentrated by evaporation or centrifugation. Preservative is added to inhibit subsequent microbial spoilage.

Synthetic Elastomers

These are manufactured by polymerization of the reactants while emulsified in a soap solution. For styrene-butadiene rubber (SBR) the reactants are styrene and butadiene. The dispersed polymer (latex) is either concentrated by the addition of salt which causes creaming, or solid obtained by addition of acid. The compositions of a number of other synthetic rubber polymer chains are also given in 7.7.

Further Processing

The polymer chains of natural rubber consist of some 1000 – 40000 isoprene units (Fig 7.8A). In common with synthetic rubber polymer chains they possess double bonds that readily oxidize on exposure to air and light. Furthermore, although the coiled and intertwined molecules unravel when the polymer is placed in tension there is slip between the chain and therefore a considerable deformation, which remains when the tension is released. The familiar elastic

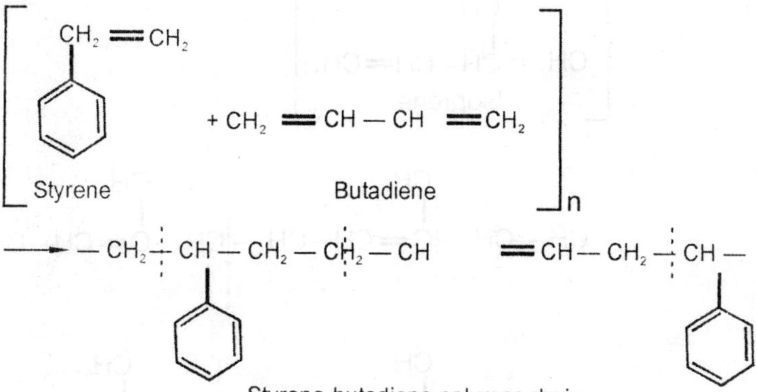

Styrene-butadiene polymer chain

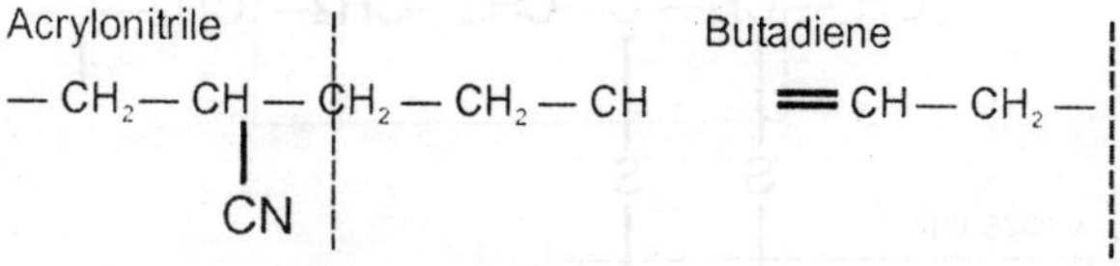

'Nitrile' rubber polymer chain

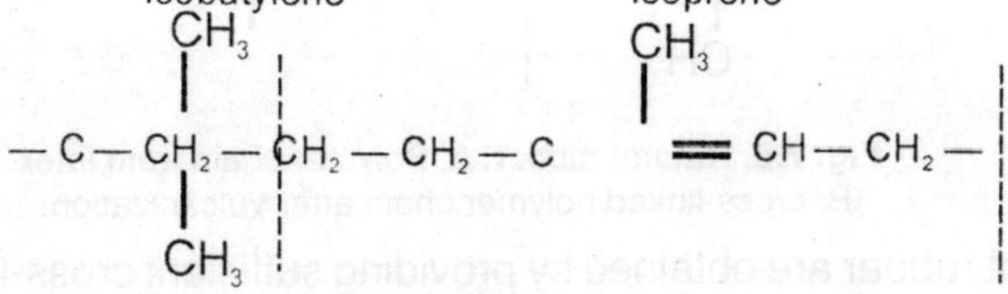

'Butyl' rubber polymer chain

Chloroprene

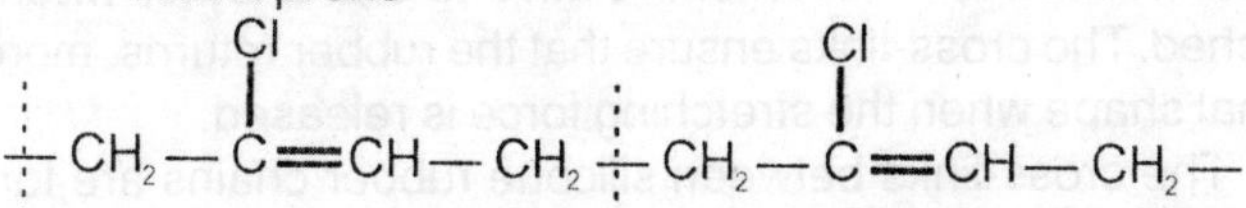

'Neoprene' rubber polymer chain

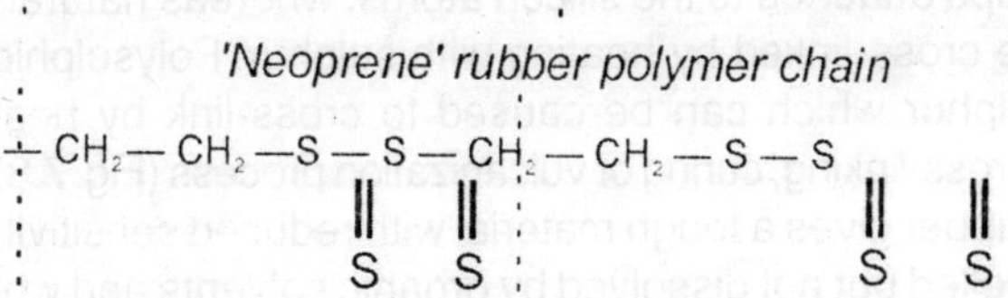

Polysulphide ('Thaikol') rubber polymer chain

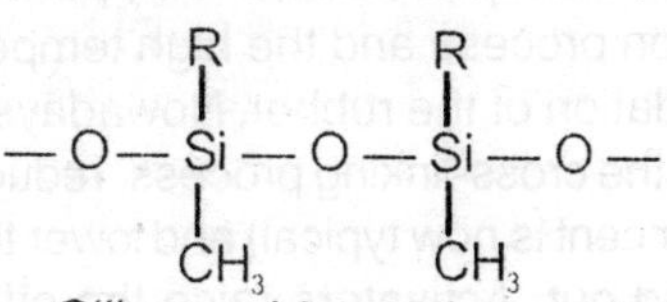

Silicon rubber polymer chain

Fig. 7.7. Synthetic rubbers.

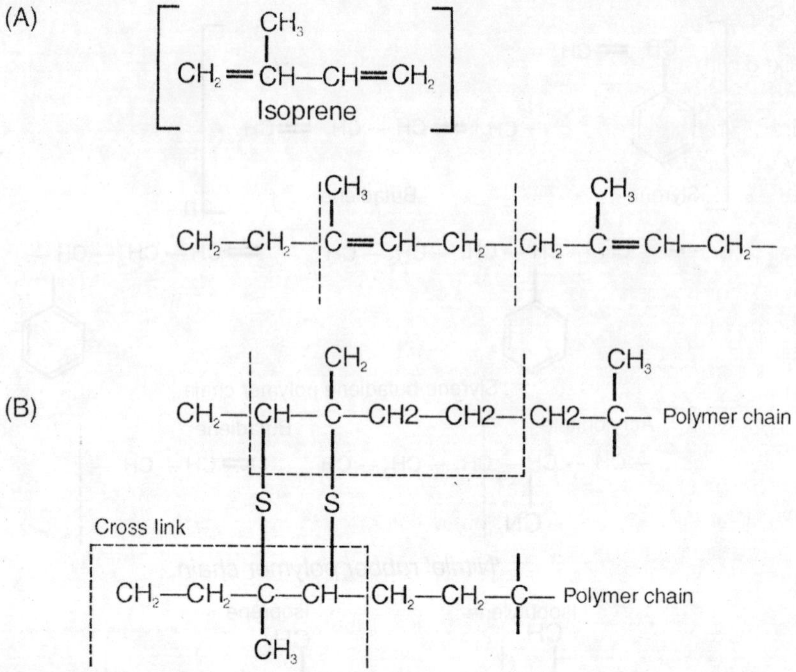

Fig. 7.8. Natural rubber: A, Polymer chain from latex. B, cross-linked polymer chain after vulcanization.

properties of rubber are obtained by providing sufficient cross-links per chain such that the product is not rigid but the chains may still uncoil although constrained in their movement relative to one another when the rubber is stretched. The cross-links ensure that the rubber returns, more or less, to its original shape when the stretching force is released.

The cross-links between silicone rubber chains are formed from the methyl groups attached to the silicon atoms, whereas natural and synthetic rubbers are cross-linked by heating with sulphur. Polysulphide rubber has 'built in' sulphur which can be caused to cross-link by heating with zinc oxide. The cross-linking, curing or vulcanization process (Fig. 7.8) when applied to natural rubber gives a tough material with reduced sensitivity to oxidation, which is swelled but not dissolved by organic solvents and which has a high degree of elasticity. As originally developed some 8 to 30 per cent of sulphur was needed for the vulcanization process and the high temperatures used brought about inevitable degradation of the rubber. Nowadays accelerators (Fig. 7.9) are added to speed up the cross-linking process, reduce the amount of sulphur required (0.5 to 3.0 per cent is now typical) and lower the temperture at which vulcanization is carried out. Activators raise the efficiency of the accelerators—zinc oxide, stearic acid or zinc stearate are commonly employed. The vulcanized rubber still possess unsaturated bonds therefore antioxidants, which persist in the final product, are added to minimize oxidation both during and subsequent to vulcanization. Traces of manganese or copper are known to catalyse the oxidation of rubber, and a sequestering agent, which may also act as an antioxidant, may be added to the compounded rubber mix prior to vulcanization. The cost of a ruber article may be reduced by using a proportion of reclaimed rubber or an extending filler such as whiting or talc. To modify the hardness or other mechanical properties, reinforcing fillers such as clays, magnesium carbonate or further quantities of zinc oxide are added as necessary to the rubber mix. These fillers are believed to combine in some way with the polymer chains (Haworth 1953; Reznek 1953b). Pigments may be added both for decorative purposes and to absorb ultraviolet radiation which promotes oxidation

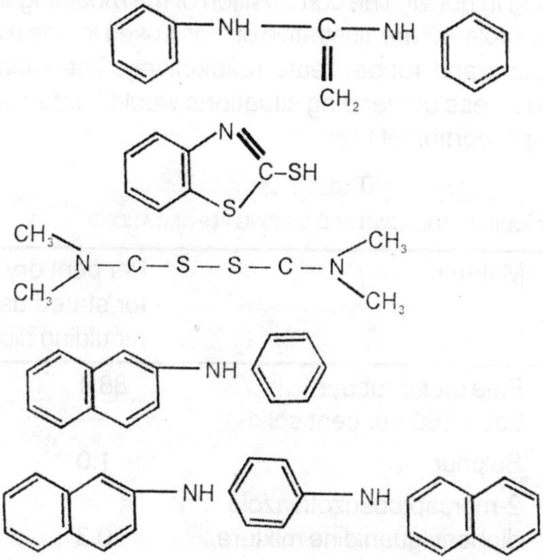

Accelerators: Diphenyl guanidine; 2-mercaptobenothiazole; Tetramethylthiuram disulphide

Antioxidant: phenyl-β-naphthylamine

Sequestering agent and antioxidant: NN′-di-β-naphthyl-*p*-phenylene diamine

Fig. 7.9. Some rubber additives.

If the article is to be made by moulding, rubber solids are finely minced in a masticator and the other compounding ingredients added. The rollers of the masticator are heated to soften the rubber but it may also be necessary to add a softener such as pine oil or tar, petroleum or coal tar fractions to obtain even dispersion. For some synthetic rubbers a plasticizer may be required. The mix has the characteristics of a dough. For dipping compounds the concentrated latex (about 60 per cent solids) is mixed with accelerators and a stabilizer to control the viscosity of the liquid so as to give the required film thickness. Foam rubber is produced by the addition to the mix of a blowing agent which decomposes during vulcanization to evolve gas (usually nitrogen). Wood and other resins may be added to provide surface stickiness or 'tack'. Small amounts of waxes that migrate to the rubber surface during vulcanization can be added to improve resistance both to water absorption and to oxidation.

To produce moulded articles a mould of the required shape and size is filled with the rubber dough which is then vulcanized by heating. It is usual to dust the surface of the dough with a mould release agent such as talc or zinc stearate so that the rubber is easily removed from the mould after vulcanization. Dipping is used where the thickness of rubber is small e.g. surgeons gloves, rubber teats. A glass or porcelain former is dipped into the compounded latex and the film coagulated in an acid bath. The process is repeated until the required thickness of rubber is built up and this is then vulcanized by heating in hot air. The composition of the moulding and dipping compounds given in Table 7.2 are illustrative of those used for the manufacture of vaccine bottle caps and rubber teats respectively. The rubber mix for closures to be used in less demanding situations would contain less rubber and a much higher proportion of filler.

TABLE 7.2

RUBBER MOULDING AND DIPPING FORMULATIONS

Function	Material	Per cent dry weight for stated use: moulding	dipping
Rubber	Pale crepe rubber	88.4	—
	Latex (60 per cent solids)	—	97.6
Vulcanizer	Sulphur	1.0	1.0
Accelerator	2-mercaptobenzothiazole diphenylguanidine mixture	0.3	—
	Zinc diethyldithiocarbamate	—	1.0
Activator	Zinc oxide	1.5	0.2
	Stearic acid	0.4	—
Antioxidant	Phenyl-b-naphthylamine	0.4	—
Filler	Zinc oxide	7.0	—
Special ingredient	Paraffin wax	1.0	—
	Film thickness stabilizer	—	0.2

For the majority of purposes natural rubber, or natural rubber with a proportion of styrene–butadiene gives the best all round performance. Synthetic rubbers are used in high proportion where special properties are at a premium. Nitrile rubber, for instance is not as resilient as natural rubber but has a very high solvent resistance that is only surpassed by the polysulphide rubbers. Butyl rubber exhibits high resistance to attack by oxygen, ozone and chemical reagents as well as very low permeability to oxygen and water vapour. Trials with butyl rubber wads (Bloom and Drennan 1957) were disappointing due to the low resilience of the rubber which led to permanent deformation and poor reseal performance. Neoprene combines good general rubber qualities with a high order of resistance to solvent and chemical attack; it is also flame resistant due to the chlorine atoms in the polymer chain. Silicone rubbers are completely saturated, inert and may be autoclaved many times, an in-use condition that would result in the rapid failure of normal rubber. They retain their resilience over a very wide range of temperature.

Rubber in the Packaging of Pharmaceuticals

Rubber is used exclusively as a closure and wad material. The specification of the B.P. 1973 is based on British Standard 3263: 1960 with certain ammendments. The specification excludes reclaimed rubber which is known to yield inferior closures and sets standards for dimensional tolerances. The force required to penetrate the closure with a hypodermic needle must not be excessive and a value for this parameter is specified. A further test limits the number of fragments of rubber detached during penetration by the hypodermic needle. Finally, if the contents of a multidose container are to remain free from microbial contamination the rubber must have good reseal properties and a test is described to assess this characteristic.

Like plastics, rubber may be regarded as a solid organic solvent and it is necessary in evaluating a particular closure to determine the oxygen and water vapour permeability, the leaching of substances from the rubber and the absorption of constituents from the product. An average value for the permeability constant P, as previously defined, is 230 for oxygen and 25000 for moisture vapour, the units being $cm^3/cm^2/mm/sec/cm\ Hg \times 10^{10}$. Since the performance of a closure probably depends more on its fit in the container (hence the standard for dimensional tolerances) than on its permeability, the British Standard describes a practical test of performance. In this test, the gain in weight of a desiccant sealed in a container by the test closure is compared with the gain in weight where the closure is one which has previously been found to be acceptable.

The process of compounding rubber suggests that two types of material which persist after the vulcanization process may be extracted, namely zinc and organic substances. Reznek (1953 a and b) studied the extraction of zinc from rubber used as the plunger in dental anaesthetic cartridges. Generally, the amount extracted from the plunger increased with the acidity of the solution, storage time and temperature and content of zinc in the rubber. With 16.1 cm^2 of rubber surface exposed to 50 ml of 0.1 N HCl for 56 days at 50° the final concentration of zinc in the solution varied from 14 to 78 ppm as the zinc oxide content of the rubber was increased from 0.41 per cent by weight. Direct experiment will show that zinc is readily extracted from closure rubber by solutions of both high and low pH and also at more neutral pH values if the leaching solution contains a substance such as citrate which is capable of complexing the zinc. Some of the organic compounds used for compounding rubber are virtually insoluble in water, while many accelerators are destroyed during the vulcanization process. Nevertheless, leaching of thiuram disulphide and other organic substances was noted by Lachman et al. (1963 b) during studies of preservative uptake by rubber closures. The toxicological significance of zinc and organic substances extracted from rubber is not clear. The British Standard limits the amount of water soluble extractive and also describes a test for the compatibility of product and closure. Natural rubber contains a proportion of protein and this has caused allergic reactions in sensitive individuals. Non-allergenic rubber is now available.

Absorption of substances from the product is, of course, very important. It may be expected that lipophilic substances are more likely to be taken up than those more polar in nature. Unfortunately, the former group includes a high proportion of the antimicrobial preservatives which depend on lipophilic properties to pass the microbial cell wall. If these are absorbed by the closure, the product is left without protection against microbial contamination. Wing (1955 and 1956) examined some thirty rubber formulations for preservative uptake and found that the initial rapid absorption slowed down with time and eventually reached an equilibrium situation. The rate of uptake increased with temperature but often the partition coefficient was less favourable to the rubber at the higher temperatures. Wing noted extremes of partition coefficient, for instance from 0.3 to 1.7 for phenol and 7 to 47 for chlorocresol depending on the rubber composition. Silica fillers and some softeners increased the partition coefficient in favour of the rubber, the former presumably by physical adsorption and the latter by providing a more favourable solvent for the preservative (Royce and Sykes 1957). Sykes (1958) and Lachman et al. (1962, 1963 a and b) have reported studies which are in general agreement if the inevitable variations in the compositions of the rubbers used by these workers are taken into account. Contact of rubber with phenol, cresol or methyl-*p*-hydoxybenzoate solutions results in the uptake of about a third of the preservative. Under similar conditions up to 90 per cent of chlorocresol, chlorbutol, cetrimide and phenylmercuric nitrate would be lost from solution. As the cetrimide would be completely ionized, adsorption rather than absorption is the most likely mechanism whereby that substance is removed from solution. The phenylmercuric nitrate is probably inactivated by –SH groups in the rubber. For the same reason specially formulated rubber caps are used for penicillin preparations. If the preservative is volatile—for example cresol—it may evaporate from the rubber surface into the atmosphere, a process that would continue until almost all the preservative has been removed from solution. Rubber also interacts with sodium with sodium metabisulphite.

Attempts to mitigate the undesirable effects that attend the use of rubber closures have involved the application of a wax or lacquer coating. Although these give short term protection they eventually flake off, or perhaps worse, may block the hypodermic needle. The most successful approach is to presaturate the rubber with those absorbable substances with which it is to come into contact. This is the official method and the reader is referred to the official monographs for details. It is sufficient here to note that the closures must be carefully washed to remove mould lubricant and dust, and that both the quantity and concentration of solution to be used for soaking is specified to ensure correct saturation of the closures.

Glass

Structures and Composition

Even the weak bonds between the molecules of a liquid will effectively permit a random disordered structure; the viscosity of a liquid is a measure of the amount of energy which must be available for disrupting the inter-molecular bonds during flow. If the viscosity exceeds some 10^{13} poises the liquid deforms so slowly under the influence of its own weight that for all practical purposes it behaves like a solid. For a liquid to crystallize, energy must also be available to break the intermolecular bonds so that these can subsequently reform to give the ordered lattice configuration of the crystal. In the case of very viscous liquids the energy required may be so large that the initial bond cleaving step is unlikely to occur and the liquid may remain more or less permanently in the supercooled state at or below the normal crystallization temperature. Technically, 'glasses' may be defined as liquids which may be supercooled to temperatures at which the viscosity exceeds 10^{13} poises, in which condition they exhibit the properties of a solid while retaining the disordered internal structure of a liquid. A large number of substances can be obtained as glasses, e.g., sulphur, many plastics, arsenic trisulphide, and these all have in common a well developed molecular network. In everyday usage, however, the term *glass* is applied to the hard, brittle, transparent material, based on a network of silicon and oxygen atoms, that is widely used for making products as diverse as electric light bulbs, windows and bottles.

Silica melts at about 1700°C and on cooling yields a glass commonly known as fused silica. This material is very resistant to the attack of all chemicals except wrong alkalis, hydrofluoric acid and related substances and, since the coefficient of linear expansion is low (0.5×10^{-6}), silica ware can be subjected to sudden large temperature changes (thermal shock) without breaking. Fused silica lacks the regular crystal lattice of quartz but possesses instead an open random three-dimensional network in which each silicon atom is surrounded by four oxygen atoms, each of the latter being shared by two silicon atoms (7.10). The high melting temperature of silica derives from the strong covalent Si—O bonds which may be pictured as radiating from the central silicon atom and directed towards the four corners of a tetrahedron so that the bond angle is fixed at about 108° (cf. carbon). The angle between the two bonds associated with each oxygen atom is not so rigidly fixed and this provides the flexibility necessary for the formation of the network. Both

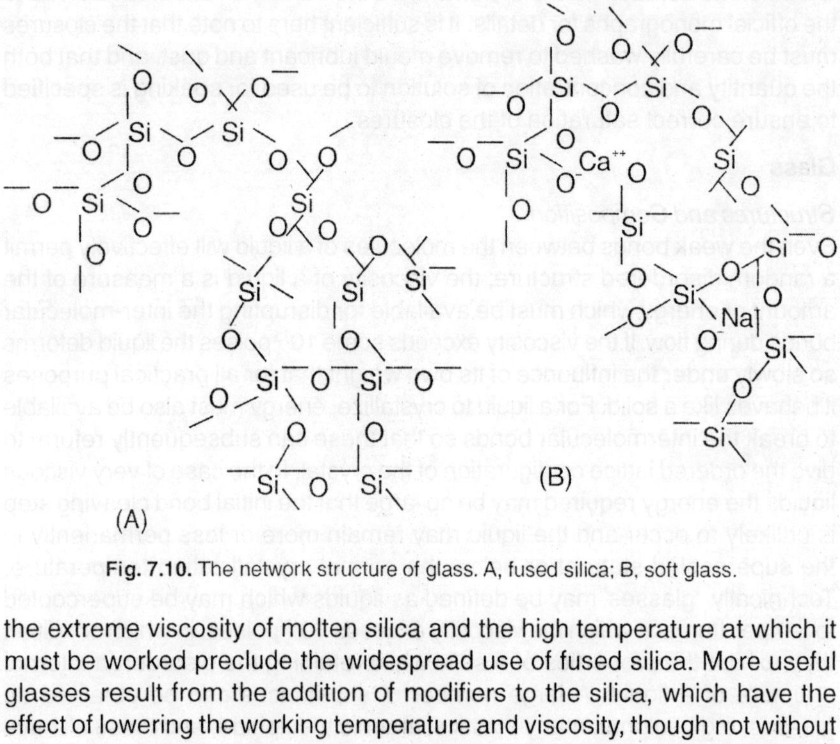

Fig. 7.10. The network structure of glass. A, fused silica; B, soft glass.

the extreme viscosity of molten silica and the high temperature at which it must be worked preclude the widespread use of fused silica. More useful glasses result from the addition of modifiers to the silica, which have the effect of lowering the working temperature and viscosity, though not without some loss of mechanical strength, resistance to thermal shock and chemical durability. Monovalent metals, e.g. Na^+ and K^+, disrupt the silica network and have the most marked effect on the working properties, but the glass has too low a resistance to chemical attack to be of any practical value. Calcium, magnesium, barium and other divalent metals can take part in the network by sharing two oxygen atoms. The structural distortion and replacement of a strong covalent bond by two weaker electrovalent bonds results in a useful reduction of working temperature without sacrificing too much chemical durability. Suitable combinations of both mono- and divalent metals yield glasses which are readily worked and yet possess adequate strength and chemical durability for use in non-critical situations (Fig.. 'Soft' or lime-soda glass is of this type and is employed in the production of many of the containers used in pharmacy. The performance of such containers falls short of the ideal when exposed to the more severe conditions encountered in, for instance, sterilization by autoclaving. In these circumstances it may be necessary to use a 'harder' glass, in which the content of mono- and divalent metals has been reduced and replaced by multivalent elements such as aluminium and boron. These elements are called network formers because they can take part in the network by covalent bonding in much the same way as silicon itself. The chemical durability, resistance to thermal shock and mechanical strength are thereby much improved but the glass is more expensive.

Four main types of glass are in common use for the production of the containers used in pharmacy. Table 7.3 gives an approximate composition, in terms of the appropriate oxide, that is representative of each type. The low values of some elements is due to their presence as contaminants in the raw materials, e.g., magnesium in limestone. It is necessary to use a high grade sand as the source of silica, as ordinary grades contain large amounts of iron, which produces a green tinge in the glass and decolorizers, usually selenium compounds, are ineffective if the ferric iron content is greater than about 0.1 per cent. Certain elements may be deliberately added to produce a coloured glass, the following being of pharmaceutical interest:

amber: carbon and sulphur or iron and manganese
green: chromium with some iron and manganese
blue: cobalt with, occasionally, some copper.

The light absorption curves for these glasses are given on page 148. At one time arsenic was used as a decolorizer. Alkaline preparations were known to dissolve glass and, to avoid contamination, arsenic free glass containers, distinguishable by their blue colour, were used to package such preparations. In this way a blue glass container has become associated with Mixture of Magnesium Hydroxide, and is still used, even though the glass employed for the fabrication of pharmaceutical containers is now arsenic (and lead) free.

TABLE 7.3

APPROXIMATE COMPOSITIONS OF SOME GLASSES USED FOR THE PRODUCTION OF CONTAINERS USED IN PHARMACY

	Soft (lime-soda)	*Neutral (for containers)*	*Neutral (for ampoules)*	*Hard (boro-silicated)*
SiO_2	73	73	67	80
Na_2O	13	7	8.5	4

K_2O	0.5	1.5	4	—
CaO	10	—	4	0.2
MgO	0.3	—	0.3	—
BaO	—	3	—	—
Al_2O3	0.5	5	8.5	2.5
B_2O_3	—	8.5	7.5	13

Container Production

Furnaces for large scale glass production are typically rectangular in shape, about a metre deep and 100 m^2 in area. For the production of soft glass, high grade sand, soda, limestone and alumina together with waste glass of the same kind are continuously fed into the furnace and heated to about 1400. The bubbles of acrbon dioxide and other gases formed during the reaction rise to the surface as the glass approaches the furnace outlet where the temperature is higher and the viscosity of the melt such reduced. A 'bridge' across the outlet skims off impurities as the melt flows into a fore-hearth at which point the temperature is about 1000° and the viscosity is suitable for the start of container manufacture. Full details of the methods used are given by Moody (1963), but in each case a preformed blank or 'parison' is blown into the final form inside a mould. A small gap between the halves of the mould allows air to escape as the container is blown to shape—its position is revealed by a fine ridge seam on the outer surface of the finished container. Careful design of the mould is necessary to ensure that the quantity of glass in the blank mould gives container walls of the correct thickness at the blowing stage.

By the time the container has been formed its external surface has cooled to approximately 300° and is rigid enough to maintain the final shape. The inside, however, is still hot and the stresses set up by uneven cooling would lead to early failure of the container in service. To overcome this problem the temperature is raised to about 550° in an annealing kiln or *lehr* so that stress dissipation by internal flow can take place. Subsequently, further stress formation is avoided by alowing the container to cool slowly and uniformly as it travels towards the exit of the kiln. Prior to entering the lehr it is usual for the moulding ridges on the rim of the neck to be removed by local heating (fire polishing).

Mechanical Strength

As the covalent Si–O bond is very strong, this should be reflected in the mechanical strength of glass. Freshly drawn fibres can support loads of the order of 1500 MNm^{-2} (15000 kg cm^{-2}) but the tensile strength of bulk glass varies from about 200 MNm^{-2} when new, to about a fifth of this value after being used for some time. The variable low value for the strength of bulk glass as compared with freshly drawn fibres is attributed to the presence of sub-microscopic cracks on the surface of bulk specimens and these will tend to be more numerous on the surface of used specimens, due to damage in service. These cracks open up under tension and, since the glass is a liquid, there are no internal boundaries to inhibit their propagation. The cracks do not open up when compressive loads are applied and glass is found to be some ten times stronger in compression than in tension.

Glass containers are subject to a number of mechanical hazards both on the filling line and in service. If they rub together abrasion scars are formed that seriously weaken the glass as described above. They are prone to fracture on impact, particularly if full of liquid and for this reason must be packed for transport and handling in cartons with shock absorbent partitions around each container. The filling and capping head may impose a vertical load on the container and this condition also obtains when the cartons of filled containers are stacked for storage or transport. The vertical load which a bottle will support without fracture is roughly proportional to the radius of curvature of the neck.

As glass is weaker in tension than in compression, the aim of modern design is to ensure that the shoulder and sides are evenly compressed by vertical loading, and tensile stresses reduced as much as possible by using the largest radius of curvature for the shoulder that is appropriate to the

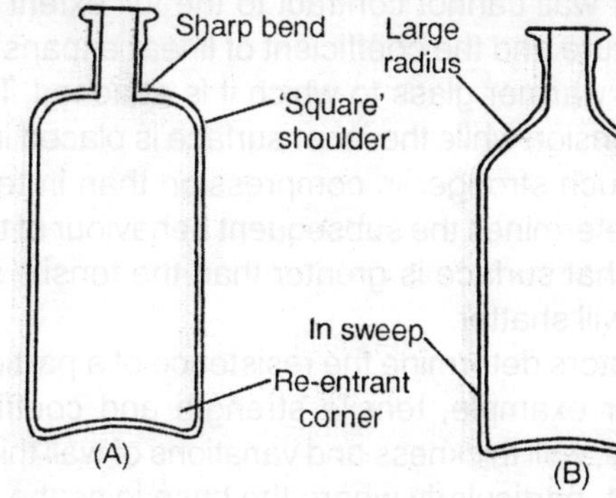

Fig. 7.11. Improvements in container design: A, old; B, new.

particular size and function of the container. In this way it has been possible to increase the vertical load resistance from some 200 kg for the older, square shouldered 'winchester' to ten times this value for its modern more rounded counterpart. Similar changes may be seen in the shape of most modern glass containers used for packaging pharmaceutical products. The modern shape also facilitates mould design to secure uniform thickness of glass at the shoulder. Finally, the shape must be considered in terms of the internal pressure that the bottle must withstand in use. The cooling of a full transfusion bottle, for instance, usually lags behind that of the autoclave. As a consequence the bottle may still be under pressure when the chamber of the autoclave has reached atmospheric pressure.

Where mechanical strength is of paramount importance it may be necessary to employ a hard glass container, but the mechanical strength of soft glass containers may be improved by a process known as titanizing. After the container has been reheated at the start of the annealing process, the outer surface is sprayed with a tin or titanium compound. This decomposes to leave an oxide film which dissolves in the glass to give a thin surface layer that significantly reduces glass-to-glass friction and the tendency to form sub-microscopic cracks. The process allows wall thickness to be reduced and yet, with suitable designs, the resistance to breakage from impact, abrasion scars and vertical loading can be better than that of similar untreated containers.

Resistant to Thermal Shock

The outside of a hot glass container cools and contracts if exposed to a cold environment, that is, to downwards thermal shock. The thicker the container wall the lower the rate of heat transfer from the warm interior and in any case this rate is low, due to the poor thermal conductivity of glass. Thus the transient temperature difference which is rapidly established between the inner and outer surfaces of the glass is greater for thick than for thin walled containers. The outer wall cannot contract to the full extent implied by the decrease in temperature and the coefficient of linear expansion, because it is constrained by the warmer glass to which it is attached. Thus, the outer surface is placed in tension while the inner surface is placed in compression but, since glass is much stronger in compression than in tension, it is the cooled surface that determines the subsequent behaviour of the container. If the tensile stress in that surface is greater than the tensile strength of the glass, the container will shatter.

A number of factors determine the resistence of a particular container to thermal shock, for example, tensile strength and coefficient of linear expansion of the glass, wall thickness and variations of wall thickness. Shape is also very important, particularly where the base joins the side-walls and the small radius of curvature at that point imposes severe bending stresses on the glass under conditions of thermal shock. Where possible these stresses are minimized by a gentle insweep of the container wall that increase the effective radius of curvature near the base. It will be clear that the calculation of the resistance to thermal shock of a given container is a matter of some complexity but an approximate value for the maximum temperature jump (T_{max} in degrees C) that may be safely imposed on a soft glass cylindrical container by chilling the outer surface is given by

$$T_{max} = 32d^{-1/2}$$

where *d* is the wall thickness in centimetres. The wal thickness of a container is inevitably a compromise between the opposing requirements of strength (thick wall) and resistance to thermal shock (thin wall). In some cases it may be necessary to use the mechanically stronger neutral or boro-silicate glasses; the latter has the particular advantage that its coefficcient of linear expansion is only a third of that of soft or neutral glass. In practice, 'winchesters' (2 litre) will survive a temperature drop of at least 30°, large (half-litre) containers about 50° and small thin-wall containers about 70°; these values may be doubled for thermal shock provided by rising temperature increments of the same order. These factors emphasize the great care that should be taken when handling hot glassware. The most serious condition arises when products which have been sterilized are prematurely removed from the autoclave. The resultant thermal shock when the container is exposed to the much colder environment outside the autoclave often leads to explosive shattering of the glass, as the container and contents will still be under pressure.

Chemical Durability

Ideally, product and package should not interact and material derived from the package that finds its way into the product must be regarded as a contaminant. Nevertheless, even the silicate glasses which are probably the most inert materials likely to be used for the fabrication of containers are attacked at all pH levels by aqueous liquids and it is necessary to apply realistic tests to ensure that the amount of contamination is within acceptable limits. Attack by alkaline solutions leads to the steady dissolution of glass, often without apparent change in appearance (Dimbleby 1953). The only visual evidence of such attack may be the formation of insoluble silicates in the product. Hydrofluoric acid and a few related fluorine containing substances also dissolve glass, but for all other acidic or neutral aqueous solution the attack proceeds by an ion exchange process in which monovalent and, later, divalent cations in the surface are replaced by hydroxonium ions. The layer of hydrated silica formed by this process affords some protection for the glass if the attacking liquid is acidic and neutralizes the cations as they diffuse from the surface. Under conditions of severe attack by water the extracted alkali may cause dissolution of the hydrated silica layer thus exposing the glass beneath to attack. The deterioration of a glass surface under adverse storage conditions involves both kinds of action. If the humidity is high; moisture condenses on the surface and extracts cations. Subsequently the flm may dry to leave behind a white deposit which contains a high proportion of sodium carbonate. When moisture again condenses on the surface the deposit dissolves and the concentrated alkaline solution attacks the silica network. The resultant loss of surface brilliance is known as weathering. In severe cases the surface acquires a white etched appearance that cannot be improved by normal washing procedures; a similar effect may be noted with soft glass containers that have been autoclaved many times.

The rate at which a glass surface is attacked depends on the type of glass and any surface treatment to which it may have been subjected, the wetted area, the type and temperature of the attacking solution and the time it has been in contact with the surface. For alkaline solutions the rate of attack falls off with time due to the accumulation of silica and other components of glass in the attacking solution. If M is the amount of material dissolved in time t from unit surface area and the amount of silica etc. accumulating in the attacking solution in proportional to M then:

$$dM/dt = K/(r + kM)$$

where K, k and r are constants. Under neutral conditions the attack is diffusion controlled by a hydrated silica layer of thickness d proportional to the amount of cations M leached from the surface that is:

$$d = k'M$$

and

$$dM/dt = P/d = P/k'M$$

where P and k' are constants. Actually, the process involves outward diffusion of Na^+ ions and inward diffusion H_3O^+ ions but if, as seems likely, only one of these processes is the rate controlling step, the foregoing treatment is valid. As with attack by alkaline solutions the rate decreases with time, in this case because of the increasing thickness of the hydrated silica layer. Both fundamental rate equations lead to a parabolic time law (M2 xt) of attack. Furthermore, as both chemical reaction leading to dissolution of the glass and loss of surface alkali by diffusion are activated processes, the Arrhenius relation may be applied, that is:

$$\log\frac{M}{\sqrt{t}} = -\frac{E}{RT} + C$$

where E is the activation energy, R the gas constant and C a constant. Hubbard and Hamilton (1941) and Douglas and Isard (1949) have confirmed that this relationship applies to the attack on a number of glasses by alkalis and by water respectively.

Surface treatment of soft glass offers a possible means for reducing the interaction with aqueous fluids. Silicons appeared to be suitable agents as they are chemically related to glass and produce water repellant films. With these substances protection was good initially, but the film tended to detach on storage or autoclaving. A more satisfactory treatment is based on the early observation that the outer surfaces of glass containers that had been annealed in a coal or gas fired lehr were more resistant to attack by water than the inner surfaces. Sulphur dioxide and other acidic components of the furnace gases had reacted with the Na^+ ions in the surface to form salts which were removed on washing the containers. The annealing process ensured that the silica rich layer which was left behind was compacted and firmly bonded to the underlying glass. Unfortunately, furnace gases do not readily penetrate the interior of a container, hence its lower resistance to attack by aqueous liquids, and in any case some lehrs are now heated electrically. To overcome these problems an acidic atomoshere is artificially formed by placing an ammonium sulphate pellet in the container prior to annealing. The process is known as *sulphating.*

Flake and Spicule Formation

The chemical durability of glass is assessed by exposing it to attack by appropriate chemical reagents and measuring the effect on that reagent or on the glass itself. The BP 1973 has adopted the tests of the European Pharmacopoeia (Vol. II) 1971. The hydrolytic resistance test sets a limit on the amount of alkali that may be extracted from the containers used to package injectable products. The containers are filled with the nominal volume of freshly distilled water and autoclaved. The alkali leached by the water from the glass and is then titrated with N/100 HCl. According to the provisions of the test for 1 ml ampoules, the extracted alkali must not exceed that equivalent to 0.02 ml of N/100 HCl. As about 5 cm^2 of internal surface is wetted by the nominal contents of 1 ml ampoules in current use the foregoing corresponds to an extraction rate of:

$$\frac{0.02}{5} \times \frac{23}{100} \times \frac{106}{1000} = 0.92\ \mu g\ cm^{-2}\ Na^+$$

Similar calculations for 10 ml (28 cm^2 wetted surface) and 50 ml (78 cm^2 wetted surface) give extraction rates of 0.82 and 0.88 $\mu g\ cm^{-2}$ respectively. Thus, the hydrolytic resistance test relates the amount of extracted alkali to the internal surface area of the container. In this way it differs from the test for alkalinity of glass in the BP 1968 which limited the concentration of extracted alkali in the container contents irrespective of the size.

A further set of tests, not previously described in a British Pharmacopoeia, but having affinities with tests in the United States is intended to distinguish between neutral, surface treated and soft glass. A crushed glass test is used to determine whether the container has been fabricated from neutral or soft glass. A further test in which the internal surface is exposed to the action of hydrofluoric acid to remove for example, the silica rich layer of a sulphated container, allows the latter to be differentiated from similar components made from neutral glass.

There is one further effect due to the reaction between the glass surface and acidic or neutral solutions. When the cations are replaced by hydroxonium ions, additional water molecules are also carried into the surface. To accommodate the hydroxonium ions and water molecules, the surface layer swells and in some cases may rupture the bonds at the interface with the unattacked glass below, so that silica rich laminae (flakes) or needle-like fragments (spicules) detach from the surface. If the attack takes place at room temperature a considerable period may elapse before flake or spicule formation becomes visible. If the temperature of the container and its contents is raised, additional stresses due to differential expansion of the glass and the hydrated silica layer causes more prompt rupture of interfacial bonds and the detachment of flakes or spicules. It is known that nearly neutral solutions containing citrates, phosphates, tartrates and bicarbonates are most prone to trouble from flake and spicule formation. Presumably, this is due to some attack of the silica network itself, in addition to the swelling and thermal effects noted above. Such products may often be packed and sterilized in new sulphated lime-soda bottles, but have a tendency to flake and spicule contamination if the bottle has been in use for some time. Although Groves and Major (1964) have confirmed the previously held view that the rubber closure, rather than the glass container was the major source of contamination in commercially available transfusion fluids, the presence of particles of any kind should be suspect as even particles smaller than 1 μm in diameter have given rise to adverse physiological effects (Stehbens & Florey 1960). Sterile pharmaceutical solutions completely free of particles could probably not be manufactured on a commercial scale.

Groves (1966) proposed a limit of not more than 50 particles greater than 5 mm in size per ml of product (see also Cooper & Barrett 1970). The BP 1973 requires that all injections must be free from particulate matter that can be observed by visual inspection. Additionally, specified products must confirm to a limit for 2 to 5 μm particles and for particles larger than 5 μm. Such products include large volume perfusion fluids containing, for example, sodium chloride and sodium lactate.

The European Pharmacopoeia distinguishes between three types of glass: type I has high hydrolytic resistance due to its composition and includes the neutral glasses; type II derives its hydrolitic resistance from surface treatment e.g. sulphating; type III includes soft glass and has only moderate hydrolytic resistance. Type III glass may be used to package a wide variety of products such as ointments, lotions, mixtures, powders for the preparation of injections and non-aqueous injections. All other parenteral products must be packaged in type I or II glass containers. Sufficient alkali could be extracted from soft glass to cause the precipitation of basic substances. Thus, strychnine has a pK_b of 6.0 and a solubility (S_O) in water of only 1 in 7000 (0.0143 per cent) at room temperature. For an aqueous injection containing, say 1 mg per ml (S = 0.1 per cent) of the alkaloid as a salt the pH at which that alkaloid will just precipitate (pH') is given by:

$$pH' = pK_w - pK_b + \log\left[\frac{S_0}{S - S_0}\right]$$

$$= 14 - 6 + \log\left[\frac{0.0143}{0.1 - 0.0143}\right]$$

$$= 7.22$$

Direct experiment shows that occasionally enough alkali may be leached from the inner surface of a soft glass ampoule to raise the pH of the contents to or above this level. Formerly, the liberation of narcotine from its salts was used in Germany as a performance test for glass containers. Many bases are sufficiently soluble in water at high pH that precipitation is unlikely to occur. Thus, with atropine, adrenaline and procaine accelerated decomposition in alkaline conditions rather precipitation is the problem. Some medicaments such as Adrenaline Acid Tartrate have inherent buffering capacity in the pH range which is optimum for stability. For Chloramphenicol Eye Drops the balance between solubility and stability is maintained by a pH 7.0 borate/boric acid buffer (Heward et al. 1970).

Another example where the extraction of alkali must be limited by the use of hard glass containers is in the packaging of Insulin Injection. The isoelectric point of this polypeptide is 5.5 to 5.6 and, although the injection is adjusted to pH 3.0 to 3.5, sufficient alkali could be extracted from unsatisfactory containers to bring the pH to the isoelectric point thus causing precipitation of insulin. The major danger with this medicament is, however, the very much accelerated degradation of the polypeptide that occurs if the pH exceeds 7.5. Borosilicate glass is too expensive for widespread use as a container material. The cheaper neutral glasses provide an acceptable alternative and are available in two grades (Table 7.1), one of which is formulated for a low fusion temperature to facilitate the sealing of ampoules (B.S. 795 : 1961). Although the coefficient of linear expansion is similar to that of soft glass, thermal shock is rarely a problem as the ampoule walls are thin. The container grade of neutral glass is employed for the production of multidose injection containers antibiotic vials, etc. Transfusion bottles (B.S. 2463 : 1962) can be made of neutral glass but sulphated lime-soda glass provides a cheaper alternative which is now much used for eye drop bottles (B.S. 1679 : 1965). To avoid the danger of flaking with repeated use, surface treated eye drop bottles are employed once only and are therefore known as 'one-trip' eye drop bottles. Some injections such as those containing apomorphine, ascorbic acid or papaveretum are light sensitive, and amber coloured ampoules have been much used for packaging them. However visual evidence of deterioration, e.g. flaking, colour changes, etc., should be readily discernible and it is now more usual to pack the product in colourless containers and exclude light by means of the ampoule box. Another reason for using colourless containers is that the product might be contaminated by the elements used to colour the glass, and Girard and Kemy (1950) have reported that iron extracted from amber glass may interfere with the stability of adrenaline solutions. For non-parenteral products the packaging requirements are less stringent and as amber container are no more expensive than the colourless variety, the majority of chemicals, galenicals, etc. are now routinely packed in amber glass bottles regardless of the light sensitivity of the packaged material.

Closures

An ideal closure will seal the container to prevent loss of product and ingress of gases or other substances. Where necessary the closure should withstand sterilizing conditions and prevent subsequent contamination by microorganisms. The closure and product must not react together. Finally, if only part of the contents of the container is to be used at a time, it should be easy to remove and replace the closure, and the reseal properties must be adequate for this purpose.

Except for this last requirement, a glass fusion seal is as perfect a seal as it is possible to make; all other seals are less satisfactory. If the product absorbs water vapour, the partial pressure for that substance inside the container will be lower than that in the environment. This provides a concentration gradient across any imperfection in the closure and leads to continuous diffusion into the container and hence into the product. Additionally, any change in ambient temperature or pressure will result in a flow of air into or out of the container via the imperfections in the closure—the container is said to 'breathe'. Over a period of storage the combined effects of breathing and diffusion may lead to the transfer of considerable quantities of water to the product and may result in instability.

The basic types of closure are folded, push-on, bung, screw-cap and fusion.

Folded Seals

These will be familiar both as the seam down the side of tinned-steel containers and as the folded end of ointment tubes. If the product inside the tube is very viscous there will be a considerable back pressure as the product is forced out of the nozzle and this will tend to unfold the seal. In commercial practice, when the folds have been formed they are crimped by corrugated jaws and this prevents unfolding of the seal (Fig. 7.12). Seepage via the folded seal may be prevented by the use of latex sealing compounds.

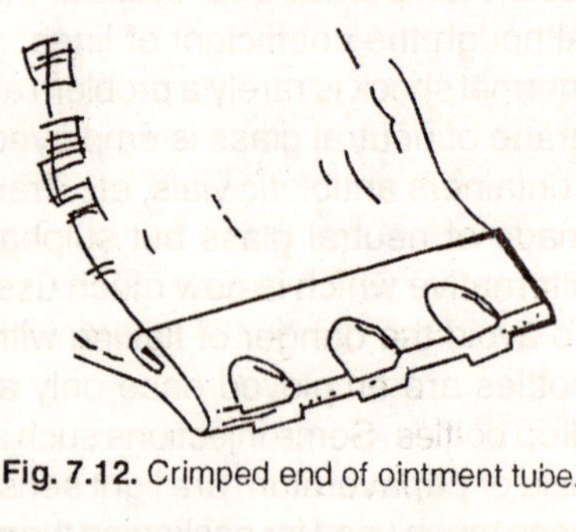

Fig. 7.12. Crimped end of ointment tube.

Push-on Seals

These are often used for tubes of lozenges and rely on the resilient distortion of the closure both for pushing the cap over the retaining ring at the rim of the tube and also for maintaining a tight seal between the neck and the rim (Fig. 7.13).

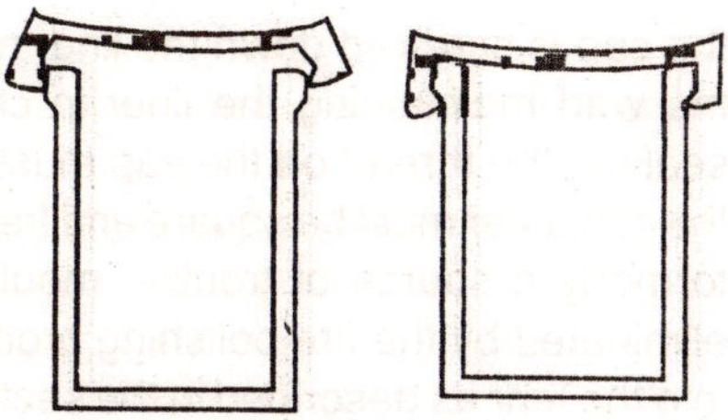

Fig. 7.13. Push-on closure.

Bung Seals

These are among the oldest known closures. They are conical and can be inserted for about half their length into the neck of the container (Fig. 7.14A). Sideways pressure due to distortion of the bung on insertion provides a seal the perfection of which depends both on the bung material and finish of the neck. Cork usually gives a good seal for general purposes but eventually becomes permanently distorted with consequent loss of reseal properties. Rubber is an excellent material for bung closures but cannot be used for oils or solvents due to swelling, or for lubricant products as the bung tends to eject from the neck of the container. There are many varieties of this type of closure. With vaccine bottle caps, bung action is assisted by a 'skirt' that folds over the outside of the neck of the bottle. A wire loop round the skirt ensures that the bung is not ejected during heat sterilization. Another type of bung closure, now much used, is that used for vials of penicillin powder. The bung is held in place by a thin aluminium cap which is spun round a retaining ring on the neck of the vial (Fig. 7.14B).

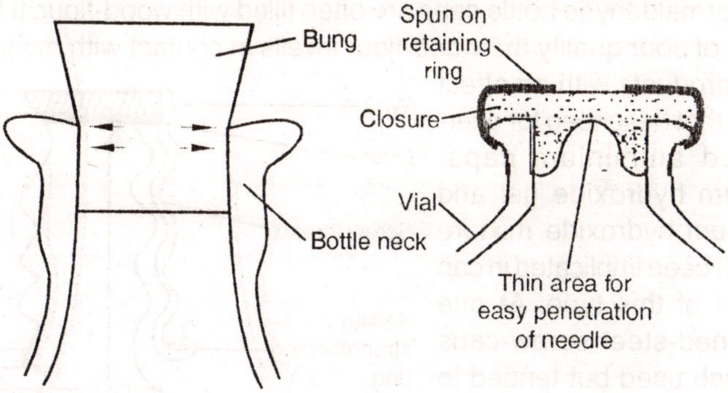

Fig. 7.14. Bung seals.

Screw-cap

The essential features (Fig. 7.15) are a cap with thread matching that of the container, and a tough linear behind which is placed a resilient wad. When the cap is screwed down the liner makes contact with the rim, distortion of the wad maintaining the liner in close contact with the rim. For efficient sealing, the thread on the cap must match that on the container; the rim of the container must be square and free from moulding imperfections. Although formerly a source of trouble, moulding imperfections have virtually been eliminated by the fire polishing process before entry of the glass container into the lehr as described in the section on glass. The performance of plastic containers in this respect has yet to be determined. The depth of the cap must be such that it does not foul the annulus on the neck of the bottle. Over-tightening must be avoided as this may crack or distort the cap. If a rubber wad is used (a liner is not required) elastic recovery from over-tightening may lead effectively to loosening of the closure. Finally, the screw-cap must be dimensionally stable. Should an aluminium cap be over-tightened the free edge may stretch and will not properly fit the screw thread on the container. Phenol-formaldehyde bottle caps are often filled with wood-flour. If the cap is basically of poor quality the wood-flour swells in contact with moisture from alkaline products with an effect similar to that described for over-tightened aluminium caps. Aluminium hydroxide gel and magnesium hydroxide mixture have both been implicated in cap distortion of this type. At one time, tinned-steel screw-caps were much used but tended to rust where friction with the thread damaged the tin coating. Both thermoplastics and thermosetting plastics are now much used for screw-cap production.

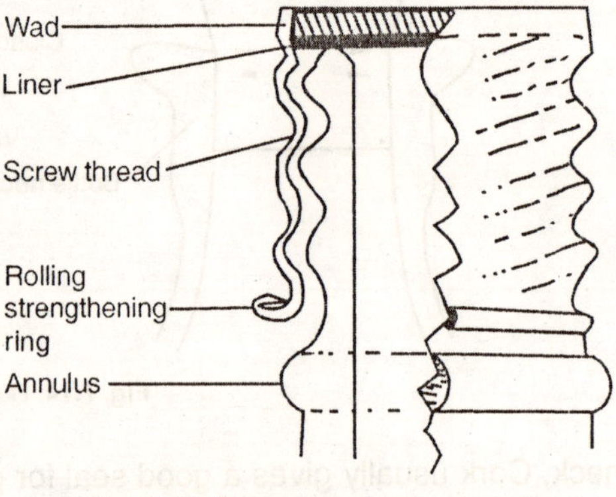

Fig. 7.15. Conventional screw-cap closure.

Liners for screw-caps must be tough. Ceresine impregnated paper, aluminium foil and plastics such as polythene are much used. Rubber is a good wad material provided it is not over-tightened; it is inert to most materials, except as described elsewhere, and does not support mould growth. Plastics share most of the properties of rubber but lack its resilience. For cheaper closures, wood pulp and felt board wads are employed but resilience is low and the reseal properties poor. Glue or resin bonded cork chips are also used but the former disintegrate in contact with aqueous liquids and support mould growth. The resin bonded variety is much better in these respects but distorts readily. Labour costs can be reduced if the wad liner are bonded together to give for instance, a polythene-faced resin-bonded cork wad. For some modern dispensing bottles the wad and the liner are replaced by a lip moulded into the screw-cap (Fig. 7.16). Rolled-on screw-caps avoid the problem of matching cap and container thread by using a straight-sided blank cap of which is held firmly against the rim of the neck while a rotating head forms the thread on the cap against that on the neck. A particular advantage of the rolled on type of seal is that provision can be made for an extended perforated skirt to fit over the annulus. The perforations must be broken before the cap may be removed. This particular system provides a pilfer-proof closure.

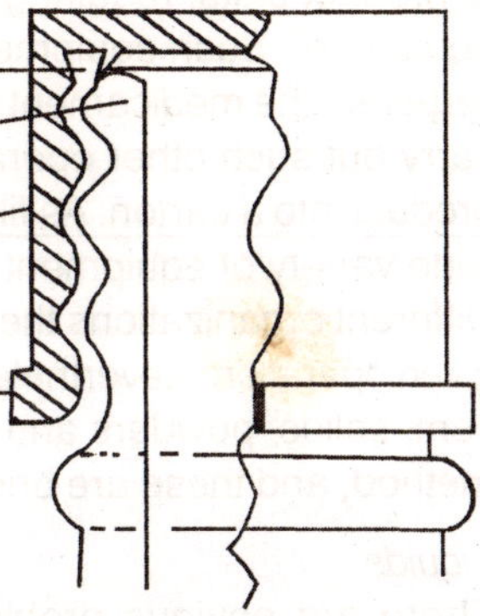

Fig. 7.16. Modern screw-cap closure.

Fusion Seals

This type of seal is used for ampoules and when properly made is hermetic. Products of the sachet type use a plastic fusion seal.

Package Testing

Each product has its own particular packaging problems, and some typical examples are discussed by Stephenson (1953). In general, it is necessary to establish:

(i) the amount, kind and toxicity of any materials that may be extracted from the package by the product and how this may be avoided,
(ii) whether any of the peofuct constituents are being absorbed and how this may be prevented or minimized,
(iii) the amount, size and kind of any particulate matter that may appear in the product and the steps necessary to prevent this,
(iv) the light transmission characteristic if the product is photosensitive,
(v) closure efficiency: this is best achieved by placing the product in the proposed package and nothig, say, weight changes over a period. An unfilled control will establish weight changes due to the package alone.
(vi) any specific interactions, how these arise and how they may be minimized, and,
(vii) whether the package satisfies legal requirements both in the country of origin and in those to which the product may be exported.

Filling

Packaging does not finish with the selection of a suitable container for the product; the latter must be filled into the container. This involves further processing and handling procedures which themselves may have an effect on the long-term stability of the product. If the batch is small, hand filling may be appropriate but on an industrial scale a batch may consist of thousands of product units, requiring for economic filling semi-automatic or automatic equipment. Such equipment would assemple the containers and closures, dispense the medicament into the conatiner, apply the closure and label and carry out such other operations as may be necessary such as placing the product into a carton. As filling operations are common to many industries, a wide variety of equipment is available to the pharmaceutical manufacturer. Different organizations therefore are unlikely to adopt the same system for a given operation. Nevertheless, there are problems basic to the filling of liquids, semi-solids, powders and unit-dose products, regardless of the production method, and these are briefly discussed here.

Liquids

There are obvious problems in filling suspensions, particularly official prepartions of kaolin, magnesium trisilicate, etc, which do not contain a suspending agent. If a product of the correct composition is to be packaged, the bulk must be continuously and thoroughly stirred throughout the entire filling operation with particular attention to the corners of the main container where stirring is relatively ineffective and where solid may accumulate. Furthermore, the transit time of the product from the bulk to the final container

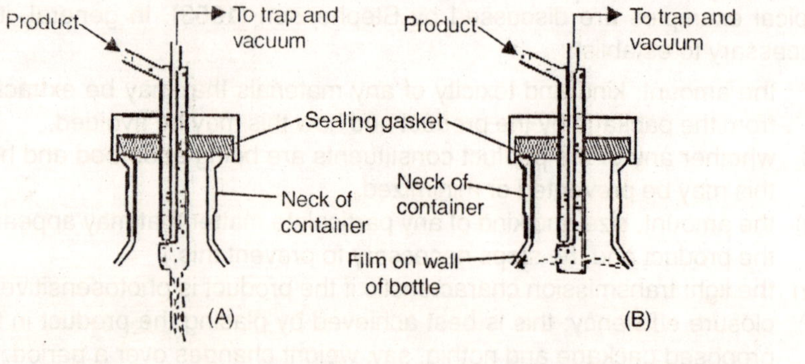

Fig. 7.17. Filing head for (A) non-foaming, and (B) foaming liquids (diagrammatic).

must be short to minimize sedimentation in the filling head. Apart from inaccuracies in the composition of the filled product, accumulating solid may jam the head mechanism. Even solutions present filing problems if the surface tension is low and the foam stability high. The liquid from the filling head (Fig. 7.17A) jetting into the product already in the bottle causes considerable agitation and build-up of a persistant froth. It is necessary for the vacuum line to suck off to the trap a large volume of froth before the bottle is properly filled with liquid product. A variant of the standard head, that is normally successful in avoiding this problem, is shown in Fig. 7.17B. The liquid jets onto the wall of the container and gently flows as a thin film without frothing. As these types of head fill to a given distance below the rim of the neck, volumetric accuracy of filling is entirely dependent on the observance of rigid tolerances during manufacture of the container. Furthermore, it is, not easy significantly to vary the filling volume from the nominal value for the container. Machine driven automatic syringes are employed if greater versatility is required, a method which finds considerable use in large scale ampoule filling. The syringe size and plunge stroke determine the volume transferred to the container.

Semi-solids

The filling of extracts, pastes, ointments, creams and other semi-solids is sometimes facilitated by warming the product to reduce viscosity. The technique must be applied with care as it may accelerate a degradative chemical reaction or have an effect on physical characteristics or stability. Sedimentation of suspended solids may occur if the viscosity of the vehicle is excessively reduced by heating, while permanent changes in consistency resulting from the breakdown of gel structure when creams are stirred or heated must be allowed for at the formulation stage. Viscous products, particularly those containing surfactants, are prone to aeration. Apart from the fact that aeration may accelerate oxidation, the entrained air bubbles are highly compressible and interfere with pumping when the product is homogenized or filled. Finally, it may not be possible to get the required amount of aerated product into the selected container.

Powders

It is often possible to resolve a powder filling problem into a powder flow problem—the subject is discussed in Chapter 17. It is worth bearing in mind, however, that the filling machine may demix the powder by stirring, may cause some particle size reduction by attrition in the feed-screw and may expose the powder to atmospheric oxygen or water vapour. If the product is particularly water sensitive, for example ampicillin, it may be necessary to provide low humidity filling conditions; it is generally accepted that, for stability, 1 per cent represents the maximum water content that may be permitted for penicillin formulations in powder form. There is often a dust hazard associated with the filling of powders and this must be carefully controlled to avoid toxic effects on the operatives and contamination of other products.

Unit-dose Products

These are usually packed in sub-multiples or multiples of a hundred. The tablets or capsules are placed in the filling machine and each unit separately interrupts a light beam or other mechanism that actuates a counting device whereby the product feed is shut off as soon as the correct number of units have been placed in the container. The filling process subjects the product to tumbling action and for this reason tablets should be formulated for high resistance to abrasion, particularly at the edges. To minimize abrasion when the tablet is in the container, the head-space is filled with 'necking' material. Formerly, cotton wool was much used but unless thoroughly dried its normal moisture content is sufficient to promote the degradation of sensitive products. Preformed polyurethane foam is now used for necking; it is easier to insert and has a very low moisture content.

Repackaging

After manufacture a product may undergo one further packaging process if prescription requirements do not match available pack sizes. The repackaging process often affects stability and poses other problems as well as those specifically associated with the correct choice of dispensing container. It might seem that these difficulties would be mitigated by the shorter period of further storage typical of dispensed items, but the prescribed quantity of drug may be intended to last the patient several months e.g. Tolbutamide or Primidone, and this factor must be assessed and taken into account. For most official preparations the packaging and storage requirements are stated in the relevant monographs. It should be noted that there are now precise meanings attached to such familiar phrases as light-resistance, freshly prepared etc.

Official directions for the preparation of creams are intended to minimize microbial contamination of the product, and this must not be increased during the repackaging operation. Additional problems are the possible interaction between the new container and the product and the selection of the correct diluent (if required) for the avoidance of incompatibilities and significant change in rheological bahaviour. The latter is also a factor to be considered in the provision of dispensing containers for mixtures and lotions. Although the original pack may serve as a guide, it is worth remembering that, even when thinned by shaking, thixotropic products such as Aluminium Hydroxide Gel and Mixture of Magnesium Hydroxide are more readily poured from a container with a wide neck. As discussed earlier, some wood-flour filled phenol-formaldehyde screw caps may swell or distort in contact with products of this type. Very thorough shaking of suspensions before dispensing is essential if the original composition is to be maintained in both the dispensed and remaining material. If the product is to be supplied in a diluted form, care must be taken that specific stabilizers and preservatives are present in sufficient quantity for efficient protective action. The oxygen permeability of a plastic container may be crucial to the stability of the product if absorption or dilution of the antioxidant has taken place.

Tablets are often repacked from bulk supplies, and the danger exists that progressive abrasion will occur as the tablets are tumbled when taken from the bulk container. The latter is frequently an aluminium or tinned-steel container or an amber glass bottle, all of which provide protection against light. The container selected for repackaging must also possess this property if the profuct is photo-sensitive drugs exhibit adequate stability if stored and dispensed in a well sealed container. More sensitive preparations—Effervescent Potassium Tablets, for example—require a much higher level of moisture exclusion. In commercial packs the tablets are sealed in a polythene bag with a desiccant sachet, enveloped in a further polythene bag and then issued in a sealed aluminium screw-capped container. Unless this order of moisture protection can be maintained in repackaging, it is probably best to obtain the prescribers agreement for the supply of the nearest size commercial pack.

It cannot be too strongly stated that thoughtful repackaging may be ruined if appropriate directions for storage and use are not given and explained to the patient.

Chapter 8

Tablets

ALUMINIUM HYDROXIDE AND MAGNESIUM TRISLICATE TABLETS

LABELLED FORMULA

Each tablet contains :

Dried Aluminium Hydroxide Gel	250 mg
Magnesium Trisilicate	500 mg

BATCH SIZE : 200,000 Tablets
PRACTICAL YIELD : 194,000 Tablets
USUAL PACKING : Strip of 10 Tablets

FORMULATION

S. No.	Ingredients	Quantity	Overages
1.	Dried Aluminium Hydroxide Gel	51.92 Kg.	
2.	Magnesium Trisilicate	100.00 Kg.	
3.	Icing Sugar	76.00 Kg.	
4.	Tricalcium Phosphate	0.50 Kg.	
5.	Starch	11.00 Kg.	
6.	Granulating Sugar	36.00 Kg.	
7.	Saccharin	174 gm.	
8.	Magnesium Stearate	6.00 Kg.	
9.	Fines	Q.S.	
10.	Menthol, Oil Peppermint & Coumarin	Q.S.	

MANUFACTURING PROCESS

1. Moisture content of granules should not be more than 4% and of Tablets not more than 6%.
2. For this product about 50% fines are required to facilitate compression.
3. Wet granulation done with boiling syrup, mixing for 10-15 minutes.
4. Dry the mass in the drier for about 6-8 hours and pass the semi dry mass through Fitz Mill or Multimill.
5. Again dry the granules and pass the dried granules through No. 18 sieve.
6. Determine the moisture content. Dry the granules till the moisture content is not more than 4%.

ALUMINIUM HYDROXIDE AND MAGNESIUM HYDROXIDE AND SIMETHICONE TABLETS

LABELLED FORMULA

Each tablet contains :

Dried Aluminium Hydroxide Gel 250 mg
Magnesium Trisilicate 250 mg
Activated Simethicone 50 mg.

BATCH SIZE : 50,000 Tablets
PRACTICAL YIELD : 48,500 Tablets
USUAL PACKING : Strip of 10 Tablets

FORMULATION

S. No.	Ingredients	Quantity	Overages
1.	Dried Aluminium Hydroxide Gel	13.10 Kg.	5%
2.	Magnesium Hydroxide	13.10 Kg.	5%
3.	Activated Simethicone	2.65 Kg.	5%
4.	Sugar Powder	17.00 Kg.	
5.	Methyl Paraben Sodium	100 g.	
6.	Propyl Paraben Sodium	50 g.	
7.	Sugar for Syrup	10.00 Kg.	
8.	Magnesium Stearate	2.00 Kg.	
9.	Talcum	2.00 Kg.	
10.	Menthol	50 g.	
11.	Essence Orange	8.40 ml.	

MANUFACTURING SPECIFICATIONS

1. Weight of granules 60 kg.
2. Weight of 20 Tablets-24 g.
3. Weight per tablet-12g.
4. Description-White round flat tablets.
5. Punch size-15 mm.
6. Weight variation about 3.5%.
7. Frability-not more than 1%.
8. Hardness-not less than 5 kg/cm^2.
9. Disintegration-does not apply.
10. Use Pharma-Grade Sugar as diluent.

MANUFACTURING PROCESS

1. Transfer Aluminium Hydroxide Gel and Magnesium Hydroxide to the mixer.

2. Add Pharma Grade Sugar.
3. Mix for 15 minutes.
4. Add Activated Simethicone and mix for another 45 minutes.
5. Prepare simple syrup with 10 kg sugar and 8 Litres water containing Methyl Paraben Sodium and Propyl Paraben Sodium. Allow the sugar syrup to cool to room temperature.
6. Add sugar syrup in the mixer and mix for 30 minutes.
7. Pass the mass through Multimill.
8. Dry the granules at 45°C.
9. Sieve the granules with Menthol dissolved in about 50 ml Chloroform. Also add 8.400 ml. of Oil Orange.
10. Lubricate the granules as usual before compression.

AMINOPHYLLINE TABLETS

LABELLED FORMULA

Each tablet contains :

Aminophylline 100 mg.

BATCH SIZE : 500,000 Tablets
STANDARD YIELD : 490,000 Tablets
USUAL PACKING : Bottle of 100 Tablets

FORMULATION

S. No.	Ingredients	Quantity	Overages
1.	Aminophylline	50.00 Kg.	
2.	Starch Talcum Granules	98.00 Kg.	
3.	Talcum	1.00 Kg.	
4.	Magnesium Stearate	1.50 Kg.	

PREPARATION OF STARCH TALCUM GRANULES

NOTE: Lactose cannot be used with Aminophylline

1. Take 70 kg. Talcum and 30 kg. Starch in a mixer and mix for ten minutes. Add Starch Paste in small portions while mixing is in operation. When the wet mass is ready, pass the same through No. 5 Mesh Stainless Steel Screen through a granulator.
2. Collect the granules and dry at 60°-7-° C for 8 hours. Pass the granules through granulator using No. 16 Mesh Screen.

MANUFACTURING SPECIFICATIONS

1.	Appearance	:	Off-white biconvex tablets
2.	Potency	:	Not less than 75% and nor more than 82% of Theophylline on anhydrous basis.
3.	Diameter	:	9 mm.
4.	Thickness	:	3.7 mm-3.9 mm.
5.	Hardness	:	5.0 to 7.0 kg/cm^2.
6.	Disintegration	:	Within 10 minutes.
7.	Moisture	:	Less than 1.5%.
8.	Weight of 20 tablets	:	6.0 g.

AMOXYCILLIN DISPERSIBLE TABLETS 125 MG.

LABELLED FORMULA

Each tablet contains :

Amoxycillin Trihydrate
equivalent to Amoxycillin 125 mg.

BATCH SIZE : 100,000 Tablets
PRACTICAL YIELD : 97,000 Tablets
USUAL PACKING : Strip of 15 Tablets
SHELF LIFE : 2 years

FORMULATION

S. No.	Ingredients	Quantity	Overages
1.	Amoxycillin Trihydrate	15.30 Kg.	
2.	Starch	1.20 Kg.	
3.	Microcrystalline Cellulose	0.37 Kg.	
4.	Sodium Saccharin	0.30 Kg.	
5.	Sodium Chloride	0.20 Kg.	
6.	Dry Flavours	0.40 Kg.	
7.	Talcum	0.16 Kg.	
8.	Magnesium Stearate	0.10 Kg.	
9.	Ethyl Cellulose	0.10 Kg.	

MANUFACTURING PROCESS

Mix all the active and inactive ingredients, granules with binder solution and prepare wet granules as usual. Dry the granules, and mix with lubricants.

TECHNICAL SPECIFICATIONS

Average weight of tablets	:	180 mg. ± 2%.
Disintegration Time	:	N.M.T. 3 minutes.
Thickness	:	3.4 mm.
Hardness	:	2.0 to 5.0 kg/cm².

AMOXYCILLIN DISPERSIBLE TABLETS 250 MG.

LABELLED FORMULA

Each tablet contains :

Amoxycillin Trihydrate
equivalent to Amoxycillin 250 mg.

BATCH SIZE	:	400,000 Tablets
PRACTICAL YIELD	:	390,000 Tablets
USUAL PACKING	:	Strip of 10 Tablets

FORMULATION

S. No.	Ingredients	Quantity	Overages
1.	Amoxycillin Trihydrate	12.00 Kg.	
2.	Microcrystalline Cellulose	13.50 Kg.	
3.	Dried Starch	8.00 Kg.	
4.	Kollidon C.L.	4.80 Kg.	
5.	Sodium Starch Glycolate	1.70 Kg.	
6.	Colloidal Silicon Dioxide	2.00 Kg.	
7.	Ethyl Cellulose	2.50 Kg.	
8.	Methanol	3.00 Kg.	
9.	Dichloromethane	140.00 Kg.	
10.	Tartrazine Yellow Colour	0.03 Kg.	
11.	Microcrystalline Cellulose	34.80 Kg.	
12.	Starch	25.00 Kg.	
13.	Starch for Paste	2.00 Kg.	
14.	Sodium Saccharin	1.60 Kg.	
15.	Collo idal Silicon Dioxide	2.00 Kg.	
16.	Pineapple Dry Flavour	2.40 Kg.	
17.	Orange Dry Flavour	2.40 Kg.	
18.	Peppermint Dry Flavour	0.24 Kg.	
19.	Kollidon C.L.	4.80 Kg.	
20.	Talcum	2.00 Kg.	
21.	Magnesium Stearate	1.20 Kg.	
22.	Purified Water	32.00 Lit.	

MANUFACTURING PROCESS

1. Mix sieved Amoxycillin Trihydrate, Microcrystalline Cellulose, Dried Starch, Sodium Starch Glycolate, Kollidon C.L., Colloidal Silicon Dioxide, Dry Flavours and collect in plastic bags.
2. Mix sifted Talcum and Magnesium Stearate and collect in separate plastic bag.
3. Charge 10.00 Kg. of Dichloromethane in S.S. container. Add Ethyl Cellulose and dissolve to get a clear solution.
4. Dissolve 22 g. Tartrazine colour in 3.0 Lit. of Methanol and filter.
5. Add solution 4 to solution 3 and add the remaining quantity of Dichloromethane mix.
6. Charge the dried mix from 1, add binder solution 5 with mixing to 6. Add more Dichloromethane to get proper wet mass. Pass the wet mass through Multimill.
7. Dry the granules at 45°C till L.O.D. at 150°C for 1 hour is N.M.T. 11%.
8. Prepare binder solution for granulation of inactive ingredients by dissolving Colour Tartrazine 10.0 g. in it. Suspend 2 kg. Starch in the purified water.
9. Transfer 30.0 Lit. of purified water to another S.S. vessel, heat to 85°C and dissolve 1.60 kg. of Sodium Saccharin.
10. Transfer Starch Slurry from 8 into hot solution 9 and stir till a uniform paste is formed. Cool to room temperature.
11. Transfer the sifted Microcrystalline Cellulose 34.8 Kg. and Starch 25 Kg. to a mass mixer and mix for 20 minutes. Add starch paste from (9) and mix for 20—25 minutes. Add more water if necessary to get a wet mass. Pass through Multimill and dry the wet granules at 50°C for 15 hours in a Tray Drier (Moisture not more than 4.0%).

Lubrication & Mixing

1. Transfer Amoxycillin granules and starch granules from (11) to a Drum Mixer, Transfer all dry flavours in Colloidal Silicon Dioxide and mix for 20 minutes.
2. Add Talcum and Magnesium Stearate mix and lubricate for 10 minutes.
3. Check for Loss on Drying (Not more than 8.5% at 105°C for 1 hour).

NOTE: Lubrication to be carried out at RH below 45% and temperature below 25°C.

AMOXYCILLIN TABLETS

LABELLED FORMULA

Each sugar coated tablet contains :

Amoxycillin Trihydrate
equivalent to Amoxycillin 250 mg.

BATCH SIZE : 100,000 Tablets
PRACTICAL YIELD : 98,000 Tablets
USUAL PACKING : Blister of 10 Tablets
SHELF LIFE : 2 Years

FORMULATION

S. No.	Ingredients	Quantity	Overages
1.	Amoxycillin Trihydrate	30.2 Kg.	5%
2.	Microcrystalline Cellulose	5.00 Kg.	
3.	Starch	5.00 Kg.	
4.	Lactose	5.00 Kg.	
5.	Polyvinylpyrrolidone	0.50 Kg.	
6.	Isopropyl Alcohol	15.0 Kg.	
7.	Sodium Starch Glycolate	2.00 Kg.	
8.	Aerosil	1.50 Kg.	
9.	Talcum	0.30 Kg.	
10.	Magnesium Stearate	0.50 Kg.	

MANUFACTURING SPECIFICATION

Punch Size : 15/32 inch.
Hardness : 3 to 4 kg/cm^2.
Weight per tablet : 500 mg. ± 25 mg.
Disintegration Time : N.M.T. 15 minutes
Friability : N.M.T. 0.5%.

MANUFACTURING PROCESS

1. Mix sifted Amoxycillin Trihydrate, Microcrystalline Cellulose, Starch and Lactose in a mass mixer and mix for 50 minutes.
2. Dissolve Polyvinylpyrrolidone in Isopropyl Alcohol.
3. Granulate the dry mix with the granulating solution.
4. Pass the wet mass through No. 8 mesh and collect sieved material.
5. Dry the wet granules in a Fluid Bed Drier without heating at room temperature till the granules are dried.
6. Pass the dried granules through 12 mesh sieve.

7. Lubricate the dried granules with sifted Aerosil, Magnesium Stearate, Talcum and Sodium Starch Glycolate in a Drum Mixer for 15 minutes.
8. The granules are ready for compression.

NOTE: These tablets can be sugar coated or film coated.

AMPICILLIN, CLOXACILLIN AND LACTOBACILLUS SPOROGENES DISPERSIBLE TABLETS

LABELLED FORMULA

Each flavoured dispersible tablet contains :

Ampicillin Trihydrate equivalent to Ampicillin	125 mg.
Cloxacillin Sodium equivalent to Cloxacillin	125 mg.
Lactobacillus Sporogenes	60 million spores

BATCH SIZE : 100,000 Tablets
PRACTICAL YIELD : 97,000 Tablets
USUAL PACKING : Blister of 10 Tablets

FORMULATION

S. No.	Ingredients	Quantity	Overages
1.	Ampicillin Trihydrate (Compacted)	14.66 Kg.	2%
2.	Cloxacillin Sodium (Compacted)	13.90 Kg.	2%
3.	Lactobacillus Sporogenes (6,000 million spores per gm.)	1.50 Kg.	50%
4.	Ethyl Cellulose	0.60 Kg.	
5.	Microcrystalline Cellulose	16.30 Kg.	
6.	Sodium Saccharin	1.00 Kg.	
7.	Menthol	0.30 Kg.	
8.	Flavouring Agent	0.50 Kg.	
9.	Crospovidone	2.00 Kg.	
10.	Colloidal Silicone Dioxide	0.40 Kg.	
11.	Magnesium Stearate	0.10 Kg.	
12.	Drymix Rasberry Flavour	0.60 Kg.	
13.	Isopropyl Alcohol	10.00 Lit.	
14.	Colloidal Silicon Dioxide	1.30 Kg.	
15.	Sodium Saccharin	1.30 Kg.	
16.	D.M. Water	20.00 Lit.	

MANUFACTURING PROCESS

NOTES:

1. Granulation of Ampicillin and Cloxacillin must be done in Flame Proof Area.

2. All operations must be carried out under relative humidity of 35—45% and temperature below 25°C.
3. Dust masks, gloves and goggles must be worn while handling the raw materials and products.

Part I: Preparation of Coating Solution

To 9.9 Lit. Isopropyl Alcohol add 0.590 Kg. Ethyl Cellulose slowly with constant stirring till a clear solution is obtained (10 Lit.).

Part II: Preparation of Ampicillin Trihydrate Granules

1. Granulate sifted Ampicillin Trihydrate with 7.5 Lit. of Coating solution from Part I.
2. Spread the wet granules on trays and dry in dehumidified area overnight.
3. Pass the dried granules through 30 mesh sieve in dehumidified area and check the moisture content. Limit N.M.T. 14%.

Part III: Preparation of Cloxacillin Sodium Granules

1. Granulate the sifted Cloxacillin Sodium with 2.5 Lit. of Coating solution from Part I.
2. Dry the granules overnight under dehumidified conditions.
3. Pass the dried granules through 30 mesh sieve and check the moisture content. Limit N.M.T. 5%.

Part IV: Preparation of Microcrystalline Cellulose Granules

1. Mix the sifted Microcrystalline Cellulose and Colloidal Silicon Dioxide in the Planetary Mixer and mix for 15 minutes.
2. Dissolve 1.30 Kg. Sodium Saccharin in 20 Lit. water and granulate the dry mix obtained in Step 1. Pass the mass through 12 mesh sieve.
3. Dry the granules at 60°C in a drier and check the moisture content (Limit 2-3% by I.R. at 100°C for 5 minutes). Sift the dried granules.

Part V: Mixing with Lactobacillus Sporogenes

1. Mix 1.5 Kg. Microcrystalline Cellulose Granules with sifted Lactobacillus spores.
2. Again mix 5.0 Kg. of Microcrystalline Cellulose Granules with granules obtained in Step 1.
3. Mix Ampicillin Trihydrate Granules from Part II with Cloxacillin Sodium Granules from Part III and Lactobacillus Granules obtained from Step 2 in a Planetary Mixer for 15 minutes at slow speed.
4. Dissolve Menthol in about 100 ml. of Isopropyl Alcohol.
5. Sift Sodium Saccharin, Crospovidone, Magnesium Stearate, Colloidal Silicon Dioxide and other dry mix flavours through 30 mesh sieve.

Part VI:

1. Add Menthol-Alcohol solution from Step 4 to the granules from Step 3 in a Planetary Mixer and mix for 5 minutes.
2. Transfer the sifted lubricants from Step 5 to a Planetary Mixer and mix with granules of Step 1 above for 10 minutes. Record the moisture content (Limit 11-13%).
3. The lubricated granules are now ready for compression.

TECHNICAL SPECIFICATIONS

Average weight of tablets	:	545mg. ± 10 mg.
Disintegration Time	:	Not more than 2 minutes.
Thickness	:	4.4-4.5 mm.
Hardness	:	2-4 kg/cm^2
Friability	:	N.M.T. 2%.

ANALGIN AND DICYCLOMINE HYDROCHLORIDE TABLETS-I

LABELLED FORMULA

Each tablet contains :

Analgin	500 mg.
Dicyclomine Hydrochloride	15 mg.

BATCH SIZE	:	100,000 Tablets
PRACTICAL YIELD	:	97,000 Tablets
USUAL PACKING	:	Strip of 10 Tablets

FORMULATION

S. No.	Ingredients	Quantity	Overages
1.	Analgin	50.00 Kg.	
2.	Dicyclomine Hydrochloride	1.50 Kg.	
3.	Starch	4.50 Kg.	
4.	Starch for Paste	1.50 Kg.	
5.	Talcum	0.50 Kg.	
6.	Magnesium Stearate	0.40 Kg.	
7.	Dried Starch	0.50 Kg.	

MANUFACTURING SPECIFICATIONS

1. Standard Wet Granulation process to be adopted.

ANALGIN AND DICYCLOMINE HYDROCHLORIDE TABLETS-II

LABELLED FORMULA

Each tablet contains :

Analgin	500 mg.
Dicyclomine Hydrochloride	10 mg.

BATCH SIZE	:	100,000 Tablets
PRACTICAL YIELD	:	98,000 Tablets
USUAL PACKING	:	Strip of 10 Tablets

FORMULATION

S. No.	Ingredients	Quantity	Averages
1.	Analgin	50.00 Kg.	
2.	Dicyclomine Hydrochloride	1.05 Kg.	
3.	Lactose	2.00 Kg.	
4.	Starch	6.25 Kg.	
5.	Gelatin	625 g.	
6.	Magnesium Stearate	625 g.	
7.	Talcum	625 g.	
8.	Menthol Carboxy Cellulose	625 g.	
9.	Aerosil	625 g.	
10.	Sodium Metabisulphite	625 g.	
11.	Methyl Paraben	11.25 g.	
12.	Propyl Paraben	1.25 g.	
13.	Colour Sunset Yellow	62.5 g.	
14.	Denatured Spirit	Q.S.	

MANUFACTURING SPECIFICATIONS

1. Description—Yellow, round, flat, uncoated tablets.
2. Total weight of granules—62.5 Kg.
3. Weight per tablet—625 mg.

MANUFACTURING PROCESS

1. Mix Analgin, Lactose and 3.5 Kg. Starch.
2. Prepare the granulating paste with 6 Lit. water, 1 Kg. Starch, 625 g. Gelatin, Methyl Paraben, Propyl Paraben and Sodium Metabisulphite, Granulate (1) with this paste and dry the granules at 60°C.
3. Granulate Dicyclomine Hydrochloride with Denatured Spirit and Sunset Yellow Colour dissolved in water. Dry the granules at 40°C.
4. Lubricate the granules as usual making up the weight to 62.5 Kg. with dried Starch.

ANALGIN TABLETS

LABELLED FORMULA

Each tablet contains :

Analgin 500 mg.

BATCH SIZE : 200,000 Tablets
PRACTICAL YIELD : 196,000 Tablets
USUAL PACKING : Strip of 10 Tablets

FORMULATION

S. No.	Ingredients	Quantity	Averages
1.	Analgin	100.0 Kg.	
2.	Starch	12.0 Kg.	
3.	Starch for paste	2.0 Kg.	
4.	Starch	4.0 Kg.	
5.	Magnesium Stearate	3.0 Kg.	
6.	Guar Gum (Dealca P)	2.0 Kg.	
7.	Talcum	2.0 Kg.	

MANUFACTURING SPECIFICATIONS

1. Punch Size : 13.3 mm Diameter bevelled punches, one punch embossed ANALGIN and other punch with divided line.
2. Potency : 98 to 102% of claim
3. Thickness : 3.7-3.9 mm.
4. Hardness : 4.0 to 6.0 kg/cm^2
5. Disintegration : Within 8 minutes
6. Moisture : Should be less than 1.5%
7. Weight of 20 tablets : 12.5 g.

ASCORBIC ACID TABLETS 100 mg.

LABELLED FORMULA

Each tablet contains :

Ascorbic Acid 100 mg.
Sodium Ascorbic 450 mg.

BATCH SIZE : 150,000 Tablets
PRACTICAL YIELD : 145,000 Tablets
USUAL PACKING : Strip of 10 Tablets

FORMULATION

S. No.	Ingredients	Quantity	Averages
1.	Ascorbic Acid	15.75 Kg.	5%
2.	Sodium Ascorbate	70.95 Kg.	5%
3.	Sugar (Pharma Grade)	55.05 Kg.	
4.	Sodium Saccharin	0.60 Kg.	
5.	Sodium Metabisulphite	0.24 Kg.	
6.	Disodium Edetate	0.15 Kg.	
7.	Sunset Yellow Colour	0.69 Kg.	
8.	Tartrazine Yellow Colour	0.25 Kg.	
9.	Polyvinylpyrrolidone	1.65 Kg.	
10.	Aerosil	1.65 Kg.	
11.	Industrial Methylated Spirit	5.00 Lit.	
12.	D.M. Water	3.00 Lit.	
13.	Orange Capsoroma	0.82 Kg.	
14.	Magnesium Stearate	2.19 Kg.	

MANUFACTURING SPECIFICATIONS

Average weight of tablet : 1000 mg.

Hardness : 4.0 to 8.0 kg/cm^2.

MANUFACTURING PROCESS

1. Pass ingredients No. 1 to No. 6 through Multimill fitted with 0.5 mm. screen.
2. Dissolve Sunset Yellow and Tartrazine colours in 3 Lit. D.M. Water.
3. Load the ingredients of (1) to a mixer and mix for 15 minutes.
4. Pour the colour solution slowly at high speed of mixer. Then add Industrial Methylated spirit slowly at slow speed till desired consistency is obtained.
5. Prepare the wet granules by passing through Multimill (10 mm sieve).
6. Dry the granules first in air for 30 minutes and then at 50° C for 16 minutes.
7. Check the moisture content. It should not be more than 1%.
8. Pass the dry granules through Multimill (2 mm sieve).
9. Remove 10 kg. fines from the granules, mix orange casoroma and Magnesium Stearate with fines and finally mix with the bulk of granules for 8 minutes.
10. The granules are ready for compression.

ASCORBIC ACID TABLETS 500 mg.

LABELLED FORMULA
Each tablet contains :
Ascorbic Acid 500 mg.

BATCH SIZE : 100,000 Tablets
PRACTICAL YIELD : 98,000 Tablets
USUAL PACKING : Strip of 10 Tablets

FORMULATION

S. No.	Ingredients	Quantity	Overages
1.	Ascorbic Acid (Coated)	52.00 Kg.	4%
2.	Lactose	2.60 Kg.	
3.	Dried Starch	2.20 Kg.	
4.	Polyvinylpyrrolidone	0.50 Kg.	
5.	Propyl Gallate	0.06 Kg.	
6.	Starch for Paste	0.50 Kg.	
7.	Methyl Paraben	0.04 Kg.	
8.	Isopropyl Alcohol	1.80 Kg.	
9.	Aerosil	0.30 Kg.	
10.	Stearic Acid	1.20 Kg.	

MANUFACTURING SPECIFICATIONS

Weight per tablet : 594 mg.
Loss on drying : N.M.T. 1%
Hardness : 2.0 Kg/cm^2
Friability : Less than 1%
Disintegration Time : 3 minutes

MANUFACTURING PROCESS

1. Dissolve Propyl Gallate in Isopropyl Alcohol.
2. Spread the solution over Vitamin C and mix well.
3. Air-dry the mix and pass through 30 mesh.
4. Sift Lactose and Dried Starch through 40 mesh.
5. Prepare a slurry of Starch for paste in double the quantity of D.M. water.
6. Dissolve Polyvinylpyrrolidone in 24 times of D.M. water, add Methyl Paraben and boil till a clear solution is obtained. Filter the solution through cloth.

7. Add the Starch Slurry from (5), heat and stir continuously to get a uniform paste.
8. Mix ingredients from (1) and (2). Add Starch Paste and mix for 10 minutes. Add the boiled and cooled D.M. water, if required, for proper wet granulation.
9. Pass the wet mass through Multimill.
10. Dry the wet granules at 40°C to 45°C inlet temperature. Sift the dry granules through No. 16 mesh.
11. Load the dry granules in a Planetary Mixer and mix for 5 minutes. Check the moisture content. It should be 0.8 to 1.2% at 60°C by Infra Red Moisture Balance.
12. Sift Aerosil and Stearic Acid through 40 mesh. Separate the fines (about 3% of total weight) by passing the granules through 40 mesh.
13. Mix these fines with Aerosil and Stearic acid and again pass through 40 mesh.
14. Add this fines mixture to the mixer and mix for 5 to 10 minutes.
15. Punching should be done under dehumidified conditions on the second day only.

ASPIRIN, PARACETAMOL AND CAFFEINE TABLETS

LABELLED FORMULA

Each tablet contains :

Aspirin	200 mg.
Paracetamol	250 mg.
Caffeine Anhydrous	30 mg.

BATCH SIZE : 100,000 Tablets
PRACTICAL YIELD : 98,000 Tablets
USUAL PACKING : Strip of 10 Tablets

FORMULATION

S. No.	Ingredients	Quantity	Overages
1.	Acetyl Salicylic Acid	20.00 Kg.	
2.	Paracetamol	25.00 Kg.	
3.	Caffeine Anhydrous	3.00 Kg.	
4.	Maize Starch for paste	1.20 Kg.	
5.	Dried Starch	2.80 Kg.	
6.	Polyvinylpyrrolidone	0.35 Kg.	
7.	Methyl Paraben	0.02 Kg.	
8.	Magnesium Stearate	0.18 Kg.	
9.	Talcum	0.44 Kg.	

MANUFACTURING SPECIFICATIONS

Weight per tablet	:	530 mg.
Punch Size	:	11.5 mm.
Hardness	:	4.0 to 5.0 Kg/cm^2
Disintegration Time	:	Less than 3 minutes
Friability	:	N.M.T. 1% for 4 minutes

MANUFACTURING PROCESS

1. Mix previously sifted Paracetamol and Maize Starch in a Planetary Mixer.
2. Dissolve Methyl Paraben and Polyvinylpyrrolidone in hot water, filter and add Maize Starch slurry to make a mucilage.
3. Granulate Paracetamol and Maize Starch mix with Polyvinylpyrrolidone-Starch Mucilage.
4. Pass the wet mass through Multimill to make the wet granules.
5. Dry the granules so that the moisture content is 1.5 to 2.0%. Pass through No. 16 mesh.
6. Lubricate Aspirin with Talcum and send the powders for slugging. Break the slugs and pass through No. 16 mesh. Store these granules in a dehumidified room at RH of less than 40%.
7. Blend the Paracetamol granules, Aspirin granules and Caffiene in/a Drum Mixer for 5 minutes. Add sifted Magnesium Stearate (100 mesh) and mix for further 2 minutes.
8. The tablets should be compressed at RH of 40 to 45% and room temperature of 18°C to 22°C.

ASPIRIN, CHLORPHENIRAMINE MALEATE AND PHENYLEPHEINE HYDROCHLORIDE TABLETS

LABELLED FORMULA

Each tablet contains :

Aspirin	300 mg.
Chlorpheniramine Maleate	2 mg.
Phenylepherine Hydrochloride	2.5 mg.

BATCH SIZE	:	100,000 Tablets
PRACTICAL YIELD	:	98,000 Tablets
USUAL PACKING	:	Strip of 10 Tablets

FORMULATION

S. No.	Ingredients	Quantity	Overages
1.	Acetyl Salicylic Acid	30.00 Kg.	
2.	Chlorpheniramine Maleate	208 g.	
3.	Phenylepherine Hydrochloride	255 g.	
4.	Dicalcium Phosphate	15.0 Kg.	
5.	Starch	16.0 Kg.	
6.	Carboxymethylcellulose Sodium	2.0 Kg.	
7.	Magnesium Stearate	700 g.	
8.	Talcum	2.8 Kg.	
9.	Gelatin	300 g.	

MANUFACTURING SPECIFICATIONS

1. Total Weight : 67 Kg.
2. Weight per tablet : 670 mg.
3. Thickness : 3.8 ± 0.2 mm.
4. Punch Size : 12.6 mm.
5. Disintegration Time : Less than 5 minutes

MANUFACTURING PROCESS

1. Mix Aspirin, 1/2 Carboxymethylcellulose Sodium, 300 gm. Talc and 300 gm. Magnesium Stearate. Feed the material to a slugging machine. Break the slugs to get granules of 16 Mesh size.
2. Mix Chlorpheniramine Maleate, Phenylephrine Hydrochloride, Dicalcium Phosphate and Starch and undertake wet granulation with a paste of Gelatin 1.2 Kg., Starch and 7.5 Litres purified water.
3. Mix granules of (1) and (2) and lubricate with Magnesium Stearate, Talcum and add balance of Carboxymethylcellulose Sodium and dry starch as disintegrating agents.
4. Compress tablets as usual.

ATENOLOL TABLETS

LABELLED FORMULA

Each tablet contains :

Atenolol 100 mg.

BATCH SIZE : 50,000 Tablets
PRACTICAL YIELD : 48,500 Tablets
USUAL PACKING : Strip of 10 Tablets

FORMULATION

S. No.	Ingredients	Quantity	Overages
1.	Atenolol	5.00 Kg.	
2.	Lactose	4.00 Kg.	
3.	Starch	4.00 Kg.	
4.	Starch for paste	0.80 Kg.	
5.	Magnesium Stearate	0.10 Kg.	
6.	Talcum	0.15 Kg.	
7.	Sodium Lauryl Sulphate	0.05 Kg.	
8.	Aerosil	0.05 Kg.	
9.	Guar Gum	0.10 Kg.	
10.	Dried Starch	0.75 Kg.	

MANUFACTURING SPECIFICATIONS

Punch Size : 11/32 inch.
Hardness : 2 to 3 kg/cm^2
Disintegration Time : N.M.T. 7 minutes

MANUFACTURING PROCESS

Follow the Standard Wet Granulation Process.

B. COMPLEX WITH VITAMIN C TABLETS

LABELLED FORMULA

Each coated tablet contains :

Vitamin B_1 10 mg.
Vitamin B_2 10 mg.
Vitamin B_6 3 mg.
Niacinamide 50 mg.
Folic Acid 1 mg.
Vitamin B_{12} 5 mcg.
Calcium Pantothenate 25 mg.
Ascorbic Acid 150 mg.

BATCH SIZE : 100,000 Tablets
PRACTICAL YIELD : 97,000 Tablets
USUAL PACKING : Bottle of 100 Tablets

FORMULATION

S. No.	Ingredients	Quantity	Averages
1.	Thiamine Hydrochloride	1.50 Kg.	50%
2.	Tartaric Acid	270 g.	-
3.	Disodium Edetate	90 g.	-
4.	Thiourea	90 g.	-
5.	Ascorbic Acid	18.00 Kg.	20%
6.	Ethyl Cellulose	180 g.	-
7.	Propyl Gallate	18 g.	-
8.	Rectified Spirit	3.0 Lit.	-
9.	Lactose	40.00 Kg.	-
10.	Pyridoxine Hydrochloride	1.15 Kg.	15%
11.	Nicotinamide	5.50 Kg.	10%
12.	Calcium Pantothenate	2.75 Kg.	10 %
13.	Polyvinylpyrrolidone	100 g.	-
14.	Starch	4.00 Kg.	-
15.	Gelatin	800 g.	-
16.	Folic Acid	150 g.	-
17.	Cyanocobalamin	1.0 g.	-
18.	Pyridoxine Hydrochloride	345 g.	-
19.	Talc	800 g.	-
20.	Magnesium Stearate	800 g.	-
21.	Aerosil	800 g.	-

MANUFACTURING SPECIFICATIONS

1.	Description	:	Sugar coated, Pink coloured and Capsule shaped tablets.
2.	Punch Size	:	Length 21.3 mm. Width 7.7 mm.
3.	Total Weight of uncoated Tablets	:	80 Kg.
4.	Weight per tablet (uncoated)	:	800 mg.
5.	Weight per tablet (coated)	:	1.2 gm.

MANUFACTURING PROCESS

1. Dissolve Tartaric Acid 270 gm., Thiourea 10 gm. and Disodium Edetate 10 gm. in water. Coat vitamin B_1 with this solution and dry at low temperature.
2. Coat the above Vitamin B_1 with M.P.S. dissolved in Chloroform and dry coated Vitamin B_1 at 50° C.

3. Mix Vitamin C with Propyl Gallate and coat with Ethyl Cellulose dissolved in Rectified Spirit. Dry at 40° C in a Tray Drier.
4. Mix Vitamin B_2, Lactose 5 kg., Calcium Pantothenate, 90g. Disodium Edetate, Thiourea, 100g Polyvinylpyrrolidone and Niacinamide 5.5 kg. Granulate the above mixture with Rectified Spirit to get a wet mass. Dry the granules at 50°C.
5. Mix 3.5 Kg. Lactose with 2 Kg. Starch and granulate with a paste of Gelatin and Starch 500 g. (4 litres) and dry the granules at 100° C in Fluid Bed Drier.
6. Mix the granules of (2), (3), (4) and (5) and lubricate with Talcum 800 g., Magnesium Stearate 800 g., and Aerosil 800 g. and the balance of dried starch.

   Total weight of Granules should be 80 Kg.

SUGAR COATING PROCESS

A. COATING MATERIALS

1.	Shellac	800	g.
2.	Denatured Spirit	1.5	Lit.
3.	Talcum	20.0	Kg.
4.	Sugar	20.0	Kg.
5.	Gelatin	1.0	Kg.
6.	Gum Acacia	1.0	Kg.
7.	Colour Erythrosine	40	g.
8.	Benzene	1.0	Lit.

B. COATING PROCESS

1. Dissolve Shellac in 1.5 Lit. Denatured Spirit and give two coats. Dry at 60° C. Weight of 20 tablets = 16.3 g.
2. Apply the sub-coating with Gelatin Paste 8 Lit. and Talcum 17 Kg. in 8 coats. Dry at 60° C. Weight of 20 tablets = 21g. Vitamin B_6, B_{12} and Folic Acid to be added in the sub-coating materials.
3. For smoothening mix 4.5 Lit. Syrup with 3 Lit. Gelatin Paste and apply 10 coats with 3 Kg. Talc. Dry at 60° C. Weight of 20 tablets = 22.5g.
4. Carry out the final smoothening with 10 Lit. simple syrup, 200g. Titanium Dioxide, Erythromysine colour 40g. and Gelatin Paste 500 ml. apply 25 coats. Dry at 60° C. Weight of 20 tablets = 24gm.
5. For polishing of tablets dissolve 20g. beeswax and 20g. carnauba wax in 1 Lit benzene.

BETAMETHASONE AND DEXCHLORPHENITRAMINE MALEATE TABLETS

LABELLED FORMULA

Each tablet contains :

Betamethasone	0.275 mg.
Dexchlorpheniramine Maleate	2.00 mg.

BATCH SIZE : 1,200,000 Tablets
PRACTICAL YIELD : 11,60,000 Tablets
USUAL PACKING : Strip of 10 Tablets

FORMULATION

S. No.	Ingredients	Quantity in Kg.			
		Sec. I	Sec. II	Sec. III	Sec. IV
1.	Betamethasone (Micronized)	0.110	0.110	0.110	0.33
2.	Dexchlorpheniramine Maleate	0.800	0.800	0.800	2.400
3.	Corn Starch	4.000	4.000	4.000	12.000
4.	Lactose	33.900	33.900	33.900	101.700
5.	Red Colour	0.030	0.030	0.030	0.090
6.	Gelatin	0.960	0.960	0.960	2.880
7.	Purified Water	3.8 L	3.8 L	3.8 L	11.4 L
8.	Magnesium	-	-	-	0.600

MANUFACTURING PROCESS

1. Mix Starch and Lactose in Planetary Mixer.
2. Prepare Gelatin - Dye active Solution by adding Red Colour and Gelatin in 2.8 Lit. distilled water. Stir and allow to soak for 10 minutes. Reserve 1.0 Lit of distilled water and maintian at 55°C for rinsing the Gelatin Dye Active Solution in Step number 3. Heat Gelatin dye water to 55°C while stirring to effect the solution.

   Section I:

   Dissolve Dexchlorpheniramine Maleate in Gelatin Dye solution, add Betamethasone and disperse in Gelatin - dye solution by stirring for 15 minutes. Repeat the process for **Section II** and **Section III**.
3. Incorporate Active Gelatin - dye solution at 55° C to mixture of Corn Starch and Lactose in Planetary Mixer and mix for 30 minutes.
4. Granulate wet mass on Multimill.
5. Semi dry the granules in a Fluid Bed Dried at 40° C for 20 minutes.

6. Pass the semi dried granules on Multimill and dry the granules in fluid bed drier at 40° C to attain the temperature of granules to 36° C.
7. Transfer the dried granules of one of the sections into the drum mixer. Add Magnesium Stearate into the section in the drum. Transfer the dried granules of the remaining two sections into the drum mixer. Mix for 25 minutes.
8. Transfer the blended granules into suitable containers for further compression.

CO-TRIMOXAZOLE TABLETS

LABELLED FORMULA

Each tablet contains :

Sulphamethoxazole 400 mg.
Trimethoprim 80 mg.

BATCH SIZE : 100,000 Tablets
PRACTICAL YIELD : 98,000 Tablets
USUAL PACKING : Strip of 10 Tablets

FORMULATION

S. No.	Ingredients	Quantity	Overages
1.	Sulphamethoxazole	40.80 Kg.	2%
2.	Trimethoprim	8.16 Kg.	2%
3.	Starch	12.50 Kg.	-
4.	Talcum	1.30 Kg.	-
5.	Magnesium Stearate	300 g.	-
6.	Gelatin	600 g.	-
7.	Methyl Paraben	11.7 g.	-
8.	Propyl Paraben	1.3 g.	-
9.	Aerosil	1.30 Kg.	-

MANUFACTURING SPECIFICATIONS

1. Prepare granules by Wet Granulation Process using Starch/Gelatin Paste.
2. Total weight of granules : 65 Kg.
3. Weight per tablet : 650 mg.

CALCIUM AND VITAMIN D TABLETS

LABELLED FORMULA

Each tablet contains :

Dicalcium Phosphate 500 mg.

Vitamin D_3 500 I.U.

BATCH SIZE : 100,000 Tablets

PRACTICAL YIELD : 98,000 Tablets

USUAL PACKING : Strip of 10 Tablets

FORMULATION

S. No.	Ingredients	Quantity	Averages
1.	Dicalcium Phosphate	50.0 Kg.	-
2.	Cholecalciferol	2.5 g.	100%
3.	Starch	4.0 Kg.	-
4.	Talcum	580 g.	-
5.	Carboxy Methyl Cellulose	580 g.	-
6.	Magnesium Stearate	580 g.	-
7.	Aerosil	580 g.	-
8.	Gelatin	580 g.	-
9.	Propyl Gallate	5.8 g.	-
10.	Sodium Chloride	58 g.	-
11.	Chloroform	100 ml.	-

MANUFACTURING SPECIFICATIONS

1. Weight of granules : 58 Kg.
2. Weight per tablet : 580 mg.
3. Thickness : 4.5 mm.
4. Tablets are round, biconvex and uncoated.

MANUFACTURING PROCESS

1. Prepare the granules by wet granulation process using Starch Gelatin Paste. Dry at 100° C in a Fluid Bed Drier.
2. Lubricate the granules with Talcum, Magnesium Stearate, Aerosil, Propyl Gallate, Carboxy Methyl Cellulose, Sodium Chloride and Dry Starch.
3. Dissolve Vitamin D_3 in 100 ml of Chloroform and add to the above lubricated granules and mix well.

CALCIUM, VITAMIN D_3 AND L-LYSINE MONOHYDROCHLORIDE TABLETS

LABELLED FORMULA

Each Film coated tablet contains :

625 mg. Calcium Carbonate from organic source (Oystershell) equivalent to elemental Calcium	250 mg.
Vitamin D_3	125 I.U.
L-Lysine Monohydrochloride	50 mg.

BATCH SIZE : 200,000 Tablets
PRACTICAL YIELD : 195,000 Tablets
USUAL PACKING : Blister of 10 Tablets
SHELF LIFE : 12 Months

FORMULATION

S. No.	Ingredients	Quantity	Averages
1.	Oystershell Powder	125.0 Kg.	
2.	Cholecalciferol (Stabilized)	0.100 Kg.	
3.	Maize Starch	38.16 Kg.	
4.	Gelatin	4.60 Kg.	
5.	Methyl Parahydroxy Benzoate	0.100 Kg.	
6.	Lake Erythrosine Colour	0.04 Kg.	
7.	Magnesium Stearate	3.00 Kg.	
8.	Talcum	1.00 Kg.	
9.	Sodium Starch Glycolate	4.00 Kg.	

For Film Coating

1.	Hydroxy Propyl Methylcellulose	2.032 Kg.
2.	Titanium Dioxide	0.466 Kg.
3.	Talcum	0.466 Kg.
4.	Polyethylene glycol	0.050 Kg.
5.	Dibutyl Phthalate	0.150 Kg.
6.	Lake Erythrosine colour	0.045 Kg.
7.	Isopropyl Alcohol	29.60 Lit.
8.	Methylene Chloride	50.00 Lit.

Note on Film Coating

Film coat the tablets as per the Standard Operating Procedure.

Film coat the tablets in two lots of 1 Lac. tablets each.

Apply 37.5 Litres of the above solution per lot of 1 Lac. Tablets.

MANUFACTURING PROCESS

NOTE:

Manufacturing process for Oystershell granules is done in 2 lots of 1 Lac. tablets each. Lubrication of both the lots of Oystershell granules is done together.

1. Prepare the Starch Gelatin Paste by boiling 10 Litres D.M. water, add 0.05 Kg. Methyl Parahydroxy Benzoate and 0.020 Kg. Colour Erythrosine, add 2.30 Kg. Gelatin previously soaked in 4 Litres of D.M. water, then add 4,400 Kg. Maize Starch in slurry form with 4,400 Litres of D.M. water with constant stirring. Cool the paste in cold water bath.
2. Sift 62.500 Kg. Oystershell Powder through 40 mesh an d14.680 Kg. Maize Starch through 100 mesh. Mix 0.020 Kg. Lake Erythrosine with 5 Kg. of sifted Maize Starch with the help of a sifter.
3. Load the sifted ingredients in the planetary mixer and mix for 20 minutes.
4. Granulate the dry powders with Starch Gelatin Paste and prepare the granules with the Multimill.
5. Dry the wet granules in Fluid Bed Drier at the inlet temperature of 70°C till the outlet temperature reaches 37° C. Pass through Multimill to obtain Oystershell Granules.
6. Take 5.00 Kg. of fines of the above granules, add 0.100 Kg. Vitamin D_3 (stabilized), mix it manually and sift through sifter twice.
7. Sift 3.00 Kg. Magnesium Stearate, 1.00 Kg. Talcum and 4.00 Kg. Sodium Starch Glycolate.
8. Load Oystershell Granules from Step 5, Vitamin D_3 mixture from Step 6, Lubricants from Step 7 together with L-Lysine Granules in a Planetary Mixer and mix at slow speed for 10 minutes. The lubricated granules are now ready for compression.

TECHNICAL SPECIFICATIONS

Average weight of the tablet	:	88 mg. ± 5%
Punch Size	:	12.75 mm. S.C.
Disintegration Time	:	N.M.T. 15 minutes.
Hardness	:	4 to 6 Kg/cm^2
Thickness	:	5.2 ± 0.2 mm.
Friability	:	N.M.T. 1%

CAPTOPRIL TABLETS

LABELLED FORMULA

Each tablet contains :

Captopril 25 mg.

BATCH SIZE : 100,000 Tablets
PRACTICAL YIELD : 98,000 Tablets
USUAL PACKING : Strip of 10 Tablets

FORMULATION

S. No.	Ingredients	Quantity	Averages
1.	Captopril	2.5 Kg.	-
2.	Lactose	9.0 Kg.	-
3.	Starch	6.0 Kg.	-
4.	Methyl Paraben Sodium	100 g.	-
5.	Propyl Paraben Sodium	50 g.	-
6.	Starch for paste	800 g.	-
7.	Magnesium Stearate	800 g.	-
8.	Talcum	300 g.	-
9.	Dried Starch	1.0 Kg.	-

MANUFACTURING SPECIFICATIONS

1. Total Weight of granules : 20 Kg.
2. Weight of 20 tablet : 4.0 gm.
3. Weight per tablet : 200 mg.
4. Do not add hot paste into the mixer for granulation.
5. Dry the granules at 60° C.
6. Moisture content of granules should be less than 0.5%.
7. Punch Size : 8 mm.
8. Weight variation about 5.0%.
9. Hardness : not less than 2 kg/cm^2.
10. Disintegration time : about 10 minutes.
11. Friability : not more than 1%.

CARBAMAZEPINE TABLETS

(Chewable Tablets 100 mg.)

LABELLED FORMULA

Each tablet contains :

Carbamazepine 100 mg.

BATCH SIZE : 100,000 Tablets
PRACTICAL YIELD : 98,000 Tablets
USUAL PACKING : Strip of 10 Tablets

FORMULATION

S. No.	Ingredients	Quantity	Averages
1.	Carbamazepine	10.00 Kg.	
2.	Aerosil 200	1.00 Kg.	
3.	Microcrystalline Cellulose	1.52 Kg.	
4.	Powdered Gum Acacia	0.40 Kg.	
5.	Powdered Stearic Acid	0.20 Kg.	
6.	Powdered Sucrose	24.50 Kg.	
7.	Sodium saccharin	0.045 Kg.	
8.	Glycerin	0.750 Kg.	
9.	Colour Sunset Yellow FCF	0.037 Kg.	
10	Dried Maize Starch	1.10 Kg.	
11.	Sodium Carboxy Methyl starch	0.40 Kg.	
12.	Magnesium Stearate	0.20 Kg.	
13.	Orange Flavour Powder	0.525 Kg.	

MANUFACTURING SPECIFICATIONS

Weight per tablet : 400 mg. (392-408 mg.)
Diameter of tablet : 11 mm.
Thickness : 3.1 mm.
Friability : Not more than 3%
Disintegration Time : N.M.T. 30 minutes

MANUFACTURING PROCESS

1. Load powdered Sucrose 22.5 Kg., Aerosil 0.45 Kg., Microcrystalline Cellulose 1.52 Kg., Gum Acacia and Stearic Acid (passed through 40 mesh) in a suitable mixer and mix for 15 minutes.
2. Triturate Sunset Yellow FCF Colour with 1.0 Kg. of the above powder mix and pass through 40 mesh. Add this colour mixture to (1) above and mix for 10 minutes.
3. Dissolve Sodium Saccharin in 1.0 Lit. of D.M. water and then add 2.0 Kg. of Powdered Sucrose. Prepare the syrup by heating. Cool down to 30° — 35°C and add 0.750 Kg. of Glycerin and mix well.
4. Granulate the powder mix with the binding solution from (3) to get a plastic mass. Add more of water if required to prepare the wet mass. Pass through No. 8 sieve.

5. Dry the granules at 50°C. Moisture content of granules should be 0.6 to 1.5%.
6. Repass the granules through No. 16 mesh and store in polythene bags tightly closed.
7. Load the dried granules in a suitable mixer and mix with 10 Kg. Carbamazepine previously passed through No. 20 mesh, for 10 minutes. Then add Sodium Carboxy Methyl Starch, 0.40 Kg. and Dried Maize Starch and mix for further 10 minutes. Now add Orange Flavour Powder and continue mixing for 10 minutes.
8. The granules are ready for compression.

CARBAMAZEPINE TABLETS 250 mg.

LABELLED FORMULA

Each tablet contains :

Carbamazepine 250 mg.

BATCH SIZE : 100,000 Tablets
PRACTICAL YIELD : 98,000 Tablets
USUAL PACKING : Strip of 10 Tablets

FORMULATION

S. No.	Ingredients	Quantity	Averages
1.	Carbamazepine	20.00 Kg.	
2.	Microcrystalline Cellulose	6.500 Kg.	
3.	Nymcel ZSB-10 modified	1.00 Kg.	
4.	Aerosil	0.200 Kg.	
5.	Magnesium Stearate	0.300 Kg.	

MANUFACTURING SPECIFICATIONS

Weight per tablet : 280 mg.
Moisture content of granules : N.M.T. 2.2%
Friability : N.M.T. 1%
Disintegration Time : 1 minute or less
Weight variation : N.M.T. 3%

CHLOROQUIN PHOSPHATE TABLETS

LABELLED FORMULA

Each sugar coated tablet contains :

Chloroquin Phosphate 250 mg.

BATCH SIZE : 100,000 Tablets
PRACTICAL YIELD : 97,000 Tablets
USUAL PACKING : Strip of 10 Tablets

FORMULATION

S. No.	Ingredients	Quantity	Averages
1.	Chloroquin Phosphate	25.00 Kg.	
2.	Lactose	2.50 Kg.	
3.	Starch	1.00 Kg.	
4.	Starch (for paste)	1.00 Kg.	
5.	Gelatin	0.10 Kg.	
6.	Aerosil	0.10 Kg.	
7.	Magnesium Stearate	0.20 Kg.	
8.	Sodium Starch Glycolate	0.40 Kg.	
9.	Starch in lubrication	1.00 Kg.	

For Sugar coating

S. No.	Ingredients	Quantity
1.	Isopropyl Alcohol	6.00 Lit.
2.	Shellac	1.20 Kg.
3.	Sugar	50.00 Kg.
4.	Talcum	20.00 Kg.
5.	Starch	8.00 Kg.
6.	Calcium Carbonate	15.00 Kg.
7.	Gelatin	1.00 Kg.
8.	Gum Acacia	1.00 Kg.
9.	Sodium Benzoate	0.22 Kg.
10.	Titanium Dioxide	1.00 Kg.
11.	Beeswax	0.09 Kg.
12.	Carnauba Wax	0.18 Kg.
13.	Carbon Tetrachloride	2.50 Lit.
14.	Colour	(as per requirement)

MANUFACTURING SPECIFICATIONS

Average weight of uncoated tablet : 300 mg.
Average weight of coated tablet : 430 mg.
Punch Size : 9.5 mm.

MANUFACTURING PROCESS

Standard wet granulation process to be adopted.

CHLORPHENIRAMINE MALEATE TABLETS

LABELLED FORMULA

Each tablet contains :

Chlorpheniramine Maleate 4 mg.

BATCH SIZE : 100,000 Tablets
PRACTICAL YIELD : 97,000 Tablets
USUAL PACKING : Bottle of 100 Tablets

FORMULATION

S. No.	Ingredients	Quantity	Averages
1.	Chlorpheniramine	416 g.	-
2.	Dicalcium Phosphate	6.0 Kg.	-
3.	Lactose	4.0 Kg.	-
4.	Starch	2.0 Kg.	-
5.	Magnesium Stearate	125 g.	-
6.	Talcum	125 g.	-
7.	Gelatin	125 g.	-

MANUFACTURING SPECIFICATIONS

1. Prepare Granules by Wet Granulation Process.
2. Total Weight of granules : 12.5 Kg.
3. Weight per tablet : 125 mg.
4. Punch size : 7.2 mm.
5. Thickness of tablets : 2.2mm.

CHLORPROMAZINE TABLETS

LABELLED FORMULA

Each coated tablet contains :

Chlorpromazine Hydrochloride 25 mg.

BATCH SIZE : 100,000 Tablets
PRACTICAL YIELD : 98,000 Tablets
USUAL PACKING : Bottle of 100 Tablets

FORMULATION

S. No.	Ingredients	Quantity	Averages
1.	Chlorpromazine Hydrochloride	2.6 Kg.	-
2.	Lactose	5.0 Kg.	-

3.	Dicalcium Phosphate	2.0 Kg.	-
4.	Starch	1.0 Kg.	-
5.	Magnesium Stearate	100 g.	-
6.	Talcum	100 g.	-
7.	Gelatin	100 g.	-

COATING MATERIALS

1.	Shellac	100 g.
2.	Denatured Spirit	200 ml.
3.	Talcum	3.0 kg.
4.	Sugar	3.0 kg.
5.	Benzene	200 ml.
6.	Gelatin	100 g.
7.	Gum Acacia	100 g.
8.	Colour Ponceau 4 R	10 g.

MANUFACTURING SPECIFICATIONS

1. Total Weight of granules : 10 Kg.
2. Weight per tablet : 100 mg.
3. Punch size : 6.6 mm.
4. Thickness of tablet : 3 mm.
5. Weight of coated tablets : 150 mg.

MANUFACTURING PROCESS

Adopt the Standard Wet Granulation Process.

CIPROFLOXACIN TABLETS

LABELLED FORMULA

Each tablet contains :

Ciprofloxacin 250 mg.
(as Hydrochloride Monohydrate)

BATCH SIZE : 100,000 Tablets
PRACTICAL YIELD : 98,000 Tablets
USUAL PACKING : Strip of 6 Tablets

FORMULATION

S. No.	Ingredients	Quantity	Averages
1.	Ciprofloxacin Hydrochloride Monohydrate	29.15 Kg.	
2.	Starch	3.20 Kg.	

3.	Magnesium Stearate	800 g.
4.	Talcum	250 g.
5.	Aerosil	270 g.
6.	Sodium Starch Glycolate	1.65 Kg.

FILM COATING MATERIALS

1.	Hydroxypropyl Methylcellulose	1.30 kg.
2.	Polyethylene Glycol	100 g.
3.	Talcum	300 g.
4.	Titanium Dioxide	370 g.
5.	Isopropyl Alcohol	15 Litres
6.	Methylene Chloride	29 Litres

MANUFACTURING SPECIFICATIONS AND PROCESS

1. Prepare the granules by Wet Granulation Process as usual.
2. Total Weight of granules : 35 Kg.
3. Weight per tablet uncoated : 350 mg.
4. Weight per tablet film coated : 375 mg.
5. Disintegration time : 30 minutes.
6. Film coat the tablets by spray coating process.

CIPROFLOXACIN AND TINIDAZOLE TABLETS

LABELLED FORMULA

Each tablet contains :

Ciprofloxacin Hydrochloride
equivalent to Ciprofloxacin 500 mg.
Tinidazole 600 mg.

BATCH SIZE : 200,000 Tablets
PRACTICAL YIELD : 194,000 Tablets
USUAL PACKING : Strip of 10 Tablets

FORMULATION

S. No.	Ingredients	Quantity	Averages
1.	Ciprofloxacin Hydrochloride	116.60 Kg.	
2.	Tinidazole	120.00 Kg.	
3.	Methyl Parahydroxy Benzoate	0.100 Kg.	
4.	Maize Starch	6.00 Kg.	
5.	Magnesium Stearate	1.50 Kg.	
6.	Sodium Starch Glycolate	2.00 Kg.	
7.	Talcum	1.50 Kg.	

Film coating material

1.	Hydroxy Propyl Methyl Cellulose	22.00 Kg.
2.	Titanium Dioxide	0.600 Kg.
3.	Talcum	0.610 Kg.
4.	Dibutyl Phthalate	0.35 Kg.
5.	Isopropyl Alcohol	31.50 Kg.
6.	Methylene Chloride	52.50 Kg.
7.	Polyethylene Glycol	0.20 Kg.

MANUFACTURING PROCESS

Manufacturing should be done in 4 lots of 50,000 tablets.

Batch Size: 50,000 Tablets.

1. Prepare Starch Paste by making a slurry of 1.50 Kg. Maize Starch in 2 Lit. D.M. water. Add this slurry to 10 Lit. of boiling D.M. water to which 0.025 Kg. Methyl Parahydroxy Benzoate has been added. Stir constantly till a thick paste is formed. Allow to cool.
2. Pulverise 30.00 Kg. Tinidazole and 29.15 Kg. Ciprofloxacin Hydrochloride through Multimill fitted with 0.5 mm sieve.
3. Load the sifted material in a planetary mixer and mix for 20 minutes.
4. Add Starch Paste to the dry mixed ingredients till a suitable mass is formed.
5. Pass the dough Multimill fitted with 10 mm sieve and collect the wet granules in clean container.
6. Dry the granules in a Fluid Bed Drier at inlet temperature of 70° C till the outlet temperature reaches 35° C.
7. Sift the dried granules through 16 mesh sieve.
8. Lubricate the granules with Magnesium Stearate 1.50 Kg., Sodium Starch Glycolate 2.00 Kg. and Talcum 0.50 Kg.

MANUFACTURING SPECIFICATIONS

Average Weight per tablet	:	1238 mg. ± 5%
Punch size	:	19 X 8.5 mm.
Disintegration time	:	Not more than 15 minutes
Hardness	:	Not less than 5 kg/cm²
Thickness	:	7.4 ± 0.2 mm.

Film Coating

Film coat the tablets in the film coating machine using the above formulation. Film coat the tablets in 2 lots of 1 Lac tablets each using 40 Lit. of the solution.

COMPOUND MAGNESIUM TRISILICATE CHEWABLE TABLETS

LABELLED FORMULA

Each uncoated chewable tablet contains :

Dried Aluminium Hydroxide Gel 120 mg.
Magnesium Trisilicate 250 mg.

BATCH SIZE : 100,000 Tablets
PRACTICAL YIELD : 99,000 Tablets
USUAL PACKING : Container of 1000 Tablets
SHELF LIFE : 3 years

FORMULATION

S. No.	Ingredients	Quantity	Averages
1.	Dried Aluminium Hydroxide Gel	13.20 Kg.	10%
2.	Magnesium Trisilicate	25.00 Kg.	
3.	Maize Starch	14.80 Kg.	
4.	Powdered Sugar	52.70 Kg.	
5.	Propyl Paraben	0.04 Kg.	
6.	Maize Starch for paste	1.00 Kg.	
7.	Saccharin Sodium	0.35 Kg.	
8.	Peppermint Oil	0.38 Kg.	
9.	Talcum	1.10 Kg.	
10.	Magnesium Stearate	1.50 Kg.	
	(Average weight per tablet)	1.10 Kg.	

MANUFACTURING PROCESS

Standard Wet Granulation process to be adopted.

DEXAMETHASONE TABLETS I

LABELLED FORMULA

Each tablet contains :

Dexamethasone 0.5 mg.

BATCH SIZE : 200,000 Tablets
PRACTICAL YIELD : 196,000 Tablets
USUAL PACKING : Strip of 10 Tablets

FORMULATION

S. No.	Ingredients	Quantity	Averages
1.	Dexamethasone	100 g.	
2.	Lactose	16.8 Kg.	
3.	Starch	6.4 Kg.	
4.	Starch for paste	800 g.	
5.	Talcum	200 g.	
6.	Magnesium Stearate	200 g.	

MANUFACTURING SPECIFICATIONS

1. Hardness : 5-8 Kg/cm^2
2. Moisture : Less than 2%.
3. Disintegration time : Less than 7 minutes
4. Weight of 20 tablets : 12 g.
5. Storage : Store in air tight containers.

DEXAMETHASONE TABLETS II

LABELLED FORMULA

Each tablet contains :

Dexamethasone 0.5 mg.

BATCH SIZE : 100,000 Tablets
PRACTICAL YIELD : 97,000 Tablets
USUAL PACKING : Strip of 10 Tablets

FORMULATION

S. No.	Ingredients	Quantity	Averages
1.	Dexamethasone	53 g.	6%
2.	Starch/Lactose Granules	14.2 Kg.	-
3.	Magnesium Stearate	150 g.	-
4.	Talcum	150 g.	-
5.	Aerosil	150 g.	-
6.	Colour Tartrazine	150 g.	-
7.	Polyvinylpyrrolidone	150 g.	-
8.	Denatured Spirit	150 ml.	-

MANUFACTURING SPECIFICATIONS

1. Prepare Granules by Wet Granulation Process.
2. Total weight of granules : 15 Kg.
3. Weight per tablet : 150 mg.

4. Disintegration time : 5 minutes.
5. Punch size : 4.2 mm.
6. Thickness : 2.6 mm.
7. Colour of Tablets : Yellow.
8. Shelf Life : 2 Years.

DIAZEPAM TABLETS

LABELLED FORMULA

Each tablet contains :

Diazepam 5 mg.

BATCH SIZE : 588,000 Tablets
PRACTICAL YIELD : 565,000 Tablets
USUAL PACKING : Strip of 10 Tablets

FORMULATION

S. No.	Ingredients	Quantity	Averages
1.	Diazepam	3.00 Kg.	2%
2.	Starch	54.00 Kg.	
3.	Lactose	54.00 Kg.	
4.	Starch (Binder)	3.00 Kg.	
5.	D.M. Water	3.00 Kg.	
6.	Talcum	7.75 Kg.	
7.	Magnesium Stearate	1.10 Kg.	

MANUFACTURING SPECIFICATIONS

1. Mix Diazepam with sifted Starch for 15 minutes. Add Lactose and again mix for 15 minutes.
2. Granulate the powders with Starch Paste prepared previously till a suitable mass is obtained.
3. Prepare the granules on the Multimill.
4. Dry the wet granules in a Fluid Bed Drier at 50° C to 60° C.
5. Lubricate the sifted dried granules with Talcum and Magnesium Stearate.

TECHNICAL SPECIFICATIONS

Weight of 20 Tablets : 4.180 g.
Punch size : 5/8th inch.
Hardness : 2.5 to 3.0 Kg/cm^2
Thickness : 2.9 to 3.1 mm.
Disintegration time : 4 to 5 minutes

DICLOFENAC SUSTAINED RELEASE TABLETS 100 mg.

LABELLED FORMULA

Each sustained release tablet contains :

Diclofenac Sodium 100 mg.

BATCH SIZE : 400,000 Tablets
PRACTICAL YIELD : 390,000 Tablets
USUAL PACKING : Strip of 10 Tablets

FORMULATION

S. No.	Ingredients	Quantity	Averages
1.	Diclofenac	40.00 Kg.	
2.	Powdered Sugar	47.60 Kg.	
3.	Cetyl Alcohol	23.60 Kg.	
4.	Aerosil	1.20 Kg.	
5.	Polyvinylpyrrolidone	2.40 Kg.	
6.	Magnesium Stearate	1.20 Kg.	

MANUFACTURING PROCESS

Caution: Use mask/gloves/goggles when handling Diclofenac Sodium. Store granules below 25°C.

1. Mix Diclofenac Sodium and Powdered Sugar in jacked Planetary Mixer and heat with hot water to 60°C.
2. Melt Cetyl Alcohol on a water bath.
3. Add the molten Cetyl Alcohol to the powder mix of (1) and mix till a homogenous mass is obtained.
4. Cool the mass to 40°C and sieve at once using 3/8" mesh.
5. Cool granules to 20°C to 25°C.
6. Check the moisture content. It should be 1.0% of 1.5%.
7. Pass the dried granules through Multimill.
8. Transfer the granules to a Drum Mixer and lubricated them with sifted Aerosil, Polyvinylpyrrolidone and mix for 5 minutes. Add sifted Magnesium Stearate and again mix for 3 minutes.
9. The granules are now ready for compression.

Film Coating of Tablets

Raw Material Requirement for Film Coating

Batch Size: 150,000 Tablets

1. Methylene Chloride 18.00 Lit.
2. Methanol 1.200 Lit.

3. Methocil 0.260 Kg.
4. Shellac 0.025 Kg.
5. Pigment Suspension Iron Oxide Red 0.041 Kg.
6. Pigment Suspension White with cellulose 0.745 Kg.
7. D.M. Water 0.030 Lit.
8. Polyethylene Glycol 0.027 Kg.
9. Sucrose 0.018 Kg.
10. Isopropyl Alcohol 0.014 Kg.

Adopt Standard Film Coating Process.

DICLOFENAC TABLETS 50 mg.

LABELLED FORMULA

Each film coated tablet contains :

Diclofenac Sodium 50 mg.

BATCH SIZE : 350,000 Tablets
PRACTICAL YIELD : 342,000 Tablets
USUAL PACKING : Strip of 10 Tablets

FORMULATION

S. No.	Ingredients	Quantity	Averages
1.	Diclofenac Sodium	17.50 Kg.	
2.	Lactose	14.00 Kg.	
3.	Microcrystalline Cellulose	14.00 Kg.	
4.	Polyvinylpyrrolidone	1.05 Kg.	
5.	D.M. Water	10.50 Kg.	
6.	Aerosil 200	0.70 Kg.	
7.	Maize Starch	14.00 Kg.	
8.	Magnesium Stearate	0.70 Kg.	
9.	Dried Maize Starch	6.30 Kg.	

For Film Coating

1.	Methylene Chloride	74.50 Kg.
2.	Methanol	5.80 Kg.
3.	Cellulose Acetate Phthalate	2.10 Kg.
4.	Diethyl Phthalate	0.66 Kg.
5.	Shellac	0.50 Kg.
6.	Iron Oxide Yellow Pigment	0.75 Kg.

7. Pigment Suspension White 0.79 Kg.
8. Pigment Suspension Iron Oxide Red 0.04 Kg.

PRECAUTIONS

1. Strictly use mask/gloves/goggles when handling Diclofenac Sodium.
2. Check dry granules to ensure complete removal of Methanol.
3. Store uncoated tablets in light resistant containers.
4. Handle organic solvents with extreme care.
5. Store film coated tablets protected from humidity.

MANUFACTURING PROCESS

1. Mix Diclofenac Sodium, Lactose (14 Kg.) and Maize Starch (14 Kg.) for 20 minutes.
2. Prepare the binding solution by dissolving Polyvinylpyrrolidone in 10.5 Lit D.M. water.
3. Add the binding solution to (1) and mix for 10 minutes to get a wet mass.
4. Immediately sieve the wet mass to prepare wet granules.
5. Dry the granules at 45°—50°C till the L.O.D. is 3.0% to 3.8%.
6. Pass the dried granules through 1.20 mm. sieve.
7. Lubricate the dried granules with Aerosil, Microcrystalline Cellulose and Maize Starch (6.3 Kg.) and mix for 10 minutes in a Drum Mixer. Add Magnesium Stearate and again mix for 5 minutes.
8. L.O.D. at 105°C for 30 minutes should be 3.5% to 4.9%.

PREPARATION OF FILM COATING SOLUTION

1. Mix Methylene Chloride and Methanol, Add Cellulose Acetate Phthalate, Shellac and Diethyl Phthalate. Dissolve by stirring to get a clear solution.
2. Disperse all the three pigments.

MANUFACTURING SPECIFICATIONS

Weight of uncoated tablet	195 mg.
Weight of coated tablet	205 mg. ± 2%
Diameter	8.0 to 8.2 mm.
Thickness	3.55 to 3.95 mm.
Resistance to Gastric Fluid	Atleast 2 hours
Disintegration in intestinal fluid	Less than 15 minutes.

ETHAMBUTOL HYDROCHLORIDE TABLETS

LABELLED FORMULA

Each tablet contains :

Ethambutol Hydrochloride 800 mg.

BATCH SIZE : 1,00,000 Tablets
PRACTICAL YIELD : 98,000 Tablets
USUAL PACKING : Strip of 10 Tablets

FORMULATION

S. No.	Ingredients	Quantity	Averages
1.	Ethambutol Hydrochloride	80.0 Kg.	
2.	Starch	2.60 Kg.	
3.	Aerosil	2.00 Kg.	
4.	Povidone	4.50 Kg.	
5.	Isopropyl Alcohol	45.0 Lit.	
6.	Talcum	1.60 Kg.	
7.	Magnesium Stearate	2.00 Kg.	
8.	Aerosil	0.80 Kg.	

MANUFACTURING SPECIFICATIONS

Average weight of 10 Tablets : 9.350 g.
Punch Size : 19.5 mm
Thickness : 6.5 ± 0.2 mm
Disintegration Time : N.M.T. 15 minutes
Hardness : 2.0 to 6.0 Kg/cm^2

MANUFACTURING PROCESS

NOTE : The product is highly Hygroscopic in nature. Compression must be carried out in an area exceeding 50% R.H.

1. Pass Ethambutol Hydrochloride, Starch and Aerosil through Multimill with no. 60 screen.
2. Blend the material in a mixer for 15 minutes.
3. Dissolve Povidone in 40 Lit. Isopropyl Alcohol. Filter the solution through cloth.
4. Granulate the powders with the Povidone solution. Add more Isopropyl Alcohol, if required, until a suitable wet mass is obtained.
5. Pass the wet mass through Multimill to make the wet granules.
6. Dry the wet granules in trays at 45°C – 50°C for 14 to 16 hours.
7. Pass the dried granules through Multimill and make up the weight of granules to 89.100 Kg. using dried starch.
8. Sift about 1.5 Kg. of 60 mesh fines from the granules and blend with

Talcum 1.60 Kg., Magnesium Stearate 2.00 Kg., and Aerosil 0.80 Kg.

9. Blend the granules with lubricant in a mixer for 15 minutes.
10. Check the granules for fines (60 mesh) N.M.T. 30% and moisture content N.M.T. 2%.
11. The granules are ready for compression.

FERROUS SULPHATE AND FOLIC ACID TABLETS

LABELLED FORMULA

Each tablet contains :

Ferrous Sulphate	200	mg.
Folic Acid	0.5	mg.

BATCH SIZE : 1,00,000 Tablets
PRACTICAL YIELD : 96,000 Tablets
USUAL PACKING : Bottle/Tin of 1000 Tablets

FORMULATION

S. No.	Ingredients	Quantity	Overages
1.	Ferrous Sulphate	20.00 Kg.	
2.	Starch	8.00 Kg.	
3.	Talcum	280 g.	
4.	Magnesium Stearate	280 g.	
5.	Sugar	1.00 Kg.	
6.	Folic Acid	70 g.	

COATING MATERIALS

1.	Sugar	9.0 Kg.
2.	Talcum	9.0 Kg.
3.	Starch	900 g.
4.	Aerosil	180 g.
5.	Shellac	300 g.
6.	Gelatin	150 g.
7.	Gum Acacia	150 g.
8.	Benzene	300 ml.
9.	Titanium Dioxide	28 g.

MANUFACTURING SPECIFICATIONS AND PROCESS

1. Prepare granules by Wet Granulation Process using Starch/Sugar Paste.
2. Lubricate the granules as usual and make up the weight to 28 Kg. with dried starch.
3. Weight per tablet (uncoated)—280 mg.
4. Folic Acid to be added during sub-coating for sugar coating.

FERROUS SULPHATE TABLETS

LABELLED FORMULA

Each tablet contains :

Ferrous Sulphate 200 mg.

BATCH SIZE : 4,00,000 Tablets
PRACTICAL YIELD : 3,88,000 Tablets
USUAL PACKING : Bottles of 100 Tablets

FORMULATION

S. No.	Ingredients	Quantity	Averages
1.	Ferrous Sulphate	84.00 Kg.	
2.	Starch	28.80 Kg.	
3.	Talcum Powder	4.60 Kg.	
4.	Liquid Glucose	4.60 Kg.	
5.	Sugar	4.60 Kg.	
6.	Magnesium Stearate	0.80 Kg.	
7.	Dealca P (Guar Gum)	1.20 Kg.	
8.	Isopropyl Alcohol	14.0 Lit.	
9.	Shellac	1.60 Kg.	
10.	Polyethylene Glycol 400	0.35 Kg.	
11.	Polyvinylpyrrolidone	0.35 Kg.	
12.	Starch	13.00 Kg.	
13.	Talcum Powder	3.40 Kg.	
14.	Calcium Carbonate	26.00 Kg.	
15.	Gelatin	1.00 Kg.	
16.	Gum Acacia	1.80 Kg.	
17.	Sugar	50.00 Kg.	
18.	Ferric Oxide Brown	0.80 Kg.	
19.	Carbon Tetrachloride	3.0 Lit.	
20.	Carnauba Wax	0.04 Kg.	
21.	Beeswax	0.04 Kg.	

NOTES : Formulation includes sugar coating material.

FRUSEMIDE TABLETS

LABELLED FORMULA

Each tablet contains :

Frusemide 40 mg.

BATCH SIZE : 1,00,000 Tablets
PRACTICAL YIELD : 97,000 Tablets
USUAL PACKING : Strip of 10 Tablets

FORMULATION

S. No.	Ingredients	Quantity	Averages
1.	Frusemide	4.2 Kg.	5%
2.	Starch	1.4 Kg.	
3.	Lactose	4.0 Kg.	
4.	Dicalcium Phosphate	4.0 Kg.	
5.	Magnesium Stearate	140 g.	
6.	Talcum	140 g.	
7.	Aerosil	140 g.	
8.	Gelatin	140 g.	

MANUFACTURING SPECIFICATIONS AND PROCESS

1. Prepare granules by Wet Granulation Process.
2. Total weight of granules : 14 Kg.
3. Punch size : 7.3 mm.
4. Thickness : 2.6 mm.
5. Weight per tablet : 140 mg.
6. Colour of tablets : White.

FURAZOLIDONE TABLETS

LABELLED FORMULA

Each tablet contains :

Furazolidone 100 mg.

BATCH SIZE : 1,00,000 Tablets
PRACTICAL YIELD : 98,000 Tablets
USUAL PACKING : Strip of 10 Tablets

FORMULATION

S. No.	Ingredients	Quantity	Overages
1.	Furazolidone	10.4 Kg.	4%
2.	Lactose	4.0 Kg.	
3.	Dicalcium Phosphate	4.0 Kg.	
4.	Gelatin	200 g.	
5.	Talcum	200 g.	
6.	Magnesium Stearate	200 g.	
7.	Starch	2.0 Kg.	

MANUFACTURING SPECIFICATIONS AND PROCESS

1. Prepare granules by Wet Granulation Process.
2. Total weight of granules : 20 Kg.
3. Punch size : 8.3 mm.

4. Thickness : 3.6 mm.
5. Weight per tablet : 200 mg.
6. Colour of tablets : Yellow.

GRIESOFULVIN TABLETS

LABELLED FORMULA

Each tablet contains :

Griesofulvin 15 mg.

BATCH SIZE : 1,00,000 Tablets
PRACTICAL YIELD : 98,000 Tablets
USUAL PACKING : Blister of 10 Tablets

FORMULATION

S. No.	Ingredients	Quantity	Averages
1.	Griesofulvin	12.50 Kg.	
2.	* Starch Lactose Granules	6.50 Kg.	
3.	Talcum	0.30 Kg.	
4.	Magnesium Stearate	0.08 Kg.	
5.	Talcum	0.87 Kg.	
6.	Magnesium Stearate	0.09 Kg.	

MANUFACTURING SPECIFICATIONS

Weight per tablet : 203 mg.
Hardness : 2.0 to 3.0 Kg/cm^2
Disintegration Time : 30 seconds

MANUFACTURING PROCESS

1. * Prepare Starch Lactose Granules by mixing 3.25 kg Starch and 3.25 kg Lactose and granulate with Starch paste of 1.625 Kg. Starch in 16.25 Lit. D.M. Water.
2. Griesofulvin tablets are prepared by slugging process. Mix Griesofulvin with Starch Lactose Granules, 300 g. Talcum and 80 g. Magnesium Stearate. Slug these powders on a slugging Machine.
3. Break the slugs and prepare granules of no. 14 mesh size.
4. Lubricate these granules with 870 g. Talcum and 90 g. Magnesium Stearate in a blender for 15 minutes.
5. The granules are ready for compression.

*** NOTE:**

1. Griesfulvin Tablets 250 mg. can also be manufactured by adjusting the weight of Starch Lactose Granules. Final weight of tablets shall be 400 mg/tablet.

2. Griesofulvin Tablets 500 mg. can also be manufactured by adjusting the weight of Starch Lactose Granules. Final weight of tablets shall be 625 mg. per tablet.

IBUPROFEN AND PARACETAMOL TABLETS

LABELLED FORMULA

Each tablet contains :

Ibuprofen 400 mg.
Paracetamol 325 mg.

BATCH SIZE : 62,500 Tablets
PRACTICAL YIELD : 60,500 Tablets
USUAL PACKING : Strip of 10 Tablets

FORMULATION

S. No.	Ingredients	Quantity	Overages
1.	Ibuprofen	25.0 Kg.	
2.	Paracetamol	20.5 Kg.	
3.	Starch	1.5 Kg.	
4.	Methyl Paraben Sodium	100 g.	
5.	Propyl Paraben Sodium	50 g.	
6.	Starch for paste	2.0 Kg.	
7.	Magnesium Stearate	700 g.	
8.	Talcum	1.5 Kg.	
9.	Dried Starch	Q.S.	

MANUFACTURING SPECIFICATIONS

1. Total weight of granules — 53.75 Kg.
2. Weight per tablet — 860 mg.
3. Moisture content of granules less than 0.5%.
4. Do not add hot paste in the mass mixer containing Ibuprofen and Paracetamol.
5. Temperature of the granules while drying should not exceed 40°C.
6. Weight of 20 Tablets — 17.2 g.
7. Weight variation within 3.5%.
8. Hardness of tablets not less than 4 Kg/cm^2.
9. Disintegration time about 10 minutes.
10. Friability should be less than 1%.

MANUFACTURING PROCESS

1. Add Ibuprofen, Paracetamol and 1.5 kg Starch to the mixer and mix for 30 minutes.

2. Add the Starch Paste containing Methyl and Propyl Paraben Sodium to form a suitable mass for wet granulation.
3. Pass through Multimill and dry the granules in a fluid bed dryer.
4. Lubricate the granules as usual and send for compression.

IBUPROFEN TABLETS

LABELLED FORMULA

Each sugar coated tablet contains :

Ibuprofen 600 mg.

BATCH SIZE : 50,000 Tablets
PRACTICAL YIELD : 49,000 Tablets
USUAL PACKING : Strip of 10 Tablets

FORMULATION

S. No.	Ingredients	Quantity	Averages
1.	Ibuprofen	30.0 Kg.	
2.	Starch	1.4 Kg.	
3.	Starch for Paste	600 g.	
4.	Magnesium Stearate	300 g.	
5.	Talcum	700 g.	
6.	Dried Starch to make	35 Kg.	

COATING MATERIAL

1.	Sugar	15.0 Kg.
2.	Talcum	6.0 Kg.
3.	Calcium Carbonate	2.0 Kg.
4.	Gelatin	500 g.
5.	Colour Erythrosine	30 g.
6.	Beeswax	20 g.
7.	Carnauba Wax	20 g.
8.	Benzene	500 ml.

MANUFACTURING SPECIFICATIONS AND PROCESS

1. Prepare granules by Wet Granulation Process.
2. Total weight of granules — 35 Kg.
3. Weight of 20 Tablets (uncoated) — 14 g.
4. Weight per tablet (uncoated) — 700 mg.
5. Donot add hot paste to Ibuprofen.
6. Punch size — 12.5 mm.
7. Friability not more than 1%.
8. Hardness not less than 4 Kg/cm^2.
9. Disintegration time (coated tablets) about 30 minutes.

10. Coat the tablets by the usual coating process. During coating the temperature should not exceed 40°C.

ISOSORBIDE DINITRATE TABLETS
(*Sublingual*)

LABELLED FORMULA

Each tablet contains :
Isosorbide Dinitrate 10 mg.

BATCH SIZE : 1,00,000 Tablets
PRACTICAL YIELD : 97,000 Tablets
USUAL PACKING : Bottle of 100 Tablets

FORMULATION

S. No.	Ingredients	Quantity	Averages
1.	Isosorbide Dinitrate	1.025 Kg.	2.5%
2.	Mannitol	17.4 Kg.	
3.	Maize Starch	2.0 Kg.	
4.	Propyl Paraben	2.0 g.	
5.	Gelatin	200 g.	
6.	Magnesium Stearate	400 g.	

MANUFACTURING SPECIFICATIONS

1. Total weight of granules — 21 Kg.
2. Weight of 20 tablets — 4.2 g.
3. Weight per tablet — 210 mg.
4. Punch size — 6.5 mm.
5. Friability of tablets less than 2%.

MANUFACTURING PROCESS

1. Pass Mannitol and Starch through no. 24 Sieve. Dissolve 2 g. Propyl Paraben in 500 ml. of boiling water. Dissolve 200 g. Gelatin in 1.25 Lit. of boiling water. Add the Gelatin solution to the Propyl Paraben Solution with constant stirring.
2. Granulate the Mannitol Starch mixture with the Gelatin Solution (add a little water if necessary).
3. Pass the mass through no. 12 sieve.
4. Dry the Granules with fan only at room temperature (not exceeding 40°C).
5. Lubricate the granules with Magnesium Stearate and compress the tablets.

MEBENDAZOLE TABLETS

LABELLED FORMULA

Each tablet contains :

Mebendazole 100 mg.

BATCH SIZE : 60,000 Tablets
PRACTICAL YIELD : 58,000 Tablets
USUAL PACKING : Strip of 10 Tablets

FORMULATION

S. No.	Ingredients	Quantity	Averages
1.	Mebendazole	6.00 Kg.	
2.	Lactose	4.20 Kg.	
3.	Starch	5.40 Kg.	
4.	Starch for Paste	0.60 Kg.	
5.	Colour Tartrazine	6.00 g.	
6.	Talcum	0.30 Kg.	
7.	Magnesium Stearate	75.00 g.	
8.	Dried Starch	0.23 Kg.	

Hardness : 2 to 3 Kg/cm^2
Disintegration Time : 5 minutes

MANUFACTURING PROCESS

Standard Wet Granulation process to be adopted.

MEFENAMIC ACID AND PARACETAMOL TABLETS

LABELLED FORMULA

Each tablet contains :

Mefenamic Acid 250 mg.
Paracetamol 500 mg.

BATCH SIZE : 1,00,000 Tablets
PRACTICAL YIELD : 98,000 Tablets
USUAL PACKING : Strip of 10 Tablets

FORMULATION

S. No.	Ingredients	Quantity	Averages
1.	Paracetamol	50.00 Kg.	
2.	Mefenamic Acid	25.00 Kg.	
3.	Polyvinylpyrrolidone	1.00 Kg.	
4.	Starch for Paste	4.00 Kg.	

5.	Dried Starch	6.20 Kg.
6.	Aerosil	0.40 Kg.
7.	Magnesium Stearate	0.40 Kg.

MANUFACTURING PROCESS

1. Mix sifted Paracetamol and Mefenamic Acid in a mixer for 15 to 20 minutes.
2. Prepare binder paste by suspending 4 Kg. Starch in 4.5 Lit. of water and 1.0 Kg. Polyvinylpyrrolidone in 16 Lit. of boiling water separately. Add the Starch suspension to the boiling solution and heat on water bath till starch gets gelatinized. Mix well and use for binding.
3. Add binder to mixed ingredients of (1) in a mixer to prepare the wet mass. Add more water if necessary.
4. Prepare the wet granules on a Multimill.
5. Dry the wet granules overnight at 50° – 60°C. Loss on drying of granules should be 2.0 to 2.5%.
6. Blend the dried granules with 4 Kg. Starch for 10 minutes. Taking remaining 2.2 Kg. Starch mix thoroughly with Aerosil. Pass this mixture through 40 mesh and mix with the above blended granules for 10 minutes. Add Magnesium Stearate and blend for 2 minutes.
   Caution: Do not mix too long after addition of Magnesium Stearate.
7. The granules are ready for compression.

METHYL DOPA TABLETS

LABELLED FORMULA

Each film coated tablet contains :

Methyl Dopa (Anhydrous) 250 mg.

BATCH SIZE : 1,00,000 Tablets
PRACTICAL YIELD : 97,000 Tablets
USUAL PACKING : Blister of 10 Tablets

FORMULATION

S. No.	Ingredients	Quantity	Overages
1.	Methyldopa (88.5% Activity)	28.3 Kg.	
2.	Citric Acid	0.43 Kg.	
3.	Calcium Disodium Edetate	0.02 Kg.	
4.	Ethyl Cellulose	2.70 Kg.	
5.	Isopropyl Alcohol	8.75 Lit.	
6.	Guar Gum	1..50 Kg.	
7.	Magnesium Stearate	0.14 Kg.	

FOR FILM COATING

1.	Cellulose Acetate Phthalate	0.10	Kg.
2.	Diethyl Phthalate	0.02	Kg.
3.	Acetone	1.00	Lit.
4.	Hydroxy Propyl Methyl Cellulose	0.76	Kg.
5.	Titanium Dioxide	1.05	Kg.
6.	Talcum	0.35	Kg.
7.	Yellow Lake colour	0.10	Kg.
8.	Isopropyl Alcohol	17.40	Lit.
9.	Chloroform	17.40	Lit.

MANUFACTURING PROCESS

1. Mix Methyldopa, Citric Acid, Calcium Disodium Edetate and Ethyl Cellulose in a mixer for 5 minutes. Pass through sifter and again mix for 5 minutes.
2. Prepare the granulating solutic n with Ethyl Cellulose 700 g. and Isopropyl Alcohol 8.75 Lit. Use slight heat to get it into solution. Cool to 25°C and filter.
3. Add 8% solution Ethyl Cellulose to the powders to make the wet mass. Pass through Multimill to get the wet granules.
4. Air-dry the wet granules overnight under controlled conditions (72° – 85°F and 45 – 65% R.H).
5. After air-drying, dry for 16–20 hours at 54°C – 59°C in forced air circulation drying cabinet. Moisture content shuld be 0.4% to 1.5%.
6. Lubricate the dried granules with Guar Gum 1.50 Kg., * Solka Floc 1.20 Kg., and * Cab-O-Sil 200 g. blend for 10 minutes. Then add Magnesium Stearate 140 g. and again mix for 5 minutes.
7. Store the lubricated granules in air-conditioned area.

* Brand names

PREPARATION OF FILM COATING SUSPENSION

1. To a mixer with high speed stirrer add 17.4 Lit. Isopropyl Alcohol and then add Hydroxypropyl Methylcellulose, Diethyl Phthalate and Chloroform. Mix until Hydroxy Propyl Methyl Cellulose is dissolved.
2. To this solution add Titanium Dioxide, Talcum and Yellow Lake Colour. Mix until a uniform suspension is formed.
3. Pass through a colloid Mill.

FILM COATING PROCESS

1. Dissolve 100 g. Cellulose Acetate Phthalate and 20 g. Diethyl Phthalate in 1.00 Lit. Acetone.
2. Apply three coatings to the pan with a paint brush.

3. Place 34.4 Kg. of tablets in the coating pan (36 inch.) and apply the film coating suspension by use of nozzles at a flow rate of 170–200 ml. per minute. Use dry air to keep the tablets dry.
4. Continue spraying till tablets are of 360 mg. each.
5. Polish the tablets as usual.

TECHNICAL SPECIFICATIONS

Weight of 10 Tablets	:	3.60 g. (3.50 – 3.70 g.)
Hardness	:	3–5 Kg/cm².
Disintegration Time	:	15 minutes.

METOCLOPRAMIDE HYDROCHLORIDE TABLETS

LABELLED FORMULA

Each tablet contains:

Metoclopramide Hydrochloride 10 mg.

BATCH SIZE	:	1,00,000 Tablets
PRACTICAL YIELD	:	97,000 Tablets
USUAL PACKING	:	Strip of 10 Tablets

FORMULATION

S. No.	Ingredients	Quantity	Overages
1.	Metoclopramide Hydrochloride	1.00 Kg.	
2.	Lactose	7.00 Kg.	
3.	Starch	7.00 Kg.	
4.	Starch for paste	0.50 Kg.	
5.	Talcum	0.20 Kg.	
6.	Magnesium Stearate	0.10 Kg.	
7.	Dried Starch	0.20 Kg.	

MANUFACTURING PROCESS

Standard Wet Granulation process to be adopted.

METOPROLOL, DIHYDRAZINE AND HYDROCHLOROTHIAZIDE TABLETS

LABELLED FORMULA

Each coated tablet contains :

Metoprolol Tartratate	100 mg.
Dihydrazine Sulphate	25 mg.
Hydrochlorothiazide	12.5 mg.

BATCH SIZE : 3,00,000 Tablets
PRACTICAL YIELD : 2,90,000 Tablets
USUAL PACKING : Strip of 10 Tablets

FORMULATION

S. No.	Ingredients	Quantity	Averages
1.	Metoprolol Tartarate	31.50 Kg.	5%
2.	Dihydralazine Sulphate	8.25 Kg.	10%
3.	Hydrochlorothiazide	4.125 Kg.	10%
4.	Starch	21.00 Kg.	
5.	Lactose	21.00 Kg.	
6.	Tartrazine Yellow Colour	0.045 Kg.	
7.	Polyvinylpyrrolidone	0.75 Kg.	
8.	Isopropyl Alcohol	15.0 Lit.	
9.	Guar Gum	3.00 Kg.	
10.	Magnesium Stearate	2.25 Kg.	
11.	Talcum	1.50 Kg.	
12.	Microcrystalline Cellulose	1.50 Kg.	

MANUFACTURING SPECIFICATIONS

Weight per tablet : 315 ± 5 mg.
Hardness : 3.5 Kg/cm²
Weight variation : ± 5%
Friability : N.M.T. 0.5%
Disintegration Time : N.M.T. 20 minutes

MANUFACTURING PROCESS

1. Pulverise all the three active ingredients and pass through No. 40 mesh sifter.
2. Load Metoprolol Tartrate, Dihydrazine Sulphate, Starch, Lactose and Hydrochlorothiazide in the Mass Mixer and mix for 45 minutes.
3. Dissolve Tartrazine Yellow colour in minimum quantity of D.M. Water and filter through muslin cloth. Mix this colour solution with a small quantity of the powder mix and add to the whole mass. Again Mix for 45 minutes.
4. Dissolve Polyvinylpyrrolidone in 15 Lit. of Isopropyl Alcohol. Filter through muslin cloth.
5. Granulate the dry mix with the granulating solution prepared above and mix for 15 minutes.
6. Pass the wet mass through no. 8 mesh sieve to prepare wet granules.
7. Air-dry the wet granules under controlled humidity conditions for 10–12 hours.

8. Pass the dried granules through no. 16 mesh of sifter.
9. Lubricate the dry granules with Guar Gum, Magnesium Stearate, Talcum and Microcrystalline Cellulose in a Drum Mixer for 15 minutes.
10. The granules are now ready for compression.

METRONIDAZOLE TABLETS

LABELLED FORMULA

Each tablet contains :

Metronidazole 200 mg.

BATCH SIZE : 1,00,000 Tablets
PRACTICAL YIELD : 98,000 Tablets
USUAL PACKING : Strip of 10 Tablets

FORMULATION

S. No.	Ingredients	Quantity	Averages
1.	Metronidazole	20.0 Kg.	
2.	Starch	10.0 Kg.	
3.	Sugar	7.0 Kg.	
4.	Liquid Glucose	1.2 Kg.	
5.	Gelatin	100 g.	
6.	Colour Ponceau 4 R	2.5 g.	
7.	Starch Dried	350 g.	
8.	Magnesium Stearate	350 g.	

MANUFACTURING SPECIFICATIONS

Weight of 20 Tablets : 7.80 g.
Diameter : 0.988 cm.
Thickness : 0.587 cm.
Disintegration Time : (a) Uncoated 11 to 15 minutes.
(b) Film coated not more than 40 minutes.
Hardness : Not less than 4 Kg/cm^2 (uncoated).
Not less than 8 kg/cm^2 (coated).
The tablets should be film coated.

MULTIVITAMIN TABLETS

LABELLED FORMULA

Each tablet contains :

Vitamin A 2000 I.U.
Vitamin B_2 0.1 mg.
Vitamin D_3 200 I.U.
Vitamin B_6 0.1 mg.

Vitamin B_1	0.5 mg.
Calcium Pantothenate	1.0 mg.
Niacinamide	5.0 mg.

BATCH SIZE : 5,00,000 Tablets
PRACTICAL YIELD : 4,80,000 Tablets
USUAL PACKING : Strip of 10 Tablets

FORMULATION

S. No.	Ingredients	Quantity	Averages
1.	Vitamin A Acetate	1.10 Kg.	
2.	Thiamine Mononitrate	0.325 Kg.	30%
3.	Riboflavine	0.05 Kg.	10%
4.	Pyridoxine Hydrochloride	0.058 Kg.	16%
5.	Cholecalciferol	5.00 g.	
6.	Nicotinamide	2.55 Kg.	2%
7.	Cetyl Alcohol	0.10 Kg.	
8.	Maize Starch	36.94 Kg.	
9.	Lactose	18.75 Kg.	
10.	Dibasic Calcium Carbonate	22.00 Kg.	
11.	Butylated Hydroxy Toluene	15.00 g.	
12.	Polyvinylpyrrolidone	1.50 Kg.	
13.	Isopropyl Alcohol	13.50 Lit.	
14.	Magnesium Stearate	0.60 Kg.	
15.	Purified Talc	1.00 Kg.	

MANUFACTURING PROCESS

1. Coat Thiamine Mononitrate with Cetyl Alcohol (melted) and cool. Sift through 40 mesh.
2. Dissolve Butylated Hydroxy Toluene in Isopropyl Alcohol and add to 2 and 3.
3. Mix ingredient 6, 8, 9, 10 with coated Thiamine Mononitrate of Step 1 and solution from Step 2. Granulate with Polyvinylpyrrolidone in Isopropyl Alcohol solution. Dry and re-size.
4. Lubricate with Magnesium Stearate and Purified Talc.

MULTIVITAMIN WITH IRON TABLETS
(*Sugar Coated*)

LABELLED FORMULA

Each tablet contains :

Vitamin A	10,000 I.U.
Vitamin D_3	400 I.U.

Thiamine Mononitrate	10	mg.
Nicotinamide	100	mg.
Riboflavin	5	mg.
Ascorbic Acid	150	mg.
Cyanocobalamin	5	mcg.
Pyridoxine Hydrochloride	3	mg.
Calcium Pantothenate	20	mg.
Iron	10	mg.
Copper	1	mg.
Iodine	150	mcg.
Manganese	1	mg.
Magnesium	5	mg.
Zinc as Zinc Sulphate	1.5	mg.

BATCH SIZE : 3,30,000 Tablets
PRACTICAL YIELD : 3,25,000 Tablets
USUAL PACKING : Bottles of 25 Tablets

FORMULATION

S. No.	Ingredients	Quantity	Averages
1.	Nicotinamide	33.00 Kg.	
2.	Riboflavine	1.65 Kg.	
3.	Calcium Pantothenate	10.00 Kg.	50%
4.	Use Sodium Ascorbate For Ascorbic Acid	63.30 Kg.	10%
5.	Calcium Phosphate Dibasic Anhydrous	79.20 Kg.	
6.	Polyvinylpyrrolidone	5.50 Kg.	
7.	Specially Denatured Alcohol	22.0 Lit.	
8.	Vitamin A Acetate (0.5 MIU/g)	8.25 Kg.	25%
9.	Cholecalciferol (0.5 MIU/g)	436 g.	50%
10.	CMC Sodium HV for tablets	1.65 Kg.	
11.	Thiamine Mononitrate	3.96 Kg.	20%
12.	Pyridoxine Hydrochloride	1.10 Kg.	10%
13.	Cyanocobalamin - Use Vit. B_{12} Oral in Mannitol (1000 mcg/g)	2.52 Kg.	40%
14.	Magnesium Stearate Powder	3.52 Kg.	
15.	Stearic Acid Fine Powder	1.65 Kg.	
16.	Talcum Powder	2.64 Kg.	
17.	Iron, Use Ferrous Sulphate Dried	10.10 Kg.	
18.	Copper, use Copper Sulphate	1.30 Kg.	
19.	Zinc use Zinc Sulphate (dry monohydrate)	2.20 Kg.	

20.	Manganese, use Manganese Sulphate Monohydrate	1.00	Kg.
21.	Magnesium, use Light Magnesium Oxide Powder	2.95	Kg.
22.	Iodine, use Calcium Iodate Powder	80	g.
23.	Light Liquid Paraffin	700	g.
24.	Chloroform	1.4	Lit.
25.	Specially Denatured Alcohol	2.8	Lit.
26.	Zein Powder	1.62	Kg.
27.	Specially Denatured Alcohol	10.0	Lit.
28.	Talcum Powder	12.00	Kg.
29.	Kaolin Light	12.00	Kg.
30.	Acacia Powder	3.00	Kg.
31.	Sugar Cane Granular	15.00	Kg.
32.	Calcium Carbonate	27.00	Kg.
33.	Talcum Powder	18.00	Kg.
34.	Kaolin Light	12.00	Kg.
35.	Gelatin Powder	1.20	Kg.
36.	Acacia Powder	1.80	Kg.
37.	Sugar Cane Granular	102.00	Kg.
38.	Iron Oxide	1.0	g.
39.	Red Ferric Oxide	620	g.
40.	Bees Wax White	50	g.
41.	Paraffin Wax White	30	g.
42.	Carnauba Wax Yellow	20	g.
43.	Carbon Tetrachloride	3.25	Lit.

NOTE: Formulation includes sugar coating materials. All materials in order of use.

NAPROXEN TABLETS

LABELLED FORMULA

Each tablet contains :

Naproxen 250 mg.

BATCH SIZE : 1,00,000 Tablets

PRACTICAL YIELD : 98,000 Tablets

USUAL PACKING : Strip of 25 Tablets

FORMULATION

S. No.	Ingredients	Quantity	Averages
1.	Naproxen	26.25 Kg.	5%
2.	Starch	4.00 Kg.	

3.	Gum Acacia	0.30 Kg.
4.	Starch for paste	2.00 Kg.
5.	Gelatin	0.50 Kg.
6.	Dried Starch	2.00 Kg.
7.	Magnesium Stearate	0.45 Kg.

MANUFACTURING PROCESS

1. Mix sifted Naproxen, Starch 4.0 Kg. and Gum Acacia in a mixer for 15 to 20 minutes.
2. Prepare the binder Starch Gelatin paste by suspending 2.0 Kg. Starch in about 2.5 Lit. of D.M. Water. Take the Gelatin 0.5 Kg. in about 6.0 Lit. of hot water and mix it well till a thick clear solution is formed. Add Starch suspension in this Gelatin solution and heat on water bath till Starch gets Gelatinized. Mix well and use for binding.
3. Add the binder solution to the powders in a Planetary Mixer. Add more D.M. water till entire mass is thoroughly wetted.
4. Pass the granulate through no. 4 mesh to prepare the wet granules.
5. Dry the wet granules in trays at a temperature of 50°C – 60°C till L.O.D. of granules is not more than 1.5%.
6. Pass the granules through no. 12 mesh.
7. Blend all the granules with Starch 2.0 Kg. in a Double Cone Blender for 10 minutes. Add Magnesium Stearate and again blend for 2 minutes.
8. The granules are now ready for compression.

NITROFURANTOIN TABLETS

LABELLED FORMULA

Each tablet contains :

Nitrofurantoin 100 mg.

BATCH SIZE : 1,00,000 Tablets
PRACTICAL YIELD : 97,000 Tablets
USUAL PACKING : Strip of 25 Tablets

FORMULATION

S. No.	Ingredients	Quantity	Averages
1.	Nitrofurantoin	10.00 Kg.	
2.	Dried Starch	8.50 Kg.	
3.	Lactose	8.50 Kg.	
4.	Starch for Paste	0.80 Kg.	
5.	D.M. Water	8.00 Kg.	
6.	Microcrystalline Cellulose	0.50 Kg.	
7.	Talcum	0.40 Kg.	

8.	Dried Starch	0.60 Kg.
9.	Magnesium Stearate	0.20 Kg.

MANUFACTURING SPECIFICATIONS

Weight per tablet	:	295 mg.
Punches	:	9 mm.
Hardness	:	3.0 to 4.5 Kg/cm^2
Thickness	:	3.3 to 3.5 mm.
Friability	:	N.M.T. 0.5%
Disintegration Time	:	5 minutes

MANUFACTURING PROCESS

Follow the Standard Wet Granulation Process.

NORFLOXACIN TABLETS

LABELLED FORMULA

Each film coated tablet contains :

Norfloxacin 400 mg.

BATCH SIZE	:	25,000 Tablets
PRACTICAL YIELD	:	24,000 Tablets
USUAL PACKING	:	Strip of 10 Tablets

FORMULATION

S. No.	Ingredients	Quantity	Averages
1.	Norfloxacin	10.0 Kg.	
2.	Starch	200 g.	
3.	Polyvinylpyrrolidone	200 g.	
4.	Isopropyl Alcohol	4.0 Lit.	
5.	Magnesium Stearate	50 g.	
6.	Talcum	200 g.	
7.	Dried Starch	850 g.	

MANUFACTURING SPECIFICATIONS

1. Total weight of granules — 11.5 Kg.
2. Weight of 20 tablets — 9.2 g.
3. Weight per tablet — 460 mg.
4. Weight variation — about 3.5%.
5. Friability less than 1%.
6. Hardness — not less than 4.0 Kg/cm^2.
7. Disintegration in N/10 HCL - 30 minutes.
8. Punch size — 12.5 mm.

MANUFACTURING PROCESS

1. Mix Norfloxacin and Starch in the mixer for 10 minutes.
2. Dissolve Polyvinylpyrrolidone in 4 litres Isopropyl Alcohol.
3. Slowly add this solution to the mixer and run the mixer for 15 minutes.
4. Lubricate the granules before compression.

FILM COATING MATERIALS

1.	Shellac	140 g.
2.	Isopropyl Alcohol	2.0 Lit.
3.	Talcum	120 g.
4.	Titanium Dioxide	100 g.
5.	Tween 80	70 g.

Tablets to be coated by spraying the solution on the tablets uniformly.

OFLOXACIN TABLETS

LABELLED FORMULA

Each film coated tablet contains :

Ofloxacin 200 mg.

BATCH SIZE : 1,00,000 Tablets

PRACTICAL YIELD : 97,000 Tablets

USUAL PACKING : Strip of 10 Tablets

FORMULATION

S. No.	Ingredients	Quantity	Averages
1.	Ofloxacin	20.0 Kg.	
2.	Micro Crystalline Cellulose	7.0 Kg.	
3.	Starch	5.5 Kg.	
4.	Dibasic Calcium Phosphate	2.5 Kg.	
5.	Talcum	200 g.	
6.	Magnesium Stearate	800 g.	
7.	Aerosil	300 g.	
8.	Sodium Starch Glycolate	2.4 Kg.	

FILM COATING MATERIALS

1.	Hydroxypropyl Methycellulose	1.35 Kg.
2.	Polyethylene Glycol 400	210 g.
3.	Titanium Dioxide	150 g.
4.	Talcum	120 g.
5.	Sodium Lauryl Sulphate	60 g.
6.	Isopropyl Alcohol	15 Lit.

7.	Methylene Chloride	30 Lit.
8.	Sunset Yellow Lake Colour	21 g.

MANUFACTURING SPECIFICATIONS AND PROCESS

1. Prepare granules by Wet Granulation Process.
2. Total weight of granules — 40 Kg.
3. Weight per tablet uncoated — 400 mg.
4. Film Coat the tablets as usual using Sunset Yellow Lake (Film Coating Grade).

PARACETAMOL TABLETS I

LABELLED FORMULA

Each tablet contains:

Paracetamol 500 mg.

BATCH SIZE : 1,00,000 Tablets
PRACTICAL YIELD : 98,000 Tablets
USUAL PACKING : Strip of 25 Tablets

FORMULATION

S. No.	Ingredients	Quantity	Averages
1.	Paracetamol	50.0 Kg.	
2.	Gelatin	300 g.	
3.	Talcum	600 g.	
4.	Magnesium Stearate	600 g.	
5.	Aerosil	600 g.	
6.	Starch	6.0 Kg.	
7.	Methyl Paraben Sodium	11.0 g.	
8.	Propyl Paraben Sodium	2.0 g.	

MANUFACTURING SPECIFICATIONS

1. Prepare the granules by Wet Granulation Process.
2. 1% moisture to be added into the dried granules to enhance the appearence of tablets.
3. Total weight of granules — 60 Kg.
4. Weight per tablet — 600 mg.
5. Punch size — 12.5 mm.
6. Preservatives to be added to prevent fungus growth.

PARACETAMOL TABLETS II

LABELLED FORMULA

Each tablet contains :

Paracetamol 500 mg.

BATCH SIZE : 1,20,000 Tablets
PRACTICAL YIELD : 1,17,000 Tablets
USUAL PACKING : Strip of 10 Tablets

FORMULATION

S. No.	Ingredients	Quantity	Averages
1.	Paracetamol	60.0 Kg.	
2.	Starch	9.0 Kg.	
3.	Starch for Paste	3.0 Kg.	
4.	Starch Dried	0.72 Kg.	
5.	Propyl Paraben	10.0 g.	
6.	Methyl Paraben	50.0 g.	
7.	Guar Gum (Dealca)	0.96 Kg.	
8.	Talcum	0.80 Kg.	
9.	Aerosil	0.72 Kg.	
10.	Magnesium Stearate	0.80 Kg.	

MANUFACTURING SPECIFICATIONS

1. Potency : 98–102%.
2. Diameter : 13.24 mm.
3. Thickness : About 4 mm.
4. Hardness : 5–7 Kg/cm^2.
5. Moisture : Less than 1%.
6. Disintegration : Less than 10 minutes.
7. Weight of 20 tablets : 12.6 g.

PARACETAMOL, CAFFEINE AND CHLORPHENIRAMINE MALEATE TABLETS

LABELLED FORMULA

Each tablet contains :

Paracetamol 500 mg.
Caffeine 30 mg.
Chlorpheniramine Maleate 2 mg.

BATCH SIZE : 1,00,000 Tablets
PRACTICAL YIELD : 97,000 Tablets
USUAL PACKING : Strip of 10 Tablets

FORMULATION

S. No.	Ingredients	Quantity	Averages
1.	Paracetamol	50.00 Kg.	
2.	Caffeine	3.06 Kg.	2%
3.	Chlorpheniramine Maleate	210 g.	5%
4.	Starch	1.50 Kg.	
5.	Methyl Paraben Sodium	200 g.	
6.	Propyl Paraben Sodium	50 g.	
7.	Starch for Paste	2.00 Kg.	
8.	Magnesium Stearate	500 g.	
9.	Talcum	500 g.	
10.	Aerosil	200 g.	

MANUFACTURING SPECIFICATIONS

1. Total weight of granules 60 Kg.
2. Weight of 0 tablets — 12 g.
3. Weight per tablet 600 mg.
4. Moisture content of tablets — 1 to 2%.
5. Weight variation — about 3.5%.
6. Hardness not less than 4 Kg/cm^2.
7. Disintegration time — about 10 minutes.
8. Friability — not more than 1%.

SALBUTAMOL AND THEOPHYLLINE SUSTAINED RELEASE TABLETS

LABELLED FORMULA

Each sustained release tablet contains :

Salbutamol (as Sulphate)	4mg.
Theophylline Anhydrous	300 mg.

Batch Size : 9,00,000 Tablets
Practical Yield : 886,000 Tablets
Usual Packing : Blisters of 10 Tablets

FORMULATION
(Salbutamol Portion)

PART I

LOT I AND II SIFTING DETAILS

S.No.	Ingredients	Per Lot.	Mesh No.
1.	Salbutamol Sulphate	2.16 Kg.	40
2.	Lactose	66.00 Kg.	40

3.	Magnesium Carbonate	8.00 Kg.	40
4.	Methyl Cellulose	1.50 Kg.	40
	(Quantities per Lot)		
	Sifting of Lubricants		
1.	Magnesium Carbonate	4.50 Kg.	40
2.	Magnesium Stearate	4.50 Kg.	100
3.	Talcum	13.68 Kg.	100

PROCESSING INSTRUCTIONS

1. Transfer all the materials of one lot into the sifting room except lubricating material.
2. Sift the materials as per the sequence and specified mesh sieves.
3. Replace the material retained over the sieve with fresh material.

PART II

BINDER PREPARATION (WAX MATRIX)
Lot I and II

1.	Stearic acid	13.50 Kg.
2.	Canauba Wax	8.50 Kg.
3.	Methyl Cellulose	1.50 Kg.
4.	Polyethylene Glycol 4000	1.50 Kg.
	(Quantities per Lit.)	

1. Transfer the binding materials for the batch to the binder preparation area.
2. Start the steam supply to a Stainless Steel Jacketed pan and load one by one the following materials :
   Stearic Acid, Carnauba Wax and Polyethylene Glycol 4000. Heat to 125°C.
3. On melting of above materials, sift the molten wax matrix through 100 mesh sieve in a suitable size S.S. vessel. Add the pre-sifted Methyl Cellulose.
4. Stir vigorously to make a homogenous suspension of Methyl Cellulose in the wax matrix.

PART-III

MIXING AND GRANULATION
For Lot I and Lot II

1.	Lactose	66.00 Kg.
2.	Salbutamol Sulphate	2.16 Kg.
3.	Molten Wax Matrix	Batch Quantity
4.	Magnesium Carbonate	8.00 Kg.

PROCESSING INSTRUCTIONS

1. Transfer sifted materials and the wax matrix to the granulation area near the Mixer.
2. Sandwitch the Salbutamol Sulphate in-between in the bowl of the Mixer.
3. Mix them for 10 minutes.
4. Add the molten wax matrix to the above dry mixed materials and further m,ix them for 5 minutes at slow speed.
   (Note: The temperature of the molten wax matrix should be between 125°C to 130°C at the time of addition).
5. Now add Magnesium Carbonate to the semisolid wet mass and continue mixing for 5 minutes or till desired consistency is achieved. Judge the end-point of granulation by manual checking.
6. Record all the observations.

COOLING OF LOT I AND II

PROCESSING INSTRUCTIONS

1. Spread the granules uniformly in the clean Fluid Bed Drier bowl.
2. Dry the granules at room temperature till the temperature of the granules reaches the room temperature.
3. Record all the observations.

PART IV SIZING

1. Transfer the dried granules into the milling area.
2. Mill the dried granules using 2mm. S.S. screen, knives forward at fast / medium speed.
3. Collect the granules in S.S. containers with status labels.
4. Weigh the granules in each container.
5. Record all the observations.

NOTE: Limits— Not less than 100.700 kg. per lot.
Not more than 101.250 Kg. per lot.

PART V LUBRICATION

1.	Unlubricated granules	Actual Quantity
2.	Magnesium Carbonate	4.500 Kg.
3.	Talcum	13.680 Kg.

PROCESSING INSTRUCTIONS

1. Transfer all the milled granules and sifted lubricants to the blending room.
2. Load the granules (Lot I and II) from Sizing into the Octagonal Blender and tick mark against each container after loading, record the observations.

3. Blend the granules for 10 minutes.
4. Load the lubricants as per the sequence specified.
5. Close the lid of the Octagonal Blender.
6. Lubricate the granules for 15 minutes.
7. Unload the granules in 6 clean aluminium containers lined with single polythene bag.
8. Record all the observations.
9. Weigh the granules and record the total weight of lubricated granules.

NOTE :

. The theoretical weights of lubricated granules is 225.00 Kg. (Limit : Not less than 223.875 Kg. i.e. 99.50%).

FORMULATION - THEOPHYLLINE PORTION

Part I Sifting Details LOT I

S.No.	Ingredients	Quantity	Mesh No.
1.	Theophylline Anhydrous	90.00 Kg.	40
2.	Lactose	32.70 Kg.	40
3.	Methocel K-4M	3.30 Kg.	40
4.	Methocel K-15M	2.70 Kg	40

PROCESSING INSTRUCTIONS

1. Transfer all the materials of one batch into sifting room except lubricating material.
2. Sift the materials as per the sequence and specified mesh sieve given.
3. Replace the material retained over the sieve with fresh material and record under remarks.

NOTE:

Same sifting details and processing instructions to be followed for LOT II and LOT III.

PART II MIXING OPERATION LOT I

PROCESSING INSTRUCTIONS

1. Mix the dry powders in a suitable mixer-grinder for 5 minutes at slow speed.
2. Add the binder solution under slow speed with granulator on and mix for 15 minutes.
3. Scrape the material from the sides and mix again. Add more D.M. water to get the wet mass of suitable consistancy. Prepare the granules with the granulator on.

NOTE:

Same processing instructions to be followed for LOT II and LOT III.

PART III DRYING LOT I
PROCESSING INSTRUCTIONS

1. Transfer the wet granules to the bowl of Fluid Bed Dryer and shift the bowl to the drying area.
2. Fix the bowl under the Fluid Bed Dryer in drying chamber.
3. Switch on the electrical heating system and set the timer at 15 minutes.
4. Switch on the dryer.
5. After initial drying for 15 minutes, remove the bowl from the drying chamber and rake the semi-dried mass.
6. Repeat Steps 2 and 3 and start the dryer.
7. Continue drying till outlet temperature indicates between 55° – 61°C.
8. Switch off the electrical heating system and allow the granules to air for 5 minutes. Switch off the Fluid Bed Dryer.
9. Remove the bowl, sample the dried granules.

NOTE:

Take the sample from different parts of the bowl and mix the sample.

10. Check loss on drying of the mixed sample using Infra-red moisture balance.
11. In case loss on drying is more than 3% continue further drying at the above outlet temperature for another 10 minutes by repeating steps 2 to 5.
12. Repeat Steps 10 to 12 to check loss on drying.
13. Record all the observations.

NOTE:

Repeat Steps 1 to 13 for the other Lots. (Lot II and Lot III)

PART -IV SIZING LOT I
PROCESSING INSTRUCTIONS

1. Transfer the Fluid Bed Dryer to the milling area.
2. Mill the dried granules using 2 mm. Stainless Steel screen, knives forward at medium/fast speed.
3. Collect the granules in a polythene bag kept in S.S. container with status labels.
4. Weigh the granules in each container.
5. Record all the observations.

NOTE: REPEAT THE PROCESS FOR LOT II AND LOT III

Weight of granules not less than 130.8 kg. /Lot and not more than 131.1 Kg. Lot.

PART V – SIFTING OF LUBRICANTS

PROCESSING INSTRUCTIONS

1. Sift 2.70 Kg. of Magnesium Stearate through Mesh No. 100.
2. Replace the material retained over the sieve with fresh material and record under remarks.

PART VI – LUBRICATION

Processing Instructions

1. Transfer all the milled granules and sifted lubricants to the blending room.
2. Load the granules of Lot I and II from Part IV into Octagonal Blender and tick mark against each container after loading and record the same.
3. Then load the lubricants (Magnesium Stearate 2.70 Kg.) and granules of Lot III into the Octagonal Blender.
4. Close the lid of the blender and lubricate the granules for 15 minutes.
5. Unload the granules in clean aluminium containers lined with single polythene bag.
6. Record the observations.
7. Weigh the granules and record the total weight of lubricated granules.
8. Check the percentage of fines (Limit 32 - 40%).
9. Check the bulk density (Limit 0.68 – 0.76 gm/ml).

SPECIFICATIONS FOR COMPRESSION

1. Punch Size : 11.0 mm.
2. Thickness : 5.4 mm.
3. Weight Variation : 2 Tabs. N.M.T. 5% from Av. wt.
4. Weight of Theophylline Portion : 440 mg./tablet (lower blue layer).
5. Weight of Salbutamol Portion : 250 mg./tablet (White layer).
6. Total compression wt. : 690 mg./tablet.
7. Friability : Not more than 3% w/w.
8. Weight of 20 tablets: 13.800 g. (Limit 13.254 - 14.076 g.)
9. Hardness : Not less than 3.0 kg./cm^2.

PROCESSING INSTRUCTIONS

1. Fix the compression machine with the dies and punches for the product.
2. Transfer the granules to the compression room.
3. Adjust the compression parameters as given above.
4. Dispose off the first two rounds of tablets at the start of the batch.
5. Check and record the parameters.
6. Set the compression machine with both blue and white layers and record the same.
7. Start the compression, if the parameters comply with standards.

SOLUBLE ASPIRIN TABLETS

LABELLED FORMULA

Each tablet contains :

Acetyl Salicyclic Acid (Aspirin) 300 mg.

Batch Size : 1,00,000 Tablets
Practical Yield : 97,000 Tablets
Usual Packing : Strip of 10 Tablets

FORMULATION

S.No.	Ingredients	Quantity		Overages
1.	Calcium Carbonate	11.5	Kg.	
2.	Citric Acid Anhydrous	1.20	Kg.	
3.	Polyvinylpyrrolidone	0.25	Kg.	
4.	Isopropyl Alcohol	Q.S	Kg.	
5.	Acetyl Salicylic Acid (Aspirin)	31.5	Kg.	
6.	Dried Starch	6.00	Kg.	
7.	Aerosil	0.20	Kg.	
8.	Talcum	0.80	Kg.	
9.	Citric Acid Anhydrous	2.40	Kg.	
10.	Aerosil	0.15	Kg.	
11.	Talcum	2.40	Kg.	
12.	Dried Starch	1.80	Kg.	

MANUFACTURING SPECIFICATIONS

Punch Diameter : 11.5 mm
Hardness : 2.0 to 5.0 Kg/cm^2
Disintegration Time : N.M.T. 3 Minutes
Weight per tablet : 582 mg.

MANUFACTURING PROCESS

1. Calcium Carbonate, Starch, Talcum and Aerosil to be dried at 105°C for 8 hours.
2. Citric Acid Anhydrous to be dried at 60°C for 3 hours.
3. Mix Calcium Carbonate and Citric Acid in a Planetary Mixer and granulate with Polyvinylpyrrolidone dissolved in Isopropyl Alcohol.
4. Pass through 12 mesh and dry the wet granules at 45°C to 50°C by fan only.
5. Mix Aspirin with Dried Starch 6 Kg. Aerosil 0.2 Kg., Talcum 0.8 Kg. and Citric Acid Anhydrous 2.4 Kg., Slug this power mix on the slugging Tablet Machine. Break the slugs and prepare granules of 12 Mesh.

6. Dry the granules of (4) and (5) for 15 to 20 minutes.
7. Lubricate the granules with Aerosil 0.150 Kg., Talcum 2.4 Kg. and Dried Starch 1.8 Kg.
8. The granules are now ready for compression.

Caution: Store the granules at all stages in double polythene bags and covered with Silica Gel Bags.

THEOPHYLLINE, EPHEDRINE AND PHENOBARBITONE SUSTAINED RELEASE TABLETS

LABELLED FORMULA

Each sustained release tablet contains :

Theophylline (Hydrated)	198 mg.
Ephedrine Hydrochloride	48 mg.
Phenobarbitone	25 mg.

Colours : Sunset yellow, Ponceau 4 R

Batch Size : 7,00,000 Tablets
Practical Yield : 6,90,000 Tablets
Usual Packing : Blister of 10 Tablets
Shelf Life : 3 years

FORMULATION

PART I SUSTAINED ACTION GRANULATION

S.No	Ingredient	Quantity	
1.	Theophylline Anhydrous	63.000	Kg.
2.	Stearic Acid	32.935	Kg.
3.	Ethyl Cellulose	0.715	Kg.
4.	Carnauba Wax	2.810	Kg.
5.	Colour Sunset Yellow	0.018	Kg.
6.	Colour Ponceau 4R	0.107	Kg.
7.	Distilled Water	0.620	Kg.
8.	Sucrose	35.000	Kg.

PART II SUSTAINED ACTION GRANULATION

S.No	Ingredient	Quantity	
1.	Ephedrine Hydrochloride	22.400	Kg.
2.	Stearic Acid	6.300	Kg.
3.	Carnauba Wax	4.720	Kg.
4.	Ethyl Cellulose	1.175	Kg.
5.	Magnesium Stearate	2.470	Kg.
6.	Colour Ponceau 4R	10	g.
7.	Distilled Water	590	ml.

PART III SUSTAINED ACTION GRANULATION

1.	Theophylline Anhydrous	63.00	Kg.
2.	Ephedrine Hydrochloride	11.200	Kg.
3.	Phenobarbitone	17.500	Kg.
4.	Starch	15.570	Kg.
5.	Lactose	12.570	Kg.
6.	Stearic Acid	4.200	Kg.
7.	Polythylene Glycol 6000	4.560	Kg.
8.	Guar Gum (140 mesh)	0.730	Kg.
9.	Stearic Acid	0.720	Kg.
10.	Guar Gum (140 mesh)	2.950	Kg.
11.	Red Starch Granules	14.00	Kg.

PART IV RED STARCH GRANULATION

Batch Size : 3 Batch of 7,00,000 Tablets each (Yield 42.250 Kg.)

		Quantity Per Batch	
1.	Starch	44.125	Kg.
2.	Starch	2.500	Kg.
3.	Distilled Water	20.00	Lit.
4.	Distilled Water	2.50	Lit.
5.	Colour Ponceau 4R	89	g.

PART V SUSTAINED ACTION GRANULATION (128.16 KG.) WITH 5% REPRODUCTION GRANULES

1.	Sucrose	33.340	Kg.
2.	Stearic Acid	31.360	Kg.
3.	Ethyl Cellulose	0.670	Kg.
4.	Carnauba Wax	2.670	Kg.
5.	Theophylline (Anhydrous)	60.000	Kg.
6.	Colour Sunset Yellow	17	g.
7.	Colour Ponceau 4R	100	g.
8.	Distilled water	590	ml.
9.	* Reproduction Granules	8.600	Kg.

* 3 Kg. Theophylline is available from 8.600 Kg. of Reproduction Granules.

PART VI SUSTAINED ACTION GRANULATION WITH 5% REPRODUCTION GRANULES

1.	Ephedrine Hydrochloride	21.335	Kg.
2.	Stearic Acid	6.000	Kg.
3.	Ethyl Cellulose	1.130	Kg.

4.	Carnauba Wax	4.500	Kg.
5.	Magnesium Stearate	2.350	Kg.
6.	Colour Ponceau 4R	9	g.
7.	Distilled Water	570	ml.

* 1.065 Kg. Ephedrine Hydrochloride is available from 8.600 Kg. of Reproduction Granules.

MANUFACTURING SPECIFICATIONS

A. Immediate Release layer

Weight per tablet	:	210 mg. (200 to 220 mg.)
Hardness	:	3 kg/cm^2
Disintergration Time	:	N.M.T 10 minutes.

B. Sustained Release Layer

Weight per tablet	:	240 mg. (228 to 252 mg.)

C. Specifications for Double-layered tablets

Weight per tablet	:	450 mg. (427 to 473 mg.)
Hardness	:	6.0 to 6.5 kg/cm^2
Thickness	:	5.7 mm. to 6.0 mm
Friability	:	N.M.T. 2%
Moisture Content	:	N.M.T. 1.0%

MANUFACTURING PROCESS

Part I Process for Sustained Action Granulation

1. Add Stearic Acid 32.935 Kg. and Ethyl Cellulose 0.715 Kg. to a oil Jacketed Planetary Mixer. Melt completely by heating the oil with immersion heaters while stirring at slow speed. Then add Carnauba Wax 2.810 Kg. and continue heating with stirring till it melts completely. Temperature should be 106º to 110ºC.
2. Powder the Sucrose 35.0 Kg. through fine mesh and add to the planetary mixer and mix untill evenly distributed. Adjust the temperature to 106º to 110ºC.
3. Add Theophylline Anhydrous 31.0 Kg. with slow mixing maintaining the temperature till the completion of Theophylline addition. Stir for 10 minutes. Now add remaining quantity of 32.0 Kg. Theophylline Anhydorus and mix for 30 minutes. Maintain the temperature of the mass between 80º - 85ºC.

   Caution: Temperature below 80ºC will affect the Theophylline release rate of the finished tablets.
4. Switch off the heating and mix till the temperature falls down to 80º - 81ºC.
5. Dissolve the colours in hot distilled water and add the colour solution

evenly on the surface of the molten mass and mix thoroughly. Temperature of mass should be 80º to 81ºC. If necessary heat the bowl to get temperature of 80º - 81ºC to release the uncoloured mass at the bottom and sides. Do not leave the mass in the bowl to fall below 72ºC.

6. Transfer the hot mass (70º to 79ºC) to aluminium trays, level it and cut into sections of 3 cm × 3 cm with a spatula while it is still soft. Keep the trays overnight in air-conditioned area (temperature 25ºC and RH 50%)
7. Pass the slabs through a granulating machine and collect the granules in ploythene lined drums. Keep the drums in air conditioned area.

Part II

PROCESS FOR SUSTAINED ACTION GRANULATION

This process is for 2 batches of 7,00,000 tablets each

1. Load Stearic Acid 12.600 Kg. and Ethyl Cellulose 2.350 Kg. to a oil jacketed Bowl of a Planetary Mixer. Melt the materials completely with heat while stirring at slow speed.
2. Add Carnauba Wax 9.440 Kg. and continue heating till it melts completely. Adujust and maintain the temperature at 106º to 108ºC.
3. Add Ephedrine Hydrochloride 44.800 kg. and mix for 5 minutes at 106º to 108ºC.
4. Mix for 30 minutes at temperature of 80º to 85ºC by switching off the heaters.
5. Stop the mixer when the temperature falls to 80º to 81ºC. Add Colour Ponceau 4 R 20 g. dissolved in hot distilled water (at 80ºC) 1.180 Lit. and spread it evenly on the molten mass.
6. Mix the mass at high speed unitl the mass is uniform and temperature is 70º to 74ºC. If necessary the bowl may be heated to release patches of uncoloured mass at he bottom. Stop the mixer and scrape the sides but temperature should not fall below 80ºC will affect the release of Ephedrine Hydrochloride in the finished product.
7. Transfer the molten mass to Aluminium Trays, flatten and cut into section of 3 cm × 3 cm. with a spatula while the mass is still soft.
8. Allow the mass to cool at room temperature for 30 minutes to 60 minutes. Store in airconditioned room at 24ºC and 50% RH.
9. Pass the cold pieces through a mill, first at slow speed with knives forward followed by medium speed with knives forward and collect. the granules in ploythene lined tared drums and check the net weight.
10. Store the drums in air conditioned area at 24ºC and 50% RH. Divide the granules in two equal parts for 2 batches.

11. On the basis of the Q.C report blend sustained release granules A and B with Magensium Stearate 2.470 Kg. for the batch of 7,00,000 tablets for 20 to 25 minutes.

Note:

The weight of granules A must be between 3.84 to 3.89 times the weight of granules B. Extract quantity depends on the assay value of granules. If the weight ratio is not within the above limits calculate the weight of excess granules (either A or B) necessary to give the desired ratio. Remove the calculated weight of excess granules either A or B and store them in polythene lined closed containers in an airconditioned area at 24ºC and 50% RH.

12. Unload the granules in ploythene lined drums tightly closed and record the weight of granules. Store the final sustained release granules A+B in an airconditioned area at 24ºC and 50% RH.

Part III
PROCESS FOR IMMEDIATE RELEASE GRANULATION
Batch size: 7,00,000

1. Mill Ephedrine Hydrochloride 11.200 Kg., Polyethene Glycol 6000 4.560 Kg., Stearic Acid 4.200 Kg. and Guar Gum 0.730 Kg. through Cadmill using screen Q.S 35 at high speed with impact forward.
2. If lumps are found sieve theophylline 63.000 Kg. Phenobarbitone 15.500 Kg. Starch 15.570 kg., Lactose 12.570 Kg., Guar Gum 0.730 Kg. through 20 mesh.
3. Transfer the powders from Step 1 except Stearic Acid 0.730 Kg. and powders of Step 2 to the blender, add Red Starch granles 14,000 Kg. into the blender and mix for 30 minutes.
4. Transfer the blended powders to tared ploythene lined drums and record the weight.

   Note : If required Theophylline 63.000 Kg. can be granulated with hot distilled water and dried in Tray Dryer followed by dry-sizing and then used for blending.
5. Compress into slughs using a compression machine with 19 mm round, flat slugging punches. Allow the slugs to harden overnight in an airconditioned area at 24ºC and 50% RH. Hardness of slugs should not be less than 5 Kg/cm².
6. Pass the slugs through cadmill using screen QS2 at slow speed, knives forward or on a granulator using 12 mesh screen. Collect in tared ploythene-lined drums and record the weight.
7. Transfer the granules to a Drum Mixer and add Steric Acid 0.730 Kg. which is milled previously and Guar Gum 2.940 Kg. and blend for 30

minutes. Unload in tared polythene lined drums and record the weight. Store in air conditioned and dehumidified area and send sample to Quality Control.

METHOD FOR RED STARCH GRANULATION

Batch size : 42.250 Kg. (equivalent to 3 batches of 7,00,000 tablets each)

1. Load Starch 14.130 Kg. in the mixer bowl.
2. Prepare coloured starch paste by adding 2.500 Kg. starch to 20 Lit. Distilled water in a stainless steel oil jacketed tank and mixing slowly.
3. Dissolve Ponceau 4R 0.089 Kg. in Distilled water 2.50 Lit. and add to Step (2). Heat the above coloured suspension to 85º to 90ºC with intermittant mixing. Maintain the temperture at 85º to 90ºC for 15 minutes. At this stage, granulating agent will attain pink colour and a very thick consistency.
4. Granulate the powders of Step (1) with coloured Starch Paste from Step 3.
5. Dry the granules at about 55º to 60ºC till the moisture content of 2% to 3%.
6. Mill the dried granules through fine mesh and collect the granules n tared ploythene lined drums. Record the weight. For every batch of 7,00,000 tablets use 14.000 Kg. of Red Starch Granules for immediate release Granulation.

Compression

Compress the blended granules into double layered tablets using 3/8 inch standard concave punches on a machine suitable for layered tablets. Immediate release layer is white with pink mottling with bisect line and the sustained release layer is pink motteled. Compression area sholld be air conditioned at 24ºC and 50% RH.

The tablets are ready for strip packing.

TINIDAZOLE AND NORFLOXACIN TABLETS

LABELLED FORMULA

Each tablet contains :

Tinidazole	600 mg.
Norfloxacin	400 mg.

BATCH SIZE	: 1.00,000 Tablets
PRACTICAL YIELD	: 97,000 Tablets
USUAL PACKING	: Blister of 10 Tablets
SHELF LIFE	: 36 Months.

FORMULATION

S. No.	Ingredients	Quantity	Overages
1.	Tinidazole	60.00Kg.	
2.	Norfloxacin	40.00Kg.	
3.	Methyl Paraben	0.05 Kg.	
4.	Polyvenylpyrrdidone	0.80 Kg.	
5.	Maize Starch	3.20 Kg.	
6.	Magnesium Stearate	1.10 Kg.	
7.	Sodium Starch Glycolate	5.00 Kg.	
8.	Aerosil	0.50 Kg.	
9.	Lactose	0.60 Kg.	
10.	Talcum	1.20 Kg.	
	Film Coating Material		
1.	Hydroxypropyl Methylcellulose	2.00 Kg.	
2.	Titanium Dioxide	0.60 Kg.	
3.	Talcum	0.60 Kg.	
4.	Lake Yellow Colour	0.10 Kg.	
5.	Dibutyl Phthalate	0.40 Kg.	
6.	Isopropyl Alcohol	30.00Kg.	
7.	Methylene Chloride	50.00Kg.	

MANUFACTURING PROCESS

NOTE : Manufacturing of Tinidazole granules and Norfloxacin granules is done separately. Norfloxacin granules to be incorporated at the time of lubrication.

A. Preparation of Tinidazole Granules

1. Prepare Starch Polyvinylpyrrolidone Paste by soaking 0.500 kg. Polyvinylpyrrolidone in 2 Lit. D.M. Water, boil 8 Lit. D.M. Water in which are dissolved Methyl Paraben, a slurry of 2.5 kg. Maize Starch and Polyvinylpyrrolidone solution with constant stirring, Cook the paste if required and cool in a cold water bath.
2. Mix Tinidazole and Lactose in the planetary Mixer and prepare the wet granules with the Starch Polyvinylpyrrolidone Paste. Pass through multimill.
3. Dry the granules in Fluid Bed Drier at inlet temnperature of 70ºC till outlet temperature reaches 37ºC. Loss of weight would be 2 to 2.5% Sift the dry granules as usual.

B. Preparation of Norfloxacin Granules

1. Dissolve 0.300 Kg. Polyvinlypyrrolidone in 10 Lit. D.M. Water.
2. Load Norfloxacin to the Planetary Mixer and make the wet mass with Plyvinylpyrrolidone solutiuon. Prepare granules on the multimill.
3. Dry the granules in Fluid Bed Drier as usual, there is gain of weight (20 to 22.5%). Sift the granules.

C. Mixing of Granules

1. Load the Tinidazole and Norfloxacin granules in the Planetary Mixer.
2. Add sifted Magnesium Stearate, Sodium Starch Glycolate, Talcum, Maize Starch 0.500 Kg. and Aerosil and mix for 10 minutes.
3. The granules are ready for compression.

Technical Specifications

Average weight of the tablet	:	1150 mg. ± 5%
Disintergration Time	:	N.M.T 15 minutes
Hardness	:	N.L.T 5 Kg/cm^2
Thickness	:	7.1 ± 0.2 mm.

TINIDAZOLE, MICANAZOLE AND NEOMYCIN TABLETS

LABELLED FORMULA

Each tablet contains :

Tinidazole	500 mg.
Micanazole Nitrate	100 mg.
Neomycin Sulphate	20 mg.

BATCH SIZE	:	75,000 Tablets
PRACTICAL YIELD	:	72,800 Tablets
USUAL PACKING	:	Strip of 10 Tablets

FORMULATION

S. No.	Ingredients	Quantity	Overages
1.	Tinidazole	37.5 Kg.	
2.	Micanazole Nitrate	7.50 Kg.	
3.	Neomycin Sulphate	1.725 Kg.	15%
4.	Lactic Acid	0.75 Kg.	
5.	Lactose	27.27 Kg.	
6.	Starch	16.12 Kg.	
7.	Polyvinylpyrrolidone	2.25 Kg.	
8.	Starch	3.15 Kg.	
9.	Talcum	0.75 Kg.	

10.	Magnesium Stearate	0.375 Kg.
11.	Isopropyl Alcohol	12.00 Lit.

MANUFACTURING PROCESS

Standard Wet Granulation Process to be adopted.

TRIMETHOPRIM AND SULPHADIAZINE TABLETS

LABELLED FORMULA

Each tablet contains :

Trimethoprim 90 mg.

Sulphadiazine 410 mg.

BATCH SIZE : 1,00,000 Tablets

PRACTICAL YIELD : 98,000 Tablets

USUAL PACKING : Blister of 10 Tablets

FORMULATION

S. No.	Ingredients	Quantity	Overages
1.	Trimethoprim	9.0 Kg.	
2.	Suphadiazine	41.00 Kg.	
3.	Maize Starch	12.20 Kg.	
4.	Polyvinylpyrrolidone	0.50 Kg.	
5.	Talcum	1.20 Kg.	
6.	Hydrogenated Castor Oil	1.95 Kg.	
7.	Magnesium Stearate	0.15 Kg.	
8.	D.M. Water	9.00 Lit.	

MANUFACTURING SPECIFICATIONS

Weight per tablet : 660 mg.

Diameter : 13 mm

Thickness : 4.2 mm

Disintergration Time : 5 minutes

MANUFACTURING PROCESS

1. Disslove Plyvinylpyrrolidone in D.M. Water on water bath. Then suspend Maize Starch in this solution. Stir well to make a slurry. Heat the slurry with stirring to form a paste.
2. Mix Trimethoprim, Sulphgadiazine and 4.0 Kg. Maize stardh in suitable mixer. Mix for 15 minutes.
3. Add the paste to the powdermixer slowly with continuousmixing. Knead the mass for about 20 minutes. Extra D.M. Water may be added to achieve thewet mass for granulation.
4. Pass the wet mass through a suitable granulator and dry the wet granuules at 50º C. The moisture content of the dry granules should not be more than 1.5%.

5. Pass the dry granules through 16 mesh sieve andlubricae the dry granules with 5.20 Kg Maize Starch, 1.20 Kg. Talcum, 1.95 Kg. Hydrogenated Castor Oil and 0.15 Kg. Magnesium Sterarate.
6. The granules are ready for compression.

TRIMETHOPRIM AND SULPHAMETHOXAZOLE DS TABLETS

LABELLED FORMULA

Each coated tablet contains :

Trimethoprim	160 mg.
Silphamethoxazole	800 mg.

BATCH SIZE	:	62,500 Tablets
PRACTICAL YIELD	:	61,000 Tablets
USUAL PACKING	:	Strip of 10 Tablets

FORMULATION

S. No.	Ingredients	Quantity	Averages
1.	Trimethoprim	10.0 Kg.	
2.	Sulphamethoxazole	50.0 Kg.	
3.	Starch	0.2 Kg.	
4.	Methyl Paraben Sodium	0.1 Kg.	
5.	Propyl Paraben Soidium	0.05 Kg	
6.	Starch for Paste	1.5 Kg	
7.	Aerosil	0.2 Kg.	
8.	Magnesium Stearate	0.3 Kg.	
9.	Talcum	0.5 Kg.	
10.	Dried Starch to make	63.75 Kg.	

MANUFACTURING SPECIFICATIONS

1. Prepare Granules by Wet Granulation Process.
2. Total weight of granules — 63.75 kg.
3. Weight of 20 Tablets — 20.4 g.
4. Weight per tablet — 1.02 g.
5. Dry the granules at 60º C.
6. Punch size — 19.8 mm.
7. Weight variation about 3.5%
8. Hardness of tablets not less than 4kg./cm^2.
9. Disintegration time about 10 minutes.

VITAMIN B. COMPLEX TABLETS

LABELLED FORMULA

Each tablet contains :

Vitamin B_1	5 mg.
Vitamin B_2	2 mg.

Vitamin B_6	2 mg.
Calcium Pantothenate	3 mg.
Niacinamide	20 mg.

BATCH SIZE : 5,00,000 Tablets
PRATICAL YIELD : 4,80,000 Tablets
USUAL PACKING : Blister of 1 Tablets

FORMULATION

S. No.	Ingredients	Quantity	Overages
1.	Thiamine Mononitrate	3.25 Kg.	30%
2.	Pyridoxine Hydrocloride	1.15 Kg.	15%
3.	Riboflavine	1.10 Kg.	10%
4.	Nicotinamide	11.00 Kg.	10%
5.	Calcium Pantothenate	1.875 Kg.	25%
6.	Lactose	10.75 Kg.	
7.	Dibasic Calcium Phosphate	30.80 Kg.	
8.	Maize Starch	22.82 Kg.	
9.	Polyvinylpyrrolidone	1.75 Kg.	
10.	Isopropyl Alcohol	11.00 Lit.	
11.	Magnesium Stearate	0.50 Kg.	

MANUFACTURING PROCESS

1. Mix 1, 2, 3, 4, 5, 6, 7, 8 and granulate with Polyvinylpyrrokidone-isopropyl Alcohol solution.
2. Lubricate with Magnesium Sterate and compress.

VITAMIN B. COMPLEX TABLETS

(Prophytlatic)

LABELLED FORMULA

Each tablet contains :

Vitamin B_1	2 mg.
Vitamin B_2	2 mg.
Vitamin B_6	0.5 mg.
Niacinamide	25 mg.
Calcium Pantothenate	1 mg.

BATCH SIZE : 1,00,000 Tablets
PRACTICAL YIELD : 97,000 Tablets
USUAL PACKING : Bottle of 1000 Tablets

FORMULATION

S. No.	Ingredients	Quantity	Overages
1.	Thiamine Hydrochloride	280 g	40%
2.	Disodium Edetate	50 g	
3.	Tarataric Acid	375 g.	
4.	Riboflavine	230 g.	15%
5.	Pyridoxine Hyarochloride	57.5 g.	15%
6.	Calcium Pantothenate	130 g.	30%
7.	Nicotinamide	2.75 Kg.	15%
8.	Dicalcium Phosphate	9.0 Kg.	
9.	Lactose	5.0 Kg.	
10.	Starch	2.0 Kg.	
11.	Talcum	200 g.	
12.	Magenesium Stearate	200 g.	
13.	Gelatin	200 g.	
14.	Thiourea	50 g.	

MANUFACTURING SPECIFICATIONS

1. Total weight of granules — 20 Kg.
2. Weight per tablet — 200 mg.
3. Punch size — 8.3 mm.

MANUFACTURING PROCESS

1. Granulate Vitamin B1 with a solution contaninng Disodium Edetate, Tartaric Acid and Thiourea dissolved in water. Dry with starch.
2. Mix (1) with methyl Ploysiloxane 5 g. dissoved in Chloroform and dry at 50º C.
3. Mix vitamin B_2, Vitamin B_6, Calcium Pantothenate, Niacinamide, Dicalcium Phosphate 9 kg. and Lactose. Granulate with 2 Lit. Starch Gelatin Paste. Dry the granules at 60º C.
4. Lubricate the granules as usual.

Chapter 9

Injectables

INTRODUCTION

This dosage form is generally available in the market in the following forms:

1. Small Volume Parenterals
2. Large Volume Parenterals
3. Powder Parenterals

SMALL VOLUME PARENTERALS

This category of parenterals include Ampoules of 1 ml., 2 ml., 3 ml., 5 ml., 20 ml., and vials of 2 ml., 5 ml., 10 ml., 15 ml., 20 ml., 30 ml. They may be suitable for intra-muscular, intravenous, intra-dermal, subcutaneous, intra-spinal, intra-cisternal or intrathecal use.

LARGE VOLUME PARENTERALS

Containers containing 100 ml or more of the injectable solution is termed as large volume. They are usually used by the intravenous route. Intravenous Fluids commonly marketed today fall under the following two categories.

A. Electrolytes
B. Non Electrolytes

Sodium Chloride and Potassium Chloride solutions are examples of Electrolytes whereas Dextrose and Mannitol Solutions are examples of Non Electrolytes.

Special purpose intravenous solutions commonly used include Peritoneal Dialysis Solution, Anti-Coagulent Citrate Dextrose Solution, Glycine Irrigation Fluid, Metronidazole in Dextrose Injection etc.

Large Volume Parenterals are usually available in containers of 500 ml or 1000 ml.

POWDER PARENTERALS

They may be defined as dry, soluble or insoluble products ready to be combined with a solvent or a vehicle just prior to use. They are usually available in vials. Examples are injections of Penicillin, Ampicillin, Chloramphenicol, Amoxycillin, Streptomycin etc.

METHODS OF MANUFACTURE

Injections are sterile and pyrogen free liquids usually in solution or suspension of drugs intended for parenteral administration. The solution or suspensions of drugs intended for injection are prepared in the same general method of manufacture of liquid oral preparations or oral suspensions with the following difference.

1. Solvents or vehicles used must meet special purity and other standards assuring their safety by injection.
2. The use of added substances as buffers, stablizers and antimicrobial preservatives fall under specific guidelines of use and are restricted in certain parenteral products.The use of coloring agents is strictly prohibited.
3. Parenteral products are always sterilzed and meet sterility standards and most of them must be pyrogen free.
4. Parenteral Solutions must be free of particulate matter.
5. Parenteral Products must be prepared in environmentally controlled areas, under strict sanitation standards.
6. Parenteral Products are packaged in special hermatic containers.
7. Each container of an injection is filled to a volume in slight excess of the labelled volume. The excess permits the ease of withdrawl and administration of the labelled volumes.
8. There are restrictions over the volume of injections permitted in multiple dose containers or even single dose containers.
9. Specific labelling regulations apply to injections.
10. Sterile powders intended for solution or suspension immediately prior to injection are frequently packaged as Lyophilized or freeze dried powders to permit ease of solution or suspension upon the addition of the solvent or vehicle.

STERILIZATION PROCESSES

Injectables are usually sterilized by the following methods :

1. By the application of heat.
2. By the use of bactericides.
3. By the application of heat in the presence of bactericides.
4. By the use of bacteria proof filters.
5. By the use of aseptic technique during processing.

PRACTICAL TIPS

1. As far as possible freshly distilled water should be used for preparation of the solutions.
2. Use of Nitrogen Gas and protection from light solves many problems of discoloration and stability.
3. Appearance of particulate matter in injectable solutions is a common problem. Usual sources are :

(a) Improper cleaning of containers.

(b) Low quality rubber closures.

(c) Use of stored distilled water.

4. Check incompatibility of the various drugs before mixing.
5. Problems of stability and hydrolysis can be solved by maintaining the desired pH.
6. Always double check the pH on different pH meters e.g., Analog and Digital.
7. Rubber Closures are the biggest source of problems in large volume parenterals and small volume vials. Selection, storage, handling and washing process must be well defined.
8. Use of Butyl or Bromobutyl rubber stoppers should be preferred than those made of natural rubber.
9. Distilled Water is the most important "Raw Material" for large volume parenterals. Ensure its quality.
10. Use aseptic technique for all injectables including those which are to undergo terminal sterilization. Let workers get used to only one standard of manufacture.
11. The most vital "ingredient" in preparation of an injectable product is the proper attitude of the pharmacist and the skilled workers. Possession and application of high moral and professional ethics is a must.
12. Special techniques are required for the manufacture of sterile preparations. They should be employed with alertness and sound judgement. They need to be constantly upgraded.
13. Special attention need to be paid to the procurement, storage and testing of raw materials used. Always insist on reliable tried sources. A raw material may meet all the prescribed standards and still be adulterated. Cost factors should be given second place in importance.
14. The stability and effectiveness of the product must be establised with substantiating data. Process variations and differences in ingredient specifications must be taken into account.
15. A well defined and controlled program must be established for the manufacture of each product.
16. It is advisable to go through prescribed "Check List" before undertaking the manufacture.
17. Always follow Standard Operating Procedures for all machinery, equipment and processes.

LIST OF PRESERVATIVES USED IN INJECTIONS

S. No.	Name of Preservative	Usual Conc.	Stability and Imcompatability
1.	Benzyl Alcohol	1.0% to 2.0%	Bacteriostatic agent, has a weak local anaesthetic action.
2.	Chlorbutol	0.2% to 0.5%	Antibacterial germicidal properties, effective against Pseudomonas aeruginosa.
3.	Chlorocresol	0.1% to 0.2%	Volatile at 100° C.
4.	Phenylethyl Alcohol	0.25% to 0.5%	More active against gram negative bacteria. Volatile, sensitive to light and oxidising agents.
5.	Phenol	0.5%	Bacteriostatic, bactericidal and fungicidal.
6.	Phenylmercuric Nit.	0.001% to 0.002%	Slow acting and toxic.
7.	Phenylmercuric Ac.	0.001% to 0.002%	Slow acting and toxic.

VOLUME OF INJECTION IN CONTAINERS

Each single dose container shall contain a volume of injection in excess of the volume which is to be withdrawn. The excess volumes specified in the following table are usually sufficient to permit withdrawl of the labelled volume:

Labelled volume	Excess Volume for Mobile Injections	Excess Volume for Viscous Injections
ml	ml	ml
0.5	0.10	0.12
1.0	0.10	0.15
2.0	0.15	0.25
5.0	0.30	0.50
10.0	0.50	0.70
20.0	0.60	0.90
50.0 or more	2 percent	3 percent

The average volume determined in ten single-dose containers does not deviate by more than 5 per cent from the requirements stated above, and in not more than one of these ten single-dose containers does the volume deviate by more than 10 per cent from the requirements stated above.

Multiple dose containers labelled to yield a specific number of doses shall contain a sufficient excess to permit the withdrawl of the designated number of doses.

CLEANING AND STERILIZATION OF RUBBER STOPPERS

1. Boil Rubber Stoppers with about 1% Liquid Detergent Solution (e.g. Teepol) for 30 minutes. Wash them well to make them free from even traces of detergent.
2. Boil washed Rubber Stoppers with 1% solution of Hydrochloric Acid for 30 minutes. Wash to make them free of acid.
3. Boil the acid washed Rubber Stoppers with 1% Sodium Carbonate Solution and wash till free of alkali.
4. Take the above treated rubber stoppers and soak them in double the concentration of bacteriostatic or bacteriocidal being used in solution, for 24 hours. Wash several times with apyrogenic water for injection.
5. Autoclave the treated Rubber Stoppers at 115° C for 30 minutes.

NOTE

If rubber Stoppers are to be used for filling of solution which has acidic pH, then treat Rubber Stoppers first with Sodium Carbonate Solution and then with acid if the pH of the solution to be filled is alkaline then treat Rubber Stoppers first with Acid followed by Alkali.

CLEANING AND STERILIZATION OF VIALS

1. Soak the vials in detergent solution overnight to make them free of sticking particles, grease etc.
2. Brush and wash with the tap water and soak in 1% Hydrochloric Acid Solution to remove surface alkalinity.
3. Wash the vials with tap water till free of alkalinity.
4. Wash the vials with Deionized water and finally with Distilled Water in a semi-automatic or automatic washing machine.
5. Arrange the vials in suitable boxes of stainless steel or aluminium and sterilize by heating in a Dry Heat Sterilizer at 200°C for 4 hours.
6. Allow to cool under closed conditions to room temperature prior to filling.

AMEKACIN SULPHATE INJECTION

LABELLED FORMULA

Each ml contains :

Amikacin Sulphate	50 mg.

BATCH SIZE	:	10 Litres
PRACTICAL YIELD	:	4500 Vials of 2 ml.
USUAL PACKING	:	2 ml. White Vials

FORMULATION

S. No.	Ingredients		Quantity	Overages
1.	Amikacin Sulphate		500 g.	
2.	Sodium Bisulphite		13 g.	
3.	Sodium Citrate		50 g.	
4.	Sulphuric Acid to adjust pH		Q.S	
5.	Water for Injection	to	10 Lit.	

MANUFACTURING PROCESS (UNDER ASEPTIC CONDITIONS)

1. Dissolve Sodium Bisulphite, Sodium Citrate and Amikacin in freshly distilled water.
2. Adjust the pH to 4.5 (limit 3.5 to 5.5) with 10% Sulphuric Acid.
3. Filter through 0.2 μ Membrane Filter and fill aseptically in 2 ml White vials.

AMINOPHYLLINE INJECTION

LABELLED FORMULA

Each 10 ml contains :

Aminophyline 250 mg.

BATCH SIZE : 200 Litres

PRACTICAL YIELD : 18500 Ampoules

USUAL PACKING : 10 ml. Ampoules

FORMULATION

S. No.	Ingredients		Quantity	Overages
1.	Theophylline		4.040 Kg.	
2.	* Ethylenediamine Anhydrous		0.980 Kg.	
3.	Water for Injection	to	200 Lit.	

* To be used not later than 2 months after the date of passing.

Safety Precautions :

1. Dust masks must be worn when handling Theophylline.
2. Skin and eyes must be protected when handling Ethylenediamine.

MANUFACTURING PROCESS

1. Transfer 50 Lit. Water for Injection in a manufacturing vessel and dissolve Ethylenediamine.
2. Add Theophylline in the above and stir till dissolved completely.
3. Make up the volume to 200 Lit. with more of water for injection and mix well.

4. Pass filtered Nitrogen gas through the bulk solution.
5. Filter the solution through pre-sterilized filter assembly using 0.2 μ Membrane Filter.
6. Fill 10.5 ml in washed and sterilized ampoules.
7. Sterilized the ampoules by heating in an autoclave at 115°C for 30 minutes.

ANALGIN INJECTION

LABELLED FORMULA

Each ml. contains :

Analgin	500	mg.
Chlorbutol	0.4	%
Benzyl Alcohol	2.0	%

BATCH SIZE : 100 Litres
PRACTICAL YIELD : 17000 Ampoules of 5 ml.
USUAL PACKING : 5 ml. Amber Ampoules

FORMULATION

S. No.	Ingredients		Quantity	Overages
1.	Analgin		50.00Kg	
2.	Chlorbutol		0.40 Kg.	
3.	Benzyl Alcohol		2.00 Lit.	
4.	Distilled Water	to	100 Lit.	

MANUFACTURING SPECIFICATIONS

1. Solution should be pale yellow sparkling clear.
2. pH — 6.8 to 7.0.
3. Potency — 98% to 105%.
4. Density — About 1.173.
5. Fill 5.3 ml. in each ampoule.
6. Use Nitrogen Gas before and after filling.
7. Sterlize the ampoules by steaming at 100° C in an autoclave for 30 minutes.
8. Ampoules to be tested for leakage.
9. Shelf Life not applicable.

MANUFACTURING PROCESS

1. Dissolve Analgin Powder in 50 Lit.of hot distilled water at a temperature of 60° C to 70° C under constant stirring till completely dissloved.
2. Add Chlorbutol and Benzyl Alcohol in succession with constant stirring.
3. When completely dissolved, cool and make up the volume with freshly distilled water.

4. Adjust pH to 6.9 (6.8 to 7.0) with 10% Hydrochloric Acid or 4% Sodium Hydroxide Solutuion.
5. Filter through Filter Paper Pad and then throughG-3 Sintered Glass Funnel or equal porocity Membrane Filter.
6. Fill ampoules under Nitrogen Gas.
7. Sterlize by steaming for 30 minutes.

Caution : At the time of filling ampoules care should be taken that the solution does not adhere to the neck as it might cause charring.

ASCORBIC ACID INJECTION 100 mg.
(Vitamin C Injection)

LABELLED FORMULA

Each ml. contains :

Ascorbic Acid 100 mg.

BATCH SIZE : 100 Litres
PRACTICAL YIELD : 18,300 Ampoules of 5 ml.
USUAL PACKING : 5 ml. Amber Ampoules
SHELF LIFE : 2 Years

FORMULATION

S. No.	Ingredients	Quantity	Overages
1.	Ascorbic Acid	10.30 Kg	3%
2.	Sodium Bicarbonate	4.94 Kg	
3.	* Sodium Hydrosulphite	0.50 Kg.	
4.	* Disodium Edetate	0.10 Kg.	
5.	Propylene Glycol	5.00 Kg.	
6.	Water for injection to	100 Lit.	

* Use Analytical Reagent Grade

MANUFACTURING PROCESS

1. Take 70 Lit. freshly distilled and cooled distilled water in a 250 Lit. stainless steel tank with 200 Lit. mark.
2. Bubble Nitrogen (oxygen free) through the bulk.
3. Dissolve Ascorbic Acid slowly under constant stirring and nitrogen bubbling.
4. Slowly add Sodium Bicarbonate under slow stirring and Nitrogen gas bubbling in order to control effervescence.
5. Dissolve Sodium Hydrosulphite in 5 Lit. of freshly distilled water in a stainless steel vessel.
6. Add this solution to the bulk.
7. Dissolve Disodium Edetate in 2 Lit. of distilled water in another vessel and add to the bulk.
8. Add and mix Propylene Glycol in the bulk solutuion under slow stirring to avoid aeration with Nitrogen bubbling.

9. Check the pH of the bulk solution and adjust to 5.70 (Limit 5.50 to 6.50) with Sodium Hydroxide soluition or Ascorbic Acid solution.
10. Make up the volume and mix for 15 minutes while avoiding aeration.
11. Transfer the bulk solution to stainless steel pressure vessel used for membrane filteration. Flush the solution with Nitrogen and close the lid tightly.
12. Filter the solutution with positive pressure of Nitrogen through sterilized 0.22µ membrane filter into sterilized filling vessel.

NOTE :

The filteration assembly should be kept in the aseptic area and suitable precautions are to be taken for the aseptic technique during filteration and all subsequent operations.

13. Fill 5.3 ml. in sterilized 5 ml. amber ampoules.

Precautions

As Ascorbic Acid is sensitive to air and rapidly oxidised, Nitrogen gas (oxygen free) should be used throughout manufacturing. Protect the solution from light.

ASCORBIC ACID INJECTION 250 mg.

LABELLED FORMULA

Each ml. contains :

Ascorbic Acid	250 mg.
Parachlorometacresol (as preservative)	0.1 %

BATCH SIZE	:	60 Litres
PRACTICAL YIELD	:	25000 Ampoules of 2 ml.
USUAL PACKING	:	2 ml. Amber Ampoules

FORMULATION

S. No.	Ingredients	Quantity	Overages
1.	Ascorbic Acid	17.25Kg.	15%
2.	Sodium Bicarbonate	8.75 Kg.	
3.	Parachlorometacresol	60 g.	
4.	Water for Injection	60 Lit.	

MANUFACTURING PROCESS

1. In about 40 Litres of Distilled Water is suspended the ?Ascorbic Acid slowly with continous stirring. This should be done in an open vessel.
2. Go on adding slowly Sodium Bicarbonate with vigorous stirring. The level of the liquid will rise considerably since profuse effervescence will be there. As this subsides add further Sodium Bicarbonate. This process is continued till Ascorbic Acid is completely dissolved.
3. Add Parachlorometacressol and stir till diossolved.

4. Make up the volume to 60 Liters with Distilled Water.
5. Adjust the pH to 5.7 (limit 5.5 to 6.4).
6. Filter through G-3 and G-4 Sintered Glass Funnels or through sutiable membrane.
7. Fill 2.15 ml. in Amber Ampoules.
8. Sterilize by Steaming for 30 minutes.

ATROPINE SULPHATE INJECTION

LABELLED FORMULA

Each ml. contains :

Atropine Sulphate 0.5 mg.

BATCH SIZE : 10 Litres
PRACTICAL YIELD : 8600 Ampoules of 1 ml.
USUAL PACKING : 1 ml. White Ampoules

FORMULATION

S. No.	Ingredients	Quantity	Overages
1.	Atropine Sulphate	5.2 g.	
2.	Acetic Acid	3.0 ml.	
3.	Sodium Acetate	12.0 g.	
4.	Sodium Chloride	65.0 g.	
5.	Sodium Metabisulphite	10.0 g.	
6.	Water for Injection to	10 Lit.	

MANUFACTURING SPECIFICATIONS

1. pH — 4.0 to 6.0
2. Terminal Sterilization by autoclaving at 116°C for 30 minutes.
3. Fill 1.1 ml in white 1 ml. Ampoules.

BUPRENORPHIN INJECTION

LABELLED FORMULA

Each ml. contains :

Buprenorphin Hydrochloride : 0.324 mg.

BATCH SIZE : 60 Litres
PRACTICAL YIELD : 53000 Ampoules of 1ml.or 27,000 Ampoules of 2 ml.
USUAL PACKING : 1 ml. White Ampoules or 2 ml. White Ampoules
SHELF LIFE : 3 years

FORMULATION

S. No.	Ingredients	Quantity	Overages
1.	Buprenorphin Hydrochloride	19.63 g.	1%
2.	Propylene Glycol	1.20 Lit.	
3.	Dextrose Anhydrous (Injectable Grade)	3.00 Kg.	-
4.	Water for Injection	60.0 Lit.	-

MANUFACTURING PROCESS

Precautions :

1. Maintain aseptic conditions throughout.
2. Temperature control 20° C – 23° C is very essential.
3. Avoid undue exposure to air during manufacturing to prevent oxidation.

Part A. Preparation of Buprenorphin Hydrochloride Solution

1. To a 2 Lit. sterile conical flask add 1.20 Lit. Propylene Glycol and heat to 50°C.
2. Add slowly with continuous stirring 19.63 g. of Buprenorphine Hydrochloride till dissolved completely.

Part B. Preparation of Dextrose Solution

1. To a 100 Lit. stainless steel vessel fitted with an overhead stirrer add 50 Lit. Sterile Water for Injection at about 50°C Then add 3.0 kg. Dextrose Anhydrous (injectable grade) and stir till a clear solution is obtained.
2. Check the pH and adjust to 3.7 with 10% Hydrochloric Acid prepared in sterile water for injection.

Part C. Mixing of Part A and B

1. To part B add slowly with constant stirring solution of Part A at a temperature 45° C – 50°C.
2. Temperature of Part A and Part B should be nearly the same while mixing otherwise precipitaion may occur.
3. Stir till a clear solution is obtained.
4. Check the pH and adjust if necessary to 3.7 with 10% Hydrochloric Acid.
5. Adjust the volume to 60 Litres with sterile water for injection.
6. Stir the solution for 10 minutes and gain check the pH. Adjust if necessary.
7. Filter the solution through 0.2μ Membrane Filter. Check the pH after filtering 15 Lit. Adjust if necessary to 3.7 and add to the bulk.
8. Fill aseptically in 1 ml. (1.1 ml.) or 2 ml. (2.15 ml.) White Ampoules previously sterilized.
9. Sterilize the ampoules by autoclaving at 121° C for 30 minutes.

CALCIUM GLUCONATE INJECTION

LABELLED FORMULA

Each 10 ml. contains :

Calcium Gluconate: 1.0 g.

BATCH SIZE : 100 Litres
PRACTICAL YIELD : 9200 Ampoules of 10 ml.of 2 ml.
USUAL PACKING : 10 ml. White Ampoules

FORMULATION

S. No.	Ingredients		Quantity	Overages
1.	Calcium Gluconate		10.0 Kg.	
2.	Calcium D-Saccharate		3.5 Kt.	
3.	Water for Injection	to	100 Lit.	

MANUFACTURING PROCESS

1. Dissolve Calcium Gluconate and Calcium D-Saccharate in freshly distilled water.
2. Adjust the pH to 6.0 to 8.2 with 10% Sodium Hydroxide solution.
3. Filter through 0.45μ Membrane Filter.
4. Fill in 10 ml. Ampoules.
5. Sterilize the ampoules by autoclaving at 120•C for 30 minutes.

CHLORAMPHENICOL INJECTION

LABELLED FORMULA

Each ml. contains :

Chloramphenicol 125 mg.
Lignocaine Hydrochloride 1.20 mg.
Chlorocresol 0.2 %
Propylene Glycol Q.S.

BATCH SIZE : 100 Litres
PRACTICAL YIELD : 9500 Vials of 10 ml.
USUAL PACKING : 10 ml. Amber Vials.

FORMULATION

S. No.	Ingredients	Quantity	Overages
1.	Chloramphenicol	12.5 Kg.	
2.	Lignocaine Hydrochloride	514 g.	
3.	Lignocaine Base	405 g.	
4.	Chlorocresol	1.0 Kg.	
5.	Distilled Water	12.0 Lit.	
6.	Propylene Glycol to	10.0 Lit.	

MANUFACTURING PRCOESS

1. Take 75 litres Propylene Glycol and steam it is an autoclave for 30 minutes.
2. Add Chloramphenicol in hot Propylene Glucol and stir till dissolved.
3. Add Lignocaine Bse to the Chloramphenicol solutionand stir till dissolved.
4. Dissolve Chlorocresol and Lignocaine Hydrochloride in 12 Litres fo freshly distilled water, add this to the bulk and stir well.
5. Allow to cool to room temperature and make up the volume to 100 Litres with steamed and cooled Propylene Glycol.
6. Check the pH of the solution. It should have the pH of 6.5 to 6.8.
7. Filter the solution under vaccum through Wattman filter paper No. 1 and then through sterile G-3 Somtered Glass Funnel.
8. Fill 10.5 ml. in dry sterile 10 ml. amber vials and flush with Nitrgen before and afterfilling. Plug the vials with washed sterile Buty Grey Plugs ans seal wigh centre tear off Aluminium seals.
9. Filling should be done under asceptic conditions.

CHLOROQUINE PHOSPHATE INJECTION

LABELLED FORMULA

Each ml. contains :

Chloroquine Base: 40 mg.
Chlorbutol 0.5 %

BATCH SIZE : 120 Litres
PRACTICAL YIELD : 3800 Vials of 30 ml.
USUAL PACKING : 30 ml. Amber Vials.

FORMULATION

S. No.	Ingredients	Quantity	Overages
1.	Chloroquin Phosphate	7.74 Kg.	-
2.	Chlorbutol	600 g.	-
3.	Benzyl Alcohol	1.20 Lit.	-
4.	Water for Injection to	120 Lit.	-

MANUFACTURING SPECIFICATIONS

1. Appearance — Clear sparkling solution.
2. Potency — 95 to 105% of claim.
3. pH — 3.5 to 4.5.
4. Fileration — Filter through G-4 and G-5 Sintered Glass Funnel.
5. Filling — Fill under asceptic conditions. Fill 30.5 to 31.0 ml. in each vial.

Note: 200 mg Chloroquine base is approximately equivalent to 322 mg. of Chloroquine Phosphate.

MANUFACTURING PROCESS

1. Take 90 Litres of freshly distilled water in a S.S. Tank and dissolve Chloroquine Phosphate.
2. Dissolve Chlorbutol in Benzyl Alcohol. Add this solution to step No.1 in small amounts till completely dissolved.
3. When the solution is clear make up the volume to 120 litres with freshly distilled water for injection.
4. Chck the pH. It should be 3.5 to 4.5.
5. Sterileze the vials by steaming.

CIPROFLOXACIN LACTATE INFUSION

LABELLED FORMULA

Each 100 ml. contains :

Ciprofloxacin 200 mg.

BATCH SIZE : 100 Litres
PRACTICAL YIELD : 970 vials of 100 ml.
USUAL PACKING : 100 ml. Vials

FORMULATION

S.No.	Ingredients	Quantity		Overages
1.	Water for Injection	90.0	Lit.	
2.	Disodium Edetate	5.0	g.	
3.	Lactic Acid	46.7	g.	
4.	Ciprofloxacin Lactate	254	g.*	
5.	Sodium Chloride	900	g.	

* Correction to be made taking into account the actual moisture content of the bulk drug.

MANUFACTURING SPECIFICATIONS

Appearance : A clear colourless liquid
pH : 3.6 to 4.0

MANUFACTURING PROCESS

1. Take 90 Litres of water for Injection and dissolve Disodium Edetate, Lactic Acid, Ciprofloxacin Lactate and Sodium Chloride one by one in this order only.
2. Make up the volume to 100 Litres with Water for Injection.
3. Filter the solution through 0.45 μ membrane filter.
4. Fill the above solution in 100 ml. washed vials and close the bottles with washed rubber plugs.
5. Autoclave the filled vials at 120°C for 30 minutes.

CLINDAMYCIN PHOSPHATE INJECTION

LABELLED FORMULA

Each ml contains :
Clindamycin Phosphate
equivalent to Clindamycin 150 mg.

BATCH SIZE : 10 Litres
PRACTICAL YIELD : 4500 Ampoules of 2 ml.
USUAL PACKING : 2 ml. White Ampoules

FORMULATION

S.No.	Ingredients	Quantity	Overages
1.	Clindamycin Phosphate	1.80 Kg.	
2.	Benzyl Alcohol	94.5 ml.	
3.	Disodium Edetate	5.0 g.	
4.	Sodium Hydroxide or Hydrochloric Acid (for pH Adjustment)	Q.S	
5.	Water for injection to	10 Lit.	

(Note : 1 mg. of Clindamycin = 1.2 mg. Clindamycin Phosphate) pH range 5.5 to 7.0.

CYANOCOBALAMIN INJECTION 1000 mcg.

LABELLED FORMULA

Each ml. contains :
Cyanocobalamin 1000 mcg.
Benzyl Alcohol 1%

BATCH SIZE : 10 Litres
PRACTICAL YIELD : 950 Vials of 10 ml.
USUAL PACKING : 10 ml. Amber Vials

FORMULATION

S.No.	Ingredients	Quantity	Overages
1.	Cyanocobalamin	12 g.	20%
2.	Sodium Chloride	75 g.	—
3.	Sodium Dihydrogen Phosphate	30 g.	—
4.	Benzyl Alcohol	100 ml.	—
5.	Water for injection to	10 Lit.	—

MANUFACTURING SPECIFICATIONS

1. pH— 4.0 to 5.5
2. Filling Aseptically in 10 ml. amber vials.

3. Use Butyl or Latex Rubber Stoppers.
4. Sterilize rubber stoppers by autoclaving at 115°C for 30 minutes.
5. Washed Vials to be sterilized at 200°C for 4 hours.
6. Filteration through G-3 Sintered Glass Funnel followed by Membrane Filteration.
7. Shelf Life - 24 Months.

CYANOCOBALAMIN INJECTION 1000 mcg.
(Vitamin B_{12} Injection)

LABELLED FORMULA

Each ml contains :

Cyanocobalamin	1000 mcg.
Benzyl Alcohol (as preservative)	1.5% v/v
Water for injection	Q.S.

BATCH SIZE : 100 Litres
PRACTICAL YIELD : 9300 Vials of 10 ml.
USUAL PACKING : 10 ml. Amber Vials

FORMULATION

S.No.	Ingredients	Quantity		Overages
1.	Cyanocobalamin	102	g.	2%
2.	Sodium Chloride	900	g.	
3.	*Sodium Acetate	370	g.	
4.	*Glacial Acetic Acid	120	g.	
5.	Propylene Glycol	2.0	Lit.	
6.	Benzyl Alcohol	1.5	Lit.	
7.	Water for injection Q.S. to	100	Lit.	

* Use Analytical Reagent Grade

NOTE: Calculate the quantity of Cyanocobalamin as per potency on anhydrous basis.

MANUFACTURING PROCESS

1. Take 90 Lit. freshly distilled water in 150 Lit. capacity stainless steel vessel with 100 Lit. marking and bubble Nitrogen gas (oxygen free) continuously.
2. Add and dissolve Sodium Chloride with stirring.
3. Add and dissolve Sodium Acetate under stirring.
4. Add and mix slowly Clacial Acetic Acid.

5. Add and Mix Propylene Glycol under stirring.
6. Check the pH of the solution, it should be 5.0 (limit 3.8 to 5.5). If required adjust the pH to 5.0 with Sodium Hydroxide solution or dilute Hydrochloric Acid or Glacial Acetic Acid.
7. Add and Mix Benzyl Alcohol in the bulk under stirring at room temperature.
8. Adjust the volume to 100 Lit. and stir for 10 minutes.
9. Filter the solution through sterile 0.22μ membrane filter under Nitrogen pressure.
10. Fill 10.5 ml. in 10 ml. Amber vials with pre and post Nitrogen flushing.

CYANOCOBALAMIN INJECTION 500 mcg.

(Vitamin B_{12} Injection)

LABELLED FORMULA

Each ml contains :

Cyanocobalamin	500 mcg.
Benzyl Alcohol	1.5% v/v

BATCH SIZE	:	100 Litres
PRACTICAL YIELD	:	9200 Vials of 10 ml.
USUAL PACKING	:	10 ml. Amber Vials

FORMULATION

S.No.	Ingredients	Quantity		Overages
1.	Cyanocobalamin	51	g.	2%
2.	Sodium Chloride	900	g.	
3.	Sodium Acetate	370	g.	
4.	Glacial Acetic Acid	120	g.	
5.	Propylene Glycol	2.0	Lit.	
6.	Benzyl Alcohol	1.5	Lit.	
7.	Water for injection Q.S. to	100	Lit.	

MANUFACTURING PROCESS (UNDER ASEPTIC CONDITIONS)

1. Take about 80 Lit. of fresh water for injection and start Nitrogen bubbling.
2. Add Sodium Chloride and dissolve.
3. Add Sodium Acetate and dissolve.
4. Add Glacial Acetic Acid under stirring.
5. In another stainless steel vessel dissolve Cyanocobalamin in fresh 10 Lit. water for injection by heating and add to the above solution.
6. Add Benzyl Alcohol and then Propylene Glycol.
7. Make up the volume and check pH. It should be 3.8 to 5.5.

8. Filter through sterile 0.2μ Membrane Filter.
9. Fill 10 ml. Amber vials under Nitrogen. Vials should be sterilized at 200°C for 2 hours and cooled to room temperature before filling.
10. Use 20 mm. Latex Rubber Plugs.

DEXTROSE INJECTION 5% and 10%
(Large Volume Intravenous Solution)

BATCH SIZE : 300 Litres.
PRACTICAL YIELD : 540 Bottles of 540 ml.
USUAL PACKING : 540 ml. White Glass Bottles

FORMULATION

S.No.	Ingredients	Quantity 5%		Quantity 10%	
1.	Dextrose Anhydrous	15.75	Kg.	31.5	Kg.
2.	Activated Charcoal	150	g.	150	g.
3.	Pyrogen Free Distilled Water to	300	Lit.	300	Lit.

MANUFACTURING SPECIFICATIONS

1. Use Bromo Butyl Grey Rubber Stoppers 31.5 mm.
2. Wash and Sterilize the Rubber Stoppers at 116°C for 30 minutes before use.
3. Use Triple Aluminium
4. Use Plastic Hangers suitable for 32 mm. vial neck Bottles
5. Sterilize the filled bottles in an autoclave at 121°C for 20 minutes. Time and Temperature should not exceed limits ± 3°C Temperature and ± 2 minutes duration.
6. Use freshly prepared water for Injection or which has been stored at 80°C for not more than 24 hours.
7. Sterilization of filled bottles should be done within two hours of its filling.
8. pH of Solution decreases on autoclaving and hence should not be adjusted. Initial pH before autoclaving is usually 5.5 to 6.5 pH after autoclaving comes to 4.0 to 4.3.
9. Autoclaving operation should be well controlled to minimise exposure to prevent excess sterilization resulting in failing of batch in 5-Hydroxy methyl furfural test of pharmacopoeia.

MANUFACTURING PROCESS

1. Add Dextrose to water for Injection at 60°C and mix for 15 minutes. Add Activated Charcoal and mix for 15 minutes.

2. Filter the solution through Filter Paper Pads to get clear charcoal free solution. Again filter through 0.45μ Membrane Filter before filling in 540 ml. Glass Bottles.
3. Fill 540 ml. of at 50° to 45°C and seal immediately.

DEXTROSE WITH SODIUM CHLORIDE INJECTION (Large Volume Intravenous Solution)

LABELLED FORMULA

Dextrose	5%
Sodium Chloride	0.9%

BATCH SIZE	:	300 Litres
PRACTICAL YIELD	:	550 Bottles of 540 ml.
USUAL PACKING	:	540 ml. White Glass Bottles

FORMULATION

S.No.	Ingredients	Quantity	Overages
1.	Dextrose	16.5 Kg.	10%
2.	Sodium Chloride	2.8 Kg.	4%
3.	Activated Charcoal	150 g.	
4.	Water for Injection to	300 Lit.	

MANUFACTURING SPECIFICATIONS AND PROCESS

1. Degradation during autoclaving in this case is more than plain Dextrose Injection. Hence 10% overages of Dextrose has been taken instead of 5%.
2. Excess sterilization to be prevented as it results in degradation and failing of the product in 5 Hydroxymethyl furfural test.

DIAZEPAM INJECTION

LABELLED FORMULA

Each ml contains :

Diazepam	5 mg.

BATCH SIZE	:	45 Litres
PRACTICAL YIELD	:	20,000 Ampoules of 2 ml.
USUAL PACKING	:	2 ml. Ampoules

FORMULATION

S.No.	Ingredients	Quantity	Overages
1.	Diazepam	229.5 g.	2%
2.	Benzyl Alcohol	675 ml.	

3.	Monobasic Sodium Phosphate	117	g.
4.	Diabasic Sodium Phosphate	4.5	g.
5.	Propylene Glycol	29.25	Lt.
6.	Water for injection to	45	Lt.

MANUFACTURING PROCESS

1. Take 29.25 Lit. Propylene Glycol and heat it to about 70°C. Start passing Nitrogen.
2. Dissolve Diazepam in Benzyl Alcohol and add to Propylene Glycol.
3. Dissolve Monobasic Sodium Phosphate and Dibasic Sodium Phosphate in 5 Lit. of fresh water for injection and add to Propylene Glycol.
4. Make up the volume to 45 Lit. and check the pH.
5. Filter through sterile 0.45µ Membrane Filter.
6. Fill 2.15 ml. in 2 ml. Amber Ampoules under Nitrogen.
7. Sterilize the ampoules before filling at 200°C for 2 hours.

NOTE:

All Manufacturing operations to be carried out under aseptic conditions.

DICLOFENAC SODIUM INJECTION

LABELLED FORMULA

Each ml contains :

Diclofenac Sodium 25 mg.

BATCH SIZE : 100 Litres
PRACTICAL YIELD : 30,700 Ampoules of 3 ml.
USUAL PACKING : 3 ml. Amber Ampoules

FORMULATION

S.No.	Ingredients	Quantity		Overages
1.	Diclofenac Sodium	2.50	Kg.	
2.	Mannitol (Pyrogen Free)	0.60	Kg.	
3.	Sodium Metabisulphite	0.30	Kg.	
4.	Benzyl Alcohol	4.00	Kg.	
5.	Propylene Glycol (Double Distilled)	20.0	Kg.	
6.	Sodium Hydrochloride (for pH adjustment)	0.11	Kg.	
7.	Water for Injection to	100	Lit.	

MANUFACTURING PROCESS

To be manufactured under aseptic conditions. Adjust the pH to 3.60 (limits 3.30 to 4.50). No special process involved in manufacturing pH to be adjusted with 10% Hydroxide.

DIGOXIN INJECTION
(For Intervenous use)

LABELLED FORMULA

Each ml contains :

Digoxin 0.25 mg.

BATCH SIZE : 100 Litres
PRACTICAL YIELD : 45,000 Ampoules of 2 ml.
USUAL PACKING : 2 ml. White Ampoules

FORMULATION

S.No.	Ingredients	Quantity		Overages
1.	Digoxin	25	g.	
2.	Propylene Glycol	50	Lit.	
3.	* Dibasic Sodium Phosphate	300	g.	
4.	Citric Acid (for pH adjustment)	80	g.app.	
5.	Water for injection to	100	Lit.	

* Use Analytical Reagent Grade

MANUFACTURING PROCESS

1. Take Propylene Glycol in 150 Lit. capacity stainless steel tank with 100 Lit. marking and bubble Nitrogen gas (oxygen free).
2. Dissolve Digoxin under stirring and Nitrogen bubbling.
3. Take 5 Lit. freshly distilled water in another vessel and dissolve Dibasic Sodium Phosphate. Add this solution to the bulk solution under stirring and Nitrogen bubbling.
4. Separately dissolve Citric Acid in 2 Lit. freshly distilled water.
5. Add this solution to the bulk under stirring and Nitrogen bubbling till pH is adjusted to 7.0 (limit 6.8 to 7.2).
6. Make up the volume to 100 Lit. with freshly distilled water and stir for 15 minutes.
7. Filter the solution aseptically with positive pressure of Nitrogen through sterile 0.22 μ membrane filter.
8. Fill 2.15 ml. in 2 ml. ampoules with pre and post Nitrogen flushing.

Note :

Nitrogen bubbling and flushing is required at every stage of manufacture. Aseptic conditions should be maintained throughout.

ELECTROLYTE MAINTENANCE I.V. FLUID
(For Peadiatric use)

LABELLED FORMULA

Dextrose Anhydrous	5%
Sodium Acetate	0.315%
Potassium chloride	0.13%
Magnesium Chloride	0.031%
Dibasic Potassium Phosphate	0.026%
Sodium Metabisulphite	0.021%
Acetic Acid	Q.S
Water for Injection to	100%

BATCH SIZE : 50 Litres
PRACTICAL YIELD : 485 Bottles of 100 ml.
USUAL PACKING : 100 ml. in 540 ml. Glass Bottles for I. V. fluids.

FORMULATION

S.No.	Ingredients	Quantity		Overages
1.	Dextrose Anhydrous	2.75	Kg.	10%
2.	Sodium Acetate	165	g.	5%
3.	Potassium Chloride	68.25	g.	5%
4.	Magnesium Chloride	16.27	g.	5%
5.	Dibasic Potassium Phosphate	13.65	g.	5%
6.	Sodium Metabisulphite	11.02	g.	5%
7.	Glacial Acetic Acid	Q.S		
8.	Water for Injection to	50	Lit.	

MANUFACTURING SPECIFICATIONS & PROCESS

1. Dissolve Sodium Acetate, Potassium Chloride, magnesium Chloride and Dibasic Potassium Phosphate in 45 Litres Water for Injection. Adjust the pH to 5.0 with Glacial Acetic Acid. Now add Dextrose Anhydrous and Sodium Metabisulphite. Make up the volume to 50 Litres and check the pH again, adjust between 4.8 and 5.0 with Glacial Acetic Acid if required.
2. Filteration, Filling and Sterilization process same as in case of other I.V. Fluids.

GENTAMYCIN INJECTION 80 mg.

LABELLED FORMULA

Each ml contains :

Gentamycin Sulphate

Equivalent to Gentamycin base 80 mg.

BATCH SIZE : 90 Litres

PRACTICAL YIELD : 2800 Bottles of 3 ml.

USUAL PACKING : 3 ml. Amber Vials

FORMULATION

S.No.	Ingredients		Quantity		Overages
1.	Gentamycin Sulphate (As base)		720	Kg.*	
2.	Propyl Paraben		0.9	g.	
3.	Methyl Paraben		72.0	g.	
4.	Disodium Edetate		9.0	g.	
5.	Sodium Metabisulphite		288.0	g.**	
6.	Water for Injection	to	90	Lit.	

* Gentamycin Sulphate Calculation

$$\text{Weight of Gentamycin Sulphate} = \frac{\textit{Weight of Gentamycin base reqd.} \times 1000}{\textit{Actual potency in mcg/mg.}}$$

** Calculation of Sodium Metabisulphite

$$\text{Wt. of Sodium Metabisulphite} = \text{Wt. of Sodium Metabisulphite reqd. on } \frac{100\%\text{ basis} \times 100}{\text{Assay}}$$

MANUFACTURING PROCESS

Same process to be adopted as given in "Gentamycin Injection 40 mg."

GENTAMYCIN INJECTION PAEDIATRIC

LABELLED FORMULA

Each ml contains :

Gentamycin Sulphate (As base) 10 mg.

BATCH SIZE : 120 Litres

PRACTICAL YIELD : 54500 Vials of 2 ml.

USUAL PACKING : 2 ml. Amber Ampoules

FORMULATION

S.No.	Ingredients		Quantity		Overages
1.	Gentamycin Sulphate (As base)		1.20	Kg.*	
2.	Methyl Paraben		156	g.	
3.	Propyl Paraben		24	g.	
4.	Sodium Metabisulphite		384	g.	
5.	Disodium Edetate		12	g.	
6.	Water for Injection	to	120	Lit.	

* Calculate the quantity of Gentamycin Sulphate as given in "Gentamycin Injection 80 mg".

MANUFACTURING PROCESS

Same process to be adopted as given in "Gentamycin Injection 40 mg.".

HYOSCINE BUTYLBROMIDE INJECTION

LABELLED FORMULA

Each ml contains :

Hyoscine Butylbromide	20 mg.
Methyl Paraben	0.1 % v/v
Water for Injection	Q.S.

BATCH SIZE : 50 Litres
PRACTICAL YIELD : 44000 Ampoules of 1 ml.
USUAL PACKING : 2 ml. Amber Ampoules

FORMULATION

S.No.	Ingredients		Quantity		Overages
1.	Hyoscine Butylbromide		1.02	Kg.	2 %
2.	Mannitol (Pyrogen free)		5.00	Kg.	
3.	Methyl Paraben		50	g.	
4.	Sodium Acetate		150	g.	
5.	Glacial Acetic Acid		25	ml.	
6.	Water for injection	to	50	Lit.	

MANUFACTURING PROCESS

1. Take 40 Lit. freashly distilled water in a stainless steel vessel with 50 Lit. marking and bubble Nitrogen gas (oxygen free).
2. Dissolve Mannitol under stirring and Nitrogen bubbling.
3. Dissolve Methyl Paraben under stirring and Nitrogen bubbling.
4. Take about 3 Lit. freshly distilled water in another vessel and dissolve

Sodium Acetate. Now mix Glacial Acetic Acid under stirring and gassing. (This is the buffering solution).

5. Slowly add the buffering solution to the bulk solution under stirring to get the pH of 5.0 (limit 3.70 to 5.50).
6. Adjust the volume to 50 Lit. and mix for 15 minutes.
7. Filter the solution aseptically through 0.22 μ membrane filter under positive pressure of Nitrogen gas.
8. Fill 1.1 ml. aspetically in 1 ml. Amber ampoules with pre and post Nitrogen flushing.
9. If required filled ampoules can also be sterilized by autoclaving at 115°C for 30 minutes.

Note : Protect the solution from light.

LIGNOCAINE AND ADRENALINE INJECTION

LABELLED FORMULA

Each ml contains :

Lignocaine Hydrochloride	20 mg.
Adrenaline Bitartrate	10 mg.

BATCH SIZE : 100 Litres
PRACTICAL YIELD : 1900 Vials of 50 ml.
USUAL PACKING : 2 ml. Amber Vials

FORMULATION

S.No.	Ingredients		Quantity		Overages
1.	Lignocaine Hydrochloride		2.00	Kg.	
2.	Adrenaline Bitartrate		1.00	Kg.	
3.	Sodium Chloride		0.60	Kg.	
4.	Sodium Bisulphite		0.015	Kg.	
5.	Chlorbutol		0.05	Kg.	
6.	Methyl Parabenq		0.10	Kg.	
7.	Water for Injection	to	100	Lit.	

MANUFACTURING PROCESS

1. No special process of manufacture is involved.
2. Keep the pH of the solution to 3.6 (3.3 to 4.5)
3. Filter and fill aseptically.

LIGNOCAINE HYDROCHLORIDE INJECTION

LABELLED FORMULA

Each ml contains :
Lignocaine Hydrochloride
equivalent to Lignocaine 10 mg.

BATCH SIZE : 100 Litres
PRACTICAL YIELD : 3200 Vials of 30 ml.
USUAL PACKING : 30 ml. Vials

FORMULATION

S.No.	Ingredients		Quantity		Overages
1.	Lignocaine Hydrochloride		1.23	Kg.	
2.	Sodium Chloride		0.60	Kg.	
3.	Methyl Paraben		0.10	Kg.	
4.	Chlorbutol		0.40	Kg.	
5.	Water for Injection	to	100	Lit.	

MANUFACTURING PROCESS

1. To 80 Lit. Water for Injection (freshly prepared) add Methyl Paraben, Sodium Chloride, Chlorbutol and Lignocaine Hydrochloride in that order. Pass Nitrogen continuously.
2. Stir till completely dissolved and check the pH. Adjust the pH between 5.0 to 7.0 with 10% Sodium Hydroxide solution.
3. Make up the volume and again check the pH.
4. Filter through 0.45 μ Membrane Filter.
5. Autoclave the filled vials at 121° C for 30 minutes.

QUININE DIHYDROCHLORIDE INJECTION

LABELLED FORMULA

Each ml. contains :
Quinine Dihydrochloride 300 mg.

BATCH SIZE : 100 Litres
PRACTICAL YIELD : 45,000 Ampoules of 2 ml.
USUAL PACKING : 2 ml. Amber Ampoules

FORMULATION

S. No.	Ingredients	Quantity		Overages
1.	Quinine Dihydrochloride	30.00	Kg.	
2.	Disodium Edetate	5.0	g.	
3.	Benzyl Alcohol	1.00	Lit.	
4.	Water for Injection to	100	Lit.	

MANUFACTURING PROCESS

NOTE: Nitrogen gas must be used throughout the manufacturing process.

1. Take 90 Lit. freshly distilled water in 150 Lit. capacity stainless steel vessel with 100 Lit. marking.
2. Dissolve Disodium Edetate under stirring.
3. Dissolve Quinine Dihydrochloride in the bulk under stirring.
4. Add Benzyl Alcohol and mix well.
5. Check the pH of the solution. It should be 3.20. If required adjust the pH with 10% Sodium Hydroxide solution (limit 2.70 to 3.50).
6. Make up the volume to 100 Lit. with freshly distilled water for injection and stir for 5 minutes.
7. Filter the solution through 0.45 μ membrane filter under Nitrogen gas pressure.
8. Fill 2.15 ml. in 2 ml. Amber Ampoules with pre and post Nitrogen flushing.
9. Sterilize the ampoules at 116°C for 30 minutes.

RANITIDINE INJECTION

LABELLED FORMULA

Each ml. contains :
Ranitidine Hydrochloride
equivalent to Ranitidine 25 mg.

BATCH SIZE : 40 Litres
PRACTICAL YIELD : 1800 Ampoules of 2 ml.
USUAL PACKING : 2 ml. Ampoules

FORMULATION

S. No.	Ingredients	Quantity	Overages
1.	Ranitidine Hydrochloride	1.145 Kg	3%
2.	Dibasic Sodium Phosphate	96.0 g.	
3.	Monobasic Potassium Phosphate	38.4 g.	
4.	Charcoal	40.0 g.	
5.	Water for injection to	40 Lit.	

MANUFACTURING PROCESS

1. Take 10 Lit. of water for injection in a mixing tank.
2. Add accurately weighed Ranitidine Hydrochloride, Dibasic Sodium Phosphate, Monobasic Potassium Phosphate and Charcoal.
3. Stir for 30 minutes.
4. Adjust the volume to 40 Lit. and filter through Whatman Filter Paper. Check the pH (6.5 to 7.5).

5. Filter through sterile G-4 sintered glass funnel and finally through 0.2 μ Membrane Filter.
6. Fill the ampoules under aseptic conditions.

PRECAUTIONS

1. Ranitidine Hydrochloride is sensitive to light. Protect the raw material from light.
2. Degradation rate fo Ranitidine Hydrochloride increases in the presence of oxygen to give a dark coloured degraded product. Nitrogen flushing should be carried out at all stages.
3. Bulk solution of Ranitidine Hydrochloride should not be stored for more than 24 hours under any circumstances.
4. Ranitidine Hydrochloride in solution form is corrosive to some extent and gives dark yellow patches after drying. Empty containers and machine parts should be washed out immediately after the work is completed.

VITAMIN B. COMPLEX INJECTION - I

LABELLED FORMULA

Each ml. contains :

Vitamin B_1	10.0 mg.
Vitamin B_2	0.5 mg.
Vitamin B_6	1.0 mg.
Niacinamide	20.0 mg.
Phenol	0.5 %

BATCH SIZE : 10 Litres
PRACTICAL YIELD : 950 Vials of 10 ml.
USUAL PACKING : 10 ml. Amber Vials

FORMULATION

S. No.	Ingredients	Quantity	Overages
1.	Thiamine Hydrochloride	125 g.	25%
2.	Riboflavin -5- Phosphate Sodium	8 g.	12.5%
3.	Pyridoxine Hydrochloride	12 g.	15%
4.	Nicotinamide	225 g.	12.5%
5.	Phenol	15 ml.	–
6.	Benzyl Alcohol	120 ml.	–
7.	Disodium Edetate	10 g.	–
8.	Thiourea	10 g.	–
9.	Tween 80	200 ml.	–
10.	Propylene Glycol	1000 ml.	–
11.	Water for Injection to	10 Lit.	–

MANUFACTURING SPECIFICATIONS

1. pH — 3.8 to 4.2.
2. Filling in 10 ml. Amber Vials.
3. Filling to be done under aseptic conditions.
4. Initial filteration through G-3 Sintered glass Funnel. Final filteration through bacteria proof membrane (0.22 μ).
5. Washed vials to be sterilized at 200°C for 4 hours and cooled to room temperature before use.
6. Rubber stoppers to be sterilized by autoclaving at 115°C for 30 minutes.
7. Aging period 7 days before filling.
8. Aseptic filling to be done with Pre and Post flushing with Nitrogen.
9. Shelf life — 18 months.

MANUFACTURING PROCESS

1. Dissolve Niacinamide and Vitamin B_2 Phosphate Sodium in sufficient Water for injection.
2. Dissolve Disodium Edetate, Thiourea, Vitamin B_1 and Vitamin B_6 in the above solution.
3. Add 175 ml. of 10% Conc. Hydrochloric Acid and mix well.
4. Add Propylene Glycol.
5. Add Benzyl Alcohol.
6. Add Phenol.
7. Add Tween 80 with vigorous shaking.

VITAMIN B. COMPLEX INJECTION - II

LABELLED FORMULA

Each ml. contains :

Vitamin B_1	10.0	mg.
Vitamin B_2	2	mg.
Vitamin B_6	2	mg.
Niacinamide	100	mg.
D-Panthenol	5	mg.

BATCH SIZE : 10 Litres
PRACTICAL YIELD : 950 Vials of 10 ml.
USUAL PACKING : 10 ml. Amber Vials

FORMULATION

S. No.	Ingredients	Quantity	Overages
1.	Thiamine Hydrochloride	150 g.	50%
2.	Riboflavin -5- Phosphate Sodium	33 g.	20%
3.	Pyridoxine Hydrochloride	24 g.	20%

4.	Nicotinamide	1.15 Kg.	15%
5.	D-Panthenol	60 g.	20%
6.	Thiourea	10 g.	–
7.	Propylene Glycol	1 Lit.	–
8.	Disodium edetate	10 g.	–
9.	Benzyl Alcohol	150 ml.	–
10.	Tween 80	200 ml.	–
11.	Phenol	50 ml.	–
12.	Water for Injection to	10 Lit.	–

MANUFACTURING SPECIFICATIONS

1. pH range — 3.8 to 4.0.
2. Use 10 ml. Amber Vials.
3. Protection from light is must.
4. Pre and Post flushing with Nitrogen Gas during filling.
5. Manufacture, filling and sealing to be done under aseptic conditions.
6. Filter through G-3 Sintered Glass Funnel and finally through 0.2 μ Membrane Filter.
7. Sterlize Vials by heating to 200°C for 4 hours.
8. Use latex Rubber Plugs.
9. Sterlize Rubber Plugs by autoclave at 115°C for 30 minutes.
10. Use Injectable Grade Niacinamide.

MANUFACTURING PROCESS

1. Dissolve Niacinamide and Vitamin B_2 Phosphate Sodium in 5 Lit. Distilled Water.
2. Dissolve Disodium Edetate, Thiourea, Vitamin B_1 and Vitamin B_6 in 3 Lit. Distilled Water.
3. Mix Solution 1 and 2.
4. Dissolve D. Panthenol in Solution 3.
5. Add 175 ml. of 10% Hydrochloric Acid.
6. Add Propylene Glycol.
7. Add Benzyl Alcohol.
8. Add Phenol.
9. Add Tween 80 with vigorous shaking.
10. Make up the volume to 10 Lit. with distilled water.
11. Keep the solution for aging for 7 days before filling.

VITAMIN B. COMPLEX INJECTION - III

LABELLED FORMULA

Each ml. contains :

Thiamine Hydrochloride 25 mg.

Riboflavin -5- Phosphate Sodium	3	mg.
Pyridoxine Hydrochloride	5	mg.
Niacinamide	60	mg.
D-Panthenol	5	mg.
Chlorbutol (as preservative)	0.5	%

BATCH SIZE : 120 Litres
PRACTICAL YIELD : 10,900 Vials of 10 ml.
USUAL PACKING : 10 ml. Amber Vials 20 mm.

FORMULATION

S. No.	Ingredients	Quantity	Overages
1.	Thiamine Hydrochloride	4.50 Kg.	50%
2.	Riboflavin -5- Phosphate Sodium	414 g.	15%
3.	Pyridoxine Hydrochloride	750 g.	25%
4.	Nicotinamide	7.92 Kg.	10%
5.	D-Panthenol	600 g.	10%
6.	Chlorbutol 0.5%	600 g.	–
7.	Water for Injection to	120 Lit.	–

MANUFACTURING SPECIFICATIONS

Description — Yellow flouroscent (green) solution.

MANUFACTURING PROCESS

1. In about 40 Litres Distilled Water dissolve Niacinamide and to this solution add Riboflavin -5- Phosphate Sodium.
2. In another 40 Litres Distilled water dissolve in succession Thiamine Hydrochloride and Pyridoxine Hydrochloride.
3. Dissolve D-Panthenol in about 15 Litres Distilled Water.
4. Add No. 3 solution to No. 2 slowly with constant stirring.
5. Add No. 4 solution to solution No. 1 slowly with constant stirring.
6. Make up the volume to 120 Litres and to it add chlorbutol.
7. Stir well to dissolve it completely.
8. Adjust pH to 5 (limit 5.0 to 5.5).
9. Keep below 10°C for 4 to 8 days and then at room temperature for the same period.
10. Filter aseptically in sterile flasks through G-5 Sintered Glass Funnels or through bacteria proof membrane filter (0.22 µ).
11. Fill 10.5 ml. in 10 ml. Amber vials under Nitrogen. Nitrogen should be passed through 1% solution of Phenol.

VITAMIN B. COMPLEX INJECTION - IV

LABELLED FORMULA

Each ml. contains:

Vitamin B_1	25 mg.
Vitamin B_2	1 mg.
Vitamin B_6	2.50 mg.
Niacinamide	50 mg.
D-Panthenol	5 mg.
Benzyl Alcohol	1.5% v/v
Water for injection	Q.S.

BATCH SIZE : 100 Litres

PRACTICAL YIELD : 9300 Vials of 10 ml.

USUAL PACKING : 10 ml. Amber Vials

FORMULATION

S. No.	Ingredients	Quantity	Overages
1.	Thiamine Hydrochloride	3.50 Kg.	40%
2.	Riboflavin	110 g.	10%
3.	Pyridoxine Hydrochloride	275 g.	10%
4.	Nicotinamide	5.25 Kg.	5%
5.	D-Panthenol	550 g.	10%
6.	Benzyl Alcohol	1.50 Lit.	
7.	Propylene Glycol	2.00 Lit.	
8.	Disodium Edetate	100 g.	
9.	Monothioglycerol	500 g.	
10.	Sodium Hydroxide (for pH adjustment)	Q.S.	
11.	Water for Injection to	100 Lit.	

MANUFACTURING SPECIFICATIONS

1. Take 10 Lit. freshly distilled water in a stainless steel vessel and bubble Nitrogen gas continuously.
2. Dissolve Niacinamide under gentle stirring to avoid aeration, with Nitrogen (Oxygen free) bubbling. Filter the solution through filter paper and collect in the same vessel.
3. Dissolve Vitamin B_2 under stirring and Nitrogen bubbling till a clear solution is obtained. Flush Nitrogen and store overnight.
4. Next day take 60 Lit. freshly distilled water in a 120 Lit. capacity stainless steel vessel with 100 Lit. marking and bubble Nitrogen.
5. Dissolve Disodium Edetate under gentle stirring.
6. Add the Niacinamide and Vitamin B_2 solution prepared earlier under

slow stirring to avoid aeration and continuous Nitrogen bubbling. Rinse the vessel with a little distilled water and add to the bulk.

7. Take about 3 Lit. of hot freshly distilled water in another vessel and bubble Nitrogen gas.
8. Dissolve Vitamin B_1 Hydrochloride, Vitamin B_6 and D-Panthenol in the above 3 Lit. of distilled water under gentle stirring and Nitrogen bubbling to get a clear solution.
9. Add this solution to the bulk and stir gently.
10. Check the pH of the bulk solution. If required adjust the pH to 4.20 (limit 4.0 to 5.0) with 10% Sodium Hydroxide solution under stirring.
11. Add Benzyl Alcohol, Propylene Glycol and Monothioglycerol to the bulk under stirring and Nitrogen bubbling.
12. Again check the pH and adjust, if required, to 4.20.
13. Make up the volume to 100 Lit. and stir for 5 minutes.
14. Filter the solution aseptically and under Nitrogen pressure through 0.22 μ Membrane Filter into a sterile filling vessel.
15. Fill 10.5 ml. Amber Vials with pre and post flushing with Nitrogen gas.

VITAMIN B_1, B_6, B_{12} INJECTION

LABELLED FORMULA

Each 3ml. ampoule contains :

Vitamin B_1	100	mg.
Vitamin B_6	100	mg.
Vitamin B_{12}	1500	mcg.
Lidocaine Hydrochloride	6	mg.
Water for Injection	Q.S.	

BATCH SIZE : 100 Litres

PRACTICAL YIELD : 30300 Ampoules of 3 ml.

USUAL PACKING : 3 ml. Amber Ampoules

FORMULATION

S. No.	Ingredients	Quantity	Overages
1.	Thiamine Hydrochloride	3.667 Kg.	10%
2.	Pyridoxine Hydrochloride	3.667 Kg.	10%
3.	Cyanocobalamin	75 g.	50%
4.	Lidocaine Hydrochloride	200 g.	
5.	Triethanolamine (for pH adjustment)	476 g. (app.)	
6.	Water for Injection Q.S.	100 Lit.	

MANUFACTURING PROCESS

NOTE:

a) The manufacturing and filling operations should be carried out under aseptic conditions.

b) Carbon Dioxide gas must be used for flushing during manufacture and filling / sealing and by passing through 0.22 μ membrane filter.

c) The manufacturing, including filling and sealing, must be completed the same day.

1. Take 85 Lit. freshly distilled water in a suitable vessel of 150 Lit. with 100 Lit. marking.
2. Bubble Carbon Dioxide at 1.5 Kg/cm^2 pressure.
3. Add and dissolve 3.667 Kg. Thiamine Hydrochloride.
4. Add and dissolve 3.667 Kg. Pyridoxine Hydrochloride.
5. Add and dissolve 200 g. Lidocaine Hydrochloride.
6. All additions should be under stirring and Carbon Dioxide gas bubbling.
7. Add and dissolve 75 g. Cyanocobalamine under stirring. Stir for 15–20 minutes.
8. Dissolve 300 g. Triethanolamine in 3.0 Lit. of water for injection.
9. Adjust the pH of the solution to 3.9 using Triethanolamine solution. Stir for 15 minutes and again check the pH.
10. Make up the volume to 100 Lit. with freshly distilled water for injection and stir for 15 minutes under CO_2 cover.
11. Check the pH and adjust to 3.9 if required.
12. Solution is preserved until filteration under Carbon Dioxide at 1.5–2.0 Kg/cm^2.
13. Filter the solution through sterile 0.22 μ membrane filter with prefilter into sterile storage vessel using CO_2 as pressure gas.
14. Fill 3.2 ml. (3.15 – 3.30 ml.) in 3 ml. Amber Ampoules with pre and post CO_2 flushing.
15. Sterilize the ampoules by autoclaving at 110°C for 30 minutes.

Chapter 10

Liquid Orals

INTRODUCTION

DEFINITIONS

Syrups : Aqueous pharmaceutical solutions containing sugar are classified as Syrups.

Elixers : Sweetened combination of water and ethyl alcohol solutions are called elixers.

Spirits : Solutions of aromatic materials in ethyl alcohol are called spirits.

Tinctures/ Extracts : Solutions prepared by extracting active ingredients are termed as tinctures or fluid extracts.

Suspensions : Prepararations containing finely divided drug particles distributed somewhat uniformly throughout a vehicle in which the drug exhibits a uniform degree of solubility are called Suspensions.

METHODS OF MANUFACTURE

The process of manufacture which is adopted in practice by the manufacturer of all the above stated dosage forms which are official in respective official Pharmacopoeias are given in the pharmacopoeias while the Patent and proprietory preparations of the said dosage forms are manufactured as per the method developed by the pharmaceutical manufacturers and approved by respective drug licencing authority of the respective State Government.

LIST OF PRESERVATIVES USED IN ORAL LIQUID AND SUSPENSIONS

S.No.	Name of Preservative	Usual Conc.	Stability and Incompatibility
1.	Benzoic Acid	0.1% to 0.2%	Ineffective at pH above.
2.	Sorbic Acid	0.1% to 0.2%	Propylene Glycol enhances activity. Most effective in acidic pH.
3.	Methyl Parahydroxybenzoate	0.25%	Less effective at pH above 8.0, Propylene

			Glycol enhances activity.
4.	Propyl Parahydroxybenzoate	0.05% to 0.25%	Less effective at pH above 8.0.
5.	Sodium Benzoate	0.1% to 0.2%	Ineffective at pH above 5.0 Antifungal and Bacteriostatic.
6.	Bronidiol	0.001% to 0.05%	Effective at pH 4.0 to 6.0.
7.	Propylene Glycol	25%	—

PRACTICAL TIPS AND NOTES

1. In order to provide acidic medium for better product stability in liquid preparations, use Acetic Acid or Hydrochloric Acid.
2. Use Nitrogen as air displacement agent to enhance product stability, specially for Vitamin Preparations. Nitrogen gas should be oxygen free.
3. Use antifungal preservatives like Benzoic Acid, Parabens, Sodium Benzoate etc. to prevent growth of Fungi.
4. Antimicrobial preservatives (list given separately) may be used in liquid and semi-liquid preparations when there is problem of growth of micro-organisms in such preparations.
5. In case alkaline medium is required in liquid preparations, use Ammonia Solution, Sodium Borate, Sodium Carbonate, Sodium Hydroxide, Potassium Hydroxide of Ammonium Carbonate to achieve the desired pH.
6. pH of almost all liquid oral preparations should be determined as a matter of routine even if the test is not prescribed in the pharmacopoeia.
7. Anti-oxidents commonly used are Propyl Gallate, Sodium Bisulphite, Sodium Metabisulphite of Monothioglycerol to prevent the deterioration of preparations by oxidative process.
8. Use of buffering agents may be necessitated to resist the change of pH upon dilution or addition of acid or alkali in pharmaceutical preparations. Usual buffering agents used are Sodium Acetate, Potassium Metaphosphate or Monobasic Potassium Phosphate.
9. Dilute solutions of sugar are more prone to fungus or bacterial contamination whereas highly concentrated sugar syrups are prone to cyrstallisation.
10. Use Stainless Steel of 304 quality or glass for all manufacturing operations.
11. All raw materials used must be approved by the Quality Control Laboratory before use.

12. All equipments should be thoroughly cleaned before use.
13. All ingredients must be weighed in clean containers or polythene bags.
14. All solid materials should be powdered and sieved before use.
15. All liquid ingredients should be passed through muslin cloth or S.S sieve before use.
16. Time taken for mixing should be recorded every time.
17. Representative samples of all finished liquids must be submitted foı approval of quality control.
18. Use only demineralised water for all manufacturing.
19. Vessels used for manufacturing should be properly marked for volume by dipstick or by other means.
20. All weighings must be checked and recorded.
21. Colours and Essences indicated in the formulations are those which were actually used. Different colours and essences may be used as per requirement.
22. Different grades of Carboxymethylcellulose Sodium are available. Selection should be based on laboratory experiments.
23. Guar Gum is also available under different brand names and quality Selection should be based on laboratory trials.
24. Sorbitol Solution where-ever mentioned means 70% solution.
25. For the manufacture of all suspensions, the raw materials should be powdered and sieved before use.
26. Hyflo Supercel wherever used is only for aid in filteration. It does not appear in the final product.
27. Containers in which solution of raw materials, colours and essences are prepared should be rinsed after transfer to the main manufacturing vessel.
28. Quantities of raw materials can vary due to moisture content and other factors. Q.C. Reports must be checked of all active raw materials before finalising the quantities.
29. Sugar Syrups should always be prepared by heating with steam in a Jacketed vessel. Direct heating may result in charring of sugar.

ABBREVIATIONS USED

Methyl Paraben	:	Methyl Parahydroxybenzoate
Propyl Paraben	:	Propyl Parahydroxybenzoate
L.O.D.	:	Loss on drying
D.M. Water	:	Demineralised Water
CMC Sodium	:	Carboxymethylcellulose Sodium
S.S.	:	Stainless Steel

Q.C. : Quality Control Laboratory
lbs : Pounds

ALBENDAZOLE SUSPENSION

LABELLED FORMULA

Each 5 ml. contains :
Albendazole 200 mg.

BATCH SIZE : 400 Litres
PRACTICAL YIELD : 39000 Bottles of 10 ml.
USUAL PACKING : 10 ml. Amber Vials

FORMULATION

S. No.	Ingredients	Quantity	Overages
1.	Albendazole (Human Grade)	16.000 Kg.	
2.	Sodium Lauryl Sulphate	0.400 Kg.	
3.	Glycerin	40.000 Kg.	
4.	Methyl Paraben	0.800 Kg.	
5.	Propyl Paraben	0.160 Kg.	
6.	Carboxymethylcellulose Sodium (Medium viscosity 700 ± 100 CPS)	*7.000 Kg.	
7.	Saccharin Sodium	0.400 Kg.	
8.	Orange Flavour	2.000 Lit.	

* On dry basis, check L.O.D.

MANUFACTURING PROCESS

1. Charge 20 Kg. Glycerin (after passing through 200 mesh nylon cloth) to a steam jacketed vessel and heat to 70°C. Add and dissolve Methyl Paraben and Propyl Paraben. Cool to room temperature and filter through 200 mesh nylon cloth.
2. Charge 240 Lit. of D.M. water to the manufacturing tank.
3. Transfer the remaining 20 Kg. Glycerine through 200 mesh nylon cloth to a 100 Lit. stainless steel vessel. Disperse Carboxymethyl Cellulose Sodium in this Glycerine and mix well. Filter through 100 mesh stainless steel screen, transfer to the manufacturing tank and mix well.
4. Transfer the solution from Step 1 to the manufacturing tank. Mix well and allow to stand overnight.
5. Dissolve Sodium Lauryl Sulphate in 60 Lit. of D.M. Water and filter through 200 mesh nylon cloth.
6. Add Albendazole to Step 5 in small portions under continuous stirring. Mix well and check the pH. Allow to stand for 1 hour to de-aerate.

Transfer to the manufacturing tank through 100 mesh stainless steel screen and mix well.

7. Dissolve Saccharin Sodium in 1.5 Lit. D.M. water. Filter through 200 mesh nylon cloth and transfer to the manufacturing tank. Mix well.
8. Filter the flavour through 200 mesh nylon cloth and transfer to the manufacturing tank. Mix well.
9. Make up the volume to 400 Lit. with D.M. water and mix well. Allow to stand overnight. Check the pH and volume.
10. Fill 10 ml. in Amber bottles.

AZATADINE MALEATE AND PSEUDOEPHEDRINE SULPHATE SYRUP

LABELLED FORMULA

Each 5 ml. contains :

Azatadine Maleate 1.0 mg.

Pseudoephedrine Sulphate 30.0 mg.

BATCH SIZE : 1600 Litres

PRACTICAL YIELD : 31300 Bottles of 50 ml.

USUAL PACKING : 50 ml. Amber Bottles

FORMULATION

S. No.	Ingredients	Quantity	Overages
1.	Azatadine Maleate	0.320 Kg.	
2.	Pseudoephedrine Sulphate	9.600 Kg.	
3.	Methyl Paraben	1.600 Kg.	
4.	Propyl Paraben	0.320 Kg.	
5.	Citric Acid	0.880 Kg.	
6.	Sugar	880 Kg.	
7.	Sorbitol Solution	320 Kg.	
8.	Propylene Glycol	80 Kg.	
9.	Glycerine	80 Kg.	
10.	Alcohol	140 Lit.	
11.	Menthol	0.192 Kg.	
12.	Orange Flavour	2.0 Lit.	
13.	Chocolate Flavour	1.6 Lit.	
14.	Raspberry Red Colour	0.080 Kg.	
15.	D.M. Water to	1600 Lit.	
16.	Hyflo Supercel (Filtering Aid)	6.000 Kg.	

MANUFACTURING PROCESS

1. Charge 400 Lit. of D.M. water to a jacketed stainless steel compounding

tank and heat the water to 70°C.

2. Add and dissolve Citric Acid and then dissolve Sugar. Ensure complete dissolution.
3. Cool to room temperature and add Sorbitol solution, Propylene Glycol and Glycerin one by one under continuous agitation till it is uniform.
4. Charge 112 Lit. of Alcohol to a suitable vessel and dissolve Methyl Paraben, Propyl Paraben, Menthol and both the flavours one by one ensuring that each ingredient is dissolved before adding the next.
5. Add the alcoholic solution from Step 4 to the bulk of Step 3 under agitation.
6. Rinse the alcoholic solution container with the remaining portion of Alcohol and add the rinse to the batch.
7. Charge 9.6 Lit. D.M. water to a suitable vessel and dissolve Azatadine Maleate under agitation. Add the active solution to the batch and mix well.
8. Rinse the active solution container and add to the batch.
9. Charge 16 Lit. D.M. water to a vessel and add Pseudoephedrine Sulphate under agitation. Add the active solution to the batch. Rinse the container and add to the batch.
10. Dissolve Raspberry Red Colour in 4.8 Lit. D.M. water and add to the bulk. Rinse the container and add to the batch. Mix until uniform.
11. Make up the volume to 1600 Lit. and allow to age for 24 hours.
12. Add Hyflo Supercel and mix for 10 minutes.
13. Filter through sparkler filter till the filterate is sparkling clear.

AZATADINE SYRUP

LABELLED FORMULA

Each 5 ml. contains :

Azatadine Maleate 0.5 mg.

BATCH SIZE : 1600 Litres

PRACTICAL YIELD : 31200 Bottles of 50 ml.

USUAL PACKING : 50 ml. Amber Bottles

FORMULATION

S. No.	Ingredients	Quantity	Overages
1.	Azatadine Maleate	0.160 Kg.	
2.	Sugar	960.0 Kg.	
3.	Sorbitol Solution	320.0 Kg.	
4.	Propylene Glycol	32.0 Kg.	

5.	Methyl Paraben	1.60 Kg.
6.	Propyl Paraben	0.320 Kg.
7.	Colour Tatrazine	0.120 Kg.
8.	Colour Sunset Yellow	0.360 Kg.
9.	Black Currant Flavour	1.60 Lit.
10.	Hyflo Supercel (Filter-aid)	1.50 Kg.
11.	D.M. Water to	1600 Lit.

MANUFACTURING PROCESS

1. Charge 400 Lit. of D.M. water to a manufacturing tank and heat to 50°C – 60°C.
2. Add and dissolve sugar and mix till dissolved. Cool at room temperature.
3. Filter the sugar solution into a suitable tank through muslin cloth.
4. Charge 10 Lit. D.M. water to a suitable vessel. Add and dissolve Azatadine Maleate.
5. Slowly add this solution to the bulk and mix well.
6. Add and mix Sorbitol solution.
7. Into a suitable container charge Propylene Glycol. Add and dissolve Methyl Paraben, Propyl Paraben and Black Current Flavour. Ensure that each ingredient is dissolved before adding the next.
8. Charge 1.5 Lit. of D.M. water in a vessel, add and dissolve both the colours completely. Add to the bulk and mix until uniform.
9. Adjust the volume to 1600 Lit. and mix well. Check the pH (limit 4.0 – 6.0).
10. Add Hyflo Supercel and mix for 10 minutes.
11. Close the tank and allow to age overnight.
12. Filter the batch through Sparkler Filter Press, circulating the batch until the filterate is sparkling clear.
13. Fill 50 ml. in Amber bottles.

CARBINOXAMINE AND DEXTROMETHORPHAN COUGH EXPECTORANT

LABELLED FORMULA

Each 5 ml contains :

Carbinoxamine Maleate	4 mg.
Dextromethorphan Hydrobromide	10 mg.
Ammonium Chloride	240 mg.
Sodium Citrate	240 mg.
Potassium Guaiacol Sulfonate	120 mg.

BATCH SIZE : 800 Litres
PRACTICAL YIELD : 7800 Bottles of 100 ml.
USUAL PACKING : 100 ml. Amber Bottles

FORMULATION

S. No.	Ingredients	Quantity	Overages
1.	Carbinoxamine Maleate	0.330 Kg	3 %
2.	Dextromethorphan Hydrobromide	0.800 Kg	
3.	Potassium Guaiacol Sulfonate	9.600 Kg	
4.	Ammonium Chloride	19.200 Kg.	
5.	Sodium Citrate	19.200 Kg.	
6.	Benzyl Alcohol	2.656 Kg.	
7.	Sodium Benzoate	0.800 Kg.	
8.	Benzoic Acid	0.960 Kg.	
9.	Citric Acid	0.200 Kg.	
10.	Sodium Saccharin	0.760 Kg	
11.	Sugar	528.0 Kg.	
12.	Sorbitol Solution (70%)	40.00 Kg.	
13.	Menthol	0.320 Kg.	
14.	Propylene Glycol	3.200 Kg.	
15.	Colour Amarnath	0.130 Kg.	
16.	Mixed Fruit Essence	2.000 Kg.	
17.	D. M. Water to	800 Litres	

MANUFACTURING PROCESS

1. Charge 40 Kg. Sorbitol solution to a processing tank.

2. Charge 310 Lit. of D.M Water to a jacketed tank and heat to boiling. Add and dissolve Sodium Benzoate, Benzoic Acid and Sugar in that order under constant stirring. Then add while mixing Citric Acid, Sodium Saccharin, Potassium Guaiacol Sulfonate, Sodium Citrate and Ammonium Chloride in that order.

   Filter while still hot through muslin cloth into the tank of Step 1. Mix for 30 minutes and allow to cool overnight.

3. Add 6.5 Lit. D.M. water to a suitable vessel and dissolve Carbinoxamine Maleate. When dissolved add to Step 1.mix .

4. Add 12 Lit. D.M. water to a suitable container and heat to 70°C–80° C. Add and dissolve Dextromethorphan Hydrobromide. Stir well to dissolve completely and add to the tank of Step 1. Mix thoroughly.

5. Add and mix Benzyl Alcohol.

6. Add 3 Lit. D.M water to a small container and dissolve Amarnath Red Colour. Mix well.
7. Dissolve Menthol in Propylene Glycol, filter through cloth and add to the bulk. Mix well.
8. Add Flavour and mix well.
9. Make up the volume to 800 Lit. and mix for 30 minutes.

CHLORAMPHENICOL PALMITATE ORAL SUSPENSION - I

LABELLED FORMULA

Each 5 ml. contains :
Chloramphenicol Palmitate
equivalent to Chloramphenicol 125 mg.
Flavoured Syrup base Q.S.

BATCH SIZE : 120 Litres
PRACTICAL YIELD : 2280 × 50 ml. (114 Litres)
USUAL PACKING : 50 ml. Amber Bottle

FORMULATION

S. No.	Ingredients	Quantity	Overages
1.	Chloramphenicol Palmitate	5.7 Kg.	10 %
2.	Carboxymethylcellulose Sodium	1.0 Kg.	
3.	Methyl Paraben Sodium	240 g.	
4.	Propyl Paraben Sodium	60 g.	
5.	Tween 80	120 ml.	
6.	Sugar	60.0 Kg.	
7.	Sodium citrate	120 Kg.	
8.	Citric Acid	200 g.	
9.	Raspberry Flavour	200 ml.	
10.	Glycerin	2.5 Lit.	
11.	Purified Water to	120 Lit.	

MANUFACTURING SPECIFICATIONS

A. 1. Heat 30 Litres of Purified Water to 60°C in a SS vessel and dissolve Methyl Paraben Sodium and Propyl Paraben Sodium (half quantity).
2. Add 60 Kg. sugar under constant stirring and raise the temperature to boiling point.
3. Add Citric Acid and Sodium Citrate to the hot syrup and filter.
4. Allow to cool to room temperature by keeping it overnight or through heat exchanger.

B. 1. Mix Glycerin with CMC Solution in an SS vessel to form a smooth paste.
2. Add Tween 80 and again stir well to form a thin paste.
3. To a SS tank transfer 50 Litres of filtered water and heat to 60°C.
4. Dissolve Methyl Paraben Sodium and Propyl Paraben Sodium (half quantity.)
5. Add 100 g. Citric Acid and 60 g. Sodium Citrate and stir till completely dissolved.
6. To this hot water solution add the Glycerin - CMC Sodium - Tween 80 paste slowly under constant stirring. Continue till completely dissolved. Allow to cool to room temperature.

C. 1. Start the stirrer in the SS vessel of Step B. In case the jelly is thick and does not move add some quantity of filtered syrup from Step A and water till the whole mass is moving with the stirrer.
2. To this mass add Chloramphenicol Palmitate in small quantities and suspend uniformly.
3. Add the syrup from Step A along with Chloramphenicol Palmitate and Purified water.
4. Pass the suspension through Colloid Mill and make-up the volume.
5. Allow to stand overnight.
6. Check the volume and adjust.
7. Add Raspberry Essence and stir thoroughly.
8. pH Should be between 4.5 and 7.0.

Note : 174 mg. of Chloramphenicol Palmitate is equivalent to 100 mg. of Chloramphenicol.

CHLORAMPHENICOL PALMITATE ORAL SUSPENSION - II

LABELLED FORMULA

Each 5 ml. contains :
Chloramphenicol Palmitate
equivalent to Chloramphenicol 125mg.

BATCH SIZE : 750 Litres
PRACTICAL YIELD : 14,500 Bottles
USUAL PACKING : 50 ml. Amber Glass Bottles

FORMULATION

S. No.	Ingredients	Quantity	Overages
1.	Chloramphenicol Palmitate	34.25 Kg.	5%
2.	Sugar	400 Kg.	

3.	Carboxymethylcellulose Sodium	5.00 Kg.
4.	Sodium Benzoate	4.00 Kg.
5.	Methyl Paraben Sodium	1.00 Kg.
6.	Propyl Paraben Sodium	100 g.
7.	Tween 80	2.50 Kg.
8.	Citric Acid	850 g.
9.	Flavour	1.00 Kg.
10.	Purified Water to	750 Lit.

MANUFACTURING SPECIFICATIONS

1. Use 50 ml. Amber Glass Bottles with 25 mm PP Caps.
2. pH range 4.5 to 7.0.

MANUFACTURING PROCESS

1. Prepare Primary Syrup as usual, filter through cloth and transfer to the mixing tank fitted with stirrer through the filter press. Transfer while hot.
2. Mix Carboxymethylcellulose Sodium with Methyl Paraben Sodium and Propyl Paraben Sodium. Add these powders to the hot syrup slowly with constant stirring. Keep overnight.
3. Add Glycerin and Tween 80 one by one.
4. Dissolve Citric Acid in 20 Lit. Water and add to the syrup.
5. Add Chloramphenicol Palmitate in small portions under constant stirring.
6. Pass the suspension through Colloid Mill. Transfer to the mixing tank and make up the volume to 750 Litres. Keep overnight. Next day make up the volume once again add the flavour and mix for 30 minutes.
7. Fill the suspension under slow stirring.

CHLOROQUIN PHOSPHATE SYRUP

LABELLED FORMULA

Each 5 ml. contains :

Chloroquin Phosphate 125 mg.
equivalent to Chloroquin Base 78 mg.

BATCH SIZE : 750 Litres
PRACTICAL YIELD : 3880 Bottles of 100 ml.
USUAL PACKING : 400 ml. Amber Glass Bottle

FORMULATION

S. No.	Ingredients	Quantity	Overages
1.	Chloroquin Phosphate	10.0 Kg.	
2.	Citric Acid	4.8 Kg.	

3.	Saccharin Sodium		1.6 Kg.
4.	Glycerin		20.0 Lit.
5.	Methyl Paraben		400.0 g.
6.	Propyl Paraben		160.0 g.
7.	Sugar		348.0 Kg.
8.	Essence Orange		2.0 Lit.
9.	Colour		Q.S.
10.	Purified Water	to	400.0 Lit.

MANUFACTURING PROCESS

1. Heat 100 Lit. water to 60°–70°C in a clean jacketed SS tank fitted with stirrer. Dissolve Citric Acid and then dissolve sugar at 60°–70°C temperature. Heat to boiling and filter hot.
2. Heat Glycerin in a S.S vessel to 60°C and dissolve first Methyl Paraben and then Propyl Paraben.
3. Add this solution to the main syrup.
4. Boil 44 Lit. water in a S.S vessel and to it add 10 Kg. Chloroquin Phosphate and stir till dissolved.
5. Add this solution to the main syrup.
6. Heat 4 Lit. water in S.S vessel and dissolve Saccharin Sodium.
7. Add this to the main syrup and stir well.
8. Make-up the volume to 400 Litres with water.
9. Heat 100 ml. water in a beaker and dissolve 4 g. colour.
10. Add this to main bulk. Stir well and allow to cool to room temperature.
11. Add Essence Orange.
12. Filter the syrup before filling.

COUGH EXPECTORANT I

LABELLED FORMULA

Each 5 ml. contains :

Ephedrine Hydrocholoride	15 mg.
Diphenhydramine Hydrochloride	15 mg.
Ammonium Chloride	150 mg.
Sodium Citrate	60 mg.
Menthol	2 mg.
Colour Amarnath	Q.S.
Flavoured Syrup	Q.S

BATCH SIZE : 100 Litres

PRACTICAL YIELD : 890 Bottles of 110 ml.

USUAL PACKING : 110 ml. Round Amber Bottle

FORMULATION

S. No.	Ingredients		Quantity	Overages
1.	Ephedrine Hydrochloride		315 g.	
2.	Diphenhydramine Hydrochloride		315 g.	
3.	Ammonium Chloride		3.0 Kg.	
4.	Sodium Citrate		1.2 Kg.	
5.	Menthol		40 g.	
6.	Sodium Benzoate		500 g.	
7.	Saccharin Sodium		250 g.	
8.	Sugar Pharm. Grade		40.0 Kg.	
9.	Sorbitol		10.0 Lit.	
10.	Propylene Glycol		10.0 Lit.	
11.	Citric Acid		500 g.	
12.	Colour Amarnath		30 g.	
13.	Essence Orange		100 ml.	
14.	D.M. Water	to	100 Lit.	

MANUFACTURING PROCESS

1. Heat 50 Lit. D.M. Water to 60°C.
2. Dissolve Ephedrine Hydrochloride, Diphenhyramine Hydrochloride, Ammonium Chloride, Sodium Citrate, Citric Acid, Sodium Benzoate and Saccharin Sodium one by one under constant stirring.
3. Dissolve Sugar at 60°C with constant stirring. Do not allow temperature to rise above 60°C.
4. Cool the Syrup Solution to room temperature (25°C).
5. Dissolve Menthol in 500 ml Alcohol and make an emulsion with Propylene Glycol.
6. Dissolve solution 5 in Syrup Solution 4 and mix thoroughly.
7. Make up the volume to 100 Lit. with D.M. Water.
8. Dissolve Amarnath Colour in water with the aid of heat and add to the bulk.
9. Add Essence Orange and stir well.
10. Filter through Filter Press.
11. Fill 110 ml. in Amber Bottles.

COUGH EXPECTORANT II

LABELLED FORMULA

Each 5 ml. contains :

Chloropheniramine Maleate	2.5 mg.
Ammonium Chloride	125 mg.

Sodium Citrate	55 mg.
Colour Amarnath	Q.S.
Flavoured Syrup	Q.S.

BATCH SIZE : 100 Litres
PRACTICAL YIELD : 890 Bottles of 110 ml.
USUAL PACKING : 110 ml. Round Amber Bottle

FORMULATION

S. No.	Ingredients	Quantity	Overages
1.	Chlorpheniramine Maleate	50 g.	
2.	Ammonium Chloride	2.5 Kg.	
3.	Sodium Citrate	1.1 Kg.	
4.	Sugar	40.0 Kg.	
5.	Methyl Paraben Sodium	200 g.	
6.	Propyl Paraben Sodium	20 g.	
7.	Sorbitol Liquid	15 Lit.	
8.	Saccharin Sodium	100 g.	
9.	Sodium Benzoate	100 g.	
10.	Citric Acid	500 g.	
11.	Colour Amarnath	30 g.	
12.	Essence Orange	100 ml.	
13.	Essence Raspberry	100 ml.	
14.	D.M. Water to	100 Lit.	

MANUFACTURING PROCESS

Same as Cough Expectorant I

COUGH EXPECTORANT III

LABELLED FORMULA

Each 5 ml. contains :

Diphenhydramine Hydrochloride	14.08 mg.
Ammonium Chloride	138.00 mg.
Sodium Citrate	57.03 mg.
Menthol	1.14 mg.
Alcohol	0.2625 ml.
(Alcohol content 5 % v/v)	
Colours- Amarnath	Sunset Yellow FCF
Erythrosine	Caramel

BATCH SIZE : 4000 Litres
PRACTICAL YIELD : 33250 x 114 ml. Bottles of 110 ml.
USUAL PACKING : 114 ml. Round Amber Bottles

FORMULATION

S. No.	Ingredients	Quantity	Overages
1.	Water	1000 Lit.	
2.	Diphenhydramine Hydrochloride	11.71 Kg.	
3.	Ammonium Chloride	110.40 Kg.	
4.	Citric Acid	8.70 Kg.	
5.	Sodium Citrate	45.62 Kg.	
6.	Saccharin Sodium	16.43 Kg.	
7.	Sugar	2397.0 Kg.	
8.	Glucose Liquid	931.4 Kg.	
9.	Glycerin	312.6 Kg.	
10.	Hot Water	200.0 Lit.	
11.	Raspberry Essence	33.3 Lit.	
12.	Red 33 D & C National Aniline	34 g.	
13.	Erythrosine Food Red 14	70 g.	
14.	Sunset Yellow	30 g.	
15.	Caramel	5,438 Kg.	
16.	Alcohol	227 Lit.	
17.	Menthol	912 g.	
18.	Water to	4000 Lit.	
19.	Hyflo Supercel (Filter-aid)	9.8 Kg.	

MANUFACTURING SPECIFICATIONS

1. Avoid contact with Brass and Copper.
2. Avoid prolonged contact with iron.
3. Protect finished product from heat and light.

pH	:	5.0 to 5.15
Specific Gravity	:	1.315 to 1.328
Alcohol Content	:	5% v/v
Diphenhydramine Hydrochloride	:	96% to 104%
Ammonium Chloride	:	97% to 105%

MANUFACTURING PROCESS

1. Transfer 1000 Lit. Water to 4000 Lit. S.S Jacketed Tank and heat upto 50°C. With constant stirring add Diphenhydramine Hydrochloride, Ammonium Chloride, Citric Acid, Sodium Citrate, Saccharin Sodium and Sugar.
2. In 200 Lit. Water add Liguid Glucose in 1000 Lit. S.S Tank and mix well. Mix it with No.1 with stirring and maintain temperature at 50° C.
3. Add Glycerin to No. 1, mix thoroughly and cool. Filter through filter press with the help of Hyflo Supercel.

4. Add Rasberry flavour into filtered liquid and mix thoroughly.
5. Dissolve Red 33 D & C National Aniline, Erythrosine, Sunset Yellow in hot 8 Lit. water and add to flavoured filtered syrup. Then add caramel which is first dissolved in 2.5 Lit. of flavoured syrup.
6. Transfer Alcohol 227 Lit. to a 250 Lit. SS Tank and dissolve menthol and then add to flavoured coloured syrup and stir well.
7. Adjust volume to 4000 Litres with D.M. water.

CYPROHEPTADINE AND L- LYSINE SYRUP

LABELLED FORMULA

Each 5 ml. contains :

Anhydrous Cyproheptadine Hydrochloride	2	mg.
(as Cyproheptadine Hydrochloride)		
L- Lysine Monohydrochloride	150	mg.

BATCH SIZE : 750 Litres
PRACTICAL YIELD : 3,600 Bottles of 200 ml.
USUAL PACKING : 200 ml. Amber Glass Bottles

FORMULATION

S. No.	Ingredients	Quantity	Overages
1.	Cyproheptadine Hydrochloride	350 g.	6%
2.	L- Lysine Monohydrochloride	23.5 Kg.	4.5%
3.	Sorbitol Liquid	30.0 Kg.	
4.	Glycerin	25.0 Kg.	
5.	Sodium Benzoate	1.0 Kg.	
6.	Methlyl Paraben Sodium	500 g.	
7.	Propyl Paraben Sodium	100 g.	
8.	Citric Acid	500 g.	
9.	Fruit Essences	1.5 kg.	
10.	Sugar	300.0 Kg.	
11.	Colour	5 g.	
12.	D.M. Water to	750 Lit.	

NOTE : 10 mg. Anhydrous Cyproheptadine Hydrochloride = 11 mg. Cyproheptadine Hydrochloride.

MANUFACTURING SPECIFICATIONS

1. Use 200 ml. Amber Glass Bottles.
2. pH range 3.5 to 4.5.

MANUFACTURING PROCESS

1. Prepare Primary Syrup as usual, filter through cloth and transfer to the mixing tank through filter press.
2. Dissolve Sodium Benzoate, Methyl Paraben Sodium and Propyl Paraben Sodium in 20 Litres of D.M Water and add to the bulk. Keep the stirrer on.
3. Add Sorbitol and Glycerin.
4. Dissolve L-Lysine Monohydrochloride in 10 Litres purified water and add to the bulk.
5. Dissolve Citric Acid in 5 Litres D.M Water and add to the bulk.
6. Dissolve Cyproheptadine Hydrochloride in 40 Litres boiling water and add to the bulk.
7. Dissolve the colour in water and add to the syrup.
8. Lastly add the flavours and make up the volume to 750 Litres.
9. Stir for 2 hours before filling.

CYPROHEPTADINE HYDROCHLORIDE ELIXER

LABELLED FORMULA

Each 5 ml. contains:
Cyproheptadine Hydrochloride 2 mg.

BATCH SIZE : 2000 Litres
PRACTICAL YIELD : 9800 Bottles of 200 ml.
USUAL PACKING : 200 ml. Amber Bottles

FORMULATION

S. No.	Ingredients	Quantity	Overages
1.	Cyproheptadine Hydrochloride (Assume 92.0% activity - adjust according to assay)	913 g.	5%
2.	Alcohol	105.0 Lit.	
3.	Flavour Tutti Frutti	0.4 Lit.	
4.	Flavour Mint	0.2 Lit.	
5.	Sugar	500.0 Kg.	
6.	Saccharin Sodium	200.0 g.	
7.	Glycerin	500.0 Kg.	
8.	Talcum (for filteration)	3.0 Kg.	
9.	Sorbic Acid	2.0 Kg.	
10.	Sodium Hydroxide (for pH adjustment)	60.0 Kg.	
11.	Tartrazine Yellow Colour	13.0 g.	
12.	D.M Water to	2000.0 Lit.	

MANUFACTURING PROCESS

Adopt the usual manufacturing process for syrups.

IBUPROFEN AND PARACETAMOL SUSPENSION

LABELLED FORMULA

Each 5 ml. contains :

Ibuprofen	100 mg.
Paracetamol	125 mg.

BATCH SIZE : 750 Litres
PRACTICAL YIELD : 12,000 Bottles of 60 ml.
USUAL PACKING : 60 ml. Amber Glass Bottle

FORMULATION

S. No.	Ingredients	Quantity	Overages
1.	Ibuprofen	15.0 Kg.	
2.	Paracetamol	19.0 Kg.	1.5%
3.	Sorbitol Liquid	200.0 Kg.	
4.	Glycerin	140.0 Kg.	
5.	Aerosil	6.0 Kg.	
6.	Sugar	150.0 Kg.	
7.	Sodium Benzoate	4.0 Kg.	
8.	Methyl Paraben Sodium	800 g.	
9.	Propyl Paraben Sodium	100 g.	
10.	Tween 80	750 g.	
11.	Citric Acid	1.9 Kg.	
12.	Colour	15 g.	
13.	Flavours	4.0 Kg.	
14.	D.M. Water to	750 Lit.	

MANUFACTURING SPECIFICATIONS

1. Use 60 ml Amber Glass Bottles with 25 mm PP Caps.
2. Stirring should be continued during filling.

MANUFACTURING PROCESS

1. Prepare the Primary Syrup as usual, filter through cloth and transfer to the mixing tank fitted with a stirrer.
2. Start the stirring.
3. Add Glycerin and then Sorbitol to the Syrup.
4. Dissolve Sodium Benzoate, Methyl Paraben Soddium and Propyl Paraben Sodium in Water and add to the syrup.
5. Add Aerosil and Tween 80.

6. Dissolve Citric Acid in water and add to the syrup.
7. Add Ibuprofen and then Paracetamol in small quantities to the syrup and mix for 30 minutes.
8. Pass the suspension through Colloid Mill, and transfer to the mixing tank.
9. Dissolve the colour in water and add to the syrup.
10. Lastly add the flavours and make up the volume to 750 Litres. Keep overnight.
11. Next day make up the volume once again and send for filling.

IRON WITH VITAMINS SYRUP

LABELLED FORMULA

Each 15 ml. contains :

Elemental Iron (as Ferrous Aminoate)	30 mg.
Protein Hydrolysate (100%) (as solution equivalent to 160 mg Nitrogen)	1.0 g.
Vitamin B_{12}	15 mg.
Vitamin B_6	1.5 mg.
Folic Acid	1.5 mg.
Flavoured Syrup base	Q.S.

BATCH SIZE : 750 Litres
PRACTICAL YIELD : 3600 Bottles of 200 ml.
USUAL PACKING : 200 ml. Amber Bottle.

FORMULATION

S. No.	Ingredients	Quantity	Overages
1.	Protein Hydrolysate	85.00 Kg.	
2.	Iron Choline Citrate	12.25 Kg.	5%
3.	Cyanocobalamin	1.5 g.	100%
4.	Folic Acid	150 g.	100%
5.	Pyridoxine Hydrochloride	225 g.	30%
6.	Sodium Benzoate	1.00 Kg.	
7.	Methyl Paraben Sodium	1.00 Kg.	
8.	Propyl Paraben Sodium	200 g.	
9.	Sugar	350.00 Kg.	
10.	Sorbitol Liquid	35.00 Kg.	
11.	Thiourea	325 g.	
12.	Colour Caramel	5.00 Kg.	

13.	Flavour		2.00 Kg.
14.	D.M Water	to	750 Lit.

MANUFACTURING PROCESS

1. Prepare the Primary Syrup as usual. Filter and transfer to the mixing tank fitted with the stirrer. Cool the syrup to room temperature and start the stirrer.
2. Dissolve Sodium Benzoate, Methyl Paraben Sodium and Propyl Paraben Sodium in 15 Litres D.M. Water and add to the bulk.
3. To 150 Litres D.M water add Protein Hydrolysate powder in small portions with continuous stirring till completely dissolved.
4. Add Iron Choline Citrate to the Syrup and mix well.
5. Dissolve Folic Acid in 5 Litres D.M water and add to the bulk.
6. Dissolve 25 to 30 g. Sodium Hydroxide in D. M Water and add to the bulk.
7. Dissolve Vitamin B_6 in 10 Litres water and add to the syrup.
8. Add Sorbitol to the syrup.
9. Dissolve Thiourea in 5 Litres water and add to the syrup.
10. Dissolve Caramel Colour in 30 Litres water and add to the syrup.
11. Dissolve Vitamin B_{12} in 15 Litres water and add to the syrup.
12. Add the flavour and make up the volume to 750 Litres with water.

IRON, CALCIUM AND VITAMINS PAEDIATRIC TONIC

LABELLED FORMULA

Each 5 ml. contains :

Ferrous Calcium Citrate	500	mg.
(equivalent to Iron 25 mg., Calcium 85 mg.)		
Vitamin A (as Palmitate)	2000	I.U.
Vitamin D_3	150	I.U.
Vitamin B_1	1.5	mg.
Vitamin B_2	2.0	mg.
Nicotinamide	20.0	mg.
L-Lysine Monohydrochloride	200	mg.

BATCH SIZE	:	1000 Litres
PRACTICAL YIELD	:	4900 Bottles of 200 ml.
USUAL PACKING	:	200 ml. Amber Bottles.

FORMULATION

S. No.	Ingredients	Quantity	Overages
1.	Ferrous Calcium Citrate	100.0 Kg.	
2.	Vitamin A Palmitate	0.600 Kg.	50%
3.	Tocopheryl Acetate	0.450 Kg.	
4.	Cholecalciferol	1.125 g.	50%
5.	Thiamine Mononitrate	0.450 Kg.	50%
6.	Riboflavine	0.480 Kg.	20%
7.	Nicotinamide	4.800 Kg.	20%
8.	L-Lysine Monohydrochloride	40.00 Kg.	
9.	Methyl Paraben	1.000 Kg.	
10.	Propyl Paraben	0.200 Kg.	
11.	Carboxymethylcellulose Sodium	6.000 Kg.	
12.	Benzoic Acid	1.200 Kg.	
13.	Sugar	300.0 Kg.	
14.	Polyvinylpyrrolidone	0.583 Kg.	
15.	Sorbitol Solution	300.0 Kg.	
16.	Glycerin	100.0 Kg.	
17.	Thioglycerol	0.150 Kg.	
18.	Butylated Hydroxy Toluene	0.050 Kg.	
19.	Disodium Edetate	0.200 Kg.	
20.	Butylated Hydroxy Anisole	0.050 Kg.	
21.	Saccharin Sodium	0.025 Kg.	
22.	Polysorbate 80	2.400 Kg.	
23.	Citric Acid	4.000 Kg.	
24.	Essence of Ripe Mango	5.000 Kg.	
25.	D.M. Water to	1000 Lit.	

MANUFACTURING PROCESS

1. Charge 140 Lit. D.M water to a jacketed manufacturing vessel. Add and dissolve Methyl Paraben and Propyl Paraben and mix till completely dissolved.
2. Filter the solution and to the filterate add Carboxymethylcellulose Sodium in small portions under constant stirring. Mix for 15 minutes to make the jelly.
3. Charge 160 Lit. D.M. water to a jacketed tank and heat to boiling. Add while mixing Benzoic Acid and Sugar till completely dissolved. Maintain at boiling temperature for 5 minutes.
4. Transfer the syrup solution to the tank containing the jelly through muslin cloth.
5. Dissolve separately Polyvinylpyrrolidone in 5 Lit. D.M. water. Transfer

to the tank containing the jelly through muslin cloth.

6. Mix the jelly and syrup for 30 minutes. Divide the jelly syrup in two equal parts A & B.
7. Charge the jelly Syrup A to a suitable container and while mixing add Glycerin 98 Kg. Keep overnight in a closed container to cool to room temperature.
8. Prepare a slurry of Butylated Hydroxy Anisole and Butylated Hydroxy Toulene with 2 Kg. Glycerin and add while mixing Thioglycerol. Mix for 10 minutes.
9. Dissolve separately Vitamin B_1 Mononitrate, Disodium Edetate and Sodium Saccharin in D.M water and add while mixing to the main tank.
10. Suspend Niacinamide, Vitamin B_2 and Polysorbate 80 0.40 Kg. in D.M water. Pass the suspension through Colloid Mill and add while mixing to the main tank.
11. Mix separately Vitamin E Acetate,Vitamin A Palmitate and Vitamin D_3 in 2.0 Kg. of Polysorbate 80. Add while mixing to the main tank.
12. Charge 65 Lit. D. M water to a suitable container and heat to 75°- 80° C. Add while stirring L-Lysine Monohydrochloride. Ensure complete dissolution and allow to cool to about 45° C. Filter and add to the main tank.
13. Add while mixing Essence of Ripe Mango to the main tank.
14. Place Jelly Syrup 'B' into a suitable container and add while mixing Sorbitol 300 Kg. and Ferrous Calcium Citrate (200 mesh) 100 Kg.
15. Dissolve separately Citric Acid 4 kg. in 2 Lit. D.M. water. Adjust the pH to about 4.0 while mixing Step 15 to Step 14. Mix for 15 minutes. Keep overnight in a closed container to cool to 40°C.
16. Transfer the Vitamin slurry and Ferrous Calcium Citrate slurry to 1000 Lit. tank through Colloid Mill.
17. Make up the volume to 1000 Lit. with D.M water and mix for one hour.

KAOLIN AND PECTIN MIXTURE

LABELLED FORMULA

Each 30 ml. contains :

Kaolin	6.0 g.
Pectin	130 mg.

BATCH SIZE	:	800 Litres
PRACTICAL YIELD	:	13120 Bottles of 60 ml.
USUAL PACKING	:	60 ml. Amber Bottles

FORMULATION

S. No.	Ingredients	Quantity	Overages
1.	Methyl Paraben	640 g.	
2.	Porpyl Paraben	160 g.	
3.	Veegum (Guar Gum)	4.80 Kg.	
4.	Kaolin Light	160.0 Kg.	
5.	Pectin	3.46 Kg.	
6.	Carboxymethylcellulose Sodium	16.00 Kg.	
7.	Saccharin sodium	808 g.	
8.	Oil Peppermint	541 g.	

MANUFACTURING PROCESS

Adopt the usual manufacturing process for suspensions.

LOPERAMIDE ORAL SOLUTION

LABELLED FORMULA

Each 5 ml. contains :

Loperamide Hydrochloride 1.0 mg.

BATCH SIZE : 800 Litres

PRACTICAL YIELD : 26000 Bottles of 30 ml.

USUAL PACKING : 30 ml. Amber Bottles with Dropper

FORMULATION

S. No.	Ingredients	Quantity	Overages
1.	Loperamide Hydrochloride	0.160 Kg.	
2.	Propylene Glycol	160.0 Kg.	
3.	Sorbitol 70% Solution	320.0 Kg.	
4.	Saccharin Sodium	2.550 Kg.	
5.	Methyl Paraben	0.575 Kg.	
6.	Propyl Paraben	0.065 kg.	
7.	* Citric Acid Monohydrate	0.047 Kg.	
8.	Supra Ponceau 4 R	0.080 Kg.	
9.	Mixed Fruit Flavour	4.000 Kg.	
10.	D. M. Water to	800 Lit.	

* For pH adjustment

MANUFACTURING PROCESS

1. Charge Propylene Glycol and Sorbitol Solution to a stainless steel tank and heat it to 60°C while stirring.
2. Add Loperamide Hydrochloride and stir till dissolved.
3. In another tank charge 230 Lit. D.M. Water and heat to 90° - 95°C.

MALT EXTRACT WITH VITAMINS

LABELLED FORMULA

Each 5 ml. contains :

Vitamin A (As Palmitate)	2500	I.U.
Vitamin D_3 (Cholecalciferol)	200	I.U.
Thiamine Hydrochloride	1.0	mg.
Riboflavin	1.0	mg.
Iron and Ammonium Citrate	45.0	mg.
Nicotinamide	16.0	mg.

In a palatable base containing Malt Extract

Colour Caramel

BATCH SIZE : 5000 Kg.

PRACTICAL YIELD : 970 Bottles of 500 g.

USUAL PACKING : 500 g.

FORMULATION

S. No.	Ingredients	Quantity	Overages
1.	Vitamin A Palmitate Synthetic	2.589 Kg.	45%
2.	Cholecalciferol In Arachis Oil	0.179 Kg.	25%
3.	Orange Oil	1.354 Lit.	
4.	Vanillin	0.568 Kg.	
5.	Acacia Powder	1.956 Kg.	
6.	D.M. Water (For Emulsion)	2.934 Lit.	
7.	Warm Water	50.00 Lit.	
8.	Thiamine Hydrochloride	1.429 Kg.	100%
9.	Nicotinamide	12.000 Kg.	5%
10.	Riboflavine	0.786 Kg.	10%
11.	Glycerin1	3000 Kg.	
12.	D.M Water q.s to make 89.29 Kg. of Oil Mixture for the product		
13.	Malt Extract (Non-Diastatic with 0.25% Sodium Benzoate)	1920 Kg.	
14.	Liquid Glucose	1062.0 Kg.	
15.	D.M. Water	438.0 Lit.	
16.	Sodium Benzoate	13.060 Kg.	
17.	Sugar	1350.0 Kg.	
18.	Caramel	54.880 Kg.	
19.	Iron and Ammonium Citrate	32.140 Kg.	
20.	Sodium Chloride	7.579 Kg.	
21.	D.M. Water	31.750 Lit.	

MANUFACTURING PROCESS

1. Transfer Vitamin A Palmitate to a suitable mixing vessel and add Cholecalciferol in Arachis Oil. Rinse out the Cholecalciferol container with Orange Oil and add to the vessel.
2. Add Vanillin and stir for atleast 15 minutes.
3. Add Acacia Powder and stir for 15 minutes.
4. Add 2.934 Lit. warm D.M. Water (for emulsion) and stir for 30 minutes.
5. Take 50 Lit. of Warm D.M. Water in a mixing vessel, add Thiamine Hydrochloride and Nicotinamide and stir until dissolved. Add sufficient warm water to make 68.33 Kg. Stir well and add to Step 4. Stir well.
6. Mix the Riboflavin thoroughly with Glycerin in a suitable blender or stirrer. Add to Step 5. Rinse the blender with sufficient D.M. water and add to Step 5.
7. Stop the stirrer and check the yield.
8. Add sufficient warm water (43°C) to make 89.29 Kg. Check the yield. Stir for 15 minutes.
9. Run this mixture through the homogeniser into a suitable container and hold as Oil Mixture for the product to add in Step 14.
10. Transfer 1200 Kg. of Malt Extract to the 4000 Lit. stainless steel reactor.
11. Add the liquid glucose.
12. Draw 438 Lit. of D.M. water to a 2400 Lit. jacketed vessel and dissolve Sodium Benzoate with the aid of heat. Add the sugar and stir until solution is complete. Do not heat over 80° C. Add the Caramel and stir. Using a Mono Pump with a 30 mesh stainless steel screen attached to the suction hose transfer to the 4000 Lit. stainless steel reactor containing the Glucose and Malt Extract in Step 10. Start the reactor.
13. Dissolve Iron and Ammonium Citrate and Sodium Chloride in 32 Lit. of D.M water and add together with the balance of Malt Extract to Step 10.
14. Add the Oil Mixture for the Product from Step 9 to the reactor and run for 30 minutes.
15. Blend thoroughly for sufficient time. Transfer the product to a 4000 Lit. stainless steel holding tank and close securely. Check the yield.
16. Specific Gravity of the product at 25° C should be 1.39 to 1.41.

MEBENDAZOLE SUSPENSION

LABELLED FORMULA

Each 5 ml. contains :

Mebendazole 100 mg.

BATCH SIZE : 400 Litres.
PRACTICAL YIELD : 13000 Bottles of 30 ml.
USUAL PACKING : 30 ml. Amber Bottles

FORMULATION

S. No.	Ingredients	Quantity	Overages
1.	Mebendazole	8.000 Kg.	
2.	Methyl Paraben	0.720 Kg.	
3.	Propyl Paraben	0.080 Kg.	
4.	Sodium Hydroxide	0.260 Kg.	
5.	Saccharin Sodium	0.100 Kg.	
6.	Carboxymethylcellulose Sodium	3.000 Kg.	
7.	Sugar	240.0 Kg.	
8.	Sorbitol 70% solution	36.00 Kg.	
9.	Polysorbate 80	0.800 Kg.	
10.	Essence American Ice Cream	1.000 Kg.	
11.	Essence Rose White	1.600 Kg.	
12.	Colour Erythrosine Supra	0.012 Kg.	
13.	Citric Acid	0.500 Kg.	

MANUFACTURING PROCESS

1. Charge 100 Lit. of D.M. water to a processing tank and heat to boiling. Dissolve Sugar in this boiling water under stirring.
2. Dissolve Methyl Paraben and Propyl Paraben in 10 Lit. D. M.Water with the help of Sodium Hydroxide.
3. Dissolve Saccharin Sodium in about 7 Lit. of D.M. Water and add to the bulk.
4. Dissolve Citric Acid in about 8 Lit. of D.M. water and add to the bulk. Stir the whole bulk for 30 minutes and allow to cool down.
5. In another tank of 200 Lit. capacity charge 80 Lit. of D.M. water and heat to 60°C–70°C. Sprinkle slowly the Carboxymethylcellulose Sodium under constant stirring till a very fine paste is obtained. Cool to room temperature.
6. To another tank transfer the filtered bulk of Step 1 and Step 5 and mix them well.
7. Make a paste of Sorbitol (previously filtered), Mebendazole and Polysorbate 80. Mix well and add to the bulk under stirring.
8. Mix the whole bulk for 30 minutes.
9. Add both the Essences and mix well.
10. Dissolve colour Erythrosine in about 7 Lit. of boiling D. M. water and add to the bulk.

11. Make up the volume and check the pH. Adjust if necessary to pH 5.5 at room temperature.

Caution : All powdered materials should be screened. All liquids should be passed through cloth before use.

METRONIDAZOLE AND FURAZOLIDONE SUSPENSION

LABELLED FORMULA

Each 5 ml. contains :

Metronidazole 100 mg.
Furazolidone 30 mg.

BATCH SIZE : 1000 Kg.
PRACTICAL YIELD : 16200 Bottles of 60 ml.
USUAL PACKING : 60 ml. Bottles

FORMULATION

S. No.	Ingredients	Quantity	Overages
1.	Metronidazole Benzoate	32.000 Kg.	
2.	Furazolidone	6.000 Kg.	
3.	Guar Gum	9.000 Kg.	
4.	Methyl Paraben	0.800 Kg.	
5.	Propyl Paraben	0.200 Kg.	
6.	Sugar	500.00 Kg.	
7.	Saccharin Sodium	1.000 Kg.	
8.	Sorbitol Solution	100.000 Kg.	
9.	Polysorbate 80 (Tween 80)	0.320 Kg.	
10.	Colour Sunset Yellow	0.050 Kg.	
11.	Mixed Fruit Flavour	2.500 Kg.	
12.	Demineralised Water Q.S	1000 Lit.	

MANUFACTURING PROCESS

1. Load about 400 Lit. D.M. Water and heat it to 90°C in a vessel 'A'. Add and dissolve 350 g. Methyl Paraben with stirring. Ensure complete dissolution. Allow to cool and add Guar Gum Slowly while stirring continously to disperse it fully. Transfer to a storage tank when the temperature falls to less than 70°C.
2. Load about 250 Lit. D.M. water to another manufacturing tank 'B' and heat to boiling point. Dissolve 450 g. Methyl Paraben and 100 gm. Propyl Paraben with stirring at 90°C. Add 500 Kg. of Sugar and dissolve by stirring. Allow to boil for some time and then cool the syrup solution. Strain the syrup into a storage tank with the help of a mono-pump through 60 mesh screen.

3. Transfer the syrup of Step (2) to the bulk of Step (1) and stir till the liquid is cooled.
4. Dissolve 1.0 Kg. Saccharin Sodium in about 2 Lit. of D.M. Water in a stainless steel vessel and add to the bulk under stirring.
5. Add 100 Kg. Sorbitol solution into the bulk syrup solution and continue stirring.
6. Dissolve 320 g. Polysorbate 80 in 1.0 Lit. of D.M. Water and add to the bulk under stirring.
7. Dissolve Sunset Yellow colour 50 g. in 500 ml. D. M. water and add to the bulk.
8. Allow the syrup to cool down to 70°C and continue the stirring.
9. Take 32 Kg. Metronidazole Benzoate and 6 kg. Furazolidone and add slowly to coloured syrup slowly with continous stirring. Avoid lumps formation during addition. Ensure complete dispersion into the syrup and continue mixing for 30 minutes.
10. Stop the stirrer and add 2.5 Lit. Mixed Fruit Flavour. Check that the temperature is below 45°C before addition. Continue mixing.
11. Stop the stirrer and add sufficient D.M. Water to make up the volume to 1000 Lit. Continue stirring for 30 minutes.
12. Pass the batch through a Colloid Mill twice.
13. Transfer the batch to the filling tank through 60 mesh screen.
14. Send a sample to Q.C for evaluation.

METRONIDAZOLE SUSPENSION - I

LABELLED FORMULA

Each 5 ml. contains :
Metronidazole Benzoate
equivalent to Metronidazole 200 mg.

BATCH SIZE : 400 Kg.
PRACTICAL YIELD : 13000 Bottles of 30 ml.
USUAL PACKING : 30 ml. Bottles

FORMULATION

S. No.	Ingredients	Quantity	Overages
1.	Methyl Paraben Sodium	400 g.	
2.	Propyl Paraben Sodium	92 g.	
3.	Guar Gum	2.0 Kg.	
4.	Sorbitol Liquid	40.0 Kg.	
5.	Polysorbate 80	400 g.	
6.	Colour Tartrazine	16 g.	
7.	Essence Mixed Fruit Conc.	800 g.	

8.	Essence Peppermint	400 g.	
9.	Sugar	200.0 Kg.	
10.	Metronidazole Benzoate (200 mg Metronidazole Benzoate is approximately equivalent to 125 mg Metronidazole)	28.1 Kg.	
11.	D.M. Water to	400 Lit.	

MANUFACTURING SPECIFICATIONS AND PROCESS

Adopt the usual process for manufacture of suspensions.

METRONIDAZOLE SUSPENSION - II

LABELLED FORMULA

Each 5 ml. contains :

Metronidazole Benzoate equivalent to Metronidazole 200 mg.

BATCH SIZE : 1000 Kg.

PRACTICAL YIELD : 16300 Bottles of 60 ml.

USUAL PACKING : 60 ml. or 30 ml. Bottles

FORMULATION

S. No.	Ingredients	Quantity	Overages
1.	Metronidazole Benzoate	64.00 Kg.	
2.	Sugar	500.00 Kg.	
3.	Methyl Paraben	0.800 Kg.	
4.	Propyl Paraben	0.200 Kg.	
5.	Guar Gum	8.000 Kg.	
6.	Disodium Hydrogen Phosphate	0.100 Kg.	
7.	Sodium Saccharin	1.000 Kg.	
8.	Sorbitol Solution (70%)	100.00 Kg.	
9.	Polysorbate 80	0.600 Kg.	
10.	Colour Tartrazine	0.050 Kg.	
11.	Pineapple Essence	2.000 Lit.	
12.	D.M. Water to	1000 Lit.	

MANUFACTURING PROCESS

1. Charge 350 Lit. D.M. water to a stainless steel tank and dissolve by heating 380 g. Methyl Paraben. Allow the solution to cool to room temperature. Add carefully with stirring 8.0 Kg. Guar Gum in small quantities and allow to stand overnight.
2. In a jacketed manufacturing vessel place 160 Lit. D.M. water and 100

Kg. Sorbitol solution. Heat to 90°C and dissolve by heating to boiling and stirring Methyl Paraben 420 g., Propyl Paraben 200 g., 500 Kg. Sugar, 100 g. Disodium Hydrogen Phosphate and 1.0 Kg. Sodium Saccharin.

3. Add 600 g. Polysorbate 80 and allow to cool to about 30°C.
4. Filter the syrup through muslin cloth.
5. Transfer the filtered syrup to the manufacturing vessel. Transfer the contents of the Step 1 to the manufacturing vessel and mix well using the disperser for 30 – 40 minutes.
6. Add 64.00 Kg. Metronidazole Benzoate (powdered) in small quantities to the manufacturing vessel and continue mixing for 30 minutes.
7. In a small container dissolve 50 g. Colour Tartrazine in 1.6 Lit. D.M. water and add to the main vessel.
8. Add 2.0 Lit. of Pineapple Essence to the main vessel.
9. Make up the volume to 1000 Lit. and mix for one hour.

MICONAZOLE ORAL GEL

LABELLED FORMULA

Miconazole Nitrate 2%

BATCH SIZE : 100 Kg.
PRACTICAL YIELD : 1950 Bottles of 50 ml.
USUAL PACKING : 50 g. Bottle

FORMULATION

S. No.	Ingredients	Quantity	Overages
1.	Glycerin	78.00 Kg.	
2.	Flavour	0.08 Kg.	
3.	Saccharin Sodium	0.13 Kg.	
4.	Tween 20	0.22 Kg.	
5.	Absolute Alcohol	0.78 Lit.	
6.	Pre-gelatinized Starch	6.00 Kg.	
7.	Miconazole Nitrate (200 mesh)	2.00 Kg.	
8.	Distilled Water to	100 Kg.	

MANUFACTURING PROCESS

1. Dissolve Saccharin Sodium in sufficient Distilled Water and add Tween-20 under constant stirring.
2. Add glycerin and flavour.
3. Suspend Miconazole Nitrate in Pre-gelatinized Starch and add sufficient

Distilled Water.

4. Mix 1, 2, 3 and add Absolute Alcohol.
5. Mix thoroughly and make up the weight to 100 Kg. with Distilled Water.
6. Mix till the Gel is formed.
7. Send a sample to Q.C for evaluation.

MULTIVITAMIN DROPS - I

LABELLED FORMULA

Each 0.6 ml. contains :

Vitamin A	3000	I.U.
Vitamin D_3	400	I.U.
Vitamin B_1	1	mg.
Vitamin B_2	1.5	mg.
Nicotinamide	15	mg.
D-Panthenol	3	mg.
Vitamin B_6	1.5	mg.
Vitamin C	40	mg.

BATCH SIZE : 100 Kg.
PRACTICAL YIELD : 9700 vials of 10 ml.
USUAL PACKING : 10 ml. Amber Vials

FORMULATION

S. No.	Ingredients	Quantity	Overages
1.	Vitamin A Palmitate (0.1 million units/g)	750 g.	50%
2.	Cholecalciferol (40000 units per g.)	1.66 g.	50%
3.	Thiamine Hydrochloride	335 g.	100%
4.	Riboflavin -5- Phosphate Sodium	471 g.	35%
5.	Nicotinamide	3.25 Kg.	30%
6.	Pyridoxine Hydrochloride	315 g.	
7.	Disodium Edetate	100 g.	
8.	Thiourea	100 g.	
9.	Methy Paraben Sodium	180 g.	
10.	Propyl Paraben Sodium	20 g.	
11.	Sorbitol	30 g.	
12.	Propylene Glycol	5 Lit.	
13.	Glycerin	15 Lit.	
14.	Tween 80	2 Lit.	
15.	Raspbery Essence	100 ml.	

16.	Tocopheryl Acetate	100	ml.	
17.	Butylated Hydroxy Toluene	50	g.	
18.	Chlorosterol	10	g.	
19.	Citric Acid	1.0	Kg.	
20.	Sodium Hydroxide	1.2	Kg.	
21.	Saccharin Sodium	500	g.	
22.	Banana Essence`	100	ml.	
23.	Ascorbic Acid (Plain)	8.65	Kg.	30%
24.	D-Panthenol	700	g.	40%

MANUFACTURING SPECIFICATIONS

1. pH range 4.0 to 4.5.
2. Shelf life 18 months.
3. Manufacturing and filling to be done under Nitrogen Gas atmosphere.
4. Use 10 ml. Amber Vials.
5. Protect from Light.
6. Use Butyl Rubber Stoppers.
7. Filling to be done after aging for 36 – 48 hours.
8. Tear down aluminium seals to be used.

MANUFACTURING PROCESS

1. Dissolve Sodium Hydroxide in water and cool to room temperature.
2. Dissolve Vitamin C in water. Add 1 to 2 with constant stirring and Nitrogen Gas flushing to obtain a clear Sodium Ascorbate Solution. Temp. not to exceed 40°C.
3. Add 3/4 of Propylene Glycol, Sorbitol and Glycerin to 2.
4. Dissolve Niacianmide, Vitamin B_2 Phosphate Sodium and D- Panthenol in water and add to the bųlk.
5. Dissolve Methyl Paraben Sodium and Propyl Paraben Sodium in water and add to the bulk.
6. Dissolve Citric Acid in water and add to the bulk.
7. Dissolve Thiourea, Disodium Edetate, Vitamin B_1 and Vitamin B_6 in water and add to the bulk.
8. Dissolve Sodium Saccharin in water and add to the bulk.
9. Mix Vitamin A Palmitate, Vitamin D_3 and Tween 80 with vigorous stirring for 2-3 hours. Dissolves Butylated Hydroxy Toulene and Chlorosterol in 1/4th Propylene Glycol and add to the Tween 80 mixture. Mix for 2 hours.
10. Fill vials with pre and post Nitrogen Gas flushing.

MULTIVITAMIN DROPS - II

LABELLED FORMULA

Each 0.6 ml. contains :

Vitamin A	5000	I.U.
Vitamin D	400	I.U.
Thiamine Hydrochloride	1.5	mg.
Riboflavine	1.2	mg.
Pyridoxine Hydrochloride	1	mg.
Ascorbic Acid	50	mg.
Nicotinamide	10	mg.

BATCH SIZE : 400 Litres.

PRACTICAL YIELD : 26300 Bottles of 15 ml.

USUAL PACKING : 15 ml. Amber Bottles

FORMULATION

S. No.	Ingredients	Quantity	Overages
1.	Glycerin	270.00 Kg.	
2.	Riboflavin -5- Phosphate Sodium	1.18 Kg.	
3.	Nicotinamide	7.00 Kg.	5%
4.	Methyl Paraben	200 g.	
5.	Benzoic Acid	400 g.	
6.	Saccharin Sodium	808 g.	
7.	Thiamine Hydrochloride	1.68 Kg.	60%
8.	Pyridoxine Hydrochloride	667 g.	
9.	Ascorbic Acid	46.70 Kg.	40%
10.	Butylated Hydroxyanisole	76 g.	
11.	Polysorbate 80 (Tween 80)	32.00 Kg.	
12.	Vitamin A, [Use Vitamin A Palmitate (1.7 miu/g)]	2.84 Kg.	45%
13.	Vitamin D_3, [Use Cholecalciferol in Arachis Oil (1 miu/g)]	410 g.	35%
14.	Oil Orange Terpeneless	104 g.	
15.	D.M. Water to	400 Lit.	

MANUFACTURING PROCESS

Adopt the same process as given in Formulation No. 1.

MULTIVITAMIN DROPS - III

LABELLED FORMULA

Each 1ml. contains :

Vitamin A	8330	I.U.
Vitamin D_3	667	I.U.
Vitamin B_1	1.67	mg.
Vitamin B_2	1.67	mg.
Vitamin B_6	1.67	mg.
Sodium Pantothenate	5	mg.
Nicotinamide	16.7	mg.
Ascorbic Acid	83	mg.

BATCH SIZE : 500 Litres

PRACTICAL YIELD : 32000 Bottles of 15 ml.

USUAL PACKING : 15 ml. Bottles with dropper.

FORMULATION

S. No.	Ingredients	Quantity	Overages
1.	Distilled Water	32 Lit.	
2.	Sodium Hydroxide	11.42 Kg.	
3.	Distilled Weter	250 Lit.	
4.	Ascorbic Acid	56.25 Kg.	
5.	Thiamine Hydrochloride	1.50 Kg.	
6.	Pyridoxine Hydrochloride	918 g.	
7.	Sodium Pantothenate	2.50 Kg.	
8.	Nicotinamide	9.20 Kg.	
9.	Riboflavin -5- Phosphate Sodium	3.50 Kg.	
10.	Sugar Pharmaceutical Grade	30.00 Kg.	
11.	Polysorbate 60 (Tween 60)	30.00 Kg.	
12.	Propyl Paraben Sodium	750 Kg.	
13.	Vitamin A Palmitate	5.63 Kg.	
14.	Calciferol in Arachis Oil (1 miu/g)	1.04 Kg.	
15.	Distilled Water to	500 Lit.	
16.	Sodium Hydroxide	15 g.	
17.	Nitrogen Gas	Q.S.	
18.	Cetite 521 (Filter Aid)	500 g.	

NOTE : Ingredients given in order of use.

MANUFACTURING SPECIFICATION

1. Take 25 Lit. of distilled water in 750 Litres jacketed S.S Tank. Cloe the tank and heat awith steam until 10 lbs. pressure is reached.Maintain

this pressure for one hour and close the steam inlet. Allow pressure to fall to zero. Prior to opening the lid allow water to go to waste.

2. Treat all the vessels and equipments with steam prior to use in manufacturing steps.
3. Protect product from light at all stages of manufacture.
4. Avoid contact with brass, copper and iron at all stages.
5. Flood product with Nitrogen Gas at all stages of production.
6. Submit a sample of distilled water to be used in manufacturing process to the laboratory to ensure the absence of Calcium.

MANUFACTURING PROCESS

1. Dissolve Sodium Hydroxide in 35 Lit. distilled water in 100 Litres S.S Tank.
2. Take 250 Lit. of distilled water in 750 Lit. S.S. Tank and dissolve Ascorbic Acid in it and then add Sodium Hydroxide solution alowly into it (from instruction No. 1).
3. Add Sugar (Pharmaceutical grade) and Riboflavin -5- Phosphate Sodium to instruction No. 2. Stir well until dissolved and adjust the temperature to 40.5°C to 44.5°C.
4. Melt Polysorbate 60 in S.S. vessel of 50 Lit. at 39°C to 41.5°C (first heat Polysorbate 60 to 85° C and then cool it to 43°C). Remove small portion for use in rinsing the container of Vitamin A and Calciferol. Add Vitamins A & D to heated Polysorbate 60 and rinse the container. Mix for not less than 10 minutes and hot more than 20 minutes. Slowly add this solution to instruction No. 3 and stir vigorously during addition so that crystal clear emulsion is formed. Check the clarity and adjust the temperature of emulsion between 39.0°C to 41.5°C.
5. Add Vitamin B_1, Vitamin B_6, Sodium Pantothenate and Nicotinamide. Stir till dissolved and cool the emulsion to 26.5°C to 29.5°C.
6. Add water to make the volume to 488 Litres. Mix thoroughly and check the pH which should be 5.0 to 5.2. If necessary adjust it with Dilute Solution of Sodium Hydroxide.
7. Dissolve Propyl Paraben Sodium in 10 Lit. of water and add to instruction No. 6 and adjust the volume with water to 500 Litres.
8. Filter bulk liquid through No. 10 μ porocity filter with Celite under Nitrogen pressure.
9. Collect filterate in a sterile clean S.S vessel. Flood with Nitrogen and close tightly.

MULTIVITAMIN DROPS WITH MINERALS

LABELLED FORMULA

Each 0.6 ml. contains :

Vitamin A	5000	I.U.
Vitamin D_3	400	I.U.
Thaimine Hydrochloride	1.5	mg.
Riboflavine	1.2	mg.
Nicotinamide	10	mg.
Ascorbic Acid	50	mg.
Pyridoxine Hydrochloride	1	mg.
Manganese Sulphate	0.92	mg.
Potassium Sulphate	3.34	mg.
Sodium Molybdate	0.38	mg.
Zinc Sulphate	1.05	mg.
Iron (As Ferrous Gluconate)	2	mg.

BATCH SIZE : 400 Litres
PRACTICAL YIELD : 26,300 Bottles of 15 ml.
USUAL PACKING : 15 ml. Amber Bottles

FORMULATION

S. No.	Ingredients	Quantity		Overages
1.	Glycerin	270.00	Kg.	
2.	Nicotinamide	7.00	Kg.	5%
3.	Riboflavin -5- Phosphate Sodium	1.25	Kg.	5%
4.	Methyl Paraben	200	g.	
5.	Benzoic Acid	400	g.	
6.	Saccharin Sodium	424	g.	
7.	Thiamine Hydrochloride	1.78	Kg.	70%
8.	Pyridoxine Hydrochloride	700	g.	5%
9.	Ascorbic Acid	53.34	Kg.	60%
10.	Oil Orange Terpeneless Sweet	104	g.	
11.	Butylated Hydroxyanisole	67	g.	
12.	Polysorbate 80 (Tween 80)	32.00	Kg.	
13.	Vitamin A Palmitate (1.7 miu/g.)	2.84	Kg.	
14.	Cholecalciferol in Arachis Oil (1 miu/g.)	426	g.	
15.	Manganese Sulphate Monohydrate	616	g.	
16.	Potassium Sulphate	2.23	Kg.	
17.	Zinc Sulphate	1.25	Kg.	
18.	Sodium Molybdate	252	g.	

19.	Ferrous Gluconate	11.98	Kg.
20.	Caramel (Acid Proof)	4.08	Kg.
21.	Distilled Water to	400	Lit.

MANUFACTURING SPECIFICATIONS AND PROCESS

Same process may be adopted as given in Formulation No. III of Multivitamin Drops.

MULTIVITAMIN SYRUP

LABELLED FORMULA

Each 5 ml. contains :

Vitamin A	3000	I.U.
Vitamin D_3	400	I.U.
Thaimine Hydrochloride	1.5	mg.
Riboflavine	1.2	mg.
Ascorbic Acid	50	mg.
Vitamin B_{12}	3	mcg.
Nicotinamide	10	mg.
Pyridoxine Hydrochloride	1	mg.

BATCH SIZE : 2000 Litres
PRACTICAL YIELD : 21,500 Bottles of 90 ml.
USUAL PACKING : 90 ml. Amber Round Bottles

FORMULATION

S. No.	Ingredients	Quantity	Overages
1.	Riboflavine	480 g.	
2.	Nicotinamide	4.40 Kg.	10%
3.	Acid Benzoic	2.00 Kg.	
4.	Menthyl Paraben	600 g.	
5.	Ascorbic Acid	28.00 Kg.	40%
6.	Thiamine Hydrochloride	945 g.	50%
7.	Pyridoxine Hydrochloride	400 g.	
8.	Cyanocobalamin (Crystals)	2.205 g.	
9.	Oil Orange Terpeneless Sweet	525 g.	75%
10.	Oil Peanut Pure Refined	4.8 Kg.	
11.	Vitamin A, (Use Vitamin A (Palmitate)	1.271 Kg.	80%
12.	Vitamin D_3, (Use Cholecalciferol in Arachis Oil (1 miu/g)	225 g.	40%
13.	Gum Acacia	2.24 Kg.	
14.	Sugar Cane Granular	312.0 Kg.	
15.	Sodium Lauryl Sulphate	163 g.	

16.	Liquid Glucose		22.5 Kg.
17.	D.M. Water	to	2000 Lit.

MANUFACTURING SPECIFICATIONS AND PROCESS

Adopt the usual process for the manufacture of Vitamin Syrups. Nitrogen bubbling to be used throughout the manufacturing process. Keep the syrup overnight in airconditioned area under Nitrogen atmosphere. Filter the lot next day, check the pH once again before filling.

PARACETAMOL SYRUP - I

LABELLED FORMULA

Each 5 ml. contains :

Paracetamol	125 mg.
Colour	Q.S.
Flavoured Syrup Base	Q.S.

BATCH SIZE : 750 Litres

PRACTICAL YIELD : 12,250 Bottles of 60 ml.

USUAL PACKING : 60 ml. Amber Glass Bottles.

FORMULATION

S. No.	Ingredients		Quantity	Overages
1.	Paracetamol		19 Kg.	1.5%
2.	Propylene Glycol		200 Kg.	
3.	Sodium Benzoate		800 g.	
4.	Methyl Paraben Sodium		800 g.	
5.	Propyl Paraben Sodium		80 g.	
6.	Sugar		450 Kg.	
7.	Glycerin		12 Kg.	
8.	Citric Acid		380 g.	
9.	Disodium Edetate		380 g.	
10.	Colour		10 g.	
11.	Flavour		2 Kg.	
12.	D.M. Water	to	750 Lit.	

MANUFACTURING SPECIFICATIONS

1. Use 60 ml. Amber Glass bottles with 25 mm PP Caps.
2. pH Range 5.4 to 6.9.

MANUFACTURING PROCESS

1. Prepare the Primary Syrup as usual, filter through cloth and transfer with filter press to the mixing tank fitted with stirrer.
2. Dissolve Sodium Benzoate, Methyl Paraben Sodium and Propyl

Paraben Sodium in 25 Litres water and add to the Syrup under stirring. Keep the stirrer on.

3. Dissolve Citric Acid in 25 Lit. water and add to the syrup.
4. Dissolve Disodium Edetate in 25 Lit. water and add to the syrup.
5. In a seperate mixing tank transfer the Propylene Glycol and add Paracetamol under stirring till completely dissolved. Add this solution to the main bulk.
6. Dissolve the colour in water and add to the syrup.
7. Add Glycerin to the syrup.
8. Lastly add the flavours and make up the volume to 750 Litres with water.

PARACETAMOL SYRUP - II

LABELLED FORMULA

Each 5 ml. contains :

Paracetamol	125 mg.
Flavoured Syrup Base	Q.S.
Colour : Erythrosine	

BATCH SIZE : 100 Litres
PRACTICAL YIELD : 1600 Bottles of 60 ml.
USUAL PACKING : 60 ml. Amber Glass Bottles.

FORMULATION

S. No.	Ingredients	Quantity	Overages
1.	Paracetamol	2.5 Kg.	
2.	Propylene Glycol	40.0 Lit.	
3.	Sugar Syrup 66%	40.0 Lit.	
4.	Saccharin Sodium	5 g.	
5.	Colour Erythrosine	20 g.	
6.	Essence Cherry	170 ml.	
7.	Essence Raspberry	170 ml.	
8.	Essence Vanilla	115 ml.	
9.	Glycerin to	100 Lit.	

MANUFACTURING SPECIFICATIONS

1. Appearance — Pink Coloured clear solution free from foreign matter.
2. Potency — 98 to 102% of lebelled claim.
3. pH — 5.6 to 6.0.

MANUFACTURING PROCESS

Adopt generally the same process as given in formulation I.

PROMETHAZINE, CODEINE AND EPHEDRINE COUGH SYRUP

LABELLED FORMULA

Each 5 ml. contains :

Promethazine Hydrochloride	3.6 mg.
Codeine Phosphate	9.0 mg.
Ephedrine Hydrochloride	7.2 mg.

BATCH SIZE : 4500 Litres
PRACTICAL YIELD : 43,800 Bottles of 100 ml.
USUAL PACKING : 100 ml. Amber Bottle

FORMULATION

S. No.	Ingredients	Quantity	Overages
1.	Promethazine Hydrochloride	3.24 Kg.	
2.	Codeine Phosphate	8.10 Kg.	
3.	Ephedrine Hydrochloride	6.48 Kg.	
4.	Sugar	3038 Kg.	
5.	Chloroform	18.00 Kg.	
6.	Caramel Colour	11.25 Kg.	
7.	Citric Acid	58.50 Kg.	
8.	Flavour	8.55 Lit.	
9.	D.M. Water to	4500 Lit.	

MANUFACTURING PROCESS

1. Charge 1500 Lit. D.M. Water to a S.S. Jacketed Tank.
2. Heat the water to 80°C and add Sugar in lots. Raise the temperature to boiling and ensure complete dissolution. Allow it to boil for 10 minutes.
3. Cool to 60°C. Add slowly Ephedrine Hydrochloride, Citric Acid and Promethazine Hydrochloride in this sequence to the syrup.
4. Dissolve the colour in 50 Lit. D.M. Water and add to the main tank. Rinse the vessel with water and add to the tank.
5. Dissolve Codeine Phosphate in 50 Lit. D.M. Water separately in a S.S. vessel, rinse the vessel and add to the tank.
6. Adjust the volume to 4500 Lit. with D.M. Water.
7. Add the flavours and Chloroform separately under stirring.
8. Mix for further 30 minutes and filter.
9. Check and adjust the pH to 1.8 – 2.4.
10. Weight per ml. at 20°C should be 1.25 – 1.26.

PYRANTEL PAMOATE SUSPENSION – I

LABELLED FORMULA

Each 5 ml. contains :

Pyrantel Pamoate
equivalent to Pyrantel base250 mg.

BATCH SIZE : 300 Litres
PRACTICAL YIELD : 36,500 Bottles of 8 ml.
USUAL PACKING : 8 ml. or 10 ml. Bottles

FORMULATION

S. No.	Ingredients	Quantity	Overages
1.	Methyl Paraben Sodium	0.300 Kg.	
2.	Propyl Paraben Sodium	0.300 Kg.	
3.	Sorbic Acid	0.450 Kg.	
4.	Carboxymethylcellulose Sodium	1.200 Kg.	
5.	Polysorbate 80	0.375 Kg.	
6.	Sorbitol Liquid 70%	45.000 Kg.	
7.	Colour Sunset Yellow	0.096 Kg.	
8.	Essence Mixed Fruit	0.105 Lit.	
9.	Essence Banana	0.300 Lit.	
10.	Sucrose	90.000 Kg.	
11.	* Pyrantel Pamoate	44.125 Kg.	2%
12.	Sodium Chloride	0.300 Kg.	

* 250 mg. Pyrantel Base = 721 mg. of Pyrantel Pamoate

MANUFACTURING PROCESS

1. Boil 60 Lit. of D.M. water in a steam jacketed vessel for 30 minutes. Add 225 g. Methyl Paraben Sodium, 225 g. Propyl Paraben Sodium and 338 g. Sorbic Acid and stir well. After the preservatives are completely dissolved add 90 Kg. Sugar with continuous stirring and boil for 10 minutes. Allow the syrup to cool to room temperature and filter through filter press and transfer to 400 Lit. stainless steel tank.
2. Boil 60 Lit. D.M. water in a steam jacketed vessel and cool to 55°C. Transfer this water to 200 Lit. tank. Add 75 g. Methyl Paraben Sodium, 75 g. Propyl Paraben Sodium and 112 g. Sorbic Acid. Stir well for 5 minutes to dissolve the preservatives completely. Slowly add Carboxymethylcellulose Sodium with continuous stirring for 2 hours. Filter the paste through muslin cloth and transfer the paste to 400 Lit. tank having sugar syrup. Mix well for 30 minutes and check the pH of the paste.

3. Weigh and pass Pyrantel Pamoate through Cadmill using 0.5 mm screen and weigh again. Weigh and transfer 45 Lit. of Sorbitol Liquid to 200 Lit. tank. Add Plysorbate 80 and 50 Lit. of sugar syrup and Carboxymethyl-cellulose Sodium paste mixture. Stir well for 5 to 10 minutes.
4. Add slowly Pyrantel Pamoate with continuous stirring and transfer to the 400 Lit. tank having mixture of sugar syrup and Carboxymethyl-cellulose Sodium paste.
5. Homogenise the suspension and pass through Colloid Mill and transfer to another 400 Lit. stainless steel tank.
6. Dissolve Sunset Yellow colour in 2 Lit. hot D.M. water (60° to 70°C), allow to cool to room temperature and add to the bulk. Mix well with the help of homogeniser.
7. Add both the Essences and mix well.
8. Make up the volume with boiled and cooled water. Homogenise the suspension for 2 hours.
9. Check the pH, it should be 5.0 to 6.0.

VITAMIN B. COMPLEX SYRUP

LABELLED FORMULA

Each 5 ml. contains :

Vitamin B_1	5 mg.
Vitamin B_2	2.5 mg.
Vitamin B_6	1.5 mg.
Niacinamide	50 mg.
D-Panthenol	5 mg.
Vitamin B_{12}	5 mcg.
Colour Carmosine	
Flavoured syrup base	Q.S.

BATCH SIZE : 750 Litres
PRACTICAL YIELD : 7,300 Bottles of 100 ml.
USUAL PACKING : 100 ml. Amber Glass Bottles

FORMULATION

S. No.	Ingredients	Quantity	Overages
1.	Thiamine Hydrochloride	825 g.	10%
2.	Riboflavine	425 g.	13%
3.	Pyridoxine Hydrochloride	250 g.	11%
4.	Nicotinamide	8 Kg.	7%
5.	D-Panthenol	825 g.	10%
6.	Cyanocobalamin	1.5 g.	100%
7.	Sodium Benzoate	800 g.	

8.	Methyl Paraben Sodium	800	g.
9.	Propyl Paraben Sodium	80	g.
10.	Sugar	400	Kg.
11.	Disodium Edetate	400	g.
12.	Thiourea	400	g.
13.	Citric Acid	400	g.
14.	Sorbitol	35	Kg.
15.	Glycerin	10	Kg.
16.	Colour Carmosine	125	g.
17.	Flavour	500	g.
18.	D.M. Water to	750	Lit.

MANUFACTURING SPECIFICATIONS

1. Use 100 ml. Amber Glass Bottles with 25 mm PP Caps.
2. pH range — 5.0 to 6.0.
3. Cool the syrup before addition of active ingredients.
4. All manufacturing should be done under Nitrogen flushing.
5. Syrup should be at room temperature before addition of Vitamins.

MANUFACTURING PROCESS

1. Prepare the primary syrup as usual, filter through cloth and transfer to the mixing tank fitted with the stirrer.
2. Dissolve Vitamin B_1 in 10 Litres water and add to the syrup. Keep the stirrer on.
3. Dissolve Vitamin B_6 in 10 Litres water and add to the syrup.
4. Dissolve Niacinamide in 40 Litres water and add to the syrup.
5. Dissolve Vitamin B_{12} in 10 Litres water and to the syrup.
6. Dissolve D-Panthenol in 15 Litres of boiling water and add to the syrup.
7. Dissolve Vitamin B_2 in 10 Litres water and add 10% Sodium Hydroxide Solution till the solution becomes transparent. Add this solution to tbe syrup.
8. Dissolve Sodium Benzoate, Methyl Paraben Sodium and Propyl Paraben Sodium in 35 Litres water and add to the syrup.
9. Dissolve Thiourea, Disodium Edetate and Citric Acid separately in 20 Litres water each and add to the syrup.
10. Dissolve the colour in 10 Litres water and add to the syrup.
11. Lastly add the flavour and make up the volume to 750 Litres.

VITAMIN B. COMPLEX SYRUP
(*Therapeutic*)

LABELLED FORMULA

Each 5 ml. contains :

Vitamin B_1	4.5 mg.
Vitamin B_2	5 mg.
Vitamin B_6	1.5 mg.
Niacinamide	45 mg.
D-Panthenol	5 mg.
Vitamin B_{12}	5 mcg.

BATCH SIZE : 100 Litres
PRACTICAL YIELD : 970 Bottles of 100 ml.
USUAL PACKING : 100 ml. Amber Bottles.

FORMULATION

S. No.	Ingredients	Quantity	Overages
1.	Thiamine Hydrochloride	135 g.	50%
2.	Riboflavine -5- Phosphate Sodium	180 g.	35%
3.	Pyridoxine Hydrochloride	35 g.	15%
4.	Cyanocobalamin	200 mg.	100%
5.	Nicotinamide	1.125 Kg.	25%
6.	D-Panthenol	125 g.	25%
7.	Disodium Edetate	100 g.	
8.	Thiourea	100 g.	
9.	Methyl Paraben Sodium	200 g.	
10.	Propyl Paraben Sodium	20 g.	
11.	Sodium Benzoate	100 g.	
12.	Sodium Chloride	25 g.	
13.	Ferric Chloride	5 g.	
14.	Sorbitol Liquid	10 Lit.	
15.	Propylene Glycol	1 Lit.	
16.	Sugar	33.5 Kg.	
17.	Colour Ponceau 4R	50 g.	
18.	Essence	500 ml.	
19.	D.M. Water to	100 Lit.	

MANUFACTURING SPECIFICATIONS

1. pH range 4.0 to 4.2.
2. Weight per ml. 1.26.
3. Fill in 100 ml. Amber Bottles.
4. Flush Nitrogen Gas for better stability.

MANUFACTURING PROCESS

1. Prepare the primary syrup, cool and mix with Sorbitol. Continue stirring during addition of materials.
2. Dissolve Sodium Benzoate in water and add to the syrup.
3. Dissolve Methyl and Propyl Paraben Sodium in water and add to the syrup.
4. Dissolve Niacinamide and Vitamin B_2 Sodium Phosphate in water and add to the syrup.
5. Dissolve D-Panthenol in water and add to the syrup.
6. Dissolve Citric Acid in water and add to the syrup.
7. Dissolve Thiourea, Disodium Edetate, Vitamin B_1 and Vitamin B_6 in water and add to the syrup.
8. Dissolve Sodium Chloride in water and add to syrup.
9. Dissolve Ferric Chloride in water and add to syrup.
10. Dissolve Vitamin B_{12} in water and add to the syrup.
11. Add Propylene Glycol.
12. Dissolve the colour in water and add to the syrup.
13. Add the essence.
14. Make up the volume to 100 Litres with water and check the pH. Adjust if necessary.

Chapter 11

Capsules and Dry Syrups

INTRODUCTION

CAPSULES

Capsules are solid dosage forms in which substance is enclosed in either a hard or soft, soluble container or shell of a suitable form of gelatin. The encapsulation of medicinal agents remains a popular method for administering drugs. Capsules have the advantage of being tasteless, easily administered and easily filled either extemporaneously or in large quantities commercially. Some patients find it easier to swallow capsules than tablets, therefore prefering to take this form when possible. This preference has prompted pharmaceutical manufacturers to market the product in capsule form even though the product has already been produced in tablet form. It may, however, be emphasised that tablets in any shape or colour are always cost effective than hard gelatin or soft gelatin capsules.

Capsules are, in some cases, the only convenient form of dosage and choice for drugs like Ampicillin, Amoxycillin, Cloxacillin, Chloramphenicol, Tetracycline, Oxytetracycline, Rifampicin etc.

It is interesting to note that Hard Gelatin Capsules contain 12-15% water. A few facts on Hard Gelatin Capsules are :

1. When humidity is very low, the capsules become brittle.
2. If sotred at high humidities, the capsules become flacid and lose their shape.
3. Storage in high temperature areas can also affect the quality of hard gelatin capsules.
4. Gelatin capsules do not protect hygroscopic materials from atomospheric water vapour as moisture can diffuse through the gelatin wall.
5. Sizes vary from 000, the largest size which can be swallowed, to 5, which is the smallest.
6. The capsules must be of Snap-Fit type or the joint must be sealed with a gelatin solution.
7. Comparatively very little machinery is required to manufacture Hard Gelatin Capsules as compared to tablets, liquid orals and injections.

DRY SYRUPS

A dry mixture of an Antibiotic e.g., Ampicillin, when mixed with one or more suitable buffers, preservatives, stabilisers, sweetening agent (usually sugar) and suspending agents, suitable for reconstitution are commonly called Dry Syrups.

AMOXYCILLIN FOR ORAL SUSPENSION

LABELLED FORMULA

Each 5 ml of reconstituted syrup contains :

Amoxycillin Trihydrate equivalent to
Amoxycillin 125 mg.

BATCH SIZE : 60 Kg.
PRACTICAL YIELD : 2,940 Bottles
USUAL PACKING : 20 g. in 70 ml. capacity glass bottle with mark of 40 ml.

FORMULATION

S.No.	Ingredients	Quantity		Overages
1.	Amoxycillin Trihydrate	3.8	Kg.	10%
2.	Carboxymethylcellulose Sodium	1.1	Kg.	
3.	Aerosil	450	g.	
4.	Colour Tartrazine	12	g.	
5.	Sodium Benzoate	270	g.	
6.	Sugar Pharm. Grade	54	Kg.	
7.	Pineapple Flavour Dry	600	g.	

MANUFACTURING SPECIFICATIONS & PROCESS

Same as in Ampicillin & Cloxacillin Dry Syrup.

AMPICILLIN AND CLOXACILLIN CAPSULES

LABELLED FORMULA

Each capsule contains :

Ampicillin Trihydrate
equivalent to Ampicillin 250 mg.
Cloxacillin Sodium
equivalent to Cloxacillin 250 mg.

BATCH SIZE	:	2,50,000 capsules
PRACTICAL YIELD	:	2,47,500 capsules
USUAL PACKING	:	Strip of 10 capsules

FORMULATION

S.No.	Ingredients	Quantity		Overages
Part A				
1.	Cloxacillin Sodium	71.75	Kg.	
2.	Methylene Chloride	8.00	Lit.	
3.	Isopropyl Alcohol	8.00	Lit.	
4.	Ethyl Cellulose	2.00	Kg.	
Part B				
1.	Ampicillin Trihydrate	72.50	Kg.	
2.	Magnesium Stearate	0.50	Kg.	
3.	Aerosil	0.25	Kg.	

MANUFACTURING PROCESS

1. Pass the Cloxacillin Sodium through 20 mesh sieve and transfer to the mass mixer.
2. Mix Methylene Chloride and Isopropyl Alcohol and pass through 120 mesh Nylon cloth.
3. Sift Ethyl Cellulose through 60 mesh sieve and dissolve slowly in the solvent mixture of Step 2. Strain this solution through No. 60 mesh sieve.
4. Solution from Step 3 is then added slowly covering all the corners of the mass mixer of Step 1. Lid of the mixer is closed and mixing operation is carried out for 5 minutes.
5. After 5 minutes mixing remaining part of the solution is poured uniformly through the half open lid of the mixer keeping the mixer on. Mixing is continued for another 5 minutes.
6. Pass the wet mass through No. 12 sieve using a sifter.
7. Granules obtained are uniformly spread into trays in the controlled temperature and humidity area against the dehumidifier for air drying for about 1 hour, keeping the exhaust and ventilators `ON'.
8. Semi-dried granules are then passed through No. 20 sieve using a sifter and spread into trays on butter paper. Finally dry the granules in a tray dryer keeping the inlet and outlet valve of thermic fluid line closed, thermostat at 0°C and ventilator open. Start only air blower and dry for about 3 hours. Transfer the dried granules to polythene lined containers.

9. Weigh the granules and transfer to the blending area.
10. Pass 72.50 Kg. Ampicillin Trihydrate through No. 20 mesh sieve and transfer to the blender.
11. Pass Magnesium Stearate and Talcum through No. 80 sieve and transfer to the blender.
12. Pass Aerosil through No. 100 mesh sieve and transfer to the blender.
13. Transfer the granules from Step 9 to the blender and blend the material for 60 minutes.
14. The material is now ready for capsule filling.

CAUTION :

Environmental conditions should be strictly followed. Temperature should be below 27°C and relative humidity 35% to 45%.

AMPICILLIN AND CLOXACILLIN DRY SYRUP

LABELLED FORMULA

Each 5 ml. of reconstituted suspension contains :

Ampicillin Trihydrate equivalent to Ampicillin	125 mg.
Cloxacillin Sodium equivalent to Cloxacillin	125 mg.

BATCH SIZE	:	6000 Bottles of 40 ml.
PRACTICAL YIELD	:	5800 Bottles of 40 ml.
USUAL PACKING	:	40 ml. Amber Bottles with Marking

FORMULATION

S.No.	Ingredients	Quantity		Overages
1.	Ampicillin Trihydrate	6.983	Kg.	
2.	Cloxacillin Sodium	6.918	Kg.	
3.	Carboxymethylcellulose Sodium	1.200	Kg.	
4.	Aerosil	0.480	Kg.	
5.	Methyl Paraben Sodium	0.240	Kg.	
6.	Sodium Chloride	1.200	Kg.	
7.	Saccharin Sodium	0.240	Kg.	
8.	Disodium Edetate	0.120	Kg.	
9.	Colour Erythrosine Supra	0.006	Kg.	
10.	Peppermint Flavour (Powder)	0.600	Kg.	
11.	Lemon Flavour (Powder)	0.600	Kg.	
12.	Sucrose (Powder)	161.456	Kg.	

MANUFACTURING PROCESS

1. Mix all the ingredients under controlled conditions of temperature and moisture for 30 minutes.
2. Use all ingredients after sifting through stainless steel sieve.
3. Fill 30 g. in each bottle and close immediately.

AMPICILLIN AND CLOXACILLIN FOR ORAL SUSPENSION

LABELLED FORMULA

Each 5 ml. of reconstituted syrup contains :

Ampicillin Trihydrate equivalent to Ampicillin 125 mg.

Cloxacillin Sodium equivalent to Cloxacillin 125 mg.

BATCH SIZE : 66 Kg.

PRACTICAL YIELD : 2600 Bottles of 40 ml.

USUAL PACKING : 24.8 g. in glass bottle of 70 ml. with mark of 40 ml

FORMULATION

S.No.	Ingredients	Quantity		Overages
1.	Ampicillin Trihydrate	3.2	Kg.	5%
2.	Cloxacillin Sodium	3.0	Kg.	5%
3.	Aerosil	900	g.	
4.	Sodium Benzoate	270	g.	
5.	Carboxymethylcellulose Sodium	900	g.	
6.	Menthol	30	g.	
7.	Methyl Paraben Sodium	100	g.	
8.	Colour Tartrazine	10.5	g.	
9.	Sugar Pharm. Grade	57.9	Kg.	

MANUFACTURING SPECIFICATIONS

1. Use Amber glass bottles of 70 ml. capacity with a mark at 40 ml.
2. Fill 24.8 g. in each bottle ± 100 mg.
3. Moisture content of the powders should be less than 1%.
4. Use completely dried and clean bottles.
5. pH of the reconstructed syrup should be between 5.0 to 7.0.
6. All process to be conducted at 20°C Temperature and less than 40% relative humidity.

MANUFACTURING PROCESS

1. Dry Pharm. Grade Sugar in a tray at 40°C for 30 minutes and add to the cone mixer.
2. Add Ampicillin Trihydrate, Cloxacillin Sodium, Sodium Benzoate, Carboxymethylcellulose Sodium, Menthol, Methyl Paraben Sodium and Colour Tartrazine to the Cone mixer. Mix for 15 minutes. Now add the balance quantity of sugar and mix for 3 hours.
3. Fill 24.8 g. in bottles with a powder filling machine.

AMPICILLIN CAPSULES 250 mg.

LABELLED FORMULA

Each capsules contain:

Ampicillin Anhydrous 250 mg.

BATCH SIZE : 1,00,000 Capsules

PRACTICAL YIELD : 98,000 Capsules

USUAL PACKING : Strip of 10 Capsules

FORMULATION

S.No.	Ingredients	Quantity		Overages
1.	Ampicillin Anhydrous	25.750	Kg.	3%
2.	Lactose	2.575	Kg.	
3.	Polyvinylpyrrolidone	0.640	Kg.	
4.	Isopropyl Alcohol	12.000	Lit.	
5.	Purified Talc	0.260	Kg.	
6.	Magnesium Stearate	0.130	Kg.	
	Total Weight	29.355	Kg.	

MANUFACTURING PROCESS

1. Mix Ampicillin Anhydrous and Lactose in a suitable mixer for 15 minutes
2. Prepare the granulating solution by dissolving 0.640 Kg Polyvinylpyrrolidone in 12.0 Lit. of Isopropyl Alcohol by stirring in suitable vessel. Filter the solution through nylon or muslin cloth.
3. Ampicillin Lactose mix is granulated in a ribbon blender with th granulating solution from Step 2. Mix for 20 minutes till a uniform w mass is obtained.
4. Initially dry the wet mass in a Fluid Bed Drier for 15 minutes at roo temperature. Rake after every 10 minutes. Dry again at 45°C for minutes.
5. Granulate through the Multimill using 1 mm sieve.

6. Dry the granules in a fluid bed drier for 30 minutes at 45°C till the material is free from solvent smell.
7. Blend the granules with Purified Talc and Magnesium Stearate in a suitable mixer.
8. Encapsulate the granules in size '1' capsules (293.55 mg.).

AMPICILLIN CAPSULES 500 mg.

LABELLED FORMULA

Each capsule contains :

Ampicillin (as Ampicillin Trihydrate) 500 mg.

BATCH SIZE	:	34,700 Capsules
PRACTICAL YIELD	:	33,600Capsules
USUAL PACKING	:	Strip of 10 Capsules

FORMULATION

No excipinents are required to be added.

MANUFACTURING SPECIFICATIONS

1. Total weight of powder — 20 Kg. (Compacted Ampicillin Trihydrate)
2. Average fill — 575 mg.
3. Weight of 20 Capsules – 13.5 g.
4. Use No. `00' Capsules.
5. Weight variation less than 5%.
6. Disintegration time – 15 minutes maximum
7. Temperature during processing 20°C.
8. Relative humidity during processing not more than 40%.

Note : 1.15 g. Ampicillin Trihydrate is equivalent to 1.00 g. Ampicillin.

AMPICILLIN FOR ORAL SUSPENSION

LABELLED FORMULA

Each 5 ml. of reconstituted syrup contains :

Ampicillin Trihydrate equivalent to Ampicillin 125 mg

BATCH SIZE	:	60 Kg.
PRACTICAL YIELD	:	2,940 Bottles of 40 ml.
USUAL PACKING	:	20g. in 70 ml. capacity bottle with at 40 ml.

FORMULATION

S.No.	Ingredients	Quantity		Overages
1.	Ampicillin Trihydrate	3.8	Kg.	10%
2.	Carboxymethylcellulose Sodium	1.1	Kg.	
3.	Aerosil	450	g.	
4.	Colour Tartrazine	12	g.	
5.	Sodium Benzoate	270	g.	
6.	Sugar Pharm. Grade	54	Kg.	
7.	Pineapple Flavour Dry	600	g.	

MANUFACTURING SPECIFICATIONS & PROCESS

Same as Ampicillin & Cloxacillin Dry Syrup.

CEPHALEXIN CAPSULES

LABELLED FORMULA

Each capsule contains
Cephalexin Monohydrate 265 mg.
equivalent to Cephalexin 250 mg.

BATCH SIZE : 1,00,000 Capsules
PRACTICAL YIELD : 98,000 Capsules
USUAL PACKING : Strip of 10 Capsules

FORMULATION

S.No.	Ingredients	Quantity		Overages
1.	Cephalexin Monohydrate	53.000	Kg.	
2.	Talcum	2.000	Kg.	
3.	Magnesium Stearate	1.000	Kg.	
4.	Capsules of Size `00'	1.00	Lac	

MANUFACTURING PROCESS

Sieve all the powders and blend for 20 minutes. Fill under controlle conditions of temperature and humidity.

CEPHALEXIN DRY SYRUP

LABELLED FORMULA

Each 5 ml. of reconstituted syrup contains :
Cephalexin Monohydrate
equivalent to Cephalexin 125 mg.

BATCH SIZE : 70.790 Kg.
PRACTICAL YIELD : 4700 Bottles of 40 ml.
USUAL PACKING : 40 ml. marked Amber Bottles

FORMULATION

S.No.	Ingredients	Quantity	Overages
1.	Cephalexin Monohydrate	5.000 Kg.	
2.	Pulverised Sugar	61.070 Kg.	
3.	Sodium Citrate	0.430 Kg.	
4.	Citric Acid	0.095 Kg.	
5.	Aerosil	0.340 Kg.	
6.	Saccharin Sodium	0.430 Kg.	
7.	Sodium Benzoate	0.330 Kg.	
8.	Disodium Edetate	0.085 Kg.	
9.	Carboxymethylcellulose Sodium	0.850 Kg.	
10.	American Ice Cream Flavour	2.150 Kg.	
11.	Colour Tartrazine Supra	0.010 Kg.	

MANUFACTURING PROCESS

Mix all the ingredients under controlled conditions of temperature and humidity. Fill 15 g. in 40 ml. amber glass bottles with mark at 40 ml.

CHLORAMPHENICOL CAPSULES 250 mg.

LABELLED FORMULA

Each capsule contains :

Chloramphenicol 250 mg.

BATCH SIZE : 100,000 Capsules
PRACTICAL YIELD : 97,000 Capsules
USUAL PACKING : Strip of 10 Capsules

FORMULATION

S.No.	Ingredients	Quantity	Overages
1.	Chloramphenicol	25 Kg.	
2.	Lactose	10 Kg.	

MANUFACTURING SPECIFICATIONS

1. Use No. '2' Capsules.
2. Total weight of powders — 35 Kg.
3. Average fill — 350 mg.

4. Weight of 20 capsules — 8.2 g.
5. Weight variation less than 5%.
6. Disintegration time 15 minutes maximum.
7. Temperature of process area 20°C.
8. Relative humidity of process area less than 40%.

ERYTHROMYCIN DRY SYRUP 100 mg.

LABELLED FORMULA

Each 5 ml. of reconstituted suspension contains
Erythromycin Ethyl Succinate
equivalent of Erythromycin Base 100 mg.

BATCH SIZE : 122.70 Kg.
PRACTICAL YIELD : 3850 Bottles of 45 ml.
USUAL PACKING : 45 ml. Bottles containing 31.17 g. granules

FORMULATION

S.No.	Ingredients	Quantity		Overages
1.	Erythromycin Ethylsuccinate (783 u/mg. potency)	4.825	Kg.	5%
2.	Pharmaceutical Grade Sugar	110.00	Kg.	
3.	Dipotassium Hydrogen Phosphate	6.400	Kg.	
4.	Carboxymethylcellulose Sodium	0.200	Kg.	
5.	Citric Acid	0.080	Kg.	
6.	Liquid Lemon Yellow	0.300	Lit.	
7.	Pineapple Powder Flavour	0.040	Kg.	
8.	Distilled Water	0.600	Lit.	

MANUFACTURING PROCESS

1. Sift sugar through sifter using 20 mesh screen. Batch of 122.7 Kg. to be processed in two parts.

PART I

1. Mix 5 Kg. Sugar, 3.2 Kg. Dipotassium Phosphate and 0.040 Kg. Citric Acid in a suitable vessel for 10 minutes manually. Mill the mixture using a suitable Milling Machine.
2. Sift Carboxymethylcellulose Sodium 0.100 Kg. and Erythromycin Ethyl Succinate 2.4125 Kg. using a hand sieve.
3. Blend the materials from Step 1 and Step 2 with 45.427 Kg. milled sugar in the mixer for 30 minutes. Total weight of materials added 61.179 Kg.

4. Add Liquid Lemon Yellow colour slowly and mix well until uniform distribution of colour takes place. Granulate further with 0.300 Lit. Distilled Water and mix until uniform cohesive mass suitable for granulation is obtained.
5. Dry the mass initially at 50°C for 40 minutes in Fluid Bed Drier.
6. Granulate through Oscillating Granulator using 20 mesh directly in another Fluid Bed Bowl.
7. Dry further in Fluid Bed Drier at 50°C for about 45 minutes to a moisture content of not more than 0.3%.
8. Unload the dried granules in double polybags in a clean container. Weight of dried granules 60.500 Kg. approx.
9. Send a sample to Q.C. for testing of loss on drying.
10. Close the bags and label the container as PART – I.

PART – II

Repeat the process as given under Part-I.

Final Blending

1. Sift Pineapple Flavour and 0.5 Kg. of fines from PART – I using hand-sieve of 60 mesh into a suitable vessel. Mix well manually for 10 minutes. Resift and divide into two equal parts. Place Part – I granules in the Drum Mixer and one lot of blended flavour and blend for 20 minutes. Load Part – II granules in the Drum Mixer and second lot of blended flavour and mix for 45 minutes.
2. Unload the blended formulated bulk from Final Blending in double polybags and weigh.
3. Submit a representative sample to Q.C. for evaluation.
4. Store the container in a cool dry place away from light in quarantine area.
5. Fill 31.17 g. in washed, dried and inspected bottles using a suitable filling machine.
6. Temperature of filling room should be 20° to 28°C and Relative Humidity 30% to 35%.

ERYTHROMYCIN DRY SYRUP 125 mg. – I

LABELLED FORMULA

Each 5 ml. of reconstituted suspension contains :

Erythromycin Estolate
equivalent of Erythromycin 125 mg.

BATCH SIZE	:	4680 Bottles of 60 ml.
PRACTICAL YIELD	:	4580 Bottles of 60 ml.
USUAL PACKING	:	60 ml. Amber Bottles with Marking

FORMULATION

S.No.	Ingredients	Quantity		Overages
1.	Erythromycin Estolate	10.615	kg	5%
2.	Carboxymethylcellulose Sodium	0.062	kg	
3.	Sodium Saccharine	0.191	kg	
4.	Sodium Citrate	6.206	kg	
5.	Sugar (Pharmaceutical Grade)	98.863	kg	
6.	Colour Erythrosine	0.016	kg	
7.	Rasberry Essence Dry Mix	0.468	kg	
8.	Aerosil	0.421	kg	
9.	Carboxymethylcellulose Sodium	2.452	kg	
10.	Sodium Benzoate	0.562	kg	
11.	Citric Acid	0.188	kg	
	Total Weight	120.042	kg	

MANUFACTURING PROCESS

1. Pass Sugar, Erythromycin Estolate, Saccharine Sodium, Sodium Citrate, Sodium Benzoate, Citric Acid and Carboxymethylcellulose Sodium through Multimill to get 40 mesh powder.
2. Dissolve the colour in 2 Lit. D.M. water, add 50% Sodium Benzoate and 2.452 Kg. C.M.C. Sodium and keep it overnight.
3. Bind material of Step 1 with paste of Step 2 and pass through Multimill to form granules.
4. Dry the granules at 50°C to 55°C to get moisture less than 0.5%.
5. Pass the granules through 18 mesh screen.
6. Add Aerosil and mix well.
7. Finally add dry flavour and mix well.
8. Fill 25.65 g. in 60 ml. marked bottles under controlled conditions of temperature and moisture.

ERYTHROMYCIN DRY SYRUP 125 mg. – II

LABELLED FORMULA

Each 5 ml. of reconstituted syrup contains :

Erythromycin Estolate
equivalent of Erythromycin — 125 mg.

BATCH SIZE	:	3510 Bottles of 25.854 gm. (60 ml)
PRACTICAL YIELD	:	3440 Bottles of 60 ml.
USUAL PACKING	:	Bottles of 60 ml.

FORMULATION

S.No.	Ingredients	Quantity	Overages
1.	Erythromycin Estolate (625 mcg. per mg. of base)	8.676 Kg.	3%
2.	Sugar Pharmaceutical Grade	74.147 Kg.	
3.	Carboxymethylcelluylose Sodium	1.839 Kg.	
4.	Sodium Benzoate	0.400 Kg.	
5.	Citric Acid Anhydrous	0.141 Kg.	
6.	Saccharine Sodium	0.143 Kg.	
7.	Sodium Citrate	4.654 Kg.	
8.	Carboxymethylcellulose Sodium	0.046 Kg.	
9.	Sodium Benzoate	0.022 Kg.	
10.	Colour Erythrosine	0.012 Kg.	
11.	Rasberry Dry Mix	0.351 Kg.	
12.	Aerosil	0.316 Kg.	
	Total Weight	90.747 Kg.	
13.	Distilled Water	3.500 Lit.	

MANUFACTURING PROCESS

1. Dissolve the colour in 3.5 Lit. of Distilled water and 46 gm. Carboxymethylcellulose Sodium and 22 g. Sodium Benzoate. Keep it aside for one hour.
2. Pass Erythromycin Estolate, Saccharin Sodium, Sodium Citrate, Sodium Benzoate, Carboxymethylcellulose Sodium and Sugar through Multimill to get 40 mesh powder.
3. Mix all the ingredients in a Planetary Mixer for 30 minutes.
4. Blend the mix from Step 3 with Step 1 to get good granules.
5. Pass the wet mass through Multimill to get 16 – 18 mesh granules.
6. Dry the sieved granules at 50° – 55°C to get moisture less than 0.5%.
7. Pass the dried granules through 18 mesh of sifter.
8. Place sieved granules in a drum mixer. Add Aerosil and Dry flavour. Mix for 15-20 minutes.
9. Fill 25.854 g. in 60 ml. Amber Bottles.

ERYTHROMYCIN DRY SYRUP 200 mg. (SACHETS)

LABELLED FORMULA

Each sachet contains:

Erythromycin (as Ethylsuccinate) 200 mg.

BATCH SIZE : 250 Kg.
PRACTICAL YIELD : 1,26,000 Sachets
USUAL PACKING : Sachets of 1.8 g. each

FORMULATION

S.No.	Ingredients	Quantity		Overages
1.	Sugar Cane Granular	199.28	Kg.	
2.	Sodium Citrate	13.20	Kg.	
3.	Veegum (Guar Gum)	2.00	Kg.	
4.	Saccharin Sodium	0.40	Kg.	
5.	Erythromycin Ethylsuccinate (850 mcg/mg)	30.96	Kg.	
6.	Flavour Cherry	1.00	Kg.	
7.	Silicone Dioxide Collodial	1.88	Kg.	
8.	Sodium Lauryl Sulphate (Acetone washed)	0.625	Kg.	
9.	Food Colour Red	22	g.	
10.	Distilled Water (Approx.)	9.0	Lit.	

MANUFACTURING SPECIFICATIONS

1. The weight of sugar is adjusted to compensate for potency variation and excess of the Erythromycin Ethylsuccinate in order to maintain the standard quantity at 230.24kg. (of Sugar and Erythromycin Ethylsuccinate).
2. Wet the mass with distilled water and prepare granules as usual.
3. Ingredients given in order of mixing.

ERYTHROMYCIN FOR ORAL SUSPENSION 100 mg.

LABELLED FORMULA

Each 5 ml. of reconstituted suspension contains :

Erythromycin Ethylsuccinate equivalent to Erythromycin Base 100 g.

BATCH SIZE : 3936 Bottles of 45 ml. (31.17 g.)

PRACTICAL YIELD : 3580 Bottles of 45 ml. (31.17 g.)

USUAL PACKING : Bottles of 45 ml. (31.17 gm.)

FORMULATION

S.No.	Ingredients	Quantity		Overages
1.	Erythromycin Ethylsuccinate (783 U/mg. Potency)	4.825	Kg.	5%
2.	Sugar Pharmaceutical Grade	110.855	Kg.	
3.	Di-potassium Hydrogen Phosphate	6.400	Kg.	
4.	Carboxymethylcellulose Sodium	0.200	Kg.	
5.	Citric Acid	0.080	Kg.	
6.	Liquid Lemon Yellow	0.300	Lit.	
7.	Pineapple Flavour	0.040	Kg.	
8.	Distilled Water	0.600	Lit.	
	Total Weight	122.70	Kg.	

MANUFACTURING PROCESS

1. The batch is to be processed in two parts.

PART A

1. Mix 5 Kg. Sugar, 3.2 Kg. Di-potassium Hydrogen Phosphate and 0.04 Kg. Citric Acid in a suitable vessel manually for 10 minutes.
2. Pass the mixture through Multimill. Rinse the Mill with 5 Kg. of Sugar to dislodge any holding material in the mill. Dismantle the screen and collect any residue left.
3. Sift Carboxymethylcellulose Sodium 0.100 Kg and Erythromycin Ethylsuccinate 2.4125 Kg. using a hand sieve.
4. Blend the material from Step 1 and Step 2 with milled sugar 45.427 Kg. in the mixer for 30 minutes. Check total weight of materials added (61.179 Kg.).
5. Add the liquid colour slowly until uniform distribution of colour takes place. Granulate further with 0.3 Lit. Distilled Water and mix until uniform cohesive mass suitable for granulation is formed.
6. Dry the mass initially at 50°C for 40 minutes in a Fluid Bed Drier.
7. Granulate through Oscillating Granulator using 20 mesh directly in another bowl.
8. Dry again at 50°C for 45 minutes in a Fluid Bed Drier to a moisture content of not more than 0.3%.
9. Unload the dried granules in a clean polythene lined container (Wt. 60.500 Kg.) and label it as Part A.

Part B

Repeat the process as given in Part A.

Final Blending

Sift Pineapple Dry Essence with 0.5 Kg. of fines from Part A using handsieve of 60 mesh into a suitable poly-lined container. Mix well manually for 10 minutes. Resift and divide into two equal parts. Place Part A granules in the drum blender and one lot of blended flavour. Blend for 20 minutes. Similarly take Part B granules in the drum blender and mix with second lot of blended flavour. Blend for 45 minutes. Unload the blended formulated batch from final blending in double polythene bags and check the weight.

Filling

Fill 31.17 g. (limit 30.6 to 31.6) in Amber Bottles on a filling machine.

Precautions

Relative Humidity of Filling Room should be 30 to 35%.
Temperature should be 20° – 28°C.
Weight variation should be checked at regular intervals and recorded.

INDOMETHACIN CAPSULES

LABELLED FORMULA

Each Capsule contains

Indomethacin 25 mg

BATCH SIZE : 50,000 Capsules
PRACTICAL YIELD : 48,500 Capsules
USUAL PACKING : Strip of 10 Capsules

FORMULATION

S.No.	Ingredients	Quantity	Overages
1.	Indomethacin	1.25 Kg.	
2.	Dried Starch	5.00 Kg.	
3.	Dried Talcum	3.75 Kg.	

MANUFACTURING SPECIFICATIONS

1. Moisture content of mixed powders should be less than 1.5%.
2. Starch should be dried at 80°C for 4 hours, sieved through 100 mesh moisture less than 1.5%.
3. Talcum should be dried at 80°C for 4 hours, sieved through 100 mesh, moisture less than 1.0%.
4. Store capsules in air-tight containers.

IRON, PROTEIN AND VITAMINS CAPSULES

LABELLED FORMULA

Each capsule contains

Protein Hydrolystate (derived from milk equivalent to 48 mg. Nitrogen)	300 mg.
Elemental Iron (as ferrous Aminoate)	60 mg.
Vitamin B_6	3 mg.
Vitamin B_{12}	15 mcg.
Folic Acid	1.5 mg.

BATCH SIZE : 81,000 Capsules
PRACTICAL YIELD : 78,500 Capsules
USUAL PACKING : Strip of 10 Capsules

FORMULATION

S.No.	Ingredients	Quantity	Overages
1.	Protein Hydrolysate with Iron	50 Kg.	
2.	Pyridoxine Hydrochloride	260 g.	7%
3.	Cyanocobalamin	2.8 g.	100%
4.	Folic Acid	250 g.	100%
5.	Methyl Paraben Sodium	200 g.	
6.	Propyl Paraben Sodium	100 g.	
7.	Thiourea	200 g.	
8.	Citric Acid	1.5 Kg.	

MANUFACTURING SPECIFICATIONS

1. Total weight of powder— 52.51 Kg.
2. Average fill — 648.27 mg.
3. Use No.'O' Capsules.
4. Weight of 20 Capsules—14.96
5. Weight variation 5% maximum.
6. Disintegaration time 15 minutes maximum.
7. Temperature of process area 20°C.
8. Relative humidity of process area less than 40%.

MANUFACTURING PROCESS

Dissolve Vitamin B_{12} in 100 ml. Alcohol and mix with 5 Kg. Protein Hydrolysate with Iron. Then mix this lot with all other ingredients. Mix for 3 hours in a double cone mixer before filling.

MEFENAMIC ACID CAPSULES

LABELLED FORMULA

Capsule contains :

Mefenamic Acid 250 mg.

BATCH SIZE : 4,00,000 Capsules

PRACTICAL YIELD : 3,92,000 Capsules

USUAL PACKING : Strip of 10 Capsules

FORMULATION

S.No.	Ingredients	Quantity		Overages
1.	Mefenamic Acid	100.00	Kg.	
2.	Lactose	38.91	Kg.	
3.	Gelatin	0.49	Kg.	
4.	Distilled Water	10.67	Kg.	
5.	Magnesium Stearate	0.40	Kg.	
6.	Sodium Lauryl Sulphate	0.20	Kg.	
7.	Empty Gelatin Capsules No. '1'	4.00	Lac.	

MANUFACTURING PROCESS

CAUTION

Protect the product from moisture and light to avoid darkening. Mefenamic Acid is irritating and care should be taken to avoid contact with eyes, face and hands.

1. Pass the Mefenamic Acid and Lactose through No. 20 mesh stainless steel screen into the planetary mixer. Blend thoroughly for 30 minutes.
2. Soak the Gelatin in 10.67 Lit. of Distilled Water in a Steam jacketed pan. After 30 minutes, heat the soaked Gelatin with stirring to aid complete dissolution.
3. Granulate the powder mixture from Step 1 with the Gelatin solution from Step 2, until the powders are thoroughly and uniformly moist. Use additional hot distilled water if necessary.
4. Pass the moist granulation from Step 3 through No. 4 mesh stainless steel screen using a suitable mill and collecting the sieved material in the basket of the Aeromatic Drier.
5. Dry the granulation in the Aeromatic Drier at a temperature not exceeding 60°C for 45 minutes.
6. Reduce the dried granulation through a 20 mesh screen using a suitable mill.

7. Transfer the granulation from Step 6 to the Planetary Mixer and add Magnesium Stearate and Sodium Lauryl Sulphate. Blend thoroughly for 20 minutes. Transfer the blended powder mixture to Polythene lined fibre drums and close tightly.
8. Fill in No. '1' Empty Hard Gelatin Capsules. 350 mg. per Capsule (Limit 237.5 mg to 262.5 mg).

OXYTETRACYLINE CAPSULES 250 mg.

LABELLED FORMULA
Each capsule contains :
Oxytetracycline Hydrochloride 250 mg.

BATCH SIZE : 100,000 Capsules
PRACTICAL YIELD : 98,500 Capsules
USUAL PACKING : Plastic Bottle of 100 Capsules

FORMULATION

S.No.	Ingredients	Quantity	Overages
1.	Oxytetracycline Hydrochloride	25.0 Kg.	
2.	Dried Starch	2.5 Kg.	
3.	Dried Talcum	2.5 Kg.	

MANUFACTURING SPECIFICATIONS

1. Moisture content of mixed powders should be less than 1.5%.
2. Starch should be dried at 80°C for 4 hours, sieved through 100 mesh, moisture less than 1.5%.
3. Talcum should be dried at 80°C for 4 hours, sieved through 100 mesh, moisture less than 1.0%.
4. Store capsules in air-tight containers.

NOTES:

PIROXICAM CAPSULES

LABELLED FORMULA
Each capsule contains :
Piroxicam : 20 mg.

BATCH SIZE : 4,00,000 Capsules
PRACTICAL YIELD : 3,90,000 Capsules
USUAL PACKING : Strip of 10 Capsules

FORMULATION

S.No.	Ingredients	Quantity	Overages
1.	Piroxicam	8.000 Kg.	
2.	Lactose	96.160 Kg.	
3.	Sodium Lauryl Sulphate	0.600 Kg.	
4.	Talcum	0.600 Kg.	
5.	Starch (Predried)	20.640 Kg.	
6.	Empty Hard Gelatin Capsules Size '2'	4.00 Lac	

MANUFACTURING PROCESS

1. Pass Lactose, Piroxicam and Sodium Lauryl Sulphate through 60 mesh sieve.
2. Pass Talcum through 80 mesh sieve.
3. Pass Starch through 100 mesh sieve.
4. Mix Piroxicam with 32 Kg. Lactose for 15 minutes.
5. Mix Starch 20.64 Kg. with 0.600 Kg. Sodium Lauryl Sulphate for 15 minutes.
6. Charge 72.16 Kg. Lactose to a suitable blender.
7. Add the Piroxicam/ Lactose Mix.
8. Add Talcum 0.600 Kg.
9. Add Starch/ Sodium Lauryl Sulphate Mix.
10. Mix all the powders for 20 minutes under controlled conditions of temperature and humidity.
11. Fill in No. '2' Capsules.

RIFAMPICIN AND ISONIAZID CAPSULES

LABELLED FORMULA

Each capsule contains :

Rifampicin	450 mg
Isoniazid	300 mg.

BATCH SIZE	:	40,000 Capsules
PRACTICAL YIELD	:	39,000 Capsules
USUAL PACKING	:	Strip of 10 Capsules

FORMULATION

S.No.	Ingredients	Quantity	Overages
1.	Rifampicin	18.00 Kg.	
2.	Isoniazid	12.25 Kg.	

MANUFACTURING SPECIFICATIONS

1. Total Weight of powder — 30.25 Kg.
2. Average fill — 756.25 mg.
3. Use No. `00' Capsules.
4. Weight of 20 capsules — 17.32 g.
5. Disintegration time 15 minutes.
6. Temperature of processing area — 20°C.
7. Relative humidity of process area less than 40%.

RIFAMPICIN CAPSULES 150 mg.

LABELLED FORMULA

Each capsule contains :

Rifampicin 150 mg

BATCH SIZE	:	100,000 Capsules
PRACTICAL YIELD	:	97,000 Capsules
USUAL PACKING	:	Strip of 10 Capsules

FORMULATION

S.No.	Ingredients	Quantity	Overages
1.	Rifampicin	15.0 Kg.	
2.	Calcium Stearate	6.5 Kg.	
3.	Sodium Lauryl Sulphate	0.2 Kg.	
4.	Carboxymethylcellulose Sodium	1.0 Kg.	

MANUFACTURING SPECIFICATION

1. Moisture content should be less than 3%.
2. During manufacturing the relative humidity should be 35–40%.

RIFAMPICIN CAPSULES 450 mg.

LABELLED FORMULA

Each capsule contains :

Rifampicin 450 mg

BATCH SIZE	:	100,000 Capsules
PRACTICAL YIELD	:	97,000 Capsules
USUAL PACKING	:	Strip of 10 Capsules

FORMULATION

S.No.	Ingredients	Quantity	Overages
1.	Rifampicin	45.0 Kg.	

MANUFACTURING SPECIFICATIONS

1. Use number '0' Capsules.
2. Fill 450 mg in each capsule without any excipients.
3. Clean the capsules before packing
4. Weight of 20 capsules 11 g.
5. Weight variation not more than 5%.
6. Disintegration time 15 minutes.
7. Relative humidity of process area less than 40%.

TETRACYCLINE CAPSULES

LABELLED FORMULA

Each capsule contains :

Tetracycline Hydrochloride 250 mg

BATCH SIZE : 100,000 Capsules
PRACTICAL YIELD : 97,500 Capsules
USUAL PACKING : Plastic bottle of 100 Capsules

FORMULATION

S.No.	Ingredients	Quantity	Overages
1.	Tetracycline Hydrochloride	25.0 Kg.	
2.	Dried Starch	2.5 Kg.	
3.	Dried Talcum	2.5 Kg.	

MANUFACTURING SPECIFICATION

1. Moisture content should be less than 1.5%.
2. Starch should be dried at 80°C for 4 hours, sieved through 100 mesh, moisture less than 1.5%.
3. Talcum should dried at 80°C for 4 hours, sieved through 100 mesh, moisture less than 1.0%.
4. Store capsules in air-tight containers.

VITAMIN B. COMPLEX CAPSULES

LABELLED FORMULA

Each capsule contains :

Vitamin B_1 4.5 mg
Vitamin B_2 5.0 mg

Vitamin B_6	1.5 mg
Vitamin B_{12}	5 mcg
Niacinamide	45.0 mg
Calcium D. Pantothenate	5.0 mg

BATCH SIZE : 100,000 Capsules
PRACTICAL YIELD : 97,000 Capsules
USUAL PACKING : Strip of 10 Capsules

FORMULATION

S.No.	Ingredients	Quantity	Overages
1.	Thiamine Hydrochloride	525 g.	15%
2.	Riboflavin	575 g.	15%
3.	Pyridoxine Hydrochloride	180 g.	20%
4.	Cyanocobalamin	1 g.	100%
5.	Nicotinamide	5.0 Kg.	10%
6.	Calcium D. Pantothenate	525 g.	20%
7.	Aerosil	100 g.	
8.	Thiourea	150 g.	
9.	Starch/ Lactose	17.5 Kg.	

MANUFACTURING SPECIFICATIONS

1. Total weight of powder — 24.55 Kg.
2. Average fill — 245.5 mg.
3. Use No. `2' Capsules.
4. Clean the capsules before packing.
5. Weight of 20 capsules — 6.11 g.
6. Weight Variation less than 5%.
7. Disintegration time 15 minutes.
8. Temperature and humidity control as usual.

MANUFACTURING PROCESS

1. Dissolve Vitamin B_{12} in 100 ml. Alcohol and mix with 5 Kg. Lactose. Alternatively use Vitamin B_{12} Triturate.
2. Mix all other ingredients and sieve all materials in double cone blender. Mix for 3 hours before filling.

VITAMIN B_1, B_6 AND B_{12} CAPSULES

LABELLED FORMULA

Each capsule contains :

Thiamine Mononitrate	10 mg.
Pyridoxine Hydrochloride	3 mg.
Cyanocobalamin	15 mcg.

BATCH SIZE : 100,000 Capsules
PRACTICAL YIELD : 98,000 Capsules
USUAL PACKING : Blister of 10 Capsules

FORMULATION

S.No.	Ingredients	Quantity		Overages
1.	Thiamine Mononitrate	1.500	Kg.	50%
2.	Pyridoxine Hydrochloride	0.330	Kg.	10%
3.	Cyanocobalamin	4.500	g.	200%
4.	Talcum	5.000	Kg.	
5.	Dried Starch	2.500	Kg.	
6.	Magnesium Stearate	0.100	Kg.	
7.	Dicalcium Phosphate	16.570	Kg.	

MANUFACTURING PROCESS

1. Take 500 g. Talcum in a suitable container. In a clean Porcelain Pestle and Mortor add Cyanocobalamin and triturate with Talcum in small lots to prepare a perfect triturate.
2. Mix the triturate with 6 Kg. of Dicalcium Phosphate in a stainless steel vessel by hand for 15 to 20 minutes. Sift through 40 mesh twice.
3. Weigh and transfer to a suitable stainless steel vessel or mixer, balance quantity of Dicalcium Phosphate, Dried Starch, Magnesium Stearate, Thiamine Mononitrate, Pyridoxine Hydrochloride and balance quantity of Talcum. Mix for 15 to 20 minutes and pass through 40 mesh twice.
4. Blend the powder mix with the triturate in a suitable blender for 15-20 minutes.
5. Fill 260 mg. in each capsule on a suitable capsule filling machine.

VITAMIN B. COMPEX WITH VITAMIN C CAPSULES

LABELLED FORMULA

Each capsule contains

Thiamine Mononitrate	10 mg
Riboflavine	10 mg
Nicotinamide	50 mg
Pyridoxine Hydrochloride	5 mg
Calcium Pantothenate	10 mg.
Cyanocobalamin	5 mcg.
Ascorbic Acid	75 mg.

BATCH SIZE : 1,20,000 Capsules
PRACTICAL YIELD : 1,17,000 Capsules
USUAL PACKING : Bottles of 25 Capsules

FORMULATION

S.No.	Ingredients	Quantity	Overages
1.	Thiamine Mononitrate	*1.800 Kg.	50%
2.	Riboflavine	1.320 Kg.	10%
3.	Nicotinamide	6.600 Kg.	10%
4.	Pyridoxine Hydrochloride	0.396 Kg.	10%
5.	Calcium Pantothenate	2.100 Kg.	75%
6.	Cyanocobalamin	2.10 g.	250%
7.	Ascorbic Acid	10.800 Kg.	20%
8.	Magnesium Oxide Light	1.680 Kg.	
9.	Dried Starch	3.000 Kg.	
10.	Magnesium Stearate	0.120 Kg.	
11.	Calcium Phosphate Dibasic	17.184 Kg.	
	Total Weight	45.000 Kg.	

MANUFACTURING PROCESS

2. Sift the blend through 30 mesh screen and transfer the sifted blend to a mixer.
3. Transfer about 5 Kg. Calcium Phosphate Dibasic to a planetary mixer. Weigh and dissolve Cyanocobalamine in about 25 ml. of distilled water. While mixing distribute in a thin stream the solution of Cyanocobalamin of Diabasic Calcium Phosphate. Rinse the container with about 5 ml. of distilled water.
4. Sift the wet mass through No. 40 screen and remix for 15 minutes.
5. Weigh and transfer the following to a planetary mixer :

Dibasic Calcium Phosphate	12.180 Kg. (app.)
Starch	3.000 Kg.
Magnesium Stearate	0.120 Kg.
Thiamine Mononitrate	0.800 kg.
Riboflavin	1.320 Kg.
Pyridoxine Hydrochloride	0.396 Kg.
Calcium Panthothenate	2.100 Kg.

Blend obtained in Step 3 and blend obtained in Step 5.

Mix for 15 minutes. Sift the blend through 40 mesh screen and remix for 15 minutes.

7. Store the blend in double polythene bag lined container until taken up for filling in capsules.
8. Fill 375 mg. in each capsule on a filling machine.

VITAMIN B_{12}, VITAMIN C, FOLIC ACID AND FERROUS FUMERATE CAPSULES

LABELLED FORMULA

Each capsule contains :

Vitamin B_{12}	15 mcg
Folic Acid	1.5 mg.
Ferrous Fumerate	300 mg.
Vitamin C	150 mcg.

BATCH SIZE : 1,20,000 Capsules

PRACTICAL YIELD : 1,17,500 Capsules

USUAL PACKING : Bottles of 50 Capsules

SHELF LIFE : 1 Year

FORMULATION

S.No.	Ingredients	Quantity		Overages
1.	Cyanocobalamin	4.0	g.	100%
2.	Folic Acid	324.0	g.	80%
3.	Ferrous Fumerate	36.0	Kg.	
4.	Vitamin C Coated	18.54	Kg.	
5.	Purified Talc	8.32	Kg.	
6.	Aerosil	60.0	g.	

MANUFACTURING PROCESS

1. Sift the entire blend through No. 14 sieve and transfer the blend to the planetary mixer.
2. Remix for 15 minutes.
3. Fill in No. '1' Capsules. Fill weight 532 mg.

Chapter 12

Eye and Ear Preparations

INTRODUCTION

Ophthalmic Preparations are sterile products, essentially free from foreign particles, suitably compounded and packaged for either topical application to the eyelids, or instillation into the space between the eyeball and eyelids. Currently available ophthalmic preparations include solutions, suspensions, ointments and flat disks. The last are designed to be held in the space between the eyeball and eyelids for continous treatment. Most ophthalmic solutions and suspensions contain an aquaous rather than oily vehicle.

Ophthalmic Solutions and suspensions for all practical purposes, should be considered at par with the parenteral preparations and all precautions taken to maintain sterility as in case of injectuons. Both classes of preparations employ similar added substances and manufacturing procedures.

In addition to therapeutic effects, topical applications to the eye may have the effect of discomfort, pain or actual tissue damage. These potential effects should be kept in mind by the manufacturing pharmascist. There are potential causes of pain reactions of many of the lacal anaesthetics, heavy metals, salts etc.

Lacrimal fluid isotonic with blood, having an isotonicity value approximately the same as that of a 0.9% Sodium Chloride Solution. It has been found, however, that in the typical occasional administration of small quantities of Ophthalmic Solutions as drops, the eye can tolerate a fairly wide range of concentration that is 0.6% to 1.5% in terms of Sodium Chloride.

Although accurate adjustment to isotonicity is obviously not necessary in many cases, especially when the Ophthalmic Solution is used in small doses, it is much more important that a solution to be used as an eye lotion be isotonic.

All solutions for use in the eye should be brilliantly clear and free from foreign particles, fibres and filaments. This is recommended from a safety as well as medicolegal point of view.

Ophthalmic Solutions are requird to be sterile when prepared, and great care must be exercised subsequently to prevent contamination is use. The common methods of sterilization are moist heat under pressure, bacterial filteration, and use of chemicals.

LIST OF PRESERVATIVES USED IN OPHTHALAMIC PREPARATIONS

S. No.	Name of Preservative	Usual Concentration	Stability and Incompatibility
1.	Benzy Alcohol	0.1% to 0.2%	Bacteriostatic agent, has a weak local anasthetic action
2.	Chlorbutal	0.2% to 0.5%	Antibacteial and germicidal properties effective against Pseudomonas aeruginosa
3.	Chlorocresol	0.1% to 0.2%	Volatile at 100°C Inactivated by Polysorbate 80
4.	Phenylethyl Alcohol	0.25% to 0.5%	More active against gram negative bacteria, volatile, sensitive to light and oxidizing agents.
5.	Benzylkonium	0.01% to 0.02%	Synergistic with Disodium Edetate
6.	Thromessal	0.05% to 0.02%	Unstable at pH lower than 7.0 Bacteriostatic and mild fungistatic.
7.	Chlorhexidine	0.01%	Effective against bith gram-positive and gram negative bacteria.
8.	Cetrimide	0.001% to 0.005%	——
9.	Phenylmercuric Nitrate	0.001% to 0.002%	Slow acting and toxic
10.	Phenylmercuric Acctate	0.001% to 0.002%	Slow acting and toxic

PRACTICAL TIPS

1. Accidental substitution of one type of drug for another can have serious consequences, as when a mydriatic is used in place of a miotic. Change the filters with the change of product.
2. Cleanliness and sterlitiy are of utmost importance in preparing ophthalmic solutions. Neglignence can lead to loss of eyes.
3. pH or hydrogen ion concentration of Ophthalmic sloutions is very important and critical. Ideal pH-7.4 (limit 6.0 to 8.0)
4. Solutions which can be autoclaved should be subjected to autoclaving at 121°C for 15 minutes.

ATROPINE EYE OINTMENT

LABELLED FORMULA

Alropine Sulphate 0.1% w/w
in a sterile eye ointment base.

BATCH SIZE : 20 Kg.
PRACTICAL YIELD : 5500 Tubes of 3.5 g.
USUAL PACKING : 3.5 g. Aluminium Collapsible Tubes

FORMULATION

S. No.	Ingredients	Quantity	Overages
1.	Atropine Sulphate	200 g.	
2.	Liquid Paraffin	1.0 Kg.	
3.	Cetostearyl Alcohol	1.0 Kg.	
4.	Hard Paraffin	1.0 Kg.	
5.	White Soft Paraffin	16.8 Kg.	

MANUFACTURING SPECIFICATIONS

1. Aluminium Collapsible Tubes should be dipped in a mixture Isopropyl Alcohol 70% containing 0.002% of Benzylkonium Chloride for 10 to 15 minutes for sterilization. Keep these tubes in previously sterilized trays.
2. Expose the washed and treated tubes to fumes of Formation Fumigation canj be dojne with Pot. Permanganate and Formalin in a chamber for 24 hours.
3. Filling of tubes to be done aseptically.

MANUFACTURING PROCESS

1. Melt Cetostearyl Alcohol, Hard Paraffin and White Soft Paraffin along with Liquid Paraffin. Heat at 150°C for atleast one hour for effective sterilization of ointment base. Allow the mass to cool to a semi solid state under aseptic conditions. Mixed base should be filtered before cooling.
2. Dissolve Atropine Sulphate in 200 ml. of Sterilized Water For Injection and add to the semi solid sterilized base under continous mixing and aseptic conditions.
3. Fill the sterile tubes.

BETAMETHASONE EYE DROPS

LABELLED FORMULA

Betamethasone Sodium Phosphate 0.1% w/v
Phenylethyl Alcohol 0.25%.

BATCH SIZE : 10 Litres
PRACTICAL YIELD : 1900 Vials of 5 ml.
USUAL PACKING : 5 ml. Amber Vials

FORMULATION

S. No.	Ingredients	Quantity	Overages
1.	Betamethasone Sodium Phosphate	11.5 g.	
2.	Creatinin	120 g.	
3.	Sodium Borate	30 g.	
4.	Sodium Citrate	100 g.	
5.	Sodium Metabisulphite	32 g.	
6.	Phenylethyl Alcohol	25 ml.	
7.	Distilled Water to	10 Lit.	

MANUFACTURING SPECIFICATIONS

1. pH range — 8.0 to 9.0.
2. Pre and Post Nitrogen Gas flushing is required.
3. Manufacture, filling and sealing under asceptic conditions.
4. Use Butyl or Latex Rubber Stoppers.
5. Use 5 ml. Amber Vials.
6. Sterilize Rubber Stoppers in autoclave at 121° C for 30 minutes.
7. Sterilize vials at 200°C for 4 hours.
8. Give pre antibacterial solution treatment before final washing.

MANUFACTURING PROCESS

1. Prepare a solution of buffer, preservative and anti-oxident in 8 Litres of Distilled Water.
2. Sterilize this solution at 121°C for 30 minutes.
3. Adjust pH with Sodium at Hydroxide Solution.
4. Dissolve Betamethasone Sodium Phosphate and Creatinin in above solution at a temperature not exceeding 40°C.
5. Make up the volume to 10 Lit. with water.
6. Filter through G-4 Sintered Glass Funnel and finally through 0.2 m Membrane Filter.
7. Fill in 5 ml. Amber Vials under Nitrogen Flushing.
8. Seal the vials immediately.

BETAMETHASONE EYE OINTMENT

LABELLED FORMULA

Betamethasone Sodium Phosphate 0.1% w/w

BATCH SIZE : 15 Kg.
PRACTICAL YIELD : 4150 Tubes of 3.5 g.
USUAL PACKING : 3.5 g. Alumininum Collapsible Tubes

FORMULATION

S. No.	Ingredients	Quantity	Overages
1.	Betamethasone Sodium Phosphate	15.75 g.	
2.	Liquid Paraffin	0.75 Kg.	
3.	Hard Paraffin	0.75 Kg.	
4.	Cetostearyl Alcohol	0.75 Kg.	
5.	White Soft Paraffin	12.75Kg.	

MANUFACTURING SPECIFICATIONS

1. Use 3.5 g. Aluminium Collapsible Tubes.
2. The tubes should be dipped in mixture of 70% Isopropyl alcohol containing 0.002% of Benzylkonium Chloride for 10 to 15 minutes for sterilization. Keep these tubes in previoulsy sterilized trays.
3. Expose the washed and treated tubes to fumes of Formalin. Fumigation can be done with Potassium Permanganate and Formalin in a chamber for 24 hours.
4. Filling of tubes to be done aseptically.

MANUFACTURING PROCESS

1. Heat Liquid Paraffin, Hard Paraffin, cetostearyl Alcohol and White Soft Paraffin to 150°C for atleast one hour for effective sterilization of the ointment base. The mas should be allowed to cool under aseptic conditions.
2. Dissolve Betamethasone Sodium Phosphate in 200 ml. of sterilezed Distilled Water 9 (Autoclave the water at 121°C for 30 minutes).
3. Add (2) to (1) with mixing for 3 to 4 hours under strict aseptic conditons.
4. Fill the ointment in 3.5 g. tubes.

BETAMETHASONE AND NEOMYCIN EYE/EAR DROPS

LABELLED FORMULA

Each ml. contains:

Betamethasone Sodium Phosphate 0.1 %w/v
Neomycin Sulphate 0.5 % w/v
Thiomersal (as preservative) 0.005 % w/v
Water for Injection Q.S.

BATCH SIZE : 210 Litres
PRACTICAL YIELD : 41000 Vials of 5 ml.
USUAL PACKING : 5 ml. Amber Vials
SHELF LIFE : 2 years

FORMULATION

S. No.	Ingredients	Quantity	Overages
1.	Betamethasone Sodium Phosphate	235.20g.	12%
2.	Neomycin Sulphate	1.103 Kg.	5%
3.	* Sodium Acid Phosphate	237.30 g.	
4.	* Disodium Phosphate	602.50 g.	
5.	Sodium Citrate	315.00 g.	
6.	Sodium Borate	120.00 g.	
7.	Disodium Edetate	21.00 g.	
8.	Sodium Chloride	997.50 g.	
9.	Thiomersal	10.50 g.	
10.	Sodium Metabisulphite (Based on 100% Assay)	67.20 g.	
11.	Water for Injection to	210 Lit.	

CHLORAMPHENICOL AND DEXAMETHASONE EYE DROPS

LABELLED FORMULA

Dexamethasone Sodium Phosphate 0.1% w/v
Chloramphenicol 1% w/v

BATCH SIZE : 10 Litres
PRACTICAL YIELD : 1920 Vials of 5 ml.
USUAL PACKING : 5 ml. Amber Glass Vials

S. No.	Ingredients	Quantity	Overages
1.	Dexamethasone Sodium Phosphate	11.5 g.	15%
2.	Chloramphenicol	105 g.	5%
3.	Creatinin	80 g.	
4.	Sodium Borate	30 g.	
5.	Boric Acid	150 g.	
6.	Disodium Edetate	10 g.	
7.	Sodium Citrate	100 g.	
8.	Phenylmercuric Nitrate	200 mg.	
9.	Phanylethyl Alcohol	25 ml.	

10.	Tween 80	200	ml.
11.	Glycerin	500	ml.
12.	Sodium Hydroxide	16	g.
13.	Water for Injection to	10	Lit.

MANUFACTURING SPECIFICATIONS

1. pH 7.2 to 7.5.
2. Use 5 ml. Amber Glass Vials.
3. Sterilize the vials at 200°C for 2 hours.
4. Use Butyl /Rubber Stoppers.
5. Sterilize the Rubber Stoppers at 116°C for 30 minutes.
6. Chloromphenicol Solution be stored for atleast 24 hours to observe for any precipitation before addition of Dexamethasone Sodium Phosphate and Creatinin.
7. Solution becomes hazy when hot. It should be allowed to attain room temperature to retain its clarity.
8. All manufacturing to be done under aseptic conditions.

MANUFACTURING PROCESS

1. Heat 6 Lit. Water for injection to 70°C and add Sodium Borate, Boric Acid, Disodium Edetate, Sodium Citrate, Phenyl Mercuric Nitrate and Phenylethyl Alcohol one by one with stirring till dissolution is complete. Add 52.5 g Chloramphenicol in small portions with stirring to dissolve it completely.
2. Mix 500 ml. Glycerin, 3 Litres of Water for injection and 200 ml. of Tween 80 continously to get a clear solution. Add 52.5g. of Chloramphenicol in very small portions with constant stirring till dissolution is complete.
3. Add solution (1) to solution (2) in small portions followed by vigorous stirring after each addition. Allow the solution to cool to room temperature to get a clear solution. Add 10 g. Sodium Hydroxide to dissolve. Adjust the pH of the solution to 7.1 to 7.2 and autoclave the solution at 116° C for 30 minutes. Allow to cool to room temperature.
4. Add 80 g. Creatinin and 11.5 g. Dexamethasone Sodium Phosphate yto dissolve completely. Check the pH and adjust the final pH to 7.2 to 7.5 with Sodium Hydroxide Solution if required.
5. Filter the solution first through Hyflosupercel Filteration Media pad followed by G-3 Sintered Glass Funnel and finally through 0.22 m Membrane Filter.
6. Fill into 5 ml. Amber Glass Vials with Pre and Post Nitrogen Gas flushing. Fix Butyl Rubber Stoppers immediately under aseptic conditions and seal.

CHLORAMPHENICOL EAR DROPS

LABELLED FORMULA

Chloramphenicol	5%
Benzocaine	1%

BATCH SIZE : 10 Litres
PRACTICAL YIELD : 970 Vials
USUAL PACKING : 10 ml. Amber Vials.

FORMULATION

S. No.	Ingredients	Quantity	Overages
1.	Chloramphenicol	510 g.	2%
2.	Benzocaine	100 g.	
3.	Propylene Glycol to	0.50 Lit.	

MANUFACURING PROCESS

1. Dissolve Benzocaine in5 Lit. Propylene Glycol at 60°C.
2. Add Chloramphenicol to (1) in small portions with stirring to dissolve completely.
3. Make up the volume to 10 Lit. with Propylene Glycol.
4. Filter the solution through G-2 Sintered Glass Funnel before filling in vials.
5. Protect the solution from light.

CHLORAMPHENICOL EYE DROPS

LABELLED FORMULA

Each ml. contains :

Chloramphenicol	0.5% w/v
Phenyl Mercuric Nitrate	0.002 % w/v

BATCH SIZE : 100 Litres
PRACTICAL YIELD : 9300 Vials of 10 ml.
USUAL PACKING : 10 ml. Amber Vials.

FORMULATION

S. No.	Ingredients	Quantity	Overages
1.	Chloramphenicol	550 g.	10 %
2.	Boric Acid	1.50 Kg.	
3.	Borax	400 g.	
4.	Phenyl Mercuric Nitrate	20 g.	
5.	Water for Injection to	100 Lit.	

MANUFACTURING PROCESS

1. Take 90 Lit. of freshly distilled water in a 150 Lit. capacity stainless steel vessel with 100 Lit. marking. Bubble Nitrogen gas in the bulk.
2. Add and dissolve Boric Acid and Borax in the bulk under stirring.
3. Add and dissolve Chloramphenicol under stirring and Nitrogen bubbling.
4. Add and dissolve Phenyl Mercuric Nitrate under stirring and Nitrogen bubbling.
5. Check the pH of the solution. It should be 7.00 to 7.50. If required adjust with Boric Acid.
6. Make up the volume to 100 Lit. with freshly distilled water. Stir for 15 minutes.
7. Filter the solution through 0.22 μ membrane filter aseptically with positive pressure of Nitrogen gas. All subsequent operations must be under aseptic conditions.
8. Fill the sterile solution into sterilized 10 ml. Amber Vials aseptically on automatic filling and sealing machine with pre and post Nitrogen flushing. Fill 10.5 ml. in each vial.
9. Stopper the vials with 20 mm. stoppers and seal with tear down aluminium seals.

CHLORAMPHENICOL AND DEXAMETHASONE EYE/EAR DROPS

LABELLED FORMULA

Each ml. contains :

Chloramphenicol	1 % w/v
Dexamethasone	0.1 % w/v

BATCH SIZE	:	20 Litres
PRACTICAL YIELD	:	3700 Vials of 5ml.
USUAL PACKING	:	5 ml. Amber Vials

FORMULATION

S. No.	Ingredients	Quantity	Overages
1.	Chloramphenicol	24 g.	20 %
2.	Dexamethasone	22 g.	10 %
3.	Phenyl Mercuric Acetate	400 mg.	
4.	Borax	60 g.	
5.	Boric Acid	300 g.	
6.	Propylene Glycol	1000 ml.	
7.	Liquid Paraffin (Light)	1000 ml.	
8.	Cetyl Alcohol	110 g.	

9.	Noigen-Cs-1000		80 g.
10.	Methyl Cellulose		6 g.
11.	Water for Injection	to	20 Lit.

MANUFACTURING PROCESS

1. Take about 15 Lit. sterile water for injection in a 20 Lit. stainless steel pressure vessel.
2. Dissolve Boric Acid and Borax at 70°C with stirring, add Chloramphenicol at 60°C with constant stirring till a clear solution is obtained. Pass Nitrogen gas for 15 to 20 minutes.
3. Collect about one Lit. fresh hot sterile water for injection in two Lit. flat bottom flask. Add and dissolve Phenyl Mercuric Acetate with vigorous shaking. Ensure complete dissolution.
4. Add the Phenyl Mercuric Acetate solution to the bulk solution with constant stirring and Nitrogen bubbling.
5. Cool the solution to room temperature and check the pH, it should be 6.0 to 7.0. Adjust if necessary with Borax solution and make the volume to 17 Lit. exactly.
6. Collect 750 ml. of Propylene Glycol in one Lit. flat bottom flask add Dexamethasone and shake well. Heat to dissolve with shaking and sterilize this solution at 121°C for 30 minutes. This is **Solution A**.
7. Collect 250 ml. of Propylene Glycol in 2 Lit. flat bottom flask and add one Lit. hot sterile water for injection. Now add Methyl Cellulose with continous shaking till uniformly dispersed and sterilize this solution at 121°C for 30 minutes. This is **Solution B.**
8. Take 1 Lit. Light Liquid Paraffin in 2 Lit. flat bottom flask then add Cetyl Alcohol (white flakes) and Noigen-CS-1000. Shake well and heat upto melting point, then filter this hot solution through sintered glass funnel by vaccum into another 2 Lit. vaccum flask. Collect this solution and sterilize at 121°C for 30 minutes. This is **Solution C**.
9. Next day filter the solution of Chloramphenicol, Borax, Boric Acid and Phenyl Mercuric Acetate through sterile 0.45 μ membrane filter in a 20 Lit. sterile filling vessel by Nitrogen gas pressure. After completion of filteration start homogenizer and then add **Solution A** and **Solution B** with continous homogenizing.
10. After 15 to 20 minutes take Solution C and melt it upto the melting point then add to the above homogenizing solution. Start the homogenizer and keep it on through out the filling process. Check bubble test before and after filteration.
11. Fill aseptically 5.3 ml. in 5 ml. sterilized amber vials with Nitrogen flushing. Stopper the vials and seal with tear down aluminium seals.

CLOTRIMAZOLE, BECLOMETHASONE AND CHLORAMPHENICOL EAR DROPS

LABELLED FORMULA

Clotrimazole	1%
Beclomethasone Dipropionate	0.025 % w/v
Chloramphenicol	5 %
Lignocaine Hydrochloride	2 %

BATCH SIZE : 250 Litres
PRACTICAL YIELD : 45800 Vials of 5 ml.
USUAL PACKING : 5 ml. Amber Vials

FORMULATION

S. No.	Ingredients	Quantity	Overages
1.	Clotrimazole	2.575 Kg.	3%
2.	Beclomethasone Dipropionate	68.75 g.	10%
3.	Chloramphenicol	13.750 Kg.	10%
4.	Lignocaine Hydrochloride	5.000 Kg.	
5.	Glycerine	60.000 Kg.	
6.	Propylene Glycol to	250 Lit.	

MANUFACURING PROCESS

Follow the usual manufacturing process of ear drops.

DEXAMETHASONE EYE/EAR DROPS

LABELLED FORMULA

Dexamethasone (as Dexamethasone Sod. Phosphate)	0.1 %
Phenylethyl Alcohol	0.25 %
Phenyl Mercuric Nitrate	0.002 %

BATCH SIZE : 10 Litres
PRACTICAL YIELD : 8750 Vials of 3 ml.
USUAL PACKING : 3 ml. Amber Glass Vials

FORMULATION

S. No.	Ingredients	Quantity	Overages
1.	Dexamethasone Sodium Phosphate	12.4 g.	
2.	Creatinin	120 g.	
3.	Sodium Metasulphite	48 g.	
4.	Sodium Borate	30 g.	

5.	Sodium Citrate		100	g.
6.	Phenyl Mercuric Nitrate		200	mg.
7.	Phenylethyl Alcohol		25	ml.
8.	Water for Injection	to	10	Lit.

MANUFACURING SPECIFICATIONS

1. pH range 7.2 to 7.8.
2. Shelf Life 18 Months.
3. Use Butyl, Latex or Neoprene Rubber Stoppers.
4. Use 3 ml. Amber Vials.
5. Sterilize Vials at 200°C for 4 hours.
6. Sterilize Rubber stoppers in autoclave at 121°C for 30 minutes.
7. Filter the solution through G-4 Sintered Glass Funnel and finally through 0.2 μ Membrane, Filter.
8. All manufacturing, filling and sealing to be done under strict aseptic conditions.

NOTE:

For manufacturing process see Dexamethasone Injection Formulation.

GENTAMYCIN EYE DROPS

LABELLED FORMULA

Gentamycin Sulphate equivalent to
Gentamycin 0.3 % w/v

BATCH SIZE : 15 Litres
PRACTICAL YIELD : 4750 Vials of 3 ml.
USUAL PACKING : 3 ml. Amber Vials

FORMULATION

S. No.	Ingredients		Quantity		Overages
1.	Gentamycin Sulphate		85	g.	10%
2.	Sodium Metasulphite		75	g.	
3.	Disodium Edetate		15	g.	
4.	Phenylmercuric Nitrate		300	mg.	
5.	Benzylkonium Chloride Solution		1.0	ml.	
6.	Phenylethyl Alcohol		30.0	ml.	
7.	Sodium Hydroxide		20	g.	
8.	Water for injection	to	15	Lit.	

MANUFACTURING SPECIFICATIONS

1. Use 3 ml. Amber Vials. Sterilize the Vials at 200°C for 2 hours.
2. Use Butyl Grey Rubber Stoppers. Wash the rubber stoppers with 1%

Teepol (a detergent) and soak for 1 day in double the strength of Preservatives and Bacteriostatics. After final washing sterilize at 116°C for 30 minutes.

MANUFACTURING PROCESS

1. Heat 14 Litres freshly distilled water for injection to 70°C and pass Nitrogen gas for 15 minutes. Dissolve Sodium Metabisulphite, Disodium Edetate, Phenyl Mercuric Nitrate, Phenylethyl Alcohol and Benzylkonium Chloride. Mix thoroughly to get a clear solution. Add 20g. Sodium Hydroxide and check the pH of the solution. Autoclave the solution at 116°C for 30 minutes.
2. Cool the solution to room temperature and dissolve Gentamycin Sulphate with stirring to get a clear solution. Check the pH of the solution and adjust to 7.0 with Sodium Hydroxide solution if required.
3. Filter the solution first through G-3 Sintered Glass Funnel and finally through 0.22 μ Membrane Filter. Fill in 3 ml. Amber Glass vials aseptically with pre and post Nitrogen gas flushing.

GENTAMYCIN AND BETAMETHASONE EYE/EAR DROPS

LABELLED FORMULA

Each ml. contains :

Gentamycin Sulphate 3.0 mg.
Betamethasone Sodium 1.3 mg.

BATCH SIZE : 170 Litres
PRACTICAL YIELD : 53500 Vials of 3 ml.
USUAL PACKING : 3 ml. Amber Glass Vials
SHELF LIFE : 3 years.

FORMULATION

S. No.	Ingredients	Quantity	Overages
1.	Gentamycin (as Gentamycin Sulphate)	* 510 g.	
2.	Betamethasone Sodium Phosphate	221 g.	
3.	Sodium Acid Phosphate	470 g.	
4.	Dibasic Sodium Phosphate`	2.710 Kg.	
5.	Anhydrous Sodium Sulphite	255 g.	
6.	Propylene Glycol	8.500 Kg.	
7.	Benzylkonium Chloride solution	68 ml.	
8.	Water for Injection to	170 Lit.	

* The weight of Gentamycin Sulphate should be calculated on the potency of the particular batch used.

MANUFACTURING PROCESS

1. In a suitable jacketed vessel of stainless steel take 120 Lit. of freshly distilled water and cool to room temperature by circulating cold water.
2. Add and dissolve under stirring the following materials one by one, dissolving each completely :
   (i) Monobasic Sodium Phosphate (Dihydrate)
   (ii) Dibasic Sodium Phosphate (Dihydrate)
3. Check the pH of the solutionl, it should be 7.40 to 7.50. Now flush with Nitrogen.
4. Add and dissolve the following in this order :
   (i) Gentamycin Sulphate
   (ii) Anhydrous Sodium Sulphate
   (iii) Betamethasone Sodium Phosphate
   (iv) Propylene Glycol
   (v) Benzylkonium Chloride Solution.
5. Make up the volume to 170 Lit. will freshly distilled and cooled distilled water and stir for 10 minutes.
6. Check the pH, it should be 7.40 to 7.60.
7. Store the solution in an airtight container under Nitrogen pressure overnight.
8. Filter the solution aseptically through sterile 0.22 μ membrane filter under Nitrogen pressure to give a clear, fibre free sterile solution.
9. Fill 3.2 ml. in 3 ml. Amber Vials (sterilized) under Nitrogen flushing.
10. Seal the vials immediately with suitable plugs with latex rubber rings and aluminium tear down seals.

GENTAMYCIN EYE/EAR DROPS

LABELLED FORMULA

Each ml. contains :

Gentamycin (as Sulphate) 3.0 mg.

BATCH SIZE : 160 Litres
PRACTICAL YIELD : 48500 Vials of 3 ml.
USUAL PACKING : 3 ml. Amber Glass Vials

FORMULATION

S. No.	Ingredients	Quantity	Overages
1.	Gentamycin Sulphate (as basic) *	528 g.	10 %
2.	Sodium Acid Phosphate	18 g.	
3.	Sodium Phosphate (Dried)	465 g.	
4.	Sodium Chloride	1.180 g.	
5.	Benzlkonium Chloride Solution (50%)	32 ml.	
6.	Water for Injection to	160 Lit.	

* Check the potency of Gentamycin Sulphate used.

MANUFACTURING PROCESS

1. Charge 150 Lit. freshly distilled water to a tank (cooled to room temperature) with Nitrogen sparging.
2. Add and dissolve Sodium Acid Phosphate.
3. Add and dissolve Dried Sodium Phosphate.
4. Add and dissolve Sodium Chloride.
5. Add and dissolve Gentamycin Sulphate.
6. Add and mix Benzylkonium Chloride solution.
7. Make up the volume to 160 Lit. with freshly distilled and cooled water for injection.
8. Check the pH. It should be 6.8 to 7.2.
9. Filter the solution through sterile 0.22 μ membrane filter aseptically.
10. Fill aseptically 3.2 ml. in 3 ml. Amber Vials and stopper immediately.

HYDROCORTISONE EYE DROPS

LABELLED FORMULA

Each ml contains :

Hydrocortisone Acetate 1%
Phenylmercuric Nitrate 0.002 %

BATCH SIZE : 10 Litres
PRACTICAL YIELD : 1900 Vials of 5 ml.
USUAL PACKING : 5 ml. Amber Vials

FORMULATION

S. No.	Ingredients	Quantity	Overages
1.	Hydrocortisone Acetate	105 g.	5 %
2.	Phenylmercuric Nitrate	200 mg.	
3.	Hydroxypropyl Methylcellulose	100 g.	
4.	Tween 80	200 ml.	

5.	Glycerin		100	ml.
6.	Water for injection	to	10	Lit.

MANUFACTURING SPECIFICATIONS

1. pH range 6.2 to 6.4.
2. Use 5 ml. Amber Vials.
3. Use Butyl or Latex Rubber Stoppers.
4. Sterilize Vials by autoclave at 121°C for 4 hours.
5. Sterilize Rubber Stoppers by autoclave at 121°C for 30 minutes.
6. Shelf life 18 months.
7. Filling done under aseptic conditions and continous mixing with stirrer.
8. No final filteration as the product is a suspension.

MANUFACTURING PROCESS

1. Suspend Hydroxypropyl Methylcellulose (HPMC) in 500 ml. water and soak overnight.
2. Sterlize Tween 80 and Glycerin.
3. Dissolve Phenyl Mercuric Nitrate in 500 ml. water for injection.
4. Incorporate Hydrocortisone Acetate in HPMC jelly, and add Tween 80 and Glycerin with the aid of trituration to get a thick paste.
5. Add 3 to 4 with Ultron Homogeniser and mix for two hours to reduce partical size.
6. Make up the volume to 10 Lit. with sterilized water and with continucus stirring with Ultron.
7. Fill in vials under aseptic conditions and continuous mixing with stirrer in bulk.

NEOMYCIN EYE DROPS

LABELLED FORMULA

Neomycin Sulphate	0.5 %
Phenyl Mercuric Nitrate	0.002 %

BATCH SIZE : 10 Litres
PRACTICAL YIELD : 3150 Vials of 3 ml.
USUAL PACKING : 3 ml. Amber Vials

FORMULATION

S. No.	Ingredients	Quantity		Overages
1.	Neomycin Sulphate	55	g.	
2.	Disodium Hydrogen Phosphate	70	g.	
3.	Disodium Phosphate	70	g.	
4.	Sodium Chloride	40	g.	

5.	Disodium Edetate		10 g.
6.	Phenyl Mercuric Nitrate		200 mg.
7.	Sodium Metabisulphite		20 g.
8.	Glycerin		500 ml.
9.	Water for injection	to	10 Lit.

MANUFACURING SPECIFICATIONS

1. pH range 6.0 to 6.5.
2. Use 3 ml. Amber Vials.
3. Sterilize vials at 200° C for 4 hours.
4. Sterilize Rubber Stoppers at 121°C for 30 minutes in an autoclave.
5. Pre and post Nitrogen flushing during filling is a must.
6. Manufacture and filling under aseptic conditions.

MANUFACTURING PROCESS

1. Dissolve Disodium Hydrogen Phosphate and Disodium Phosphate in 5 Litres of water for injection.
2. Dissolve Neomycin Sulphate in 1 Lit. of water.
3. Add solution 2 to solution 1 with stirring.
4. Dissolve Disodium Edetate and Sodium Metabisulphite in 1 Lit. water.
5. Add solution 4 to solution 3.
6. Dissolve Sodium Chloride in 500 ml. water and add to Solution 6.
7. Dissolve Phenyl Mercuric Nitrate in 500 ml. water and add to Solution 6.
8. Add Glycerin to Solution 7.
9. Make up the volume to 10 Litres and check the pH. Adjust if necessary.

SULPHACETAMIDE EYE DROPS 10%

LABELLED FORMULA

Sulphacetamide Sodium 10 %

BATCH SIZE : 10 Litres
PRACTICAL YIELD : 950 Vials of 10 ml.
USUAL PACKING : 10 ml. of Amber Vials

FORMULATION

S. No.	Ingredients	Quantity	Overages
1.	Sulphacetamide Sodium	1 Kg.	
2.	Sodium Metabisulphite	20 g.	
3.	Disodium Edetate	10 g.	
4.	Phenylethyl Alcohol	20 ml.	

5.	Activated Charcoal		10	g.
6.	Phenyl Mercuric Nitrate		0.2	g.
7.	Water for Injection	to	10	Lit.

MANUFACTURING SPECIFICATIONS

1. pH range 7.6 to 7.8.
2. Adjust pH with 5% Sodium Hydroxide Solution.
3. Use 10 ml. Amber Vials.
4. Fill under pre and post Nitrogen Gas Flushing.
5. Filter first through Filter Pad with the aid of Hyflo Supercel and then through G-3 and G-4 Sintered Glass Funnels, or membrane filter.
6. Sterilize Vials at 200°C for 4 hours.
7. Sterilize Rubber Stoppers in autoclave at 116°C for 30 minutes.
8. Charcoal treatment should be given with vigorous shaking for atleast 30 minutes before filteration through pad.
9. Use freshly distilled water free from dissolved CO_2.
10. Sterilize filled vials by steaming at 116° C for 30 minutes.

Chapter 13

Topical Preparations

INTRODUCTION

Topical administration is employed to deliver a drug at or immediately beneath the point of application. Although occasionally enough drugs is absorbed into the systemic circulation to cause systemic effects, absorption is too erratic for the topical route to be used for systemic therapy. A large number of topical medicaments are applied to the skin, although topical drugs are also applied to the eye, nose, throat, ear, vagina etc.

In man, percutaneous absorption probably occurs mainly from the surface. Absorption through the hair follicles occurs, but the follicles in man occupy too small a portion of the total integument to be of primary importance. When the medicament is rubbed on vigorously, the amount of the preparation that is forced into the hair follicles and glands is increased. Since much of a drug that is absorbed through the epidermis diffuses into the circulation without reaching a high concentration in some portions of the dermis, systemic administration may be preferred in lieu of or in addition to topical administration.

Briefly, topical preparations fall into the following categories

— Protectives and Absorbents
— Mechanical and Chemical Protectives
— Demulcents
— Emollients
— Astringents and Antiperspirants
— Irritants, Rubefacients and Vesicants
— Sclerosing Agents
— Caustics and Escharotics
— Keratolytics
— Cleansing Preparations

Most commonly used topical preparations are Creams, Ointments and Lotions. In the Ointments category the bases used may be:

1. Hydrocarton Bases
    - They are non-water washable.
2. Absorption Bases
    - They absorb water.

3. Emulsion Bases or Creams
   - They may be water in oil or oil in water type.
4. Water Soluble Bases
   - They are nongreasy, water soluble and washable.

Lotions are usually liquid suspensions or dispersions intended for external application to the body. They may be prepared in general by triturating the ingredients to a smooth paste and then cautiously adding the remaining liquid phase. High speed mixers or homogenizers produce better dispersions and are, therefore, the tools of choice in the preparation of larger quantities of lotions. A Colloid Mill is still better machine which can be very effectively used in the commercially stable lotions and suspensions for topical use.

LIST OF PRESERVATIVES USED IN TOPICAL PREPARATIONS

S. No.	Name of Preservatives	Usual Conc.	Stability and Incompatibility
1.	Benzoic Acid	0.1% to 0.2%	Ineffective at pH above 5.0
2.	Sorbic Acid	0.1% to 0.2%	Most effective in acidic pH
3.	Methyl Parahydroxybenzoate	0.25%	Less effective at pH above 8.0
4.	Propyl Parahydroxybenzoate	0.05% to 0.25%	Less effective at pH above 8.0
5.	Chlorocresol	0.1% to 0.2%	Volatile at 100°C Inactivated by Polysorbate 80
6.	Cresol	0.3%	Bactericide.

BETAMETHASONE AND CLOTRIMAZOLE CREAM

LABELLED FORMULA

Each g. contains :

Betamethasone	0.5 mg.
Clotrimazole	10.0 mg.

BATCH SIZE : 180 Kg.
PRACTICAL YIELD : 17500 Tubes of 10 g.
USUAL PACKING : 10 g. Tubes

FORMULATION

S. No.	Ingredients	Quantity
1.	Betamethasone Dipropionate (Micronized)	115.74 g.
2.	Clotrimazole	1.80 Kg.
3.	Liquid Paraffin	10.80 Kg.
4.	White Soft Paraffin	27.00 Kg.
5.	Cetostearyl Alcohol	12.96 Kg.
6.	Cetomacrogol 1000	4.05 Kg.
7.	Benzyl Alcohol	1.80 Kg.
8.	Sodium Acid Phosphate	539.27 g.
9.	Phosphoric Acid	3.60 g.
10.	Propylene Glycol	18.00 Kg.
11.	Distilled Water to * 106.0 Litres app.	*180.0 Kg.

MANUFACTURING PROCESS

1. Charge 82.8 Lit. of Distilled water to a jacketed S.S. Kettle fitted with Agitator and cover. Heat the water to 70°C while mixing. Add and dissolve Sodium Phosphate.
2. Dilute Phosphoric Acid with 270 ml. of distilled water in a separate vessel. Add the diluted Phosphoric Acid to the aquous solution of Step 1 and mix until uniform.
3. Add Propylene Glycol and Benzyl Alcohol in a separate vessel and mix well. Add the mixture to the aquous mixture of Step 2. Rinse the vessel with 1.35 Lit. of water and add to the aquous phase.
4. In a separate pre-mix vessel equipped with a mixer, charge White Soft Paraffin, Liquid Paraffin, Cetostearyl Alcohol and 3.96 Kg. of Cetomacrogol. Melt and mix thoroughly at 70°C and maintain this temperature.
5. Add the wax phase from Step 4 at 70°C through a 80 mesh S.S. screen into the aquous phase also at 70°C of Step 3. Mix rapidly for 15 minutes.
6. Check the pH of the cream base, it should be 4.5 to 5.5. Adjust the pH if necessary with 10% Sodium Hydroxide or 10% Phosphoric Acid solution.
7. Cool the cream base to 60°C under rapid agitation. Continue cooling to 42°C ± 2°C with moderate agitation to avoid air entrapment. Maintain this temperature.
8. In a suitable S.S. vessel add 18 Lit. of Distilled water and heat to 65°C.

Add and dissolve the remaining 90 g. of Cetomacrogol 1000. Cool the solution to 25°C-30°C.

9. Add Betamethasone Dipropionate and Clotrimazole to the solution of Step 8 and mix with a small Turbo Disperser for about 30 minutes. Ensure that the dispersion is complete by absence of grittiness on feel.
10. Add the milled slurry to the batch of Step 7 with slow agitation.
11. Rinse the Turbo Disperser and the container used to prepare the slurry with 3.6 Lit. of Distilled water.
12. Add the rinses to the batch and mix for 30 minutes or until uniform. Continue cooling the batch with slow agitation until the temperature reaches 34°C to 36°C.
13. Send a sample to Q.C. for evaluation.

BETAMETHASONE AND GENTAMYCIN CREAM

LABELLED FORMULA

Betamethasone Valerate	0.12 mg.
Gentamycin Sulphate (as base)	0.10 mg.

BATCH SIZE : 40 Kg.
PRACTICAL YIELD : 1950 tubes of 20 g.
USUAL PACKING : 20 g. Collapsible Tubes

FORMULATION

S. No.	Ingredients	Quantity	
1.	Betamethasone Valerate	48.80	g.
2.	Gentamycin Sulphate (as base)	* 40.00	g.
3.	Chlorocresol	40.00	g.
4.	Sodium Acid Phosphate	138.65	g.
5.	Phosphoric Acid	0.80	g.
6.	White Soft Paraffin	6.00	Kg.
7.	Liquid Paraffin	2.40	Kg.
8.	Cetomacrogol 1000	0.90	Kg.
9.	Cetostearyl Alcohol	2.88	Kg.
10.	Distilled Water	28.40	Kg.
11.	** 5% or 5N Sodium Hydroxide Solution or Phosphoric Acid Solution	Q.S.	

* Calculation Gentamycin Sulphate

$$\frac{1000 \times 40}{X} = \text{----------} \text{ g. Gentamycin Base}$$

Where X = Potency of Gentamycin Base

** for pH adjustment.

MANUFACTURING PROCESS

1. **Part I - Oil Phase**

   Take White Soft Paraffin, Liquid Paraffin, Cetamacrogol 100 and Cetostearyl Alcohol in a suitable vessel. Melt and maintain a temperature of 70°C-75°C.

2. **Part II - Aquous Phase**

   Dissolve Sodium Acid Phosphate, Chlorocresol and Phosphoric Acid in Distilled water and maintain a temperature of 65°C-70°C.

3. Add the oil phase to the aquous and stir for 15 minutes. Start cooling and cool to 45°C-46°C.
4. **Slurry Preparation**: Take Distilled water and add 10 g. of Cetomacrogol 1000 and Betamethasone Valerate. Stir well and add the slurry to the batch which is at a temperature of 45°C-46°C.
5. Cool the batch to a temperature of 40°-42°C.
6. Dissolve Gentamycin Sulphate in water and add to the batch which is at 40°C-42°C.
7. Stir for 1 to 11/2 hour. Mix well and unload the batch.
8. Check the pH, it should be 4.8 to 4.9 (Limit 4.5 to 5.5).

BETAMETHASONE AND GENTAMYCIN OINTMENT

LABELLED FORMULA

Betamethasone Valerate	0.12 %
Gentamycin (as Sulphate)	0.10 %

BATCH SIZE : 300 Kg.
PRACTICALYIELD : 19500 tubes of 15 g.
USUAL PACKING : 15 g. Tubes

FORMULATION

S. No.	Ingredients	Quantity
1.	Betamethasone Valerate	0.366 Kg.
2.	* Gentamycin Sulphate (as base)	0.300 Kg.

3.	White Soft Paraffin	299.300 Kg.

* Gentamycin Sulphate Calculation

$$\frac{1000 \times 300}{X}$$

Where X = Potency of Gentamycin Base.

MANUFACTURING PROCESS

1. Melt the White Soft Paraffin before use.
2. Charge 299.334 Kg. of melted White Soft Paraffin to a Planetary Mixer by passing through 80 mesh S.S. Screen.
3. Remove 6 Kg. of White Soft Paraffin from Step 1 for use in Steps 4 and 7.
4. In a suitable S.S. container, charge 4 Kg. of melted White Soft Paraffin from Step 3. Add Betamethasone Valerate and mix until a slurry is obtained. Now add Gentamycin Sulphate and mix with the help of a small Turbo Disperser. Ensure complete homogenization.
5. Cool the batch of Step 2 by passing water through the jacket while mixing at slow speed. Cool to 47°C-48°C.
6. While the mixing is on add the Betamethasone Valerate and Gentamycin Sulphate slurry form Step 4. Mix slowly to disperse.
7. Rinse the container and Turbo Disperser with the remaining 2.0 Kg. of melted White Soft Paraffin from Step 3 and add to the batch of Step 5.
8. Cool the product over a period of 2 hours to 30°C ± 3°C using constant agitation.
9. Send a sample to Q.C. for evaluation.

BETAMETHASONE AND IODOCHLOROHYDROXYQUINOLINE CREAM

LABELLED FORMULA

Each g. contains:

Betamethasone Dipropionate	0.64 mg.
Iodochlorohydroxyquinoline	30.0 mg.

BATCH SIZE	:	180 Kg.
PRACTICAL YIELD	:	17500 Tubes of 10 g.
USUAL PACKING	:	10 g. Tubes

FORMULATION

S. No.	Ingredients	Quantity
1.	Betamethasone Dipropionate (Micronized)	115.20 g.
2.	Iodochlorohydroxyquinoline	5.400 Kg.
3.	Chlorocresol	0.180 Kg.
4.	Sodium Acid Phosphate	610.40 g.
5.	Phosphoric Acid	3.60 g.
6.	White Soft Paraffin	27.000 Kg.
7.	Liquid Paraffin	10.800 Kg.
8.	Cetomacrogol 1000	4.050 Kg.
9.	Cetostearyl Alcohol	12.960 Kg.
10.	Distilled Water	*122.450 Kg.

* Contains 3% excess for evaporation.

MANUFACTURING PROCESS

1. Charge 59.65 Lit. of Distilled water to a jacketed S.S. Kettle and heat to 65°C. Add and dissolve Chlorocresol, Sodium Acid Phosphate and Phosphoric Acid. Mix well till completely dissolved.

   NOTE: Cover the batch whenever possible too avoid excessive loss due to evaporation. Do not add additional water to make up the total weight.

2. To a suitable S.S. vessel add White Soft Paraffin, Light Liquid Paraffin, 3.404 Kg. of Cetomacrogol and Cetostearyl Alcohol. Heat to 70°C and mix immediately. Continue heating and mixing until all the ingredients are completely melted and the mixture is uniform.

3. Pass the melted waxes through 120 mesh S.S. screen into the batch of Step 1 while maintaining the temperature of 65°C. Mix for 20-30 minutes. Continue mixing at fast speed and cool by circulation of water till the temperature is 50°C. Stop circulation of water and allow the temperature to drop to 47°C ± 1°C. Check and adjust the pH to 5.3 ± 0.1 with 0.1 N. Phosphoric Acid solution or 0.1 N Sodium Hydroxide solution.

4. In a suitable S.S. container charge 62.8 Lit. of Distilled water and heat to 65°C. Add and dissolve remaining 646 g. of Cetomacrogol under stirring. Cool to 47°C. Remove 20 Lit. for rinsing etc. Disperse Betamethasone Dipropionate and Iodochlorohydroxyquinoline in the remaining solution by using Turbo Disperser or Colloid Mill set at 0.005" gap. Add to the batch which is also at 47°C ± 1°C and mix until dispersed uniformly.

5. Rinse the container used to prepare the slurry and the Colloid Mill with remaining 20 Lit. of Step 4.Continue slow mixing. Check the final pH and allow to cool overnight.
6. Send sample to Q.C. for evaluation.

BETAMETHASONE AND NEOMYCIN SKIN OINTMENT

LABELLED FORMULA

Betamethasone Valerate	0.12% w/w
Neomycin Sulphate	0.5% w/w
in an ointment base	

BATCH SIZE : 15 Kg.
PRACTICAL YIELD : 4100 tubes of 3.5 g.
USUAL PACKING : 3.5 g. Aluminium Collapsible Tubes

FORMULATION

S. No.	Ingredients	Quantity	
1.	Betamethasone Valerate	18.5	g.
2.	Neomycin Sulphate	80	g.
3.	Cetostearyl Alcohol	1.5	Kg.
4.	Cetomacrogol 1000	750	g.
5.	White Soft Paraffin	11.25	Kg.
6.	Liquid Paraffin	1.5	Kg.

MANUFACTURING SPECIFICATIONS

1. Use 3.5 g. Aluminium Collapsible Tubes.
2. Pass Nitrogen Gas through melted waxes to improve stability.
3. Antioxidants like Propyl Gallate or Sodium Metabisulphite may be incorporated in the formulation to protect the deterioration of Neomycin Sulphate.

MANUFACTURING PROCESS

1. Heat Cetostearyl Alcohol, Cetomacrogol 1000, White Soft Paraffin and 1/2 Liquid Paraffin to 100°C filter through cloth.
2. Allow the melted waxes to cool to room temperature.
3. Triturate Betamethasone Valerate and Neomycin Sulphate with 1/2 Liquid Paraffin to form a smooth paste.
4. Add (3) to (2) with stirring at a Temperature not exceeding 40°C. Carry out mixing for 2 hours.

5 Pass the ointment through Triple Roller Mill to minimise particle size.

6. Send a sample to Q.C. for evaluation.

BETAMETHASONE AND SALICYLIC ACID OINTMENT

LABELLED FORMULA

Each g. contains :

Betamethasone Dipropionate	0.64 mg.
Salicylic Acid	30.00 mg.

BATCH SIZE : 150 Kg.
PRACTICAL YIELD : 14600 Tubes of 10 g.
USUAL PACKING : 10 g. Tubes

FORMULATION

S. No.	Ingredients	Quantity
1.	Betamethasone Dipropionate (Micronized)	0.096 Kg.
2.	Salicylic Acid (Micronized)	4.500 Kg.
3.	Liquid Paraffin	7.500 Kg.
4.	White Soft Paraffin	38.500 Kg.

MANUFACTURING PROCESS

1. Charge 70 Kg. White Soft Paraffin to a jacketed vessel and heat to 60°C till completely melted. Filter through 120 mesh screen into a compounding vessel and mix until homogenous. Maintain at 55°C to 60°C.
2. Add 68.5 Kg. White Soft Paraffin into the same vessel and repeat Step1. Filter through 120 mesh stainless steel screen into the compounding vessel. Mix until homogenous. Maintain at 55° to 60°C.
3. Charge 40 Kg. of the base in a clean jacketed bowl. Disperse Salicylic Acid maintaining the temperature at 55°-60°C. Mix with the Turbo Disperser until a uniform slurry is obtained.
4. Take out 10 Kg. of molten base from Step-2 and keep aside.
5. Add the Salicylic Acid slurry to the compounding tank. Rinse the turbo disperser and the container in which the slurry was prepared with the molten base set aside in Step 4. Add the rinsings to the batch.
6. Mix with anchor type beater of a mixer at slow speed till the batch attains a temperature of 45°C.

7. Charge 5 Kg. of Liquid Paraffin into a suitable steel vessel and slurry of Betamethasone Dipropionate using a small turbo disperser. Mix until a uniform slurry is obtained.
8. Add the slurry to the batch of Step 6. Rinse the disperser and the vessel with the remaining 2.5 Kg. of Liquid Paraffin. Add the rinsing to the batch.
9. Mix using fast speed till a homogenous mass is obtained. Continue mixing at slow speed till the ointment attains a temperature of 34°C-36°C. Discontinue the mixing.
10. Transfer the batch into clean drums lined with double polythene bags and record the weight.
11. Submit a sample to Q.C. for evaluation.

BETAMETHASONE CREAM

LABELLED FORMULA

Each g. contains :

Betamethasone Dipropionate 0.64 mg.

BATCH SIZE : 180 Kg.
PRACTICAL YIELD : 17500 Tubes of 10 g.
USUAL PACKING : 10 g. Tubes

FORMULATION

S. No.	Ingredients	Quantity	Overages
1.	Betamethasone Dipropionate (Micronized)	126.72 g.	10%
2.	Titanium Dioxide	0.900 Kg.	
3.	Carbopol 940	2.700 Kg.	
4.	Sodium Hydroxide (Pellets)	0.072 Kg.	
5.	Propylene Glycol	126.000 Kg.	
6.	Distilled Water	*51.300 Kg.	

* Includes 2% excess to compensate estimated loss on evaporation.

MANUFACTURING PROCESS

1. Charge 82.8 Kg. Propylene Glycol and 49.5 Lit. Distilled water to jacketed compounding vessel equipped with two stirrers of 930 RPM and 1440 RPM of 2.5 H.P. and 3.5 H.P. respectively and mix well. Set aside 10 Kg. of this mixture for preparation of Titanium Dioxide slurry and rinsing etc. of Step 2.

2. Transfer 6.5 Kg. of the reserved Propylene Glycol/Water mixture from Step 1 (out of 10 Kg.) and 9.0 Kg. of Propylene Glycol to a suitable container equipped with Turbo Disperser. Add Titanium Dioxide and mix until a uniform slurry results. Add to the bulk of Step 1 under continuous agitation. Rinse the Turbo Disperse and the container used to prepare the slurry with remaining 3.5 Kg. of Propylene Glycol/Water mixture and add the rinsings of the batch in Step 1.
3. Heat the resultant mixture of Step 1 to 50°C under continuous mixing and maintain the temperature of 50°C ± 1°C.
4. Position the stirrer with 2.5 H.P. Motor at 45°-50°C in such a way that sufficient vortex is generated without aeration. Slowly sift the carbopol-940 through a 10 mesh S.S. screen directing the powder to the vortex. After the Carbopol is added stop the agitation and take out the stirrer held vertically. Continue mixing until a uniform lump-free dispersion is obtained. Discontinue heat and agitation. Ensure that there are no lumps.
5. Dissolve Sodium Hydroxide in 1.8 Lit. of Distilled water and add the solution to 12.6 Kg. of Propylene Glycol and mix until uniform.
6. Add the Sodium Hydroxide/Propylene Glycol solution slowly at a rate of about 50 ml. per minute under slow agitation. Continue mixing until a smooth white gel is formed. Check the pH, it should be 4.7 to 5.0.
7. Remove about 20 Kg. of the gel formed is Step 6 and transfer to a suitable sized planetary mixer.
8. Charge 20 Kg. of Propylene Glycol to a suitable jacketed S.S. container. Heat the Propylene Glycol to 40°C and then dissolve Betamethasone Dipropionate with agitation. Cool to room temperature. Charge the Active/ Propylene Glycol solution to the gel in Step 7 in small lots under continuous agitation. Rinse the container with 1.6 Kg. of Propylene Glycol. Continue mixing till it is homogenous.
9. Transfer the active gel to the bulk dispersion of Step 1 and mix for about one hour till it is homogenous.
10. Send a sample to Q.C. for analysis.

BETAMETHASONE, CLOTRIMAZOLE AND GENTAMYCIN CREAM

LABELLED FORMULA

Betamethasone	0.5 mg.
Clotrimazole	10.0 mg.
Gentamycin Sulphate	1.0 mg.

BATCH SIZE : 20 Kg.
PRACTICAL YIELD : 1950 Tubes of 10 g.
USUAL PACKING : 10 g. or 5 g. Collapsible Tubes

FORMULATION

S. No.	Ingredients	Quantity	
1.	Betamethasone Dipropionate (Micronized)	12.86	g.
2.	Clotrimazole (Micronized)	200.00	g.
3.	Mineral Oil (Heavy)	1.20	Kg.
4.	White Soft Paraffin	3.00	Kg.
5.	Cetostearyl Alcohol	1.44	Kg.
6.	Cetomacrogol 1000	0.45	Kg.
7.	Benzyl Alcohol	200.00	g.
8.	Sodium Acid Phosphate	60.00	g.
9.	Propylene Glycol	2.00	Kg.
10.	Purified Water	11.98	Kg.
11.	Phosphoric Acid	0.60	g.
12.	Gentamycin Sulphate equivalent to 20 g. Base, Potency 541.6 mcg/mg.	36.92	g.

MANUFACTURING PROCESS

1. Charge White Soft Paraffin, Liquid Paraffin, Cetostearyl Alcohol and 0.40 Kg. of Cetomacrogol 1000 to a suitable container, heat and maintain the temperature at 70°C.
2. Into the main compounding vessel charge 9.98 Lit. of Purified water. Heat the water to 70°C while mixing. Add and dissolve Sodium Acid Phosphate. Add diluted Phosphate Acid with 30 ml. of water and mix until uniform.
3. In a separate vessel add Propylene Glycol and Benzyl Alcohol and mix until uniform. Add the mixture to the aquous mixture in Step 2. Rinse the vessel with 150 ml. of water and add the rinse to the aquous phase.
4. Maintain both aquous phase of Step 3 and Wax phase of Step-1 at 70°C. approx. Add the wax phase from Step 1 through a 80 mesh stainless steel screen into the aquous phase of Step 2. Mix rapidly for 15 minutes maintaining the batch temperature at 70°C.
5. Check the pH of the cream base. The specified range is 4.5 to 5.5. Adjust if necessary with 10% Sodium Hydroxide or 10% Phosphoric Acid Solution.

6. Cool the cream base to 60°C while maintaining rapid agitation. Continue cooling to 30°C ± 2°C with moderate agitation to avoid air entrapment. Maintain this temperature.
7. In a suitable vessel take 1.0 Lit. of water and heat to 65°C. Add and dissolve the remaining 50 g. of Cetomacrogol 1000.
8. Add the Betamethasone Dipropionate and the Clotrimazole to above in 1.5 Lit. and mix thoroughly in Turbo Disperser for 30 minutes. Check the slurry.
9. Add the milled slurry to the batch in Step 6 with slow agitation at 50°C-55°C to the cream base at 60°C.
10. Rinse the vessel and Turbo Disperser used to prepare active slurry with 400 ml. of solution from Step 7. Add the rinses to the batch and mix.
11. Begin cooling the batch while mixing to 42°C-44°C.
12. Charge 200 ml. of Purified Water, add and dissolve the calculated amount of Gentamycin Sulphate. Rinse the container used to prepare the solution with the remaining water to 200 ml. Mix at high speed for about 20 minutes or until uniform.
13. Transfer the batch to suitable holding container.
14. Send a representative sample to Q.C. for evaluation.

BETAMETHASONE, GENTAMYCIN, TOLNAFTATE AND IODOCHLOROHYDROXYQUINOLINE CREAM

LABELLED FORMULA

Betamethasone Valerate	0.05%
Gentamycin Sulphate (as base)	0.10%
Tolnaftate	0.10%
Iodochlorohydroxyquinoline	1.00%

BATCH SIZE : 360 Kg.
PRACTICAL YIELD : 35000 Tubes of 10 g.
USUAL PACKING : 10 g. or 5 g. Tubes

FORMULATION

S. No.	Ingredients	Quantity
1.	Betamethasone Valerate (Micronized)	230.6 g.*
2.	Tolnaftate	3.600 Kg.
3.	Gentamycin Sulphate (as base)	0.360Kg.**

4.	Iodochlorohydroxyquinoline	3.600 Kg.
5.	Chlorocresol	0.360Kg.**
6.	Cetomacrogol 1000	7.560 Kg.
7.	Cetostearyl Alcohol	25.920 Kg.
8.	White Soft Paraffin	54.000 Kg.
9.	Liquid Paraffin	21.600 Kg.
10.	Sodium Acid Phosphate	1.224 Kg.
11.	Distilled Water	252.00Kg.***

* Includes 5% overages

** 0.600 Kg. Gentamycin Base would be required if potency of Gentamycin in Gentamycin Sulphate is 60%.

*** Contains about 4.4% excess water to compensate for estimated loss due to evaporation.

MANUFACTURING PROCESS

1. Charge 204 Lit. D.M. water to a jacketed Planetary Mixer and heat to 65°C-70°C. Add and dissolve Chlorocresol and Sodium Acid Phosphate and mix well.
2. To a separate vessel equipped with a suitable mixer charge White Soft Paraffin, Liquid Paraffin, Cetostearyl Alcohol and 6.480 Kg. of Cetomacrogol 1000, melt and mix thoroughly at 90°C-95°C. Add and dissolve Tolnaftate. Cool the wax solution to 80°C.
3. Transfer the molten waxes with Tolnaftate through 120 mesh into the aquous phase of Step 1 and maintain a temperature of 65°C-70°C. Mix for 5 to 7 minutes at high speed during the transfer of waxy phase and after that for 15 minute at slow speed.
4. Cool the batch by passing water through the jacket while mixing at slow speed. Cool to 47°-48°C.
5. Side by side charge 40 Lit. D.M. water to a suitable vessel and heat to 65°C-70°C. Add and dissolve 1.080 Kg. of Cetomacrogol 1000.
6. To a separate vessel charge 30 Lit. of solution from Step 5 and disperse Betamethasone Valerate and Iodochlorohydroxyquinoline. Mix well until a uniform slurry is obtained. Add the slurry to the batch at 47°C-48°C of Step 4 and mix slowly to disperse.
7. Rinse the container of slurry and the stirrer with remaining portion of Cetomacrogol 1000 solution from Step 5 and add to the batch. Continue mixing for 20 minutes without water circulation and then with cooling.
8. While the batch is cooling in Step 5 and after the slurry preparation, charge 4.0 Lit. of D.M. water to a suitable container. Add and dissolve

Gentamycin Sulphate. Add it to the batch in Step 7 at 41°C-42°C. Rinse the container with 4.0 Lit. of D.M. water and add the rinsing to the batch with regular mixing.

9. Check the pH and adjust to 4.8 ± 0.1 if necessary with 1% Phosphoric Acid or 1% Sodium Hydroxide Solution.
10. Continue the slow mixing for about 60 minutes. When the batch is homogenous, increase the flow of water in the jacket. Cool the batch by agitating for 30 seconds every 5 minutes till the batch reaches a temperature of 34°C to 36°C.
11. Transfer the cream into heavy double polythene bags lined containers.
12. Send a representative sample to Q.C. for evaluation.

BETAMETHASONE GEL

LABELLED FORMULA

Betamethasone Dipropionate 0.055%

BATCH SIZE : 400 Kg.
PRACTICAL YIELD : 26000 Tubes of 15 g.
USUAL PACKING : 15 g. Collapsible Tubes

FORMULATION

S. No.	Ingredients	Quantity
1.	Betamethasone Dipropionate	0.260 Kg.
2.	Butylated Hydroxytoluene	0.400 Kg.
3.	Benzyl Alcohol	8.000 Kg.
4.	Cetomacrogol 1000	0.800 Kg.
5.	Cetostreayl	3.200 Kg.
6.	Chlorocresol	0.400 Kg.
7.	Cetyl Alcohol	16.000 Kg.
8.	Carbopol 940	2.000 Kg.
9.	Disodium Edetate	0.200 Kg.
10.	Glycerin	12.000 Kg.
11.	Propylene Glycol	12.000 Kg.
12.	Sodium Hydroxide	0.600 Kg.
13.	Titanium Dioxide	1.400 Kg.
14.	Distilled Water	342.74 Kg.

MANUFACTURING PROCESS

1. Charge 342.740 Kg. Distilled water to a manufacturing tank and dissolve Disodium Edetate and Titanium Dioxide.

2. Pass Carbopol through No. 10 sieve and charge to the tank with propeller stirrer. Slowly heat upto 70°C.
3. In a separate vessel charge Propylene Glycol and heat upto 70°C. Add to the manufacturing tank of Step 1 under continuous stirring.
4. In a separate vessel charge Cetyl Alcohol, Cetostearyl Alcohol, Cetomacrogol 1000, Chlorocresol and Butylated Hydroxy Toluene. Heat upto 70°C.
5. Add this oil phase to the manufacturing tank under constant stirring. Pass the material through No. 60 mesh sieve and maintain the temperature of 65°C to 70°C.
6. Cool the batch upto 50°C-55°C.
7. In a separate vessel charge Benzyl Alcohol and dissolve Betamethasone Dipropionate.
8. Add the slurry of Step 7 in the manufacturing tank at 50°C-55°C. Rinse the vessel with small quantity of Benzyl Alcohol.
9. Add slowly Glycerin in the manufacturing tank under continuous stirring. Cooling is to continue.
10. In a separate vessel charge 8 Lit. Distilled water and dissolve Sodium Hydroxide. Add this solution to the manufacturing tank very slowly under continuous stirring and cooling.
11. After 15 minutes start the Homogenizer. After 10 minutes take the whole assembly 7-8 inches up and keep it there for 3 minutes and homogenize the bulk. Again repeat the process for 10 minutes.
12. Check the pH, it should be 5.5 to 6.5.
13. Cool the batch to 34°C-36°C till it is homogenous.
14. Transfer the batch to holding container with double lined polythene bags, then record the bulk yield.
15. Send a sample to Q.C. for evaluation.

CLOTRIMAZOLE CREAM

LABELLED FORMULA

Clotrimazole 1% w/w

BATCH SIZE : 100 Kg.
PRACTICAL YIELD : 4900 Tubes of 20 g.
USUAL PACKING : 20 g. Tubes

FORMULATION

S. No.	Ingredients		Quantity
1.	Clotrimazole		1.00 Kg.
2.	Liquid Paraffin (Heavy)		6.00 Kg.
3.	White Soft Paraffin		15.00 Kg.
4.	Cetostearyl Alcohol		7.20 Kg.
5.	Cetomacrogol 1000		2.25 Kg.
6.	Propylene Glycol		10.00 Kg.
7.	Benzyl Alcohol		1.00 Kg.
8.	Sodium Acid Phosphate		0.30 Kg.
9.	Distilled Water	to	100 Kg.

MANUFACTURING PROCESS

1. Prepare the Oil Phase by melting at 60°C, White Soft Paraffin, Cetostearyl Alcohol, Cetomacrogol 1000 and 3 Kg. of Liquid Paraffin. Keep this Oil Phase at 55°C.
2. Prepare a slurry of Clotrimazole with 3 Kg. Liquid Paraffin with a homogenizer type stirrer and add to the mixture of Step 1.
3. Prepare the water phase by heating distilled water to 60°C and add Benzyl Alcohol, Sodium Acid Phosphate and Propylene Glycol.
4. Mix the oil phase with the water phase at 55°C to 60°C. Allow the cream to cool slowly. Add Liquid Paraffin slurry of Clotrimazole at about 45°C. Mix well for 10 minutes at fast speed and then at slow speed for 30 minutes.
5. Make up the weight to 100 Kg. with calculated quantity of Distilled Water.

CROTAMITON CREAM

LABELLED FORMULA

Crotamiton 10% w/w

BATCH SIZE : 180 Kg.
PRACTICAL YIELD : 8800 Containers of 20 g.
USUAL PACKING : 20 g. and 60 g. Containers

FORMULATION

S. No.	Ingredients	Quantity
1.	Crotamiton	18.000 Kg.
2.	Chlorocresol	0.180 Kg.
3.	Sodium Acid Phosphate	0.610 Kg.

4.	White Soft Paraffin	24.530	Kg.
5.	Cetomacrogol 1000	3.680	Kg.
6.	Liquid Paraffin	9.810	Kg.
7.	Cetostearyl Alcohol	11.780	Kg.
8.	Butylated Hydroxy Toluene	3.60	g.
9.	Distilled Water	113.60	Lit.

MANUFACTURING PROCESS

1. Change Distilled Water to a jacketed S.S. Kettle fitted with agitation and cover. Heat the water to 65°C-70°C. Add and dissolve Chlorocresol and Sodium Acid Phosphate and continue mixing.
2. In a separate pre-mix vessel equipped with a mixer, charge White Soft Paraffin, Liquid Paraffin, Cetostearyl Alcohol, Cetomacrogol 1000 and Butylated Hydroxy Toulene and while mixing heat to 65°C-70°C.
3. Warm and add Crotamiton to the molten waxes and continue mixing till completely homogenous.
4. Cool and maintain the oil phase at 65°C to 70°C.
5. Strain the oil phase from Step 4 through 80 mesh S.S. screen into the aquous phase of Step 1 while maintaining the batch temperature at 65°C to 70°C.
6. Check and adjust the pH to 5.0 ± 0.2 if necessary with 1.0% Phosphoric Acid or 1.0% Sodium Hydroxide solution.
7. Cool the batch with slow mixing to 34°C to 36°C.
8. Transfer the batch into suitable holding containers and send a sample to Q.C. evaluation.

DEXAMETHASONE, CLOTRIMAZOLE AND AZIDAMPHENICOL CREAM

LABELLED FORMULA

Each 15 g. contains :

Dexamethasone Acetate equivalent to Dexamethasone	6.0 mg.
Clotrimazole	150 mg.
Azidamphenicol	150 mg.

BATCH SIZE : 100 Kg.
PRACTICAL YIELD : 6500 Tubes of 15 g.
USUAL PACKING : 15 g. Tubes

FORMULATION

S. No.	Ingredients	Quantity	Overages
1.	Dexamethasone Acetate	0.049 Kg.	10%
2.	Azidamphenicol	1.100 Kg.	10%
3.	Clotrimazole	1.000 Kg.	
4.	Liquid Paraffin (Heavy)	6.000 Kg.	
5.	White Soft Paraffin	15.000 Kg.	
6.	Ceto Stearyl Alcohol	7.200 Kg.	
7.	Cetomacrogol 1000	2.250 Kg.	
8.	Propylene Glycol	10.000 Kg.	
9.	Benzyl Alcohol	1.000 Kg.	
10.	Distilled Water to	100 Kg.	

MANUFACTURING PROCESS

Follow the same process as given under Clotrimazole Cream.

DICLOFENAC GEL

LABELLED FORMULA

Diclofenac Diethylammonium Salt
equivalent to Diclofenac Sodium 1% w/w

BATCH SIZE : 150 Kg.
PRACTICAL YIELD : 4850 Tubes of 30 g.
USUAL PACKING : 30 g. Tubes

FORMULATION

S. No.	Ingredients	Quantity	Overages
1.	Liquid Paraffin	3.75 Kg.	
2.	White Petroleum Jelly	5.00 Kg.	
3.	Diclofenac Diethylammonium Salt	1.74 Kg.	
4.	Isopropyl Alcohol	15.00 Lit.	
5.	Propylene Glycol	15.00 Kg..	
6.	Carbopol 934 P	1.50 Kg.	
7.	Sodium Hydroxide 10% Solution (for pH adjustment)	Q.S.	
8.	Flavours (Lavender, Cologne)	300 ml.	
9.	Distilled Water	Q.S.	

MANUFACTURING PROCESS

1. Charge 110 Lit. Distilled water to a S.S. Tank and suspend Carbopol 934 P by adding slowly under Homogenizer Typer Stirrer with fast stirring.
2. Prepare a solution of Isopropyl Alcohol, Diethylammonium Salt Diclofenac and Propylene Glycol.
3. Add slowly solution of Step 2 to Carbopol suspension of Step1.
4. Melt White Petroleum Jelly and mix with Liquid Paraffin and add to the Carbopol Jelly. Mix well.
5. Add Sodium Hydroxide 10% solution to adjust the pH to 7.0. Add the flavours and mix well.
6. Adjust the final weight with Distilled water and mix well.

EMOLIENT CREAM

LABELLED FORMULA

Mephenesin	5% w/w
Capsicum Oleoresin	0.05% w/w
Methyl Salicylate	4% v/w
Menthol	1% w/w
Methyl Nicotinate	1% w/w

BATCH SIZE : 15 Kg.
PRACTICAL YIELD : 730 Tubes of 20 g.
USUAL PACKING : 20 g. Collapsible Aluminium Tubes

FORMULATION

S. No.	Ingredients	Quantity
1.	Mephenesin	765 g.
2.	Capsicum Oleoresin	8 g.
3.	Methyl Salicylate	630 g.
4.	Methyl Nicotinate	153 g.
5.	Menthol	150 g.
6.	Emulsifying wax	900 g.
7.	Cetostearyl Alcohol	3.35 Kg.
8.	White Soft Paraffin	6.25 Kg.
9.	Liquid Paraffin	1.1 Kg.
10.	Hard Paraffin	1.75 Kg.

MANUFACTURING PROCESS

1. Heat Emulsifying wax, Cetostearyl Alcohol, White Soft Paraffin, Hard Paraffin and Liquid Paraffin to 100°C and filter through cloth.

2. Dissolve Mephenesin in the above mass at 70°C with stirring.
3. Add Capsicum Oleoresin.
4. Dissolve menthol in Methyl Salicylate with stirring.
5. Melt Methyl Nicotinate on a water bath.
6. Add (5) to (4) at 40°C.
7. Mix for atleast two hours.
8. Send a sample to Q.C. for evaluation.

FLUOCINOLONE CREAM

LABELLED FORMULA

Fluocinolone Acetonide 0.025% w/v

BATCH SIZE : 225 Kg.
PRACTICAL YIELD : 14600 Tubes of 15 g.
USUAL PACKING : 15 g. Tubes

FORMULATION

S. No.	Ingredients	Quantity	Overages
1.	Fluocinolone Acetonide	16.875 g.	10%
2.	Cetostearyl Alcohol	18.000 Kg.	
3.	Cetomacrogol 1000	5.998 Kg.	
4.	Light Liquid Paraffin	9.000 Kg.	
5.	White Soft Paraffin	33.750 Kg.	
6.	Hard Paraffin	4.500 Kg.	
7.	Propylene Glycol	6.750 Kg.	
8.	Sorbitol	4.500 Kg.	
9.	Butylated Hydroxy Anisole	22.500 g.	
10.	Butylated Hydroxy Toluene	22.500 g.	
11.	Disodium Edetate	22.500 g.	
12.	Propylene Glycol	2.250 Kg.	
13.	Sorbitol	1.500 Kg.	
14.	Methyl Paraben	0.150 Kg.	
15.	Propyl Paraben	37.500 g.	
16.	Sodium Acid Phosphate	0.180 Kg.	
17.	Disodium Phosphate	0.135 Kg.	
18.	Benzyl Alcohol	0.150 Kg.	
19.	Distilled Water to (Approx. 75 Kg. used)	225 Kg.	

MANUFACTURING PROCESS

1. Melt Cetostearyl Alcohol, Cetomacrogol 1000, Light Liquid Paraffin, White Soft Paraffin and Hard Paraffin at 65°C.
2. Mix Propylene Glycol, Sorbitol, Butylated Hydroxy Anisole & Butylated Hydroxy Toluene. Prepare a slurry of Fluocinolone Acetonide in Step 1. Heat to 65°C.
3. Mix Step 1 and Step 2 and keep it at 60°C.
4. Dissolve Methyl Paraben, Propyl Paraben and Sodium Acid Phosphate in required quantity of Distilled water. Add Benzyl Alcohol and mix properly. Add Sorbitol 1.5 Kg. and Propylene Glycol 2.25 Kg. Heat to a temperature of 60°C.
5. Add slowly under stirring mixture of Step 1 and 2 under fast speed stirrer for 10 minutes. Then mix at slow speed for 20 minutes and allow to cool down.

FLUOCINOLONE SKIN LOTION

LABELLED FORMULA

Fluocinolone Acetonide 0.01% w/v

BATCH SIZE : 300 Kg.
PRACTICAL YIELD : 19500 Bottles of 15 ml.
USUAL PACKING : 15 ml. Plastic Squeez Bottie.

FORMULATION

S. No.	Ingredients		Quantity
1.	Fluocinolone Acetonide		31.50 g.
2.	White Soft Paraffin		2.28 Kg.
3.	Cetyl Alcohol		5.70 Kg.
4.	Propylene Glycol		17.10 Kg.
5.	Methyl Paraben		0.45 Kg.
6.	Propyl Paraben		0.15 Kg.
7.	Sodium Lauryl Sulphate		0.85 Kg.
8.	Sutable Perfume		0.20 Kg.
9.	D.M. Water	to	300 Kg.

MANUFACTURING PROCESS

1. Charge 274 Lit. of D.M. water to suitable a vessel. Add Methyl Paraben and Sodium Lauryl Sulphate. Heat upto 70°C-75°C under stirring.

2. Weight White Soft Paraffin, Cetyl Alcohol, Propylene Glycol, Propyl Paraben and Fluocinolone Acetonide in a suitable vessel. Melt and heat upto 60° to 65°C till everything melts.
3. Filter the mix from Step 2 to a mixing tank through muslin cloth and while stirring add D.M. water through filter cloth. Continue stirring for about 4 hours and if required pass tap water through the jacket.
4. Next day add the Perfume and stir for 15 minutes and send a sample for testing.

FLUOCINOLONE LOTION

LABELLED FORMULA

Fluocinolone Acetonide 0.01%

BATCH SIZE : 300 Litres
PRACTICAL YIELD : 19500 Bottles of 15 ml.
USUAL PACKING : 15 ml. Bottles

FORMULATION

S. No.	Ingredients	Quantity	Overages
1.	Fluocinolone Acetonide	0.0315Kg.	5%
2.	White Soft Paraffin	2.280 Kg.	
3.	Cetostearyl Alcohol	5.700 Kg.	
4.	Propylene Glycol	17.100 Kg.	
5.	Methyl Paraben	0.450 Kg.	
6.	Propyl Paraben	0.150 Kg.	
7.	Sodium Laurayl Sulphate	0.850 Kg.	
8.	Perfume	0.200 Kg.	
9.	Distilled Water to	300 Lit.	

MANUFACTURING PROCESS

1. Dissolve Methyl Paraben, Propyl Paraben and Sodium Lauryl Sulphate in required quantity of Distilled water and heat to 60°C.
2. Melt White Soft Paraffin, Cetostearyl Alcohol and dissolve Fluocinolone Acetonide. Cool to 45°C, add Propylene Glycol and Perfume.
3. Mix Step 1 and Step 2 and make up the volume to 300 Lit. with Distilled water.

FLUOCINONIDE AND NEOMYCIN GEL

LABELLED FORMULA

Fluocinonide	0.025%
Neomycin Sulphate	0.050%

BATCH SIZE : 200 Kg.
PRACTICAL YIELD : 19500 Tubes of 10 g.
USUAL PACKING : 10 g. Collapsible Tubes

FORMULATION

S. No.	Ingredients	Quantity
1.	Fluocinonide	50.0 g.
2.	Neomycin Sulphate	110.0 g.
3.	Propylene Glycol	120.0 Kg.
4.	Propyl Gallate	200.0 g.
5.	Sodium Metabisulphite	200.0 g.
6.	Disodium Edetate	200.0 g.
7.	Carbopol 940	2.0 Kg.
8.	Triethanolamine	1.5 Kg.
9.	Distilled Water	75.8 Kg.
	Total Weight	200.0 Kg.

MANUFACTURING PROCESS

1. Charge 75.8 Lit. Distilled water to a manufacturing tank. Add and dissolve Sodium Metabisulphite, Disodium Edetate and Neomycin Sulphate under continuous stirring.
2. In a separate vessel charge Propylene Glycol and heat upto 50°C. Add and dissolve Propyl Gallate. Heat the solution to 80°C and dissolve Fluocinonide. Cool this solution to 40°C.
3. Charge active slurry from Step 2 in the manufacturing tank at 40°C temperature under constant stirring.
4. Charge and disperse Carbopol 940 through No. 10 mesh sieve to the manufacturing tank. Continue stirring till the batch is homogenous.
5. Charge Triethanolamine to the Planetary Mixer of 400 Lit. Capacity stirring is continued till the batch is clear and transparent. Scrape all the sides.
6. Check the pH, it should be 5.5 to 6.5.
7. Send the sample to Q.C. for evaluation.

GENTAMYCIN CREAM

LABELLED FORMULA

Gentamycin 0.1% w/w

BATCH SIZE : 40 Kg.
PRACTICAL YIELD : 2600 Tubes of 15 g.
USUAL PACKING : 15 g. Collapsible Tubes

FORMULATION

S. No.	Ingredients	Quantity
1.	Gentamycin Base (as Sulphate)	* 40.00 g.
2.	Chlorocresol	40.00 g.
3.	Sodium Acid Phosphate	135.65 g.
4.	Phosphoric Acid	0.80 g.
5.	White Soft Paraffin	6.00 Kg.
6.	Liquid Paraffin	2.40 Kg.
7.	Cetomacrogol 1000	0.90 Kg.
8.	Cetostearyl Alcohol	2.88 Kg.
9.	Distilled Water	28.40 Kg.
10.	** 1% Sodium Hydroxide Solution	Q.S.

** (For pH adjustment)

* Calculation for Gentamycin Sulphate

$$\frac{1000 \times 40}{\text{Potency of Gentamycin Base}} = \text{Gentamycin Sulphate}$$

MANUFACTURING PROCESS

Part I - Oil Phase

Charge White Soft Paraffin, Liquid Paraffin, Cetomacrogol and Cetostearyl Alcohol to a suitable vessel. Heat to melt and maintain a temperature of 70°-75°C.

Part II - Aquous Phase

Dissolve Sodium Acid Phosphate, Chlorocresol and Phosphoric Acid in the Distilled water and maintain a temperature of 65°-70°C.

1. Add Oil Phase to Aquous Phase and stir for 15 minutes. Start cooling and cool to 45°C-46°C.
2. Cool the batch by further cooling and attain a temperature of 40°C-42°C.

3. Dissolve Gentamycin Sulphate in water and add to the batch at 40°-42°C.
4. Stir for 90 minutes, mix well and unload the batch.
5. Check the pH and adjust to 4.8 to 4.9 (limit 4.5 to 5.5).
6. Send a sample to Q.C. for evaluation.

HYDROCORTISONE CREAM 1%

ABELLED FORMULA

Hydrocortisone 1% w/w

BATCH SIZE : 100 Kg.
PRACTICAL YIELD : 9750 Tubes of 10 g.
USUAL PACKING : 10 g. Tube

FORMULATION

S. No.	Ingredients		Quantity	Overages
1.	Hydrocortisone (Fine Powder)		1.10 Kg.	10%
2.	Liquid Paraffin		6.00 Kg.	
3.	White Soft Paraffin		15.00 Kg.	
4.	Cetostearyl Alcohol		7.20 Kg.	
5.	Cetomacrogol 1000		1.80 Kg.	
6.	Propylene Glycol		10.00 Kg.	
7.	Chlorocresol		0.10 Kg.	
8.	Sodium Metabisulphite		0.20 Kg.	
9.	Distilled Water	to	100 Kg.	

MANUFACTURING PROCESS

1. Prepare the Oil Phase by melting at 65°C, White Soft Paraffin, Cetostearyl Alcohol, Cetomacrogol and half quantity of Liquid Paraffin (3 Kg.).
2. Prepare a slurry of Hydrocortisone in 3 Kg. Liquid Paraffin with Homogenizer Type Stirrer.
3. Prepare the water phase by dissolving Chlorocresol in Propylene Glycol. Dissolve Sodium Metabisulphite in Distilled water. Calculate the balance quantity of Distilled water required and heat to 65°C. Add Chlorocresol solution and Sodium Metabisulphite solution.
4. Mix the Oil phase and the water phase at about 60°C. Mix well with slow stirring.

5. Add the Hydrocortisone slurry to the above, and mix well for 10 minutes with fast speed mixing.
6. Add Propylene Glycol and make up the total weight with calculated quantity of Distilled water.

MEPHENESIN, METHYL NICOTINATE AND CAPSICUM OLEORESIN OINTMENT

LABELLED FORMULA

Mephenesin	10% w/w
Methyl Nicotinate	1% w/w
Capsicum Oleoresin	0.05% w/w

BATCH SIZE : 100 Kg.
PRACTICAL YIELD : 4850 Tubes of 20 g.
USUAL PACKING : 20 g. Tubes

FORMULATION

S. No.	Ingredients		Quantity
1.	Mephenesin		10.00 Kg.
2.	Methyl Nicotinate		1.00 Kg.
3.	Capsicum Oleoresin		0.05 Kg.
4.	Lanolin Anhydrous		2.00 Kg.
5.	Hard Paraffin		2.00 Kg.
6.	Cetostearyl Alcohol		2.00 Kg.
7.	White Soft Paraffin	to	100 Kg.

MANUFACTURING PROCESS

1. Heat Hard Paraffin, Cetostearyl Alcohol with White Soft Paraffin and Lanolin Anhydrous to 80°C.
2. Strain the mixture through 100 mesh S.S. sieve to another vessel.
3. Add Mephenesin (sifted through 40 mesh) to Step 2 and stir well till dissolved.
4. Start the homogenizer and cooling.
5. Cool to 60°C with Homogenizer.
6. Melt Methyl Nicotinate and Capsicum Oleoresin and add to Step 5.
7. When the temperature reaches to 45°C take out the homogenizer and mix with the simple blade stirrer. Cool to room temperature.

NOTE:

Mephenesin precipitates out at 50°-60°C, so keep continuous stirring with homogenizer to avoid lumps of Mephenesin.

MICONAZOLE AND HYDROCORTISONE GEL

LABELLED FORMULA

Miconazole Nitrate	2% w/w
Hydrocortisone Acetate	1% w/w

BATCH SIZE : 300 Kg.
PRACTICAL YIELD : 58500 Tubes of 5 g.
USUAL PACKING : 5 g. Tubes

FORMULATION

S. No.	Ingredients	Quantity
1.	* Miconazole Nitrate (200 mesh)	6.000 Kg.
2.	Hydrocortisone Acetate (200 mesh)	3.000 Kg.
3.	Carbopol 934 (40 mesh)	4.500 Kg.
4.	Triethanolamine	4.500 Kg.
5.	Disodium Edetate	0.015 Kg.
6.	Propylene Glycol	15.00 Kg.
7.	D.M. Water	267.000 Kg.

* Miconazole Nitrate powder should be passed through 200 mesh sieve just before the manufacture of the product.

MANUFACTURING PROCESS

1. Charge 160 Lit. D.M. water to a suitable vessel fitted with Lightening Stirrer (1200-1600 RPM). Add while stirring Miconazole Nitrate, Hydrocortisone Acetate and Carbopol 934 in that order. Add all ingredients in small portions only when the first portion of powder is completely dispersed. Add the powder to an area of vigoruous agitation at the centre of the vortex. Avoid agglomaration of Carbopol 934.
2. Continue stirring for 20 minutes.
3. Pass the above slurry through Colloid Mill (in a tight position), filter through muslin cloth and transfer into a mixing vessel fitted with agitator and scrapper blades.

3.1 Rinse the container and Colloid Mill with 20 Lit. D.M. water. Filter through muslin cloth and add to the mixing vessel. Allow the slurry to stand for 8 hours to de-aerate.

3.2 Start stirring of slurry at 15 RPM.

4. Prepare the following solution:

4.1 Into a suitable vessel take 40 Lit. D.M. water. Add and dissolve Disodium Edetate and when completely dissolved add Triethanolamine. Mix well and filter through muslin cloth.

4.2 Into a suitable vessel take 27 Lit. D.M. water and 15 Kg. Propylene Glycol. Mix well and filter through muslin cloth.

5. Formation of Gel.

5.1 Increase speed of stirring to 25 RPM (Step 3.2).

5.2 Add solution 4.1 slowly in a fine stream.

5.3 Rinse the container with 10 Lit. D.M. water. Filter through muslin cloth and add to the batch.

5.4 Add solution 4.2 slowly in a fine stream.

5.5 Rinse the container with D.M. water 10 Lit. Filter through muslin cloth and add to the batch.

6. Continue stirring of the batch for 2 hours at 15 RPM.

7. Stop stirring and pass the Gel through Colloid Mill, setting the opening to the minimum.

8. Store the product into suitable container in an airc onditioned room.

9. Intimate the Q.C. to collect the sample and await report.

MICONAZOLE GEL

LABELLED FORMULA

Miconazole Nitrate 2% w/w

BATCH SIZE : 500 Kg.
PRACTICAL YIELD : 24500 Tubes of 20 g.
USUAL PACKING : 20 g. Tubes

FORMULATION

S. No.	Ingredients	Quantity
1.	* Miconazole Nitrate (200 mesh)	10.000 Kg.
2.	Carbopol 934 (40 mesh)	7.500 Kg.
3.	Triethanolamine	7.500 Kg.
4.	Disodium Edetate	0.025 Kg.
5.	Propylene Glycol	25.000 Kg.
6.	D.M. Water	449.975 Kg.

* Miconazole Nitrate powder should be passed through 200 mesh just before the manufacture.

MANUFACTURING PROCESS

1. Charge 300 Lit. D.M. water to a suitable vessel fitted with two lightening stirrers (1500 RPM). Add Miconazole Nitrate under stirring. Continue stirring for 30 minutes.

NOTE:

a. Add Miconazole Nitrate in small portions. Ensure that the first portion is fully dispersed before adding the next.

b. Add Miconazole Nitrate into the centre of vortex for vigorous agitation.

2. Pass Miconazole Nitrate suspension through the Colloid Mill and collect in another container. Rinse the vessel and Colloid Mill with 10 Lit. D.M. water. Add the rinse to the suspensions after passing through the mill.
3. Transfer the Miconazole suspension again to the mixing vessel and rinse the container with 10 Lit. D.M. water. Add the rinse to the suspension.
4. Start stirring with both the lightening stirrers and add through 40 mesh Carbopol 934. Avoid agglomeration of Carbopol 934. Continue stirring for further one hour. Stop the stirring, cover the container with lid and allow to stand for 8 hours.
5. Pass the above slurry through Colloid Mill (in a tight position) and filter through muslin cloth.
6. Place the slurry into the stainless steel kettle equipped with agitation and fitted with Ebonite scraper blades. Rinse the vessel with 10 Lit. D.M. water. Add to the slurry.
7. Start the stirring and continue for 10 minutes.
8. Meanwhile prepare the following solutions:

(a) Dissolve Disodium Edetate in 50 Lit. of water. When completely dissolved, add and dissolve Triethanolamine. Mix well and filter through muslin cloth.

(b) Mix Propylene Glycol with 60 Lit. water, mix well and filter through muslin cloth.

9. Increase the speed of stirring to 30 RPM. Add Disodium Edetate and Triethanolamine solution 8 (a) into the slurry in a fine stream. Rinse the container with 5 Lit. water, filter through muslin cloth and add to the batch.

10. Add solution 8 (b) into the batch in a fine stream. Rinse the container with 5 Lit. water, filter through muslin cloth and add to the batch.
11. Continue stirring of the batch for 2 hours at 20 RPM.
12. Stop stirring and pass through Colloid Mill keeping the opening at 10 mm.
13. Store the product into a stainless steel container in an air-conditioned room.
14. Send a sample to Q.C. for evaluation.

MICONAZOLE OINTMENT

LABELLED FORMULA

Miconazole 2% w/w

BATCH SIZE : 150 Kg.
PRACTICAL YIELD : 9750 Tubes of 15 g.
USUAL PACKING : 15 g. Tubes

FORMULATION

S. No.	Ingredients	Quantity	Overages
1.	Miconazole Nitrate	3.150 Kg.	5%
2.	Cetostearyl Alcohol	12.000 Kg.	
3.	Cetomacrogol 1000	4.050 Kg.	
4.	Light Liquid Paraffin	6.000 Kg.	
5.	White Soft Paraffin	22.500 Kg.	
6.	Hard Paraffin	3.000 Kg.	
7.	Propylene Glycol	75.000 Kg.	
8.	Sorbic Acid	0.150 Kg.	
9.	Butylated Hydroxy Anisole	0.015 Kg.	
10.	Butylated Hydroxy Toluene	0.015 Kg.	
11.	Disodium Edetate	0.015 Kg.	
12.	Sodium Acid Phosphate	0.360 Kg.	
13.	Disodium Phosphate	0.230 Kg.	
14.	Flavour	0.375 Kg.	
15.	Distilled Water to	150 Kg.	

MANUFACTURING PROCESS

1. Melt Cetostearyl Alcohol, Cetomacrogol 1000, White Soft Paraffin, Hard Paraffin, Butylated Hydroxy Anisole and Butylated Hydroxy Toluene at 60°C.

2. Prepare a slurry of Miconazole Nitrate in Liquid Paraffin and heat to 60°C.
3. Add Step 2 to Step 1 of molten mass and stir well.
4. Heat the required quantity of Distilled water to 55°C, add and dissolve Sodium Acid Phosphate, Disodium Phosphate & Sorbic Acid. Mix Propylene Glycol with the flavour.
5. Add Step 3 to Step 4 slowly under stirring and cool down to room temperature.

MICONAZOLE SOLUTION

LABELLED FORMULA

Miconazole 2% w/v

BATCH SIZE : 400 Litres.
PRACTICAL YIELD : 39000 Bottles of 10 ml.
USUAL PACKING : 10 ml. Amber Bottles

FORMULATION

S. No.	Ingredients		Quantity
1.	Miconazole Base		8.00 Kg.
2.	Polyethylene Glycol 400		233.64 Kg.
3.	Butylated Hydroxy Toluene		0.09 Kg.
4.	Propylene Glycol	to	400 Lit.

MANUFACTURING PROCESS

1. Charge 175 Kg. Propylene Glycol and 233.64 Kg. Polyethylene Glycol 400 to a steam jacketed stainless steel vessel fitted with a stirrer. Heat the mixture to 65°-70°C. Start stirring and add the following:

   Butylated Hydroxy Toluene 0.08 Kg.
   Miconazole 8.00 Kg.

   Continue stirring and maintain the temperature for 30 minutes. Stop heating and cool the solution to 30°-35°C.
2. Adjust the volume to 400 Lit. with Propylene Glycol.
3. Filter the solution through suitable filter press.
4. Send a sample to Q.C. for evaluation.

MICONAZOLE TALC POWDER

LABELLED FORMULA

Miconazole Nitrate 2% w/w

BATCH SIZE : 80 Kg.
PRACTICAL YIELD : 7500 Bottles of 10.5 g.
USUAL PACKING : 10.5 g. Bottles

FORMULATION

S. No.	Ingredients	Quantity
1.	Miconazole Nitrate	1.60 Kg.
2.	Zinc Oxide	4.00 Kg.
3.	Aerosil	0.80 Kg.
4.	Talcum	73.44 Kg.

MANUFACTURING PROCESS

1. Mix Miconazole Nitrate in 2 parts with 50% of all inactive ingredients.
2. Mix both the parts for 30 minutes in a powder mixer.
3. Send a sample to Q.C. for evaluation.

NEOMYCIN AND BACITRACIN OINTMENT

LABELLED FORMULA

Each g. contains:
Neomycin Sulphate 5 mg.
Bacitracin Zinc 500 I.U.

BATCH SIZE : 100 Kg.
PRACTICAL YIELD : 27000 Tubes of 3.5 g.
USUAL PACKING : 3.5 g. Aluminium Collapsible Tubes

FORMULATION

S. No.	Ingredients	Quantity	Overages
1.	Bacitracin Zinc (69 Units/mg.)	780 g	8%
2.	Neomycin Sulphate	540 g.	8%
3.	White Soft Paraffin	85 Kg.	
4.	Hard Paraffin	5 Kg.	

5.	Liquid Paraffin	10 Kg.
6.	Disodium Edetate	100 g.

MANUFACTURING SPECIFICATIONS

1. Moisture content of the Ointment should be less than 0.2%.
2. Bacitracin Zinc is incompatible with Cetostearyl Alcohol, Cetomacrogol, Propylene Glycol, Polyethylene Glycol, Sodium Lauryl Sulphate and Glycerin.
3. Neomycin Sulphate and Bacitracin Zinc should be added at a temperature not exceeding 35°C.
4. The Ointment must be protected from light for better stability.

MANUFACTURING PROCESS

1. Heat White Soft Paraffin, Hard Paraffin and 3/4 Liquid Paraffin to 100°C for atleast 30 minutes to remove any moisture. Pass Nitrogen Gas through the melted waxes for 30 minutes.
2. Triturate Neomycin Sulphate, Bacitracin Zinc and Disodium Edetate with balance of Liquid Paraffin to form a paste.
3. Add (2) to (1) in a planetary mixer at a temperature not exceeding 35°C and mix for atleast 2 hours.
4. Send a sample to Q.C. for evaluation.

NITROFURAZONE CREAM

LABELLED FORMULA

Nitrofurazone 0.2%

BATCH SIZE : 100 Kg.
PRACTICAL YIELD : 3450 Tubes of 28 g.
USUAL PACKING : 28 g. Aluminium Collapsible Tubes

FORMULATION

S. No.	Ingredients	Quantity
1.	Nitrofuazone	208 g.
2.	Cetostearyl Alcohol	7.2 Kg.
3.	Cetomacrogol 1000	1.8 Kg.
4.	Liquid Paraffin	6.0 Kg.
5.	White Soft Paraffin	15.0 Kg.
6.	Propylene Glycol	1.0 Kg.

7.	Chlorocresol	20 g.
8.	Purified Water	69.0 Kg.

MANUFACTURING PROCESS

1. Melt together and mix Cetostearyl Alcohol, Cetomacrogol 1000, Liquid Paraffin, White Soft Paraffin and filter the molten mass through cloth.
2. Heat Purified water to 50°—60°C and add to (1) with Emulsifier.
3. Mix Nitrofurazone with Propylene Glycol and add to (2) with stirring.
4. Allow to cool under constant mixing till the consistency is right for filling in tubes.
5. Store the material in a cool dark place.
6. Send a sample to Q.C. for evaluation.

POVIDONE IODINE OINTMENT

LABELLED FORMULA

Each g. contains:
Povidone Iodine 5.0% w/w
(0.5% Available Iodine)

BATCH SIZE : 600 Kg.
PRACTICAL YIELD : 20800 Tubes of 28 g.
USUAL PACKING : Tubes of 10 g. & 28 g. Jar of 250 g.

FORMULATION

S. No.	Ingredients	Quantity	Overages
1.	Povidone Iodine	31.50 Kg.	5%
2.	Polyethylene Glycol 4000	180.00 Kg.	
3.	Polyethylene Glycol 400	385.50 Kg.	
4.	Distilled Water	30.00 Lit.	

MANUFACTURING PROCESS

1. Charge Polyethylene Glycol and Distilled water to a jacketed stainless steel manufacturing tank through 100 mesh sieve and heat to 60°C-65°C by passing steam.
2. Add Povidone Iodine slowly with regular stirring until Povidone Iodine is completely dissolved in the mixture. Take a sample to ensure complete dissolution.
3. To another jacketed tank add Polyethylene Glycol 4000 and melt by

heating to 60°C-65°C with steam. Filter the Polyethylene Glycol through 100 mesh sieve and add to the manufacturing tank containing Povidone Iodine mixture. Ensure that the temperature of both the phases is 60°C to 65°C. Stir well to ensure proper mixing.

4. Stir the batch for one hour then start the cooling by passing water in the jacket. After attaining the temperature of 30° to 35°C take out the batch and store in a closed container in an air-conditioned room.
5. Send the sample to Q.C. for evaluation.

POVIDONE IODINE TOPICAL SOLUTION

LABELLED FORMULA

Povidone Iodine (1.0% Available Iodine) 10.0% w/v

BATCH SIZE : 600 Lit.
PRACTICAL YIELD : 5800 Bottles of 100 ml.
USUAL PACKING : 100 ml. Bottles

FORMULATION

S. No.	Ingredients		Quantity
1.	Povidone Iodine		60.00 Kg.
2.	Disodium Hydrogen Phosphate		23.00 Kg.
3.	Citric Acid		6.600 Kg.
4.	Sodium Lauryl Sulphate		3.00 Kg.
5.	Distilled Water	to	600 Lit.

MANUFACTURING PROCESS

1. Transfer about 150 Lit. of Distilled water in 750 Lit. jacketed manufacturing tank. Add gradually Disodium Hydrogen Phosphate and stir till dissolved. Add Citric Acid gradually and stir till dissolved. Check the pH, it should be 4.0 to 6.0.
2. Transfer 150 Lit. Distilled water to another 300 Lit. jacketed tank. Add Povidone Iodine slowly with constant stirring. Ensure complete dissolution of Povidone Iodine.
3. Transfer Povidone Iodine solution to the main manufacturing tank containing the buffer solution. Stir the solution for 30 minutes.
4. Make up the volume to 550 Lit. with Distilled water.
5. Transfer 25 Lit. distilled water to another vessel and add Sodium Lauryl Sulphate and stir till completely dissolved. Transfer this solution to the main tank.

6. Make up the final volume to 600 Lit. and stir well for 20 minutes.
7. Filter the solution through 100 mesh stainless steel sieve.
8. Check the pH, it should be 4.0 to 6.0.
9. Send a sample to Q.C. for evaluation.

SISOMICIN CREAM

LABELLED FORMULA

Sisomicin Sulphate equivalent to Sisomicin — 0.1%

BATCH SIZE : 360 Kg.
PRACTICAL YIELD : 23500 Tubes of 15 g.
USUAL PACKING : 15 g. or 7.5 g. Tubes

FORMULATION

S. No.	Ingredients	Quantity
1.	Sisomicin Sulphate (360 g. Base)	*648.20 g.
2.	White Soft Paraffin	54.00 Kg.
3.	Liquid Paraffin	21.60 Kg.
4.	Polyoxyethylene Stearyl Ether	6.48 Kg.
5.	Cetyl Alcohol	25.92 Kg.
6.	Methyl Paraben	72.00 g.
7.	Butyl Paraben	648.00 g.
8.	Lactic Acid	3.60 Kg.
9.	Sodium Hydroxide of 2N Sol.	16.51 Lit.
10.	Distilled Water to (238 Kg. approx.)	360 Kg.

* Sisomicin Sulphate Calculation

$$\text{Weight of Sisomicin Sulphate} = \frac{\text{Weight of base required} \times 1000}{\text{Actual potency in mcg.}}$$

$$\frac{360 \times 1000}{555.48} = 648.20 \text{ g.}$$

* Include 2.1% overages to compensate for estimated losses during manufacture due to evaporation.

MANUFACTURING PROCESS

1. Preparation of Sodium Hydroxide solution. — (a) Dissolve 1.440 Kg. of

Sodium Hydroxide in 2.0 Lit. of Carbon Dioxide free water (Boil the Distilled water for 10 minutes to make it free of Carbon Dioxide). (b) Cool the solution to room temperature and filter through Whattman Filter No. 1. (c) Transfer 50% Filterate to a 2 Lit. volumetric flask and dilute with Carbon Dioxide free water and make up the volume to 2.0 Lit. (d) Similarly transfer the balance quantity of filterate and make up the volume to 2.0 Lit.

2. Charge Distilled water to jacketed stainless steel compounding tank equipped with agitator and heat to 75°-80°C. Add and dissolve Methyl Paraben and then Lactic Acid. Adjust the pH to 5.50 with 2N Sodium Hydroxide solution (about 16.50 Lit.).

3. Simultaneously in a separate compounding jacketed vessel equipped with stirrer, charge White Soft Paraffin and heat to 80°C ± 2°C. Add Cetyl Alcohol gradually to avoid lump formation. Mix well to dissolve. Add Polyoxyethelene Stearyl to avoid lump formation. Mix well to dissolve. Add Polyoxyethelene Stearyl Ether and stir till dissolved. Add Butyl Paraben and stir to dissolve. Add Liquid Paraffin and mix well till uniform mixture is obtained. Maintain temperature to 80°C ± 2°C during the addition of all the above ingredients.

4. Strain the melted waxes from Step 3 through 80 mesh screen into a jacketed vessel equipped with Turbo Disperser. Maintain the contents at 80°C ± 2°C.

5. Remove a portion of aquous mixture obtained in Step 2 for preparing Sisomicin Sulphate solution and rinsing the container. Cool to room temperature. Dissolve Sisomicin Sulphate and check the pH. Adjust the pH to 5.5 using 2 N Sodium Hydroxide solution. Add gradually the aquous phase from Step 2 into the oil phase of Step 4 under constant stirring at high speed. Maintain the temperature at 80°C ± 2°C. Mix well to obtain a smoothe emulsion.

6. Cool the emulsion gradually to attain 60°C temperature under continuous mixing at slow speed (discontinue mixing by Turbo Disperser). Charge Sisomicin Sulphate solution prepared is Step 5 to the emulsion obtained. Rinse the container with aquous mixture and add the rinse to the emulsion. Continue mixing at slow speed till the cream attains room temperature. Check and record the pH of the cream.

7. Drop the cream without agitation into double polythene lined bag container and check the weight. Submit sample to Q.C. for evaluation.

TOTAL CAPITAL INVESTMENT

TOTAL FIXED CAPITAL	Rs.	19,06,500.00
TOTAL WORKING CAPITAL FOR 3 MONTHS	Rs.	53,21,032.13
TOTAL	Rs.	72,27,532.13

TURN OVER/ANNUM

1. By sale of 6,00,000 packs Castor oil.
2. 3,00,000 Glucose D packs
3. 1200000 Glycerine Packs
4. 600000 Petroleum Jelly Packs

TOTAL	Rs.	3,81,00,000.00

PROFIT SALES RATIO = Profit / Sales x 100 = 41.41 %
RATE OF RETURN = Operating profit / T.C.I x 100 = 218.27 %
BREAK EVEN POINT (B.E.P) = 8.29 %

Chapter 21

Plant Economics of Saline & Dextrose - Saline & PVC Containers

Rated Plant Capacity	=		9000.00 NOS/Day
LAND & BUILDING (1500 sq.mt.)	=	Rs.	25,00,000.00

PLANT & MACHINERY

1. Water distillation unit (pyrogen free) consists of 3 distillation columns in series
2. Water storage tank
3. Covered storage tank made of polypropylene
4. Stainless steel storage tank
5. Rotary washing machine
6. Bottle drier
7. Mixing tank for mixing distilled water with ingredients
8. Sterilizing unit
9. Stainless steel filling tank 200 & 400 litres
10. Fitter press Horizontal plate type
11. Laminar air flow meter horizontal type, Various type
12. Instrument trolley
13. pH meter
14. Automatic,Volumetric liquid filling cap sealing machine
15. Automatic gumming and labeling machine
16. Aerosolve (Fusigator)
17. Load bearing trolley
18. Polarimeters
19. Membrane filtration unit
20. Baby boiler
21. Ultrviolet lamps for testing purposes
22. Equipment accessories, steel vessal containers etc.
23. Miscellaneous equipments including storage vessals for various raw materials
24. Laboratory equipments & Pumps
25. PVC Bottle/Container manufacturing Machine (Blow Moulding)
26. Injection Moulding Machine for Caps
27. Moulds

FIXED CAPITAL

1.	LAND & BUILDING	Rs.	25,00,000.00
2.	PLANT & MACHINERY	Rs.	40,97,000.00
3.	OTHER FIXED ASSETS	Rs.	6,10,000.00
	TOTAL	Rs.	72,07,000.00

RAW MATERIALS

1. PVC Granules
2. Misc like plug caps hangers,labeles
3. Dextrose (I.P. grade) 3 MT
4. Sodium chloride (I.P. Grade) 9.6 MT
5. Packing materials card board boxes 18750 boxes
6. Miscellaneous including KMnO4 (Sodium Hydroxide) and Sterillizing Agents

TOTAL WORKING CAPITAL/MONTH

1.	RAW MATERIAL	Rs.	8,71,275.00
2.	SALARY & WAGES	Rs.	1,19,494.00
3.	UTILITIES & OVERHEADS	Rs.	1,83,000.00
	TOTAL	Rs.	11,73,769.00

TOTAL CAPITAL INVESTMENT

TOTAL FIXED CAPITAL	Rs.	72,07,000.00
TOTAL WORKING CAPITAL FOR 1 MONTH	Rs.	11,73,769.00
TOTAL	Rs.	83,80,769.00

TURN OVER/ANNUM

1. By the sale of 900000 bottles of Dextrose I.V. Fluid
2. By the sale of 900000 bottles of Dextrose-Sodium chloride I.V. Fluid
3. By the sale of 900000 bottles of Sodium Chloride I.V. Fluid

TOTAL	Rs.	1,84,50,000.00

PROFIT SALES RATIO = Profit / Sales x 100 = 13.66 %

RATE OF RETURN = Operating profit / T.C.I x 100 = 30.21 %

BREAK EVEN POINT (B.E.P) = 56.42 %

Chapter 22

Plant Economics of Surgical Cotton and Bandage (EOU)

Rated Plant Capacity =		0.30 TON/Day
LAND & BUILDING(350 sq. mt.) =	Rs.	5,37,500.00

FIXED CAPITAL

1. LAND & BUILDING	Rs.	5,37,500.00
2. PLANT & MACHINERY	Rs.	23,72,000.00
3. OTHER FIXED ASSETS	Rs.	4,23,000.00
TOTAL	Rs.	33,32,500.00

RAW MATERIALS

1. Surgical Bandage good quality cloth bleached gauge cloth width 34" Reed picks 155000 meter
2. Expenditure on soap and other Chemical
3. Raw material for surgical cotton Gnjk 797 or MAHA Varalaxmi, 110 mt
4. Kraft paper and labels

TOTAL WORKING CAPITAL/ANNUM

1. RAW MATERIAL	Rs.	14,75,750.00
2. SALARY & WAGES	Rs.	3,94,500.00
3. UTILITIES & OVERHEADS	Rs.	7,25,000.00
TOTAL	Rs.	25,95,250.00

TOTAL CAPITAL INVESTMENT

TOTAL FIXED CAPITAL	Rs.	33,32,500.00
TOTAL WORKING CAPITAL FOR 3 MONTHS	Rs.	6,48,812.50
TOTAL	Rs.	39,81,312.50

TURN OVER/ANNUM

1. By sale of 90 T of Surgical Cotton
2. 8 lakh number of different sizes of Bandages

TOTAL	Rs.	51,66,667.00

PROFIT SALES RATIO = Profit / Sales x 100 = 28.31 %

RATE OF RETURN = Operating profit / T.C.I x 100 = 36.74 %

BREAK EVEN POINT (B.E.P) = 51.56 %

Chapter 23

Plant Economics of Pharmaceutical Unit Tablet, Capsules, Syrups, Lotion Etc.

Rated Plant Capacity	=		4000.00 NOS/Day
LAND & BUILDING (500 sq.mt.)	=	Rs.	15,25,000.00

PLANT & MACHINERY

1. FOR TABLET & CAPSULE MAKING MACHINE
2. Powder Mixing Machine
3. Automatic tablet/capsule making machine
4. Packaging Machine (Automatic)
5. FOR SYRUP SECTION :S.S.Tank Mixer with stirrer bottom
6. Automatic bottle washing & drying machine
7. Automatic bottle filling machine
8. Conveyer
9. Distillation Plant for distilled water
10. Misc. Machinery
11. Contingency & escalation

FIXED CAPITAL

1. LAND & BUILDING	Rs.	15,25,000.00
2. PLANT & MACHINERY	Rs.	19,15,000.00
3. OTHER FIXED ASSETS	Rs.	1,93,000.00
TOTAL	Rs.	36,33,000.00

RAW MATERIALS

1. Paracetamol
2. Chlorpheniramine Maleate
3. Caffeine
4. Phenyl propanolamine hydrochloride
5. Refampiun
6 Malt disatage
7. Papain
8. Vitamin B1
9. Vitamin B2
10. Vitamin B6
11. Niacihamide

12. 1-Lysine mono Hcl
13. Cardamon-Co-tine
14. Thymol
15. Alcohol
16. Paracetamol
17. Alcohol
18. Packaging material

TOTAL WORKING CAPITAL/MONTH

1.	RAW MATERIAL	Rs.	6,95,743.75
2.	SALARY & WAGES	Rs.	97,350.00
3.	UTILITIES & OVERHEADS	Rs.	3,62,500.00
	TOTAL	Rs.	11,55,593.75

TOTAL CAPITAL INVESTMENT

TOTAL FIXED CAPITAL	Rs.	36,33,000.00
TOTAL WORKING CAPITAL FOR 2 MONTHS	Rs.	23,11,187.50
TOTAL	Rs.	59,44,187.50

TURN OVER/ANNUM

1. TABLETS:Koldech Type 3x10^6 Tablets per annum
2. Paracetamol 3x10^6 tablets/annum
3. Refampicin 3x10^6 Tablets/annum
4. SYRUPS: Enzymol tonic 1500000 bot. each capacity 110 ml syrup,
5. Paracetamol tonic 1500000 bottles each capacity 110 ml bottles

TOTAL Rs. 1,67,00,000.00

PROFIT SALES RATIO = Profit / Sales x 100 = 8.26 %
RATE OF RETURN = Operating profit / T.C.I x 100 = 23.21 %
BREAK EVEN POINT (B.E.P) = 72.63 %

Chapter 24

Suppliers of Pharmaceutical Chemicals

Sri Krishna Drugs Ltd.
C-4, Indl. Area, Uppal
Hyderabad,
Andhra Pradesh-500039
India
TEL : +91 (0) 40 7201101
FAX : +91 (0) 40 7204470
E-mail:
skg@gnhyd.sk.group.global.net.in

Andhra Chemical Industries
B-63 & 64, APIE
Balanagar, Hyderabad,
Andhra Pradesh-500037
India
TEL : +91 (0) 40 3770625
FAX : +91 (0) 40 3771865

Arandy Laboratories Ltd.
6-3-1090/1/A, 2nd Flr.
Pancom Chmbrs.,
21,Somajiguda,
Hyderabad, Andhra
Pradesh-500082
India
TEL : +91 (0) 40 3311563
FAX : +91 (0) 40 3311517
E-mail:
arandy@hd2.vsnl.net.in

Bacto Chem Laboratories
14, 15, 14 A, IDA
Balanagar
Hyderabad, Andhra
Pradesh-500037
India
TEL : +91 (0) 40 3078690
FAX : +91 (0) 40 3078269
E-mail: itsvasu@hotmail.com

Chemtech Acids & Chemicals Pvt. Ltd.
Flat No. 119, Sanali
Heavens Apts.,
Nagarjuna Ngr.,Hyderabad,
Andhra Pradesh-500073
India
TEL : +91 (0) 40 3748372
FAX : +91 (0) 40 3748374
E-mail:
chemtechltd@yahoo.com

Dolphin Drugs Pvt. Ltd.
C 10, Madhura Ngr.
Hyderabad, Andhra
Pradesh-500038
India
TEL : +91 (0) 40 3732787
FAX : +91 (0) 40 3733816
E-mail:
bsgopal@hd1.vsnl.net.in

Ekasila Chemicals Ltd.
Plot No. 77
Road No. 1, IDA
Mallapur
Nacharam IE (PO)
Hyderabad, Andhra
Pradesh-500076
India
TEL : +91 (0) 40 7755457
FAX : +91 (0) 40 7752194
E-mail:
ekasilachem@yahoo.com

Focus Interchem Pvt. Ltd.
Plot No. 31, E C Extn.
ECIL (Post),
Kushaiguda
Hyderabad,
Andhra Pradesh-500062
India
TEL : +91 (0) 40 7120458
FAX : +91 (0) 40 7121353
E-mail:
sudhirl@hd1.vsnl.net.in

Godavari Drugs Ltd.
Mayfair, S P Rd.
Secunderabad,
Andhra Pradesh-500003
India
TEL : +91 (0) 40 7849700
FAX : +91 (0) 40 7849859
E-mail:
godavari@hd1.vsnl.net.in

Harika Drugs Pvt. Ltd.
36/A, Vengal Rao Ngr.
Hyderabad,
Andhra Pradesh-500038
India
TEL : +91 (0) 40 3700915
FAX : +91 (0) 40 3700731
E-mail:
amarbabu@hd1.vsnl.net.in

Anuja Impex Pvt. Ltd.
SCO 912, 1st Flr.
NAC, Manimajra
Chandigarh,
Chandigarh (UT)-160055
India
TEL : +91 (0) 172 735690
FAX : +91 (0) 172 735690
E-mail:
anuradha2000@glide.net.in

Surya Medicare Ltd.
110, Phase-I,
Indl. Area
Chandigarh,
Chandigarh (UT)-160002
India
TEL : +91 (0) 172 655166
FAX : +91 (0) 172 655377
E-mail:
surya.com@rme.sprintrpg.ems.vsnl.net.in

Surya Pharmaceuticals Ltd.
1232, Sector 18-C
Chandigarh,
Chandigarh (UT)-160018

India
TEL : +91 (0) 172 779635
FAX : +91 (0) 172 779639
E-mail:
sales@suryapharma.com

Ace Laboratories Ltd.
C-52, Phase-I
Okhla Indl. Area
New Delhi,
NCT of Delhi-110020
India
TEL : +91 (0) 11 6819192
FAX : +91 (0) 11 6811831
E-mail:
acelab@del.vsnl.net.in

Bharat Starch Industries Ltd.
N-75, Connaught Circus
New Delhi,
NCT of Delhi-110001
India
TEL : +91 (0) 11 3313195
FAX : +91 (0) 11 3325289
E-mail: bsil@nda.vsnl.net.in

Chemicals & Associates
27, Ashoka Chambers
Opp. Rachna Cinema,
5-B, Rajendra Park
Pusa Rd., New Delhi,
NCT of Delhi-110060
India
TEL : +91 (0) 11 5735151
FAX : +91 (0) 11 5755507
E-mail: chemika@vsnl.com

Daurala Sugar Works
A Divn. Of DCM Shriram Industries
Kanchenjunga Bldg.,
18, Barakhamba Rd.
New Delhi,
NCT of Delhi-110001
India
TEL : +91 (0) 11 3321413
FAX : +91 (0) 11 3315424
E-mail:
chemicalsud@dcmsr.com

Fanny Pharmaceuticals
105, UGF,
World Trade Centre
Barakhamba Lane
New Delhi,
NCT of Delhi-110001
India
TEL : +91 (0) 11 3317774
FAX : +91 (0) 11 3414774
E-mail: meditron@vsnl.net

Geoffrey Manners & Company Ltd.
Lakshmi Insurance Bldg.
Asaf Ali Rd.New Delhi,
NCT of Delhi-110002
India
TEL : +91 (0) 11 3238187
FAX : +91 (0) 11 3237176

Jagsonpal Pharmaceuticals Ltd.
T-210J, Shahpur Jat
New Delhi,
NCT of Delhi-110016
India
TEL : +91 (0) 11 6473708
FAX : +91 (0) 11 6213519

JG Works
B-1191, Phase-I
Okhla Indl. Area
New Delhi,
NCT of Delhi-110020
India
TEL : +91 (0) 11 6811719

Paam Pharmaceuticals (Delhi) Ltd.
13, Exchange Store Bldg.
Alipur Rd., Civil Lines
New Delhi,
NCT of Delhi-110054
India
TEL : +91 (0) 11 2918490
FAX : +91 (0) 11 2937857
E-mail:
paamco@del2.vsnl.net.in

Ranbaxy Laboratories Ltd.
19, Nehru Place
New Delhi,
NCT of Delhi-110019
India
TEL : +91 (0) 11 6415522
FAX : +91 (0) 11 3476288

Aico Agencies Pvt. Ltd.
75, Outside Raipur Gate
New Cloth Mkt.
Ahmedabad,
Gujarat-380002
India
TEL : +91 (0) 79 2166482
FAX : +91 (0) 79 2145207
E-mail: aico@ad1.vsnl.net.in

Balco Chemicals
859/4/D, GIDC
Makarpura Indl. Est.
Vadodara,
Gujarat-390017
India
TEL : +91 (0) 265 561275
FAX : +91 (0) 265 648102

Cadila Pharmaceuticals Ltd.
Bhat Village
Sharkhej-Dholka Rd.
Dholka, Ahmedabad,
Gujarat-382500
India
TEL : +91 (0) 79 3825001
FAX : +91 (0) 79 1

Dada Chemicals Ltd.
P.O. Box No.4
Nr. Chikhora Crossing
Chikhora, Ahmedabad,
Gujarat-388320
India
TEL : +91 (0) 79 24892
FAX : +91 (0) 79 41193

Elam Pharma Pvt. Ltd.
Plot No. 3709/4
B/h New Auto Telephone
Exch., GIDC Est.
Ankleshwar,
Gujarat-393002
India

TEL : +91 (0) 2646 21825

Gujarat Alkalies & Chemicals Ltd.
P.O. Petrochemicals
Vadodara, Gujarat-391346
India
TEL : +91 (0) 265 372681
FAX : +91 (0) 265 372130
E-mail:
nksachar@gujaratalkalies.com

Halcyon Labs Pvt. Ltd.
409, Phase-IV, GIDC Est.
Naroda Ahmedabad,
Gujarat-382330
India
TEL : +91 (0) 79 2811132

Indon Healthcare Ltd.
Cadila House, Drive-In Rd.
Ahmedabad,
Gujarat-380001
India
TEL : +91 (0) 79 7410861
FAX : +91 (0) 79 7410870

JS Chemicals
4801/A-8
GIDC Est.
Ankleshwar,
Gujarat-393002
India
TEL : +91 (0) 2646 51419
FAX : +91 (0) 2646 52663
E-mail:
jollyc8@narmada.net.in

Maruti Chemicals
15-16-17, 1st Flr.,
Yogeshwar Cmplx.
Nr. Sola Over Bridge
Approach, Gulab Tower Rd.
Thaltej
Ahmedabad,
Gujarat-380054
India
TEL : +91 (0) 79 7482072
FAX : +91 (0) 79 7482072
E-mail:
marutichem@icenet.net

Ind-Swift Laboratories Ltd.
No. 382, Sect. 6
Panchkula,
Haryana-134109
India
TEL : +91 (0) 172 550503
FAX : +91 (0) 172 550504
E-mail: isll@chl.vsnl.net.in

Anglo-French Drugs & Industries Ltd.
41, 3rd Cross, SSI Aera,
V Block, Rajaji Ngr.
Bangalore,
Karnataka-560010
India
TEL : +91 (0) 80 3356757
FAX : +91 (0) 80 3389963

Bal Pharma Ltd.
Ravi Kiran Apts.
12, Plain St., Bangalore,
Karnataka-560001
India
TEL : +91 (0) 80 2860394
FAX : +91 (0) 80 2867734
E-mail:
balpharm@blr.vsnl.net.in

Kemwell Ltd.
11, Tumkar Rd.
Yeshwanthpur
Bangalore,
Karnataka-560022
India
TEL : +91 (0) 80 3376724
FAX : +91 (0) 80 3379152

Micro Labs Ltd.
No. 3, Queens Rd.
Bangalore,
Karnataka-560001
India
TEL : +91 (0) 80 2269609
FAX : +91 (0) 80 2266323

Recon Ltd.
16/2, OVH Rd.
Basavanigudi
Bangalore,
Karnataka-560004
India
TEL : +91 (0) 80 6612792
FAX : +91 (0) 80 6522566
E-mail:
wintacltd@hotmail.com

Somu Organo-Chem Pvt. Ltd.
25, S G N Layout
Lalbagh Rd.
Bangalore,
Karnataka-560027
India
TEL : +91 (0) 80 2241085
FAX : +91 (0) 80 2235754
E-mail: somusols@vsnl.com

Superfine Aromatic Company Pvt. Ltd.
157, K Kamaraj Rd.
Bangalore,
Karnataka-560042
India
TEL : +91 (0) 80 5561144
FAX : +91 (0) 80 5560894

Suprajit Chemicals Pvt. Ltd.
No. 100
Bommasandra Indl. Area
Bangalore,
Karnataka-560158
India
TEL : +91 (0) 80 8422689
FAX : +91 (0) 80 8423279

GRD Chemicals Pvt. Ltd.
25 A/26-B, Sect. E
Sanwer Rd., Indl. Est.
Indore,
Madhya Pradesh-452003
India
TEL : +91 (0) 731 421933
FAX : +91 (0) 731 701905

Malwa Oxygen & Industrial Gases Pvt. Ltd.
Sect. 'C', Indl. Area
Ratlam,
Madhya Pradesh-457001
India

TEL : +91 (0) 7412 60840
FAX : +91 (0) 7412 60667
E-mail:
malwache@sanchrnet.in

Medilux Laboratories Pvt. Ltd.
201, B C Chmbrs.,
47, Jaora Compound
Indore,
Madhya Pradesh-452001
India
TEL : +91 (0) 731 702891
FAX : +91 (0) 731 463188
E-mail:
medilux@bom4.vsnl.net.in

Pan India Drugs & Chemicals Ltd.
415-416, Manas Bhawan,
11, RNT Marg
Indore,
Madhya Pradesh-452001
India
TEL : +91 (0) 731 512548
FAX : +91 (0) 731 521503
E-mail:
dhanshree@vsnl.com

Ava Chemicals Pvt. Ltd.
1/20 B, Narayan Plaza
26-A, Chandivli Rd.
Mumbai,
Maharashtra-400072
India
TEL : +91 (0) 22 8523955
FAX : +91 (0) 22 8525790
E-mail:
ava@bom2.vsnl.net.in

Multi Organics Pvt. Ltd.
503, Keshava
Bandra-Kurla Cmplx.
Bandra (E)
Mumbai,
Maharashtra-400051
India
TEL : +91 (0) 22 6590118
FAX : +91 (0) 22 6590358
E-mail:
mumbai@multiorganics.com

Nitika Chemicals
FO-05, Amarjyoti Palace
Wardha Rd.
Dhantoli, Nagpur,
Maharashtra-440012
India
TEL : +91 (0) 712 542870
FAX : +91 (0) 712 534055
E-mail:
nitika@nagpur.dot.net.ir

Aarti Drugs
Plot No. 109-D,
Mahendra Indl. Est.
Rd. No. 29, Sion East
Mumbai,
Maharashtra-400022
India
TEL : +91 (0) 22 4072249
FAX : +91 (0) 22 4073462
E-mail:
sales@aartidrugs.com

Alpha Bond Enterprise
202/5530
Amar Jyot, 3rd Flr.,
Opp. Odeon Cinema
90, Feet Rd., New Pant Ngr.
Ghatkopar (E)
Mumbai,
Maharashtra-400075
India
TEL : +91 (0) 22 5160195
FAX : +91 (0) 22 5106582

Amritlal Chemaux Ltd.
Rang Udyan, Sitla Devi Rd.
Mahim (W)
Mumbai,
Maharashtra-400016
India
TEL : +91 (0) 22 4449401
FAX : +91 (0) 22 4449059
E-mail: amritlalltd@vsnl.com

Bakul Aromatics & Chemicals Ltd.
Sterling Centre, 4th Flr.
16/2, Dr A B Rd., Worli
Mumbai,
Maharashtra-400018
India
TEL : +91 (0) 22 4934638
FAX : +91 (0) 22 4932623
E-mail: bakulin@vsnl.com

Camlin Ltd.
Camlin House, J B Ngr.
Andheri (E)
Mumbai,
Maharashtra-400059
India
TEL : +91 (0) 22 8360302
FAX : +91 (0) 22 8366579
E-mail: art@camlin.com

Deepak Nitrite Ltd.
A Deepak Group Of Industries Company
Deepak Cmplx.
National Games Rd.
Yerawada
Pune, Maharashtra-411006
India
TEL : +91 (0) 20 6689265
FAX : +91 (0) 20 6685448
E-mail:
export@deepaknitrite.com

Eagle Chemical Works
205, New Apollo Est.
Mogra Lane
Andheri (E)
Mumbai,
Maharashtra-400069
India
TEL : +91 (0) 22 8365699
FAX : +91 (0) 22 8218869
E-mail: eaglechem@vsnl.net

Fancy Industrial Corp.
405, Veena Chmbrs.
Clive Rd.,
Dana Bunder
Mumbai,
Maharashtra-400009
India
TEL : +91 (0) 22 3738244
FAX : +91 (0) 22 3738304
E-mail: fancy@vsnl.com

Ganesh Anhydride Ltd.
Ganesh House,
PMC Cmplx.
Andheri (E)
Mumbai,
Maharashtra-400059
India
TEL : +91 (0) 22 8502096
FAX : +91 (0) 22 8391529
E-mail: rkp1@vsnl.com

Ganesh Benzoplast Ltd.
Ganesh House
Off Andheri Kurla Rd.,
Marol Naka
Andheri (E)
Mumbai,
Maharashtra-400059
India
TEL : +91 (0) 22 8502096
FAX : +91 (0) 22 8504412
E-mail: rkp1@vsnl.com

Gitanjali Chemicals Pvt. Ltd.
Madhukunj
Shankar Ghanekar Marg
Prabhadevi
Mumbai,
Maharashtra-400025
India
TEL : +91 (0) 22 4370553
FAX : +91 (0) 22 2041255
E-mail:
gcpl@bom3.vsnl.net.in

Halides Chemicals Pvt. Ltd.
W-118, S-Blk., MIDC
Bhosari
Pune,
Maharashtra-411026
India
TEL : +91 (0) 20 7121774
FAX : +91 (0) 20 7121182
E-mail: aroon@vsnl.com

Hindustan Antibiotics Ltd.
Bombay-Pune Rd.
Pimpri
Pune,
Maharashtra-411018
India
TEL : +91 (0) 20 776511
FAX : +91 (0) 20 772327
E-mail:
hapune@pn3.vsnl.net.in

Interchemie
246/3-B, Mangaldas Bldg.
Mangaldas Rd.
Mumbai,
Maharashtra-400002
India
TEL : +91 (0) 22 2017409
FAX : +91 (0) 22 2064688
E-mail:
interchem@giasbmol.vsnl.net.in

Jaya Oil Fields Chemical Industries Pvt. Ltd.
Jaya Talkies Bldg.
S V Rd., Borivili (W)
Mumbai,
Maharashtra-400092
India
TEL : +91 (0) 22 8981134
FAX : +91 (0) 22 8985708
E-mail: viren@vsnl.com

Jovin Chemical Industries
4th Flr., 65, Kazi Sayed St.
Masjid
Mumbai,
Maharashtra-400003
India
TEL : +91 (0) 22 3415558
FAX : +91 (0) 22 3444413
E-mail: krunald@vsnl.com

Khatau Agrotech Ltd.
Khatau House
Mogul Lane, Mahim
Mumbai,
Maharashtra-400001
India
TEL : +91 (0) 22 4450050

Lupin Chemicals
CST Rd., Kalina
Santacruz (E)
Mumbai,
Maharashtra-400098
India
TEL : +91 (0) 22 6526122
FAX : +91 (0) 22 6119984

Lupin Ltd.
159, Kalina, CST Rd.
Santacruz (E)
Mumbai,
Maharashtra-400098
India
TEL : +91 (0) 22 6528311
FAX : +91 (0) 22 6114008

Metal Salts & Catalyst (I) Pvt. Ltd.
310/3, Jawahar Ngr.,
Rd. No. 16, Goregaon (W)
Mumbai,
Maharashtra-400062
India
TEL : +91 (0) 22 8730294
FAX : +91 (0) 22 8724940
E-mail: eastmen@vsnl.net.in

Natasha International
4-Bunglow, 162, Park St.
Andheri (W)
Mumbai,
Maharashtra-400053
India
TEL : +91 (0) 22 6313195
FAX : +91 (0) 22 6311395
E-mail: ninte@roltanet.com

Navnidh Pharma Lab.
Bharat House, 3rd Flr.,
104, Mumbai Samachar
Marg, Fort
Mumbai,
Maharashtra-400023
India
TEL : +91 (0) 22 2672356
FAX : +91 (0) 22 8510870

New Generic Drug House Ltd.
41, Damji Shamji Indl. Est.
LBS Marg, Vikhroli (W)
Mumbai,
Maharashtra-400083

India
TEL : +91 (0) 22 5771104
FAX : +91 (0) 22 5792358
E-mail:
ngdh@bom8.vsnl.net.in

Oceanic Laboratories Pvt. Ltd.
9, Nandini Krupa
Subhash Rd., Vile Parle (E)
Mumbai,
Maharashtra-400057
India
TEL : +91 (0) 22 8212833
FAX : +91 (0) 22 8369624
E-mail:
oceaniclabs@hotmail.com

Padarsh Pharmaceuticals Pvt. Ltd.
59-C, Maker Arcade
Cuffe Parade
Mumbai,
Maharashtra-400005
India
TEL : +91 (0) 22 2182424
FAX : +91 (0) 22 2189500
E-mail:
muneesh_chadda@vsnl.net

Pfizer Ltd.
Pfizer Centre, Patel Est.
Patel Estate Rd., Off S V Rd.
Jogeshwari (W)
Mumbai,
Maharashtra-400102
India
TEL : +91 (0) 22 6785511
FAX : +91 (0) 22 6781766

Quimica India A Divn. of Emtex Industries (I) Ltd.
413, G, 5th Flr., Basantwadi
Kalbadevi Rd.
Mumbai,
Maharashtra-400002
India
TEL : +91 (0) 22 2014745
FAX : +91 (0) 22 2032106
E-mail:
maliram@bom3.vsnl.net.in

Alpha Drug India Ltd.
Villages Kohlim Ajra &
Smalheri, Lalru,
Punjab-160019
India
TEL : +91 (0) 171 2779210
FAX : +91 (0) 171 2779308
E-mail:
alphadrug@alphadrug.co.in

Caliron Chemicals Pvt. Ltd.
5, Nirankari St., Miller Ganj
Ludhiana,
Punjab-141003
India
TEL : +91 (0) 161 534753
FAX : +91 (0) 161 533203

Himachal Pharmaceutical Industries
E-71, Focal Point
Ludhiana,
Punjab-141010
India
TEL : +91 (0) 161 671247
FAX : +91 (0) 161 671621

Sterling Chemicals
Patiala Rd.
Rajpura,
Punjab-140401
India
TEL : +91 (0) 1762 22316

Asian Organo Industries
E-79, IPIA
Kota,
Rajasthan-324005
India
TEL : +91 (0) 744 432276
FAX : +91 (0) 744 427109
E-mail:
domains24hrs@yahoo.com

Guljag Industries Ltd.
Nahata Bhawan
Chopasni Rd.
Jodhpur,
Rajasthan-342003
India
TEL : +91 (0) 291 435581
FAX : +91 (0) 291 435670
E-mail: guljag@jp1.dot.net.in

Mithila Drugs Laboratories
F-70, M I Area
Rd. No. 2, Udaipur,
Rajasthan-313001
India
TEL : +91 (0) 294 491271
FAX : +91 (0) 294 492780

Mittal Enterprises (Regd.)
E-81 (A)
Indraprastha Indl. Area
Kota, Rajasthan-324005
India
TEL : +91 (0) 744 425973
FAX : +91 (0) 744 500748
E-mail:
info@metalsoaps.com

Aktive Products
125, Amman Koil St.
Chennai,
Tamil Nadu-600079
India
TEL : +91 (0) 44 516627

Amrutanjan Ltd. Fine
Chemicals Divn.
42-45, Luz Church Rd.
Mylapore
Chennai,
Tamil Nadu-600004
India
TEL : +91 (0) 44 4994164
FAX : +91 (0) 44 4994585
E-mail:
finechem@md3.vsnl.net.in

Maruthi Industrial Carbohydrates Ltd.
9, Kasturba Ngr.
1st Cross St., Adyar
Chennai,
Tamil Nadu-600020
India
TEL : +91 (0) 44 4414419

FAX : +91 (0) 44 4414419
E-mail: marutilab@eth.net

Maruti Laboratories Pvt. Ltd.
Kasturba Ngr., 9
1st Cross St., Adyar
Chennai,
Tamil Nadu-600020
India
TEL : +91 (0) 44 4414419
FAX : +91 (0) 44 4414419
E-mail:
maruti.labs@elnet.ems.vsnl.net.in

Mohan Pharma
129, Nyniappa Naick St.
Chennai,
Tamil Nadu-600003
India
TEL : +91 (0) 44 5352758
FAX : +91 (0) 44 5354759
E-mail:
mohanpharma@satyam.net.in

Orchid Chemicals & Pharmaceuticals Ltd.
1, 6th Flr., Crown Court, 34
Cathedral Rd.
Chennai,
Tamil Nadu-600086
India
TEL : +91 (0) 44 8284776
FAX : +91 (0) 44 8284983

Advance Inorganics
B-6, Sect. I, Noida,
Uttar Pradesh-201301
India
TEL : +91 (0) 120 4542494
FAX : +91 (0) 120 4542494

Paras Chemical Industries
20/4, Maruti Towers
Telephone Exch. Lane
Sanjay Place
Agra,
Uttar Pradesh-282002
India
TEL : +91 (0) 562 351640
FAX : +91 (0) 562 351650
E-mail:
paras_chem@vsnl.com

Vam Organic Chemicals Ltd.
Plot No. 1-A,
Institutional Area,Sect. 16-A
Noida,
Uttar Pradesh-201301
India
TEL : +91 (0) 120 4516682
FAX : +91 (0) 120 4516627

Adcco Ltd.
11, Camac St.
Kolkata,
West Bengal-700017
India
TEL : +91 (0) 33 2827530
FAX : +91 (0) 33 2293187
E-mail:
pentex@cal2.vsnl.net.in

Bengal Chemicals & Pharmaceuticals Ltd.
6, Ganesh Chandra Avenue
Kolkata,
West Bengal-700013
India
TEL : +91 (0) 33 2259502
FAX : +91 (0) 33 2257697
E-mail:
bengchem@cal.vsnl.net.in

Bihani Chemical Industries Pvt. Ltd.
Stephen House,
Room No. 11, 1st Flr.
4, BBD Bagh (E)
Kolkata,
West Bengal-700001
India
TEL : +91 (0) 33 2104586
FAX : +91 (0) 33 4641530
E-mail:
bihanibm@cal.vsnl.net.in

Dey's Medical Stores (Manufacturing) Ltd.
3rd Flr., 17, Collin Lane
Kolkata,
West Bengal-700016
India
TEL : +91 (0) 33 2446107
FAX : +91 (0) 33 2452348

Rishi Chemical Works Pvt. Ltd.
56/1, Room No. D-23
BRB Basu Rd.
Kolkata,
West Bengal-700001
India
TEL : +91 (0) 33 2356153
FAX : +91 (0) 33 2255785
E-mail:
bharech@cal.vsnl.net.in

The Oriental Chemical Works Pvt. Ltd.
1/1B,Govinda Auddy Rd.
Chetla, Kolkata,
West Bengal-700027
India
TEL : +91 (0) 33 4799385
FAX : +91 (0) 33 4796723

Bihar Caustic & Chemicals Ltd.
A J.V. Of Aditya Birla Group
& Bihar SIDC
Ghanshyamkunj,
Garhwa Rd., P.O. Rehla
Palamau,
Jharkhand-822124
India
TEL : +91 (0) 6584 87221
FAX : +91 (0) 6584 87205

DRUG GLASSWARE

Jain Scientific Glass Works
2580/29
B/h S D Public School
Gian Marg
Ambala Cantt.,
Haryana-133001
India
TEL : +91 (0) 171 643090
FAX : +91 (0) 171 643246
E-mail: jsgw@sancharnet.in

The Popular Science
Apparatus Workshops
3724
Opp. Kalibari Mandir
Ambala Cantt.,
Haryana-133001
India
TEL : +91 (0) 171 641462
FAX : +91 (0) 171 641462
E-mail:
psawindia@satyam.net.in

Gujarat Glass Ltd.
A Piramal Enterprise
100, Centrepoint
Morarjee Mills Compound
Dr. Ambedkar Rd.
Parel, Mumbai,
Maharashtra-400012
India
TEL : +91 (0) 22 4134653
FAX : +91 (0) 22 4146006
E-mail:
gglass@bom3.vsnl.net.in

Ablaze Glass Works Pvt. Ltd.
E/52-2, Sardar Indl. Est.
Ajwa Rd., Vadodara,
Gujarat-390019
India
TEL : +91 (0) 265 561241
FAX : +91 (0) 265 564341
E-mail:
ablaze@satyam.net.in

Holy Scientific
C-2(6), 67/3
GIDC Est., Phase-I,
Nr. Manekchaw's Co-op.
Bank, Vatva
Ahmedabad,
Gujarat-382445
India
TEL : +91 (0) 79 5831006
FAX : +91 (0) 79 5834006
E-mail:
holuscientific@yahoo.com

Star Scientific Glass Co.
C-14 A, Sardar Est.
Ajwa Rd., Vadodara,
Gujarat-390019
India
TEL : +91 (0) 265 564159
FAX : +91 (0) 265 514417
E-mail:
info@starscientificindia.com

Chapter 25

Suppliers of Plant & Machineries

PHARMACEUTICAL MACHINERY

Vascon Engineering Equipments
C-31/1, Indl. Est.
(Nr. SBH, Opp. RMSC Stockyard)
Sanathnagar
Hyderabad,
Andhra Pradesh-500018
India
TEL : +91 (0) 40 3708586
FAX : +91 (0) 40 3708586
E-mail:
vasconengg@yahoo.com

Fine Fab Pvt. Ltd.
319, Amrutha Ville
Raj Bhavan Rd.
Somajiguda
Hyderabad,
Andhra Pradesh-500082
India
TEL : +91 (0) 40 3403050
FAX : +91 (0) 40 3313050

Premier Industrial Equipments Pvt. Ltd.
A-4
Yousufguda Rd.
Madhuranagar
Hyderabad, Andhra Pradesh-500038
India
TEL : +91 (0) 40 3736150
FAX : +91 (0) 40 3744822
E-mail:
metal.eqip@rmm.sprintrpg.ems.vsnl.net.in

Sneha Engg. Equipment Pvt. Ltd.
D-12, Phase-IV Extn.,
IDA, Jeedimetla
Hyderabad,
Andhra Pradesh-500055
India
TEL : +91 (0) 40 3096386
FAX : +91 (0) 40 3091065
E-mail:
chidkuri@hd2.vsnl.net.in

Sreenex Machines Pvt. Ltd.
2-1-460/1, Nallakunta
Hyderabad,
Andhra Pradesh-500001
India
TEL : +91 (0) 40 7662606
FAX : +91 (0) 40 7619475
E-mail:
sreenex@hd2.dot.net.in

Yen Plas Pvt. Ltd.
Shed No. 14 & 27
Nr. CIPET, IDA,
Phase-II, Cherlapally
Hyderabad,
Andhra Pradesh-500051
India
TEL : +91 (0) 40 7260851
FAX : +91 (0) 40 7264310
E-mail: info@yenplas.com

Propac Enterprises
B2C/23B, Janak Puri
New Delhi,
NCT of Delhi-110058
India
TEL : +91 (0) 11 5610240
FAX : +91 (0) 11 5550443
E-mail:
propac@del3.vsnl.net.in

Precious Fab-Cast Pvt. Ltd.
4809, Nr. Water Tank,
Phase-IV, GIDC, Vatva
Ahmedabad,
Gujarat-382445
India
TEL : +91 (0) 79 5842237
FAX : +91 (0) 79 5840026
E-mail:
precifab@yahoo.com

Balkrishna Boilers Inds.
Plot No. 14
Jay Khodiyar Indl. Est.
Nr. Subhash Est.
Ramol Rd.
Ahmedabad,
Gujarat-380026
India
TEL : +91 (0) 79 5855883
E-mail: info@balkrishn.com

Aahan Engineers Pvt. Ltd.
4906/15, GIDC Est.
Ankleshwar,
Gujarat-393002
India
TEL : +91 (0) 2646 21757
FAX : +91 (0) 2646 50719

Aaren Engineers Pvt. Ltd.
27/69, Opp. Govt. Press
Indl. Area
Faridabad,
Haryana-121001
India
TEL : +91 (0) 129 5237132
FAX : +91 (0) 129 5281812
E-mail:
aaren@del3.vsnl.net.in

Kishore & Co.
344, Udyog Vihar
Indl. Cmplx., Phase-II
Dundehera
Gurgaon,
Haryana-122016
India
TEL : +91 (0) 124 6340410
FAX : +91 (0) 124 6340615

E-mail:
kishoreb@nda.vsnl.net.in

Artech Engineering Works
23/B, Sect. A
Sanwer Rd., Indore,
Madhya Pradesh-452003
India
TEL : +91 (0) 731 247449
FAX : +91 (0) 731 421099
E-mail:
artechengg@rediffmail.com

Pharma Engg. Industries
146-B, 147-A
Sect. F, Indl. Area
Sanwer Rd., Indore,
Madhya Pradesh-452001
India
TEL : +91 (0) 731 721863
FAX : +91 (0) 731 721863

Kaps Engineers
Samraat Silk Mills
Compound
LBS Marg, Vikhroli (W)
Mumbai,
Maharashtra-400079
India
TEL : +91 (0) 22 5781933
FAX : +91 (0) 22 5785741
E-mail:
vmsrehls@bom4.vsnl.net.in

Aeolus Technovations Pvt. Ltd.
13/14, 'Avanti' 'B'
1st Flr., Above Rithik Hotel
Haridas Ngr., Shimpoli Rd.
Borivali (W)
Mumbai,
Maharashtra-400092
India
TEL : +91 (0) 22 8994582
FAX : +91 (0) 22 8994584
E-mail: aeolus@vsnl.com

BMT Industrial Machines Ltd.
15-16-17
Neelkanth Shopping Arcade,
1st Flr., Nr. Vijaya Bank,
R C Marg, Chembur
Mumbai,
Maharashtra-400071
India
TEL : +91 (0) 22 5288035
FAX : +91 (0) 22 5281136
E-mail:
bmt@bom2.vsnl.net.in

Bright India Enterprises
Sanjay Bldg. No. 5, A/9
Mittal Indl. Est.
Andheri Kural Rd.
Andheri (E)
Mumbai,
Maharashtra-400059
India
TEL : +91 (0) 22 8506097
FAX : +91 (0) 22 8502815

Chhaya Enterprises
C-14, Mohammed Ali Est.
Salim Compound,
Chimatpada, Marol Naka
Andheri (E)
Mumbai,
Maharashtra-400059
India
TEL : +91 (0) 22 8329259

Dabir Industries
Shed No. 11,Parag Indl. Est.
Pokhran Rd. No. 1, Upvan
Thane,
Maharashtra-400608
India
TEL : +91 (0) 22 5440524
FAX : +91 (0) 22 5440524
E-mail:
dabir_ind@rediffmail.com

Dhruv-Deep Engg.
Gala No. 35
Islam Compound, Opp.
Sanghvi Indl. Est.
Off M G Rd., Charkop
Kandivili (W)
Mumbai,
Maharashtra-400067
India
TEL : +91 (0) 22 8630544
FAX : +91 (0) 22 8679420
E-mail:
ddengg.vjp@bol.net.in

El-And-Bee Industries
189/3/5, Ganesh Ngr.
Rehmat Masjid Rd.,
Charkop Linking Rd.
Kandivli (W)
Mumbai,
Maharashtra-400067
India
TEL : +91 (0) 22 8620019
FAX : +91 (0) 22 8659672
E-mail:
elandbee@maharashtradirectory.com

Fit-Well Engg. Co.
Opp. Oswal Park
2nd Pokhran Rd.
Thane,
Maharashtra-400601
India
TEL : +91 (0) 22 5346436
FAX : +91 (0) 22 5333632
E-mail:
fitwell@bom3.vsnl.com

Gansons Engineers Pvt. Ltd.
Shantinagar Indl. Est.
Vakola, Santacruz (E)
Mumbai,
Maharashtra-400055
India
TEL : +91 (0) 22 5524548
FAX : +91 (0) 22 5526788

Gansons Ltd.
C-5/2, MIDC, Ambad
Nasik,
Maharashtra-422010
India
TEL : +91 (0) 253 383352
FAX : +91 (0) 253 382401

Indo German Pharmachem Equipments
Kothari House,
Plot No. A-13, St. No. 5,
MIDC Area, Marol

Andheri (E)
Mumbai,
Maharashtra-400093
India
TEL : +91 (0) 22 8323615
FAX : +91 (0) 22 8374426

Internet Macphar Pvt. Ltd.
49, Chandragupta Est.
New Link Rd.,
Andheri (W)
Mumbai,
Maharashtra-400053
India
TEL : +91 (0) 22 6331650
FAX : +91 (0) 22 6317872

Jaico Metals
Mathuradas Mill Compound
Lower Parel,
Mumbai, Maharashtra-400013
India
TEL : +91 (0) 22 4923259
FAX : +91 (0) 22 4943409
E-mail:
vshah@bom4.vsnl.net.in

Kalina Engg. Pvt. Ltd.
34, Suryakirti Indl. Est.,
Chinchpada, Gokhiware
Vasai,
Maharashtra-401208
India
TEL : +91 (0) 250 453212
FAX : +91 (0) 250 8165840
E-mail:
kalinaengg@maharashtradirectory.com

Kothari Pharma
C-11, M K Brothers Indl. Est., Jarimari
Andheri-Kurla Rd.
Andheri (E)
Mumbai,
Maharashtra-400072
India
TEL : +91 (0) 22 8510837
FAX : +91 (0) 22 8513584
E-mail:
chandrakant@kothariapharma.com

Dhiman Engineers (Regd.)
Dakhni Gate
Nakodar, Punjab-144040
India
TEL : +91 (0) 1821 20300
FAX : +91 (0) 1821 22300
E-mail:
dhiman@jla.vsnl.net.in

Trover Pharmamach (Regd.)
6214, Kapurthala Rd.
Nakodar, Punjab-144040
India
TEL : +91 (0) 1821 20318
FAX : +91 (0) 1821 23599
E-mail:
sanjeev@troverindia.com

Doris (India) Engineers Pvt. Ltd.
No. 389, 390, Arcot Rd.
Kodambakkam
Chennai,
Tamil Nadu-600024
India
TEL : +91 (0) 44 4801098
FAX : +91 (0) 44 4815652
E-mail:
machines@dorisindia.com

Alpha Process Engineers
312/2/5, Nehru Ngr.
Kottivakkam
Chennai,
Tamil Nadu-600041
India
TEL : +91 (0) 44 4925294
FAX : +91 (0) 44 8283122
E-mail: apeepa@vsnl.com

The Royal Scientific Industries
TS-74A, SIDCO Indl. Est.
Ekkattuthangal
Chennai,
Tamil Nadu-600097
India
TEL : +91 (0) 44 2324749
FAX : +91 (0) 44 4831748

Sharp Engineering Corporation
A-17, B/h Shiva Scooter Agency
Meerut Indl. Area
New Arya Ngr.
Ghaziabad,
Uttar Pradesh-201003
India
TEL : +91 (0) 120 4720290
FAX : +91 (0) 120 4719024
E-mail:
sharpec@satyam.net.in

Hindustan Pharmaceutical Equipments Co.
49, B T Rd.
Narendra Ngr.
Kolkata,
West Bengal-700056
India
TEL : +91 (0) 33 5532701
FAX : +91 (0) 33 5531436
E-mail:
hinphar@cal.vsnl.net.in

Pasteur Engg. Company Pvt. Ltd.
15/8/A, The Mall
Dum Dum
Kolkata,
West Bengal-700080
India
TEL : +91 (0) 33 5593015
FAX : +91 (0) 33 5593015

Pharma-Mach
10, Chaulpatty Rd.
Beliaghata
Kolkata,
West Bengal-700010
India
TEL : +91 (0) 33 3502567
FAX : +91 (0) 33 4756187

Sunita Impex Pvt. Ltd.
36-A, Bentinck St.
Kolkata,
West Bengal-700069
India
TEL : +91 (0) 33 2481986

FAX : +91 (0) 33 2483664
E-mail:
sunita.impex@gems.vsnl.net.in

PHARMACEUTICAL MIXERS

Enfab Industries Pvt. Ltd.
C-2, Shanthi Niwas
Mettuguda
Secunderabad,
Andhra Pradesh-500017
India
TEL : +91 (0) 40 7824343
FAX : +91 (0) 40 7830010
E-mail:
enfabs@hd1.vsnl.net.in

Anand Reinforced Systems
Plot No. 44, IDA,
Opp. BEL
Mallapur, Hyderabad,
Andhra Pradesh-501507
India
TEL : +91 (0) 40 7157316
FAX : +91 (0) 40 7159618
E-mail:
ars26@rediffmail.com

Dhopeshwar Engineering Pvt. Ltd.
A-16, CIE, Balanagar
Hyderabad,
Andhra Pradesh-500037
India
TEL : +91 (0) 40 3771579
FAX : +91 (0) 40 3772450
E-mail:
dhopesh@hd2.dot.net.in

Karamson Engineering Corporation
3/24, Kirti Ngr. Indl. Area
New Delhi,
NCT of Delhi-110015
India
TEL : +91 (0) 11 5417621
FAX : +91 (0) 11 5433577
E-mail: kencor@sify.com

Rank & Co.
A-95/3, Wazirpur Indl. Est.
Delhi,
NCT of Delhi-110052
India
TEL : +91 (0) 11 7456101
FAX : +91 (0) 11 7234126
E-mail:
vkmrank@del3.vsnl.net.in

Sukriti Engineers Pvt. Ltd.
55, Phase-I, DSIDC
Okhla Indl. Area
New Delhi,
NCT of Delhi-110020
India
TEL : +91 (0) 11 6817546
FAX : +91 (0) 11 6821812

Techmac Engg. Works
325, Usha Kiran Bldg.
Azadpur, Delhi,
NCT of Delhi-110033
India
TEL : +91 (0) 11 7137027
FAX : +91 (0) 11 7137027
E-mail:
techmac@mantraonline.com

Kevin Engineering Pvt. Ltd.
A/1/3706, GIDC, Phase-IV
Vatva, Ahmedabad,
Gujarat-382445
India
TEL : +91 (0) 79 5841503
FAX : +91 (0) 79 5841243
E-mail: info@kevinindia.com

Mecon Engineering
Opp. IIM
Bannerghatta Rd.
Bangalore,
Karnataka-560076
India
TEL : +91 (0) 80 6581217
FAX : +91 (0) 80 6580614
E-mail: kanal@vsnl.net

Molly Enterprises
Major Indl. Est., Ollur
Thrissur,
Kerala-680306
India
TEL : +91 (0) 487 352446

Arihant Engineering Works
124, Guru Nanak
Timber Mkt., Dhar Rd.
Indore,
Madhya Pradesh-452002
India
TEL : +91 (0) 731 380535
FAX : +91 (0) 731 380537
E-mail:
arihantengineering@epatra.com

Pharmaceutical Machinery Manufacturing Works
47/B, Laxmibai Ngr.
Indore,
Madhya Pradesh-452006
India
TEL : +91 (0) 731 410963
FAX : +91 (0) 731 410071
E-mail:
pharmamach@satyam.net.in

Hindustan Equipment Craft
D-74, MIDC Indl. Est.
Hingna Rd., Nagpur,
Maharashtra-440028
India
TEL : +91 (0) 7104 37742
FAX : +91 (0) 7104 37740
E-mail:
hecraft@nagpur.dot.net.in

Bright Pharma Machinery
37-A, New Empire Indl. Est.
Kondivita Rd., J B Ngr.
Andheri (W)
Mumbai,
Maharashtra-400059
India
TEL : +91 (0) 22 8214341
FAX : +91 (0) 22 8210190
E-mail:
brightpharma@hotmail.com

Adam Fabriwerk Pvt. Ltd.
203, Rajguru Apts.
New Nagardas Rd.
Andheri (E)
Mumbai,
Maharashtra-400069
India
TEL : +91 (0) 22 8380548
FAX : +91 (0) 22 8390195
E-mail: adamfab@vsnl.com

Associated Technocrats
R-423, TTC Indl. Area
Thane-Belapur Rd.
Rabale
Navi Mumbai,
Maharashtra-400701
India
TEL : +91 (0) 22 7691617
FAX : +91 (0) 22 7691954

Grovers International
3, F4, Shankardham
Sundervan Cmplx.
Off Lokhandwala Cmplx.
Rd.
Andheri (W)
Mumbai,
Maharashtra-400059
India
TEL : +91 (0) 22 6313092
FAX : +91 (0) 22 6313014
E-mail:
OFFICE@groversequip.com

Kothari Pharma
C-11
M K Brothers Indl. Est.,
Jarimari
Andheri-Kurla Rd.
Andheri (E)
Mumbai,
Maharashtra-400072
India
TEL : +91 (0) 22 8510837
FAX : +91 (0) 22 8513584
E-mail:
chandrakant@kothariapharma.com

Paresh Engg. Co.
74-B, Sanjay Bldg. No.5
Mittal Indl. Est., Marol Naka
M V Rd.
Andheri (E)
Mumbai,
Maharashtra-400059
India
TEL : +91 (0) 22 8501794
FAX : +91 (0) 22 8509193
E-mail:
pecmarol@vsnl.net.in

Rama Pharma Process Engineers
A/3, Amdekar Ngr.
G D Ambekar Rd.
Parel, Mumbai,
Maharashtra-400012
India
TEL : +91 (0) 22 4160983
FAX : +91 (0) 22 4149754
E-mail:
rampharm@bom5.vsnl.net.in

Dhiman Udyog
6026, Opp. Residence
(S. Gurbachan Singh
Dhiman)
Nr. Dakhni Gate
Nakodar,
Punjab-144040
India
TEL : +91 (0) 1821 20891
FAX : +91 (0) 1821 22891

Trover Pharmamach (Regd.)
6214, Kapurthala Rd.
Nakodar,
Punjab-144040
India
TEL : +91 (0) 1821 20318
FAX : +91 (0) 1821 23599
E-mail:
sanjeev@troverindia.com

Chetan Enterprise
No. 6, Nehru Ngr.
Old Mahabalipuram Rd.
Kottivakkam
Chennai,
Tamil Nadu-600041
India
TEL : +91 (0) 44 4925547
FAX : +91 (0) 44 4925030
E-mail:
dhaman_a@hotmail.com

Raviraj Industries
W450, New No. 11
4th St., Anna Ngr. West
Extn.
Chennai,
Tamil Nadu-600101
India
TEL : +91 (0) 44 6250894
FAX : +91 (0) 44 6252865
E-mail: rajshree1@vsnl.com

Iyappan Engg. Industries Pvt. Ltd.
107-A. SIDCO Indl. Est.
Ambattur
Chennai,
Tamil Nadu-600098
India
TEL : +91 (0) 44 6252073
FAX : +91 (0) 44 6250192
E-mail: iyappan@vsnl.com

Seba Engineers Pvt. Ltd.
D-26, Indl. Area
Bulandshahr Rd.
Ghaziabad,
Uttar Pradesh-201009
India
TEL : +91 (0) 120 4703703
FAX : +91 (0) 120 4703703

Advance Equipment
B-18, Sect.7
Noida,
Uttar Pradesh-201301
India
TEL : +91 (0) 120 4545560
FAX : +91 (0) 120 4535160
E-mail:
meera@del3.vsnl.net.in

Neomachine Mfg. Company Pvt. Ltd.
39/2A, Purna Das Rd.
Kolkata,

West Bengal-700029
India
TEL : +91 (0) 33 4644568
FAX : +91 (0) 33 4647254
E-mail:
neocota@satyam.net.in

Precision Balance (I)
6, Wood St.
Kolkata,
West Bengal-700016
India
TEL : +91 (0) 33 2403476
FAX : +91 (0) 33 2402427

PHARMACEUTICAL OVENS

Sreenex Machines Pvt. Ltd.
2-1-460/1, Nallakunta
Hyderabad,
Andhra Pradesh-500001
India
TEL : +91 (0) 40 7662606
FAX : +91 (0) 40 7619475
E-mail:
sreenex@hd2.dot.net.in

Karamson Engineering Corporation
3/24, Kirti Ngr. Indl. Area
New Delhi,
NCT of Delhi-110015
India
TEL : +91 (0) 11 5417621
FAX : +91 (0) 11 5433577
E-mail: kencor@sify.com

SMID Engineering Co.
25-A
Rama Park Bus Stop,
Nr. Medicine Factory
Uttam Ngr.
New Delhi,
NCT of Delhi-110059
India
TEL : +91 (0) 11 2351450
FAX : +91 (0) 11 5649879

Cadmach Machinery Company Pvt. Ltd.
3604 & 3605
GIDC Indl. Est., Phase-IV
Vatva
Ahmedabad,
Gujarat-382445
India
TEL : +91 (0) 79 5831491
FAX : +91 (0) 79 5842602
E-mail:
cadmach@ndl.vsnl.net.in

Infra Control Systems
B-7, Sahyog Soc.
Refinery Rd., Gorwa
Vadodara,
Gujarat-390016
India
TEL : +91 (0) 265 387826
FAX : +91 (0) 265 387723
E-mail: infra@bnpl.com

Karnavati Engineering Ltd.
S. No. 342, Nani Kadi
Taluka-Kadi
Mehsana,
Gujarat-382715
India
TEL : +91 (0) 2764 62463
FAX : +91 (0) 2764 42608
E-mail:
karnavati@wilnetonline.net

Febchem Engineering Works
Plot No. A/2
Sect. A, Indl. Area
Sanwer Rd.
Indore,
Madhya Pradesh-452003
India
TEL : +91 (0) 731 720467
FAX : +91 (0) 731 723087
E-mail:
febchem@yahoo.com

AMI Industries
8, Surve Indl. Est.
1st Sonawala Cross Rd.
Goregaon (E)
Mumbai,
Maharashtra-400063
India
TEL : +91 (0) 22 8727120
FAX : +91 (0) 22 8734753
E-mail:
oven@bom5.vsnl.net.in

Saiman Engineers Pvt. Ltd.
D/3, Hari Bhakti Indl. Est.
Old Ghod Bunder Rd.
P.O. Mira
Thane,
Maharashtra-401104
India
TEL : +91 (0) 22 8458206
FAX : +91 (0) 22 8458466
E-mail:
saimanengg@hotmail.com

Grovers International
3, F4, Shankardham
Sundervan Cmplx.
Off Lokhandwala Cmplx. Rd.
Andheri (W)
Mumbai,
Maharashtra-400059
India
TEL : +91 (0) 22 6313092
FAX : +91 (0) 22 6313014
E-mail:
OFFICE@groversequip.com

Indlab Equipment Corp.
403, Binu Apt., 4th Flr.
Section 25
B/h Venus Cinema
Ulhasnagar,
Maharashtra-421004
India
TEL : +91 (0) 251 534246
FAX : +91 (0) 251 524685
E-mail: indlab@hotmail.com

Lab Control Equipment Co.
B/50, Akurli Indl. Est.
Akurli Rd., Kandivali (E)

Mumbai,
Maharashtra-400101
India
TEL : +91 (0) 22 8874328
FAX : +91 (0) 22 8864948
E-mail:
lab_mumbai@yahoo.co.in

Malhotras Bombay Engg. Works
116, Gambhir Indl. Est.
Off Aarey Rd.,
Goregaon (E)
Mumbai,
Maharashtra-400063
India
TEL : +91 (0) 22 8754383
FAX : +91 (0) 22 8749142
E-mail:
bomengg@bom3.vsnl.net.in

Ravi Industries
B/17, Adke Compound
Surya Ngr., Opp. Western
Paper Mill, LBS Marg
Vikhroli (W)
Mumbai,
Maharashtra-400083
India
TEL : +91 (0) 22 5776356
FAX : +91 (0) 22 5776356
E-mail:
sales@ravipharma.com

Shirsat Electronics
133, Dewan Indl. Est.
No. 6, Navghar
Vasai (East)
Thane,
Maharashtra-401210
India
TEL : +91 (0) 22 392946
FAX : +91 (0) 22 390793
E-mail: sakav@vsnl.com

Tempo Instruments & Equipments (I) Pvt. Ltd.
1, Lamington Chmbrs.,
394, Dr. Bhadkamkar Marg
Mumbai,
Maharashtra-400004
India
TEL : +91 (0) 22 3855674
FAX : +91 (0) 22 3855708
E-mail: tempo@vsnl.com

The Bombay Engg. Works
1, Navyug Indl. Est.
T J Rd., Sewree (W)
Mumbai,
Maharashtra-400015
India
TEL : +91 (0) 22 4137094
FAX : +91 (0) 22 4135828
E-mail:
bomeng@bom3.vsnl.net.in

Thermex Industrial & Laboratory Instrument Co.
113, Satyam Indl. Est.
Govandi Stn. Rd.
Deonar
Mumbai,
Maharashtra-400088
India
TEL : +91 (0) 22 5512070
FAX : +91 (0) 22 5584519

Unique Mixers & Furnaces Pvt. Ltd.
Plot No.B-95, MIDC
Rd. No.27
Wagle Indl. Est.
Thane,
Maharashtra-400604
India
TEL : +91 (0) 22 5820172
FAX : +91 (0) 22 5820992

Gambaks Instruments Co.
5 Brindavan Ngr.
Door No. 20,
Venkateswara Ngr.
Main Rd.
Valasaravakkam
Chennai,
Tamil Nadu-600087
India
TEL : +91 (0) 44 4869541
FAX : +91 (0) 44 4867044
E-mail:
gambaks@md3.vsnl.net.in

Precision Balance (I)
6, Wood St.
Kolkata,
West Bengal-700016
India
TEL : +91 (0) 33 2403476
FAX : +91 (0) 33 2402427

The Wesman Engg. Company Ltd.
"Wesman Center",
8, Mayfair Rd.
Kolkata,
West Bengal-700019
India
TEL : +91 (0) 33 2405320
FAX : +91 (0) 33 2478050
E-mail:
mailbox@wesman.com

PHARMACEUTICALS STILLS

Dipesh Engineering Works
3, Sheroo Villa
87, J P Rd.
Andheri (W)
Mumbai,
Maharashtra-400053
India
TEL : +91 (0) 22 6336729
FAX : +91 (0) 22 6315507
E-mail:
kjpatel_71@hotmail.com

Pragati Engineering Works
Plot No. 114
New Chikhloli, MIDC
Ambernath,
Maharashtra-421505
India
TEL : +91 (0) 251 687407
FAX : +91 (0) 251 685054
E-mail:
shantaflaker@vsnl.com

Febchem Engineering Works
Plot No. A/2
Sect. A, Indl. Area
Sanwer Rd.
Indore,
Madhya Pradesh-452003
India
TEL : +91 (0) 731 720467
FAX : +91 (0) 731 723087
E-mail:
febchem@yahoo.com

PHARMACEUTICAL TESTERS

Bright Pharma Machinery
37-A
New Empire Indl. Est.
Kondivita Rd., J B Ngr.
Andheri (W)
Mumbai,
Maharashtra-400059
India
TEL : +91 (0) 22 8214341
FAX : +91 (0) 22 8210190
E-mail:
brightpharma@hotmail.com

Electrolab
401, Tirupati Indl. Est.
I B Patel Rd., W E Highway
Goregaon (E)
Mumbai,
Maharashtra-400063
India
TEL : +91 (0) 22 6904080
FAX : +91 (0) 22 6904083
E-mail: electrolab@vsnl.com

Indlab Equipment Corp.
403, Binu Apt., 4th Flr.
Section 25
B/h Venus Cinema
Ulhasnagar,
Maharashtra-421004
India
TEL : +91 (0) 251 534246
FAX : +91 (0) 251 524685
E-mail: indlab@hotmail.com

JR Industrial Corp.
Osworld House
Ramkrishna Mandir Rd.
Kondivita
Andheri (E)
Mumbai,
Maharashtra-400059
India
TEL : +91 (0) 22 8320880
FAX : +91 (0) 22 8390487
E-mail: osworld@vsnl.com

Polyplast Equipments & Accessories
104, KK Gupta Indl. Est.
Dr. RP Rd.
Mulund (W)
Mumbai, Maharashtra-400080
India
TEL : +91 (0) 22 5617126
FAX : +91 (0) 22 5649567
E-mail:
mercaso@bom7.vsnl.net.in

TABLET MACHINERY

Kelleys Engg. Works
24-B/6 Indl. Area
Faridabad,
Haryana-121001
India
TEL : +91 (0) 129 5233251
FAX : +91 (0) 129 5233251
E-mail: kelleysvib@usa.net

Septu (India) Pvt. Ltd.
"Septu House", 12/7
P.O. Box 4
Urban Est., Gurgaon,
Haryana-122001
India
TEL : +91 (0) 124 6373010
FAX : +91 (0) 124 6322997
E-mail:
septu@del3.vsnl.net.in

Pharmaceutical Machinery Manufacturing Works
47/B, Laxmibai Ngr.
Indore,
Madhya Pradesh-452006
India
TEL : +91 (0) 731 410963
FAX : +91 (0) 731 410071
E-mail:
pharmamach@satyam.net.in

Precision Gears (Indore) Pvt. Ltd.
8, Indl. Area, Laxmibai Ngr.
Indore,
Madhya Pradesh-452006
India
TEL : +91 (0) 731 224070
FAX : +91 (0) 731 413445
E-mail:
pglind@bom4.vsnl.net.in

Bright Pharma Machinery
37-A, New Empire Indl. Est.
Kondivita Rd., J B Ngr.
Andheri (W)
Mumbai,
Maharashtra-400059
India
TEL : +91 (0) 22 8214341
FAX : +91 (0) 22 8210190
E-mail:
brightpharma@hotmail.com

Gaylord Engineers
Opp. Chandi Karkhana
Mogra, Amboli Phatak
Andheri (E)
Mumbai,
Maharashtra-400069
India
TEL : +91 (0) 22 8200093
FAX : +91 (0) 22 8216032
E-mail:
gaylord@bom8.vsnl.net.in

Indo-German Pharma Pvt. Ltd.
Plot No. A-13,
Kothari House
Off Cross Rd. B, MIDC
St. No. 5, Andheri (E)
Mumbai,
Maharashtra-400093
India

TEL : +91 (0) 22 8323615
FAX : +91 (0) 22 8374426
E-mail:
indogmbh@bom3.vsnl.net.in

Kamal Export Industries
Datta Bhavan
Kashinath Dhuru Rd.
Dadar (W), Mumbai,
Maharashtra-400028
India
TEL : +91 (0) 22 4221555
FAX : +91 (0) 22 4373474
E-mail: kei@vsnl.com

Leoscor Exports
3 & 19, Ashok Indl. Est.
L B S Marg
Mulund (W)
Mumbai,
Maharashtra-400080
India
TEL : +91 (0) 22 5612165
FAX : +91 (0) 22 5685241
E-mail:
magnus@bom2.vsnl.net.in

Misido Pharma Machinery
B/2, Sahyadri Soc.,
Lallubhai Park, Rd. No. 2
Andheri (W)
Mumbai,
Maharashtra-400058
India
TEL : +91 (0) 22 6282330
FAX : +91 (0) 22 8151592

Pharmachine India
103
Hindustan Kohinoor Cmplx.
LBS Marg, Vikhroli (W)
Mumbai,
Maharashtra-400082
India
TEL : +91 (0) 22 8408789
FAX : +91 (0) 22 8408018
E-mail:
pharmchn@giasbm01.vsnl.net.in

Precision Gears Ltd.
G-1, Everest Apts.
156, Tardeo
Mumbai,
Maharashtra-400038
India
TEL : +91 (0) 22 4949196
FAX : +91 (0) 22 4950592
E-mail:
sales@precisiongears-ima.com

Rama Pharma Process Engineers
A/3, Amdekar Ngr.
G D Ambekar Rd., Parel
Mumbai,
Maharashtra-400012
India
TEL : +91 (0) 22 4160983
FAX : +91 (0) 22 4149754
E-mail:
rampharm@bom5.vsnl.net.in

Dhiman Udyog
6026, Opp. Residence
(S. Gurbachan Singh Dhiman)
Nr. Dakhni Gate
Nakodar, Punjab-144040
India
TEL : +91 (0) 1821 20891
FAX : +91 (0) 1821 22891

Trover Pharmamach (Regd.)
6214, Kapurthala Rd.
Nakodar, Punjab-144040
India
TEL : +91 (0) 1821 20318
FAX : +91 (0) 1821 23599
E-mail:
sanjeev@troverindia.com

Modern India Machine Tools Pvt. Ltd.
18/1/6, Canal West Rd.
Kolkata,
West Bengal-700009
India
TEL : +91 (0) 33 3504395
FAX : +91 (0) 33 2484840
E-mail:
oriental1919@yahoo.com

National Engg Industries Ltd.
2/2
Shashi Bhusan Basak Lane
Kolkata,
West Bengal-700036
India
TEL : +91 (0) 33 5578652
FAX : +91 (0) 33 5288458
E-mail:
neiupmt@yahoo.com

Neo Machine Manufacturing Company Pvt. Ltd.
39/2A
Purna Das Rd.
Kolkata,
West Bengal-700029
India
TEL : +91 (0) 33 4647253
FAX : +91 (0) 33 4647254

Aalmach Machinery
L/4103/2, Phase-IV, GIDC
Vatva, Ahmedabad,
Gujarat-382445
India
TEL : +91 (0) 79 5833034
FAX : +91 (0) 79 5833034
E-mail:
aalmach@yahoo.com

Bright Sun Pharma Machinery
B-3
Jayshree Shesh Est.,
Narayan Ngr., Bapu Ngr.
Ahmedabad,
Gujarat-380024
India
TEL : +91 (0) 79 2891028
FAX : +91 (0) 79 2726158

CAPSULE FILLING MACHINERY

Chemac Equipments Pvt. Ltd.
M J D'Souza Compound
Safed Pool, Sakinaka
Mumbai,
Maharashtra-400072
India
TEL : +91 (0) 22 8510777
FAX : +91 (0) 22 8516986
E-mail:
chemac@bom4.vsnl.net.in

Techmac Engg. Works
325, Usha Kiran Bldg.
Azadpur, Delhi,
NCT of Delhi-110033
India
TEL : +91 (0) 11 7137027
FAX : +91 (0) 11 7137027
E-mail:
techmac@mantraonline.com

Meta Photo Manufacturing Co.
Plot No. 15
GIDC, Nr. CMC, Odhav Rd.
Ahmedabad,
Gujarat-382415
India
TEL : +91 (0) 79 2872798
FAX : +91 (0) 79 2871814
E-mail:
metaphoto@rediffmail.com

Reva Pharma Machinery
Plot No. 492/4
GIDC, Makarpura
Vadodara,
Gujarat-390010
India
TEL : +91 (0) 265 640082

Riddhi Pharma Machinery Ltd.
2, Riddhi Est.,
B/h Manish Est.
Gulab Ngr., Amraiwadi
Ahmedabad,
Gujarat-380026
India
TEL : +91 (0) 79 2740683
FAX : +91 (0) 79 2740737

Septu (India) Pvt. Ltd.
"Septu House", 12/7
P.O. Box 4, Urban Est.
Gurgaon, Haryana-122001
India
TEL : +91 (0) 124 6373010
FAX : +91 (0) 124 6322997
E-mail:
septu@del3.vsnl.net.in

Bright Pharma Machinery
37-A, New Empire Indl. Est.
Kondivita Rd., J B Ngr.
Andheri (W)
Mumbai,
Maharashtra-400059
India
TEL : +91 (0) 22 8214341
FAX : +91 (0) 22 8210190
E-mail:
brightpharma@hotmail.com

Tooltronics
C-6, Udyog Sadan No. 1,
MIDC, Marol
Andheri (E)
Mumbai,
Maharashtra-400093
India
TEL : +91 (0) 22 8327148
FAX : +91 (0) 22 8365026
E-mail: ttarbes@vsnl.com

Alps Containers Pvt. Ltd.
Plot No. 16-B
Govt. Indl. Est.
Kandivali (W), Mumbai,
Maharashtra-400067
India
TEL : +91 (0) 22 8689522
FAX : +91 (0) 22 8670891
E-mail:
shobi@indiatimes.com

Apex Electromec Pharma Pvt. Ltd.
8, Hare Rama Hare Krishna
Indl. Est., I B Patel Rd.
Goregaon(E)
Mumbai,
Maharashtra-400063
India
TEL : +91 (0) 22 8960263
FAX : +91 (0) 22 8116196
E-mail:
apexin@bom2.vsnl.net.in

Automatic Devices
105 A
Hind Saurashtra Indl. Est.,
Marol
Andheri-Kurla Rd.
Andheri (E)
Mumbai,
Maharashtra-400059
India
TEL : +91 (0) 22 8501376
FAX : +91 (0) 22 8593042
E-mail:
autodevices@vsnl.com

Kamal Export Industries
Datta Bhavan
Kashinath Dhuru Rd.
Dadar (W)
Mumbai,
Maharashtra-400028
India
TEL : +91 (0) 22 4221555
FAX : +91 (0) 22 4373474
E-mail: kei@vsnl.com

Magnose Engineering Co.
Gali No. 3 & 19
Ashok Indl. Est.
LBS Marg, Mulund (W)
Mumbai,
Maharashtra-400080
India
TEL : +91 (0) 22 5612165
FAX : +91 (0) 22 5914218

Pam Pharmaceutical & Allied Machinery Company Ltd.
127, Kandivli Indl. Est.
Kandivli (W)
Mumbai,

Maharashtra-400067
India
TEL : +91 (0) 22 8682650
FAX : +91 (0) 22 8683091
E-mail:
pam.ppamc@gems.vsnl.net.in

Precision Gears Ltd.
G-1, Everest Apts.
156, Tardeo
Mumbai,
Maharashtra-400038
India
TEL : +91 (0) 22 4949196
FAX : +91 (0) 22 4950592
E-mail:
sales@precisiongears-ima.com

Ravi-Kiran Industries
213, Mittal Indl. Est. No-2,
Marol Naka,
Andheri (E)
Mumbai,
Maharashtra-400059
India
TEL : +91 (0) 22 8506569
FAX : +91 (0) 22 8506135
E-mail: ravikiran@vsnl.com

Sagar Pharma Industries
Unit No. 34, Ground Flr.
Akshay Indl. Est.,
Navghar Village,
Vasai (E)
Thane,
Maharashtra-401210
India
TEL : +91 (0) 250 391202
FAX : +91 (0) 250 390207

Softesule Ltd.
86-A, LBS Marg
Mulund (W)
Mumbai,
Maharashtra-400080
India
TEL : +91 (0) 22 5601202
FAX : +91 (0) 22 5646276
E-mail:
softesul@bom3.vsnl.net.in

Sri Rudran Instruments Co.
56, Vaikundapuram 2nd St.
Nungambakkam
Chennai,
Tamil Nadu-600034
India
TEL : +91 (0) 44 8172803
FAX : +91 (0) 44 8175843
E-mail: srico@satyam.net.in

Sharp Engineering Corporation
A-17, B/h Shiva Scooter Agency
Meerut Indl. Area
New Arya Ngr.
Ghaziabad,
Uttar Pradesh-201003
India
TEL : +91 (0) 120 4720290
FAX : +91 (0) 120 4719024
E-mail:
sharpec@satyam.net.in

SYRUP MACHINERY

Capco Engg. Pvt. Ltd.
2-27-16, Gokul St.
Srinagar
Kakinada,
Andhra Pradesh-533005
India
TEL : +91 (0) 884 8311
FAX : +91 (0) 884 72100

Ashoka Technologies
A-15, Phase-I
Mayapuri Indl. Area
New Delhi,
NCT of Delhi-110064
India
TEL : +91 (0) 11 5135308
FAX : +91 (0) 11 5138250
E-mail:
amtc@ndb.vsnl.net.in

Triveni Engg. Works Ltd.
D-196, Phase-I
Okhla Indl. Area
New Delhi,
NCT of Delhi-110020
India
TEL : +91 (0) 11 6811878
FAX : +91 (0) 11 6812280
E-mail:
bkagrawal@projects.trivenigroup.com

Triveni Engg. & Industries Ltd.
D-196, Phase-I
Okhla Indl. Area
New Delhi,
NCT of Delhi-110020
India
TEL : +91 (0) 11 6811878
FAX : +91 (0) 11 6812280
E-mail:
bkagrawal@projects.trivenigroup.com

Gayatri Engg. Works
139, Navi Chawl
B/h Police Chowki
Dudheshwar Rd.
Dudheshwar
Ahmedabad,
Gujarat-380004
India
TEL : +91 (0) 79 5625751

Chanderpur Works
Village Jaoria
Radour Rd. Yamuna Nagar,
Haryana-135001
India
TEL : +91 (0) 1732 50964
FAX : +91 (0) 1732 79852
E-mail:
sudhiryn@sancharnet.in

Kaps Engineers
Samraat Silk Mills Compound
LBS Marg, Vikhroli (W)
Mumbai,
Maharashtra-400079
India
TEL : +91 (0) 22 5781933
FAX : +91 (0) 22 5785741
E-mail:
vmsrehls@bom4.vsnl.net.in

Chapter 26

Suppliers of Packaging Materials

Daman Foils Pvt. Ltd.
Bhenslore Indl. Est.
Kunta Rd.
Daman, Daman (UT)-396210
India
TEL : +91 (0) 260 262004
FAX : +91 (0) 260 263522
E-mail: damanfoils@vsnl.net

SMB Polymers Pvt. Ltd.
4805/24, Bharat Ram Rd.
Darya Ganj
New Delhi,
NCT of Delhi-110002
India
TEL : +91 (0) 11 3273775
FAX : +91 (0) 11 3289806
E-mail: bengani@vsnl.com

Ahlcon Parenterals (I) Ltd.
3rd Flr., 4, Comm. Centre
Saket
New Delhi,
NCT of Delhi-110017
India
TEL : +91 (0) 11 6514262
FAX : +91 (0) 11 6852036
E-mail:
ahlcon@gndel.globalnet.ems.vsnl.net.in

Owens Brockway (I) Ltd.
Glass Divn.
Thapar House, 1st Flr.
Western Wing, 124
Janpath
New Delhi,
NCT of Delhi-110001
India
TEL : +91 (0) 11 3342611
FAX : +91 (0) 11 3367981

Plasto Packs
1314, Pharilmli
Matia Mahal, Jama Masjid
Delhi,
NCT of Delhi-110006
India
TEL : +91 (0) 11 3261575

Royal Thermoformers
72, Village Patpar Ganj
Delhi,
NCT of Delhi-110092
India
TEL : +91 (0) 11 2754531
FAX : +91 (0) 11 2754531

Angel Articles
Plot No. 2804
Phase IV, GIDC
Wadhwan,
Gujarat-363030
India
TEL : +91 (0) 2752 51335

Avichal Press Pvt. Ltd.
703/2, Phase-IV
GIDC Est.
Vithal Udyognagar,
Gujarat-388121
India
TEL : +91 (0) 2692 35290
FAX : +91 (0) 2692 38836

Navrang Plastic
Plot No. 243/21/22
GIDC
Waghodia,
Gujarat-391760
India
TEL : +91 (0) 26682 62314

Plastopack Containers
64, GIDC Est.
Makarpura
Vadodara,
Gujarat-390010
India
TEL : +91 (0) 265 646714
FAX : +91 (0) 265 637669
E-mail:
plastopackcontainers@yahoo.com

Plus Point Foils & Strips
32, Kasturi Layout
Nr. Minerva Mills
MSR Deviation Rd.
Bangalore,
Karnataka-560023
India
TEL : +91 (0) 80 3200929
FAX : +91 (0) 80 3108891
E-mail:
pluspoint@yahoo.com

Victory Glass & Industries Ltd.
205, 2nd Flr., Midford House
(Off M G Rd.)
Midford Gardens
Bangalore,
Karnataka-560001
India
TEL : +91 (0) 80 5589475
FAX : +91 (0) 80 5584064
E-mail:
vgil.glass@gems.vsnl.net.in

Excell Glasses Ltd.
Udaya Ngr.
Pathirappally
Alapuzha,
Kerala-688521
India
TEL : +91 (0) 477 258671
FAX : +91 (0) 477 258670
E-mail:
mail@excelglasses.com

SG Plast Pvt. Ltd.
E 1/4, Arera Cly.
Bhopal,
Madhya Pradesh-462016
India

TEL : +91 (0) 755 566329
FAX : +91 (0) 755 585549

Perfect Containers Pvt. Ltd.
205, Anand Est.
189-A Sane Guruji Rd.
Nr. Kasturba Hospital
Mumbai,
Maharashtra-400011
India
TEL : +91 (0) 22 3003961
FAX : +91 (0) 22 3052726
E-mail:
srk@perfecttubes.com

Bharat Rubber Works
B-16, Girikunj Indl. Est.
Off Mahakali Caves Rd.
Andheri (E)
Mumbai,
Maharashtra-400093
India
TEL : +91 (0) 22 8378915
FAX : +91 (0) 22 8367442
E-mail:
bharatb@bom8.vsnl.net.in

Surya Papers Ltd.
B/18, Rasulgarh Indl. Est.
Bhubaneshwar,
Orissa-751010
India
TEL : +91 (0) 674 587486

Ashirwad Plastic Industries
Blow Moulding & Injection Moulding Divn.
2417/1, St. No. 9
Janta Ngr., Gill Rd.
Ludhiana,
Punjab-141003
India
TEL : +91 (0) 161 490939

Singh Plastics
392, New Jawahar Ngr.
Jalandhar,
Punjab-144001
India
TEL : +91 (0) 181 239050

Noble Packaging
71-A, Sect. II
Pithampur,
Rajasthan-454773
India
TEL : +91 (0) 7292 63055
FAX : +91 (0) 7292 40425
E-mail:
noblepet@yahoo.com

Srinivasa Cartons & Containers Pvt. Ltd.
305, T T K Rd.
Alwarpet
Chennai,
Tamil Nadu-600018
India
TEL : +91 (0) 44 4991653
FAX : +91 (0) 44 4992153
E-mail: corrobox@vsnl.net

Vikaash Packaging
120, Mugappair Rd.
Padi, Chennai,
Tamil Nadu-600050
India
TEL : +91 (0) 44 6521703
FAX : +91 (0) 44 6521703
E-mail: rvs@eth.net

Baijal Packaging Industries Pvt. Ltd.
D-6, Sect. 7
Noida,
Uttar Pradesh-201301
India
TEL : +91 (0) 120 4553548
FAX : +91 (0) 120 4544678
E-mail:
sharadbaijal@vsnl.com

Flex Industries Ltd.
A-107, Sect. IV
Noida,
Uttar Pradesh-201301
India
TEL : +91 (0) 120 4522558
FAX : +91 (0) 120 4520877

Injex Poly Products Pvt. Ltd.
D-136, Bulandshahr Rd.
Indl. Area
Ghaziabad,
Uttar Pradesh-201002
India
TEL : +91 (0) 120 700886
FAX : +91 (0) 120 702668

Alufoil Products Pvt. Ltd.
208, Mukit Chmbr.
(South Wing), 2nd Flr.
4, Clive Row
Kolkata,
West Bengal-700001
India
TEL : +91 (0) 33 2214989
FAX : +91 (0) 33 2214988
E-mail:
alufoil@giascl01.vsnl.net.in

Hindustan Seals Ltd.
8/1, Lal Bazar St.
Kolkata,
West Bengal-700001
India
TEL : +91 (0) 33 2210050
FAX : +91 (0) 33 2200336
E-mail: info@manaksia.com

India Foils Ltd.
A Sterlite Group Company
1, Sagore Dutta Ghat Rd.
Kamarhati
Kolkata,
West Bengal-700058
India
TEL : +91 (0) 33 5532317
FAX : +91 (0) 33 5834419
E-mail:
corporate@indiafoils.com

Precision Balance (I)
6, Wood St.
Kolkata,
West Bengal-700016
India
TEL : +91 (0) 33 2403476
FAX : +91 (0) 33 2402427

117. MANUFACTURE OF TIN CONTAINERS
118. MANUFACTURE OF STORAGE TANKS, PRESSURE VESSELS, HEAT EXCHANGERS
119. MARK II HAND PUMPS
120. MARUTI WORKSHOP CUM - SERVICE STATION
121. MECHANICAL JACKS
122. METAL CUTTING DIE DESIGN
123. METAL CUTTING OF AND GRINDING WHEELS (ABBRASIVE CUTTING WHEELS)
124. METAL HOOKS & CLIPS
125. METAL SEPARATION (COPPER, TIN, LEAD) FROM SPENT WASH ACID
126. METALLIC RING JOINTS
127. METALLIC GASKET (SPIRAL WOUND)
128. MICROVEE & ABSOLUTE FILTER
129. MICROWAVE OVEN
130. MILD STEEL INGOTS
131. MINI STEEL PLANT
132. MODERN VEHICLE WORKSHOP
133. MOPED
134. M.S.HINGES
135. M.S.INGOT AND HR. STEEL STRUCTURALS
136. M.S.INGOT BY INDUCTION FURNACES
137. M.S.PIPES
138. M.S. WELDING ELECTRODE
139. MUFFLERS & SILENCERS FOR THREE WHEELERS
140. NAIL CUTTER WITH FILER & MANICURE
141. NICHROME WIRE
142. NICKEL LINED SCREENS
143. NON-FERROUS ALLOY ROLLING
144. NON-FERROUS FORGING
145. NON-FERROUS FOUNDRY
146. NON PRESSURE
147. INCANDESCENT LAMP
148. NUMBER COMBINATION LOCKS FOR LUGGAGES
149. NUTS & BOLTS
150. PAPER COATED ALUMINIUM AND COPPER WIRE
151. PETROMAX CONTAINER
152. PHOTO ETCHING OF STAINLESS STEEL PLATES
153. PIPE GALVANIZING PLANT
154. PISTON RING-AUTOMOBILE
155. PLANT PROTECTION EQUIPMENTS
156. PLATINUM LABORATORY APPARATUS
157. PRESSURE COOKER & ALUMINIUM UTENSILS
158. PRESSURE COOKER (ALUMINIUM)
159. PRESSURE DIE CASTING
160. PRINTED ALUMINIUM COLLAPSIBLE TUBES
161. PRINTED TIN CONTAINERS
162. PRINTING PRESS (CYLINDER MACHINE)
163. PUMPS FOR CHEMICAL INDUSTRY (SPECIAL)
164. RAILWAY SLEEPERS (M.S.)
165. RAZOR TWIN BLADE
166. R.C.C SPUN PIPES
167. RECONDITIONING OF M.S. DRUMS/BARRELS
168. RE-ROLLING COPPER AND BRASS SHEET AND RODS
169. RE-ROLLING MILLS
170. RESIN COATED SAND
171. RESIN CORED SOFT SOLDER WIRES
172. ROLLING MILL (BY INDUCTION FURNACE) & MANUFACTURE OF BARS, ANGLES, SQUARES, TUBES AND OTHERS
173. ROLLER BEARING & FORGING
174. ROLLING OF STAINLESS STEEL PATTA
175. RUBBER INSULATED PLIERS (HAND TOOLS)
176. RUBBING COMPOUND FOR AUTOMOBILES
177. SCIENTIFIC LABORATORY EQUIPMENTS
178. SCOOTER ASSEMBLING
179. SECONDARY LEAD EXTRAC-TION BY SCRAP BATTERY PLATES,PIPES & SHEET
180. SEAMLESS M.S. TUBES & PIPES
181. SELF TAPPING STEEL SCREW
182. SEWING NEEDLES
183. S.G. IRON & ALLOY STEEL
184. SHEET METAL PRODUCTS, (FERROUS/NON-FERROUS)
185. SHIP/MARINE CONTAINER
186. SHOCK ABSORBERS
187. SHOE EYELETS
188. SHOT AND GRITS BY AUTOMIZATION PROCESS
189. SHOVELS
190. SILICO MANGANESE ALLOYS
191. SILENCERS (MUFFLERS) EXHAUST & TAIL PIPE FOR ALL TYPES OF VEHICLES
192. SINTERED BEARING
193. SINTERED BUSHES
194. SINTERED METAL PRODUCTS
195. SOFT AND HARD FERRITES
196. SPANNERS
197. SPARK PLUGS
198. STEEL PLANT (ELECTRIC ARC FURNACE BASED- EAF)
199. SPHERIODAL GRAPHITE CAST IRON
200. SPRAY DRYER
201. STAINLESS STEEL HINGES
202. STAINLESS STEEL SHEET ROLLING TO PRODUCE STAINLESS STEEL UTENSILS
203. STAINLESS STEEL UTENSILS
204. STAPLE PINS,PAPER PIN, GEM CLIPS ETC.
205. STEEL CASTINGS
206. STEEL CHAIN
207. STEEL FOUNDRY
208. STEEL FURNITURES AND ELECTRICAL APPLIANCES
209. STEEL PLANT (MINI)
210. STEEL RODS AND COILS FROM SCRAPS
211. STEEL ROLLING MILL
212. STEEL STRIPS (COLD ROLLED) SILICON WITH GRAIN RIENTED FOR ELECTRIC USE
213. STEEL TRANSMISSION LINE TOWERS & ROLLING MILL TO PRODUCE STEEL SECTION
214. STEEL FURNITURES AND ELECTRICAL APPLIANCES
215. STEEL WIRE DRAWING AND GALVANIZING
216. STEEL WOOL
217. SUBMERGED ARC WELDED PIPES
218. SUBMERSIBLE PUMP MANUFACTURING
219. SUPER ENAMELLED COPPER WIRE
220. THREE WHEELERS
221. TIE-ROD ENDS
222. TIN CONTAINERS
223. TOOLROOM AND SHEET METAL PRODUCTS
224. TRACTOR TRAILERS
225. TRANSMISSION POWER FITTING
226. TUBULAR POLES
227. SUPER ENAMELLED COPPER WIRES
228. TUBULAR POLES FOR ELECTRICAL TRANSMISSION (BY FABRICATION PROCESS)
229. TUBULAR POLES OF M.S. & HIGH TENSILE STEEL
230. VACUUM CLEANERS
231. VACUUM FLASK (STAINLESS STEEL)
232. VALVES FOR REFRIGERA TION AND AIR-CONDITION
233. VEHICLE WELDING & PAINTING
234. VENETION BLIND
235. WASHING MACHINES (AUTOMATIC & COMPUTERISED)
236. WATER CONTROLLER (AUTOMATIC)
237. WATCH STRAPS/CHAINS/BRACELETS/BELT BRASS & STAINLESS STEEL
238. WATER COOLERS
239. WELDED WIRE MESH
240. WELDING ELECTRODES
241. WICK STOVES
242. WIND MILL WINDOW FRAME (FERROUS & NON-FERROUS)
243. WRIST WATCH

359. DI ETHYL OXALATE
360. DI METHYL ORTHOPHTHALATE
361. DI-METHYL PHTHALATE
362. DICLOFENAC GEL
363. DIOCTYL PHTHALATE (DOP)
364. DI PHENYL GLYCERINE
365. DI PHENYL OXIDE
366. DINITRO-CHLORO BENZENE
367. DISTILLED WATER
368. DODECYL BENZENE SULPHONATE
369. DUSTLESS CHALK
370. EDTA & ITS SALTS
371. ELECTROLESS NICKEL PLATING ON PLASTICS
372. ENDOSULFAN
373. EPOXY RESIN BASED COMPOUND
374. ETHYL ACETATE
375. EHTYL ETHER
376. ETHYL ALCOHOL (POTABLE LIQUOR)
377. ETHYL HEXANOL
378. EXTRACTION OF ESSENTIAL OILS BY SUGAR CRITICAL FLUID (CARBON DIOXIDE) METHOD FROM FLOWERS, HERBAL & SPICES
379. FERRIC ALUM
380. FERRO CHROME LIGNO SULPHONATE
381. FERRO MANGANESE
382. FERRO SILICONE
383. FERRO VANADIUM FROM VANADIUM SLUDGE
384. FERROUS SILICATE
385. FERROUS SULPHATE
386. FERTILIZER FROM ANIMAL BLOOD & LEATHER WASTE
387. FLUORESCENT TUBE LIGHT POWDER
388. FOAMED PVC COMPOUNDING & ITS PRODUCTS
389. FORMALDEHYDE
390. FRACTIONAL DISTILLATION OF D.M.O (DEMENTHOLIZED OIL)
391. FRACTIONAL DISTILLATION OF ESSENTIAL OIL & MEDICINAL PLANT EXTRACT
392. FRICTION DUST (LIQUID & POWDER) FROM CNSL
393. FRUIT FLAVOURS
394. FURFURAL FROM RICE HUSK
395. GARLIC ACID
396. GASKET SHELLAC COMPOUND
397. GEAR OIL
398. GIBBERELLIC ACID
399. GLASS PUTTY
400. GLYCERINE
401. GOSSYPOL (POLY PHENOL) FROM COTTON SEED OIL
402. GUAR GUM POWDER
403. HAIR FIXER (HAIR GEL TYPE)
404. H - ACID
405. HENNA PASTE MAKING
406. HEPTAL DEHYDE
407. HIGH CARBON FERRO CHROME
408. HYDRATED CALCIUM SILICATE BRICK
409. HYDRATED LIME FROM SEA SHELL
410. HYDROCHLORIC ACID
411. HYDRO FLUORIC ACID
412. HYDROGEN PEROXIDE (BY AUTO-OXIDATION PROCESS)
413. ICE PACKS (SOLUTIONS TYPE, WHITE GEL TYPE, VIOLET SEMI SOLID POLYMER TYPE)
414. IMPROVING DROP POINT PARAFFIN WAX FROM 45-50ºC TO 75-80ºC
415. INDUSTRIAL ALCOHOL
416. INTEGERATED COMPLEX OF EASTER & ALLIED PRODUCTS (D.O.P, D.B.P, ETHYL ACETATE WIRE ENAMEL & CABLE JELLY)
417. IMFL (WHISKY) & COUNTRY LIQUOR
418. IRON OXIDE FOR MAKING FERITTE
419. IRON SULPHIDE
420. JUTE BATCHING OIL
421. KESH KALA TEL (HAIR DYE LOTION) (VASMOL 33, BLACK NITE TYPE)
422. L-LYSINE MONOHYDROCHLORIDE
423. LACTIC ACID FROM WHITE SUGAR BY FERMENTATION PROCESS
424. LDPE GRANULES FROM VIRGIN (LDPE RESIN)
425. LEAD EXTRACTION FROM BATTERY SCRAP
426. LEAD OXIDE (A) LEAD MONOXIDE (B) LEAD TETRA OXIDE (C) GREYLEAD OXIDE
427. LIQUID GLUCOSE & ITS BY PRODUCTS
428. LIQUID OXYGEN BOTTLING PLANT
429. LIQUID SHOE POLISH
430. LIQUID FLOOR POLISH
431. LUBE OIL VISCOSITY IMPROVED FOR P.P.G/P.E.G.
432. LUBRICANTS ASHLESS 100% COMBUSTION
433. MAGNESIUM CARBONATE AND MAGNESIUM BICARMONATE
434. MAGNESIUM HYDROXIDE POWDER
435. MAGNESIUM SILICATE
436. MAGNESIUM SULPHATE
437. MALACHITE GREEN
438. MALEIC ANHYDRIDE
439. MANGANESE SULPHATE
440. MANUFACTURING OF CARBON MONO-OXIDE WATER GAS
441. MENTHOL BOLD CRYSTALS FROM FLAKES
442. MENTHOL CRYSTAL & MENTHA OIL
443. MERCURIC OXIDE
444. METAL PRE-TREATMENT CHEMICALS
445. METHANE GAS BY SODIUM ACETATE & SODA LIME
446. METHYL ACETYL RICINOLATE
447. METOL
448. METOL FROM HYDROQUINONE & METHYLAMINE
449. MICANITE
450. MICRO NUTRIENT MIXTURE
451. MINERAL WATER
452. MINERAL WATER AND PET BOTTILNG PLANT
453. MINERAL WATER IN BOTTLES, GLASS AND POUCHES
454. MINI CEMENT PLANT (BY ROTARY KILN PROCESS)
455. MIXED FERTILIZER
456. MOSQUITO & FLIES REPELLENT AGARBATTI (INCENSE STICKS)
457. MONO CHLORO ACETIC ACID
458. MONOCROTOPHOS (TECHNICAL)
459. MOSQUITO COIL
460. MOSQUITO COIL & MAT
461. MOSQUITO MAT
462. MOTHER TINCTURE & BIO CHEMIC MEDICINES
463. NAPHTHALENE & PHENYL (INTEGRATED UNIT)
464. NATURAL MINERAL WATER BY REVERSE OSMOSIS PROCESS
465. NICKEL PLATING BRIGHTNER (PRIMARY OR CARRIER BRIGHTNER & SECONDARY BRIGHTNER)
466. NICKEL SULPHATE
467. NICOTINE FROM TOBACCO WASTE
468. NICOTINE SULPHATE FROM TOBACCO WASTE
469. NITRO BENZENE
470. NITRO CELLULOSE SANDING SEALER/LACQUER
471. NITRO MUSK
472. NITROGEN & OXYGEN GAS PLANT
473. NON-IONIC SURFACTANT (WETTING AGENT)
474. NO-CARB PASTE
475. OCTANOL
476. ORTHO NITRO PHENOL
477. OXALIC ACID FROM MOLASSES
478. OXALIC ACID FROMRICE HUSK
479. OXALIC ACID FROM TREE BARK
470. OXALIC ACID FROM WASTE VEGETABLES
471. OXYGEN GAS PLANT
472. OXYGEN GAS PLANT (AIR SEPERATION METHOD)
473. PARA-AMINO BENZOIC ACID
474. PARA-AMINO PHENOL
475. PARA TOLUENE SULPHONIC ACID
476. PECTIN FROM RAW PAPAYA
477. PERFUME (LEMON & OTHERS)

CRUDE NAPHTHA
570. TRIMETHYL AMMONIUM CHLORIDE
571. TRIPHENYL PHOSPHITE (T.P.P)
572. ULTRAMARINE BLUE (LIQUID)
573. UREA FORMALDEHYDE & MELAMINE FORMALDEHYDE POWDER
574. UNDECYLINIC ACID
575. VINYL ACETATE MONOMER
576. VITAMIN C
577. VITAMIN E
578. WASTE WATER TREATMENT PLANT FOR INDUSTRIAL SECTOR IN INDIA (ONLY MARKER SURVEY)
579. WIRE DRAWING LUBRICANT
580. WIRE ENAMEL
581. XANTHATES
582. YELLOW DEXTRIN
583. ZINC CHLORIDE
584. ZINC OXIDE
585. ZINC PHOSPHATING BY COLD PROCESS
586. ZINC SILICATE
587. ZINC STEARATE
588. ZINC SULPHATE
589. ZINC SULPHATE MONOHYDRATE
590. ACID BLACK
591. AURAMINE'O'
592. AZO DYES STUFF
593. DYE & DYE INTERMEDIATE
594. DYE INTERMEDIATES
595. MALACHITE GREEN
596. METHYLENE BLUE
597. PHTHALOCYANINE BLUE
598. PHTHALOCYANINE BLUE & GREEN
599. REACTIVE DYES
600. SULPHUR BLACK DYE
601. VAT DYES
602. WATER CHILLING PLANT
603. WADDING OIL (100%) FOR WADDING OF COTTON HOSIERY CLOTH IN THE DYEING PROCESS
604. WHITE OIL
605. WAX FLOOR POLISH

ELECTRICAL, ELECTONICS, COMPUTERS AND INFOTECH/IT PROJECTS

606. AIR CONDITIONING
607. ALUMINIUM ALLOY CONDUCTOR
608. ALUMINIUM CABLE
609. ALUMINIUM ELECTROYTIC CAPACITORS
610. AUDIO CASSETTE ASSEMBLING & RECORDING
611. AUDIO CASSETTES DUPLICATING RECORDING
612. AUDIO CASSETTES & AUDIO STUDIO
613. AUDIO CASSETTES PLANE & RECORDED
614. AUDIO MAGNETIC HEADS
615. AUDIO MAGNETIC TAPE
616. AUDIO/VIDEO CASSETTES
617. AUTO BULB/LAMPS
618. AUTOMATIC VOLTAGE STABILIZER
619. BATTERY PLATES
620. BACK OFFICE (Rs. 5000/-)
621. B/W TV & COMPUTER MONITOR PICTURE TUBE
622. BREAD BOARDS
623. CALL CENTRE
624. CAMERA (35 MM)
625. CAPACITORS
626. CARBON ELECTRODE USED FOR BATTERY CELL
627. CARBON POTETIOMETERS
628. CEILING FAN
629. CERAMIC INSULATOR
630. CHILDREN INFOTECH TRAINING INSTITUTE (Rs. 5000/-)
631. CHOKE AND PATTI
632. CHOKE AND STARTER
633. CHOKE USED FOR FLUORESCENT LAMPS
634. COLOUR TELEVISION
635. COLOUR AND BLACK & WHITE TELEVISION
636. COMPACT DISC
637. COMPACT DISC PLAYER (AUDIO/VIDEO)
638. COMPUTER EDUCATION INSTITUTE
639. COMPUTER ASSEMBLY
640. COMPUTER HARDWARE
641. COMPUTER KEYBOARD
642. COMPUTER PERIPHERALS
643. COMPUTER PRINTERS
644. COMPUTER RIBBON
645. COMPUTER RIBBON REINKING OR REFILLING
646. COMPUTER STATIONERY
647. COMPUTER STATIONERY &

IMPORTED HARDWARE PARTS
648. COMPUTER TERMINALS
649. COMPUTERISED WASHING MACHINE (AUTOMATIC)
650. COMPUTER SOFTWARE
651. CONDENSER FOR MOTOR USING MPP FILM
652. CONTENT DEVELOPMENT CENTRE (EOU) (Rs. 5000/-)
653. CONTROL PANEL BOARD
654. COOLING COIL FOR AIR CONDITIONERS
655. COPPER STRIP COIL FROM SCRAP
656. CORDLESS TELEPHONES
657. CYBER CAFE
658. CYBERKIOSK (Rs. 5000/-)
659. DATA PROCESSING CENTRE (Rs. 5000/-)
660. D.C. MICRO MOTORS
661. D.G.SETS
662. DISH ANTENNA AND CABLE T.V. NETWORK EQUIPMENT
663. DISTRIBUTION TRANSFORMERS & REPAIRS
664. DOMESTIC ELECTRICAL APPLIANCES- ROOM COOLER, WASHING MACHINE, WATER HEATER, ELECTRIC ROOM HEATER
665. E-SCHOOL
666. E-COMMERCE/BUSINESS
667. ELECTRIC ENERGY METER
668. ELECTRIC FANS
669. ELECTRIC HORN FOR AUTOMOBILE
670. ELECTRIC LAMP/GLS (INCANDESCENT LAMP)
671. ELECTRIC MIXER
672. ELECTRIC MOTORS UP TO 10 HP. REWINDING OF ALL TYPES OF MOTORS WATER PUMPS
673. ELECTRIC MOTOR WINDING (FOR FAN, MIXIES, ETC.)
674. ELECTRIC STEAM IRON
675. ELECTRICAL APPLIANCES
676. ELECTRICAL FIXTURES
677. ELECTRICAL STAMPING
678. ELECTROLYTIC CAPACITORS
679. ELECTROMAGNETIC RELAY
680. ELECTRONIC BALAST/CHOK
681. ELECTRICAL CHOKE
682. ELECTRONIC DIGITAL WATCHES
683. ELECTRONIC DIGITAL WEIGHING MACHINE
684. ELECTRONIC FIRE ALARM
685. ELECTRONIC GAS STOVE LIGHTERS
686. ELECTRONIC PRESSURE INDICATORS, ELECTRICALS, ELECTRONIC LIQUID LEVEL INDICATORS, ELECTRONIC TEMPERATURE INDICATOR, DIGITAL TACHOMETER
687. ELECTRONIC TELEPHONE INSTRUMENTS
688. ELECTRONIC TOYS
689. ELECTRONIC WATCHES & CLOCKS
690. FAX MACHINES
691. F.H.P MOTORS
692. FLOPPY DISKETTES
693. FLUORESCENT LAMP STARTER
694. FLUORESCENT TUBULAR

LAMPS WITH INTRODUCTION TO MERCURY VAPOUR LAMP
695. FRANCHISEE COMPUTER EDUCATION CENTRE (Rs. 5000)
696. GAS DETECTOR (L.P.G)
697. GENERATOR SET & PUMP SETS
698. GENERATOR (BATTERY OPERATED)
699. GIS SERVICE CENTRE (GEOGRAPHICAL INFORMATION SYSTEMS)
700. HARDWARE FITTING FOR TRANSMISSION LINE OVERHEAD LINE MATERIAL
701. HEADERS FOR TRANSISTOR ICS SEMI CONDUCTOR
702. H.T & L.T INSULATORS
703. H.T & M.V INDUSTRIAL CUBICAL SWITCH BOARD
704. INFORMATION MOVING DISPLAY (L.E.D TYPE)
705. INSURANCE CLAIM PROCESSING CENTRE (EOU) (Rs. 5000/-)
706. INTEGRATED CIRCUITS
707. INTERNET BASED STOCK TRADING (Rs. 5000/-)
708. INTERNET SERVICE PROVIDER (I.S.P.)
709. JELLY FILLED TELEPHONE CABLES
710. LAP TOP COMPUTERS
711. LEAD ACID BATTERIES
712. LEAD ACID BATTERY PLATES AND ASSEMBLING OF BATTERY
713. LEGAL TRANSCRIPTION & SECRETARIAL SERVICES CENTER (EOU)(Rs. 5000/-)
714. LIGHT EMITTING DIODES (L.E.D)
715. LINEAR ICS TRAINER KIT
716. LOUD SPEAKER
717. L.T TRANSFORMER REPAIRING
718. MEDICAL TRANSCRIPTION CENTRE
719. METAL FILM RESISTORS
720. METALLISED POLYPROPYLENE, POLYESTER FILM CAPACITOR
721. MICA BASE ELECTRONIC COMPONENTS
722. MICA PAPER WASTE PAPER FROM MICA WASTE
723. MICRO PROCESSORS TRAINER KITS BASED ON MICRO PROCESSORS
724. MINI COMPUTER (PERSONAL COMPUTER)
725. MINIATURE CIRCUIT BREAKER (M.C.B)
726. MINIATURE WATCH BATTERIES (BUTTON CELL)
727. MIXER/GRINDER (MIXI)
728. MONO CHROME COMPUTER MONITOR
729. MOTOR START ELECTROLYTIC CAPACITOR
730. MULTI LAYER P.C.B
731. MULTIPLE RELAY FOR LOW VOLTAGE
732. NEON INDICATOR
733. NEON SIGN MANUFACTURE
734. OPTICAL FIBRE CABLES
735. ON LINE SHOPPING MALL (Rs. 5000/-)
736. OPTO MECHANICAL & ELECTRICAL EQUIPMENTS
737. PHOTO COLOUR LAB
738. PICTURE TUBE (B/W)
739. PLAIN PAPER COPIER
740. PLASTIC FILM CAPACITORS
741. POLYESTER CAPACITORS
742. PORTABLE GENERATOR SET
743. PORTAL
744. PORTABLE TELEVISION(TV)
745. POWER CAPACITORS
746. POWER INVERTERS
747. POWER PLANT
748. POWER TRANSFORMERS UP TO 600 KVA
749. PRINTED CIRCUIT BOARD
750. PVC WIRES & CABLES
751. RE-CONDITIONING OF PICTURE TUBE
752. RESIN CAST CT & PT (1 KV)
753. SEMI CONDUCTOR DEVICE
754. SEMI CONDUCTORS FOR TRANSISTORS & DIODES
755. SETTING UP OF A VIDEO STUDIO
756. SMOKE DETECTORS
757. SOLAR CELLS
758. SOLAR MODULES
759. SOLAR PHOTO VOLTAIC SYSTEM
760. SOLDER FLUXES
761. SOLAR WATER HEATING PANELS
762. STEEL FURNITURE & ELECTRICAL APPLIANCES
763. STEREO AMPLIFIERS
764. STEREO CASSETTE RECORDERS/PLAYERS
765. STREET LIGHT FITTINGS SURGE SUPPRESSOR
766. TANTALUM CAPACITORS
767. TEFLON COATED ELECTRIC CABLE
768. TELEMEDICINE (DISTANCE HEALTH CARE) (Rs. 5000/-)
769. TELEPHONE CORD/CABLE
770. TELEPHONE (PUSH BUTTON TYPE)
771. TELEPHONE (PUSH BUTTON & CORDLESS)
772. TELEVISION (CTV & B/W)
773. TELEVISION (3-D)
774. TELEVISION DEFLECTION COMPONENTS
775. TELEVISION SIGNAL BOOSTERS
776. TELEVISION TUNERS
777. TRACTION BATTERIES
778. TRAINING INSTITUTE OF MEDICAL TRANSCRIPTION
779. TRANSFORMER FOR B/W TV
780. TRANSFORMER FOR VOLTAGE STABILIZER & E.H.T
781. TRANSMISSION POWER LINE FITTING
782. TRANSMISSION TOWER FITTING
783. TV AUDIO EQUIPMENT CABINETS & THEIR ASSEMBLING UNIT
784. UN-INTERRUPTED POWER SUPPLY (U.P.S)
785. VARIABLE FREQUENCY
786. VARIABLE VOLTAGE A.C. DRIVE
787. VIDEO CASSETTES (COMPLETE MANUFACTURING & ASSEMBLING)
788. VIDEO CASSETTES RECORDER (V.C.R)
789. VIDEO FILM STUDIO
790. VOLTAGE REGULATOR FOR AUTOMOBILES
791. VOLTAGE STABILIZERS
792. VOLTAGE STABLIZER & T.V. GAIN BOOSTER
793. WAX AND CHEMICAL COATED, BRAIDED TINSEL WIRE
794. WEBSITE DESIGN & E-MAIL REGISTERING
795. WELDING ELECTRODES
796. WIND ENERGY POWER PROJECT (10 MW)
796A WIRES (METAL)

FOOD, AGRO FOOD, PROCESSED FOOD, AGRO PLANTATION, CULTIVATION, FARMING, DAIRY/MILK, TOBACCO/PAN MASALA, BREWERY & DISTILLERY, EDIBLE OILS, EOU FOOD PRODUCTS AND ALLIED PRODUCTS

797. ALCOHOLIC BEVERAGES & VENEGAR FROM COCONUT WATER
798. ALCOHOL DRINKS FROM ETHYL ALCOHOL BY MIXING OF VARIOUS FLAVOURS
799. ANTI SCALE COMPOUND FOR ADDING INTO SUGAR JUICE BOILING
800. APPLE JUICE CONCENTRATED & DEHYDRATED FRUIT & VEGETABLES
801. ARTIFICIAL FISH MEAL FOR POULTRY FEED
802. AUTOMATIC BISCUIT PLANT
803. BABY CEREAL FOOD AND MILK POWDER
804. BACTERIA FOR CANE JUICE
805. BAKER'S YEAST
806. BAKERY INDUSTRY
807. BANANA PUREE
808. BEER & WINE
809. BEER PLANT (BREWERY)
810. BIDI
811. BIDI & CIGARETTE
812. BISCUIT PLANT

813. BREAD (AUTOMATIC PLANT)
814. BLACK PEPPER (SPICES)
815. BREAD AND BISCUITS
816. BREEDING FARM
817. BROILER CHICKEN
819. BUTTON MUSHROOM CULTIVATION & PROCESSING
820. CANNING OF RASAGULLAS IN METAL CANS
821. CAFFEIN FROM TEA WASTE
822. CANNING OF FRUITS & VEGETABLES
823. CASEIN AND BY-PRODUCTS
824. CASHEW FRUIT JUICE FROM CASHEW FRUIT APPLE
825. CASHEWNUT KERNEL EXTRACTION FROM CASHEWNUT FRUIT
826. CASHEWNUT SHELL LIQUID & KERNEL PROCESSING
827. CASHEW FENI
828. CATECHEU (BY CHEMICAL PROCESS)
829. CATTLE FEED FROM TAPIOCA
830. CHEWING & BUBBLE GUM
831. CHICKEN/SHEEP MEAT PROCESSING
832. CHOCOLATE (MILK)
833. CIGARETTE AND BEEDIES
834. COCOA BUTTER FROM COCOA MASS
835. COCONUT PRODUCTS & BY PRODUCTS PROCESS COMPLEX
836. COLD/SOFT DRINKS
837. COLLECTION OF MILK AND MILK MAKING POWDER
838. COLLECTION OF MILK AND PACKING IN POLYTHENE POUCH (1/2 KG.1 KG. & 2 KG.)
839. CONDENSED MILK (SWEETNED)
840. CONFECTIONERY INDUSTRY (TOFFEE & CANDY, SEMI-AUTOMATIC PLANT)
841. COUNTRY LIQUOR FROM MOLASSES
842. CIGARETTE
843. DAIRY FARM AND DAIRY (MILK) PRODUCTS (PASTEURISED MILK, BUTTER, GHEE, PANEER)
844. DAIRY FARM TO PRODUCE MILK & PACKING IN POUCHES (50%) & CAN(50%)
845. DAIRY FOR MILK PROCESSING
846. DAIRY FARM (BUFALO)
847. DAL (PULSE) MILL UNIT
848. DEHYDRATION OF CARROT & GARLIC
849. DEHYDRATION & CANNING OF FRUITS & VEGETABLES
850. DEHYDRATION OF FIGS
851. DEHYDRATION OF FRUITS AND VEGETABLES
852. DEHYDRATED ONIONS AND ONION POWDER
853. DRY ICE BY BREAKING OF AIR
854. DRYING OF RED CHILLIES, HALDI, DHANIA, AND GREEN PEAS
855. EGG POWDER (40,000 EGGS PROCESSING PER DAY)
856. EXPORT OF PROCESSED FOODS AND MARINE PRODUCTS
857. FISH CANNING & POUCHING
859. FISH FARMING (PRAWN & OTHER MARINE PRODUCTS)
860. FISH MEAL
861. FLOUR MILL AND MUSTARD OIL
862. FOOD COLOUR & ORASTED GROUNDNUT GRAM PEAS, ETC IN POUCHES
863. FROG LEGS PROCESSING
864. FROZEN MEATS PROCESSING
865. FOOD FLAVOURS (WHISKY) VODKA, GRAPE, BUTTER SCOTCH)
866. FOOD PRODUCTS COMPLEX (DEHYDRATED ONIONS, GARLIC POWDER & FLAKES, CATTLE FEED, TOMATO POWDER, TOMATO PRODUCTS, CANNED FRUITS & VEGETABLES, TOMATO PURE, GROUN NUT OIL, REFIND OIL, DEHYDRATED GRAPES, BANANA POWDER & WAFFERS)
867. FRUIT JUICE, JAM, JELLIES & ALLIED PRODUCTS
868. FRUIT JUICE, PICKLES PROCESSING AND CANNING
869. FRUIT JUICE MAKING & PACKING IN PLASTIC CONTAINER/POUCHES
870. FRUIT PROCESSING (JAM & JELLIES)
871. FRUIT PULP & JUICE CONCENTRATES
872. FRUIT & VEGETABLE DRYING (FREEZE DRYING METHOD)
873. GOAT & SHEEP FARMING
874. GRAM DALL/PULSE MILL
875. GRAPE DEHYDRATION
876. HARD BOILED CANDY (TOFFEE & CANDY)
877. HERBAL CIGARETTES
878. HONEY PROCESSING & PACKAGING
879. ICE CREAM OF DIFFERENT FLAVOURS
880. ICE CREAM STABILIZER
881. ICE MAKING PLANT
882. INDIAN MADE FOREIGN LIQUOR (I.M.F.L)
883. INSTANT FOOD (IDLI MIX, DOSA MIX, GULAB JAMUN MIX)
884. INSTANT FOOD (INSTANT FOOD & FAST FOOD PARLOUR)
885. INSTANT NOODLES
886. INSTANT TEA
887. INSTANT TEA FROM BLACK TEA
888. INTEGERATED STARCH BAKING POWDER/YEAST INDUSTRY
889. IODIZED SALT
890. IODIZED SALT (ORDINARY MOISTURE-LESS/FREE FLOWING IN PLASTIC BAGS AND CONTAINERS)
891. JAM, JELLIES, FRUIT JUICE & ALLIED PRODUCTS
892. KATHA AND CUTCH
893. KHANDSARI SUGAR
894. KHANDSARI SUGAR & IMFL
895. LACTIC ACID FROM WHITE SUGAR BY FERMENTATION PROCESS
896. LACTOSE & BY PRODUCTS PROCESSING FROM MILK
897. LIQUID GLUCOSE AND ITS BYE PRODUCTS
898. MACRONI AND VERMICILLI
899. MALT EXTRACTION FROM BARLEY
900. MANGO PROCESSING (MANGO PULP, JUICE & SLICES)
901. MAYUR BRAND TYPE CHEWING TOBACCO
902. MINERAL WATER
903. MILK PRESERVATION & MARKETING TO WHOLE SELLERS (INPOUCH PACKING BY UHT TECHNOLOGY)
904. MILK PROCESSING AND PACKAGING OF MILK PRODUCTS
905. MILK PRODUCTS (CASEIN, LACTOSE, GHEE & WHEY POWDER)
906. MILK TOFFEE
907. MINI FLOUR MILL
908. MINI SUGAR PLANT
909. MISRI (PEARL SUGAR CANDIES)
910. MODERN RICE MILL
911. MURABBA
912. MUSTARD OIL EXTRACTION & REFINING
913. MUTTON TALLOW
914. NAMKEEN INDUSTRY (BHUJIA, CHANA CHUR ETC.)
915. NAMKEEN & SWEETS
916. NON-BASMATI RICE FROM PADDY
917. OLEORESIN, ESSENTIAL OIL, DYES & POWDER OF SPICES
918. OLEORESIN EXTRACTION FROM DIPTERO-CARPUT TURMINATUS AND PINUS KHASYANA
919. OLEORESIN EXTRACTION FROM CHILLI
920. PAN MASALA AND POUCH

1059. BUFFALO HORN TIP, HOOF
1060. BANQUET HALL
1061. BUTTON
1062. CALCINED PETROLEUM (C.P) COKE
1063. CANVAS SHOES
1064. CANVAS SHOES, JUNGLE BOOTS
1065. CARBON BRUSH, BRUSH HOLDER & SLIP RING
1066. CEMENT SHEETS WITH COIR FIBRE & OTHER SEGMENTS
1067. CERAMIC TILES (GLAZED) BY DOUBLE FIRING/HEATING
1068. CHILDREN RECREATION CENTRE
1069. COAL BRIQUETTES
1070. COLD STORAGE & ICE
1071. COLD STORAGE FOR FRUITS AND VEGETABLES
1072. COMPRESSOR (HERMETIC) FOR AIR CONDITIONER
1073. COSTUME JEWELLERY/ IMITATION JEWELLERY
1074. DECORATIVE LAMINATED SHEET (SUNMICA)
1075. DIAMOND CUTTING & EXPORTS
1076. DRINKING STRAW FROM PROPYLENE
1077. ENGINEERING COLLEGE
1078. ENTERTAINMENT CLUB
1079. FASHION TECHNOLOGY INSTITUTE
1080. FAST FOOD PARLOUR
1081. FAST FOOD (INSTANT FOOD & FAST FOOD PARLOUR)
1082. FIRE EXTINGUISHERS (SODA ACID TYPE)
1083. FISH NET
1084. FLORICULTURE (CUT FLOWER ROSE) WITH GREEN HOUSE
1085. FLOOR COVERING SHEET
1086. FILM STUDIO (VIDEO)
1087. FLUSH DOOR, CHIP BOARD, WOOD WOOL & OTHER INSULATING BOARDS
1088. GAS DETECTORS OF L.P.G
1089. GEMS MANUFACTURING
1090. GLASS BOTTLE BY SCRAP
1092. GOAT & SHEEP FARMING
1093. GOLD ELECTROPLATING
1094. GOLD JEWELLERY (E.O.U)
1095. GOLD PLATED SILVER JEWELLERY & CUTLERY
1096. GRANITE SLAB AND TILES
1097. GREEN HOUSE
1098. HARD CHROMIUM PLATING
1099. HEALTH CLUB AND BEAUTY PARLOUR CUM HAIR SALOON WITH SONA BATH
1100. HEALTH CLUB CUM BEAUTY PARLOUR TRAININGINSTITUTE
1101. HORN TIP,HOOVE BUTTON
1102. HOSPITAL
1103. HOSPITAL (100 BEDS)
1104. HOSPITAL (200 BEDS)
1105. ICE MAKING PLANT
1106. IMITATION AND COSTUME
1107. JEWELLERY (NECKLACE, EARRINGS EAR TOP ETC.)
1108. INITMATE SCENT CHEMICALS FROM ALL TYPES OF FLAVOUR
1109. INVESTMENT CASTING
1110. JUTE, COIR, GLASS ROPE/ SUTLI
1111. JUTE TWINE
1112. L.P.G BOTTLING PLANT
1113. L.P.G REGULATOR (DOMESTIC PURPOSE)
1114. LAMINATED PARTICLE BOARD & HARD BOARD
1115. LAMINATED SAFETY AND TOUGHENED GLASS
1116. LEASING & HIRE PURCHASE
1117. LICHEN (CHARILA)
1118. MANILA ROPES
1119. MEDICAL COLLEGE
1120. MATCH UNIT FROM WAXED PAPER
1121. MEDIUM DENSITY FIBRE BOARD
1122. MELAMINE CROCKERY
1123. MINERAL WATER
1124. MINI CEMENT PLANT
1125. MIRROR SILVER, GOLDEN, PINK, BLACK & SMOKES
1126. MODERN ADVERTISING AGENCY WITH DTP & FILM STUDIO
1127. MOTEL/SMALL HOTEL
1128. MULTI COLOUR PRINTING
1129. MULTI STOREY COMMERCIAL COMPLEX ALONGWITH RESIDENTIAL AND DELUX FLATS FOR FOREIGN TOURISTS & REVOLVING RESTAURENT AT THE TOP
1130. MULTIPLE LAMINATION INDUSTRY
1131. MUSHROOM GROWING AND PROCESSING (BY DEEP FREEZING METHOD)
1132. NEWS PAPER PRINTING
1133. NICKEL LINED INDUSTRIAL SCREEN
1134. OFFSET COLOUR PRINTING PRESS (SIX COLOUR)
1135. OFFSET PRINTING PRESS
1136. P.C.C ELECTRIC POLES
1137. PHOTOGRAPHIC DEVELOPER & FIXER
1138. PVC EXTRUSION PROFILE (DOOR & WINDOWS)
1139. POP-CORN
1140. PHOTO ETCHING OF S.S.
1141. PRE STRESSED CEMENT CONCRETE PIPES
1142. PILFER PROOF CAPS
1143. PILFER PROOF CAPS AND CROWN CAP
1144. POUCH MAKING & GRAVURE PRINTING (ROTO PRINTING)
1145. POULTRY & FISH FARMING (INTEGERATED UNIT)
1146. PRINTING OF TIN SHEETS
1147. READYMADE GARMENTS
1148. RESTAURANT
1149. ROSE PLANTATION AND ROSE OIL EXTRACTION
1150. ROTOGRAVURE PRINTING
1151. SAFETY BELTS
1152. SAFETY MATCHES
1153. SHOE LACES
1154. SILKCOCOON CULTIVATION (GROWING OF SILK COCOON WARM)
1155. SILK SCREEN PRINTING FORMULATIONS FOR PLASTIC, PAPER & CLOTH
1156. SPIKENARD (JATAMANSI)
1157. STENCIL COATING SOLUTION
1158. SUGAR CANDY (MISRI)
1159. SUGAR CANE PLANTATION
1160. SUGAR CANE JUICE PRESERVATION
1161. SURAT ZARI
1162. SYNTHETIC SHOES & SOLES
1163. TEA PACKAGING INDUSTRY
1164. TENNIS BALLS
1165. THREE STAR HOTEL
1166. TRAVELLING AGENCY
1167. TRAYS, TROLLEYS FOR HOSPITAL WITH SCRATCHLESS COATING
1168. WAX EXTRACTS (TANNING POWDER)
1169. WIRE ROPE SLINGS
1170. WOOD WOOL SLAB
1171. WOODEN CANE FURNITURE WITH EXPORT POTENTIAL
1172. WOODEN FURNITURE
1173. WOODEN PANEL INCLUDING KILN SEASONING
1174. WOODEN FURNITURE
1175. WATCH CASE BUFFING
1176. WATCH DIAL
1177. WRIST WATCHES
1178. WATCHES (ELECTRONIC)
1179. ZEDOARY (KACHUR)

EDIBLE OILS, ESSENTIAL OILS LURICATIING OILS, GREASES, VEGETABLE OILS, WAXES, CAMPHOR, PERFUMES & PERFUMERY COMPOUNDS AND REFINED OILS ETC.

1180. AROMATIC PERFUMERY COMPOUND
1181. AEROSOL
1182. AGARBATTI PERFUMERY COMPOUND
1183. BEES WAX MANUFACTURE
1184. CAMPHOR
1185. CARDANOL FROM CASHEW NUT SHELL LIQUID
1186. CASTOR OIL
1187. CASTOR OIL DERIVATIVE OLEORESINS
1188. CHILLI OIL
1189. CITRONELLA OILS
1190. CLOVE OIL
1191. CONCENTRATE OF ROSE JASMINE & LILY ETC.
1192. COLOURED FLAME CANDLE

1193. CANDLES (SEMI-AUTOMATIC)
1194. CORN OIL (MAIZE OIL)
1195. DEHYDRATED CASTOR OIL
1196. EUGENOL FROM CINNAMON LEAF OIL
1197. EXTRACTION OF ESSENTIAL OIL (CARDAMON, JEERA, AJOWAN, GINGER OILS ETC. & PACKAGING OF GROUND SPICES)
1198. EXTRACTION OF JASMINE ESSENCE
1199. EXTRACTION OF ESSENTIAL OILS BY SUPER CRITICAL FLUID METHOD FROM FLOWERS, HERBS & SPICES
1200. EUCALYPTUS OIL
1201. EXTRACTION OF OIL FROM OIL SEED EXPANDEREXTRUSION TECHNOLOGY)
1202. FAT LIQUOR SULPHATED OIL
1203. FLAVOURS FOR FOOD
1204. GARLIC OIL & POWDER
1205. GINGER OIL, SANDALWOOD OIL AND NAGARMOTHA OIL
1206. GINGER OIL
1207. GINGER OIL & GINGER DUST
1208. INTEGERATED WAX COMPLEX
1209. IONONE FROM LEMON GRASS OIL
1210. JASMINE & LILLY FLOWER OIL
1211. LEMON GRASS OIL
1212. LIQUID PARAFFIN
1213. LUBE OIL & GREASE
1214. LUBRICATING OIL
1215. MENTHOL CRYSTALS
1216. MENTHOL OIL & CRYSTAL
1217. MICRO CRYSTALLINE WAX
1218. MUSTARD OIL (EDIBLE OIL)
1219. OIL FROM ARTEMISIA HERBS
1220. PALM OIL CRUSHING UNIT
1221. PAN MASALA
1222. PARAFFIN WAX
1223. PARAFFIN WAX FROM SLACK WAX
1224. REFINED OIL-SUN FLOWER OIL, GROUNDNUT OIL, STAFF FLOWER OIL & COTTON SEED OIL
1225. REFINED VEGETABLE OIL
1226. RECLAMATION OF USED ENGINE OIL
1227. RICE BRAN OIL (R.B.O)
1228. ROSE OIL EXTRACTION
1229. SMOKE LESS CANDLE
1230. SPICE OIL & OLEORESINS
1231. SOLVENT EXTRACTION PLANT (OIL CAKE BASED)
1232. SYNTHETIC ALMOND OIL
1233. SYNTHETIC TALLOW
1234. SYNTHETIC GHEE
1235. VEGETABLE OIL EXTRACTION & REFINING
1236. WADDING OIL (100%) FOR WADDING OF COTTON HOSIERY CLOTH IN DYEING PROCESS
1237. WAX EMULSION FOR TEXTILE
1238. WAX FLOOR POLISH

PAINT, ENAMEL, SOLVENTS, THINNERS, INKS & VARNISH

1239. ACRYLIC EMULSION PAINTS
1240. ALUMINIUM PAINT
1241. AUTOMOBILE PAINTS
1242. BALL POINT PEN REFILL INK
1243. BITUMINIOUS ROAD EMULSION
1244. BITUMEN
1245. BITUMINIOUS FELTS FOR WATER & DAMP PROOFING
1246. BITUMINIOUS ROAD EMULSION RAPID MEDIUM & SLOW SETTING
1247. BUFFING & POLISHING
1248. CEMENT PAINT FOR WHITE & GREY CEMENT

1249. DISPERSANT
1250. DRY DISTEMPER
1251. DRY DISTEMPER & CEMENT PAINT
1252. DUPLICATING INK BLACK FOR GESTNER DUPLICATOR
1255. EMULSION PAINTS (WATER BASED)
1256. HAMMERTONE PAINT
1257. INSULATING VARNISH & WIRE ENAMEL
1258. IRON OXIDE PIGMENTS
1259. INSULATING VARNISH (POLY VINYL BUTYRAL BASED, FFC GRADE)
1260. LIME COLOUR (CEMENT COLOUR)
1261. SYNTHETIC RED OXIDE FOR FLOORINGS
1262. SOLVENT & THINNERS
1263. MARKING INKS (WATER PROOF)
1264. METAL NAPHTHANATE (AS DRIER FOR PAINTS)
1265. N.C.PUTTY
1266. OFFSET PRINTING INK
1267. OIL BOUND DISTEMPER PAINT
1268. PAINT BRUSHES
1269. PAINT REMOVERS
1270. PAINT INDUSTRY
1271. PAINT & VARNISH
1272. PICTURE VARNISH
1273. POWDER COATING PAINT
1274. PRINTING INKS (OFFSET, FLEXO & ROTO GRAVURE)
1275. PRIMER PAINT & ENAMEL PAINT
1276. PUTTY & WATER PROOFING PAINT
1277. PRINTING INKS (FLEXO-GRAPHIC INK)
1278. PUTTY (METAL CASEMENT)
1279. RED OXIDE PRIMER (ANTI CORROSIVE)
1280. REFRECTORY PAINT (GRAPHITE BASED)
1281. SCREEN PRINTING INKS
1282. SILK SCREEN PRINTING INK FORMULATION FOR PLASTIC, PAPER, CLOTH
1283. STAMP & PAD INK
1284. STOVING PAINT
1285. SPIRIT SOLUBLE MALEIC RESIN
1286. TEXTURE PAINT
1287. THINNERS AND ITS ALLIED PRODUCTS
1288. TONER INK
1289. VARNISH THINNER (SOLVENT)
1290. VACUUM METALLIZING LACQUERS
1291. WOOD PRIMER

PHARMACEUTICAL, DRUGS, AYURVEDIC/HERBAL COSMETICS & MEDICINES, HOMOEOPATHIC MEDICINES, DISPOSABLE SYRINGE, DENTAL COLLEGE & FINE CHEMICALS ETC.

1292. AROMATIC PILLS
1293. ASPIRIN
1294. AYURVEDIC PAIN BALM OINTMENTS
1295. AYURVEDIC CHURAN AND TABLETS
1296. AYURVEDIC TABLETS (HAJMOLA TYPE)
1297. AYURVEDIC/HERBAL PHARMACY
1298. AYURVEDIC SHERBATS
1299. AYURVEDIC PRODUCTS
1300. BULK DRUGS (E.O.U)
1301. BLOOD BAGS
1302. CALCIUM GLUCONATE
1303. CAPSULE, TABLET & INJECTION WITH MODERN INSTRUMENTS
1304. CASHEW FENI
1305. CHLOROQUINONE PHOSPHATE (BULK DRUGS)
1306. CLINICAL THERMOMETER
1307. DENTAL CLINIC

Price Rs. 4200/- for each "Detailed Project Report" Payable in advance through Draft/Cash/ M.O. in favour of *"ENGINEERS INDIA RESEARCH INSTITUTE"*. 4449, Nai Sarak (D), Main Road Delhi - 110 006 *OR Ask by V.P.P.* ● Ph : 23918117, 2391 6431, 23840361 ●Fax : 91-11- 2391 6431 ●E-Mail : eirisidi@bol.net.in ● WebSite : www.startindustry.com

1308. DENTAL COLLEGE
1309. DENTAL GRADE EUGENOL
1310. DEXTROSE MONOHYDRATE, LIQUID GLUCOSE
1311. DEHYDRATED ONION & ONION POWDER
1312. DEXTROSE POWDER (ANHYDROUS FROM STARCH)
1314. DEXTROSE SALINE SOLUTION
1315. DISTILLERY (I.M.F.L)
1316. DISPOSABLE NEEDLES FOR SYRINGES
1317. DISPRIN
1318. DISTILLED WATER
1319. EMPTY HARD GELATINE CAPSULES
1320. FILLING & PACKING OF CAPSULES
1321. GLUCOSE - D - POWDER
1322. GLYCERINE
1323. HERBAL COSMETICS
1324. HERBAL SHAMPOO
1325. HERBAL HAIR OILS (AYURVEDIC)
1326. HOMOE & BIO-MEDICINES WITH MOTHER TINCTURE
1327. HOMOEPATHIC MEDICINES
1328. HYPODERMIC NEEDLES
1329. I.V. FLUIDS
1330. IBUPROFEN
1331. INFUSION & TRANSFUSION SETS (I.V. SET)
1332. INJECTABLE FOR PHARMACEUTICALS
1333. INJECTION AMPOULES PACKAGING,BOX
1334. INTEGERATED SURGICAL COTTON
1335. ICE MAKING PLANT
1336. ICE & COLD STORAGE
1337. LACTOSE & BY PRODUCTS PROCESSING FROM MILK
1338. LICHEN (JATAMANSI CHARILA)
1339. LIQUID GLUCOSE AND ITS BY-PRODUCTS
1340. L-LYSINE MONOHYDRO CHLORIDE
1341. LIQUID GLUCOSE FROM POTATOES
1342. MEDICAL COLLEGE
1343. NICOTINE FROM TOBACCO WASTE
1344. OINTMENT-AYURVEDIC (YELLOW & WHITE)
1345. PHARMACEUTICAL AND FOOD GRADE GELATINE
1346. PHARMACEUTICAL INDUSTRY (TABLETS, CAPSULES, LIQUID, GEL, OINTMENT POWDER INJECTABLE)
1347. PHARMACEUTICAL UNIT (EOU) WITH FORMULA TIONS, INJECTABLES, ETC. PYRIDINE & DERIVATIVES
1348. SALT (IODIZED SALT)
1349. SALINE & INJECTION WATER
1350. SALINE WATER & DEXTROSE SOLUTION (I.V.FLUID IN PLASTIC BOTTLES)
1351. SORBITOL
1352. STARCH (MAIZE)
1353. SURGICAL ADHESIVE PLASTER
1354. SURGICAL BANDAGES
1355. SURGICAL GLOVES
1357. SURGICAL COTTON
1358. SURGICAL COTTON AND BANDAGE
1359. SYNTHETIC CAMPHOR POWDER
1360. TABLETS & CAPSULES
1361. TISSUE CULTURE
1362. TINCTURE FROM RECTIFIED SPIRIT
1363. TRIMETHOPIME
1364. VETERENARY MEDICINES (ONLY FORMULATIONS)
1365. VITAMIN 'C', SORBITOL' ANHYDROUS DEXTROSE, STARCH

PULP, PAPER, STRAW/GREY BOARD, KRAFT PAPER, PACKAGING, PAPER CARRY BAGE, PAPER FROM AGRO WASTE & STATIONERY ETC.

1366. AMMONIA PAPER
1367. AUTOMATIC BOOK BINDING
1368. ADHESIVE (FEVICOL TYPE)
1369. ALL PIN & GEM CLIPS
1370. CARBON PAPER
1371. CARD BOARD
1372. CARBON LESS PAPER
1373. CELLPHANE PAPER
1374. COMPUTER FORMS & SECURITY PRINTING PRESS
1375. CORRUGATED BOARD & BOX (PRINTED & LAMINATED)
1376. CORRUGATED BOARD AND BOXES FROM FROM CARD BOARDS
1377. CORRUGATED CARTONS FROM PLAIN PAPERS
1378. CORRUGATRED PACKING & MATERIAL (BULB & TUBES PACKING)
1379. DESK TOP PUBLISHING
1380. DEFOAMING AGENT FOR PAPER PLANT
1381. DRINKING STRAW PAPER
1382. D.T.P CUM OFFSET PRESS
1383. EGG TRAYS
1384. EXERCISE NOTE BOOK, REGISTER AND PAD
1385. FLEXOGRAPHIC INK
1386. GREETING CARD BY OFFSET PRESS
1387. HAND MADE PAPER FILTER PAPER
1388. HARD BOARD
1389. INJECTION AMPOULES PACKAGING BOXES
1390. INSULATIING PAPER
1391. KRAFT PAPER
1392. KRAFT PAPER FROM BAGASSE
1393. LAMINATED PACKAGING PAPER WITH PRINTING
1394. LAMINATION & COATING ON PAPER
1395. M.G. PAPER FROM WASTE PAPER
1396. MILL PAPER FROM WASTE PAPER
1397. MILL BOARD FROM RICE & WHEAT STRAWS
1398. MILL BOARD FROM WASTE PAPER
1399. MINI PAPER PLANT FROM SISAL
1400. MINI PAPER PLANT
1401. MULTI WALL PAPER SACKS
1402. NEWS PAPER FOR CHILDREN
1403. NEWS PRINT PAPER FROM RICE STRAW BAGASSE
1404. NEWS PAPER CHILDRENS
1405. NEWS PRINT PAPER
1406. OFFSET AND TREADLE TYPE PRINTING PRESS
1407. MILL BOARD BASED ON RICE STRAW
1408. PAPER AND BOARD FROM STRAW
1409. PAPER & PAPER PRODUCTS
1410. PAPER ENVELOPES
1411. PAPER CARRY BAGS
1412. PAPER BOARD CARTON
1413. PAPER CONES FOR LOUD SPEAKERS
1414. PAPER FROM AKRA
1415. PAPER FROM BAGASSE WITH CORRUGATED BOARD & BOXES
1416. PAPER FROM BAMBOO
1417. PAPER GLASSES FOR BEVERAGES
1418. PAPER FROM RICE HUSK & WHEAT HUSK
1419. PAPER FROM TREE BARK, EUCALYPRUS WOOD
1420. PAPER PRODUCTS.
1421. PAPER PLANT (WHITE WRITING & NEWS PAPER FOR PULP & WASTE PAPER)
1422. PAPER PLATES, PAPER GLASS
1423. PAPER CONES & TUBES
1425. PAPER PLANT WITH DTP & PRINTING & PUBLISHING UNIT
1426. PAPER BASED PHENOLIC SHEET
1427. PAPER CUP FOR ICE CREAM
1428. PAPER TUBES SPIRAL WINDING COMPOSIT CONTAINER
1429. PAPER LABLE FOR BEER BOTTLES
1430. PARTICLE BOARD & BLACK BOARD WITH SANDING & LAMINATION OF PARTICLE BOARD
1431. PARTICLE BOARD FROM RICE HUSK
1432. POUCH FILLING & MAKING FOR TOMATO SAUCE
1433. POUCH MAKING &

GRAVURE PRINTING
1434. PROCESSING OF PAPER FOR FEEDING IN COMPUTER
1435. PULP FROM BAMBOO & WOOD
1436. PAPER FILES
1437. PLAYING CARDS
1438. ROSIN SIZING AGENT (FOR PAPER PLANT)
1439. SAND PAPER
1440. SANITRY NAPKINS
1441. SILICON COATED PAPER
1442. STENCIL PAPER
1443. STRAW BOARD AND GREY BOARD
1444. STRAW BOARD & MILL BOARD
1445. STRAW BOARD AND PAPER BOARD
1446. TISSUE PAPER FACIAL
1447. TISSUE MOIST TOILETERY CLEANSING TISSUE AND RELATED PRODUCTS
1448. TISSUE PAPER ROLLS
1449. TETRA PACK FOR MILK PACKAGING, GHEE & OTHER LIQUIDS
1450. TOILET PAPER ROLLS
1451. TOILET PAPER & NAPKINS
1452. WAX COATED PRINTED PAPER
1453. WET FACE FRESHNER TISSUE
1454. WHITE WRITING & PRINTING PAPER
1455. WRITING & PRINTING PAPER (PAPER MILLS)

PLASTIC, B.O.P.P, ACRYLIC, DISPOSABLE PLASTIC PRODUCTS, PET PRODUCTS, P.V.C, H.D.P.E, P.P, L.D.P.E., P.U, A.B.S, THERMOFOARMING, MASTER BATCHES, & POLYMER AND RUBBER PRODUCTS, TYRE, TUBE, ADHESIVE, SHEET, COIR & MANY OTHERS

1456. ABS GRANULES FROM ABS SCRAPS FROM OLD T.V. CABINETS, WHITE GOODS ETC.
1457. ACRYLIC BEADS
1458. ACRYLIC COPOLYMER EMULSION
1459. ACRYLIC LATEX
1460. ACRYLIC SHEET
1461. ACRYLIC SHEET & MOULDED PRODUCTS
1462. ACRYLIC TEETH
1463. AUTO TUBES
1464. AUTO FLAPS FOR TRUCKS & BUSES
1465. AUTO TYRES & TUBES
1466. BABY BOTTLES (PLASTIC) WITH WHITESILICON RUBBER NIPPLES
1467. B.O.P.P. FILM
1468. B.O.P.P. PRESSURE SENSITIVE SELF ADHESIVE TAPE
1469. BABY NIPPLE (SILICON)
1470. BABY NIPPLE (BIG SIZE)
1471. BALLOON PLASTIC ADVERTISING
1472. BLISTER FILM PVC
1473. BLISTER PACKAGING & POUCH PAKAGING
1474. BLOW MOULDING PLASTIC CONTAINER
1475. COATING ON METALIZED POLYESTER FILM/METALISED PAPER/ ALIMINIUM FOIL
1476. COATING ON PLASTIC (ELECTROLYSIS) & GLASS
1477. COIR FOAM (RUBBERISED)
1478. COLOUR COATING ON PLASTICS
1479. COLOUR MASTER BATCHES FOR VARIOUS PLASTICS
1480. CYCLE TYRES AND TUBES
1481. DISPOSABLE PLASTIC CUPS GLASSES, ETC.
1482. DISPOSABLE PLASTIC SYRINGES & NEEDLES
1483. DISPOSABLE PLASTIC SYRINGES
1484. DOUGH MOULDING COMPOUND (D.M.C)
1485. EPOXY RESIN
1486. EXPANDED POLYESTRENE MOULDING (THERMOCOLE)
1487. F.R.P AUTO,SCOOTER ROOFS & CEILINGS
1488. F.R.P PRODUCTS (HELMET, WASHBASIN SHEETS, ROOFING SHEETS)
1489. FIBRE REINFORCED PLASTIC (HIGH PRESSURE MOULDING WITH SMC BMC AND DMC)
1490. FIELD RUBBER CONVERTED TO THE 60% LATEX RUBBER
1491. FLEXIBLE P.U. FOAM
1492. FORMALDEHYDE CROCKERY & OTHER ITEMS
1493. FORMALDEHYDE RESIN (UREA, PHENOL,MELEMINE)
1494. GASKET SHEET
1495. GUM BOTTLE (PVC)
1496. GLASS BEADS
1497. HDPE COATED PAPER SACK
1498. H.D.P.E. BAGS
1499. H.D.P.E. CONTAINERS (BLOW MOULDING)
1500. H.D.P.E. CONTAINER, POLY JARS BY INJECTION MOULDING (FOOD GRADE)
1501. H.D.P.E. JERRY CANS
1502. HDPE MANUFACTURING FROM ETHYLALCOHOL
1503. H.D.P.E PIPE AND FITTINGS
1504. H.D.P.E. PIPES
1505. H.D.P.E PRINTED BAGS
1506. H.D.P.E TWINES AND ROPES
1507. H.D.P.E. & L.D.P.E PIPES AND FITTINGS
1508. H.D.P.E/PP BOX STRAPPING
1509. H.D.P.E/PP WOVEN SACKS USING PLAIN LOOMS
1510. HOLOGRAM STICKERS-3D
1511. H.M BAG PLANT WITH PRINTING UNIT
1512. HAWAI CHAPPALS (RUBBER)
1513. I.V PLASTIC BOTTLE
1514. ICE CREAM CUP (PLASTIC)
1515. INJECTION MOULDED AUTO COMPONENTS
1516. INJECTION & BLOW MOULDED PLASTIC PRODUCTS
1517. INJECTION MOULDED PLASTIC PRODUCTS
1518. INTEGERATED COMPLEX ESTER'S & ALLIED PRODUCTS (D.O.P,D.B.P, & ETHYL ACETATE, BUYTL ACETATE, WIRE ENAMELS, JELLY CABLE COMPOUND)
1519. L.D.P.E. (LOW DENSITY POLY ETHYLENE) GRANULES FROM VIRGIN (L.D.P.E. RESIN)
1520. INTEGERATED SURGICAL RUBBER GOODS INDUSTRY
1521. INJECTION MOULDED PLASTIC BALLS
1522. L.D.P.E FROM ETHYL ALCOHOL
1523. LDPE MOULDED PRODUCTS
1524. LAMINATION OF COEXTRUSION MULTILAYER FILM IN ROLL FORM
1525. LATEX RUBBER
1526. LATEX RUBBER CONDOM
1527. MASTER BATCHES (COLOURED, P.V.C, L.D.P.E, H.D.P.E, ETC.)
1528. MELAMINE FORMALHYDE RESIN
1529. MOULDED LUGGAGE
1530. MULTI-LAYER (3 LAYER BAGS)
1531. MULTI-LAYER (3 LAYER) FILM WITH LAMINATION & PRINTING
1532. OIL SEAL
1533. PET BOTTLE/CONTAINERS
1534. PET BOTTLES FROM PRE FORM
1535. PET BOTTLE & MINERAL WATER
1536. PET PRE-FORM FROM PET RESIN
1537. PET PRE-FORM CUM PET BOTTLES
1538. PET PRE-FORM PET BOTTLES CUM MINERAL WATERS
1539. POLY CARBONATE RESIN
1540. PTFE COMPONENTS
1541. PU/PVC SOLE FOR SPORT SHOE BY IMPORTED M/C.
1542. PVC BATTERY SEPARATOR
1543. P.V.C COMPOUNDS (FRESH)
1544. P.V.C COMPOUNDS (SCRAP)
1545. P.V.C ELECTRICAL INSULATING TAPE
1546. P.V.C. EXTRUSION PROFILES
1547. P.V.C FITTINGS
1548. P.V.C FLEXIBLE FUSIBLE POWDER HEAT FUSIBLE POWDER
1549. P.V.C GRANULES (FOR

INSULATION & SHEETS GRADES)
1550. P.V.C GRANULES FROM PVC SCRAPS (WITH POLLUTION CONTROL)
1551. P.V.C HOSES
1552. P.V.C LEATHER CLOTH
1553. P.V.C FLEXIBLE PIPES
1554. P.V.C PIPES AND FITTINGS
1555. POLYTHENE BAGS (PRINTED)
1556. PVC PLASTICS FILM SHEET SOFT/RIGID
1557. PVC RESIN AND COMPOUND
1558. PVC RULAR
1559. PVC STABLIZERS (SINGLE PACK SYSTEM)
1560. PVC WIRE AND CABLES
1561. PAPER BASED PHENOLIC SHEET FOR ELECTRICAL
1562. PHENOL FORMALDEHYDE RESIN
1563. PHENOLIC RESIN
1564. PLASTIC BEADS FROM PLASTIC SCRAPS
1565. PLASTIC BUTTONS
1566. PLASTIC CANS
1567. PLASTIC COLLAPSIBLE TUBE
1568. PLASTIC CORRUGATED SHEET & BOXES
1569. PLASTIC FILM AND SHEETS WITH PRINTING FLEXO & ROTO/LDPE/HDPE/PP/HM/PVC
1570. PLASTIC FILTER MASTER BATCH & OTHER MASTER BATCHES FOR VARIOUS PLASTICS
1571. PLASTIC JERRY CANS
1572. PLASTIC GRANULES OR POWDER FROM PLASTIC SCRAP
1573. PLASTIC INJECTION MOULDED T.V. CABINETS
1574. PLASTIC ITEMS MANUFAC TURE FROM POWDER MELAMINE
1575. PLASTIC GOODS
1576. PLASTIC PIPES & TARPAULINES
1577. PLASTIC SHEET FROM SCRAP
1578. PLASTIC PLANT (BLOW MOULDING & INJECTION MOULDING)
1579. PLASTIC PRODUCTS (GOLD, SILVER, NICKEL)
1580. PLASTIC TOYS
1581. POLYESTER BEADING
1582. POLYESTER FILM
1583. POLYTHENE BAGS & AUTOMATIC PRINTING
1584. POLYTHENE PRINTED BAGS
1585. POLYURETHANE FOAM AND ITS PRODUCTS
1586. PROPYLENE FILM (PRINTED) & BAG MANUFACTURING
1587. PLASTIC MATS
1588. RAINBOW COLOUR ON PVC FILM & SHEET
1589. RED MUD PVC PIPES AND FITTINGS
1590. RE-RUBBERISED OF SOLID TYPE
1591. RESIN COATED SAND REXINE
1592. REXINE CLOTH & ALLIED PRODUCTS
1593. RUBBER ADHESIVE
1594. RUBBER AUTO PARTS
1595. RUBBER BELTING
1596. RUBBER MOULDING UNIT INCLUDING LINING RUBBER SHEETING
1597. RUBBER RECLAIMING
1598. RUBBER ROLLERS FOR TEXTILE MILLS & PAPER INDUSTRIES
1599. RUBBER & PLASTIC SHEETS, MATS & FLAPS
1600. RUBBER SHEET AND ALLIED HOSPITAL RUBBER GOODS
1601. RUBBERIZED PVC GASKET
1602. RUBBERISED COIR
1603. RUBBER COMPOUND FOR AUTOMOBILES
1604. SAFETY BELTS
1605. SILVER AND GOLD PLATING ON PVC AND NYLON-6
1606. SILICONE RUBBER NIPPLES/ TEATS
1607. SPECTACLE FRAMES (PLASTIC)
1608. SPUNGE RUBBER
1609. SURGICAL EXAMINATION GLOVES
1610. SYNTHETIC PEARL COATING ON POLYSTYRENE BEADS
1611. SYNTHETIC RUBBER ADHESIVE
1612. TEFLON MANUFACTURING
1613. TEFLON TAPE
1614. TEFLON TAPES & CABLES
1615. THERMOCOLE SHEET AND MOULDED PRODUCTS EXPANDED POLYESTERENE EXTRUSION PROFILES
1616. THERMOFORMED PACKAGING (BLISTER PACKAGING & POUCH PACKAGING)
1617. THERMOPLASTIC POLYURETHANE
1618. THERMOFORMED CUPS, PLATES & GLASS WITH HIPS SHEET
1619. THERMOCOLE
1620. THERMOCOLE BASED DISPOSABLE GLASS, CUPS & PLATES
1621. TOOTH BRUSHES
1622. TOY BALLOON, DECORA TIVE & INDUSTRIAL BALLOONS
1623. TREAD RUBBER
1624. TYRE RETREADING (HOT)
1625. TYRE RETREADING BY COLD PROCESS
1626. TYRE TUBES & FLAPS
1627. TYRE & TUBES
1628. UNSATURATED POLYESTER FOR REXINE
1629. V-BELT AND FAN BELT
1630. VINYL ASBESTOS AND PVC WALL PAPER
1631. VITON (FLUORO ELASTOMER)

SOAP, COSMETICS & PERFUMS

1632. ACID SLURRY, SYNTHETIC DETERGENT POWDER
1632. ACID SLURRY
1633. AGARBATTI SYNTHETIC, PERFUMERY COMPOUND
1634. AFTER SHAVE LOTION
1635. ANTISEPTIC CREAM
1636. BETA IONONE
1637. BLEACHING POWDER
1638. BLUE DETERGENT POWDER
1639. CLEANING POWDER (VIMTYPE)
1640. COLD CREAM
1641. COLOURED FLAME & PERFUMED CANDLES (RED, BLUE, GREEN FLAME)
1642. COSMETIC INDUSTRY (MODERN)
1643. COSMETIC INDUSTRY (SHAMPOO, SPRAY PERFUME, TALCUM POWDER
1644. DETERGENT POWDER (ARIEL TYPE)
1645. DETERGENT POWDER (NIRMA TYPE) FULLY AUTOMATIC PLANT
1646. DETERGENT WASHING POWDER
1647. FISH OIL SOAP
1648. GLYCERINE TRANSPARENT SOAP
1649. HAIR REMOVING CREAM
1650. HERBAL COSMETICS
1651. HERBAL SHAMPO & CREAM
1652. HERBAL/AYURVEDIC COSMETICS
1653. INCENSE POWDER, INCENSE STICKS & INCENSE CAKE
1654. OPTICAL WHITENERS
1655. ROSE OIL EXTRACTION
1656. SHAMPOOS (COCONUT OIL BASED COLD PROCESS)
1657. SHAVING CREAM
1658. SINDUR (KUMKUM)
1659. SOAP COATED PAPER
1660. SPRAY DRIED DETERGENT POWDER
1661. STAIN REMOVER
1662. TALCUM POWDER (FACE & TOILET POWDER)
1663. TOILET AND HERBAL SOAP
1664. TOOTH PASTE & POWDER
1665. WASHING DETERGENT POWDER AND WASHING SOAP
1666. WASHING POWDER LIQUID DETERGENTS, LOTION & SHAMPOO

TEXTILE INDUSTRIES, READYMADE GARMENTS, COTTON, DYEING, BLEACHING, CLOTH, HOSIERY, POWER LOOM, HAND LOOM, WOOLLEN, SILK, SOCKS, SURGICAL COTTON & MANY OTHERS

1667. ANGORA RABBIT WOOL
1668. BUCKRAM
1669. CANVAS SHOES, JUNGLE BOOT, BOOT RUBBER KNEES & BOOT COMBAT
1670. CARPET FROM COTTON WASTE
1671. CERAMIC THREAD GUIDE
1672. COTTON BUDS/SWABS
1673. COTTON FROM WASTE YARN
1674. COTTON ROLLS
1675. COTTON SPIDERS FOR LOUD SPEAKERS
1676. DENIM CLOTH
1677. DENIM CLOTH (INTEGERATED UNIT WITH BLEACHING, DYEING AND PRINTING)
1678. DISPERSENT FOR TEXTILE
1679. DYEING & BLEACHING
1680. DYEING OF HANK YARN
1681. EMULSIFIER FOR WOOL BATCHING OIL
1682. EMBROIDERY ON FABRICS
1683. GARMENT DYEING, WASHING & STITCHING (JEANS, JACKETS, SKIRTS & SHIRTS)
1684. GOVES KNITTING
1685. GUNNY BAGS
1687. HDPE WOVEN SACKS
1688. HDPE TARPAULINS USING PLAIN LOOM WITH LAMINATION
1689. HDPE/PP WOVEN SACKS USING CIRCULAR LOOMS
1690. HOSIERY CLOTH (COTTON) PROCESSING (BLEACHING, DYEING, FINISHING OF CLOTH)
1691. HOSIERY INDUSTRY
1692. HOSIERY MERCERISING
1693. HOSIERY PRODUCTS LIKE VEST, BRIEF, T-SHIRTS & SOCKS
1694. JACQUARD FABRICS
1695. JUTE COIR, GRASS ROPE/ SUTLI MAKING
1696. JUTE FELT
1697. JUTE TWINES
1698. KNITTED FABRICS
1699. LAMINATED JUTE BAGS
1700. LAMINATION OF HDPE WOVEN CLOTH (JUTE,COTTON, PAPER)
1701. NYLON YARN CRIMPING, DOUBLING AND BLEACHING
1702. PIGMENT BINDER FOR TEXTILE PRINTING
1704. POLYESTER RESIN FOR WIRE ENAMEL
1705. POLYESTER RESIN
1706. POLYESTER YARN FROM WASTE POLYESTER ZIP FASTENERS
1707. POWER LOOM
1708. READYMADE GARMENTS & HOSIERY
1709. READYMADE GARMENTS MERCHANDISE
1710. READYMADE GARMENTS & COVERS
1711. READYMADE GARMENTS & EMBROIDERY OF GOWNS, SHIRTS, BLOUSES, T-SHIRTS ETC. (ONLY LADIES)
1712. READYMADE SALWAR SUIT
1713. RECOVERY OF NYLON FROM NYLON WASTE
1714. ROTARY PRINTING AND DYEING ON COTTON, SYNTHETIC TEXTILE
1715. SANITARY NAPKINS
1716. SCREEN PRINTING ON COTTON CLOTH
1717. SEWING THREAD REELS & BALLS MAKING INDUSTRIES
1718. SCREEN PRINTING ON COTTON, POLYESTER & ACRYLIC
1719. SHAWLS (WOOLLEN)
1720. SHOE LACES
1721. SILK FABRICS ON HANDLOOM
1722. SOCKS KNITTING
1723. SPINNING, DOUBLING DYEING MERCERISING & BLEACHING OF COTTON YARN
1724. SPINNING & CARDING OF WOOL INTO YARNS
1725. STARCH BOOK BINDING CLOTH
1726. SURAT JARI
1727. SURGICAL COTTON & BANDAGE
1728. SYNTHETIC TEXTILE INDUSTRY(SUITING, SHIRTING, SAREES) TERRY CLOTH
1729. T-SHIRTS
1730. TOWELS, BED SHEET COVERS
1731. TERRY TOWEL
1732. TERRY FABRICS WEAVING UNIT
1733. TEXTILE AUXILLIARIES & CHEMICALS
1734. TEXTILE BLEACHING, DYEING & FINISHING & PRINTING OF COTTON FABRICS
1735. TEXTILE (HOSIERY)
1736. TEXTILE MILL
1737. TEXTILE DYEING & PRINTING
1738. TEXTILE PRINTING (JOB WORK)
1739. TEXTILE PIGMENT PRINTING BINDER
1740. TOWEL (TERRY)
1741. VELVET CLOTH BY FLOCKING PROCESS
1742. VISCOSE STAPLE FIBRE
1743. WADDING OIL (100%) FOR WADDING OF COTTON HOSIERY CLOTH IN THE DYEING PROCESS
1744. WEAVING OF DASUTI CLOTH WITH PRINTING, DYEING, EMBROIDERY & FINISHING
1745. WASHING OF JEANS & OTHER GARMENTS
1746. WORSTED WOOLLEN YARN CLOTH
1747. ZARI GLITTER SALMA SITARA OF PLASTIC FILM

INFOTECH/IT, HOSPITALITY, HOSPITAL, COLLEGE, SCHOOL, MEDICAL, ENTERTAINMENT CLUB, WARE HOUSING & REAL ESTATE, PROJECTS

1748. AMUSEMENT PARK
1749. AMUSEMENT PARK CUM WATER PARK
1750. BANQUET HALL
1751. CALL CENTER (DOMESTIC)
1752. CALL CENTER (INTERNATIONAL)
1753. CHILDREN RECREATION CENTRE
1754. COLD STORAGE
1755. COMMUNITY HALL
1756. COMPUTER EDUCATION INSTITUTE
1757. COMPUTER SOFTWARE
1758. COLLEGE
1759. CYBER CAFE
1760. DENTAL CLINIC
1761. DENTAL COLLEGE
1762. DIAGONOSTIC CENTRE
1763. E-COMMERCE/BUSINESS
1764. E-SCHOOL (Rs. 5000/-)
1765. ENGINEERING COLLEGE
1766. ENTERTAINMENT CLUB
1767. ENTERTAINMENT CLUB, HOLIDAY RESORT, 4 STAR HOTEL, AMUSEMENT PARK CUM WATER PARK, MUSHROOM & ITS PRODUCTS, FISH FARMING, LAKE FOR BOATING, DEER PARK
1768. FASHION TECHNOLOGY INSTITUTE
1769. FAST FOOD PARLOUR
1770. FIVE STAR HOTEL
1771. FOOD PARLOUR
1772. FRANCHISE TRAINING PROGRAMME FOR IIT & ENGINEERING ENTRANCE EXAMS.
1773. GOLF COURSE
1774. HEALTH CLUB, BEAUTY PARLOUR
1775. HEALTH CLUB AND FITNESS CENTER
1776. HEALTH RESORTS
1777. HOLIDAY RESORTS
1778. HOLIDAY RESORT CUM

ENTERTAINMENT CLUB WITH 4 STAR HOTEL
1779. HOSPITALS
1780. ICE CREAM PARLOUR
1781. INTERNET SERVICE PROVIDER (I.S.P.)
1782. MEDICAL COLLEGE
1783. MEDICAL COLLEGE, HOSPITAL & RESEARCH INSTITUTE
1784. MEDICAL TRANSCRIPTION CENTRE
1785. MENTAL RETARDATION HOSPITAL & CEREBRAL PALSY
1786. MOTEL/SMALL HOTEL
1787. MULTISTOREY COMMERCIAL COMPLEX
1788. MULTISTOREY RESIDENTIAL COMPLEX
1789. NURSERY SCHOOL
1790. NATURE CARE CENTRE
1791. NURSING HOME
1792. ONLINE SHOPPING MALL (RS. 5000/- REPORT)
1793. PORTAL
1794. REHABILITATION CENTRE FOR AGED & NEEDY PERSONS
1795. RESIDENTIAL CUM COMMERCIAL COMPLEX
1796. RESTAURANT
1797. RESTAURANT WITH PUB
1798. SCHOOL (PRIMARY)
1799. SCHOOL (HIGHER SECONDARY)
1800. THREE STAR HOTEL
1801. TOURIST CLUB
1802. TRAINING INSTITUTE FOR MEDICAL TRANSCRIPTION
1803. VIDEO FILM STUDIO
1804. WARE HOUSE
1805. WEBSITE DESIGN & E-MAIL REGISTERING

AGRO BASED INDUSTRIES

1806. COAL BRIQUETTES FROM AGROWASTE
1807. FURFURALFROM RICEHULL
1808. MUSHROOM CULTIVATION & PROCESSING (BUTTON)
1809. MUSHROOM GROWING & PROCESSING WITH AIR CONDITIONING
1810. MUSHROOM CULTIVATION & PROCESSING UNIT DEHYDRATION & PACKAGING OF OYSTER & PADDY STRAW MUSHROOMS
1811. ORGANIC MANURE
1812. PAPAYA CULTIVATION
1813. PAPAYA & TOMATO CULTIVATION
1814. PROCESSING & UTILISATION OF COCONUT
1815. PROCESSING OF SHEEP HAIR TO PRODUCE WOOL

BAKERY, CONFECTIONERY & FOOD PRODUCTS

1816. AGROLACTOR SOYA MILK
1817. APPLE FRUIT JUICE WITH CANNING BOTTLING
1818. AYURVEDIC SHARBAT
1819. BAKERY UNIT (PASTRIES, BREAD, BUNS, CAKE, TOFFEE ETC.)
1820. BAKING POWDER
1821. BANANA & ITS BY PRODUCTS
1822. BANANA POWDER
1823. BANANA WAFERS
1824. BANANA CULTIVATION
1825. BEER INDUSTRY
1826. DEHULLING OF JAUN FOR BEER
1827. BEER & WINE
1828. BEER, ALCOHOL, IMFL
1829. BESEN PLANT
1830. BISCUIT PLANT
1831. BREAD & BISCUIT PLANT
1832. BOTTLING PLANT COUNTRY LIQUOR FROM RECTIFIED SPIRIT
1833. BRANDY
1834. BREAD RUSKS
1835. CANNED FRUITS & VEGETABLES
1836. CANNING & PRESERVATION OF MEAT
1837. CANNING & PRESERVATION OF VEGETABLES
1838. CANNING OF MANGO PULP & MANGO SLICES
1839. CARBONATED BEVERAGS
1840. CASHEW FENI
1841. CASHEW NUT (DRIED & FRIED)
1842. CATTLE BREEDING
1843. CATTLE BREEDING & DAIRY FARM TO PRODUCE MILK
1844. CATTLE FEED FROM TAPIOCA
1845. CHEWING GINGER & AMLOKI
1846. CHEWING GUM
1847. CHILLI SAUCE
1848. CHILLI POWDER
1849. CHOCOLATE
1850. CIDER PLANT
1851. COCOA POWDER
1852. COCOA BUTTER & COCOA POWDER
1853. COCONUT SHELL POWDER
1854. COCONUT WATER
1855. COCONUT SWEET (WATERY)
1856. COCONUT MILK POWDER (DEHYDRATED)
1857. COCONUT PRODUCTS & BY PRODUCTS (INTEGRATED PLANT)
1858. COLD DRINK
1859. CURRY POWDER
1860. DAIRY FOR MILK PROCESSING (GHEE, BUTTER & PANEER)
1861. DAIRY PRODUCTS
1862. DAIRY PRODUCTS MILK PACKAGING IN POUCH (GHEE, BUTTER, ETC.
1863. DAIRY FARM TO PRDUCE MILK WITH PACKAGING (COW)
1864. DAIRY FARM TO PRDUCE MILK WITH PACKAGING (BUFALLOE)
1865. DAIRY FARM & MILK PRODUCTS
1866. DAL MOTH, CHANACHUR & BHUJIYA
1867. DEHYDRATION OF FRUITS & VEGETABLE
1868. DESICCATED COCONUT POWDER FROM COCONUTS
1869. DEHYDRATION & CANNINGOF FRUITS & VEGETABLES
1870. DRY FRUIT ROASTING & PACKAGING
1871. DRYING OF RED CHILLIES, HALDI, DHANIYA, PEAS & GROUND NUT
1872. EGG POWDER
1873. FISH CANNING IN TIN & POUCHES
1874. FISH DEHYRATION (DRYING OF FISH)
1875. FISH MEAL
1876. FISH PROCESSING (BEAST FREEZING PROCESSES)
1877. FLAVOURS FOR FOOD INDUSTRIES
1878. FLOUR MILL (ROLLER)
1879. FROZEN MEAT
1880. FOOD DEHYDRATION (FRUITS & VEGETABLES)
1881. FRIED & ROASTED GROUND NUT, GRAMS, PEAR ETC.
1882. FRUIT JUICE MAKING & PACKAGING IN PLASTIC CONTAINER
1883. FRUIT JUICE IN TETRA PACK (DRINKS)
1884. FRUIT JUICE, SQUASHES, SAUCE & KETCHUP, JAM, JELLY, VINEGAR ETC.
1885. GARLIC FLAKES
1886. GARLIC POWDER
1887. GHEE & BUTTER
1888. GINGER (PULVERISED)
1889. GINGER GLAZING & PRESERVATION
1890. GINGER STORAGE
1891. GINGER PROCESSING
1892. GINGER OIL & GINGER DUST
1893. GINGER POWDER (DRY) & OLEORESIN
1894. GRAPE DEHYDRATION
1895. GRAPE CULTIVATION
1896. GRAPE JUICE
1897. HONEY PROCESSING & PACKAGING
1898. ICE CREAM & ICE CANDY
1899. ICE CUBE
1900. INVERT SUGAR
1901. IDLI MIX, DOSA MIX SAMBHAR MIX, VADA MIX,GULAB JAMUN MIX
1902. INSTANT COFFEE & INSTANT TEA

1903. INSTANT NOODLES
1904. INSTANT SOUPS
1905. IODIZED SALT FROM CRUDE SALT
1906. JAM CHUTNEY PICKLES & SQUASHES
1907. KATHA MANUFACTURING
1908. LECITHIN (SOYA BASED)
1909. LEMON & ITS PRODUCTS
1910. MACARONI MANUFACTURING
1911. MACARONI, SPAGHETTI, VERMICELLI & NOODLES
1912. MAIZE & ITS BY PRODUCTS MALTING PLANT
1913. MANGO PAPPAD (AAM PAPPAD)
1914. MANGO POWDER RIPE
1915. MANGO POWDER
1916. MANGO PROCESSING & CANNING (MANGO PULP)
1917. MEAT PROCESSING (CHICKEN MUTTON)
1918. MEAT PROCESSING (BUFFALO)
1919. MENTHOL BOLD FROM MENTHOL FLAKES
1020. MILK POWDER
1921. MILK POWDER & GHEE
1922. MILK POWDER, GHEE & SPICES
1923. MILK PRESERVATION & MARKETING TO WHOLE SELLERS
1924. MILK PRESERVATION & MARKETING TO WHOLE SELLERS (IN POUCHES)
1925. MILK TOFFEE MANUFACTURES
1926. MINERAL WATER
1927. MINERAL WATER IN POUCHES
1928. MINI FLOUR MILL ATTA MAIDA, SUJI & WHEAT BRAN
1929. MITHAI/HALWAI (SWEET & NAMKEEN)
1930. MUTTON PROCESSING
1931. PAN MASALA (MEETHA, SADA, ZARDA) MAKING & PACKING
1932. PAN MASALA AND POUCH MAKING
1933. PANEER (CHEESE)
1934. PAPAD & BARIYAN
1935. PAPAD PLANT
1936. PEPSICOLA IN POLYTUBES
1937. PETHA PACKAGING
1938. PICKLES
1939. PIGGERY/MEAT/CHICKEN PROCESSING
1940. PINE APPLE JUICE CANNING
1941. POTATO & ONION POWDER
1942. POTATO & ONION FLAKES
1943. POTATO CHIPS
1944. POTATO GRANULES
1945. POUCH FILLING FOR SAUNF SUPARI ILAICHI ETC.
1946. PRESERVATION OF RAWS MANGO JUICE
1947. PROCESSED CHEESE & MARINE PDTS.
1948. PULP FROM TARMARIND
1949. READYMATE PROCESSED FOOD
1950. RICE & CORN FLAKES
1951. RICE BASMATI (TRADING)
1952. RICE POLISHING & PACKAGING IN POUCH
1953. ROASTED/SALTED/MASALA/ CASHEW NUTS ALMONDS & PEA NUT
1954. ROLLER FLOUR MILL

INFOTECH/IT PROJECTS

1955. MEDICAL TRANSCRIPTION
1956. E-COMMERCE
1957. CYBERCAFE
1958. INTERNET SERVICE PROVIDER (ISP)
1959. COMPUTER EDUCATION CENTRE
1960. PORTAL (WEBSITE DESIGN)
1961. CALL CENTRE

TERMS AND CONDITIONS

FOR INDIA

1. Price Rs. 4200/- (Rs. Four Thousand Two Hundred Only) for Each *Market Survey Cum Detailed Techno Economic Feasibility Report.* Payable in advance through Draft/M.O./Cash in favour of 'ENGINEERS INDIA RESEARCH INSTITUTE', Delhi. Delivery by Regd.post within 2 Days. (Postage Free)

2. Reputed Firms/Companies may place their orders by V.P.P. for full amount in India Only.

FOR OVERSEAS

1. Price US $ 250/- (US Dollars Two Hundred Fifty Only) for Each *Market Survey Cum Detailed Techno Economic Feasibility Report.*

2. Payable fully in advance through Draft in favour of 'ENGINEERS INDIA RESEARCH INSTITUTE', Delhi (Payable in India) Delivery by Regd. Air Mail Post within 2 Days.

ENGINEERS INDIA RESEARCH INSTITUTE

4449, Nai Sarak (D), Main Road, Delhi - 110 006 (India)
Ph:. 91-11-23918117, 23916431, 23840361
Fax: 91-11-23916431 E-Mail : eirisidi@bol.net.in
Website:www.startindustry.com
Also at : 4/27, Roop Nagar, Near Roop Nagar No. 1 School, Delhi - 110 007 (India) Ph:. 23840361